AF722460

MERCHANTS OF LEGALISM

As the doctrine of international law that regulates international rights and wrongs, state responsibility represents the potency of international law. When it set out to codify state responsibility in 1948, the United Nations hoped the doctrine would establish once and for all that states could settle their disputes by binding each other to an international rule of law. Since the Draft Articles on the Responsibility of States for Internationally Wrongful Acts were finalized in 2001, most of the attention has been on the codification history of the topic. Alan Nissel widens the historic lens to include the pre-United Nations origins, offering the first extensive study on the American contribution to the modern law of state responsibility. The book examines the recurring narrative of lawyers using international law to suit the particular needs of their clients in three key contexts: the US turn to international arbitration practice in the New World, the German theorization of public law in the setting of its national unification, and the multilateral effort to codify international law within world bodies. This expanded historical framework not only traces the pre-institutional origins of the code but also highlights the duality of state responsibility doctrines and the political environments from which they emerged.

ALAN TZVIKA NISSEL is an assistant professor at the Pepperdine Caruso School of Law where he teaches international and property law–related courses. He is also CEO of Wilshire Skyline, a Los Angeles–based investment firm. Nissel received his LLD in international law from Helsinki University under the supervision of Martti Koskenniemi.

CAMBRIDGE STUDIES IN INTERNATIONAL AND COMPARATIVE LAW: 190

Established in 1946, this series produces high quality, reflective and innovative scholarship in the field of public international law. It publishes works on international law that are of a theoretical, historical, cross-disciplinary or doctrinal nature. The series also welcomes books providing insights from private international law, comparative law and transnational studies which inform international legal thought and practice more generally.

The series seeks to publish views from diverse legal traditions and perspectives, and of any geographical origin. In this respect it invites studies offering regional perspectives on core *problématiques* of international law, and in the same vein, it appreciates contrasts and debates between diverging approaches. Accordingly, books offering new or less orthodox perspectives are very much welcome. Works of a generalist character are greatly valued and the series is also open to studies on specific areas, institutions or problems. Translations of the most outstanding works published in other languages are also considered.

After seventy years, Cambridge Studies in International and Comparative Law sets the standard for international legal scholarship and will continue to define the discipline as it evolves in the years to come.

Series Editors

Larissa van den Herik
Professor of Public International Law, Grotius Centre for International Legal Studies, Leiden University

Jean d'Aspremont
Professor of International Law, University of Manchester and Sciences Po Law School

A list of books in the series can be found at the end of this volume.

MERCHANTS OF LEGALISM

A History of State Responsibility (1870–1960)

ALAN TZVIKA NISSEL
Pepperdine Caruso School of Law

CAMBRIDGE
UNIVERSITY PRESS

CAMBRIDGE
UNIVERSITY PRESS

Shaftesbury Road, Cambridge CB2 8EA, United Kingdom

One Liberty Plaza, 20th Floor, New York, NY 10006, USA

477 Williamstown Road, Port Melbourne, VIC 3207, Australia

314–321, 3rd Floor, Plot 3, Splendor Forum, Jasola District Centre, New Delhi – 110025, India

103 Penang Road, #05-06/07, Visioncrest Commercial, Singapore 238467

Cambridge University Press is part of Cambridge University Press & Assessment, a department of the University of Cambridge.

We share the University's mission to contribute to society through the pursuit of education, learning and research at the highest international levels of excellence.

www.cambridge.org
Information on this title: www.cambridge.org/9781009378642

DOI: 10.1017/9781009378659

© Alan T. Nissel 2024

This publication is in copyright. Subject to statutory exception and to the provisions of relevant collective licensing agreements, no reproduction of any part may take place without the written permission of Cambridge University Press & Assessment.

When citing this work, please include a reference to the DOI 10.1017/9781009378659

First published 2024

A catalogue record for this publication is available from the British Library.

Library of Congress Cataloging-in-Publication Data
Names: Nissel, Alan T., author.
Title: Merchants of legalism : a history of state responsibility (1870-1960) / Alan Tzvika Nissel, Dudley Lotus LLP.
Description: Cambridge, United Kingdom ; New York, NY : Cambridge University Press, 2024. | Series: Cambridge studies in international and comparative law ; 190 | Includes bibliographical references and index.
Identifiers: LCCN 2024002319 (print) | LCCN 2024002320 (ebook) | ISBN 9781009378642 (hardback) | ISBN 9781009378628 (paperback) | ISBN 9781009378659 (ebook)
Subjects: LCSH: Government liability (International law)–History. | Government liability.
Classification: LCC KZ4080 .N57 2024 (print) | LCC KZ4080 (ebook) | DDC 341.26–dc23/eng/20240129
LC record available at https://lccn.loc.gov/2024002319
LC ebook record available at https://lccn.loc.gov/2024002320

ISBN 978-1-009-37864-2 Hardback

Cambridge University Press & Assessment has no responsibility for the persistence or accuracy of URLs for external or third-party internet websites referred to in this publication and does not guarantee that any content on such websites is, or will remain, accurate or appropriate.

Steven T. Katz
with gratitude for being my first academic rebbe, for teaching me that synthesis requires tension and for showing me how to remain loyal to the law while questioning the arguments lawyers make.

Sarah, Zelig, Orly, Moshe and Zev
for inspiring me to create my best work and for indulging me in the process.

[T]he lawyer's job is selling legitimacy: reassurance to the client and its potential regulators, investors, or business partners that what it wants to do is basically all right.

Robert W. Gordon, *'The Ideal and the Actual in the Law': Fantasies and Practice of New York City Lawyers, 1870–1910.*

♦

The study of international commercial arbitration allows us to see how competition among key actors and groups serves to construct legal legitimacy and at the same time promote law in the service of merchants.

Yves Dezalay and Bryant Garth, "Merchants of Law as Moral Entrepreneurs: Constructing International Justice from the Competition for Transnational Business Disputes," *Law & Society Review* (1995).

CONTENTS

ACKNOWLEDGMENTS

Ultimately, this is a project about enterprising lawyers using the law to engineer certain social ends. It has very much been a shared labor, so I am eager to acknowledge the broad assistance from which I have benefited over the past decade. During this time, I have come across many such lawyers and must thank them for guiding me along this ongoing journey. Writing and thinking within the warm intellectual community that is NYU's law school was one of the most romantic professional experiences of my life. I have many people to thank for that gift, including the late Thomas M. Franck for taking the time to meet with me on several occasions even when his health was failing him, and for schmoozing with me about the challenges of enforcing international law without a police force. Thank you, Sam Estreicher, for helping me write like a lawyer, for always picking up the breakfast tab and for introducing me to Tal Becker, a paradigmatic lawyer-diplomat and, in many ways, a living personification of this project. Special thanks must go out to my old partner in the trenches, Doreen Lustig (now at Tel Aviv University) for making history present, for helping me with my most challenging chapter, for connecting the dots between corporate immunity and state responsibility and for our "International Law & History" sessions; there were moments in those McDougal Street cafes during which I felt hints of *fin-de-siècle* Vienna.

It was in my residence at NYU that I met two mentors who would set my life on an academic trajectory that I am still navigating. One could say (without much exaggeration) that my master's degree there was in Professor Joseph Weiler. I enrolled in every class that he offered with the simple objective of absorbing as much wisdom (on law, morality, pedagogy, psychology, theology, etc.) as I could. During that year and subsequent years as Professor Weiler's teaching assistant and researcher, I benefited from a relationship that has yielded more than any apprenticeship in lawyering could. I acquired a mentor and collaborator whose advice and friendship I look forward to relying upon for many years to come. Thank you, Professor Weiler, for bringing me into your space, for opening your home to me and for demonstrating how to live a complete life. Relatedly, thank you Claudia Golden, who continues to run Professor Weiler's office with the highest degree of care.

When you are in NYU Law, there is no telling into whom you may run or what you will learn. So, it is perhaps not surprising that I audited (and subsequently enrolled in) a class taught by a visiting law professor that would result in a decision to pursue a doctoral degree in Scandinavia. Professor Martti Koskenniemi's seminar on International Law & Politics was my introductory course on international law and common sense. After the ten-week seminar was complete, I picked up the *Gentle Civilizer of Nations* and began to dream of a future in which I was continuously engaging with the past. A couple of years later, I was sitting in Professor Koskenniemi's office talking a big game about what a doctoral thesis should be. Professor Koskenniemi guided me through close readings of Hohfeld, Kelsen, Lauterpacht, Miéville and Strupp. He lent me books, marked up outlines, critiqued drafts, talked through challenges and did everything I could ask of him over a decade (yes, a decade) of supervision. Perhaps it would not have taken as long if I had not insisted on reading John Bassett Moore's six-volume *History and Digest of the International Arbitrations to which the United States Has Been a Party* (1898), which led me down one of several international rabbit holes! Sitting at a coffeehouse on Robertson and Beverly every morning for several months while marking up my copy of Moore's arbitrations was an exercise in time-travel worth taking. Since I didn't live in Helsinki for most of this project, we had to coordinate supervision meetings in Boston, Cambridge, Helsinki, New York, Oslo, Toronto and elsewhere. Supervising a student with full-time professional responsibilities could not have been easy. It certainly took patience, perseverance and a lasting good will. Thank you for insisting that I complete this project with the same ambition that we articulated in our first meeting. Thank you for introducing me to Jean d'Aspremont, the Series Editor of Cambridge Studies in International and Comparative Law. Thank you for your kind and generous Preface. Thank you for being the ultimate supervisor.

While in Helsinki, I enjoyed the intellectual comradery of Martin Björklund, Joakim Frande, Monica Garcia-Salmones, Tina Pajuste, René Uruena and Sanna Villikka. In particular, the late nights and protracted discussions with Jan Klabbers, Anne Charlotte Martineau and Jarna Petman shined much-needed light during some dark Helsinki winters. In Columbia, I give thanks to Kent McKeever for his research guidance (and his salty stories about a former law professor, John Bassett Moore). At UCLA, I would like to thank Richard Steinberg, Kal Raustiala and Jonathan Zasloff for critiquing early versions of chapters as well as Tiffany Parnell and Kathy Stone for making me feel so welcome in Westwood. While editing the manuscript in UCLA, I made many research visits to the Huntington Library, which has a surprisingly wonderful archive of post-bellum diplomacy (in addition to its fabulous botanical gardens); Olga Tsapina was extremely helpful and patient with me.

Many civil servants in various research positions enabled my ongoing needle-in-haystack searches to find "the beginning" of modern international arbitration. Thank you to Elizabeth Gray, Richard McCulley and Rodney Ross, National Archives and Records Administration (NARA); Lewis Wyman at the Library of Congress; Katherine Scott of the US Senate Historical Office; Daniel Holt of the Federal Judicial Center; Joshua Botts, Tiffany T. Hamelin and Aaron Marrs at the Office of the Historian, Department of State; Michael Belgrade of Homeland Security (previously with the State Department) – your patience with reading my manuscript will always be remembered; Jack Guggenheim at the United States Foreign Claims Settlement Commission; and the indefatigable Daniel Silverberg at Capstone but previously on the Committee on Foreign Affairs of the US House of Representatives.

A slew of historians from various disciplines were instrumental in fleshing out preliminary arguments and reviewing portions of the draft. These generous souls include Arnulf Becker Lorca (King's College London), Emmett H. Buell Jr. (Denison University), Johannes Birke (University of Maryland), Dean Christopher (Spin), Benjamin Coates (Wake Forest College), Gidi Cohen (CGI), Harlan Grant Cohen (University of Georgia School of Law), Ron Crane (UCLA), Isser Elishis (Waterton Global), Kellen R. Funk (Princeton University), Joyce Goldberg (University of Texas at Arlington), Ryan Goodman (NYU School of Law), Kathryn Greenman (University of Technology Sydney), Nienke Grossman (University of Baltimore School of Law), John D. Haskell (Mississippi College School of Law), Jonathan Horn (Pepperdine University), Daniel Hulsebosch (NYU School of Law), Robert Howse (NYU School of Law), David Hugh-Jones (University of East Anglia), Mark Weston Janis (University of Connecticut School of Law), Benedict Kingsbury (NYU School of Law), Brian Loveman (San Diego State University), Ruth Mullin, Yasmin Mohammad (Fortress Investment Group), Cynthia Nicoletti (Mississippi College School of Law), Simon Olleson (Thirteen Old Square Chambers), Martins

Paparinskis (University College London), Reut Yael Paz (Justus-Liebig-Universität Gießen), Eran Shamir-Borer (Israel Democracy Institute), Allen Shamooilian (King's Arch), Richard Shamooilian (King's Arch), Marina Spinedi (University of Florence), Samuel Spinner (Johns Hopkins University), Eli Stern (Yale University), Avi Stieglitz, Allison Powers Useche (University of Wisconsin-Madison), Stephen Wertheim (Carnegie Endowment for International Peace) and José Manuel Álvarez Zárate (Alvarerez Zárate & Asociados).

Here, in the Pepperdine Caruso School of Law, I am thankful for my colleagues Michael Avi Helfand, Donald Trey Childress, Jack Coe, David Feingold, Colleen Graffy, Barry McDonald, Greg McNeal, Sarah Nissel, Shelley Saxer and Victoria Schwartz for helping make Malibu a beautiful intellectual home. In Wilshire Skyline, I would like to thank Silva Gabrielyan, Kenia Garnica, Nona Ghulian, Danielle Gross, Joseph Kaplan, Adley Morison and Dina Robles for supporting my research and teaching addictions.

The editing process with Cambridge University Press included substantive comments from three excellent anonymous reviewers – thank you for this unacknowledgable sacrifice. Your comments were largely incorporated and helped rework the project from a dissertation into a book. Within Cambridge University Press, thank you to my editors, Tom Randall, Marianne Nield and Aiswarya Narayanan, for shepherding this project to completion and a warm thank you to the series editors, Jean d'Aspremont and Larissa van den Herik, for encouragement and advice. It is so difficult to convert footnotes from a doctoral dissertation into references within a new monograph and this, among other great edits, was the task that was elegantly accomplished by our copy editor, Ian Pickett.

Last, but not least, I am indebted to my family who enabled me to ride out this beast of a project over the course of many hours and years. Thank you Mami, Aba, Chaimi, Dahlia, Erez, Rikki, Elke, Daphne, Dukie and Shari for your constant encouragement and support. I am thrilled beyond words to thank my stalwart wife, Sarah. Like state responsibility, you are "so easy to look at, so hard to define."[1] Thank you for always illuminating the path out of my many research caverns. Thank you for being my mate, for raising a wonderful family and for partnering with me on this brief and beautiful adventure we call "2020." *What's next?*

[1] Bob Dylan, "Sarah," by Bob Dylan, Desire, Ram's Horn Music, 1975.

Prologue

State responsibility is that oddest of international legal institutions, theoretically omnipresent but rarely visible as practical implementation. There is a sense in which the institution appears simply tautologous with the totality of international law itself. Isn't every legal subject "responsible" for carrying out their obligations? Isn't it part of the very definition of a legal rule – in contrast to other rules – that it is accompanied by the "responsibility" of the one who breaches them? The word plays tricks on its users: it designates both the rule ("you have a responsibility to do this") and the consequences of the rule ("breach of obligation entails responsibility"). In such ways, responsibility penetrates all legal thinking and practice, underlining the seriousness of the legal system and the duty of the subjects of that system to comply. And yet it is seldom applied as such. States may readily agree to ex gratia payments to settle disputes with their neighbours – but responsibility is seldom recognized, perhaps to avoid the tone of moral condemnation it may engage.

Like "state sovereignty," state responsibility appears as a necessary part of any serious description of international law, a structural feature without which popular doubt about international law's character as "law" would be so much harder to dispel. But owing to its legalistic tenor, it does not appear often in diplomatic correspondence. Its place has in practice been largely taken by specific treaty regimes that address the implementation of the treaty rules, regimes or process and of civil liability, of non-compliance as well as, recently, criminal enforcement. Or then it is reduced to the technical question about measuring the liability to pay compensation for some damage. Nevertheless, it is a favourite topic of doctrine and of textbooks and every international lawyer is to some extent at least familiar with the saga about the codification of the topic by the International Law Commission and perhaps also of the culmination of that process in the 2001 Draft Articles on State Responsibility.

Bearing all that in mind, it may seem astonishing that there has not, until now, been a comprehensive history of that notion. This may be precisely because the topic seems so amorphous, hard to compress in few succinct statements or an easily identifiable pattern of state practice. Our debt to Tzvika for having done this is therefore all the greater. Pulling together the different strands that have made state responsibility in modern international law what it is, he has been able to give credit to its abstract complexity while simultaneously offering an excellent account of the legal contexts where our professional ways to address the phenomenon have been forged. It will become no surprise, then, that as an important aspect of the structure of "modern" international law, the notion arose in the latter part of the nineteenth century and that this took place in the context of the efforts by the US government to deal with problems emerging from its relations with its Latin American neighbours. Nor, in view of the many recent retellings of international law's recent history, can it come as a surprise that these practices were eventually given a doctrinal articulation within German public law. The Latin American pedigree of the notion then follows into the early efforts in the 1950s at the International Law Commission to give it legal form as the law covering the treatment of aliens, a kind of predecessor to international human rights law, weighted towards the question of the status of foreign property. And yet, the author of this work ends his history quite properly at the very point where the doctrine comes to its own as a combination of what he calls ad hoc legalism focusing on investment protection and a more theoretically imbued effort to give international law meaning as the general law applicable in a society of states, or a *lex generalis.*

This is an erudite, occasionally also in places a provocative work on an excellent topic that provides a welcome description of the type of *bricolage* in which ambitious lawyers engage so as to provide workable legal solutions to new problems. Operating between concrete problem–solution and efforts at doctrinal articulation, a history of the institution of state responsibility provides a powerful insight into the character of legal work, both as diplomacy and as academic reflection. It also interestingly highlights the presence within state policy of private interests of various sorts, especially those of foreign investment, as formative elements behind ostensibly public law doctrines such as state responsibility. To have given such a lucid articulation of that feature of the practical operation of their field, Tzvika deserves the gratitude of all international lawyers.

Martti Koskenniemi, FBA
Professor of International Law (Emeritus, University of Helsinki)

1

The Responsibilities of States in International Law

An Overview

Mending Femurs

As long as humans have occupied this earth, they have fought and sought to make amends. A student once asked Margaret Mead (1901–1978), an American anthropologist, when exactly civilization began. In a response that must have surprised her student, Mead said that the history of socialization began 15,000 years ago, the age of an excavated human skeleton containing a broken femur that was healed. To Mead, the fact of the mended femur established that humans had begun caring for one another. Without the social support to mend it, a broken leg was a death sentence carried out by roaming predators. As intertribal contacts increased, humans developed further rules of cooperation such as the fair treatment of travelers. Abraham of Ur, the patriarch of three world religions, was known for his generosity to strangers. Upon the arrival of guests to his tent, Abraham is said to have washed their feet, provided cooked food and offered a place to sleep.[1] Over time, the custom grew into a broader duty of hospitality imposed upon individuals and communities alike.

Fast forward to the modern era of nation-states when governments employed international law to mandate a minimum standard of care to foreigners. It was the legalized duty of hospitality that would form the basis of state responsibility, the modern set of enforcement rules that is the subject of this study. This history is an account of how a handful of American and European lawyers established the first mechanisms of legality to hold states accountable for failing to mend the broken femurs of foreigners.

[1] *See* Genesis 18:4.

A Sacred Doctrine

To international lawyers, state responsibility is a sacred doctrine. As the legal framework that determines whether a state has breached its international duties, and what can be done about such a breach, the existence of state responsibility underpins our hope of ordering the world through law. It is one of the most frequently referenced doctrines of international law. Yet, unlike other international legal norms, state responsibility is a relatively young one. Whereas the concept of state sovereignty was in wide usage since the sixteenth century,[2] the term "state responsibility" was rarely used before the late nineteenth century and had no effective meaning prior to 1930.[3] How could it be that such a fundamental doctrine of international law is of such recent origin?[4] The law of nations has existed for as long as there have been nations. But there was never any technical framework to regulate international disputes until the expansion of US and German territories in the nineteenth century.

I trace the creation of state responsibility through three narratives: (1) the US arbitral practice in the New World; (2) the German theorization of public law in the setting of its national unification and (3) the institutional effort to codify state responsibility within world bodies. As a legal framework for resolving interstitial disputes, state responsibility was created sometime in the late nineteenth century. The US and Germanic conceptions of state responsibility, however, were very different. When the League of Nations, and later the United Nations (UN), undertook to codify the field, they had two credible sources upon which to base their work: (1) The US practice of alien protection and (2) German theories of public international responsibility. The UN ultimately codified state responsibility based on German theory, but international practice is still mostly in the field of alien protection.[5] One was

[2] Jean Bodin, *Les Six Livres de la République* (Paris: J. Du Puys, 1576) (sets out classical principles of absolute state sovereignty).

[3] *See* Martti Koskenniemi, "Doctrines of State Responsibility" in James Crawford, Alain Pellet and Simon Olleson (eds.), *The Law of International Responsibility* 45–51 (Oxford: Oxford University Press, 2011) (there is no concept of state responsibility that would not be connected to or seek justification from its recent manifestation as a doctrine of international law); *see also* Table 1.1.

[4] *See* Jean d'Aspremont, *International Law as a Belief System* (Cambridge: Cambridge University Press, 2017), especially at p. 4 (state responsibility as a "fundamental" doctrine of international law).

[5] As will be explained below, the term "alien protection" originated from the Latin "alienus," which means of or belonging to another; namely, something not shared or someone different. The idea of the term is that the law of nations required different protection for Westerners because they were deemed to be different from natives. See Julia Cresswell (ed.), *Oxford Dictionary of Word Origins* (Oxford: Oxford University Press, 2010), at p. 11.

codified by the UN and the other continues to be practiced ad hoc. According to both the narrow (US) and broad (UN) approaches, the existence of state responsibility asserts the legitimacy of international law as the appropriate forum for international dispute resolution.[6]

In sum, this history is a phenomenology of and not a treatise on state responsibility. State responsibility is impossible to define. Despite the legal citations to and commentaries associated with the doctrine, it is important to recognize at the outset of this project that there is no objective thing called "state responsibility."[7] This history is but a series of stories about how merchants and their advocates used legalism to protect private investments abroad. And it is about the unintended consequences of this turn to legalism on fundamental doctrines of international law.

Table 1.1 *State responsibility in books (1800–2008)*[8]

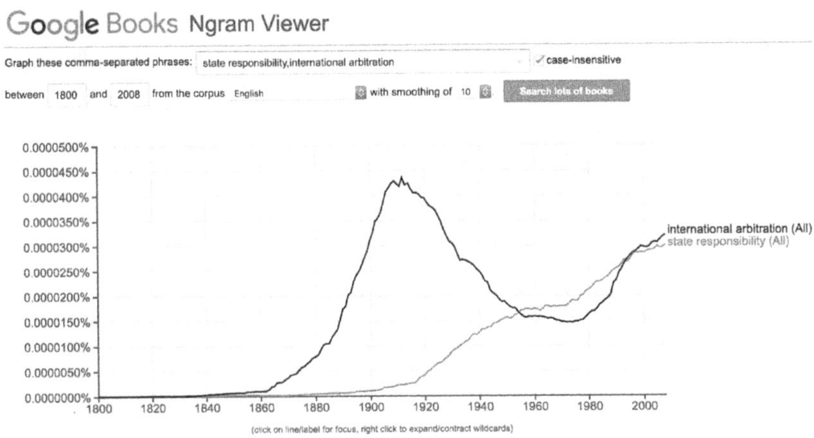

6 Legitimacy is particularly important to international law because of its "flat," non-hierarchical nature; *see* Alexis Galán, "The Search for Legitimacy in International Law: The Case of the Investment Regime," 43 *Fordham International Law Journal* 79 (2019), at p. 84 ("There is no field in which legitimacy does not appear."). Galán convincingly argues that legitimacy as a concept is a purely evaluative one (as opposed to also being descriptive); it is a thin concept that helps make simple judgments (such as "good" and "bad") as opposed to a thick one (such as "friendly" and "rude"), *ibid* at p. 91.

7 *See* Yves Dezalay and Bryant Garth Law, "Merchants of Law as Moral Entrepreneurs: Constructing International Justice from the Competition for Transnational Business Disputes," 29(1) *Law & Society Review* 27 (1995), at p. 31 (from where I borrowed this turn of phrase).

8 This rise in usage is similar in French (though in French there is a higher spike in the 1960s) – Google Ngrams: Jean-Baptiste Michel, Yuan Kui Shen, Aviva Presser Aiden, Adrian Veres, Matthew K. Gray, William Brockman, The Google Books Team, Joseph P. Pickett, Dale Hoiberg, Dan Clancy, Peter Norvig, Jon Orwant, Steven Pinker, Martin A. Nowak and Erez Lieberman Aiden.

Of Modern Origins

The existing literature contains no monographs on the origins of state responsibility.[9] This is the first book-length attempt to provide a history of the topic.[10] What explains this apparent lack of attention to such an important doctrine of international law? One reason is that there is a

[9] Commentators have written histories by way of "introduction" to other agenda, but not as a stand-alone monograph. Existing histories of state responsibility include introductory sections to lengthier studies as well as article-length discussions. *See* Edwin M. Borchard, *The Diplomatic Protection of Citizens Abroad or The Law of International Claims* (New York: The Banks Law Publishing Company, 1915), ∫17; Clyde Eagleton, *The Responsibility of States in International Law* (New York: New York University Press, 1928), ch. 1; Roberto Ago, *L'origine de la responsabilité internationale*, Yearbook of the International Law Commission, 1970, Vol. II, U.N. Doc. A/CN.4/233; Ian Brownlie, "The History of State Responsibility," in R. G. Girardot, H. Ridder, M. L. Sarin and T. Schiller (eds.), *New Directions in International Law: Essays in Honour of Wolfgang Abendroth – Festschrift zu seinem 75. Geburtstag* 19 (Frankfurt: Campus, 1982); Shabtai Rosenne (ed.), *The International Law Commission's Draft Articles on State Responsibility, Part 1, Articles 1–35* (Dordrecht: Nijhoff, 1991), at p. vi; Pierre-Marie Dupuy, "Dionisio Anzilotti and the Law of International Responsibility of States," 3(1) *European Journal of International Law* 139 (1992); Georg Nolte, "From Dionisio Anzilotti to Roberto Ago: The Classical International Law of State Responsibility and the Traditional Primacy of a Bilateral Conception of Inter-State Relations," 13(5) *European Journal of International Law* 1083 (2002); Jan Arno Hessbruegge, "The Historical Development of the Doctrines of Attribution and Due Diligence in International Law," 36 *New York University Journal of International Law & Politics* 265 (2004); Jan Paulsson, *Denial of Justice in International Law* (Cambridge: Cambridge University Press, 2005), ch. 2; James Crawford, Thomas Grant and Francesco Messineo, "Towards an International Law of Responsibility: Early Doctrine," in Laurence Boisson de Chazournes and Marcelo Kohen (eds.), *International Law and the Quest for Its Implementation* 377–402 (Leiden: Brill, 2010); N.D. Gowda, *State Responsibility in the Present Context: A Critical Study with Reference to the Contemporary Issues under International Law* (Thesis Submitted to University of Mysore, May 2010); Borzu Sabahi, *Compensation and Restitution in Investor-State Arbitration* (Oxford: Oxford University Press, 2011), ch. 2; James Crawford, *State Responsibility: The General Part* (Cambridge: Cambridge University Press, 2013), ch. 1; Robert Kolb, *The International Law of State Responsibility: An Introduction* (Cheltenham: Edward Elgar, 2017), ch. 1; Kathryn Greenman, "Aliens in Latin America: Intervention, Arbitration and State Responsibility for Rebels," 31 *Leiden Journal of International Law* 617 (2018); Katja Creutz, *State Responsibility in the International Legal Order: A Critical Appraisal* (Cambridge: Cambridge University Press, 2020), ch. 2.

[10] Given the immense volume of data through which I had to sift for this study, several historical works and styles have informed my analysis; but none provided a direct road map or methodological framework for researching the history of state responsibility. On the methodology of my research for this book, see chapter 1 of my doctoral dissertation, Alan Tzvika Nissel, *A History of State Responsibility: The Struggle for International Standards (1870–1960)*, dissertation submitted to Helsinki University in satisfaction of LLD degree, 2016, available online at www.stateresponsibility.com/2016/02/blog-post.html, last visited February 2, 2019.

certain level of inevitability to the concept.[11] The idea that a person (or nation) should be responsible for breaking the law is as old as *lex talionis* and inherent in the idea of law as law.

When the twentieth-century dean of legal positivism H. L. A. Hart (1907–1992) set out to write a clear introduction for first-year law students, his resulting work, *The Concept of Law*, became one of the most influential law books of the twentieth century. For Hart, what is critical to the concept of law is its consequentiality. There must be socially acceptable and predictable consequences when the law is broken: "it has consequences definable in terms of the rules, which the system enables persons to achieve."[12] In international law, if states were not held accountable for breaching their international obligations, "then it would be questionable whether anything worthy of the name of international law – and *a fortiori* international responsibility – would be left."[13]

A second reason why the history of state responsibility is so understudied is the *complexity* of the concept. As the late James Crawford (1948–2021) has written, "[r]esponsibility has a bewildering array of meanings, each of which occupies a distinctive role in legal and moral reasoning."[14] State responsibility exercises multiple functions in the institutionalized regime of international law. Its rules determine the following:

1. Existence of an attributable international wrong;
2. Extent to which a State is liable for an international wrong; and
3. Manner in which a State may act to remedy that international wrong.

These multiple roles of responsibility – culpability, imputability and implementation – are unique to international law. In domestic law, culpability rules govern the extent to which the law can impute a civil

[11] According to Clyde Eagleton (1891–1958), "If one inquires as to the origin of obligation in jurisprudence, he is forced back to moral axioms" (*supra* note 9; Eagleton cites Thomas Atkins Street, *The Foundations of Legal Liability* (Northport: Edward Thompson Company, 1906) at p. 67).

[12] Herbert Lionel Adolphus Hart, *The Concept of Law* (3rd ed., Oxford: Oxford University Press, 2012), at p. 31. *See generally* Anthony Townsend Kronman, "Hart, Austin, and the Concept of a Legal System: The Primacy of Sanctions," 84(3) *Yale Law Journal* 584 (1975).

[13] James Crawford and Jeremy Watkins, "International Responsibility" in Samantha Besson and John Tasioulas (eds.), *The Philosophy of International Law* 283 (Oxford: Oxford University Press, 2010), at p. 292.

[14] *Ibid.* I come back to discuss this point further in the Epilogue.

or criminal wrong to the respondent. Punishment generally reflects a level of fault.[15] A legal remedy will generally be justified to the extent that it "fits" the wrong that was done. It is the task of law enforcement institutions to safeguard the justness of domestic law by implementing legal acts consistently and in a like manner. This is the rule of law.

Considering the function of responsibility in the domestic law highlights the problem of responsibility in international law.[16] There are no formal civil or criminal distinctions of international law. The extent to which civil and criminal (or even private and public) remedies are available is a matter of ongoing debate.[17] The nature and purpose of state responsibility are equally open to controversy. Are they based on utilitarian or deontic principles? Are they limited to compliance, or do they extend to retributive elements? Each adjudicator is left to select the particular nature of the responsibility to apply on a case-by-case basis – with little guidance from positive sources. Indeed, even the nomenclature of "state responsibility" conflates the distinction between a state's duties and the legal consequences of breaching them. International lawyers use "responsibility" to mean either and both.[18]

A related explanation for the lack of attention to the doctrine's history is the confusion over its applicability. In 2001, the International Law Commission of the UN (ILC) finalized its draft articles on state responsibility (Draft Articles).[19] The lengthiness and inclusiveness of this international codification process commanded considerable attention from law scholars, many of whom believe that the resulting code has attained

[15] Obligations of result and strict liability concepts, of course, exist as well as an exception to this rule.

[16] *See* Amanda Perreau-Saussine, "A Case Study on Jurisprudence as a Source of International Law: Oppenheim's Influence," in Matthew Craven, Malgosia Fitzmaurice and Maria Vogiatzi (eds.), *Time, History and International Law* 100 (2007); Arthur Nussbaum, *A Concise History of the Law of Nations* (New York: Macmillan, 1947), at p. 61.

[17] As discussed in Chapters 3–5.

[18] As discussed in the Epilogue.

[19] International Law Commission, *Responsibility of States for Internationally Wrongful Acts 2001*, Text adopted by the Commission at its fifty-third session, in 2001, and submitted to the General Assembly as a part of the Commission's report covering the work of that session. The report, which also contains commentaries on the draft articles, appears in Yearbook of the International Law Commission, 2001, vol. II (Part Two). Text reproduced as it appears in the annex to General Assembly resolution 56/83 of December 12, 2001 and corrected by document A/56/49(Vol. I)/Corr.4; reproduced in James Crawford, *Commentaries to the Draft Articles on Responsibility of States for Internationally Wrongful Acts* (Cambridge: Cambridge University Press, 2001).

the reified status of customary international law.[20] But this acceptance has led to a misconception about the relevance of the ILC rules to actual disputes.[21] The Draft Articles were intended to apply only by default, where no other special laws hold force.[22] The ILC code does not apply when there are other, specific rules that do pertain, based on the general principle of *lex specialis derogat legi generali*; namely, when in conflict, specific rules trump general ones.[23] The fact that the ILC doctrine is

[20] *See, e.g.*, Kaj Hobér, "State Responsibility and Attribution," in P. Muchlinski *et al.* (eds.), *The Oxford Handbook of International Investment Law* (Oxford: Oxford University Press, 2008), at p. 553; *Noble Ventures, Inc. v. Romania*, Award, ICSID Case No. ARB/01/11, para. 69 (October 12, 2005). According to Judge James Crawford (1948–2021), "They have been referred to as often as any treaty of the same sort in the period in question, and much more often than most." (Jack Taylor, "Inside the ICJ: Interview with Judge James Crawford," *Harvard Political Review*, May 11, 2020, available online at https://harvardpolitics.com/interviews/interview-with-judge-james-crawford/, last visited June 2, 2020). In a 2017 report, the UN identified at least 392 decisions including those of the ICJ, the ICC and the WTO that authoritatively reference the Draft Articles (UNSG-UNGA, 'Responsibility of States for internationally wrongful acts – Compilation of decisions of international courts, tribunals and other bodies – Report of the Secretary-General – Addendum' (June 27, 2017) A/71/80/Add.1); The report identifies 264 arbitral decisions referencing the Draft Articles. On the total number of investment arbitrations leading to a decision since 2000, see: UNCTAD, Investment Dispute Settlement Navigator (UNCTAD Investment Policy Hub, December 31, 2019) https://investmentpolicy.unctad.org/investment-dispute-settlement/ as cited in Sotirios-Ioannis Lekkas, "The Uses of the Work of the International Law Commission on State Responsibility in International Investment Arbitration: Maintaining the Unity of the Law of State Responsibility through Interpretation?" in J. M. Alvarez Zarate, Panos Merkouris, Andreas Kulick and Maciej Zenkiewicz (eds.), *The Rules of Interpretation of Customary International Law* 93 (Cambridge: Cambridge University Press, 2024), at p. 93. *The Rules of Interpretation of Customary International Law*, available online at SSRN: https://ssrn.com/abstract=3719456, last visited May 5, 2021, at p. 1.

[21] *See, e.g.*, my discussion of how four Argentinian gas cases (*CMS Transmission Co. v. Argentine Republic*, ICSID Case No. ARB/01/8, Award (May 12, 2005); *LG&E Energy Corp. v. Argentine Republic*, ICSID Case No. Arb/02/1, Decision on Liability (October 3, 2006); *Enron Corp., Ponderosa Assets, L.P. v. Argentine Republic*, ICSID Case No. Arb/01/3, Award (May 22, 2007); *Sempra Energy Int'l v. Argentine Republic*, ICSID Case No. Arb/02/16, Award, P 391, September 28, 2007) approach the ILC Draft Articles – Alan Tzvika Nissel, "The Duality of State Responsibility," 44(3) *Columbia Human Rights Law Review* 793 (2013), at p. 853. As Martins Paparinskis states: "there is something to be said against the excessive enthusiasm of adopting the ILC formulae wholesale." (Martins Paparinskis, "Circumstances Precluding Wrongfulness in International Investment Law," 31(2) *ICSID Review – Foreign Investment Law Journal* 484 (2016), at p. 488).

[22] *See* para. 1 of the Introduction to the Draft Articles, *supra* 19.

[23] *See* Draft Article 55 ("These Articles do not apply where and to the extent that the conditions for the existence of an internationally wrongful act or the content or implementation of the international responsibility of a State are governed by special rules of international law").

residual in nature[24] seems to have been overlooked in the literature.[25] There is, thus, a duality of state responsibility doctrines: one general and codified, and the specific and largely uncodified.

Since most of the academic attention has focused on the UN, its codification of state responsibility has become identified as *the* doctrine of state responsibility,[26] and its history as *the* history of state responsibility. However, the majority of doctrines of state responsibility – including those regarding the use of force, regional human rights regimes, environmental law, consular law and alien protection – remain either expressly or implicitly outside its purview.[27] Recently, international scholars have begun to question the relevance of the ILC Draft Articles to all international disputes.[28] Some have critiqued its eloquent simplicity

[24] See para. 5 of the Introduction to the Draft Articles, *supra* 19: "In principle, States are free, when establishing or agreeing to be bound by a rule, to specify that its breach shall entail only particular consequences, and thereby to exclude the ordinary rules of responsibility."

[25] In their recently edited book on "Exceptions in International Law," while Lorand Bartels and Federica Paddeu analyze the exceptional structure of ILC doctrine of state responsibility, almost no attention is paid to the biggest loophole of the project – *i.e.*, the distinction between *lex specialis* and *lex generalis* in Draft Article 55 (Lorand Bartels and Federica Paddeu (eds.), *Exceptions in International Law* (Oxford: Oxford University Press, 2020). To Lorand Bartels and Federica Paddeu, "In its simplest form, a rule is a norm that, when its preconditions and international conditions are satisfied, generates a specified outcome" (*ibid* at p. 1). They continue, "Rules regulating conduct, for example, typically state that when a given event occurs (the antecedent), a given legal person must (obligation) or may (a right) engage in a certain type of conduct (the consequent)." Is the exception a part of or a deviation from the rule? Cambridge University criminal law professor Glanville Williams argued that it was the former. To him there really is "no intrinsic difference between the elements of an offence and an exception (or defence) to that offence" (Glanville Williams, "The Logic of 'Exceptions,'" 47 *Cambridge Law Journal* 261 (1988), at pp. 277–278).

[26] James Crawford, "The International Court of Justice and the Law of State Responsibility" in Christian J. Tams and James Sloan (eds.), *The Development of International Law by the International Court of Justice* 71 (Oxford: Oxford University Press, 2013), at p. 81 (it has "encoded" the manner in which we think about *all forms* of international responsibility).

[27] *See* Katja Creutz, *State Responsibility in the International Legal Order: A Critical Appraisal* (Cambridge: Cambridge University Press, 2020), at p. xi ("State responsibility is a blunt tool." "This is why in practice, state responsibility has been taken over by special . . . regimes").

[28] *See, e.g.*, Lekkas, *supra* note 20; The Rules of Interpretation of Customary International Law series, available online at SSRN: https://ssrn.com/abstract=3719456, last visited May 5, 2021 (the ILC Articles on state responsibility "constitute an experiment in international law-making" (p. 1)).

as breeding professional (if not intellectual) laziness.[29] Indeed, the Draft Articles are clearly written and seem easy to apply. Of course, they are not – state responsibility, as Crawford noted, is a particularly loaded doctrine that international courts and tribunals have inconsistently applied in practice.[30]

This book is a critique of the ILC doctrine as well as of the existing academic literature in two important ways: (1) I trace the legal doctrine of state responsibility to its pre-institutional origins in nineteenth-century US and Germany and (2) I explain that development in terms of a *duality of doctrines*. I note that the existing literature's focus on the ILC and its unified doctrine of state responsibility makes it difficult to appreciate how to apply the law to general *as well as to* specific situations, as I will explain in the next section. As such, this book is a *counter-history* of sorts regarding state responsibility – one that complements current accounts of the codified doctrine, but also one that helps situate it within the overall spectrum of international law enforcement theories. It will

[29] *See, e.g.*, Sotirios-Ioannis Lekkas, *ibid* at p. 6 (often times tribunals cite to the Draft Articles axiomatically, as reflective codified law; however, only rarely do tribunals understand or explain why – *e.g.*, as a work of highly qualified writers.) and *ibid* at pp. 10–11 (there is an abundance of decisions in which tribunals proceed to apply the Draft Articles "as self-explanatory to the facts of the case"); Martins Paparinskis, "The Once and Future Law of State Responsibility," 114(4) *American Journal of International Law* 618 (2020), at pp. 624–625 ("A critical reading of practice in support of the ILC Articles may suggest that impressive numbers are not always matched by the quality of reasoning, approval in state and institutional practice, and representativity of the international community. Concerted practice could attempt to reshape, for example, the rule of necessity around the gravity-of-peril axis, or relax the 'only available means' to 'reasonable means,' or relax or even drop altogether the qualification as to contribution.").

[30] It seems that all an attorney has to do is to input the facts of state conduct and out from the court or tribunal comes the ILC's equation of responsibility. As discussed in Chapter 5, "The success of an ideology consists precisely in its ability to make its assumptions seem natural or transparent to the mind" (Jack M. Balkin, "The Rhetoric of Responsibility," 76(2) *Virginia Law Review* 197 (1990), at p. 201, internal citations omitted). More critically, according to David Caron, the ILC Articles engender intellectual laziness and practice has shown a marked increase in citations of articles without further analysis – as though the ILC Articles are already customary international law – which they are not entirely. *See* David D. Caron, "The ILC Articles on State Responsibility: The Paradoxical Relationship Between Form and Authority," 96a *American Journal of International Law* 857–873 (2002).

provide a broader context for studying the history of this continuously practiced field of international law.[31]

An Exceptional Nature

It is easy to appreciate the exceptional nature of state responsibility. To begin with, international law itself is often perceived as somehow different from *normal*, domestic types of law.[32] Generally, *for law to be law* (*e.g.*, something more binding and different than social mores), it needs to be enforced by a sovereign power with the authority and ability to do so. Philosophers from the English legal theorist John Austin[33]

[31] For one such "blinded" history, *see* Florian Grisel, "Arbitration as a Dispute Resolution Process: Historical Developments," in Andrea Bjorklund, Franco Ferrari and Stefan Kröll (eds.), *Cambridge Compendium on International Commercial and Investment Arbitration* 1 (Cambridge: Cambridge University Press, 2019), which declines to trace a history of international arbitration and instead opts to examine international arbitration's developments in the twentieth century by studying Filip Batselé, "Foreign Investors of the World, Unite! The International Association for the Promotion and Protection of Private Foreign Investments (APPI) 1958–1968," 34(2) *European Journal of International Law* (2023), pp. 415–447 and the International Centre for the Settlement of Investment Disputes. For a recent history on the rise of arbitration and international arbitration, *see* Michaël Schinazi, *The Three Ages of International Commercial Arbitration* (Cambridge: Cambridge University Press, 2021), ch. 1.

[32] Regarding the anxiety of state responsibility in particular, and of international law in general, *see* Martti Koskenniemi, "Law of Nations and the 'Conflict of the Faculties,'" *The Intersection of Theory and History* (Spring 2018), at pp. 4–28, at p. 1, available online at www.academia.edu/39100486/LAW_OF_NATIONS_AND_THE_CONFLICT_OF_THE_FACULTIES_?auto=download&email_work_card=download-paper, last visited July 4, 2020 ("Histories of international law rarely engage with what experts – teachers and practitioners – feel as the existential insecurity of the field. Is there such a thing as 'international law'? What sort of thing is it? Engaging with the 'deniers' is a traditional textbook topos and every international lawyer knows half – dozen ways to defend the existence or relevance of the field, as well as some rejoinders' 'to those responses'"). Tangentially, Viktor E. Frankel once wrote: "An abnormal reaction to an abnormal situation is normal behavior" (*Man's Search for Meaning: An Introduction to Logotherapy* (Boston: Beacon Press, 2006 [1959]), at p. 20).

[33] This is often referred to as the "Austinian Critique." Traditionally, positivists have viewed international law as being less law-like than municipal law. John Austin first articulated this view – A rule is usually considered to be a "law" when issued by a sovereign and backed by sanctions. *See* John Austin, "The Province of Jurisprudence Determined" in *The Province of Jurisprudence Determined and the Uses of the Study of Jurisprudence* (Introduction by H.L.A. Hart, Indianapolis: Hackett, 1954 [1832]), at pp. 141–142. Perhaps ironically, it was his mentor, Jeremy Bentham (1748–1832), who first coined the term "International Law" (Jeremy Bentham, *An Introduction to the Principles of Morals and Legislation* (Burns and Hart, eds. 1970 [1789]), at p. 6). In response, international jurists (often ritualistically) begin their monographs with a statement of faith on

(1790–1859) to contemporary Israeli positivist Joseph Raz[34] (1939–2022) have noted international law's *special* character. However, even granting the "law-ness" of international law, enforcing that "law" is quite another matter. How is state responsibility to be implemented in a world without an effective international judiciary or police force? A rule-of-law environment is a society that is constrained by a framework of predictable rules. Disputes are resolved according to those rules, and usually resolved when they are followed.[35]

But international disputes are relatively infrequently resolved by the UN or the International Court of Justice (ICJ or World Court). Most are settled on a case-by-case basis by diplomats or international arbitrators.[36] International claims are resolved in a less rule–like manner than the otherwise traditional doctrine of state responsibility would provide. The process is inherently fluid and dependent upon state consent. It operates by hired attorneys using fountain pens and wearing tailored suits rather than civil servants with their familiar gowns and gavels.

Viewed through the lens of international law, the world is flat. There is no hierarchy of governing entities overseeing states to ensure their

the bindingness of international law – *see* Glanville L. Williams, "International Law and the Controversy Concerning the Word 'Law,'" 22 *British Yearbook of International Law* 146 (1945). For a recent discussion on the relevance of this critique, *see* Jean d'Aspremont, "Bindingness," in Jean d'Aspremont and S. Singh (eds.), *Fundamental Concepts for International Law* (Cheltenham: Edward Elgar, 2016), Amsterdam Law School Research Paper No. 2015-44; Amsterdam Center for International Law No. 2015-19, available at http://ssrn.com/abstract=2690155 (the paradox of bindingness has endured since the nineteenth century).

34 Joseph Raz, "The Law's Own Virtue," *Columbia Public Law Research Paper* No. 14-609, at p. 1, available online at https://ssrn.com/abstract=3262030, last visited on February 28, 2019 ("The Law is a structure of rules, institutions, practices and the common understandings that unite them, which normally are an aspect of some social organization: state, city, university, corporation. International Law is a possible exception, not being united by its relation to a single organization").

35 It is outside the scope of this project to discuss the rule of international law, the international rule of law, etc., but *see further* Sir Arthur Watts, "The International Rule of Law," 36 *German Yearbook of International Law* 15 (1993); Jeremy Waldron, "The Rule of International Law," 30 *Harvard Journal of Law & Public Policy* 15 (2006); Carmen Pavel, "International Rule of Law," 23(3) *Critical Review of International Social and Political Philosophy* 332 (2020).

36 Yves Dezalay and Bryant G. Garth have famously written on how "The abstraction of the rule of law, for example, draws from what could be termed the rule of business and especially from the rule of lawyers who serve business interests" (*Dealing in Virtue International Commercial Arbitration and the Construction of a Transnational Legal Order* (Chicago: University of Chicago Press, 1996), at p. 3).

compliance. This horizontality inevitably fosters an environment of auto-interpretation,[37] the pre-modern environment in which states were constantly at risk of other states unilaterally imposing their rights when and how they so desire.[38] Today, international law generally requires lawyers rather than soldiers to resolve international disputes. This is by necessity as there is no international court or police to enforce the law of nations. It is this aspect of international life that is most often critiqued as its structural weakness. As the Finnish law professor Martti Koskenniemi writes, it is precisely this difficulty that "always made the distance between domestic and international law seem greatest."[39]

With this gulf in mind, Sir Hersch Lauterpacht (1897–1960) drafted the legislative agenda for the newly formed International Law Commission in 1948. He recommended codifying state responsibility as a kind of *ersatz* criminal law, a regime of international sanctions modeled as similarly as possible on its domestic *doppelganger*.[40] The ILC was to establish a doctrine of state responsibility that provides for the possibility of international law, one that could control international relations by binding nations to an international rule of law. This was not, of course, a modest goal. And the first *Special Rapporteur* of state responsibility, Cuban diplomat Francisco "Paco" V. García Amador (1917–93), was unable to secure a majority view within the newly formed ILC.

A decade later, however, the second *Special Rapporteur*, Roberto Ago (1907–95), was able to implement Lauterpacht's view by reconceiving the codification project of state responsibility as a set of abstract principles that could regulate any occurrence of international wrong; it would implicitly depend on the content of whatever primary obligation was alleged to have been breached. Ago's abstract division between primary

37 *See generally*, Leo Gross, "States as Organs of International Law, and the Problem of Auto-Interpretation," in G. A. Lipsky (ed.), *Law and Politics in the World Community* (Berkeley: University of California Press, 1953), at p. 59. *See also* James Leslie Brierly, *The Basis of Obligation in International Law, and Other Papers* (Hersch Lauterpacht and C. H. M. Waldock, eds., Oxford: Clarendon Press, 1958), at p. 230.

38 On the horizontality of international law, *see further* Christopher Whytock. "From International Law and International Relations to Law and World Politics" *Oxford Research Encyclopedia of Politics*, 2018, UC Irvine School of Law Research Paper No. 2018-29, available at https://ssrn.com/abstract=3170066 last visited February 16, 2019.

39 Martti Koskenniemi, "Solidarity Measures: State Responsibility as a New International Order?" 72 *British Yearbook of International Law* 337 (2001), at p. 337.

40 Koskenniemi, *supra* 39, at p. 339. *See generally*, Alan Tzvika Nissel, "The ILC Articles on State Responsibility: Between Self-Help and Solidarity," 38 *N.Y.U. Journal of International Law & Politics* 355 (2006).

obligations and secondary responsibilities was broadly accepted within the ILC; if a government fails to meet its primary obligation to protect aliens in its territory, this automatically triggers its secondary responsibility to repair that wrong. In Ago's worldview, when one state violates one international law, *all* states have an interest in ensuring that the responsible state will be brought to justice. A state's responsibility is not owed just to the directly injured state; it extends to all states because of their innate interest in international order. It was this sweeping idea of state responsibility as a set of rules that was generally applicable *to all nations for all nations* that was codified by the UN between 1948 and 2001.[41]

A Fragile Norm

As the general legal basis upon which states could assert their international rights, state responsibility has come to represent both the potency as well as frailty of international law. The everyday practice of state responsibility continues to reflect the disparity of power possessed by states; the impossibly complex matter of law enforcement still depends on a state's ability and willingness to compel compliance.[42] North American states are, not surprisingly, more likely to be plaintiffs and South American states defendants in such actions. This inequality has posed obvious challenges to the legitimacy, and illustrates the inherent fragility, of the doctrines. On the one hand, the code is broadly recognized as a juridical milestone.[43] It is rare for an international court or tribunal to issue a decision or award without citing to the Draft

[41] The ILC finalized its *Draft Articles on the Responsibility of States for Internationally Wrongful Acts* (ILC Articles) in 2001: Text adopted by the International Law Commission at its fifty-third session, in 2001, and submitted to the General Assembly as a part of the Commission's report covering the work of that session (A/56/10), available online at http://legal.un.org/ilc/texts/instruments/english/commentaries/9_6_2001.pdf, last visited November 12, 2018; reprinted as James Crawford (ed.), *The International Law Commission's Articles on State Responsibility: Introduction, Text and Commentaries* (Cambridge: Cambridge University Press, 2002).

[42] For a classical statement, *see* Alwyn V. Freeman, "Responsibility of States for Unlawful Acts of their Armed Forces," 88(2) *Recueil de Cours* 267 (1955), at pp. 15 ("If reprisals and war are construed as sanctions for the realization of the rule of law, the international legal structure at once takes on the appearance of an uncentralized system which delegates the task of enforcing its rules to the individual States").

[43] On the customary international legal status of the Draft Articles, *see* Fernando Lusa Bordin, "Reflections of Customary International Law: The Authority of Codification Conventions and ILC Draft Articles in International Law," 63(3) *International and*

Articles.[44] On the other hand, it does not seem to actually regulate state behavior. The force of the ILC code seems more in its symbolic than its predictive nature. While the doctrine of state responsibility is applicable to any violation of international law *in theory*, it does not seem to prevent the most notorious international violations – or even portend their consequences – *in practice*. Where was it in the aftermath of the 9/11 attacks that occurred just after the ILC finalized its codification of state responsibility on August 9, 2001?

Parallel Histories

The duality of state responsibility[45] is reflected in its parallel histories. One arc follows the pre-codified history of the doctrine from US diplomacy to European theory in the nineteenth century; the other tracks the effort to legislate a code of international enforcement within world bodies in the twentieth century. There is no singular history that covers both paths of its journey. While there are several overviews of state responsibility in the literature, the historical accounts within these works largely fixated on the ILC's five-decade effort to codify the field.[46] This is not

Comparative Law Quarterly 535 (2014); *see also* Kaj Hobér, "State Responsibility and Attribution," in P. Muchlinski *et al.* (eds.), *The Oxford Handbook of International Investment Law* (Oxford: Oxford University Press, 2008), at p. 553. For caselaw on the status, *see Noble Ventures, Inc. v. Romania*, Award, ICSID Case No. ARB/01/11, para. 69 (October 12, 2005) ("While those Draft Articles are not binding, they are widely regarded as a codification of customary international law"); United States – Definitive Anti-dumping and Countervailing Duties on Certain Products from China WT/DS379/AB/R (adopted March 25, 2011) or regarding Draft Article 25, *see, e.g., LG&E Energy Corp. et al. v. Argentine Republic*, ICSID Case No. ARB/02/1, Award of July 25, 2007. As James Crawford and Simon Olleson have written, "responsibility is the necessary corollary of obligation: every breach by a subject of international law of its international obligations entails international responsibility" ("The Nature and Forms of International Responsibility," in Malcolm Evans (ed.), *International Law* (2nd ed, Oxford: Oxford University Press, 2006), at p. 451).

44 On how the world court operates within the ILC framework since the 1970s, *see* Christian J. Tams, "Law-Making in Complex Processes: The World Court and the Modern Law of State Responsibility," in Christine Chinkin and Freya Baetens (eds.), *Sovereignty, Statehood and State Responsibility: Essays in Honour of James Crawford* 287 (Cambridge: Cambridge University Press, 2015) at p. 297.

45 As mentioned above, one doctrine is a general rule and the other its exception – *see further* Alan Tzvika Nissel, "The Duality of State Responsibility," 44(3) *Columbia Human Rights Law Review* (2013).

46 Commentators have written histories by way of "introduction" to other agenda, but not as a stand-alone monograph. Existing histories of state responsibility include

surprising given that general understanding that, *by default*, international law enforcement is governed by the ILC doctrine.[47] However, it is an unfortunate oversight since the ILC Articles are not – nor were they intended to be – the final word on state responsibility.[48]

introductory sections to lengthier studies as well as article-length discussions: Edwin M. Borchard, *The Diplomatic Protection of Citizens Abroad or the Law of International Claims* (New York: The Banks Law Publishing Company, 1915), ∫17; Clyde Eagleton, *The Responsibility of States in International Law* (New York: New York University Press, 1928), ch. 1; Roberto Ago, *L'origine de la responsabilité internationale*, Yearbook of the International Law Commission, 1970, Vol. II, UN Doc. A/CN.4/233; Ian Brownlie, "The History of State Responsibility," in R. G. Girardot, H. Ridder, M. L. Sarin and T. Schiller (eds.), *New Directions in International Law: Essays in Honour of Wolfgang Abendroth – Festschrift zu seinem 75. Geburtstag* 19 (Frankfurt: Campus, 1982); Shabtai Rosenne (ed.), *The International Law Commission's on State Responsibility, Part 1, Articles 1–35* (Dordrecht: Nijhoff, 1991), at p. vi; Pierre-Marie Dupuy, "Dionisio Anzilotti and the Law of International Responsibility of States," 3(1) *European Journal of International Law* 139 (1992); Georg Nolte, "From Dionisio Anzilotti to Roberto Ago: The Classical International Law of State Responsibility and the Traditional Primacy of a Bilateral Conception of Inter-State Relations," 13(5) *European Journal of International Law* 1083 (2002); Jan Arno Hessbruegge, "The Historical Development of the Doctrines of Attribution and Due Diligence in International Law," 36 *New York University Journal of International Law & Politics* 265 (2004); Jan Paulsson, *Denial of Justice in International Law* (Cambridge: Cambridge University Press, 2005), ch. 2; James Crawford, Thomas Grant and Francesco Messineo, "Towards an International Law of Responsibility: Early Doctrine," in Laurence Boisson de Chazournes and Marcelo Kohen (eds.), *International Law and the Quest for Its Implementation*, 377–402 (Leiden: Brill, 2010); N.D. Gowda, *State Responsibility in the Present Context: A Critical Study with Reference to the Contemporary Issues under International Law* (Thesis Submitted to University of Mysore, May 2010): Borzu Sabahi, *Compensation and Restitution in Investor-State Arbitration* (Oxford: Oxford University Press, 2011), ch. 2, James Crawford, *State Responsibility: The General Part* (Cambridge: Cambridge University Press, 2014), ch. 1; Katja Creutz, *State Responsibility in International Law: From Paradigm to Periphery*, ch. 2 (Doctoral Thesis Submitted to the Faculty of Law at the University of Helsinki, August, 2015); Antal Berkes, "The League of Nations and the International Law of State Responsibility," (May 31, 2020). *International Community Law Review*, vol. 22, nos. 2–3, at pp. 332–333. Available at https://ssrn.com/abstract=3680512, last visited September 2, 2021.

47 *See* Christian J. Tams, "Law-Making in Complex Processes: The World Court and Modern Law of State Responsibility," in Christine Chinkin and Freya Baetens (eds.), *Sovereignty, Statehood and State Responsibility: Essays in Honour of James Crawford* 287 (Cambridge: Cambridge University Press, 2015), at p. 289: "so completely have we internalised the ILC's approach that it has become quite a challenge to identify the choices made on the journey towards the ILC's 2001 text."

48 The ILC designed its code as default principles to be triggered in the event that no other specific law applied (*lex specialis*) according to Draft Article 50. According to *Special Rapporteur* Crawford, the reason for codifying state responsibility as a set of abstract "secondary rules" of general application was: "[T]o formulate, by way of codification and progressive development, the basic rules of international law concerning the

Due to the lack of historical scholarship on this topic, in researching this project, I found it challenging to systematically follow a particular historiographical approach. What I can state categorically is this is no attempt at providing *the* history of state responsibility, as though the topic is some stable object that can be "found" and provided to readers.[49] This book employs a quilted historical approach relying upon many methodological threads: Biographical,[50] Chronological,[51] Critical,[52] Diplomatic,[53] Epochal,[54]

responsibility of States for their internationally wrongful acts. The emphasis is on the secondary rules of State responsibility: that is to say, the general conditions under international law for the State to be considered responsible for wrongful actions or omissions, and the legal consequences which flow therefrom. The articles do not attempt to define the content of the international obligations, the breach of which gives rise to responsibility. This is the function of the primary rules, whose codification would involve restating most of substantive customary and conventional international law." This is the first sentence of the first paragraph of "General Commentary" to *Draft Articles on Responsibility of States for Internationally Wrongful Acts, supra* note 19.

49 Anne Orford, *International Law and the Politics of History* (Cambridge: Cambridge University Press, 2021), at pp. 253–257 (international lawyers often support claims of substantive legal content based on "finding" evidence for such positions in the history of international law). No attempt here is made at "method laundering" (*ibid* at p. 286).

50 *See, e.g.*, Simone Lässig, "Biography in Modern History – Modern Historiography in Biography," in V. R. Berghahn and Simone Lässig (eds.), *Biography between Structure and Agency: Central European Lives in International Historiography* 1–27 (Oxford: Oxford University Press, 2008).

51 *See, e.g.*, Robert L. Beisner, *From the Old Diplomacy to the New 1865–1900* (2nd ed., Arlington Heights, IL: Harlan Davidson, 1986), at p. 2: "A strictly chronological narrative ... would not adequately clarify some of the sharpest and most bewildering differences among historians."

52 *See, e.g.*, Jack M. Balkin, "The Rhetoric of Responsibility," 76(2) *Virginia Law Review* 197 (1990), at p. 210.

53 *See, e.g.*, Charles A. and Mary R. Beard, *The Rise of American Civilization* (New York: Macmillan, 1927), at p. vii: "To put in the presidents and the leading senators ... and leave out such prime actors in the drama is to show scant respect for the substance of life. Why, moreover, should anyone be interested in the beginnings of the House of a Howard or Burleigh and indifferent to the rise of the House of Morgan or Rockefeller?"

54 This history contains multiple narratives, not a linear sequence of "epochs," that show the development of state responsibility. In contrast to, *e.g.*, Wilhelm Georg Grewe, *The Epochs of International Law* (transl. Michael Byers, Berlin; New York: Walter de Gruyter, 2000); Hessbruegge, *supra* note 9; Brownlie, *supra* note 9; Ole Spiermann, *International Legal Argument in the Permanent Court of International Justice: The Rise of the International Judiciary* (Cambridge: Cambridge University Press, 2005); Jean d'Aspremont, "Time Travel in the Law of International Responsibility," in Samantha Besson (ed.), *Theories of International Responsibility Law* (Cambridge: Cambridge University Press, 2022) at p. 257, available online at ssrn.com, at p. 6 ("the present, built on a past, is now working for the future; the future has already begun in the past"). *See further* David Schneiderman, *Investment Law's Alibis: Colonialism, Imperialism, Debt and*

Geological,[55] Political,[56] Sociological,[57] *etc.* On the historiographical continuum, examining realist and idealist accounts of international law, I have borrowed from both with an appreciative but wary eye.[58] Realist histories tend to focus on state power,[59] whereas geopolitical and idealist histories concentrate on lawyers, philosophers, and institutions.[60] To date, historical writing on state responsibility has been the purview of idealists, those with a distinctly legalist bias, giving little validity towards the pragmatic nature of diplomacy. Chapters 2, 3 and 5, which emphasize the importance of particular power structures, are a counterpoint to such views.

An influential example of the doctrinal pull of idealist accounts is Sir Ian Brownlie's *System of the Law of Nations: State Responsibility Part I* (1983).[61] The former Chichele Professor at Oxford University, Brownlie (1932–2010) describes state responsibility as inherent to international society:

Development (Cambridge: Cambridge University Press, 2022), at p. 7 and accompanying notes; Michaël Schinazi, *The Three Ages of International Commercial Arbitration* (Cambridge: Cambridge University Press, 2021), at pp. 39–40.

55 More than any other, I have borrowed Professor Weiler's "geological" mode of historiography – J. H. H. Weiler, "The Geology of International Law-Governance," 64 *Heidelberg Journal of International Law* 547 (2004).

56 I have sought to use a form of "analytical narrative" pioneered by political scientists in the late 1990s – Robert H. Bates, Avner Greif, Margaret Levi and Jean-Laurent Rosenthal, *Analytic Narratives* (Princeton, NJ: Princeton University Press, 1998). This model helped me combine vast quanta of data with general legal theories.

57 *See, e.g.*, Louis Henkin, *How Nations Behave: Law and Foreign Policy* (2nd ed., New York: Columbia University Press, 1979), at p. 7.

58 *See* Martti Koskenniemi, "Histories of International Law: Dealing with Eurocentrism" Inaugural Lecture delivered on November 16, 2011 on the occasion of accepting the Treaty of Utrecht Chair at Utrecht University (on file with author), at p. 9. A similar (but earlier) draft of the piece was published in *Zeitschrift des Max-Planck-Instituts für europäische Rechtsgeschichte*, Rg 19/2011. For an excellent if brief historiographic discussion on "scientism," the empiricist turn in the scholarship of the history of international law (and the critical response to that turn), *see* Jean d'Aspremont, "International Law and the Rage against Scienticism. Review of Anne Orford, International Law and the Politics of History," 33(2) *European Journal of International Law* 679 (2021).

59 Exemplary is Jonathan Zasloff's history of US diplomatic legalism in the late-nineteenth and early-twentieth centuries (Jonathan Zasloff, "Law and the Shaping of American Foreign Policy: From the Gilded Age to the New Era," 78 *New York University Law Review* 239 (2003) and Jonathan Zasloff, "Law and the Shaping of American Foreign Policy: The Twenty Years' Crisis," 77 *Southern California Law Review* 583 (2004)).

60 Representative is Jan Arno Hessbruegge's "The Historical Development of the Doctrines of Attribution and Due Diligence in International Law," a thoughtful and detailed history of two crucial doctrines related to state responsibility (Hessbruegge, *supra* note 9).

61 Brownlie, *supra* note 9.

> The essential idea of responsibility is simple and has its basis in religious thought or secular morality of which law is the outwork . . . Consequently, responsibility is an inherent element in any community based upon some system . . . of morality, religion or law, or several of these.[62]

To Brownlie, the idea of responsibility is both unitary and innate, no matter its form or function (penal, compensatory, strict, domestic, international, *etc.*). He suggests that only an intellectual curiosity – and a childlike one at that – would lead one to investigate the historical origins of state responsibility. More interestingly, Sir Ian actually wrote a paper on the history of state responsibility, *except it was not a history at all*, since

> 'Tracing the origins' of legal concepts and institutions can be an artificial and practically fruitless endeavour . . . In the case of state responsibility, the task is complicated by two peculiarities of the genre. The first lies in the fact that the concept of responsibility is both very simple and yet sophisticated. It is both a fundamental moral idea common to laymen and lawyers, and a concept which legal experience calls for considerable study and refinement, involving nice problems of measure of damages, liability of 'moral damage' and so forth.[63]

While I have been mindful of various approaches to the histories of diplomacy and international law, I have customized my methodology to suit the needs of this study.[64] I have presented this history as three overlapping narratives, reflecting how three groups of professional lawyers – practitioners, philosophers and publicists – have coped with the problem of state responsibility in international law.[65] A common

62 *Ibid*, at p. 19.

63 *Ibid*, at pp. 19–20. Similarly, Jean d'Aspremont in a recent book review of Crawford *supra* note 9, wrote that "It obviously is impossible to trace and establish precisely the conceptual and functional variations that affected the development of the law of state responsibility over the last centuries." http://dev.sharesproject.nl/book-review-james-crawford-state-responsibility-the-general-part-cup-2013, last visited March 12, 2024.

64 For example, in order to locate the early positive sources of state responsibility (discussed in Chapter 3), I turned to the world of international arbitration. The result is Chapter 2, which is not about substantive international law at all, but Chapter 3 would make little political sense without it. Thus, my effort to explain why the US professionalization of international arbitration was a necessary (albeit unforeseen) offshoot of this project. What emerges from these sources is a history of international law based on my several research methodologies. This decision reflects the various observational standpoints at play in the creation of state responsibility.

65 I hasten to note that this trichotomy is similar to but is perhaps slightly more precise than the influential dichotomy presented by Dezalay and Garth in 1995: "The field of international commercial arbitration is given its structure and its logic of transformation through oppositions and complementarities that we shall now begin to map. The key

theme is the motivation to *show* the consequentiality of breaching international law. American, German and other lawyers debated the relevance of law to the resolution of international disputes. By the 1930s, a rough consensus had emerged about the existence of an international doctrine that governs the resolution of (at least some) international disputes.

Three Observational Standpoints

That state responsibility existed as a doctrine became increasingly uncontroversial, but when and how it applied remained contested, depending on the professional viewpoint taken.[66] I present the history of this doctrine through the lens of three archetypes of international lawyers: (1) practitioners like the US lawyer-diplomats; (2) philosophers like the European professor-diplomats and (3) publicists like those institutional-diplomats who comprised the ILC.

Practitioners

From the practitioner's observational standpoint, state responsibility is a weak but important legal tool that helps validate their clients' claims of redress. State responsibility is a technical term they invoke when it is appropriate to address international claims – especially international investment disputes. Practitioners understand why, while there are the thousands of annual claims in the dockets of international tribunals, there is a relatively meager caseload within international courts; this is because international doctrines do not account for international power,

source of conflict, and also of transformation, is that between two generations 'grand old men' versus 'technocrats'" (Yves Dezalay and Bryant Garth, "Merchants of Law as Moral Entrepreneurs: Constructing International Justice from the Competition for Transnational Business Disputes," 29(1) *Law & Society Review* 27 (1995), at p. 35). I also note that Jean d'Aspremont uses a "hall of mirrors" to illustrate "the three distinct images of the international lawyer" (*see* Jean d'Aspremont, "Three International Lawyers in a Hall of Mirrors," 32(3) *Leiden Journal of International Law* 367 (2019), available online at https://papers.ssrn.com/sol3/papers.cfm?abstract_id=3334075, last visited on May 3, 2021, at p. 1); to d'Aspremont, the hall of mirrors "refers to the extent to which international legal discourses are built on self-referential mechanisms tantamount to mutually reflecting mirrors, by virtue of which movements and postures are reproduced ad infinitum without disclosing the origin thereof" (*ibid*).

66 The extent to which the doctrine actually reflected diplomatic practice exposed international law to criticisms ranging from apology to utopia. *See generally* Martti Koskenniemi, *From Apology to Utopia: The Structure of International Legal Argument* (Helsinki: Finnish Lawyers' Publishing Company, 1989).

Figure 1.1 Hans Joachim Morgenthau[67]

which is an inherent element to the resolution of international disputes. This perspective privileges the everyday practice of international lawyers without denying the value of doctrine, but almost certainly minimizing the relevance of theory. A leading voice within this group is the German-born US international lawyer Hans Morgenthau (1904–80) (Figure 1.1), for whom *diplomatic practice* counts as a source of law far more than either doctrine or theory.[68] Some commentators refer to this group somewhat cynically as "managerialists," for whom international law need not – perhaps even ought not – resemble the theoretical rigors of domestic law.[69] In the international system, observed practice is a strong

[67] Photo courtesy: Getty Images, www.gettyimages.no/detail/news-photo/morgenthau-hans-news-photo/162084772?adppopup=true.

[68] *See, e.g.*, Hans Joachim Morgenthau, *Die internationale Rechtspflege. Ihr Wesen und ihre Grenzen* (Leipzig: Noske, 1929); *see also, e.g.*, Jack L. Goldsmith and Eric A. Posner, *The Limits of International Law* (Oxford: Oxford University Press, 2006).

[69] On "managerialism" in international law generally, see Martti Koskenniemi, "The Politics of International Law – 20 Years Later," 20 *European Journal of International Law* 7 (2009); Michaël Schinazi, *The Three Ages of International Commercial Arbitration* (Cambridge: Cambridge University Press, 2021), at pp. 11, 15. (It was during the third generation of arbitrators that investment protection became secured as a technical, specialized practice to be legalistically upheld by the "Managers" of investment protection (what Schinazi calls the "age of Autonomy").)

normative component that usually serves to limit doctrinal or theoretical formulations of the law.

Each area of practice comprises its own reality: environmental law employs the "responsibility" or "liability" of states differently than, for example, investment protection law. Environmental lawyers and commercial arbitration lawyers know this well and act accordingly. They are, thus, careful to rely on "international law" to the extent that its rules further their clients' interests. This stream of international law is sometimes associated with the Anglo-American culture of legal pragmatism.[70]

Philosophers

To philosophers, in contrast to practitioners, *theory* is the best device for explaining the inherent completeness of international law.[71] Philosophers search for the fundamentals of international society, seeking to provide the preconditions and the relevance of just what we mean when we say a state is "responsible." This group consists exclusively of law professors who tend to be more concerned with *examining the criteria* for the possibility of law than with the substance of its doctrine.[72] The most important of the philosophers, or theorists, is Austrian public

[70] Yves Dezalay and Bryant G. Garth, *Dealing in Virtue: International Commercial Arbitration and the Construction of a Transnational Legal Order* (Chicago: University of Chicago Press, 1996), at p. 56 ("the conflict specialists from the United States (or elsewhere) do not feel any responsibilities except to their client."); Joseph R. Stromberg, "Sovereignty, International Law, and the Triumph of Anglo-American Cunning," 18(4) *Journal of Libertarian Studies* 29 (2004).

[71] I use the term "theory" in the broad, Kantian sense of: "A collection of rules, even of practical rules, is termed a *theory* if the rules concerned are envisaged as principles of a fairly general nature, and if they are abstracted from numerous conditions which, nonetheless, necessarily influence their practical application" (Immanuel Kant, "On the Common Saying: 'This May Be True in Theory, But It Does Not Apply in Practice,'" in H. Reiss (ed.), *Kant's Political Writings* (Cambridge: Cambridge University Press, 1970), at pp. 61–62). I do not, however, employ the term "practice," in the circular manner prescribed by Kant in the continuation of the above-quoted passage: "Conversely, not all activities are called *practice*, but only those realisations of a particular purpose which are considered to comply with certain generally conceived principles of procedure" (*ibid*).

[72] *See* Jörg Kammerhofer, "The Interaction of Doctrine and Theory in (International) Legal Scholarship," in Pauline Westerman, Kostiantyn Gorobets and Andreas Hadjigeorgiou (eds.), *Conceptual (De)Constructions of International Law* (Cheltenham: Edward Elgar, 2022), at p. 9, available online at SSRN: https://ssrn.com/abstract=3777918, last visited May 3, 2021, at p. 1 ("Legal theory is the key to understanding what it means to engage in legal scholarship. It partakes both of the realm of philosophy and of law and links them as well as the human activities, discourses and jargons centred around them").

Figure 1.2 Georg Jellinek[73]

lawyer Georg Jellinek (1851–1911) (Figure 1.2), who constructed the concept of *Selbstverpflichtungslehre* (self-limitation) to explain how international law binds sovereigns. In Jellinek's view, the starting point was simple: state responsibility *must exist* – even if inconsistently in practice – for international law to exist at all.

The fact that the theory of international law was more unified or complete than diplomatic practice would allow was easily explained. Compared to civilized domestic societies, the international community of nations was in an earlier stage of legal development. To the philosophers, the inadequacies of international practice was a temporary problem that should not hinder the formulation of a robust theory of state responsibility. As a younger legal system, international law would require more time to produce more sophisticated bodies of norms as found in

[73] Photo courtesy: Wikimedia commons, available online at https://commons.wikimedia.org/wiki/File:Georg_Jellinek_%28HeidICON_28827%29_%28cropped%29.jpg, last visited May 24, 2023.

domestic societies. In the meantime, when legitimating their systems, theorists rely on authoritative legal sources rather than provisional political acts. As such, domestic laws and international treaties will be more valuable than *ad hoc* arbitrations. This view of international law is often associated with the German-speaking approach to public law.[74]

Publicists

From the perspective of this third group of lawyers, state responsibility is constitutive of international law. From their experience with constitutional law, it is the role to help explain the capriciousness of state practice.[75] Paradigmatic of this group is Roberto Ago (1907–95) (Figure 1.3), the Italian jurist who led the ILC's successful codification of state responsibility in the 1960s (until he was appointed to the bench of the World Court). Doctrinalists employ doctrine to describe legal rules in a predictable and coherent form – despite the vicissitudes of practice. To them, *the overarching ideal is the rule of law.* According to Ago,

> there is not a single judgment of the Permanent Court of International Justice or of the International Court of Justice, nor of a single international arbitral award, that explicitly or implicitly recognizes the existence of international obligations the breach of which would not be a wrongful act and would not entail international responsibility.[76]

This approach to international law is often associated with international lawyers operating within the League of Nations and later the United Nations.[77] Like theorists, they share an optimistic faith in history, one that will lead to a more full and consistent judicial practice. Thus,

74 *See* Martti Koskenniemi, "Between Coordination and Constitution: International Law as a German Discipline," 15 *Redescriptions. Yearbook of Political Thought, Conceptual History and Feminist Theory* 45–70 (2011).

75 Perhaps another way to label this group is as the "Global Administrative Lawyers." In this study, I use the term "doctrine" in the manner Judge Harry T. Edwards suggests in "The Growing Disjunction between Legal Education and the Legal Profession," 91 *Michigan Law Review* 34 (1992), at p. 43: "the various sources of law (precedents, statutes, constitutions) that constrain or otherwise guide the practitioner, decisionmaker, and policymaker."

76 Roberto Ago, "Fifth Report on State Responsibility," *Yearbook of the International Law Commission*, Vol. II, (1976), Part One at para. 74, p. 25.

77 See Bardo Fassbender, "The United Nations Charter as Constitution of the International Community," 36(3) *Columbia Journal of Transnational Law* 529 (1998); *see generally* Moshe Hirsch, *Invitation to the Sociology of International Law* (Oxford: Oxford University Press, 2016).

Figure 1.3 Roberto Ago[78]
Roberto Ago, 5th President of the Italian Republic, 1965

when appointed to global bodies such as the ILC, they see their roles as progressive developers of international law. To them, once practitioners are set on the correct course of international law (as articulated in doctrine), the system will settle into a sophisticated structure that resembles its domestic counterpart.

Merchants of Legalism and Purveyors of Legitimacy

Viewing the history of state responsibility through these three lenses helps situate its multi-branched development within specific social and political contexts. These include reunification in the US after the Civil War of 1861–1865; unification in Germany following the Franco-Prussian War of 1870–1871; and the establishment of world bodies in the wake of two catastrophic world wars in 1914–1918 and 1939–1945. These lawyers wielded principles of law and philosophy to solve diplomatic disputes in Latin America, to understand the rapid growth of a federating empire

[78] Photo courtesy: https://en.wikipedia.org/wiki/Roberto_Ago.

and to design a system of international law enforcement that could appeal to a postcolonial audience.

While each of these models represents a different observational standpoint, what is common to all of them is a struggle to justify their expansive view of international law.[79] Yale legal historian Robert Gordon describes late-nineteenth century lawyers as purveyors of legitimacy on behalf of their clients:

> The law ... is an artificial utopia of social harmony ... The lawyer's job, thus, is to mediate between the universal vision of legal order and the concrete desires of his clients, to show how what the client wants can be accommodated to the utopian scheme.
>
> The lawyer, thus, has to find ways of squeezing the client's plan of action into the legally recognized categories of approved conduct. Of course, the law's view of the client's reality is often a highly distorted one, since its categorizing forms are administratively manageable only if they drastically abstract and simplify for that reality, and legitimate only if they seem to be part of the system of universal normative order. Even so, *the lawyer's job is selling legitimacy*: reassurance to the client and its potential regulators, investors, or business partners that what it wants to do is basically all right ...[80]

There is a theme of norm entrepreneurship in these stories. State responsibility emerged through the creative efforts of professional lawyers.[81] In

[79] For a recent articulation of this struggle for binding international standards, described in the literature as a "battle for international law," *see* Jochen von Bernstorff and Philipp Dann (eds.), *The Battle for International Law: South–North Perspectives on the Decolonization Era* (Oxford: Oxford University Press, 2019).

[80] Robert W. Gordon, "'The Ideal and the Actual in the Law': Fantasies and Practice of New York City Lawyers,1870–1910," in Gerard W. Gawalt (ed.), *The New High Priests: Lawyers in Post-Civil War America*, 53 (Westport, CT: Greenwood Press, 1984), at pp. 53–54 (emphasis added). Katja Creutz explores difference standards for assessing the legitimacy of state responsibility (Katja Creutz, *State Responsibility in the International Legal Order: A Critical Appraisal* (Cambridge: Cambridge University Press, 2020), at pp. 43–52).

[81] Attorneys are a professional group that has historically worked magic through the abstraction of rules. As Dezalay and Garth argue, they often draw "from what could be termed the rule of business and especially from the rule of lawyers who serve business interests" (Yves Dezalay and Bryant G. Garth, *Dealing in Virtue International Commercial Arbitration and the Construction of a Transnational Legal Order* (Chicago: University of Chicago Press, 1996), at p. 3). On the role of "norm entrepreneurs" in norm creation, *see* Cass R. Sunstein, "Social Norms and Social Roles," 96 *Columbia Law Review* 903 (1996), at p. 909. *See also* Richard Abel, "Speaking Law to Power: Occasions for Cause Lawyering," in Austin Sarat and Stuart Scheingold (eds.), *Cause Lawyering: Political Commitments and Professional Responsibilities* (Oxford: Oxford University Press, 1998).

the US, lawyer-diplomats used state responsibility as a loose framework of remedies borrowed from domestic law that could be imposed on states for alien injuries; states, *as states*, were liable for damages when they failed to provide international standards of protection to aliens in their territory. Latin American lawyer-diplomats, also, viewed state responsibility as a characteristic of statehood; but the US model of the field was an acceptable double-standard of protection in their eyes.

This international standard of care seemed to apply more frequently to new states than it did to established ones. To Latin Americans, the appropriate form of state responsibility would have to be more general than one field of law and it would have to apply equally to the North and South. Hence their affinity for German theory. German public lawyers contemplated state responsibility similarly to the Latin Americans – as a unified, overarching theory of public law, one that could be used both as a tool for civilizing their expanding colonial governments, and a standard for measuring the liability of all states.

These norm entrepreneurs did not describe their projects as legislative in nature. This would have been an impractical position to take, and they were professional attorneys after all. US lawyer-diplomats described their government's allegations of state responsibility for alien injuries as consistent with existing legal doctrine and based on general principles of law.[82] German philosophers articulated their expectations of public responsibility in terms of a valid system of public law; and even though such a system did not yet exist, they would invent one to address the

Martti Koskenniemi sketches four standard roles for international lawyers: the judge, the adviser, the activist and the academic in "Between Commitment and Cynicism: Outline of a Theory of International Law as Practice," in *Collection of Essays by Legal Advisors of States, Legal Advisors of International Organizations and Practitioners in the Field of International Law* 495 (New York: United Nations, 1999). On interpretative entrepreneurship, *see* Melissa (MJ) Durkee, "Interpretive Entrepreneurs," 107 *Virginia Law Review* (2021), available online at https://ssrn.com/abstract=3782643, last visited May 3, 2021, at p. 1 ("Private actors use interpretation to influence legal rules. Interpretive entrepreneurship is particularly significant in the international context, where many disputes are not subject to judicial resolution, and there is no official system of precedent."). For David Schneiderman's description of norm entrepreneurs in this context, *see* his *Investment Law's Alibis: Colonialism, Imperialism, Debt and Development* (Cambridge: Cambridge University Press, 2022), at p. 1 (lawyers, arbitrators and scholars promoted and participated in the spread of international investment law).

82 *See* Martti Koskenniemi, *To the Uttermost Parts of the Earth: Legal Imagination and International Power, 1300–1870* (Cambridge: Cambridge University Press, 2021) at p. 9 (how lawyers adapted and reused existing domestic legal terminologies and applied them at the international level, referring to the phenomenon as *lawyers building vocabularies*).

needs of modern society. International lawyers within world bodies sought to draw up a code that was a hybrid of the above two models: it was purportedly based on the actual practice of states as well as conceptualized using existing theories of public law. It is important to emphasize that all three groups overlapped in varying degrees, especially the doctrinalists.[83] This account of their efforts is not my attempt to provide a neat history of state responsibility.[84] The best I can hope for is to offer a contextual account of its origins while avoiding oversimplifying what is one of the most intricate fields of international law.

In the next and final section of this introduction, I preview the six chapters that comprise this book. For the reader's convenience, I provide summaries at the end of each substantive chapter. Further, I wrote Chapter 6 as an "epilogue" to state responsibility's history that both summarizes the first five chapters and conceptualizes some lasting legacies.

Road Map

Chapter 1 – In the introductory chapter, I introduce the norm of international responsibility and describe it as an exceptional doctrine that is easy to oversimplify. I presented my thesis on the recent origins of state responsibility, which was "born" sometime between 1870 and 1930 to American and German parents. I discussed the problems with state responsibility that are unique to international law – at the same time, it could seem like everything and nothing at all. Lawyers have coped with this in very different ways. This book is structured to reflect three such perspectives: (1) International practitioners in the US, (2) Philosophers based in German-speaking countries and (3) Publicists within international institutions. I set out to trace the pre-institutional origins of state responsibility and connect these narratives to existing doctrines. This expanded historical framework highlights the non-unified doctrine of state responsibility as well as the political contexts from which they emerged.

[83] For example, many ILC commissioners (including Roberto Ago) were not just institutional codifiers (doctrinalists); they were also governmental lawyers (practitioners) and law school professors (philosophers).

[84] As Cass Sunstein writes, causal claims of this kind "inevitably involve counterfactual history" (though, he continues, "there is nothing dishonorable about that fact") – *see* Cass R. Sunstein, "Historical Explanations Always Involve Counterfactual History," 10(3) *Journal of the Philosophy of History* 433 (2016), at p. 436.

Chapters 2 and **3** – In the first narrative, I describe state responsibility as the enforcement of the age-old rules regarding hospitality to strangers that have come to really mean *investment protection*. In the New World, international arbitrators employed the word "responsibility" in the many different settings of diplomatic protection claims: European-Latin American,[85] Anglo-American[86] and intra-American.[87] However, "responsibility" did not refer to a singular legal idea at the time. It was a word that connoted many legal and moral ideas about state rights vis-à-vis alien injuries. I identify the first modern usages of responsibility – that is, the legalistic consequences of a state's breaching its international obligations – in the diplomatic practice of the US Government following the Civil War.[88]

At that time, US nationals flooded the State Department with claims for diplomatic protection. To resolve international claims efficiently with scant political or human resources, the State Department began delegating the resolution of these disputes to professional international arbitrators. In so doing, US lawyers firmly established international arbitration as the forum for resolving alien injuries. The US staffed these tribunals with likeminded lawyers who would base their awards on international, rather than local, standards of protection. This manner of litigating alien protection claims generated a body of positive law on state responsibility for alien injuries.[89] US lawyers did not set out to create a doctrine of state

[85] *Cotesworth & Powell* (Great Britain v. Colombia), John Bassett Moore, *History and Digest of the International Arbitrations to which the United States has been a Party, Together with Appendices Containing the Treaties relating to such Arbitrations, and Historical Legal Notes* (Washington, DC: Government Printing Office, 1898) (hereinafter *History and Digest*), at p. 2081.

[86] *The Alabama Claims (United States of America v. Great Britain)*, Moore, *History and Digest*, at pp. 655, 656.

[87] *Tomas Marin v. The United States*, No. 751 of the Lieber Tribunal (United States v. Mexico), Moore, *supra* note 85, at pp. 2889–2891.

[88] I discuss the concept of "legalism" further in Chapters 2 and 3. I prefer the term "legalistic" to the term "modern" in reference to the law of state responsibility. However, I could use the term "modern" in the sense that Professor Michael Levenson uses it (*see generally*, Michael Levenson, *Modernism* (New Haven: Yale University Press, 2011)). To slightly paraphrase Levenson, religion in the past and politics in the present have failed to become "a sphere of conviction and a site of shared value" (Michael Levenson, "Why We're Still Struggling to Make Sense of Modernism," *The Atlantic* (October 2013), at p. 39).

[89] Not just for the protection of property claims *stricto sensu* but for a broad range of property rights including contract, personal injury, etc. *See further* Jean Ho, *State Responsibility for Breaches of Investment Contracts* (Cambridge: Cambridge University Press, 2018), at p. 3.

responsibility, but to use international law *as a tool for securing better than local protection* of property in the New World. But the unavoidable result was a set of precedents that would ultimately become applicable to the US as well. By internationalizing alien protection claims, the US unwittingly positioned itself to be judged in the same manner. Such is the power of law.

Chapter 4 – In the second narrative, I describe state responsibility as a theory for holding states accountable for their actions. In nineteenth-century Germany, academic lawyers applied a "juristic method" to construct theories of public law to account for expanded governmental powers that resulted from political unification. German legal scholar August Wilhelm Heffter (1796–1880) is often cited as the first to articulate principles of state liability, but it was Georg Jellinek (1851–1911) who offered its first theoretical basis, *Selbstverpflichtungslehre.* German public lawyers did not base their theories on international awards from the New World. To them, international arbitration did not produce law in the technical sense. They viewed liability under international law primarily as an iteration of state liability under *domestic* public law. In this way, fledgling international practice did not prevent them from articulating comprehensive theories extrapolated from their domestic legal experience. In the end, the German theorization of state responsibility had a far greater impact upon lawyers within international institutions (*e.g.*, ILC) than it did within Germany (*e.g.*, *Auswärtiges Amt*).

Chapter 5 – In the third narrative, I explain how and why the United Nations first sought to codify state responsibility based on the US practice and later, on German theory. This decision was neither simple nor obvious. The world body had two choices: interpret state responsibility narrowly as alien protection, or broadly as a general code of international enforcement. On one level, the codification question was structural: should world bodies codify a fragmented law of state responsibility (akin to the domestic analogy) or a unified law of state responsibility (unique to international law)? On another level, the legislative question was one of scope: should it be limited to past practice, or should it provide a doctrine that addresses longer-term institutional needs? Finally, the issue was a political one as well that pitted two groups of litigants – North and South Americans – against each other within world legislative bodies. Going into the 1930 Hague Codification Conference, US diplomats were optimistic about limiting the codification of state responsibility to alien protection. However, they sobered up soon thereafter. By 1960, it was clear that any endeavor to base the UN's work on the US practice amounted to codification suicide.

By that time, five attempts to codify state responsibility as alien protection had already failed. This is because Latin American lawyers had finally accumulated sufficient voting power within international institutions to oppose US efforts to entrench an imperialistic practice. A turning point came in the early 1960s under the stewardship of Special Rapporteur Roberto Ago, who untethered the UN's codification from past practice and set out to draft a general code of international enforcement. In contrast to German theory, however, Ago drafted the code to allow for specific regimes of practice to remain as exceptions to its rule. In this way, both North and South America could claim victory. The US could maintain its arbitral practice of alien protection while Latin America secured a general code of international enforcement that applied, technically speaking, to the North and South equally. As such, the ILC doctrine of state responsibility is both a rejection as well as a validation of the US practice of alien protection.

Chapter 6 – In this final chapter, I take a step back to offer a few generalizations about state responsibility and its historic role of selling legitimacy. I reconceptualize the growth of state responsibility in terms of three overlapping phases: (1) pre-legalism, (2) *ad hoc* legalism and (3) institutional legalism.[90] The continuously fertile field of alien protection has survived beyond the ILC's codification. There remains a duality of doctrines of state responsibility, one specific and one general. While these doctrines are, of course, very different in scope and content, I identify several motifs that are present across the spectrum of state responsibility doctrines. *One idea that runs through all three narratives of this history is the consequentiality of breaking international law.* A second theme is the habitual reliance on legalism as the appropriate process for resolving international claims. Another motif is the exceptional nature of state responsibility; it is a doctrine in which the exceptions are more applicable than its rules. While, as a doctrine of international law enforcement, it

[90] Interestingly, the structure of this historic and normative development seems to conform with Max Weber's analysis that new legal norms have two primary sources: the standardization of certain consensual understandings and judicial precedent – Max Weber, *Economy and Society: An Outline of Interpretive Sociology* [1921] (Guenther Roth and Claus Wittich (eds.), Ephraim Fischoff, et. al., trans. Berkeley and Los Angeles: University of California Press, 1968, reprinted 2012), Vol. II, at p. 759.

does not predict state behavior well, it remains a crucial symbol about the relevance of international law to world affairs. The codification of state responsibility as secondary rules has provided international society with an argumentative tradition for questioning and judging any type of state conduct. We begin in the US, where lawyer-diplomats in the White House turned to law as a tool of diplomatic power.

2

The US Turn to the Technique of International Arbitration

1869: Fish Enters the White House

After losing his reelection bid for the US Senate in 1856, Hamilton Fish (Figure 2.1) decided to retire from political life. He had been elected as Lieutenant Governor and then Governor of the State of New York. He had also represented New York in both the House and the Senate. Despite his comparative youth – still only forty-eight – Fish was politically depleted; he longed to return home to his family and his legal practice in Manhattan. Fish was an excellent attorney, but an ineffective politician. He never managed to win reelection to political office. This is not to say that Fish was to leave the world of politics. Given his deep Federalist roots, Fish's social and vocational life all but mandated public service.[1] In addition to providing legal services to the political Brahmins of New York and Washington, DC, Fish would become the President General of the Society of the Cincinnati, President of the New York Historical Society, President of the Union League Club, trustee of what was to become the New York Public Library and Chairman of the Board of Trustees of Columbia University. Fish simply could not walk away from politics since his life was a fundamentally political one.

So, it was no great surprise when Ulysses S. Grant, inaugurated as the eighteenth US President on March 4, 1869, sent him a letter later that month, requesting that Fish become his Secretary of State. It did not take long for Fish to politely decline the offer. In his mind, he was through with Washington.

The surprise came the next day, when Fish received a letter informing him that the new Administration was in a vulnerable position and that

[1] His father was Colonel Nicholas Fish, a comrade of Lafayette. He was named after his father's good friend, Alexander Hamilton, the first US Secretary of the Treasury. *See* Allan Nevins, *Hamilton Fish: The Inner History of the Grant Administration* (New York: Dodd, Mead & Co., 1936), at p. 12.

Figure 2.1 Hamilton Fish[2]

Grant desperately needed Fish to[2] accept the offer. The President had already bungled his first pick, Elihu B. Washburne (1816–87), who resigned after eleven days in office. Further, without consulting him, President Grant had already passed Fish's "acceptance" on to Congress for confirmation. If Fish refused the position, the Grant Administration would be humiliated before he began office. For Fish, the choice between personal inconvenience and national misfortune was no real choice at all. His dutiful nature overcame his reluctance to re-enter public life. Within a mere seventy-two hours of Grant's first note, Fish was sitting at his desk on the second floor at the southwest corner of the State Department, then housed in the Washington City Orphan Asylum building.[3] It was without political ambitions that Fish began the final and most influential stage of his public life. The appointment of Fish to Grant's cabinet proved to be a monumental turning point in US diplomatic history. Fish's eight years in office laid much of the groundwork for what we now know and recognize as international arbitration.

2 Photo courtesy of Getty images, www.gettyimages.com/detail/news-photo/hamilton-fish-united-states-senator-and-secretary-of-state-news-photo/102321725?adppopup=true.

3 Fittingly, Fish moved into a building designed by Charles Bulfinch, the first native-born American to practice architecture as a profession. *See* Edward Digby Baltzell, *Puritan Boston & Quaker Philadelphia* (New Brunswick: Transaction Publishers, 1996), at pp. 322–324.

As Secretary of State, Fish reshaped his department into a professional diplomatic service provider to the White House. He also resolved the famous *Alabama Claims* dispute with Great Britain[4] and began the process of displacing Great Britain as the dominant power in Latin America. A potent tool that Fish relied on to accomplish these goals was international law. Fish used arbitration to settle the *Alabama Claims* ("Alabama Tribunal"), an event that remains a focal point for international law historians.[5] Much less appreciated is Fish's use of arbitration in the Latin American context, where he replaced a haphazard diplomatic process of alien protection with a reliable, professional one. By accustoming States to arbitration, Fish secured better-than-local protection for US nationals abroad. Also, by inserting the technique of arbitration into the process of diplomatic protection, Fish and his successors all but prohibited European powers from engaging in reprisals to redress injuries to their nationals in Latin America. This maneuver diluted the potency of the Royal Navy in the New World and helped the US take its place as regional hegemon (né, protector).

This newfound power was clearly evident by the turn of the twentieth century. It was not a diplomatic aberration when, in 1902, US President Theodore Roosevelt prevented a British intervention in Venezuela by requiring the two states to delegate the resolution of their diplomatic spat to a panel of professional lawyers. The dispute, which concerned injuries to British nationals arising out of the Venezuelan Civil War, was the second case in the docket of the newly established Permanent Court of Arbitration (PCA).[6] This chapter describes how the US, under Secretary Fish, normalized and professionalized the process of international arbitration during its postbellum era.[7]

[4] The *Alabama Claims* (United States of America v. Great Britain) (1872) in John Bassett Moore (ed.), *History and Digest of the International Arbitrations to Which the United States Has Been a Party*, Vol. I (Washington, DC: Government Printing Office, 1898) (hereinafter, *History and Digest*), ch. XIV, at p. 495.

[5] *See infra* note 256 and accompanying text.

[6] Preferential Treatment of Claims of Blockading Powers against Venezuela (Germany, Great Britain and Italy v. Venezuela) constituted in virtue of the Protocols signed at Washington on May 7, 1903 (Arbitrators: N. Mourawieff and H. Lammasch Martens). Tellingly, the PCA's first case involved the US and Mexico, as I will discuss further below.

[7] On the formation of the US practice into an international legal custom, *see* Frank Griffith Dawson and Ivan L. Head, *International Law, National Tribunals, and the Rights of Aliens* (Syracuse: Syracuse University Press, 1971), at p. 9. My argument is not that the US was the only frequent user – but the US *professionalized* a preexisting practice – of international arbitration. On one count, the most frequent users between 1794 and 1900 were Great Britain (70 instances) and the US (56 instances), following by Chile and France (26 instances

A New Variation on an Ancient Theme

The US narrative beings with the US–Mexico Mixed Claims Commission of 1868 (the "Lieber Tribunal").[8] In selecting his friend Francis Lieber (1798–1872) to head the commission, Fish appointed the first professional international lawyer to umpire an international arbitration.[9] The intra-American narrative of arbitration ends with the Spanish American War of 1898, by which time the US reliance on international law in Latin America was eclipsed by its willingness to use force to further its interests.[10] In the same year that the US forcibly conquered Cuba, Tsar Nicholas II circulated a letter inviting other nations to form the Permanent Court of Arbitration. The turn to the technique of arbitration expanded beyond the New World. A new practice had been consecrated, one that differed in many critical respects from the old usage.[11]

International arbitration has existed for millennia, as chronicled in Greek mythology, Mesopotamian history,[12] the Bible,[13] the

apiece) – Henri La Fontaine, *Pasicrisie Internationale: Histoire Documentaire des Arbitrages Internationaux (1794–1900)* (Berne: Imprimerie Stampelli & CIE, 1902), at p. ix.

[8] Convention between the United States of America and United States of Mexico, signed in Washington, DC on July 4, 1868, 15 Stat. 679.

[9] The Commissioners of the US–Ecuadorian Mixed Claims Commission of November 25, 1862 first selected Andres Bello, the Chilean international lawyer to umpire the commission, but Bello turned it down. Dr Alcides Destruge was ultimately selected as umpire. The first *ad hoc* arbitral tribunal umpired by a professional attorney was the *Hudson's Bay and Puget's Sound Agricultural Companies* (US and Great Britain) of July 1, 1863. The umpire was Benjamin Robbins Curtis (the first Associate Justice of the US Supreme Court with a formal law degree, from Harvard), who issued reasoned awards. Caleb Cushing served as counsel for the US (on Cushing, *see infra* 192 and accompanying text).

[10] In diplomatic historical terms, this era is generally seen as being bookended by the end of the Civil War in 1865 to the beginning of the Spanish-American War of 1898. The period also coincides with a break in US territorial expansionism: between the annexations of Alaska and Hawaii. *See* Milton Pelsur, *America's Outward Thrust: Approaches to Foreign Affairs, 1865–1890* (DeKalb: Northern Illinois University Press, 1971), at pp. 7–10; Charles De Benedetti, "Peace History, in the American Manner," 18(1) *The History Teacher* 75–110 (1984), at p. 94, Marshall C. Eakin, *The History of Latin America: Collision of Cultures* (New York: Palgrave, 2007), at p. 245.

[11] As James Crawford has written, "there already existed a fully modern conception of arbitration at the beginning of the 20th century" (James Crawford, "Continuity and Discontinuity in International Dispute Settlement," 1(1) *Journal of International Dispute Settlement* 3 (2010), at p. 12).

[12] Hittites used it for boundary disputes among its cities. See L. W. King and Harry Reginald Hall, *Egypt and Western Asia: In Light of Recent Discoveries* (London: Society for Promoting Christian Knowledge, 1907) at p. 171.

[13] See 1 Kings 3:16–28; 1 Corinthians 6:1–8. *See further* K. J. Tromp, *Aliens and Strangers in the Old Testament in Vox Reformata* 4 (2011), at pp. 17–18 (the resident alien, based on a

Quran,[14] *etc.*[15] However, the content and form of arbitration was categorically different from the practice as we know it today. It was not only unlegalistic, as will be discussed; it was also infrequently employed. Premodern disputes were usually resolved without third parties as they were self-judged.[16] What changed in the nineteenth century was the professionalized procedure of third-party attorneys, which produced the body of law and doctrine that became known as "state responsibility."

Ancient societies employed forms of arbitration in their inter-city relations, as did the Holy Roman Empire and other nations.[17] The

variety of passages, is supposed to be incorporated into the house of Israel – this is largely based on the Israelites' identity being shaped by their history of transient existence and God's concern for the alien as shown through the laws).

14 See, e.g., 4:105; 5:42.

15 For an overview of the history of international arbitration *see* Gary B. Born, *International Arbitration: Cases and Materials* (New York: Aspen, 2010), ch. 1. For the classical histories, in English, *see* John Bassett Moore, *International Adjudications, Ancient and Modern* (Oxford: Oxford University Press, 1937) and Robert Clark Morris, *International Arbitration and Procedure* (New Haven: Yale University Press, 1911), chs 1–2; in French, Alftandre Giraud and J. A. Merignac, *Traité théorique et pratique de l'arbitrage international* (Paris: Larose, 1895); in German, Heinrich Lammasch, *Die lehre von der schiedsgerichtsbarkeit in ihrem ganzen umfange* (Stuttgart: W. Kohlhammer, 1914). In the words of Westlake, "There has never been a time in history when they [third-party dispute resolution mechanisms] were unknown, and they had often been the instruments of maintaining peace" (John Westlake, "International Arbitration," *International Journal of Ethics* (October 1896), reprinted in Appendix of Lassa Oppenheim, *International Law, Vol I (Peace)*, 1st ed. (London: Longmans, Green and Co., 1905), at p. 333). See, in the Bible, for example, 1 Kings 3:16, Job 9:33. See also Louise E. Matthaei, "The Place of Arbitration and Mediation in Ancient Systems of International Ethics," 2(4) *The Classical Quarterly* 241–264 (October 1908), at p. 241; Charles H. Brower, II, "The Functions and Limits of Arbitration and Judicial Settlement under Private and Public International Law," 18(2) *Duke Journal of Comparative & International Law* 259–309 (2008), at p. 270; Steven C. Bennett, *Arbitration: Essential Concepts* (New York: ALM Publishing, 2002), at p. 9.

16 This problem, known as "auto-interpretation," has been a key obstacle to the development of international legal responsibility – *see* Leo Gross, "States as Organs of International Law, and the Problem of Auto-Interpretation, in Law and Politics in the World Community," in G. A. Lipsky (ed.), *Law and Politics in the World Community* (Berkeley: University of California Press, 1953), at p. 59; James Leslie Brierly, "The Basis of Obligation in International Law, and Other Papers," in Hersch Lauterpacht and C. H. M. Waldock (eds.), *The Basis of Obligation in International Law and other Papers by the late James Leslie Brierly* (Oxford: Oxford University Press, 1958), at p. 230. The political theory of "just war," while relevant to the problem of premodern dispute resolution and auto-interpretation, is outside the scope of this book.

17 There were at least eighty-one arbitrations between Greek towns – *see* Jackson H. Ralston, *International Arbitrations from Athens to Locarno* (Stanford: Stanford University Press,

Greeks assumed its existence even among disputing gods.[18] By one count, the ancient Greeks used international mediation and arbitration seven hundred times.[19] Thucydides (circa 460 BCE – 395 BCE) praised arbitration in his *History of the Peloponnesian War*, and praises the words of the King of Sparta, who said, "It is impossible to attack as a transgressor him who offers to lay his grievance before a tribunal of arbitration."[20] Ancient Sumerians, Persians and Egyptians also had a tradition of arbitration.[21] These ancient societies practiced arbitration mainly among themselves (*e.g.*, as between Greek city-states) since they regarded aliens as lawless, as barbarians.[22] On those rare occasions when international arbitration *was* practiced in the ancient world, it was based on Delphic or other divine sources and not on adjudication.[23]

1929), at p. 154. Since the Greeks only used arbitration amongst themselves, according to Lassa Oppenheim: "The Jewish ideal of perpetual peace and the union of all mankind under One God, foreseen in prophetic vision by Isaiah (ii. 2-4), may be taken as the first formulation of pacificist doctrine, which of course implies a community of law between all states, but the prophet does not apprehend this community of law as an independent idea" (*The Future of International Law* (Oxford: Clarendon Press, 1921) at pp. 1–2).

18 Ralston, *supra* note 17, at p. 153. Compared to the Greeks, however, arbitration declined with the Romans. See Henry Salmon Fraser, "A Sketch of the History of International Arbitration," 11 *Cornell Law Quarterly* 179 (1925–26), at p. 190.

19 Kaja Harter-Uibopuu, "Anthropological and Historical Foundations: Ancient Greek Approaches toward Alternative Dispute Resolution," 10 *Willamette Journal of International Law and Dispute Resolution* 47 (2002), at p. 67.

20 *See* John Bassett Moore, "International Arbitration: Historical Notes and Projects," in *The American Conference on International Arbitration, Washington, April 22 and 23, 1896* (New York: The Baker & Taylor Company, 1896) reprinted in *The Collected Papers of John Bassett Moore*, II 27–83 (New Haven: Yale University Press, 1944), at pp. 28–29. *See also* Alexandre Mérignhac, *Traité théorique et pratique de l'arbitrage international* (Paris: Larose, 1895); Ralston, *supra* note 17, at p. 158.

21 See Will Durant, *The Story of Civilization: Our Common Heritage* (New York: Simon and Schuster, 1935), at pp. 127, 361; Catherine A. Rogers, "Fit and Function in Legal Ethics: Developing a Code of Conduct for International Arbitration," 23 *Michigan Journal of International Law* 341 (2002), at p. 348 note 27.

22 According to the historian Stephen Neff, "There would appear to be no record of a Greek *polis* ever concluding a treaty with a barbarian State" (Stephen C. Neff, *Justice among Nations: A History of International Law* (Cambridge, MA: Harvard University Press, 2014), at p. 35). *See also* Moore, *supra* note 20, at p. 28.

23 Marcus Niebuhr Tod, *International Arbitration amongst the Greeks* (Oxford: Clarendon Press, 1913), at p. 95; *See* Moore, *supra* note 20, at p. 27: "In ancient times, when war constituted the normal state of peoples and the foreigner was everywhere treated as an enemy, arbitrations were necessarily rare, and we do not find either a general system or harmonious rules governing the subject."

International arbitration became less uncommon in the Middle Ages.[24] Inadequate domestic protection of foreign commerce was a major impetus for increased arbitration.[25] Roman Pontiffs were appointed (and sometimes even self-appointed) as arbitrators. By virtue of their divinely accorded positions, Christian religious leaders were broadly recognized as delegates of God and, thus, authorized to issue binding resolutions for international disputes. Innocent III (circa 1160–1216), for example, declared that the Pope was "the sovereign mediator on earth."[26] Kingdoms turned to religious leaders to arbitrate their claims based on their perceived "divine mandate" – as opposed to a specific expertise in international arbitration. Consequently, pontifical awards were not always binding upon subsequent Popes. For example, in 1481, Pope Sixtus IV (1414–1484), as arbitrator, legitimated Portugal's territorial claims south of the Canary Islands;[27] and in 1493, Pope Alexander VI (1431–1503) decreed that those lands west and south of the Cape Verde Islands belonged to Spain.[28]

Though some papal bulls were binding forms of third-party dispute resolutions, recourse to them was a religious ritual, based more on religious than civil legal principles. Though not infrequently employed by European powers,[29] this *ad hominem* approach to international arbitrations was unstable. In the Spanish–Portuguese example above, the parties ultimately negotiated a separate convention (the Treaty of

[24] According to Mérignhac, there were at least one hundred arbitrations in thirteenth-century Italy between princes and communes of that country. Mérignhac, *supra* note 20 at p. 38. *See also* J. Verzijl, *International Law in Historical Perspective*, Vol. 8 (Leiden: A. W. Sijthoff, 1974), at pp. 189–190; Born, *supra* note 15, at p. 14. On the early history of the legal profession within the Church, *see* Thomas J. McSweeney, *Priests of the Law: Roman Law and the Making of the Common Law's First Professionals* (Oxford: Oxford University Press, 2020).

[25] Born, *supra* note 15, at p. 12.

[26] Moore, *supra* note 20, at p. 32.

[27] The papal bull *Aeterni regis* was issued June 21, 1481.

[28] The papal bull *Inter caetera* was issued May 4, 1493. Later that year, on September 25, 1493, another bull, *Dudem siquidem*, was issued, granting the mainlands and islands then belonging to India to Spain.

[29] Indeed, papal arbitration had a palpable impact on the form of modern arbitration. See Ralston, *supra* note 17, at p. 174; Moore, *supra* note 20, at p. 37: "Let us finally add that in arbitrations anterior to the seventeenth century, it is difficult, sometimes impossible, clearly to separate cases of mediation from those of arbitration, either because the terminology was not very definite or the expressions used were equivocal, or because the distinction was not clear to the minds of the negotiators."

Tordesillas) in 1494 to resolve the contradiction created by the bulls.[30] The extent to which pontifical awards were enforceable often depended upon the fear inspired by that Pope (or his force of arms).[31] Further, because the medieval practice of papal arbitration was religious,[32] it is difficult to draw the line between arbitration and other, non-binding, dispute resolutions such as mediation during the Middle Ages.[33] Hugo Grotius (1583–1645) and other the early international lawyers adapted the Law of Nature in large part to fill the vacuum created by the extinction of supreme religious authorities.[34] Papal arbitration, while not modern, did have a lasting influence on international law. For example, it was during this era that the enforceability of arbitration awards became increasingly recognized.[35]

If the late nineteenth-century Americas represents the high point of international arbitration, the preceding period – that of the *ancien régime* – was its low point.[36] This era of the formation of states in Europe consisted of many aspirational but few actual arbitral arrangements. For example, the conception of French King Henri IV "le Grand" (1553–1610) of a grand Christian Republic of fifteen states[37] and his

30 Signed on June 7, 1494 (which was confirmed by Pope Julius II in his bull *Ea quae* of January 24, 1506).

31 Premodern international awards also imposed liability upon States; however, this was done primarily by being based on the authority of the international tribunal – usually a respected religious figure – rather than on general legal authority. Like its Greek predecessor, pontifical forms of arbitration were often more of a fetial procedure than one based on the Law of Nations – *see* David J. Bederman, "The Foundations of Law: World Law Transcendent," 54 *Emory Law Journal* 53 (2005), at pp. 61–62; Moore, *supra* note 20, at p. 37; Ralston, *supra* note 17, at pp. 175, 187 and 188 (a typical sanction provided by treaty for the violation of an arbitration was excommunication).

32 On medieval monk arbitration, see Amelia J. Uelmen, "A View of the Legal Profession from a Mid-Twelfth-Century Monastery," 71 *Fordham Law Review* 1517 (2003), at p. 1540.

33 Born, *supra* note 15, at p. 4.

34 Discussed further in Chapter 4.

35 *See* Born, *supra* note15, at p. 12 ("This result was generally based on the principle of *pacta sunt servanda* … developed and applied by canonical jurists…" (internal citations omitted).

36 C. G. Roelofsen, "The Jay Treaty and All That': Some Remarks on the Role of Arbitration in European Modern History and its 'Revival' in 1794," in Alfred H. A. Soons (ed.) *International Arbitration: Past and Prospects* 201–210 (1990), at p. 201.

37 Maximilien de Béthune duc de Sully, *Grand Design of Henry IV* (reprinted, London: Sweet & Maxwell, 1921).

scheme of international arbitration, were deemed by contemporaries as too remote from daily realities.[38] Bentham, Kant, Penn, Rousseau and other eighteenth-century European thinkers put forth similar elaborate plans.[39] Such idealism, while ineffective in the near-term, did have an impact on the education of US lawyers and, consequentially, on modern arbitration.[40]

Typical of Latin American arbitration with Western States prior to 1868 was the French intervention in Buenos Aires (1838). For two years, France forcefully intervened in the province of Buenos Aires to ensure that French nationals were treated with the same protections as British nationals, who, for example, were not forcibly conscripted. A series of tit-for-tat reactions ensued.[41] In the end, the two countries signed an arbitration treaty that established a six-person commission.[42] Under the treaty, France secured all its demands of alien protection and returned Martín García Island from Uruguay to Argentina. The purpose of the mixed commission was to set the amounts of injuries to be paid, but not to establish the liability of Argentina. Since state responsibility was already pre-negotiated in the *compromis,* the tribunal was tasked

38 *See* Eleanor Louisa Lord, "International Arbitration," 2(4) *Annals of the American Academy of Political and Social Science* (1892): too remote, writes Lord, "not to have been regarded either as the dreams of a visionary fanatic or as a subtle attempt at the aggrandizement of France."

39 Early examples include Emeric Cruce (1623), Grotius (1625), William Penn (1693), Abbe de Saint-Pierre (1718), Jean Jacques Rousseau (1872), Jeremy Bentham (1789), Immanuel Kant (1795); *see further* Céline Spector, "The Plan for Perpetual Peace: From Saint-Pierre to Rousseau," 39(3) *History of European Ideas* 371 (2013).

40 In *Le droit de gens,* Vattel presented a progressive view of arbitration just a few decades before the US and the United Kingdom signed the Jay Treaty (1794) – *Le droit de gens,* Book II, §329. The views of Vattel had a profound impact on the writers of the US Constitution *See* David Armitage, "Declarations of Independence, 1776–2011: From The Law of Nature to International Law," Paper presented to NYU Legal History Colloquium on November 22, 2011, available online at www.law.nyu.edu/sites/default/files/ECM_PRO_073173.pdf, last visited December 22, 2011 ("The US Declaration of Independence was the most enduring product of that Vattelian moment"). *See also* David Golove and Daniel Hulsebosch, "The Law of Nations and the Constitution: An Early Modern Perspective," (NYU Sch. of Law Pub. Law & Legal Theory Research Paper Series, Working Paper No. 18-45, 2018), pp. 1593, 1616–1623.

41 For an account of the French intervention and its context, *see* Horacio A. Grigera-Naon, "Arbitration and Latin America: Progress and Setbacks," 21 *Arbitration International* 27 (2005).

42 Article 1 of the Arana-Mackau Treaty, signed October 29, 1840.

with quantifying the financial extent of – rather than the legal existence of – liability.[43] Indeed, more often than not, international claims for diplomatic protection were not resolved by international arbitration.[44] They were, as their name suggests, resolved diplomatically – as was seen in the *María Luz* dispute between Japan and Peru (1873)[45] and the South Oran affair between Spain and France (1881).[46]

Before the twentieth century, holding a State responsible for violating international law was not accepted by Western publicists as an attribute of sovereignty. Rather than search for legal determinations, European powers preferred to rely on Popes, sovereigns or direct diplomacy to settle disputes. Conceptually, indemnifications arising out of Old World diplomacy were based on negotiation rather than adjudication. This is why, prior to the New World practice, lawyers did not typically employ the term "responsibility" to describe the legal consequences of an international breach. The legal discourse revolved around the rights more than the duties of States.

[43] Argentina entered into a similar arbitration agreement with France and Great Britain with the President of Chile appointed as sole arbitrator in 1864 – *see* Alexis Mourre, "Perspectives of International Arbitration in Latin America," 17 *American Review of International Arbitration* 597 (2006), at p. 597. The Chilean president issued his award on August 1, 1870, rejecting British demands and finding that a nation in a state of war is free to close its ports to commerce.

[44] The first monograph on diplomatic protection was by Edmond Pittard, the future Swiss delegate to the League of Nations, in *La protection des nationaux à l'étranger* (Geneva: W. Kündig, 1896).

[45] Alexander Marie Stuyt, *Survey of International Arbitrations* (3rd ed, The Hague: Nijhoff, 1990), at p. 104 (Friedrich de Martens, on behalf of the Russian Tsar, ruled in favor of Japan). On influence of Martens on the procedure of international arbitration, *see* W. E. Butler and V. S. Ivanenko, "Fedor Fedorovich Martens: Russian Legal Scholar, Diplomat, Arbitrator," 4 *Jus Gentium: Journal of International Legal History* 145 (2019) ("It is no accident that Martens became widely known as an international arbitrator through his successful resolutions of complex inter-State disputes: England and France concerning fishing around Newfoundland in 1891; United States and England on catching fur seals in the Bering Sea in 1893; England and the Netherlands concerning the arrest by Dutch authorities of the Costa Rica Packet in 1897; England and Venezuela concerning the boundary between Venezuela and British Guiana near the Orinoco River, in 1899. . ." (at p. 172)).

[46] 2(7) *Archives diplomatiques* 59; for a discussion, *see* Julius Goebel, Jr., "The International Responsibility of States for Injuries Sustained by Aliens on Account of Mob Violence, Insurrections and Civil Wars," 8(4) *American Journal of International Law* 802 (1914) (adapted from his master's thesis in Political Science from the University of Illinois, 1913)), at p. 826 ("The present case was clearly one of an eye for an eye, and, for this reason, whatever expressions of principle were made, were not of great importance").

Modern Arbitration as *Ad Hoc* Legalism

What stands out as unique about the US turn to international arbitration is its legalism, even if it was *ad hoc* and not institutionalized. By "legalism" I refer to both its technical and philosophical elements.[47] Legalism connotes a belief in *the* utility of law – that the law should regulate certain social conduct and that third parties should be the final arbiters of that law. Lawyers who shared these assumptions played a critical role in the reconstruction and expansion of the postbellum US economy.[48] The idea of legalism also implies the propriety of using a specific form of dispute resolution that features four basic elements: (1) third-party tribunals, (2) comprised of professional lawyers, (3) who are authorized to issue binding awards, (4) based on legal principles or rules. *None of these elements were original in themselves.* However, they were uncommonly employed and rarely employed together prior to the New World practice.[49]

[47] Judith Shklar has described legalism's two elements as, respectively, "rule-oriented thinking" and "tribunalism" (*Legalism: Law, Morals, and Political Trials* (2nd ed., Cambridge, MA: Harvard University Press, 1986), at p. viii). Regarding US legalism in diplomacy, *see* Benjamin Brake and Peter J. Katzenstein, "The Transnational Spread of American Law: Legalization as Soft Power," Institute of International Law & Justice Presentation of June 2010, available online at iilj.org/courses/documents/HC2010Oct22.Katzenstein.pdf, last visited on June 23, 2013, at p. 2. Coates, *infra* note 69, at p. 2, note 7. On the premodern legalism of *lex mercatoria*, *see* Paul R. Milgrom, Douglass C. North and Barry R. Weingast, "The Role of Institutions in the Revival of Trade: The Law Merchant, Private Judges, and the Champagne Fairs," 2(1) *Economics and Politics* 1 (1990); the *lex mercatoria* (or law merchant) of premodern times employed lawyers but not legalism in the modern sense of the term (as employed in this book).

[48] As Francis Boyle has written, "lawyers were the best trained and equipped group of professionals to govern both domestic affairs and international relations in the United States at that time" (Francis Anthony Boyle, *Foundations of World Order: The Legalist Approach to International Relations (1898–1922)* (Durham, NC: Duke University Press, 1999), at p. 17). Note: Boyle's discussion of legalism is broader than the concepts deliberated in this study.

[49] Georg Schwarzenberger assesses the "juridical" character of modern international arbitrations (such as, for him, the Jay Treaty) based on six tests: the professional qualifications of their members, the degree of autonomy granted to and exercised by the commissions, the rules applied by the commissions, the technical standards of their awards, their legal effects and the overall structure of the commissions. *See* Georg Schwarzenberger, "Present-Day Relevance of the Jay Treaty Arbitrations," 53 *Notre Dame Law Review* 715–733 (1977–78). For a more recent categorization, *see* The Project on International Courts and Tribunals, Oxford's new *Handbook on International Adjudication* by Cesare P. R. Romano, Karen J. Alter, and Chrisanthi Avgerou, *The Oxford Handbook of International Adjudication* (Oxford: Oxford University Press, 2013), at ch. 1.

The US use of international law and lawyers was pragmatic. Legalism is not a neutral idea, but an instrument of specific policies. The US was interested in bolstering its foreign investment and political control in a region where diplomacy required a tactful approach to local sovereignty. The inequalities inherent in Old World protection (*e.g.*, extraterritoriality) were repulsive to the newly recognized governments in Latin America. The US needed a new framework to redress injuries to its nationals in the region. As Richard Steinberg and Jonathan Zasloff have written, "They found that paradigm in law."[50] For the US in the New World, international arbitration provided some of the benefits of colonial rule – such as effective economic protection – without some of its costs – such as political domination. Respecting the political sovereignty of weak local governments was a pragmatic tool in helping the US tighten its regional control.[51] Latin American governments received the promise of recognition in return for accepting responsibility for injuries suffered by aliens in their territory.[52]

A foreign policy of almost every US President during the nineteenth century was first formalized in President James Monroe's Annual

[50] Richard H. Steinberg and Jonathan Zasloff, "Power and International Law," 100 *American Journal of International Law* 64 (2006), at p. 65. *See also* Gráinne de Búrca, Robert O. Keohane and Charles Sabel, "New Modes of Pluralist Global Governance," 45 (3) *New York University Journal of International Law & Politics* 723 (2013) (when private individuals are involved in international disputes new "experimentalist" models for transnational governance may arise), as cited in Gregory Shaffer, "Theorizing Transnational Legal Ordering," 12 *Annual Review of Law and Social Science* 231 (2016). *See also* Coates, *infra* note 136, at p. 83 ("Legalism provided language and concepts that helped the United States resolve a tricky ideological problem: how can a nominally anti-imperialist republic be an empire?" and Coates, *infra* note 69, at p. 85 (US international lawyers "recast the civilizing mission, not as the conversion of savages at gunpoint, but as the leadership of a world movement toward a legalized world order of justice and peace." *See also* Francis A. Boyle, "American Foreign Policy toward International Law and Organizations: 1898–1917," 6 *Loyola of Los Angeles International and Comparative Law Review.* 185 (1983).

[51] After all, "In civilized countries one of the most incontestable of the rights of the sovereign state is to render justice" (Chester Lloyd Jones, *The Consular Services of the United States: Its History and Activities* (Philadelphia: The John C. Winston Co., 1906), at p. 46).

[52] For a discussion of the same issue but from the perspective of the international law of recognition, *see* James Crawford, *The Creation of States in International Law* (2nd ed., Oxford: Oxford University Press, 2016), at p. 44. Thus, whereas the withholding of recognition enabled Western imperialism in Asia and Africa, the providing of recognition allowed the same in Latin America – *see* Antony Anghie, "Finding the Peripheries: Sovereignty and Colonialism in Nineteenth-Century International Law," 40 *Harvard International Law Journal* 1–80 (1990), at pp. 29–30.

Message to Congress on December 2, 1823. The Monroe Doctrine, as the policy became known, asserted certain "rights and interests of the United States" regarding the non-colonization of the region.[53] The policy is now closely associated with US diplomacy, but it was actually derivative of British imperial "fair field and no favor" policy in the region.[54] Both major political powers in the region, the US and Great Britain, agreed that imperialism in Latin America had to be different – it had to be indirect, more informal – than in the rest of the world. The US iteration of its policy was intentionally ambiguous: it neither defined intervention nor specified if the prohibition was to apply to European nations alone. It thus lent itself to regular manipulation. There were several common features to the way the US applied the Monroe Doctrine. US politicians invoked the doctrine defensively – rather than as a justification for conquest – by tapping into domestic fears of the Old World's continuing influence.[55] With its ever-expanding economies and its balance of power-wielding monarchies, Europe appeared to the US public as an ongoing existential threat to the political experiment known as the United States of America.

Another common element in the use of the Monroe Doctrine was the US insistence that its role in the region was strictly commercial in nature. The postbellum era began a new stage of US foreign relations in the region. Secretary of State Seward made it clear in his diplomatic instructions to his Mexican consulate that the US had no interest in territorial

[53] To Monroe, "American continents, by the free and independent condition which they have assumed and maintain, are henceforth not to be considered as subjects for future colonization by any European powers…" He further stated that: "It is only when our rights are invaded or seriously menaced that we resent injuries or make preparation for our defense … We … declare that we should consider any attempt on their part to extend their [political and diplomatic] system to any portion of this hemisphere as dangerous to our peace and safety…" (James Monroe, "7th Annual Message (02 December 1823)," reprinted in Alfred A. Stockton (ed.), *The Monroe Doctrine and Other Addresses* (London: McMillan, 1898), at pp. 1–5).

[54] For an excellent discussion on the topic, *see* Charles Lipson, *Standing Guard: Protecting Foreign Capital in the Nineteenth and Twentieth Centuries* (Berkeley: University of California Press, 1985), at pp. 3–61: London understood that Amsterdam's model of *merchant* capitalism was dead; the new model of *industrial* enterprise required an economic infrastructure rather than a political one (*ibid* at p. 5, italics in original). According to Anne Orford, however, mercantilism, like empire, never died – *see* Anne Orford, "Food Security, Free Trade, and the Battle for the State," 11(2) *Journal of International Law and International Relations* 1 (2015), at p. 42.

[55] *See, e.g.*, Joshua Leavitt, *The Monroe Doctrine* (New York: Sinclair Tousey, 1863).

"aggrandizement" and sought the "perfect liberty" of Mexico.[56] Hamilton Fish[57] and Francis Lieber[58] often spoke of the undesirable costs of territorial expansion. Latin American diplomats, especially liberal-minded ones, shared this view and also described commercial expansion themselves as a way of "obtaining all of the advantages ... without suffering any of the inconveniences."[59] The rhetoric of US–Mexican relations was one of "good neighbors."[60]

An Effective Tool for an Emerging Power

In the 1870s, the US was a wealthy but still a weak power.[61] Though it was not a major capital exporter to Latin America – in fact, it was still a net importer – the US acted with greater diplomatic vigor than the dominant economic power of the day, Great Britain.[62] In European

56 Seward to Campbell, October 26, 1866, as quoted in J. Fred Rippy, *The United States and Mexico* (New York: Alfred A. Knopf, 1928), at p. 276.

57 *See* James Burke Chapin, *Hamilton Fish and American Expansion* (Ph.D. dissertation, Cornell University, 1971) at pp. 17, 65. To Fish, international law doctrines that legitimated territorial annexation were "dangerous" (Letter of Hamilton Fish to Daniel Lord, October 22, 1852, as cited in Chapin at p. 65). Indeed, one of his first memories was his father's violent opposition to the War of 1812 (*ibid* at p. 132).

58 For a discussion, *see* Frank Freidel, *Francis Lieber: Nineteenth-Century Liberal* (Baton Rouge: Louisiana State University Press, 1947), at pp. 395–397.

59 Schoonover, *infra* note 76, at p. 256.

60 *See* Brian Loveman, *No Higher Law: American Foreign Policy and the Western Hemisphere Since 1776* (Chapel Hill: University of North Carolina, 2010), at p. 119 (a policy originating with President Buchanan in 1859, authorizing US force in Mexico to extend "a helping hand to save her"). According to Chapin, who wrote his doctoral dissertation on Fish's diplomacy, "The nature of American expansion was changing in this period. The old idea of direct annexation was giving way to a more subtle form of expansion through protectorates or economic control" (Chapin, *supra* note 57, at p. *vi)*. Clearly, to sound credible as regional "protectors," the US often insisted that its regional interests, as expressed in the Monroe Doctrine, were commercial and defensive in nature. As I will discuss, this changed around the turn of the century. Poignantly, President Grant's two most important foreign policy goals were accomplished in 1898 – war (Cuba) and peace (Britain). *See* Gregg Jones, *Honor in the Dust: Theodore Roosevelt, War in the Philippines, and the Rise and Fall of America's Imperial Dream* (New York: New American Library, 2012).

61 On the structural weakness of the US in the late nineteenth century, *see* Fareed Zakaria, *From Wealth to Power: The Unusual Origins of America's World Role* (Princeton: Princeton University Press, 1998), at p. 56. The US was, in Zacharias' words, a "strong nation" but a "weak State." Prior to the 1890s, the US had the domestic wealth but not diplomatic power with which to project that wealth abroad (*ibid* at p. 181).

62 With regards to the weak economic ties between the US and Mexico as of 1870, *see* U.S. For. Rel., 41 Cong., 3rd Sess., 1445, No. 212, Mr. Nelson to Mr. Fish; Minnie McDonald

terms, the US was not quite yet a Great Power in the middle of the nineteenth century. However, in American terms, the US was a country to be feared, a brawn adolescent newcomer, one that had already appropriated massive swaths of Mexican territory. Although the US was an early recognizer of Latin American sovereignty, it walked a spurious line between aggressor and defender in the region. This was a strategy of having one's cake (respecting sovereignty) and eating it whole (piercing said sovereignty).

During the first century of its existence, the US lacked an effective framework for protecting its nationals abroad. Since 1776, US nationals struggled to secure the diplomatic protection abroad that they previously enjoyed under the pre-Revolutionary British flag.[63] Arbitration was not the only solution to this problem. Other means of protection – such as negotiation, annexation and extraterritoriality – were more traditionally employed, especially by Great Britain. Extraterritorial jurisdiction was a formal procedure for protecting nationals abroad through bilateral agreements.[64] These treaties usually included three elements: (1) most-favored-nation clauses, (2) a lack of tariff autonomy for non-Western partners and (3) consular jurisdiction for Westerners.[65] Given the

Paisley, *Relations between the United States and Mexico from 1868 to 1882* (Masters Dissertation, UC Berkeley, September 1913) at p. 80; *see also* Chapin, *supra* note 57; Joseph Smith, *Illusions of Conflict: Anglo-American Diplomacy toward Latin America, 1864–1896* (Pittsburgh: University of Pittsburgh Press, 1979), at p. 45 (70–80 percent of US exports were destined for Europe and little more than 10 percent for Latin America).

63 *See* Leandro Prados de la Escosura, "Lost Decades? Economic Performance in Post-Independence Latin America," 41 *Journal of Latin American Studies* 279 (2009), at p. 283: (on the "scramble to preserve colonial protection and privileges or to secure new powers").

64 Historians of imperialism generally categorize European economic expansion in terms of formal and informal protection. Becker Lorca identifies two forms of such protection: formal colonial conquest and informal expansion and three forms of informal protection (Arnulf Becker Lorca, "Universal International Law: Nineteenth-Century Histories of Imposition and Appropriation," 51 *Harvard Journal of International Law* 475 (2010), at p. 481). On the origins of international commercial arbitration being found in early mixed claims and consular cases based on the principle of territoriality, *see* Willem Theus, "There and Back Again: From Consular Courts through Mixed Arbitral Tribunals to International Commercial Courts," in Hélène Ruiz Fabri and Michel Erpelding (eds), *The Mixed Arbitral Tribunals, 1919–1939: An Experiment in the International Adjudication of Private Rights* 29 (Baden-Baden: Nomos, 2023).

65 Kal Raustiala, *Does the Constitution Follow the Flag? The Evolution of Territoriality in American Law* (Oxford: Oxford University Press, 2009), at p. 17. For an overview of the US consular courts, *see* Chester Lloyd Jones, *The Consular Services of the United States: Its History and Activities* (Philadelphia: The John C. Winston Co., 1906), at pp. 54–58.

efficacy of this practice – and its use by the US in other parts of the world – why did the US not protect its nationals in Latin America through "unequal treaties"?[66] Such arrangements would have obviated arbitration and allowed for the domestic or consular resolution of alien injuries. Another related possibility to "unequal treaties" was territorial annexation. Like extraterritorial protection, this option would provide access to domestic courts for injured US nationals.

US racism towards their darker-skinned neighbors presented a practical obstacle to maintaining a democracy within expanded territories.[67] Also, such treaties were unlikely to be ratified by the uncooperative US Congress.[68] Even the domestic protection of its own nationals was largely in the hands of the judicial rather than the legislative branch of the US Government.[69] The US did enter into a few unequal treaties with the Barbary States, Turkey, China and other so-called non-civilized countries. But the Monroe Doctrine meant that American states were all brothers and brothers are all equal, right?[70]

[66] For a clear summary of this form of property protection abroad, *see* Kate Miles, *The Origins of International Investment Law* (Cambridge: Cambridge University Press, 2013), at pp. 25–28.

[67] *See* Eric T. L. Love, *Race over Power: Racism and US Imperialism, 1865–1900* (Chapel Hill: University of North Carolina Press, 2004). This reason also partially explains why, in 1898, after the US conquered Cuba, it opted instead to install a puppet government in Havana rather than annex it.

[68] It was difficult to get Congress to ratify bilateral commercial treaties – *see* Osgood Hardy, "Ulysses S. Grant, President of the Mexican Southern Railroad," 24(2) *Pacific Historical Review* 111 (1955), at p. 117; Burdette Gibson Lewis, "Our Trade Relations with Latin America," 14(10) *Journal of Political Economy* 602 (1906), at p. 606.

[69] The fact of legislative inaction in the late nineteenth century created a real opportunity for judicial protection of rights – *see* Larry D. Kramer, *The People Themselves: Popular Constitutionalism and Judicial Review* (New York: Oxford University Press, 2000), at p. 213; Zakaria, *supra* note 61, at p. 105; Benjamin Allen Coates, *Transatlantic Advocates: American International Law and US Foreign Relations, 1898–1919*, Doctoral Dissertation submitted to Columbia University, 2010 (on file with author, at p. 6, internal citations omitted).

[70] While the US did sign an "unequal treaty" with Colombia, those circumstances were distinct in that they were related to US interests in a specifically strategic area. The Mallarino–Bidlack Treaty with New Granada (now Colombia) was signed December 12, 1846. Charles I. Bevans, *Treaties and Other International Agreements of the United States of America 1776–1949* (Washington, DC: Government Printing Office, 1971), vol. VI, at pp. 865–881. This was the only collective security agreement that the US signed with a Latin American country in the nineteenth century. It granted the US, among other things, the authority to intervene with force to suppress local conflicts. Not surprisingly, the US intervened militarily several times during the second half of the nineteenth century. *See further* Raustiala, *supra* note 65, at p. 17.

The US was a loud supporter of all things republican and anti-colonial. With its Monroe Doctrine, the US recognized the sovereignty of its Latin American brothers, which effectively foreclosed the possibility of unequal treaties with them. International sovereignty implied equality.[71] Wheaton's *Elements of International Law* expresses this US policy as a fundamental principle of international law:

> The first general principle on this subject results immediately from the fact of the independence of nations. Every nation possesses and exercises exclusive sovereignty and jurisdiction throughout the full extent of its territory. The second general principle is 'that no State can, by its laws, directly affect, bind, or regulate property beyond its own territory, or control persons who do not reside within it, whether they be native-born subjects or not.'[72]

This position permeated its entire legal community – commentators as well as courts. According to the Supreme Court, US nationals could not expect the US Constitution or courts to apply to them abroad.[73]

Post Facto Protection

Given the wild expansion of its economy and boundaries at the time, the US Government was not yet able to foster – let alone control – private investment abroad.[74] The US employed legalism as a practical tool to

[71] Entrance to the club of Christian civilization came with the national right to jurisdictional sovereignty. As Secretary of State Bayard wrote to his minister in Spain, "Such a doctrine has never been suggested in the case of Spain, which is not classed as a non-Christian country, in which Christian nations have asked for the exemption of their citizens from the local law" (Letter from Secretary of State Thomas Bayard to his minister to Spain, J. L. M. Curry, October 20, 1886, *Foreign Relations of the United States: 1892–1893* (Washington, DC, Government Printing Office, 1893), at p. 413). It is noteworthy that the recognition policy did not preclude US suppression of Native American sovereignty in the 1870s (see the act of March 3, 1871, 16 Statutes at Large, 566), which prohibited the recognition of Native American tribes – *see* Hunter Miller (ed.), *Treaties and Other International Acts of the United States of America*, Vol. 1 (Washington, DC: Government Printing Office, 1931), at p. 5. *See generally* Julius Goebel, Jr., *The Recognition Policy of the United States* (New York: Columbia University Press, 1915).

[72] *Ibid* at 10. Henry Wheaton, *Elements of International Law* (8th ed., Richard Dana, ed., Philadelphia: Carey, Lea & Blanchard, 1866), at ʃ78, internal citation omitted.

[73] *Cherokee Nation v. Georgia*, 30 US 1 (1831).

[74] The US Government could barely control its own consuls abroad. On the difficulties of controlling diplomatic representatives abroad, but not one which yields a great deal in the way of tangible results, *see* Nick Cleaver, "Wagging the Dog: The Influence of American Representatives Overseas on the Evolution of US Foreign Policy in the Late 19th

address diplomatic problems created by the international exploits of its nationals. Understaffed and underfunded, Fish's State Department was overwhelmed by claims for diplomatic protection, and he needed to find an effective way to address them. As I will explain below, the US professionalization of international arbitration was motivated less by regional solidarity than by political pressure by adventurous nationals who lost money abroad. International lawyers followed that financial trail.[75]

In the aftermath of its Civil War, the US essentially demobilized its military and primarily focused on domestic reconstruction.[76] Yet, the years were far from economically anemic. During the postbellum era, US Gross National Product quadrupled[77] and its Production Index quintupled.[78] Additionally, the 1848 Treaty of Guadalupe Hidalgo that ended the US-Mexican War transferred more than half of Mexico's territory – over 500,000 square miles – to the US This acquisition took several decades to incorporate through infrastructural improvements. Railroad construction, both domestic and foreign, became a major source of private US speculation.[79] With the backing of local governments, US

Century" (2013), available online at www.academia.edu/3391328/Wagging_the_Dog_The_Influence_of_American_Representatives_Overseas_on_the_Evolution_of_US_Foreign_Policy_in_the_Late_19th_Century, last visited June 13, 2021.

75 On the "professionalization" of international commercial arbitration, *see* Mikaël Schinazi, *The Three Ages of International Commercial Arbitration* (Cambridge: Cambridge University Press, 2021), at pp. 195–201.

76 *See* Christian G. Samito, *Changes in Law and Society during the Civil War and Reconstruction* (Carbondale: Southern Illinois University Press, 2009), at pp. 59–99. For contrasting views (on the "second American Revolution"), *see* Charles R. Morris, *The Tycoons: How Andrew Carnegie, John D. Rockefeller, Jay Gould, and J.P. Morgan Invented the American Supereconomy* (New York: Times Books, 2005), at p. 10; T. J. Stiles, *The First Tycoon: The Epic Life of Cornelius Vanderbilt* (New York: Knopf, 2009), at p. 70; Joseph Smith, *Illusions of Conflict: Anglo-American Diplomacy Toward Latin America, 1864–1896* (Pittsburgh: University of Pittsburgh Press, 1979), at p. 33 ("American naval action after the mid-1860s was limited to 'showing the flag' and to surveys and explorations of potential canal routes and naval harbors); Thomas David Schoonover, *Dollars over Dominion: The Triumph of Liberalism in Mexican–United States Relations, 1861–1867* (Baton Rouge: Louisiana State University Press, 1978), at p. 250 (the US had little need for a standing army, given the US' commercial and not territorial expansionist aims).

77 From US$ 9,110,000,000 for 1869–73 to US$ 37,100,000,000 for 1897–1901.

78 From seventeen in 1865 to 100 in 1900.

79 The railroad industry grew from 35,085 of miles of railway under operation in 1865 to 250,103 miles in 1899. US Bureau of the Census, *Historical Statistics of the United States, Colonial Times to 1957* (Washington, DC: Government Printing Office, 1961), at pp. 139, 284, 427, 429, 409 as cited in Campbell, *infra* note 169, at p. 84. In the words of Consul Foster, "The most necessary feature in building up commerce between our countries is

investors such as Cornelius Vanderbilt (1794–1877) and William Aspinwall (1807–75) built up passage routes throughout the Americas. These one-off arrangements were very effective.[80] As production efficiencies yielded an overabundance of goods, new infrastructure provided easier and greater access to new markets. As a result, the US economy was heavily dependent on international trade, especially with Latin America.[81]

Private entrepreneurs, rather than government subsidies, drove foreign trade.[82] In contrast to Europe, this was a bottom-up phenomenon. Political instability and domestic regulatory reforms in Latin America created economic opportunities for US entrepreneurs (*e.g.*, Henry Meiggs) and corporations (*e.g.*, United Fruit Company).[83] Of course, these investments were highly speculative and when they soured, the State Department became inundated with requests for alien protection.[84] So much so that the focus of the State Department's work during the second half of the nineteenth century would be to manage those claims. As legal historians Benjamin Coates and Christopher Casey write, lawyers in the US State Department were more concerned with the

the construction of an international railroad" (Statement made by Consul Foster–Ex. Doc. 45 Cong., 3 Sess., Serial No. I8X2, doc. 15, p. 5, Mr. Poster to Mr. Mason as cited in Paisley, *supra* note 62, at p. 98).

80 For example, trade with Mexico increased from about US$ 7,000,000 to US$ 63,000,000 between 1860 and 1900 (Walter LaFeber, *The New Empire: An Interpretation of American Expansion 1860–1898* (Ithaca: Cornell University Press, 1963), at pp. 51–52).

81 US trade jumped 18,158 percent in three decades: from US$ 13,305,000 in 1870 to US$ 2,429,233,000 in 1900. Bureau of the Census, *Historical Statistics of the Units Stats, 1789–1945* (Washington, DC: Government Printing Office, 1949), at p. 244 as cited in Milton Pelsur, *America's Outward Thrust: Approaches to Foreign Affairs, 1865–1890* (Dekalb: Northern Illinois University Press, 1971), at p. 16.

82 *See generally* Naomi R. Lamoreaux and John Joseph Wallis, "States, Not Nation: The Sources of Political and Economic Development in the Early United States," 1 *American Capitalism* 1 (2016): "The federal government played essentially no role in this process [of financial modernization] until the Civil War, and even then it played only a bit part," available online at https://sites.krieger.jhu.edu/iae/files/2017/04/Lamoreaux_and_Wallis_States_Not_Nation.pdf, last visited May 7, 2017.

83 Thomas F. O'Brien, *The Century of US Capitalism in Latin America* (Albuquerque: University of New Mexico Press, 1999), at p. 16.

84 Christopher A. Casey, *National Abroad: Globalization, Individual Rights, and the Making of Modern International Law* (Cambridge: Cambridge University Press, 2020), at p. 38 (Foreign offices "buried under an avalanche of correspondence relating to the protection of nationals abroad"); regarding a similar experience in the British Foreign Office, *see* Van Hulle, *Britain and International Law in West Africa: The Practice of Empire* (Oxford: Oxford University Press, 2020), at p. 81.

protection of private property abroad than anything else.[85] The State Department was the only major foreign ministry that kept indexed records of all claims for diplomatic protection brought by nationals abroad.[86] Thus, the most protection the US Government could afford its nationals was *post facto* protection coming after-the-fact of injury.[87]

The most successful US exporting companies achieved their status primarily through aggressive organization rather than governmental support.[88] In fact, the US economy was being steered by private actors such as John Davison Rockefeller (1839–1937) and Cornelius Vanderbilt, whose sophisticated use of corporations and consolidations jangled both domestic markets and courts. In the words of Charles Francis Adams Jr. (1835–1915), Vanderbilt "introduced Caesarism into corporate life."[89] Corporate responsibility law was constantly being rewritten by the courts,[90] which had to react to a market that federal regulators failed to control.[91] The Federal Government had even less control over investors' conduct abroad.[92] US protection abroad was *ad hoc* and *post facto*.[93] It was unsynchronized with the activities of private actors and

[85] Christopher A. Casey, *National Abroad: Globalization, Individual Rights, and the Making of Modern International Law* (Cambridge: Cambridge University Press, 2020), at p. 39; Coates, *supra* note 69, at p. 256.

[86] Casey, *supra* note 85, at p. 38.

[87] When the Examiner of Claims bureau of the State Department was created in 1866 (Act of July 25, 1866, c. 233, sec. 2, 14 Stat. L, 226), it was tasked not with stemming the tide of alien protection claims, but with responding to them, discussed further below.

[88] Joseph A. Fry, "Phases of Empire: Late Nineteenth-Century US Foreign Relations," in Charles W. Calhoun (ed.), *The Gilded Age: Perspectives on the Origins of Modern America* 283 (Lanham: Rowman & Littlefield Publishers, 2007), at p. 264.

[89] Charles Francis Adams, Jr., "A Chapter of Erie," 109 *North American Review* (1869), at p. 38.

[90] In the early nineteenth century, as Morton J. Horwitz describes it, a corporation was perceived as an "association between state and private interests for public purposes" (Morton J. Horwitz, *The Transformation of American Law, 1780–1848* (Cambridge, MA: Harvard University Press, 1977), at pp. 136–137) (after the Civil War, corporations were seen as separate entities from their stockholders).

[91] On the change of corporate structure in the US economy, *see* Horwitz, *supra* note 90, ch. 5.

[92] Early-nineteenth century usage of the word "company" was as a plural noun, as a gathering of individuals akin to a partnership (Stiles, *supra* note 76, at p. 168).

[93] US private entrepreneurs too were distinguishable from their European counterparts because the former wielded more risky and innovative technologies – *see* O'Brien, *supra* note 83, at pp. 56, 59; Robert Kagan, *Dangerous Nation: America's Foreign Policy from Its Earliest Days to the Dawn of the Twentieth Century* (New York: Alfred A. Knopf, 2006) at pp. 128, 137); James C. Knarr, *Uruguay and the United States, 1903–1929: Diplomacy in the Progressive Era* (Kent: Kent State University Press, 2012), at p. 5.

investments in Latin America. The few diplomatic and consular posts of the US abroad were all subject to the spoils system of appointments.[94] US investment abroad, especially in the case of Mexico, was driven by private businessmen.[95]

US investors abroad included both individual expeditionists as well as corporate entrepreneurs. There was no private–public partnership with the US Government to compare with, say, the Dutch East India Company. A well-known example of corporate entrepreneurialism is Cornelius Vanderbilt, who eschewed public participation in his own business affairs. While Vanderbilt enjoyed cordial relationships with governmental officials, he viewed the legal and political systems as "too slow" for resolving corporate business issues.[96] "The Commodore," as he was known for his role in the steamship industry, often challenged and overtook his government-subsidized competition. Vanderbilt was Economic Man, an "anti-aristocrat . . . who never felt the tug of *noblesse oblige*."[97] An example of the other type of trader, the "filibusterer,"[98] was William Walker (1824–1860). Expeditionists were backed not by the US Government but by private US banks. Walker, for example, was supported by Charles Morgan (1795–1878).[99] Walker was particularly precocious and adventurous – graduating *summa cum laude* from the University of Nashville at age fourteen and with a medical degree from the University of Pennsylvania at age nineteen. At twenty-nine, he declared himself the first president of the "Republic of Lower California" (Baja California). Within months, Walker was hauled off to

94 William Barnes and John Heath Morgan, *The Foreign Service of the United States: Origins, Development, and Function* (Washington, DC: Department of State, 1961), at pp. 133–134.

95 Schoonover, *supra* note 76, at p. 275: "United States economic expansion into Mexico between 1861 and 1867 was largely the work of a highly active private business sector that was quietly encouraged by Congress and the State Department and welcomed by Mexico."

96 Stiles, *supra* note 76, at pp. 346, 357 (during the Civil War, Secretary of War Stanton asked Vanderbilt to seek and destroy the *C.S.S. Virginia and C.S.S. Alabama*).

97 Stiles, *supra* note 76, at p. 58.

98 Filibustering is a term that was originally used with a derogatory association and was synonymous with pirating or buccaneering. It is a variant of freebooter (Dutch vrijbuiter) – William O. Scroggs, *Filibusters and Financiers* (New York: Macmillan, 1916), at p. 4.

99 John M. Belohlavek, *Broken Glass: Caleb Cushing and the Shattering of the Union* (Kent: Kent State University Press, 2005), at p. 265.

California, where he was tried for waging an illegal war.[100] The US Government was neither willing nor able to control the actions of its private citizens in Latin America.

Vanderbilt himself had stronger naval capabilities than the entire Federal Government.[101] Even when the paths of the two types of traders collided, the US government remained impassive on the sidelines. In 1855, Walker intervened in a civil war in Nicaragua and installed himself as the country's President. He then seized the property of the Accessory Transit Company,[102] an act that displeased its owner, Cornelius Vanderbilt. When US Secretary of State William Marcy rejected Vanderbilt's request to put down the Walker rebellion in Nicaragua, the industrialist was forced to pursue "an independent foreign policy."[103] Vanderbilt assembled his own private army and successfully uprooted Walker from Nicaragua. Given the aggressiveness of such independent-minded investors, "It is a remarkable fact," writes Vanderbilt's biographer T. J. Stiles, "that the only foreign conflict involving the United States during the fifty years between the Mexican and the Spanish American wars was fought by a private army of American civilians."[104] As Attorney General, Caleb Cushing was so frustrated by his government's inability to regulate these activities that he was prompted to draw "heavily upon his extraordinary vocabulary of expletives whenever the subject was mentioned."[105]

[100] Considering that the US public generally approved of filibustering, it is not surprising that Walker was acquitted of all charges by the California jury after minutes of deliberations.

[101] *See further* Joseph Smith, *Illusions of Conflict: Anglo-American Diplomacy Toward Latin America, 1864–1896* (Pittsburgh: University of Pittsburgh Press, 1979), at p. 33.

[102] The Accessory Transit Company was set up by Vanderbilt after the California gold rush to provide transit from New York to San Francisco via Nicaragua (a route that was quicker and cheaper than the government subsidized route that ran through Panama).

[103] Stiles, *supra* note 76, at p. 281. Arguably, the federal government lacked the financing and organization to undertake a major war; the federal budget in 1860 was US$ 63 million (*ibid* at p. 341).

[104] Stiles, *supra* note 76, at p. 341. Costa Rican national identity was forged in the private international battle against William Walker – *see further* Aviva Chomsky, *West Indian Workers and the United Fruit Company in Costa Rica, 1870–1940* (Baton Rouge: Louisiana State University Press, 1996), at p. 209 (viewed as its "National War"). This led, writes Chomsky (without irony), to a national movement of "liberal anti-imperialism" and later "radical anti-imperialism" by the early twentieth century (*ibid* at pp. 212–220). Providing foreign companies such as the United Fruit Company with concessions was equated "with a complete loss of sovereignty" (*ibid* at p. 213).

[105] Belohlavek, *supra* note 99, at p. 266, internal citations omitted.

In addition to providing *post facto* protection to its nationals, by insisting on international arbitration, the US also ensured that its nationals be protected using international rather than local standards of care. In a circulated memo, Secretary Fish stated his intention to use triadism, including "good offices," to resolve regional disputes.[106] It soon became clear that by "good offices," the US did not mean peaceful diplomacy but the imposition of international arbitrations.[107] Fish's memorandum spelled out his determination "to secure to the United States that proportionate share of the trade of this continent to which their close relations of geographical contiguity and political friendship with all the states of America justly entitle them."[108] International arbitration not only protected aliens abroad but it also began to exclude European intervention in the region.[109] An important aim of the Monroe Doctrine was to prevent just that – and to enable the US to secure a larger share of the British-dominated international trade.[110] By mitigating the influence of the British Navy, the US increased its opportunity to expand its foreign investment in Latin America.

[106] Hamilton Fish, "Circular – Department of State to Ministers and Consuls in Spanish-American States and Brazil," July 14, 1870, *FRUS* (1870), 254–261, at p. 257, emphasis added.

[107] *See* Judith Ewell, *Venezuela and the United States: From Monroe's Hemisphere to Petroleum's Empire* (Athens: University of Georgia Press, 1996), at p. 21. Latin Americans were eager to have the Monroe Doctrine be followed by military support against European intervention. The fact that this did not happen led Simón Bolívar to withhold an invitation to the US to the first Pan-American Congress in 1826 (Alan McPherson, "Forget the Maine! The Legacy of 'The United States and the Americas'," 35 (4) *Diplomatic History* 709–728 (2011), at pp. 713–714).

[108] Hamilton Fish, "Circular – Department of State to Ministers and Consuls in Spanish-American States and Brazil," *FRUS* (1870), July 14, 1870, 254–261, at p. 254.

[109] Like Fish, for example, Blaine, in his 1881 Pan-American Conference invitation, announced that it was a consensually acknowledged fact among American governments that the US was the regional protector: "It has been . . . a source of profound satisfaction to the government of the United States to see that this country is in a large measure looked to by all the American powers as their friend and mediator. . ." (A. Curtis Wilgus, "James G. Blaine and the Pan American Movement," 5(4) *The Hispanic American Historical Review* 662 (1922), at pp. 670–671).

[110] Arthur P. Whitaker, *The United States and the Independence of Latin America, 1800–1830* (New York: W. W. Norton & Co., 1964 [1941]), at p. 530 ("These facts suggest the nature of the most important immediate result of Monroe's declaration, namely, that it opened a new and more intense phase of Anglo-American rivalry over Latin America").

The Willingness of Latin Americans to Arbitrate

While alien protection and regional hegemony explain US motivations to employ international arbitration, what explains the Latin American willingness to participate in this process? After all, Latin American governments agreed to 154 arbitral agreements during the nineteenth century.[111] Was it a naïve belief in Pan-American solidarity? Not likely, since by the mid-nineteenth century, Latin American diplomats were already critical of the Monroe Doctrine as enabling US intervention.[112] The Mallarino–Bidlack Treaty of 1846 had demonstrated the US willingness to resort to traditional imperialistic means in the region.[113] By the 1870s, the US had expressly interpreted the Monroe Doctrine as prohibiting *European* but not *US* force in the region. Although the US did not frequently make actual recourse to force in the mid-nineteenth century (*see* Table 2.1), the fact that it could – and that it occasionally would – was enough to intimidate its southern neighbors.[114] The military

[111] William R. Manning (ed.), *Arbitration Treaties among the American Nations to the Close Year 1910* (New York: Oxford University Press, 1924). *See also* regarding why Latin American nations agreed to arbitrate Christopher R. Rossi, *Whiggish International Law: Elihu Root, the Monroe Doctrine, and International Law in the Americas* (Leiden: Brill, 2019), at p. 53 (citing to an unpublished paper by Matthias Packeiser, Rossi writes that "a constellation of economic and political insecurities foisted a condition of Latin American dependency on foreign capital, making practical if not necessary the embrace of European value standards to achieve diplomatic status and acceptance as sovereign equals").

[112] Some Latin American historians appropriated the Monroe Doctrine as a Hispanic American doctrine based on Francisco de Vitoria's belief that America could not be the subject of European occupation nor colonization – *e.g.*, Camilo Barcia Trelles, *Doctrina de Monroe y cooperación internacional* (Madrid: Editorial Mundo Latino, 1931). *See further* Samuel Flagg Bemis, *The Latin American Policy of the United States: An Historical Interpretation* (New York: Harcourt, Brace and Company, 1943), at p. 49.

[113] I note here what is now increasingly commonly appreciated, namely, that "empire" is neither necessarily "good" or "bad" and that international law itself, in its apathy toward national law and in its unwillingness to allow for states to remove themselves from the international rule of law, is imperialistic – *see further* Ian Hurd, "The Empire of International Legalism," 32 *Ethics and International Affairs* 265 (2018).

[114] Until the mid-twentieth century, the US invoked its right to forcefully intervene to take over customs houses and insert New York banks to administer them until sovereign debt was repaid. On one account, between 1869 and 1897, the US had sent warships into Latin American ports 598 times (Greg Grandin, *Empire's Workshop: Latin America, the United States, and the Rise of the New Imperialism* (New York: Henry Holt and Co., 2007) at p. 20). Still, the US waged no major wars between 1865 and 1898 and its military interventions were comparatively few – mostly in Mexico and rarely south of Colombia – *see* Albert Bushnell Hart, "The Experience of the United States in Foreign Military Expeditions," *Harper's Magazine* 618–628 (September 1860), at p. 625.

Table 2.1 *Number of forceful US foreign interventions*[115]

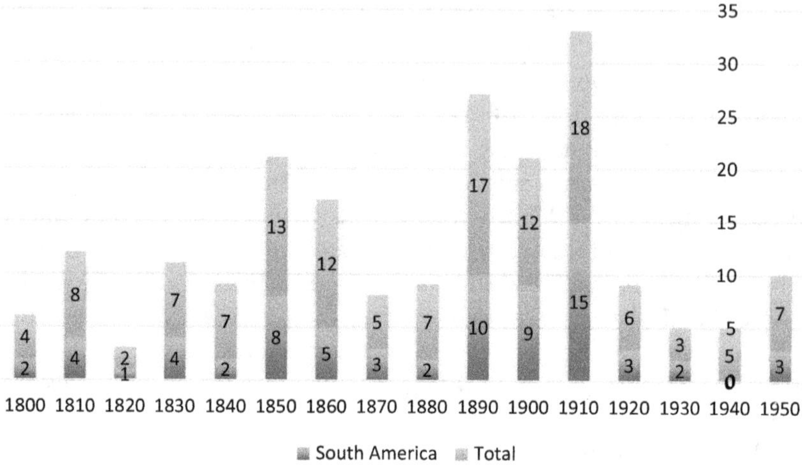

and geopolitical reality was clear. Although its global standing was weak, the US was steadily becoming the dominant power in Latin America.[116]

When the US pressed Latin American governments to arbitrate international claims, there was rarely much choice in the matter. Formally, international law recognized both the absolute right both to request arbitration and to reject such an offer.[117] Informally, the US would habitually direct men-of-war toward respondent States to facilitate a "peaceful resolution" of their disputes.[118] The first US–Mexico Mixed

[115] Source: Ellen C. Collier, *Instances of the Use of Force by United States' Forces Abroad, 1783–1993* (Washington, DC: Congressional Research Services, October 7, 1993).

[116] *See* Smith, *supra* note 314, at p. 25; Montt, "Latin American Position," *infra* note 351, at p. 10.

[117] *See* Anthony J. Bellia, Jr. and Bradford R. Clark, "The Federal Common Law of Nations," 109(1) *Columbia Law Review* 1–93 (2009), at p. 18.

[118] *See* Andreas H. Roth, *The Minimum Standard of International Law Applied to Aliens* (Leiden: Sijthoff, 1949), at p. 88; Alwyn V. Freeman, *The International Responsibility of States for Denials of Justice* (London: Longmans, Green & Co., 1938), at pp. 497–530; William Marion Gibson, *Aliens and the Law: Aspects of the National Treatment of Aliens in the United States* (Chapel Hill: Chapel Hill Press, 1940), at pp. 1–18; Clyde Eagleton, *The Responsibility of States in International Law* (New York: New York University Press, 1928), at pp. 82–87; Frederick Sherwood Dunn, *The Protection of Nationals: A Study in the Application of International Law* (Baltimore: The Johns Hopkins Press, 1932), at pp. 113–172.

Claims Commission was established (in 1839)[119] only after Congress authorized President Andrew Jackson to initiate reprisals against Mexico, unless the latter agreed to settle claims.[120] The *Water Witch* affair also illustrates this point. In that case, President Buchanan dispatched nineteen vessels and 2,500 men (the largest naval force that had ever been sent from the US until that time)[121] to the Río de la Plata to secure a conciliatory solution.[122] After Paraguay agreed to arbitrate, President Buchanan reported the "happy effect" of this expedition.[123]

Even an offer of arbitration had the ironic effect of threatening military intervention.[124] The right to arbitrate was described in the nineteenth century as a "perfect right," the refusal of which could justify war. In 1797, the London Telegraph invoked the phrase to explain that because of the "perfect equality" of nation, each "has a perfect right to … honourable negotiation, which in the practice of nations is employed for the pacific adjustment of their contested claims." The refusal to arbitrate, thus understood, would make the refusing state "responsible for a war which that refusal makes on their part unjust."[125] Thus, the relationship between arbitration and force was not always a simple one. The ever-present threat of forceful intervention makes it impossible to ascertain how much "consent" was ever given by Latin

[119] The first US–Mexico Mixed Claims Commission was established by the Convention for Adjustment of Claims of Citizens of the United States on Mexico, signed April 11, 1839; Moore, *supra* note 3, p. 1218.

[120] From Washington: Message in Relation to Mexico, Virginia Free Press (Charlestown, WV), Issue 3, col. E (February 16, 1837) as cited in John D. Rosero, *Private v. Public Authority in NAFTA: The Procyclicality of Investor Protections and Global Governance Issues* (Ph.D. diss., Rutgers the State University of New Jersey, 2010), at p. 91.

[121] Harold F. Peterson, "Edward A. Hopkins: A Pioneer Promoter in Paraguay," 22(2) *The Hispanic American Historical Review* 245 (1942), at p. 258.

[122] On the east coast of Argentina, from where the landlocked Paraguay is reachable via the Parana River. Alien protection was one of three outstanding issues between the US and Paraguay - the other being a treaty ratification and the *Water Witch* incident itself (Moore, *supra* note 3, at pp. 1489–1493).

[123] Peterson, *supra* note 120, at pp. 258–259 and Moore, *supra* note 3, Vol. II, at p. 1494. Interestingly, Cornelius Vanderbilt *both built and sold* the *Water Witch* for the US Government. I discuss this case further in Chapter 3.

[124] Since intervention increasingly required justification (beyond the assertion of right). As late as 1955, Lauterpacht wrote that intervention would only be appropriate when a debtor state refuses to arbitrate a dispute (Hersch Lauterpacht, *Oppenheim's International Law* (8th ed., London: Longmans, Green & Co., 1955), at p. 309.

[125] Origin and Principles of the War, *Telegraph* (London), Jan. 17, 1797, at 3, as cited in Anthony J. Bellia, Jr. and Bradford R. Clark, "The Federal Common Law of Nations," 109(1) *Columbia Law Review* 1–93 (2009), at p. 18.

American nations to arbitrate alien protection claims.[126] Between 1830 and 1900, the US used military force abroad more than seventy-five times, of which nearly sixty was to protect private property of US nationals abroad. According to Casey, "*nearly* every trans-hemispheric conflict in the nineteenth century (that was not explicitly an independence movement) involved the protection of nationals abroad."[127] It seemed that, "Virtually everywhere they looked, Latin Americans saw US warships off their coasts. . ."[128]

Recognition as Motivation for Arbitration

The threat of force alone does not fully explain why Latin American governments agreed to arbitrate alien protection claims. In the case of Mexico, international and US arbitration were closely related: eleven of the seventeen compromissory agreements that Mexico entered into during the nineteenth century were with the US (see Table 2.2). Many of the arbitral agreements coincide with the formation of new national governments. Thus, another compelling factor was that international arbitration facilitated recognition by other states.[129]

Though Latin American independence began as early as 1808, recognition of these new states commenced only in 1822, with US recognition of Gran Colombia and Mexico.[130] The US, through its espousal of the Monroe Doctrine and promotion of international arbitration, became a strategic (if not ideological) partner in the decolonization of Latin America. In the first half of the nineteenth century, Latin American governments looked to the US as a guarantor of their political independence. As diplomatic historian Thomas David Schoonover observed, "Time and time again, the Central American, Mexican, or

[126] When an international lawyer attempted to classify the early arbitrations according to whether "they had been entered into willingly or unwillingly," he concluded that it was impossible to make such a distinction (Lionel M. Summers, "Arbitration and Latin America," 3 *California Western International Law Journal* 1 (1972), at p. 5, note 15).

[127] Christopher A. Casey, *National Abroad: Globalization, Individual Rights, and the Making of Modern International Law* (Cambridge: Cambridge University Press, 2020), at pp. 39, 49.

[128] Loveman, *supra* note 60, at p. 153 (internal citations omitted).

[129] Liliana Obregón, *Completing Civilization: Nineteenth Century Criollo Interventions in International Law*, SJD Dissertation submitted to Harvard Law School (September 2002), on file with author, at p. 70.

[130] Frederick Waymouth Gibbs, *Recognition: A Chapter from the History of the North American & South American States* (London: W. Ridgway, 1863), at p. 1.

Table 2.2 *Mexican arbitrations in the nineteenth century*

No.	Year	Participating states		Topic
1	1823	Mexico	Colombia	General
2	1839	Mexico	US	Mixed
3	1848	Mexico	US	General
4	1853	Mexico	US	General
5	1868	Mexico	US	Mixed
6	1871	Mexico	US	Mixed
7	1872	Mexico	US	Mixed
8	1874	Mexico	US	Mixed
9	1876	Mexico	US	Mixed
10	1882	Mexico	Guatemala	Other: Treaty Interpretation
11	1888	Mexico	Guatemala	Mixed
12	1888	Mexico	Ecuador	General
13	1889	Mexico	US	Other: Boundary
14	1891	Mexico	Guatemala	Mixed
15	1893	Mexico	Salvador	General
16	1895	Mexico	Guatemala	Other: Boundary
17	1897	Mexico	US	*Ad hoc*

other Latin American liberals were compelled to recall to the United States its role in defending the liberal New World institutions from Old World attack."[131]

Thomas Jefferson, author of the US Declaration of Independence, forged the early US foreign policy of recognition. The third US President was also a trained lawyer with a detailed understanding of legal and political sovereignty. Internally, sovereignty was a question of law. The US Government had the rights and duties set out in its constitutional norms. Externally, however, sovereignty was a question of fact. Jefferson based this view on the same natural law faith upon which he based his Declaration of Independence: "We hold these truths to be self-evident, that all men are created equal, that they are endowed by their Creator with certain unalienable Rights, that among these are Life,

[131] Schoonover, *supra* note 76, at p. 167. For example, the US mediated the Latin American "War of the Pacific" in inviting delegates from Peru, Chile and Bolivia to hold a five-day conference aboard the USS Lackawanna in 1800. In that example, the mediation failed.

Liberty and the pursuit of Happiness."[132] Like men under domestic law, states were equal under international law. To Jefferson, the US had no right to judge the legitimacy of a foreign government.[133]

The progressiveness of this foreign policy notwithstanding, the US did not apply it consistently in the nineteenth century.[134] In the first round of Latin American independence, the US was quick to recognize the new nations, beginning in 1822 with Gran Colombia and Mexico.[135] As noted above, in the first half of the nineteenth century, Latin American governments often looked up to the US as a guarantor of their political independence.[136] This changed by the second half of the century, when recognition became associated with acknowledging a new government's ability to protect aliens. Western investors in developing regions did not want to limit their protection to local law (why would they?). Aliens and their governments insisted on international standards of protection (the "Standard of Civilization").[137] In order to build up domestic infrastructure, newly formed governments needed to attract foreign investors who might be worried about the risk of revolutions and expropriations.[138] Thus, when it came to recognizing the government of General Porfirio Díaz (1830–1915) in Mexico, Hamilton Fish instructed his Minister there to withhold US recognition until the latter was assured that the Díaz Government had "sufficient strength to carry out its international

[132] Jefferson believed that "the Catholic principle of republicanism, to wit, that every people may establish what form of government they please, and change it as they please" (Instructions to Mr. Pinckney of December 30, 1792 as cited in Julius Goebel, Jr., *The Recognition Policy of the United States* (New York: Columbia University Press, 1915), at p. 104).

[133] *See* Goebel, *supra* note 133.

[134] According to Goebel, "No doctrine . . . bears more deeply the imprint of his [Jefferson] political thinking than does our recognition policy" (Goebel, *supra* note 133, at p. 98).

[135] Gibbs, *supra* note 130, at p. 1.

[136] See Schoonover, *supra* note 76, at p. 167 (as diplomatic historian Thomas David Schoonover observed, "Time and time again, the Central American, Mexican, or other Latin American liberals were compelled to recall to the United States its role in defending the liberal New World institutions from Old World attack").

[137] *See* Leandro Prados de la Escosura, *supra* note 63, at p. 281 ("integration into the world economy brought net gains to Latin American economies over the long run"). The Standard of Civilization is discussed further in the next chapter.

[138] Andrew T. Guzman, "Why LDCs Sign Treaties That Hurt Them: Explaining the Popularity of Bilateral Investment Treaties," 38 *Virginia Journal of International Law.* 639 (1998), at pp. 687–688 (Latin American states needed – and still need – a credible way to attract foreign investment).

obligations."[139] Gonzalo de Quesada (1868–1915), a Peruvian diplomat, expressed the geopolitical position of Latin America as follows:

> In our continent for reasons known by all, the difficulties which history has accumulated in the Old World do not exist. There is no system of international balance of power, nor has there elapsed sufficient time for our nationalities to form strong sentiments of exigent time for our nationalities to form strong sentiments of exigencies.[140]

In fact, governments resorted to desperate means to raise capital. General Santa Anna of Mexico (1794–1876) took the highly unpopular step of selling nearly 30,000 square miles of territory to the US for US$ 10,000,000.[141] In retrospect, foreign capital did not solidify even the countries with the best economic outlooks, such as Argentina. This is because the investments in domestic infrastructure were designed to develop foreign rather than domestic needs; railroads connected ports with products rather than governments with their citizens. Latin American industry, as the historian David Landes (1924–2013) writes, "was not a driver but a passenger of growth."[142]

Cultural reasons also explain the Latin American motivation to arbitrate. In the late nineteenth century, Liberals were in power in many Latin American countries, including Mexico. These politicians were guided by Auguste Comte's (1798–1857) positivism and, to some meaningful degree, welcomed the civilizing mission of imitating Western culture and laws. Center-right elites were ideologically compatible with the application of international law to alien claims. The applicability of international law to what otherwise would be private domestic claims was one among many concessions – including the suppression of their populations – that Liberal governments were willing to make in order to press ahead with their agendas of material progress.[143] As Arnulf Becker

139 1877 For. Rel., pp. 385 *et seq.* as cited in Goebel, *supra* note 133, at p. 203.

140 Gonzalo de Quesada, *Arbitration in Latin America* (Rotterdam: Wyt, 1907), at p. 72.

141 The Gadsden Purchase was of a 29,670-square-mile region of present-day southern Arizona and southwestern New Mexico that was signed on December 30, 1853. According to Schoonover, US imperialism "was not the product of undesired United States penetration or of United States international power politics, but rather, initially at least, a phenomenon heartily welcomed by the governing liberal elite in Mexico" (*supra* note 76, at p. *xx*).

142 David S. Landes, *The Wealth and Poverty of Nations: Why Some Are So Rich and Some So Poor* 327 (New York: W.W. Norton, 1999).

143 O'Brien, *supra* note 83, at p. 55.

Lorca writes, the Latin American push for independence relied on international law:

> [F]or the endeavor ... symbolized broader allegiances with the liberal ideals of progress and civilization generated by the independence movement. International law proved critical in providing Latin American politicians with a discourse to bolster the claim of sovereign autonomy for the new nations, and the attainment of international legal autonomy emerged as a prized benchmark for civilization.[144]

In sum, there were several reasons why Latin American governments agreed to international arbitration with the US and other Western powers. First and foremost, these decisions were made in the shadow of the US Navy. However, international arbitration also bolstered their sense of independence from European political domination. Further, agreeing to arbitrate ensured the continued flow of foreign capital into Latin American markets, which was crucial given the formative state of their fledgling infrastructures. Though agreeing to arbitrate exposed Latin American governments to state responsibility, the amounts in question were frequently low and were an acceptable price for recognition. Finally, the acceptance of international arbitration played into the strategy among Liberal rulers in Latin America who believed that international law would strengthen the positions of their governments.

Claims Flood the State Department

By the late 1860s, appeals for diplomatic protection had created a massive backlog in the State Department, which lacked the human and political resources to resolve them. The vast majority of these claims being alleged by US nationals was that they had been denied justice while abroad. Prior to the Fish regime, clerks had been passively logging such claims in the event that an international commission would eventually be established to resolve them.[145] With increased international intercourse came

[144] Arnulf Becker Lorca, "International Law in Latin America or Latin American International Law? Rise, Fall, and Retrieval of a Tradition of Legal Thinking and Political Imagination," 47(1) *Harvard International Law Journal* 283 (2006), at p. 300 (internal citations omitted).

[145] Secretary of State Edward Livingston inaugurated the creation of America's first global bureaucracy, the US consulship. But this was not enough to administer the task of managing international claims of diplomatic protection. *See* Simeon Andonov Simeonov, "The United States' First Global Bureaucrats: Consuls and the Making of the Global American State, 1833–1856," SHAFR 2020 Annual Conference Panel 60:

increased disputes. US nationals, often with little appreciation for the fragility of local infrastructures, were making large investments in new countries with dissimilar legal systems to that of the US. When local jurisdictions failed to deliver results that met their expectations, these aliens would inundate their foreign offices with applications for diplomatic protection. As soon as he took office in 1861, Secretary of State Seward (1801–1872) wrote to Minister Thomas Corwin (1794–1865) in Mexico,

> I find the archives here full of complaints against the Mexican government for violations of contracts and spoliations and cruelties practiced against American citizens.[146]

Seward explained that these complaints against Mexico were being filed away until such time as Mexico regains "sufficient solidity to assume *a character for responsibility*."[147] Secretary of State Seward deferred his interposition for seven years. It was up to each state when or whether to accept private requests for protection.

Technically, the international right of protection was not triggered every time an alien alleged a denial of justice claim. By the nineteenth century, it was already an established rule of international law that the right of diplomatic protection was triggered only upon the exhaustion of local remedies.[148] However, in practice, this general rule allowed for a very important exception: when making recourse to local law enforcement would clearly be ineffective, as I discuss further below.[149] This exception was not infrequently applicable in Latin America, where a combination of fiscal and political weakness often undermined the domestic rule of law.

The two decades of the 1850s–1860s saw internal wars being fought in several Latin American nations, including Argentina, Chile, Venezuela, Colombia, Central America (now Guatemala, El Salvador, Honduras,

Citizens Without Borders: Extraterritoriality, Citizenship, and the Origins of the Global American State, 1815–1860, available online at https://shafr.memberclicks.net/assets/docs/Simeonov%2C%20Simeon%20Andonov.pdf, last visited June 2, 2021.

146 Seward to Corwin, Letter of April 6, 1861, *FRUS* (1861), at p. 65.

147 Seward to Corwin, *supra* note 147, at p. 65, emphasis added.

148 Discussed substantively further below.

149 The rule originated in premodern Europe as a basis for legal reprisals, the historical origins – *see* A. A. Cançado Trindade, "Origin and Historical Development of the Rule of Exhaustion of Local Remedies in International Law," 12 *Belgian Review of International Law* 499 (1976), at p. 501; Chittharanjan Felix Amerasinghe, *Local Remedies in International Law* (2nd ed., Cambridge: Cambridge University Press, 2004), at ch. 2.

Nicaragua and Costa Rica), Paraguay, Mexico and Brazil. While a government is occupied with suppressing a military rebellion – such as the US during its civil war – it was usually not expected to indulge claimant states with diplomatic protection.[150] During such times, foreign offices tended to defer their diplomatic interpositions until it was known which government represented the state and it was shown that the government had attained a modicum of domestic stability. All of the abovementioned states entered into international arbitral agreements only after their internal victories.

Claimant states used the political weakness of local governments to insist on international arbitration. As Yale law professor Edwin M. Borchard (1884–1951) wrote in his 1915 monograph on alien protection,

> However just it may be to confine the alien to the rights granted by local law, predicating state liability merely upon the state's failure to make its grant effective, *practice has shown* that *nations of the Western European type are unwilling unreservedly to concede the application of this principle* to some of the weaker countries of the world.[151]

US diplomats often behaved this way. As Secretary Seward complained, "We are unfortunately too familiar with complaints of the delay and inefficiency of the courts in the South American republics."[152]

The Diplomatic Importance of Alien Protection

Diplomatic protection was one of the most important issues in US–Mexican relations during the nineteenth century and beyond. In the four decades between 1825 and 1868, the US and Mexico entered into five claims conventions. In the first half of the century, it was Mexico who

[150] The US signed a *compromis* regarding alien injuries arising out of its civil war with France, Great Britain and Spain. For a list of arbitrations, *see* John Barrett, *The Pan American Union: Peace, Friendship, Commerce* (Washington, DC: Pan American Union, 1911).

[151] Borchard, *infra* note 218, at p. *vi*.

[152] Seward to Burton (US Minister to Colombia), April 27, 1866, in United States Department of State, *Papers Relating to the Foreign Relations of the United States* (Washington, DC: Government Printing Office, 1867), at p. 433). US officials viewed the Mexican infrastructure as corrupt and unreliable (House Ex. Doc. No. 2, Part III, 34 Cong., I Sess. (Ser. 844), p. 191) and as based on the "erroneous conception" that it was a "civilized country" (Report of February 24, 1858, Sen. Ex. Doc. No. 37, 35 Cong., 2 Sess. (Ser. 991).

proposed arbitration and the US who reluctantly agreed.[153] In the second half of the century, the dynamic shifted; now the US was asking for arbitration, and it was Mexico who had to be cajoled into agreement.[154] After the 1848 Treaty of Guadalupe Hidalgo, there was considerable foreign pressure on the Mexican Government regarding foreign claims. The US severed its diplomatic relations with the Juárez Administration owing to the lack of alien protection in Mexico.[155]

In 1861, Mexico entered into a treaty with France, Great Britain and Spain regarding improved alien protection, the enforcement of which could be coercive.[156] But the US declined to sign the treaty and Great Britain and Spain refused to participate in the coercive measures. This left France to act forcefully on its own. Six years later, writing to his minister in Mexico, Seward was still waiting patiently: "In the present unsettled condition of the government of Mexico, it is not deemed compatible with the interests of this government nor conducive to an establishment of friendly understanding with the Republic of Mexico to press with importunity the pecuniary claims of citizens of the United States."[157] The fact that Seward waited as long as he did to negotiate with Mexico led to much public criticism. In particular, the business community, of which Hamilton Fish was then a leading attorney, was dissatisfied with its government's protection of transnational investments.[158]

153 Abraham H. Feller, *The Mexican Mixed Claims Commission 1923–1934: A Study in the Law and Procedure of International Tribunals* (New York: Macmillan, 1935), at pp. 1–7. The French Government rejected the original Mexican proposal to arbitrate the Pastry War dispute as "laughable" given that the dignity of France "could not permit it to leave to a third party" (Ultimatum of March 21,1838, as quoted in Lapradelle and Politis, *infra* note 333, at p. 546).

154 In the spring of 1858, the subject of a United States protectorate for Mexico was discussed in both countries – *see* James Morton Callahan, *Evolution of Seward's Mexican Policy* (West Virginia University Studies in American Diplomatic Relations, 1909), at p. 5.

155 Moore, *supra* note 3, at p. 1289. Similarly, the US withheld its recognition of the Díaz Government in Mexico until it proved it had "sufficient strength to carry out its international obligations." Seward's policy was not to recognize a government that is not "approved by the people" or does not have "sufficient strength to carry out its international obligations" (*FRUS* (1877) at p. 404).

156 Moore, *supra* note 3, at pp. 1290–1291.

157 Letter of Seward to Otterborg, August 8, 1867, Messages and Documents, Dept. of State, Part 2, 1867–8, p. 388 as cited in Paisley, *supra* note 62, at p. 12.

158 In 1866, Fish criticized Seward's meek handling of the "Mexican Question" (Hamilton Fish to Dr. Niles, January 1, 1866, as quoted in Chapin, *supra* note 57, at p. 149). In addition to Fish, Grant was tied closely to the business community. Grant was the Chairman of the Mexican Southern Railroad. This is a relatively unexplored area of

By 1868, the situation changed: the Maximilian rebellion was defeated, and President Juárez began his new administration. Seward commenced negotiations with a view to stopping forced loans and military service.[159] The US had given up its territorial interests in Mexico and focused instead on securing special (international) protection of its nationals. Seward, in particular, after the Civil War, was keen to reopen the Mexican market to the US. As *The New York Times* observed, Seward went from defensively protecting the region from European intervention to proactively seeking "with extraordinary success to extend American influence around the globe, and to negotiate treaties of commerce, amity and relationship with all those powers and peoples with which we have heretofore had no intercourse, or with which it has been limited and imperfect."[160] Mexico, in turn, agreed to arbitrate out of the need for recognition, as well as its gratitude to the US for helping oust Maximilian.[161] Interestingly, what is clear is that the 1868 *compromis* had nothing to do with Article XXI of the 1848 treaty between the US and Mexico, which provided for the general arbitration of all international claims between the two countries.

Fish Reshapes the State Department

The rise in international claims arrived at a State Department in a period of transition. In the first half of the century, it was seen as the most critical arm of the executive branch and a stepping-stone to the Presidency.[162] The last Secretary of State to rise to the US Presidency was James Buchanan, in 1857. In the second half of the century, the

diplomatic history – *see* Hardy, *supra* note 68; Bruce Benson, "An Exploration of the Impact of Modern Arbitration Statutes on the Development of Arbitration in the United States," 11 *Journal of Law, Economics and Organization* 479 (1995), at p. 482; John Y. Simon (ed.), *The Papers of Ulysses S. Grant*, Vol. 30 (Carbondale: Southern Illinois University, 1967), at pp. 156–1157.

159 Messages and Documents, Dept. of State, Part 2, 1867–8, pp. 388, 544 as cited in Paisley, *supra* note 62, at pp. 7–8, 11–12.

160 *The New York Times*, December 16, 1867, as cited in Walter Stahr, *Seward: Lincoln's Indispensable Man* (New York: Simon & Schuster, 2012), at p. 503.

161 Stahr, *ibid*, at p. 535 (Mexicans credited Seward with forcing French and Austrian troops to leave their country); *see* Feller, *supra* note 205, at p. 6.

162 In 1849, Congress created the Department of the Interior to carve out the administration of domestic concerns from the State Department. The latter was denied jurisdiction over "great national objects" and was to focus on settling "private complaints against foreign powers" (Gaillard Hunt, *The Department of State of the United States: Its History and Functions* (New Haven: Yale University Press, 1914), at pp. 26–27).

Secretary position evolved into a hybrid legal-diplomatic advisory post. Secretary Fish was instrumental in the reorganization of his department into an international law bureau supporting the White House.[163]

Hamilton Fish accomplished this institutional change while serving as Secretary of State during both of Grant's administrations (1869–1877). Historians have remembered Fish more for reshaping the State Department than for any of his specific diplomatic feats (even the Treaty of Washington).[164] When Fish first took the reins of the State Department, it was unprofessional and disorganized – qualities opposite to those that characterized its new chief. The department was still saddled with the "spoils system" (appointments made based on political influence) initiated by President Andrew Jackson and notoriously maintained by Grant.[165] Fish's diary includes the following conversation: "Do you really wish George S. Fisher of Georgia given a place?" "Yes," the President responded, "I want to get him out of the country." "Well," Fish concluded, "La Guayra will do."[166]

During the nineteenth century, US diplomacy was more personal than institutional; it depended more on the skill of its highest diplomats than on institutionalized policies or practices.[167] During his term as Secretary, Fish molded the State Department in his image of bureaucratic professionalism.[168] He established a more efficient bureaucracy for processing

[163] The catalogue of books of the legendary Alvey A. Adee that were purchased over his half century of service to the State Department shows a number of acquisitions in the late 1870s in diplomatic history and international law (Peter Bridges, "An Appreciation of Alvey Adee," 10(1) *Diplomacy and Statecraft* 31 (1999), at p. 38).

[164] Convention between the United States of America and Great Britain signed in Washington, DC on May 8, 1871 ("Treaty of Washington"), 17 Stat. 863.

[165] Barnes and Morgan, *supra* note 94, at p. 68.

[166] *Ibid*, at p. 134, emphasis added.

[167] This was especially the case with Latin America, regarding which the US lacked any overall policy in Latin America – *see* Henry Adams, "The Session," *North American Review* 29–62 (July 1870). Anton-Hermann Chroust has described US diplomacy at the time as "not so much the story of institutions, organizations, or policies as it is a running account of individual lawyers who by their determination and astounding competence shaped not only the history of American law and jurisprudence but also the fate and fortune of the profession itself and, indeed, of the whole young nation" (*infra* note 339 at p. 284).

[168] On Fish's bureaucratic personality, *see* Stuart, *infra* note 341 at p. 142 ("a stickler for accuracy and regularity"); Charles S. Campbell, *The Transformation of American Foreign Relations 1865–1900* (New York: Harper & Row, 1976), at p. 25 (Fish was "unimaginative"); Nevins, *supra* note 1, at p. 19 (Fish "was quiet to a fault – a lover of study, of home, and of dignified employments; he hated contention; he was a natural conservative").

international claims and otherwise supporting the President's foreign policy.[169] He doubled the number of clerks in the department[170] and created a Bureau of Law to manage them.[171] Fish tasked this bureau with examining "all questions of law submitted by the Secretary or the Assistant Secretaries, and . . . all claims."[172] This ensured that the department would serve not only as administrator of alien protection claims but, more broadly, as a professional in-house advisory body on international law.[173] Additionally, Fish instituted a series of other reforms

[169] A telling story is that shortly after hearing of his nomination to the post of Secretary of State, George Strong, a leading lawyer and diarist, described Fish as the ultimate bureaucrat: "He sees everything, great and small, essential and non-essential, *of the same size*, and as Secretary of State, would put a dispatch sealed with wax in the same category with the *Alabama* piracies" (George Templeton Strong, Diary, March 11, 1869 as reproduced in Chapin, *supra* note 57, at p. *iv*).

[170] An increase of 80 percent, from 25 to 45 clerks – Nevins, *supra* note 1, at p. 864. Charles Morris labeled this development as the "Conquest of the Clerks" (Charles Morris, *The Tycoons: How Andrew Carnegie, John D. Rockefeller, Jay Gould, and J. P. Morgan Invented the American Supereconomy* (New York: Macmillan, 2006), at pp. 188–196). When Jefferson became the first Secretary of State in 1790, he had a total staff of nine and a combined salary quota of US$ 7,000 – *see* Barnes and Morgan, *supra* note 94, at p. 81.

[171] While the Department grew steadily from its inception, structural changes to the manner in which it handled international claims began with the creation of the Claims Clerk position in 1848 (the first semblance of legal counsel to Secretary of State) – *see* Richard B. Bilder, "The Office of the Legal Adviser: The State Department Lawyer and Foreign Affairs," 56 *American Journal of International Law* 633–684 (1962), at p. 634; *see also* (generally) John R. Crook, "Practicing International Law for the United States," 6 *Journal of Transnational Law & Policy* 1 (1996), at p. 2; Michael J. Powell, *From Patrician to Professional Elite: The Transformation of the New York City Bar Association* (New York: Russell Sage, 1988). In 1866, Seward created the "Examiner of Claims" position, which is the predecessor of today's "Office of the Legal Advisor." In 1891, the title was changed to "Solicitor for the Department of State." *See further* Hunt, *supra* note 163, at p. 202; William Henry Michael, *History of the Department of State of the United States* (Washington, DC: Government Printing Office, 1901), at pp. 26–27; Michael P. Scharf and Paul R. Williams, *Shaping Foreign Policy in Times of Crisis: The Role of International Law and the State Department Legal Adviser* (Cambridge: Cambridge University Press, 2010).

[172] Benjamin Perley Poore, *Congressional Directory*, 1st ed. (Washington, DC: Government Printing Office, 1881), at p. 122.

[173] It loosely corresponded to what was known in most Foreign Offices as the Bureau de Contentieux – see Eugene Schuyler, *American Diplomacy and the Furtherance of Commerce*, Vol. III (New York: Scribner, 1886), at pp. 11–12. The first occupant of this position was Erasmus Peshine Smith, who soon left and became an advisor to Japan's Ministry of Foreign Affairs. E. Peshine was a journalist and newspaper editor, a professor of mathematics, and a public education official and court reporter in the state of New York – in addition to being a student of law and economics. In *A Manual of Political*

relating to document organization (*e.g.*, duplication and indexing) and hiring processes (*e.g.*, professional examination) in the State Department.[174] These changes meant greater institutional strength as well as autonomy for the State Department.[175]

Fish viewed his role as providing a fiduciary service to the President. In this sense, he was a prototypical lawyer-diplomat: lawyer first, diplomat second.[176] I distinguish lawyer-diplomats from the lawyer-politicians who immediately preceded Fish in office. These were lawyers who used their posts as a springboard for their political aspirations.[177] Fish saw himself more as a lawyer than a politician.[178] Lawyer-diplomats

Economy (Philadelphia: Baird, 1872), Smith considered the "American" (as opposed to British) style of capitalism.

174 Amos Elwood Corning, *Hamilton Fish* (New York: Lanmere Publishing Co., 1918), at pp. 53–54.

175 *See* Nick Cleaver, *Grover Cleveland's New Foreign Policy: Arbitration, Neutrality, and the Dawn of American Empire* (New York: Palgrave MacMillan, 2014), at p. 64. According to Cleaver, the late nineteenth-century State Department often used legal structures – most notably treaty rights and the international law relating to neutrality in wars – as a basis for policy and a means of maintaining distance from events in foreign nations (*ibid* at pp. 63–64).

176 On the term "lawyer-diplomat," see Gerald Fitzmaurice, "Legal Advisers and Foreign Affairs," 59 *American Journal of International Law* 72 (1965). Michael Young calls them "Attorney-Advisers," which for "somewhat obscure historical reasons" retains the British spelling (rather than the more common American "Advisor") – Michael K. Young, "The Role of the Attorney-Adviser in the US Department of State: Institutional Arrangements and Structural Imperatives," 61 *Law and Contemporary Problems* 133 (1998), note 1. Robert Gordon uses "lawyer-statesmen" – Robert W. Gordon, "The Legal Profession," in Austin Sarat, Bryant Garth and Robert A. Kagan (eds.), *Looking Back at Law's Century* 287 (Ithaca: Cornell University Press, 2002), at p. 287. For a similar concept to lawyer-diplomats in the postwar context, *see* Afroditi Giovanopoulou, "Pragmatic Legalism: Revisiting America's Order after World War II," 62(2) *Harvard International Law Journal* 325 (2021), available online at https://ssrn.com/abstract=3708235, last visited February 23, 2021.

177 This distinction is somewhat arbitrary. Lawyer-diplomats and politicians alike used their positions for self-promoting purposes. Yet, there is a meaningful distinction here. Lawyer-politicians such as Daniel Webster (1782–1852) were regularly in the public eye – in Webster's case, both as Secretary of State and prior to that as a US Senator and Representative from Massachusetts and as a Supreme Court litigator. Webster's two professions were often in conflict. As an attorney, he often championed public causes at the cost of his duties toward paying private clients – *see* R. Kent Newmyer, "Daniel Webster as Tocqueville's Lawyer: The Dartmouth College Case Again," 11(2) *American Journal of Legal History* 127–147 (1967), at p. 143. Similarly, William Seward, Fish's predecessor, was another famous lawyer-politician.

178 Fish preferred the role of political professional to political activist – even Fish's most famous biographer subtitled his book: *The Inner History of the Grant Administration* (Nevins, *supra* note 1).

like Fish were a new breed of diplomats who played an important – if unnoticed – role in the transitional state of late nineteenth-century US diplomacy. The Fish–Grant team was the first lawyer–client relationship of its kind in the White House. Grant would express his foreign policy expectations to Fish, who would implement them as best he could.

Lieber Becomes Umpire in 1870

When Fish took up the reins of the State Department as Seward's successor, one of his early decisions was to select an umpire for the Mexico tribunal. Rather than appoint a local minister or sovereign to act as arbitrator – as was then the custom – Fish chose Francis Lieber (Figure 2.2), a professional international lawyer with famously progressive views about international arbitration. This selection was based on the personal relationship between the two men as well as on Lieber's views and stature as well. Lieber advocated for a larger role for lawyers in resolving international disputes. This would require the ability to delegate diplomatic disputes to independent tribunals composed of technical experts. The gaps in existing international laws were not an obstacle. Lieber did not believe that international arbitration required multilateral codification. The professionalism of lawyers – such as himself and his close colleague in Germany, Johann Casper Bluntschli (1808–1881) – was sufficient for settling most international disputes.[179]

In early 1869, Columbia University Trustee, Samuel Ruggles, presented President Grant with a petition that was signed by leading New York Republicans. It urged the newly elected President to appoint Lieber "abroad in a representative capacity or in international arbitrations."[180]

179 *See, e.g.*, Bluntschli to Lieber, May 25, 1866; Lieber to Bluntschli, December 8, 1867. In a letter to Dufour, Lieber writes: "one of the most promising things in matters of internationalism would be the meeting of the most prominent jurists of the Law of Nations, of our Cis-Caucasian Race – one from each country – in their individual and not in any public capacity, to settle among themselves certain great questions of the Law of Nations, as yet unsettled" (Lieber to General G. H. Dufour, April 10, 1872, Lieber Papers, Huntington Library, Box 26, emphasis in original). Lieber would refer to his relationship with Bluntschli in Heidelberg (and Laboulaye in Paris) as a "scientific clover leaf" (Johann Casper Bluntschli, "Lieber's Service to Political Science and International Law," in Francis Lieber (ed.), *Miscellaneous Writings* 7 (Philadelphia: J. B. Lippincott, 1880), Vol. II, at p. 13); *see further* Betsy Röben, *Johann Caspar Bluntschli, Francis Lieber und das modern Völkerrecht 1861–1881* (Baden-Baden: Nomos, 2003).

180 Ruggles and others to the President of the United States, April 8, 1869, copy. The signatories were J. A. Roosevelt, Wm. T. Blodgett, Francis C. Barlow, George Cabot

Figure 2.2 Francis Lieber[181]

This document, which by "abroad" implied Europe, underlines how much Lieber did not expect to be appointed to umpire some Latin American tribunal.[182] Lieber's primary international focus, even in his frequent communications with Fish, was European diplomacy.[183] Lieber

Ward, C. E. Detmold, J. S. Schultz, Joseph H. Choate, Theodore W. Dwight, Wm. C. Brian, Henry W. Bellows and LeGr. B. Cannon. Lieber to Thayer, February 12, 1868 and May 7, 1869; Lieber to Sumner, April 16 and December 11, 1869, Lieber papers, Lieber to Fish, April 23, 1869, Fish papers, Library of Congress reproduced in Freidel, *supra* note 58 at p. 404. Lieber forwarded the letter on to Sumner, not knowing that the latter had fallen out of favor with Fish and Grant's Administration.

181 Photo courtesy of Wikimedia Commons, https://en.wikipedia.org/wiki/Francis_Lieber#/media/File:Francis_Lieber_-_Brady-Handy.jpg.

182 *See also* Lieber to Fish, May 15, 1870 (microfilm, reel 1), wherein which Lieber asks Fish to have him appointed to fill the vacant ministerial position in Madrid or otherwise in central Europe: "I know that in such a place I would do some good in the promotion of the Law of Nations – the jural church of good will among Men." Note the date is months after his appointment to the Mexican tribunal.

183 In one letter, Lieber wrote "That is the thing I should have promoted with all my soul, could I have been sent diplomatically to Europe. *It would have been the last work of my life*" (Letter of Lieber to Judge Thayer of May 7, 1869, Huntington Library, MSS MFILM 00003, Reel 1, emphasis added).

regularly advised Fish on the Alabama Tribunal.[184] Ultimately, it was Lieber's suggestion to arbitrate with Great Britain that Fish realized in the Treaty of Washington.[185] Fish also sought out Lieber and his European contacts in order to legitimate other US policies.[186] Lieber, who was regularly in communication with Fish, had no expectation of being offered the Mexican umpireship. Fish, however, declined to appoint Lieber to a diplomatic or arbitral position in Europe; he needed Lieber to implement US policy in Latin America.

Justice, Delegated

The Lieber Tribunal was established by a *compromis* between the US and Mexico signed on July 4, 1868 by William Seward, Fish's predecessor.[187] The 1868 treaty was neither particularly novel nor the first of its kind between the two countries. However, in contrast to the 1839 and 1853 mixed claims commissions with Mexico and Great Britain, respectively, the Lieber Tribunal was legalistic (*see* Table 2.3).[188] No substantive laws were specified in any of the arbitral agreements; no general or specific

[184] Lieber to Fish, March 12, 1869, Fish Papers, Library of Congress; Fish to Lieber, March 24, 1869; Fish to Lieber, June 10, 1869, Lieber papers; Lieber to Fish, June 8, 1869, Fish Papers, Library of Congress; Lieber to Fish, May 31 and June 20, 1869, Fish Papers, Library of Congress.

[185] Lieber to Fish, May 31 and June 20, 1869, Fish Papers, Library of Congress.

[186] Lieber to Bluntschli, May 29, 1869. Shortly thereafter, Lieber penned an editorial in the *Evening Post* under his favorite nom de plume, "Americus" – "The Alabama or Laird Principle," *New York Evening Post*, May 29, 1869 (the *Post* incorrectly attributed the editorial to "Americanas"). Also, Lieber to Fish, September 15, 1870, Fish to Lieber, September 12, 1870 and October 4, 1870. Bluntschli published his indictment of Sumner in "Opinion Impartiale sur la Question de l'Alabama et sur la Maniére de la Résoudre," 2 *Revue de droit international et de législation comparé* 452–479 (1870). Bluntschli's view was also translated as a letter to the *New York Times* of May 3, 1872.

[187] Claims of Mexican and American citizens under the convention of July 4, 1868, 44 Cong., 2 Sess., No. 31 (1720), discussed further in the next chapter.

[188] The *compromis* was ostensibly based on the 1853 London Convention between the US and Great Britain (Convention of 1853 Between Great Britain and the United States signed February 8, 1853; Moore, *supra* note 3, at p. 1292). The awards were to be final and binding, "without appeal and in writing" (Article 2). Arbitrators were merely asked to "designate whether any sum which may be allowed shall be payable in gold or in the currency of the United States" (*ibid* at pp. 1294–1295). The 1839 treaty did not allow for any Mexican claims to be considered by the arbitral tribunal; only US claims were admissible. The 1838 compromis also include twice the number of commissioners (four instead of two in 1868), making it more difficult to reach a consensus. Otherwise, the arbitral agreements were not very different.

Table 2.3 *Comparison of three US Mixed Claims Commissions*

	1839 (Mexico)	1853 (Britain)	1868 (Mexico)
A third-party tribunal	X	X	X
Authorized to issue binding awards	X	X	X
Tribunal comprised of attorneys			X
Awards based on legal reasoning		X	X

principles of state responsibility were pre-agreed upon. Instead, *the focus was on the procedure of arbitration.*

The first US–Mexico tribunal was umpired by Baron Von Róenne, the Prussian minister to Washington. Von Róenne's decisions "were expressed in the form of simple awards, state his conclusions, but not the reasons upon which they were based."[189] The US–British commission was umpired by Joshua Bates (1788–1864), a US-born financier (with Baring Brothers & Co.) in London. Though not a lawyer, Bates' awards did include some reasoning based on legal principles.[190] The second US–Mexico tribunal was umpired by Francis Lieber and included awards based on legal analysis. The 1868 *compromis* contained a new provision regarding each state's right to appoint an agent to argue its case before the tribunal. (This nuance was so subtle that Seward's own biographers barely mention the 1868 treaty at all.[191]) The US chose William Henry Wadsworth (1821–1893) as its Commissioner and Joseph Hubley Ashton (1836–1907) (former Assistant Attorney General) as its agent and counsel. Mexico appointed its *chargé d'affaires*, Francisco Gómez Palacio, as Commissioner and Caleb Cushing (1800–1879) (former US Attorney General) as its agent and counsel.[192] Through this provision

[189] Moore, *supra* note 3, at p. 1238. Secretary of State Webster insisted that Berlin show the reasoning in at least one particular decision – *ibid* at pp. 1238–1239.

[190] Interestingly, like Lieber in 1870, Bates was not the first choice; it was former-US President Martin Van Buren, who declined the offer.

[191] Ferris, for example, does not even mention it at all – Norman B. Ferris, *Desperate Diplomacy: William H. Seward's Foreign Policy, 1861* (Knoxville: University of Tennessee Press, 1976).

[192] Cushing (1800–1879) was educated at Harvard (he enrolled at age thirteen). He entered politics at the early age of twenty-five and fifty years later was tapped by President Grant to become a Supreme Court justice in 1874 (he withdrew his nomination). Cushing was also a diplomat, appointed the first US minister to China in 1843. After returning to the

of the 1868 *compromis*, attorneys began to play a quiet but critical role in arbitral proceedings.

The selection of Cushing as Mexican agent is particularly remarkable. Cushing was not only a racist,[193] he was specifically scornful of Mexicans themselves, citing "the intolerant spirit of the Mexicans, and their ignorance, passion, or indiscretions in dealing with foreigners and foreign governments."[194] Cushing partook in the filibustering activities of a group of private businessmen who sought control of Lower California (actually, with approval of the Juárez regime as a balance to the French threat).[195] Finally, Cushing had several financial investments in Mexico, including the American and Mexican Railroad and Telegraph Company, which sought to build a railroad and telegraph connecting the states of Sonora and Chihuahua with Texas and the Gulf of Mexico.[196]

Cushing's conflict of interest could hardly have been more apparent. He turned down the offer to be named US Minister to Mexico so that he could advance his own financial interests as Mexico's agent in the Lieber Tribunal.[197] Cushing had little faith in the Mexican administration and openly predicted *in 1868* that Mexico's "northern provinces cannot fail to be . . . possessed by us, sooner or later." The only reason he limited his comments to northern Mexico is because he thought more territorial annexations would result in a "savage," British-like rule.[198] It is unclear how much of this information was available to Mexico at the time of Cushing's appointment. What is known is that Cushing spoke Spanish fluently and was a close friend of Secretary of State William Seward.

Fish appointed Lieber to umpire the 1868 tribunal in order to provide a level of dignity to its proceedings. Lieber initially declined the offer but

US, he became a judge on the Massachusetts Supreme Court and later the Attorney General of the US. In 1869, he was appointed Commissioner to serve on the US–Mexico Mixed Claims Commission by Mexico. Two years later, President Grant appointed him as US Counsel for the Alabama Tribunal.

193 *See* Belohlavek, *supra* note 99, at pp. 325, 335.

194 Caleb Cushing, "Memoir on the Mexican Republic," Washington, March 22, 1845, to James Buchanan, as cited in Belohlavek, *supra* note 99, at p. 192.

195 Belohlavek, *supra* note 99, at p. 336.

196 American and Mexican Railroad and Telegraph Company, *Prospectus and Act, Incorporating the American and Mexican Railroad and Telegraph Company, for Building a Railroad and Establishing Telegraph Lines through the States of Chihuahua and Sonora, with Copies of the Grants from said States and the General Government of Mexico* (New York: Frank McElroy, Steam Book and Job Printer, 1865), at p. *v*.

197 Belohlavek, *supra* note 99, at p. 337. For example, Cushing argued the Mexican claims throughout the period, receiving a US$ 4,000 annual retainer.

198 Belohlavek, *supra* note 99, at p. 336.

Table 2.4 *The claims of the Lieber Tribunal*[199]

Claims against the US (including *Aguirre* cases)	998
Claims allowed against the US	167 (16.7%)
Claims against the US (excluding *Aguirre* cases)	631
Claims allowed against the US	167 (26.5%)
Claims against Mexico	1,017
Claims allowed against Mexico	186 (18.3%)

after a few months of negotiations concerning his salary and a personal visit from Minister Mariscal, he accepted the position.[200] However, from Mexico's perspective, Lieber was a controversial choice. Soon after beginning his umpireship, Mexico expressed its regret over agreeing to Lieber's appointment. In 1871, Cushing wrote to Joseph Hubley Ashton complaining about Lieber's lack of judicial independence and pro-US bias. Mexico requested to disqualify Lieber, but Ashton declined to even consider the request.[201] At one point, Lieber also intended to resign his umpireship and travel to Europe in his final days. Before doing so, however, Lieber died on October 2, 1872. He was succeeded a year later by a dignified British attorney, Sir Edward Thornton (1817–1906), then serving as Minister to Washington.

The Lieber Tribunal adjudicated 1,017 claims against Mexico and 998 against the US. The claims against Mexico, including interest and damages, amounted to US$ 470,126,613.40; those against the US equaled US$ 86,661,891.15 (see Table 2.4).[202] Claims included wrongful death, forced loans, impressment into Mexican military service and wrongful

[199] Report of House Com. 27, 45 Cong., 2 Sess., Serial No. 1822. The *Aguirre* cases also concerned Indian depredations that were released under Article 2 of the US–Mexico Treaty of 1853, which abrogated the Treaty of Guadalupe Hidalgo, by which the US was obligated to prevent Indian incursions into Mexico from the US.

[200] Thomas Sergeant Perry (ed.), *Life and Letters of Francis Lieber* (Boston: James R. Osgood and Co., 1882), at pp. 394–395.

[201] Thus, neither Mexico nor Lieber himself wanted Lieber to be appointed to the umpireship. Bizarrely, Mexico's first choice was William Cullen Bryant, who was a lawyer in his youth but then became editor of the *New York Evening Post*. Lieber was only offered the umpireship after Bryant (incidentally, Lieber's friend) rejected it on January 12, 1870 (Moore, *supra* note 3, at pp. 1299–1300). Though I have not seen any evidence to support the intuitive hypothesis that Bryant declined the position to make room for Lieber, Bryant did sign the Ruggles petition (*supra* note 182).

[202] Report of House Com. 27, 45 Cong., 2 Sess., Serial No. 1822; Ex. Doc. 48 Cong., 1 Sess. doc. 103, Serial No. 2205 as cited in Moore, *supra* note 3, at pp. 1314–1320.

imprisonment. The vast majority of its claims concerned property rights. The awards were reasoned and often nuanced. A relatively publicized example was the case of *Rafael Aguirre*, one of 366 claims of Mexican citizens against the US for injuries caused by Indian depredations (amounting to US$ 31,813,053.64). The claim was dismissed by Umpire Thornton based on a prior US–Mexican treaty.[203]

In disposing of such a high volume of claims by employing the professional tools of attorneys, the Lieber Tribunal made an early and important contribution to the laws regarding citizenship,[204] the definition of injury,[205] causation,[206] attribution,[207] recognition[208] and belligerency.[209] The Tribunal also contributed to international procedural matters, including the admissibility of an alien injuries claim and the local remedies rule. For present purposes, the most important legal impact of the Lieber Tribunal was its establishment of the "international minimum standard," as I will discuss in the next section.[210]

The General Rule of Location Protection

As mentioned, when US nationals crossed borders, they were generally subject to local laws; however, exceptions could apply to this rule that would see the applicability of an international standard of care. In 1851, Secretary of State Daniel Webster (1782–1852) said:

> Our citizens who resort to countries where the trial by jury is not known ... frequently imagine when the laws of those countries are administered in the forms customary therein, that they are deprived of rights to which they are entitled, and therefore may expect the interference of their own Government. But it must be remembered, in all such cases, that they have of their own free will elected a residence out of their

[203] Award of Sir Edward Thornton of April 16, 1874, Moore, *supra* note 3, at pp. 2443–2447. Regarding the 1853 treaty, *see supra* note 246, Article 2.
[204] *See, e.g.*, Moore, *supra* note 3, at pp. 2862–2863.
[205] *Ibid*, at pp. 2432–2433.
[206] Discussed in Chapter 3.
[207] Discussed in Chapter 3.
[208] *See, e.g.*, Moore, *supra* note 3, at pp. 2873–2877.
[209] *Ibid*, at p. 2938.
[210] I later discuss the procedural and substantive laws to which the Lieber Tribunal contributed. In Chapter 3, I discuss the content of a state's responsibility that was triggered for violating those international laws.

> native land, and preferred to live elsewhere, and under another Government, and in a country in which different laws prevail.[211]

In 1873, Secretary Fish made a subtle qualification to Webster's position:

> It may, *in general*, be sure that when foreigners take up their abode in a country they must expect to share the fortune of the other inhabitants, and cannot expect a preference over them.[212]

The Lieber Tribunal affirmed the US position that *generally* international tribunals would not hear claims in which local remedies were not first exhausted; however, exceptions could apply.[213] In dismissing the case of *Jennings, Laughland & Company*, the tribunal reasoned, "The umpire does not conceive that any government can thus be made responsible for the misconduct of an inferior judicial officer when no attempt whatever has been made to obtain justice from a higher court. The umpire therefore awards that the claim be disallowed."[214] An exception that affirmed this rule was the case of *Ulrich and Langstroth*, a claim against Mexico for losses inflicted, and forced loans imposed, by Monterey insurgents. The US argued that the claimants had no practicable means of exhausting local remedies prior to the existence of the Lieber Tribunal.[215] The award affirmed that states may interpose diplomatically on behalf of their citizens abroad *if* the local remedies rule had either been complied with *or* could not be complied with because no local remedies were effectively available. The Lieber Tribunal extended this right of interposition to include corporations.[216]

211 Report of Webster to President, December 23, 1851, 6 Websters Works, pp. 527–528, *Thrasher's Case* as cited in Francis Wharton, *A Digest of the International Law of the United States, Taken from Documents Issued by Presidents and Secretaries of State, and From Decisions of Federal Courts and Opinions of Attorney-General* (Washington, DC: Government Printing Office, 1886), §223.

212 Fish to Foster, December 16, 1873 as cited in Wharton, *supra* note 213, §223.

213 For an overview of Lieber Tribunal awards, *see* Rosero, *supra* note 119, at pp. 107–118.

214 *Case of Jennings, Laughland & Co.*, Thornton, umpire, November 5, 1874, as reproduced in Moore, *supra* note 3, at p. 3136. For more examples of the Lieber Tribunal's contribution to the general obligation of states to protect aliens, *see* the *William W. Mills* case, *John Bensley's* case (*ibid* at pp. 3017–3033).

215 Moore, *supra* note 3, at pp. 678–680.

216 In the *Delagoa Bay* case, involving US shareholders in a foreign (Mexican) company, the Lieber Tribunal accepted the US argument that "a government may intervene on behalf of a company incorporated under its laws or under the laws of a constituent state or province" (Moore, *supra* note 3, at pp. 1865–1899; see also, Edwin M. Borchard, *The Diplomatic Protection of Citizens Abroad or The Law of International Claims* (New York: The Banks Law Publishing Co., 1915), at §279.

Officially, *Ulrich and Langstroth* was the exception to the general rule of international law regarding local laws and legal systems. However, in retrospect, the case represented *the rule rather than the exception* of diplomatic protection within Latin America. As the aforementioned US Attorney-General (and frequent diplomat and international litigator) Caleb Cushing writes:

> As to exceptions to the general rule [on local remedies], they have grown up chiefly in Spanish America in consequence of the unsettled condition of the new American Republics. Great Britain, France, and the United States, have each occasionally assumed, on behalf of their subjects or citizens in those countries, rights of interference, which neither of us would tolerate at home – in some cases from necessity, in others with very questionable discretion or justification, so as greatly to aggravate the evils of misgovernment therein, as will plainly appear on a careful study of the internal condition of the South American republics.[217]

Early Awards Yielded Inconsistent Results

As was often the case with mixed claims commissions, the Lieber Tribunal rarely probed deeply into the factual evidence supporting the claims. For example, in the case of *Benjamin Weil,* the injury claimed was US$ 334,950 for wrongfully seized cotton being exported to Mexico in transit by a General of the Liberal Mexican forces. According to US Commissioner Wadsworth, "In the face of so many witnesses of respectability, I am unwilling to decide that the facts detailed by them are not true." The umpire awarded US$ 285,000 plus interest.[218] In the *La Abra Silver Mining Company* case, the fraud with which the claim was put forward went entirely unnoticed by the US commissioner and the umpire. Mexican Commissioner Zamacona insisted that the evidence was fabricated.[219] However, the umpire awarded US$ 358,791, believing that Mexican authorities had constructively expropriated US property.[220] After the award was rendered and paid, Mexico continued its protest diplomatically. When Chester A. Arthur became US President in 1881,

217 *Official Opinions of the Attorneys General of the United States Advising the President and Heads of Departments in Relation to their Official Duties*, Vol. VII: Opinions of Hon. Caleb Cushing (C. C. Andrews, ed., Washington: W. H. & O. H. Morrison, 1871), at p. 234–235, internal citations omitted.

218 Moore, *supra* note 3, at pp. 1324–1347.

219 *Ibid*, at pp. 1326, 1327.

220 *Ibid*, at pp. 1328–1329.

his Secretary of State, Frederick T. Frelinghuysen suspended the payments until an investigation was concluded. The petitioner, Mr. Weil, filed a mandamus to the Supreme Court compelling the government to continue distributing the award. It was rejected.[221]

The Lieber Tribunal made specious conclusions about the intent behind domestic legislation. In the *Anderson and Thompson* case, the claimants sought indemnification for losses to properties they had developed in Mexico. The properties were damaged by the Mexican army while resisting French attacks. Mexico expropriated a plantation owned by the claimants and sought to dismiss their claim based on a lack of citizenship. Umpire Lieber dismissed this argument. According to Mexican law, by default, every purchaser of local property triggers Mexican citizenship unless the purchaser simultaneously and expressly disavows the citizenship. Lieber interpreted the purpose of the domestic law as to confer a benefit upon the foreign purchaser of land. Thus, to use the law to bestow a penalty upon the purchaser would be an inequitable usurpation of property rights. Thornton reaffirmed this award, adding his interpretation that the Mexican law was simply permissive in nature. It allowed for but did not necessarily require the replacement of US with Mexican citizenship.[222]

In addition to property loss cases, the US brought several claims for wrongful death as well as wrongful imprisonment.[223] Interestingly, the US seems to have considered continuing injuries (such as wrongful imprisonment) as more pressing diplomatic matters than completed injuries (such as wrongful death).[224] One such case involving a US national wrongfully imprisoned by Mexico that mobilized Congress into

[221] "The government assumed the responsibility of presenting his claim, and made it its own in seeking redress in respect to it" (Per Fuller CJ, November 23, 1889 as cited in *United States ex rel. Boynton v. Blaine*, 139 *US* 306, as cited in *ibid*, at pp. 1328–1329). On "Assumed Responsibility" as distinct from "responsibility" properly so-called, *see* Bin Cheng, *General Principles of Law as Applied by International Courts and Tribunals* 165–170 (London: Stevens & Sons, Ltd., 1953).

[222] Lieber umpire April 24, 1871, *Benjamin Elliott v. Mexico* No 460 Am Docket convention of July 4, 1868; Moore, *supra* note 3, at p. 2481. Thornton reaffirmed Lieber's ruling–Thornton umpire November 5, 1874, *Fayette Anderson and WM Thompson v. Mexico* No. 333.

[223] In 1874, US Minister to Mexico, Mr. Poster, stated that in the short time he had been in charge of the legation, he had been officially informed by United States' consuls of thirteen murders of American citizens, no one of which to his knowledge had been punished. FRUS, 43 Cong., 2 Sess., Serial No. 1634, doc. at pp. 489, 490, 491.

[224] *See* Gerald G. Eggert, *Richard Olney: Evolution of a Statesman* (University Park: Pennsylvania State University Press, 1974), at p. 192 (even bureaucrats such as

action was that of John Jay Smith. Smith was a US citizen arrested and charged with espionage and selling arms to General Cortina while in Brownsville. The evidence presented by Mexican authorities was scant and his treatment was viewed as "undignified." The US Consul interceded unsuccessfully for the release of Smith. Pressure from the US public was intense and included letters in national newspapers imploring Secretary Fish to have Smith released from prison. After several months of Smith's imprisonment – and almost daily exchange of diplomatic notes – Fish succeeded in securing Smith's release.[225] The State Department in the *Smith* case expressly rejected the possibility of threatening force.

The *Smith* case contrasts with that of *Julio Romano Santos*, in which the US did use force. Santos was a naturalized US citizen with no strong political connections or wealth. Born in Ecuador in 1852, Santos was sent by his family at age thirteen to the US for his secondary and graduate education. He took up teaching positions at the University of Virginia and later the Medical College of Alabama, during which time he became naturalized as a US citizen. In 1879, he returned to Ecuador to help his ailing mother and her business. In 1884, Ecuadorian officials arrested and imprisoned Santos for alleged complicity in a revolutionary movement. After a protracted incarceration, Santos was tried but not granted a "fair hearing."[226] The US presented a request for diplomatic protection, but Ecuador did not respond. The US then dispatched a Navy ship to Ecuador whose mission was "one of peace and good will … [and] of exerting the moral influence of our flag toward a discreet and mutually honorable solution."[227] Ecuador still did not respond. After another letter was sent, this time threatening military action to enforce its international claim, Ecuador released Santos after 226 days in prison and agreed to arbitrate his claim (he received an award of US$ 40,000).[228] The continuing nature of Mr. Santos' plight, it seems, though a private one in

Assistant Secretary Alvey A. Adee sent warships to seek their redemption as a matter of course, without even consulting the Secretary or President).

225 Reports of Com., 45 Cong., 2 Sess., at pp. 356–367. For a discussion, *see* Paisley *supra* note 62, at pp. 52–60.

226 There were no records of any sentence, conviction or acquittal of Mr. Santos – Moore, *supra* note 3, at pp. 1583–1585. In response, the US Congress passed two resolutions in relation to the case, one of which requested the President to use his efforts to secure a speedy and fair trial and to protect the life and property of the prisoner.

227 Moore, *supra* note 3, at p. 1581, note 2.

228 *Ibid*, at pp. 1583, 1591.

itself and without much of an imperial stake, mobilized both branches of the US Congress as well as the State Department into action.

Why such political and military drama to address a relatively minor injury to a naturalized citizen? The stakes for the US in the *Santos* case were similar to those of Britain in the *Don Pacifico* affair a few decades earlier.[229] British nationals residing in Greece were protected by the Crown because the fact of British nationality – even when possessed by a Jew – was an asset worth defending even at a high diplomatic cost. US Presidents often took such positions for the sake of shoring up the value of US citizenship, even abroad.[230] However, diplomatic and military pressures are two different weapons. Even though John Jay Smith had strong political ties to the US establishment, the military option was rejected. In contrast, when Julio Romano Santos was wrongfully imprisoned, without any such ties, the US sent in the Navy to secure the "consent" for his release. Clearly, then, the US was prepared to use force to protect the person and property of its citizens abroad – any of its citizens, by virtue of their citizenship. However, this practice was country specific. With Mexico, it was rejected, while with Ecuador, it was accepted. The US was careful to emphasize its non-forceful, commercial intentions with Mexico, whereas this was less important with Ecuador.[231]

Many of the Lieber Tribunal's awards imposed liability upon Mexico and upon the US for injuries to aliens. However, as discussed in the next chapter, the awards offer few definitive doctrines of international law. There are several reasons for this inarticulateness – both within the Lieber Tribunal specifically and in early international awards generally. International arbitrations were *ad hoc* adjudications and decades from institutionalization.[232] Tribunals lacked both the incentive and

[229] Discussed further in Chapter 3.

[230] For a discussion of President Cleveland's version of Palmerston's speech, *see* Loveman, *supra* note 60, at p. 161.

[231] *See* 44th Congress 2nd Session, Ex. Doc. No. 31. And *see* Denys P. Myers, "Violation of Treaties by Adverse National Action," 12 *American Journal of International Law* (1918) (private disputes of alien protection claims are appropriately non-public and susceptible to arbitration).

[232] On the institutionalization of *ad hoc* international arbitration through, among other bodies, the International Chamber of Commerce, *see* Paul R. Milgrom, Douglass C. North and Barry R. Weingast, "The Role of Institutions in the Revival of Trade: The Law Merchant, Private Judges, and the Champagne Fairs," 2(1) *Economics and Politics* 1 (1990). On the history of the ICC as an ostensible vehicle of peace, *see* George L. Ridgeway, *Merchants of Peace: Twenty Years of Business Diplomacy Through the International Chamber of Commerce 1919–1938* (New York: Columbia University

bureaucratic opportunity to establish or maintain a rule of law. Umpires were concerned with settling disputes and, to that end, would rely on anything from general principles and partial evidence to personal intuition.

According to the Mexican Commissioner (Palacio) in the *Rafael Aguirre* case, the normative basis for a claim can range from "the law of nature in its application to international relations" to "international law, as established by the consent of civilized nations and the opinions of writers" and even general maxims such as "*Quod tibi non vis fieri, alteri ne facias*" (do not do to others that which you would not have done to you).[233] In the *Emilio Roberts* case, the Lieber Tribunal admitted: "It is much more difficult for us to fix the amount of the claim... than to give judgment about the justice of the same claim." The tribunal continued: "[W]e, the Commissioners, are compelled to proceed solely by simple conjectures and inferences, drawn from the very few facts we have before us, and to make a very ample use of the discretionary power which pertains to our office."[234]

Existing international laws – including arbitral agreements – were porous.[235] The 1868 *compromis* establishing the Lieber Tribunal only required its commissioners to "impartially and carefully examine and decide, *to the best of their judgment*, and according to public law, justice, and equity, without fear, favor, or affection to their own country, upon all such claims above specified."[236] Lieber openly applied principles of equity in order to avoid the "painful psychological itching . . . an umpire

Press, 1938). More recently, on the relationship during the postwar era between lawyers and investors such as bankers in shaping the international protection of property abroad, *see* Filip Batselé, "Foreign Investors of the World, Unite! The International Association for the Promotion and Protection of Private Foreign Investments (APPI) 1958–1968" 34(2) *European Journal of International Law* 415–447(2023).

233 Moore, *supra* note 3, at pp. 2432–2433.

234 Memorial and Opinion, docket 594, MS., US Department of State as cited in Cheng, *supra* note 223, at p. 239, note 18.

235 To Lieber, the decisions of local courts were generally dispositive of the matter. Exceptionally, when a local decision was "so unfair" that it amounted to a "denial of justice," Lieber allowed himself to review the lower court (*Case of Frederic Bronner v. Mexico*, Thornton umpire November 04, 1874, Moore, *supra* note 3, at p. 3135).

236 Emphasis added. Similarly, Article 3 of the US–Paraguay treaty of February 4, 1859 simply required the commissioners to "fairly and impartially investigate the said claims, and a just decision thereupon render, to the best of their judgment and ability." Article 6 of the US–Venezuela *compromis* of December 5, 1885, stated that "The Commissioners shall make such decision as they shall deem in reference to such claims, conformable to justice" (Manning, *supra* note 111, at p. 147).

feels when he does not see a loophole through which he can escape assigning a monstrously large sum to a vile widow of a swindler who cheated every creditor of his."[237] Article 2, however, did include a novel procedure: the appointment of agents – that is, litigators.[238] Before and after 1868, arbitrators had wide discretionary powers.[239] They could consider anything – whether matters of law, politics or equity – when considering their decisions. However, by setting up international tribunals with lawyers and appointing umpires who were also lawyers, the US practice of alien protection yielded an increasing number of awards articulating general principles of liability. These awards became important sources of international law, especially in areas such as alien protection and state responsibility.

Because international arbitration relied heavily on general principles of law, the resulting awards depended heavily on each arbitrator's personal background.[240] This was no coincidence. By packing international tribunals with Western-trained attorneys, the US could ensure that the resulting awards would be based on Western expectations of legal protection. International arbitration was more than just an effective procedure of dispute resolution. It also solidified the US position concerning the substantive legal standard that international arbitrators were to apply in their awards. As I will discuss in the next chapter, international adjudication repackaged US iterations of those standards as "international" in nature. Late nineteenth-century lawyers were trained to wield general principles of law in litigation and that is what professional arbitrators did in international tribunals.[241] In his final report on the Lieber Tribunal to Hamilton Fish, the US agent, Joseph Hubley Aston, wrote:

[237] Lieber to Thomas C. Reynolds, June 15, 1872, Lieber papers, Library of Congress. *See also* Janis, *infra* note 346.

[238] "It shall be competent for each government to name one person to attend the commissioners as agent on its behalf, to present and support claims on its behalf, and to answer claims made upon it, and to represent it generally in all matters connected with the investigation and decision thereof." This provision was also included as Article 2 of the US–Peru *compromis* of December 4, 1868. But it was not in the US–Brazil *compromis* of March 14, 1870 or the US–Columbia *compromis* of August 17, 1874, which is noteworthy because the former was entered into by Seward and the latter by Fish.

[239] The idea of *kompetenz-kompetenz* was repeated in a number of Mexican arbitrations in the nineteenth century in which, again, it was very clearly articulated. *See* Georges Berlia, "Jurisprudence, des tribunaux internationaux en ce qui concerne leur compétence" 88 *Recueil de Cours* 105 (1955) at pp. 120–121; Crawford, *supra* note 52, at p. 15.

[240] Martti Koskenniemi, "General Principles: Reflexions on Constructivist Thought in International Law," 18 *Oikeustiede-Jurisprudentia* 117 (1985), at p. 141.

[241] I discuss this point further in Chapter 3.

> The commissioners deemed it proper, at the outset of their labors, to give reasons for their judgments and action, in carefully prepared opinions; and this practice was followed by each of the gentlemen who acted as umpire. The opinions of the commissioners and the umpire are recorded, and they will be found to contain valuable contributions to the law of international reclamations.[242]

A Legacy of Legalism

Above, I have focused on the workings of the Lieber Tribunal not only because it was an important precedent for intra-American arbitration, but as a representative example of that practice as well.[243] Indeed, the unexpectedly high volume of its caseload – 2015 submitted claims – establishes the tribunal as an important source of international law.[244] The awards have often since been relied upon by subsequent arbitrations.[245] This legacy of Lieber's is relatively understudied.

Francis Lieber is known for his early codification of the *jus in bello*, which instituted a minimum standard of treatment of prisoners during the US Civil War.[246] His other, lesser-known legacy is his contribution to a minimum standard of treating nationals abroad during times of peace.

242 Moore, *supra* note 3, at p. 1299.

243 On the general importance of the US–Mexico mixed claims commissions, *see* Feller, *supra* note 153, at p. *iiv*. As discussed in Chapter 6, the delegation of alien protection claims to professional international tribunals began with the appointment of Francis Lieber and has continued ever since. Even the specific procedure of selecting a third-party arbitrator used in the Lieber Tribunal became standardized around the world. Article 37(1) of the first Hague Treaty entrenched the original Article 2 of the 1868 US–Mexico *compromis*, which permitted States to appoint agents to represent them before the arbitral tribunal (Convention for the Pacific Settlement of International Disputes, July 29, 1899, 187 CTS 410). On this legacy in the international bar, or lack thereof, *see* James Crawford, "The International Law Bar: Essence Before Existence?," ESIL 2013 5th Research Forum: International Law as a Profession Conference Paper No. 11/2013, available at SSRN: http://ssrn.com/abstract=2364104 or http://dx.doi.org/10.2139/ssrn.2364104.

244 This was a much higher number than that expected by the signers of the 1868 *compromis* – *see* Moore, *supra* note 3, at pp. 1313–1314.

245 Ralston, *supra* note 17, at p. 204.

246 He was widely known as the international lawyer who authored the "Lieber Code," also known as the "Lieber Instructions," which were the Instructions for the Government of Armies of the United States in the Field, General Order № 100, issued on April 24, 1863. *See* John Fabian Witt, *Lincoln's Code: The Laws of War in American History* (New York: Free Press, 2010). For a discussion, *see* Georg Schwarzenberger, "The Standard of Civilisation in International Law," 8 *Current Legal Problems* 212 (1955), at pp. 221–222.

International arbitration was a cause Lieber actively supported. The *ad hoc* delegation of diplomatic disputes to dignified international lawyers became Lieber's last mission in life, occupying much of his final decade.[247] Like his other legacy, the legalism of his US–Mexico tribunal became a common feature in international arbitrations.[248] Going forward, international claims would be resolved by recourse to third-party tribunals (*1st element*) composed of one or more professional lawyers (*2nd element*) who are authorized to issue binding awards (*3rd element*) based on legal rules (*4th element*). In the next few paragraphs, I will elaborate upon each of these elements.

US legalism was triadic – Old World findings of international violation were usually made dyadically and not triadically.[249] Once a State alleged a violation, it could commence enforcement actions immediately – without negotiation, let alone arbitration.[250] The Old World approach was inappropriate in Mexico and much of the New World. In the Americas, increased foreign investment (and consequent claims) had to be complemented with greater sensitivity to the sovereignty of newly formed governments. As arbitration replaced traditional diplomatic protection, forceful intervention became a less acceptable means of redressing private injuries.[251] *The triadism of arbitration was premised upon the sovereign equality of states and the primacy of international law.* By referring legal disputes to third-party tribunals, international arbitration bypassed a major obstacle to the development of state responsibility: auto-interpretation.

US legalism relied on professional lawyers – Old World diplomacy did include examples of binding arbitration, but these were not professional. Triadic dispute resolution included "sovereign" and "papal," "*ad*

247 *See, e.g.*, Letter of Francis Lieber to Charles Sumner of December 27, 1861, Huntington Library Archives: "International law is the greatest blessing of modern civilization, and every settlement of a principle in the law of nations is a distinct, plain step in the progress of humanity."

248 Moreover, early twentieth-century international awards made frequent reference to and were often modeled after the 1868 *compromis* – *see* Feller, *supra* note NOTEREF _Ref380324105 \h 153, at p. 33.

249 This move from dyadic to triadic dispute resolution in diplomacy is clearly recognizable. As opposed to "bilateral" or "trilateral," "dyadic" and "triadic" emphasize delegation (as opposed to collaboration, such as in a treaty negotiation).

250 Premodern dispute resolution and state responsibility is further discussed in Chapter 5.

251 In one modern day practitioner's words, "The history of denial of justice is happily one of declining violence" (Jan Paulsson, *Denial of Justice in International Law* (Cambridge: Cambridge University Press, 2005), at p. 36).

hoc," "mixed claims" and "institutional" arbitral tribunals.[252] Sovereign or papal arbitration was the process wherein emperors and princes delegated their disputes for resolution by other heads of state or religious figures.[253] However, the level of professionalism expected of Old World arbitrators was not proportionate to the level of discretion that a *compromis* granted them. The first international mixed claims commission was the US–British commission established under the Ghent Treaty of 1814. The first *ad hoc* professional arbitral tribunal was in the *Hudson's Bay and Puget's Sound Agricultural Companies* case (1863).[254] *Ad hoc* arbitrations were comparatively diplomatic and mixed claims commissions more professional, given the broader discretion involved in resolving a more mixed bag of claims. Roughly half of US claims for alien protection in Latin America were determined by mixed commissions and it was in these commissions that many rules of international law were first attempted.

US legalism authorized arbitrators to issue binding awards – Arbitration was not the only form of triadism favored by Hamilton Fish, but it was a binding form of international dispute resolution. Non-binding forms of third-party assistance included good offices, mediation, conciliation and inquiry. While it is difficult to draw a bright line between these categories – the main difference being the level and scope of third-party involvement – they all share one common characteristic: they were voluntary triadic processes, the results of which were not necessarily binding upon disputing parties. They allowed the disputing parties to retain the maximum amount of control over their dispute through continued negotiation. International arbitration, in contrast, was a final process in which direct state involvement ended with the execution of the compromissory agreement. In the words of Secretary of State Richard Olney, arbitration that does not end in a final award "is no arbitration at all."[255]

[252] For a similar classification, see Merrills, *infra* note 337, at pp. 83–86.

[253] On the downsides of "sovereign" international arbitration, see Francis Lieber, *The Miscellaneous Writings of Francis Lieber*, Vol. II (Philadelphia: J. B. Lippincott & Co., 1881), at pp. 325–326: "So far, however, monarchs have been almost exclusively chosen as arbiters, which is inconvenient on several accounts."

[254] The first ad hoc arbitral tribunal umpired by a professional attorney was the Hudson's Bay and Puget's Sound Agricultural Companies (US and Great Britain) of July 01, 1863. The umpire was Benjamin Robbins Curtis (1809–1874).

[255] Richard Olney to Hoke Smith, February 14, 1912; Richard Olney to Grover Cleveland, March 19, 1896, OP, LC, as cited in Gerald G. Eggert, *Richard Olney: Evolution of a Statesman* (University Park: Pennsylvania State University Press, 1974), at p. 235.

US legalism was based on legal rules – Unlike the authority of papal or sovereign arbitrators, the normative basis of professional arbitrations was pre-existing law. These sources included, treaties, customs, general principles of law, and equity. In *Cotesworth & Powell*, Colombia was held responsible for the wrongful acts of municipal courts.[256] The tribunal, umpired by French *Chargé d'Affaires* Casimir Troplong (1824–87), listed ten "principles of responsibility"[257] but also stated:

> It is . . . necessary at the outset to reject the idea that denial of justice and state responsibility are co-extensive, and to put the discussion of the meaning of denial of justice on its true basis, which is one of terminology rather than of substantive rights.[258]

International tribunals were quick to rely on principles of liability before issuing awards, but slow to refer to them in substantive terms such as "state responsibility." The manner in which arbitrators applied general principles, was anything but declarative in nature. It was a creative process that began with the establishment of the Lieber Tribunal.

The Alabama as a Precedent of International Diplomacy

Why is the Alabama Tribunal and not the Lieber Tribunal remembered as the prototype of modern international arbitration? For one thing, until then, the US did not employ international law or legalism consistently. Another reason for this conflation is the widespread optimism left in the wake of the Alabama Tribunal. As soon as the Treaty of Washington was signed, the resulting *Alabama Claims* arbitration was spoken of as the harbinger of a new era of peaceful diplomacy. This optimism, however, was misplaced because the thrust of the political dispute had been eliminated by Fish and his British counterpart prior to the treaty's signing in Washington. There was little in the way of a legal dispute remaining for the arbitrators to resolve in Geneva. It certainly was critical in the history of international arbitration – but more because of its popularity than its technique of arbitration.

[256] Moore, *supra* note 3, Ch. XLIX. Arbitrations before United States Ministers.

[257] Moore, *supra* note 3, at pp. 2064–2065.

[258] Moore, *supra* note 3, at pp. 2081, 2085, respectively. But, which injury, then, was the indemnification aimed at remedying: the wrongful seizure, the subsequent cover-up or both? Of the ten "principles of responsibility" articulated by the international tribunal, none addressed this basic question.

The *Alabama Claims* captured the public's imagination on both sides of the Atlantic. To resolve a complex political clash over the role of Great Britain in supporting the Confederacy during the US Civil War, the two nations appointed an arbitral tribunal composed entirely of international lawyers. Periodicals such as *The New York Times, The North American Review* and the *London Standard* followed the back-and-forth diplomatic correspondence between both governments. What the excitement surrounding the Alabama Tribunal hides, however, is that its reliance on international arbitration was more a continuation of, than a break from, Old World diplomacy.

The facts of the *Alabama Claims* are well known and continue to be commented upon.[259] The dispute concerned British neutrality during the US Civil War. Had Great Britain breached international law by not diligently preventing a Liverpudlian ship builder from constructing the *CSS Alabama* (Figure 2.3), a Confederate raider? Most commentators agreed that Great Britain had not met its international obligations. Though several peculiar facts led to its inaction, the crucial diplomatic question was whether a Great Power would either admit any liability for its actions or expose itself to the possibility of being held accountable by an international tribunal. This was clearly understood by both US and British diplomats to be a political question.

Great Britain refused to apologize, leading many in the US to demand the concession of Canada to the US as a remedy.[260] US Minister to the Court of St. James Charles Francis Adams (1807–1886) offered to have the *Alabama Claims* arbitrated as early as 1863. But Lord John Russell (1792–1878) declined on the grounds that only the British were "the sole guardians of their own honor."[261] Arbitrating "high" political disputes was still considered a remote, if utopian notion. Thomas Balch (1821–1877), an American internationalist, had an opportunity to discuss the

[259] *E.g., see* Awalou Ouedraogo, "La neutralité et l'émergence du concept de due diligence en droit international. L'affaire de l'Alabama revisitée," 13(2) *Journal of the History of International Law* 307–346 (2011); The Rt Hon Lord Bingham of Cornhill, "The Alabama Claims Arbitration," 54 *International and Comparative Law Quarterly* 1 (2005); T. de Kay, *The Rebel Raiders: The Warship "Alabama," British Treachery and the American Civil War* (London: Pimlico, 2003); Eric Bruggink, "The 'Alabama' Claims," *The Alabama Lawyer* 339 (1996); A. Cook, *The Alabama Claims* (Ithaca: Cornell University Press, 1975); Doris W. Dashew, "The Story of an Illusion: The Plan to Trade Alabama Claims for Canada," 15(4) *Civil War History* 332 (1969).

[260] *See* Dashew, *supra* note 321, at p. 332.

[261] Moore, *supra* note 86, at p. 77.

Figure 2.3 CSS Alabama[262]

idea of arbitration directly with President Lincoln. The President, recalled Balch, replied:

> the idea was a good one in the abstract, but that in the then temper of the American people it was neither possible nor popular. In fact, as he quaintly expressed it, we were not near enough to the millennium for such methods of settling international quarrels.[263]

Several events changed the Anglo-American dynamic in 1869. Politically, the US was not the only Western power on the rise. Britain kept a wary eye on the newly federated Germany. The Franco-Prussian War of 1870 demonstrated Germany's military strength and its willingness to use it. This triggered a wave of diplomatic optimism in the US, where it was hoped that Britain was able to compromise on the *Alabama*

[262] Photo courtesy of Wikimedia Commons, painting of C.S.S. Alabama by J.W. Schmidt (1961), https://www.ibiblio.org/hyperwar/OnlineLibrary/photos/images/h85000/h85593k.jpg.

[263] Thomas Balch, *International Courts of Arbitration* (Philadelphia: Henry T. Coates & Co., 1899), at pp. 8–11.

Claims dispute. Referring to Shakespeare's *Richard III*, Lieber wrote to Fish: "Richard called, 'A Kingdom for a horse!' Our call now will be, 'An empire for the Law of Nations!'"[264]

Another factor in the establishment of the Alabama Tribunal was the personal relationships among Lieber, Fish and British Minister to the US, Sir Edward Thornton.[265] Through their meetings together, Fish and Thornton came to a realistic understanding of how to reach a settlement of claims. For example, Thornton appreciated the popular need for a public concession of some sort from Great Britain.[266] And Fish fully realized that Britain would never release Canada as a concession.

The idea of arbitration was much discussed at the time. Initially, Fish and Thornton were even open to Lieber's idea of referring the *Alabama Claims* to a European law faculty.[267] But when the *London Standard* found out about this possibility and denounced the plan, it was dropped.[268] Writing to each other regularly and confidentially, Fish and Lieber also discussed sending a High Commission of "special ministers" to negotiate an arbitral agreement – similar to how peace treaties were negotiated in the Old World.[269] However, Fish also wanted an apology from Britain. But to get one, he would have to address Britain's need of an honorable settlement. Fish wrote to John C. Hamilton (1792–1882), the lawyer and historian whose father was Alexander Hamilton, that a British apology could even be putative: "It may be said by a definition of what shall be maritime international law in the future,

264 Lieber to Fish, July 20, 1870, Lieber Papers, Huntington Library, Box 7. Perhaps it was not by chance that the Treaty of Washington was signed on May 8, 1871, two days before the Treaty of Frankfurt was signed, on May 10, 1871.

265 Interestingly, Thornton succeeded Lieber as umpire on the US–Mexican tribunal.

266 As he wrote in his diary, "Some kind expressions of regret, and a competent indemnity, are indispensable" (Diary of Hamilton Fish, July 9, 1869, Fish Papers, Library of Congress). Fish actually opposed Sumner's approach for indirect claims. See Diary of Hamilton Fish, June 11, 1869; Letter from Fish to Lieber, June 10, 1869. Fish also directed Balch to explain to British parliamentarians that Americans thought they suffered to the extent of Sumner's claims. Fish to Balch, June 12, 1869, Huntington Library Archives, Microfilm Reel 1.

267 Fish to Lieber, October 4, 1870, Lieber Papers, Huntington Library, Box 7.

268 Fish to Lieber, September 12, 1870, September 18, 1870 and October 4, 1870. Lieber to Fish, December 30, 1870 and May 25, 1871, Lieber Papers, Huntington Library, Box 7: In the final section of the September 18 letter to Lieber, labeled "confidential," Fish writes that he met with Edward Thornton about the Alabama who "insists on arbitration and nothing else."

269 Fish to Lieber, June 10 and August 27, 1869, Confidential, Lieber Papers, Huntington Library, Box 7.

and a few kind words; she will want in the future what we have claimed; thus she will be benefited – we satisfied."[270] This idea of a hypothetical apology was what Great Britain in fact ended up agreeing to in Washington.

In a mid-summer talk with Sir John Rose (1820–1888), a Canadian lawyer and unofficial representative of the Crown in the US, Fish planted the seeds for a Joint Commission between the two nations.[271] Nothing came of this plan until Sir Edward Thornton called upon Fish at the Secretary's home.[272] That evening, the two diplomats worked out a detailed compromise in which the US agreed to lower tariffs on Canadian goods, surrender its claim for Canadian territory and arbitrate the *Alabama Claims*, while Great Britain agreed to also arbitrate outstanding boundary disputes and to open Canadian fisheries to the US.[273] Over the course of a few months, the two lawyer-diplomats came to terms on a "High Commission" that was to convene in Washington, DC to negotiate a resolution to the *Alabama Claims* with all the pomp of Old World diplomacy.[274]

Fish led the US delegation in Washington. He drafted rules of neutrality upon which the international tribunal was to issue its award. The US refused to arbitrate without first clarifying precisely which laws would predetermine the dispute's resolution.[275] The British delegation, led by

270 Fish to John C. Hamilton, September 4, 1869, emphasis in original. Fish outlines his expectations of Great Britain: 1. Payment of an agreed upon sum of money. 2. Expression by Great Britain of some kind of apology. 3. A declaration of the principles of Maritime laws – see Fish to Lieber, October 4, 1870, Lieber Papers, Huntington Library, Box 7.

271 Diary of Hamilton Fish, November 20, 1870. The meeting was arranged at Rose's initiative – J. C. Bancroft Davis, *Mr. Fish and the Alabama Claims: A Chapter in Diplomatic History* (Cambridge: Riverside Press, 1893), at p. 44.

272 Sir Edward Thornton served as attaché in Mexico in 1845 and Secretary of the Legation to Mexico in 1851. He was also appointed *Chargé d'affaires* and Consul General to the Republic of New Granada and later the Republic of Uruguay in 1854 and was appointed Minister Plenipotentiary to the Argentine Confederation in 1859. In 1865 he was appointed Envoy Extraordinary and Minister Plenipotentiary to the Emperor of Brazil. In 1867 he was transferred to Washington. Sir Edward was a barrister (admitted at the Middle Temple in 1842). See "The Right Hon. Sir Edward Thornton, K.C.B.," in Foreign Office, Diplomatic and Consular Sketches (London: W.H. Allen & Co., 1883).

273 Diary of Hamilton Fish, September 26, 1870, Library of Congress.

274 The High Commission was entirely composed of attorneys on the US but not British side.

275 Without these substantive rules agreed upon by Great Britain, the US would not agree to arbitration (*FRUS* 1872, Pt. II at p. 10 as cited in Campbell, *supra* note 170, at p. 33), contrasts with the US insistence that Latin American countries arbitrate alien protection

Thornton, accepted three of the four US-proposed rules (known as the "Three Rules"); the fourth would have Great Britain formally accept state "responsibility" for violations of the three substantive rules.[276] Fish, who had already anticipated this reaction, suggested a compromise: Britain was to authorize an international tribunal to apply the Three Rules as the applicable law during the conduct in question *without actually conceding that they in fact were responsible.* Any adjudicated responsibility would be of a hypothetical nature.[277] The most explosive US claim, that Great Britain had "indirectly" caused the prolongation of the Civil War, Fish decided to omit from the Treaty of Washington. He felt certain that, notwithstanding any political merit they might have, these national claims for damages would certainly result in a British rejection of the High Commission. It was neither included nor excluded in the final draft of the treaty.[278]

> According to Fish's biographer, the signing of the Treaty of Washington on May 8, 1871 was the proudest moment of the Secretary of State's life.[279] Fish saw it as inaugurating "a new era in the relations of the two governments, and possibly (even beyond that) in the mode of settlement of grave questions between great Powers."[280] Both High Commissions

claims without first codifying the relevant international laws underlying those claims – discussed above.

276 Gladstone did not see the arbitration as righting a wrong. Rather, "He saw the process as exemplifying the means by which two civilized nations could settle differences, without either having to admit being in the wrong." Gladstone considered the award "harsh in its extent and punitive in its basis" yet "as dust in the balance compared with the moral example set" of two proud nations going "in peace and concord before a judicial tribunal" rather than "resorting to the arbitrament of the sword" (Bingham, *supra* note 264, at p. 24). *See also* Nevins, *supra* note 1, at pp. 482–486. In retrospect, the Alabama affair was widely known for enshrining these "three rules" of due diligence, approved by the Institut de Droit international in its 1874 session. For recent iterations of the rule *see* International Law Commission, 56th Sess., Supp. No. 10, at 59–62, UN Doc. A/56/10 (Responsibility of States for Internationally Wrongful Acts), Art. 2(b); James Crawford, "First Report on State Responsibility," International Law Commission, 50th Sess., ~ 2, UN Doc. A/CN.4/490 (1998), para. 122 (addendum 4); International Law Commission, 56th Sess., Supp. No. 10, at 59–62, UN Doc. A/56/10, at 69 (article 2, commentary para. 3).

277 For a discussion on the inclusion and limitation of the general rule of the law of nations regarding the liability of states, *see* Davis, *supra* note 276, at pp. 75–76.

278 Thus, though the *Alabama Claims* dispute concerned elements of "high" politics (such as "indirect claims"), these were not delegated by the disputing parties to an arbitral tribunal in Geneva. Even the exceptional case of "indirect claims" by the US.

279 Hamilton Fish Diary, May 2–5, 1871, Library of Congress.

280 Letter to Truman Smith, May 27, 1871, Letterbooks, Library of Congress, as cited in Nevins, *supra* note 1, at p. 490.

Figure 2.4 The Alabama Room in the Hôtel de Ville, Ghent (photo courtesy of Geneva.com)

> were self-conscious of their historical positions. The treaty itself opens with the following proclamation: "The United States of America and Her Britannic Majesty, being desirous to provide for an amicable settlement of all causes of difference between the two countries. . .." Article 1 delegated the resolution of the *Alabama Claims* to an arbitration tribunal in Geneva that would be comprised of five international lawyers.[281] The tribunal sat in the Hôtel de Ville (the city hall) (Figure 2.4), which still has an "Alabama room" that is open to visits by guests. This is the same room in which the first Geneva Convention was adopted in 1864.[282]

Fish has rightly received credit for the success of the Treaty of Washington[283] and the ensuing arbitral tribunal in Geneva.[284] It is not

[281] *See* Geneva Convention Commemoration.

[282] ICRC, "Geneva Convention Commemoration," 42 *International Review of the Red Cross* 466 (1964), at p. 466, note 2.

[283] There were several outstanding disputes between America and Britain, the most famous of which was the *Alabama Claims*. Others were: disputes over Canadian fisheries, ownership of San Juan, navigation of the St. Lawrence River and compensation for Fenian raids (by Irish Americans into Canada).

[284] Charles Francis Adams, *Before and After the Treaty of Washington: The American Civil War and the War in the Transvaal* (New York: New York Historical Society, 1902), at

clear whether Lieber expected to be appointed as one of its arbitrators. Given his already-accepted position as Umpire of the Mexican tribunal, this would not have been likely. One thing, however, is evident: Fish insisted that the American arbitrator be an international lawyer with strong diplomatic experience and language skills.[285] Fish overcame strong opposition from President Grant in order to appoint Charles Francis Adams to the Alabama Tribunal.[286] The rest of the star-packed tribunal was composed of Sir Alexander Cockburn (Britain), Count Federico Sclopis (Italy), Jakob Stämpfli (Switzerland) and the 2nd Baron of Itajubá, Marcos Antônio de Araújo (Brazil). After nine months, at the tribunal's final session on September 14, 1872, it issued an award in English by a vote of four to one (Sir Alexander refused to sign it) granting the US US$ 15,500,000.[287] The award was paid on September 9, 1873 (a day after the founding of the *Institut de Droit international*) in British Treasury Bonds.[288]

"Arbitration in the Air"

The tribunal's award was an international event. President Grant was so taken by the award that he predicted "an epoch when a court recognized by all nations will settle international differences instead of keeping large standing armies."[289] The historian Thomas Balch (1821–77), declared that international arbitration was a "sign of the times."[290] The euphoria was transatlantic. Francis Lieber wrote, "My letters from Germany show

p. 7: According to Adams, "So far as any considerable political or diplomatic result can be said to be the work of one man, the Treaty of Washington was the work of Hamilton Fish."

285 Diary of Hamilton Fish, June–September 1871, Library of Congress.

286 Charles Francis Adams, the son of John Quincy and the grandson of John, received his legal training from Daniel Webster: three generations of Adams were lawyer-politicians. On Grant's pushback, *see* Nevins, *supra* note 1, at pp. 511–512.

287 The details as to how Stämpfli and the tribunal came to the figure of US$ 15,500,000 are obscure. According to Lord Tenterden, the final amount was a compromise between eight and fifteen million dollars, plus interest. The US claimed about US$ 21,000,000 in direct and US$ 4,000,000 in indirect damages caused by Confederate ships. The UK acknowledged about US$ 8,000,000. It seems that the arbitrators pretty much split the difference by issuing an award for US$ 15,500,000 – Nevins, *supra* note 1, at p. 560.

288 Janis, *infra* note 351, at p. 137.

289 C. D. Davis, *The United States and the First Hague Peace Conference* (Ithaca: Cornell University Press, 1962), at pp. 13–14; Janis, *infra* note 351, at p. 137.

290 Thomas Balch, "International Courts of Arbitration," 3 *The Law Magazine and Review* 1026–1046 (1874), at pp. 1038, 1044.

me that they are getting there an *Alabama feeling* toward England too. Even the highest German jurists feel very strong about it."[291] Premier Gladstone (1809–1898) himself was proud of the "losing" result. The British Premier hung the US receipt of the award on the walls of 10 Downing Street.[292] Westlake and other European international lawyers credited the peace movement for popularizing the idea of arbitration:

> But for the encouragement of the lovers of peace ... international *arbitration is in the air*. When this happens to an idea ... the idea for good cannot be measured by logic, necessary as it is that we should do our best to understand the conditions in order to work with them. It is the season to raise our hopes, and do our utmost to try what the idea of international arbitration can accomplish.[293]

Peace activists and publicists alike lauded the tribunal in historical terms.[294] There was a general sense that Old World diplomacy was no longer adequately equipped for the pressing necessities of modern business.

The international system needed a more effective method of dispute resolution, one that worked, just as arbitration had for the United States and Great Britain. In the public imagination, the Alabama Tribunal has come to represent the modern ideas of professional arbitration and state accountability in international affairs. The late James Crawford (1948–2021) cites the *Alabama Claims* "axiomatic" principle that a state's national laws will not shield it from international responsibility whenever

[291] Letter of Francis Lieber to J. C. Bancroft Davis of August 27, 1870, in Chester Squire Phinney, *Francis Lieber's Influence on American Thought* (Philadelphia: International Printing Company, 1918), at p. 79, emphasis added.

[292] Janis, *infra* note 351, at p. 137.

[293] John Westlake, *International Law, Part I: Peace* (Cambridge: Cambridge University Press, 1904), at p. 350, emphasis added. *See also* F. Peter Phillips, "Ancient and Comely Order: The Use and Disuse of Arbitration by New York Quakers," 2016 *Journal of Dispute Resolution.* 81 (2016). According to Phillips, from the late seventeenth century until the early twentieth century, Quakers observed a method of resolving disputes that culminated in final and binding arbitration (based on their scripture). Members of the community applied distinct standards of conduct, rather than general legal codes, to resolve disputes. Further, arbitration awards were self-executing, and resorting to court enforcement could not be done. The author explains that attributes such as mutual accountability, closed communities and shared behavioral expectations are distinctive hallmarks of the arbitration process.

[294] *See generally* Alan Nissel, "Arbitration Is in the Air: A Moment of Contact between Anglo-American Peace and International Arbitration (1864–1871)," (unpublished paper on file with author).

it fails to perform its international obligations.[295] The primacy of international over national law was affirmed by high courts around the world, including the US Supreme Court.[296]

To publicists as well, the success of the Alabama Tribunal represented a turning point in the history of international law enforcement. James Bassett Moore (1860–1947), the first holder of the Hamilton Fish Professorship of International Law and Diplomacy at Columbia Law School, regarded it as the greatest arbitration in history.[297] To Moore, the Alabama Tribunal was the "final vindication of the system as the ultimate standard of international obligation and responsibility was made in the case of the *Alabama* claims."[298] Writing on the origins of international law several decades later, Sir Hersch Lauterpacht identifies the legacy of the Alabama Tribunal as being the prototype of modern international dispute resolution both in term of its substantive responsibility and arbitral procedure.[299] In other words, what Moore's generation

[295] James Crawford, "State Responsibility," in Anne Peters (ed.), *Max Planck Encyclopaedia of Public International Law* (Oxford: Oxford University Press, 2006), at §17. For a similar statement from the mid-twentieth century, *see* George A. Finch, "The American Society of International Law 1906–1956," 50 *American Journal of International Law* 293–312 (1956), at p. 293. *See also* Janis, *infra* note 351, at p. 117: the years between the Civil War and the Great War were "the most optimistic years of all for American international law." Janis considers the Alabama Tribunal to be probably the most influential international law event of the nineteenth century (*ibid*, at p. 135).

[296] In the case of *United States v. Arjona*, Chief Justice Morrison R. Waite (who also argued for the US before the Alabama Tribunal) determined that "The national government is . . . made responsible to foreign nations for all violations by the United States of their international obligations, and because of this, Congress is expressly authorized 'to define and punish . . . offenses against the law of nations'" (120 US 479 (1887)).

[297] To Moore, "The right of this treaty to be regarded as the greatest treaty of arbitration the world had yet seen was only emphasized by the fact that it provided for four distinct arbitrations, the largest number ever established under a single convention" (John Bassett Moore, *The United States and International Arbitration* (Boston: American Peace Society, 1896), at pp. 11–12). He makes a similar statement in Moore, *supra* note 3, at pp. 652–653. A contemporary of Moore and another great US historian of international arbitration, Jackson Harvey Ralston, also deemed it "by far the greatest of all" (*supra* note 17, at p. 197); similarly, James Brown Scott, another influential US international lawyer, asserted, "The case of the Alabama is . . . the classic arbitration of the nineteenth century" (*The Spanish Conception of International Law and of Sanctions* (Washington, DC: Carnegie Endowment for International Peace, 1934), at p. 39).

[298] John Bassett Moore, *Progress of International Law in the Nineteenth Century* (New York: 1901), reprinted in *The Collected Papers of John Bassett Moore*, Vol. II, 437–449 (New Haven: Yale University Press, 1944), at p. 440.

[299] Hersch Lauterpacht, *Private Law Sources and Analogies of International Law: With Special Reference to International Arbitration* (London: Longmans, Green and Co., 1927), at p. 216: the Alabama Tribunal standing "on the threshold of modern

remembered but was lost by Lauterpacht's time, was that the Treaty of Washington was more a feat of diplomacy than adjudication.[300] While the Alabama Tribunal itself paved little international ground, its *compromis* was certainly a work of unprecedented diplomatic success.[301]

Moore's colleague, Jackson Harvey Ralston (1857–1945), credits the *Alabama Claims* for inspiring further attempts to promote international arbitration around the world, especially in Latin America.[302] By the first Pan-American Conference of 1889 in Washington, DC, arbitration was a recognized "principle of American international law."[303] Inspired – and, in some cases, pressured – by US diplomatic actions,[304] Old World powers upped their practice of international arbitration. Frederic René Coudert (1832–1903) wrote that "War, logically speaking, is an anachronism."[305] Coudert was not a peace activist or utopian idealist. He and his two younger brothers founded one of the largest US law firms of his time, Coudert Brothers.[306] In sum, the Alabama Tribunal soon represented *an idealized form of international dispute resolution* rather than a model of future international legalism.

An Illusion of Legalism

The Alabama Tribunal more closely resembles Old World arbitration than it does the modern international arbitration of the twentieth century and beyond. The memory of the Alabama Tribunal as demonstrating the arbitrability of vital state interests, is overstated. The High Commission in Washington ensured that no open legal issues of weight would be left

international arbitration . . ., not only owing to the importance of the legal questions which it had to answer, and to the application, on an unprecedented scale, of a well-ordered arbitral procedure, but also owing to its political importance as the first instance of settling a dispute which raised high national feeling on both sides," emphasis added.

300 So much so that "The prior work rendered the labors of the Geneva tribunal little more than that of a jury of award" (Ralston, *supra* note 17, at p. 199).

301 Ralston, *supra* note 17, at pp. 198–199.

302 *Ibid*, at pp. 141–142. *See also ibid*, at p. 108: "We only reach a period of real activity consequent upon the reference of the *Alabama* claims to arbitration. Then for the first time men opened their eyes to the possibility of wide application of judicial methods to the settlement of international disputes and commenced to devote volumes to its history and theory."

303 *See* Ralston, *supra* note 17, at p. 143.

304 *See* Edmund Morris, "'A Matter of Extreme Urgency': Theodore Roosevelt, Wilhelm II, and the Venezuela Crisis of 1902," 55(2) *Naval War College Review* 73–85 (2002).

305 F. R. Coudert, "Arbitration," 87 *Harper's Monthly* 918–927 (1893), at p. 918.

306 According to some, it was the first international law firm – *see* Veenswijk, *infra* note 334.

to the tribunal in Geneva.[307] The members of its commission did not believe that international law contained preexisting answers to public international problems.[308] The illusion of legalism in the Alabama Tribunal was critiqued by British legal historian Sir Henry Maine (1822–1888) as a "precedent likely to exercise serious influence on the whole law of nations, . . . it was dangerous, as well as reactionary and retrogressive."[309] The fact was that Great Britain and the US never referred the underlying Civil War dispute to Geneva; yet that was precisely how the event was remembered.[310]

The Treaty of Washington was a political solution that touched on the most sensitive of humanitarian issues: Britain's alleged prolonging of the institution of slavery.[311] International arbitration enabled Britain to avoid any direct apology for its wrongful conduct and allowed the US to claim that the British were liable: but this was state liability without

[307] On the Alabama Tribunal's early rejection of Alexander Cockburn's suggestion of determining the applicability of overarching general principles, *see* Nevins, *supra* note 1, at p. 557.

[308] On the contrary, they accepted Wheaton's view that international law was an "imperfect" form of positive law: "both on account of the indeterminateness of its precepts, and because it lacks that solid basis on which rests the positive law of every particular nation" (Wheaton, *supra* note 72, at pp. 21–22). Interestingly, it was the Richard Henry Dana (eighth) English edition of *Elements of International Law* in 1866 that served as the definitive text in Clarendon Press' Classics of International Law series issued in 1936.

[309] John Bassett Moore, *International Adjudication – Ancient and Modern History and Documents: Together with Mediatorial Reports, Advisory Opinions and the Decisions of Domestic Commissions on International Claims*, Modern Series Vol. I (New York: Oxford University Press, 1929), at p. *lxviii*; for an analysis of the British criticism of the award, *see ibid*, at pp. *lxii, lxiii, lxviii. See further* Westlake, *supra* note 298, at pp. 342–345; Frederick Edwin Smith (The Right Honourable Lord Birkenhead), *International Law* (4th ed., London: J. M. Dent & Sons, Ltd, 1911), at p. 316; Letter from James Lorimer to Thomas Balch, February 10, 1874, reprinted in Thomas Balch, "International Courts of Arbitration," 3 *The Law Magazine and Review* 1026–1046 (1874), at p. 1041.

[310] To Westlake, "as soon as the parties agreed on the Three Rules as applicable to the case, it only remained to apply those rules to the facts; in other words, the difference became a legal one and suitable for arbitration" (*supra* note 298, at p. 341).

[311] *See* Eugene Kantorovich, "The Constitutionality of International Courts: The Forgotten Precedent of Slave Trade Tribunals," 158(39) *University of Pennsylvania Law Review* 39–115 (2009), at pp. 114–115; Jenny S. Martinez, "Anti-Slavery Courts and the Dawn of International Human Rights Law," 117 *Yale Law Journal* (2007). The abolition of slavery was a stated US and British foreign policy goal – Jay Sexton, "The United States, the Cuban Rebellion, and the Multilateral Initiative of 1875," 30(3) *Diplomatic History* 335–365 (2006), at p. 339.

moral culpability.[312] The establishment of an international tribunal in Geneva muddled these dynamics. The Geneva tribunal was really a juridical cover for the political compromises set out in the Treaty of Washington.[313]

Fish and Thornton's distracting legal spectacle gave their employers just enough legal cover to put the affair to rest. Even years after the treaty was concluded, Prime Minister Gladstone continued to emphasize the moral and civilizational (rather than legal) example that was set by the treaty.[314] Fish did not employ international arbitration more than once with Western nations in matters of "high" politics. To take the example of Spain: Fish agreed to send private US and Spanish claims arising out of the Civil War to a mixed claims tribunal.[315] But he refused to have the *Virginius* affair – in which Spain captured a ship waving the American flag – delegated to a third party.[316] Similarly, claims from France and Spain were usually resolved diplomatically, the exceptions being a couple

312 While it allowed for the question of "indirect claims" to be submitted for adjudication, the issue was not actually left to the tribunal, which refused to adjudicate the matter until it received backdoor assurances from Fish through Adams that even he saw "indirect claims" as being based on "equity" and not law. Adams saved the tribunal by preventing the British from postponing inevitably the arbitration and agreeing to take up and reject the question of indirect claims the next day (prior to postponement, which was then cancelled). *See* Nevins, *supra* note 1, at pp. 521, 546–550.

313 The myth of Alabama is still repeated by respected international law commentators today – *see, e.g.*, Bingham, *supra* note 264; James Crawford, "State Responsibility," in Rüdiger Wolfrüm (ed.) *Max Planck Encyclopedia of Public International Law* (Oxford: Oxford University Press, 2012).

314 Hansard, Debates, Third Series, Commons, 6 Feb. 1873, ccxiv. 114–115 as cited in Maureen M. Robson, "Liberals and 'Vital Interests': The Debate on International Arbitration, 1815–72," 32(85) *Bulletin of the Institute of Historical Research* 38–55 (1959), at p. 41; Finch, *supra* note 300, at p. 293.

315 Signed on February12, 1871. The tribunal was another example of US professionalism: M. Bartholdi (the French minister to the US) was appointed Umpire but was later replaced by Baron A. Blan (the Italian minister to the US) and then Count Carl Lewenhaupt (the Swedish and Norwegian minister to the US). The US Commissioner was William Tod Otto (former Second Circuit judge and Assistant Secretary of the Interior and later US Supreme Court Reporter and diplomat) who was succeeded by Kenneth Rayner (House Representative and later judge on the domestic Alabama Claims Court) and then by Joseph Segar, Joseph J. Stewart and James Lowndes. The US agent was initially Caleb Cushing.

316 Fish rejected arbitration due to the question of national honor at hand. If the demand was not met in twelve days, the US would resort to forceful measures against Spain (though it was widely conceded that the latter had "not for some time past been able to control" Cuba. When it was determined that the ship had falsely obtained US papers, the demand for the salute was dropped. Instead, an indemnity was pressed for and received in 1875 (US$ 80,000). Great Britain also demanded and received reparation. No one was

of incidents arising out of the US Civil War and Franco-Prussian War (leading to the US–France mixed claims commission from 1880).[317]

Perhaps this is why European diplomats viewed US legalism as a trojan horse. To Gladstone, the interventionism of US lawyer-diplomats lacked "European manners."[318] During the Trent Affair, for example, the British minister in Washington was warned by the Foreign Office about the "ingenuity of American lawyers" seeking "to entangle you in endless arguments" especially when it came to Seward, who had "all the genius of a country attorney."[319] Whereas Latin Americans, at least at first, welcomed international arbitration as a principle of *American international law*, Europeans often viewed it in extra-legal terms. Intra-American arbitration delegated general jurisdiction to tribunals to set a state's liability, Anglo-American arbitrations had little creative role in the development of international law.[320]

A Tale of Two Tribunals

In retrospect, Fish's two separate approaches to international arbitration with Great Britain and Mexico reflect the different strategies US diplomacy took with those two countries (*see* Table 2.5). The Alabama Tribunal is representative of nineteenth-century Anglo-American arbitration: famous, dignified personalities addressing matters of national importance, but with very limited judicial discretion. With Great Britain, the US made a grand effort to dress up arbitration in the traditional Old World garb. Fish created a "High Commission" composed of celebrity diplomats tasked with negotiating a dignified outcome. By contrast, with Mexico, all the US had to do to secure a *compromis* was to ask. Mexico was willing to establish a mixed claims commission and

punished. *See* John Norton Pomeroy, "The Virginius," 17 *Nation* 332–334 (1873); John Norton Pomeroy, "The Virginius Case," 8 *American Law Review* 470 (1874).

317 Moore, *supra* note 298, at p. 14.

318 Nevins, *supra* note 1, at p. 526.

319 Cowley to Russell, December 5, 1861, Palmerston to Russell, December 27, 1861, Russell to Palmerston, December 27, 1861, as cited in Ferris, *supra* note 193, at p. 159. The British saw "International Law" as the mechanism of this US trick that would have the US avoid an apology or giving up the Confederate men by offering "to leave it to some Third Power or somebody to decide" (Westbury to Palmerston, January 3, 1862, as cited in Ferris, *supra* note 193, at p. 160).

320 Johann Caspar Bluntschli pointed this out when he provided his own "scientific" analysis of the *Alabama Claims* – Johann Caspar Bluntschli, "An Impartial Opinion on the Alabama Question and the Manner of Settling It," *II Revue de droit international et de législation comparée* (1870), Part IIID (reprinted in Washington, DC: Government Printing Office, 1871), at p. 15.

Table 2.5 *Comparison of Lieber and Alabama Tribunals*

The Lieber Tribunal	The Alabama Tribunal
Established in 1870	Established in 1871
Staffed and led by professional lawyers	Staffed and led by professional lawyers
Resulted in binding international awards	Resulted in binding international awards
Based on general principles of law	Based on general principles of law
Between the US and a Latin American country	Between the US and a European country
"Low" commission resolving property claims	"High" commission addressing vital state interests
Mixed claims tribunal with broad authority to adjudicate	*Ad hoc* tribunal with little authority to adjudicate
Little-known tribunal	Famous tribunal
Lasting impact on international arbitration and state responsibility	Limited legal influence

practically allowed the US to choose its umpire. These regular commissions addressed technical property matters by and large.[321] Fish and his successor Secretaries of State designed tribunals to depoliticize the injustices of international claims *via* market value compensation.[322] He set up the Mexican tribunal as a "Low Commission" and balanced out its lack of pomp with the inclusion of Francis Lieber (already famous for his code on the laws of war in 1870) as its umpire.

The distinction between "high" and "low" commissions reflected Anglo-American diplomacy generally with Latin America. When, as part

[321] Georg Schwarzenberger opens his article on "The Protection of British Property Abroad" with the following: "In every mature legal system, the law of property counts among the most technical branches of law. It is lawyer's law *par excellence.*" He continues: "Behind the technicalities of every existing system of property law lie, shrewdly hidden, the fundamental political, social and economic decisions on which these legal rules are based. Once these are laid bare, it becomes evident that we have uncovered one of the deepest roots of the law, and we readily understand why a subject that, on the surface, is merely technical is extremely bound up with the most crucial decisions that every community has to make" (5(1) *Current Legal Problems* 295 (1952), at p. 295).

[322] On how the US pressed for the international "standard of civilization" as the technocratic basis for these claims, *see* Allison Powers Useche, "The Standard of Civilization on Trial at the United States/Mexico Claims Commission 1923–1937," 1 *Jus Gentium: Journal of International Legal History*. 391 (2016), at pp. 398–399. I also discuss this further in the next chapter.

of his internal professionalization program, Hamilton Fish rearranged the State Department in 1870, he assigned the First Diplomatic Bureau to cover relations with Europe and a Second (separate) Diplomatic Bureau to the developing world.[323] Similarly, British nationals in Latin America were protected by the same division within the Foreign Office that included much of Asia.[324]

The differences between the Lieber and Alabama Tribunals overall are indicative of the Victorian division between law and politics, that not all international problems could be solved by legal rules or courts.[325] Especially after the trauma of the Civil War, many in the US felt resigned to the uncomfortable reality that certain political questions could be resolved only by force. The repression of the Confederate rebellion demonstrated that sometimes war was the ultimate arbiter even of law.[326] Conversely, Anglo-American lawyers viewed alien injuries as a matter of "low" legalism: that is, the technical, non-political fixing of private wrongs. As British legal historian Nick Cleaver notes, this approach was largely limited to the resolution of simpler, more private claims but was not able to effectively manage more extended diplomatic disputes.[327] Even though the motivation for creating "low commissions" was not one-sided, it was clearly driven by Northern rather than Southern needs.[328]

Anglo-American arbitrations were media sensations. The public followed them as a type of "legal Olympics." Every few years, countries sent their best and brightest attorneys to compete on the international stage, with the proceedings and judgments carefully scrutinized by the popular press on

323 Hunt, *supra* note 163, at p. 222.

324 Smith, *supra* note 314, at pp. 9, 21, 24.

325 See Lord Salisbury in Moore, *supra* note 3, at 964 (two types of diplomatic disputes).

326 *See* Cynthia Nicoletti, "The American Civil War as a Trial by Battle," 28(1) *Law and History Review* 71 (2010) (article is a synopsis of Nicoletti's doctoral thesis on the topic).

327 Nick Cleaver, *Grover Cleveland's New Foreign Policy: Arbitration, Neutrality, and the Dawn of American Empire* (New York: Palgrave MacMillan, 2014), at p. 192. Similarly, Steve Harris writes that international arbitration was never a means of preventing war in the nineteenth century but was merely a "regular and increasingly used tool in the international system, not a means of controlling that system or its components" ("Arbitration at Vienna: Recasting the History of International Dispute Resolution," 3 *Jus Gentium: Journal of International Legal History* 391 (2018), p. 393).

328 *See* Frédéric Mégret, "Mixed Claim Commissions and the Once Centrality of the Protection of Aliens," *in* Ignacio de la Rasilla and Jorge E. Viñuales (eds.), *Experiments in International Adjudication: Historical Accounts* 127–149 (Cambridge: Cambridge University Press, 2019), at p. 1: (on conflict between globalization and nationalization that created an ideological and economic problem for local governments for whom the US proposal of using a depoliticized framework for the settlement of investment disputes was also practical).

a regular – sometimes daily – basis.[329] Less well known is that several months earlier, Hamilton Fish had appointed Lieber to umpire a commission tasked with resolving several thousand diplomatic protection claims between the US and its southern neighbor. But the Lieber Tribunal was not only the first professional international arbitration.[330]

[329] Specific "superstar" international arbitrators such as Fedor Fedorovich Martens (1845–1909) had a disparate influence on the procedure of international arbitration; *see, e.g.,* W. E. Butler and V. S. Ivanenko, "Fedor Fedorovich Martens: Russian Legal Scholar, Diplomat, Arbitrator," 4 *Jus Gentium: Journal of International Legal History* 145 (2019), at p. 172 ("It is no accident that Martens became widely known as an international arbitrator through his successful resolutions of complex inter-State disputes: England and France concerning fishing around Newfoundland in 1891; United States and England on catching fur seals in the Bering Sea in 1893; England and the Netherlands concerning the arrest by Dutch authorities of the Costa Rica Packet in 1897; England and Venezuela concerning the boundary between Venezuela and British Guiana near the Orinoco River, in 1899; to the first two disputes in the Permanent Court of International Arbitration: between the United States and Mexico concerning the 'Pious Fund,' in 1902; and between England, Germany, Italy and Venezuela regarding violations of the rights of citizens, in 1905; and others. Martens' role as arbitrator led to him being called in the United States 'the chief arbitrator of the Christian world.'") For a discussion of the US sending Frederic René Coudert to its Bering Sea arbitration with Great Britain and to sit on the Venezuela and British Guiana border commission *see* Virginia Kays Veenswijk, *Coudert Brothers: A Legacy in Law: The History of America's First International Law Firm: 1853–1993* (New York: Dutton, 1994), p. 107. Other examples include the *Alabama Claims*, as well as the early PCA disputes.

[330] In the literature, most see the Jay Treaty of 1794 as the genesis of modern international arbitration (*See, e.g.,* Henri La Fontaine, *Pasicrisie Internationale: Histoire Documentaire des Arbitrages Internationaux (1794–1900)* (Berne: Imprimerie Stampelli & CIE, 1902); Albert G. de Lapradelle and Nicolas Politis, *Recueil des Arbitrages Internationales* (Paris: Pedone, 1905); John Barrett, *The Pan American Union: Peace, Friendship, Commerce* (Washington, DC: Pan American Union, 1911), at p. 192; William L. Griffin, "International Claims of Nationals of Both the Claimant and Respondent States – The Case History of a Myth," 1 *International Lawyer* 400 (1967), at p. 400; Georg Schwarzenberger, "Present-Day Relevance of the Jay Treaty Arbitrations," 53 *Notre Dame Law Review* 715 (1977–78), at p. 716; Maureen M. Robson, "Liberals and 'Vital Interests': The Debate on International Arbitration, 1815–72," 32(85) *Bulletin of the Institute of Historical Research* 38 (1959), at p. 42; Jackson Harvey Ralston, *International Arbitration from Athens to Locarno* (New York: Garland, 1972), at p. 191; C. G. Roelofsen, "'The Jay Treaty and All That'; Some Remarks on the Role of Arbitration in European Modern History and Its 'Revival,'" in L. B. Sohn, *International Arbitration in Historical Perspective: Past and Present* 201–210 (1990); Roger P. Alford, "The American Influence on International Arbitration," 19(1) *Ohio State Journal on Dispute Resolution* 69 (2003), at p. 70; Judge Stephen W. Schwebel, "The Reality of International Adjudication and Arbitration," 12 *Willamette Journal of International Law and Dispute Resolution* 359 (2004), at p. 363. Even histories of specifically intra-American arbitration point to the Jay Treaty as the "time zero" of contemporary international arbitration. Guerra Everett, "International Arbitration in the Americas," 17 *New York University Law Quarterly Review* 617 (1939–40), at p. 618. As recently as 2023, one author writes that "the Jay Treaty does remain the breakthrough that launched modern day inter-state

It represents the American model of international arbitration: unrecognized, unremarkable, focusing on matters of private concern, but with broad judicial powers. The Lieber Tribunal presented itself as an international tribunal of private law. Umpires Lieber and Thornton were careful not to stress issues of public law. Concepts such as "sovereignty" and "responsibility" are rarely mentioned in their awards. Yet, the tribunal's underlying ethos was clearly a public one that addressed fundamental rights and minimum standards. The public issue of state responsibility that

arbitration and dispute resolution ... [that] eventually led to the establishment of institutions such as the Permanent Court of Arbitration" (Willem Theus, "There and Back Again: From Consular Courts through Mixed Arbitral Tribunals to International Commercial Courts," in Hélène Ruiz Fabri and Michel Erpelding (eds.), *The Mixed Arbitral Tribunals, 1919–1939: An Experiment in the International Adjudication of Private Rights* 29 (Baden-Baden: Nomos, 2023), at pp. 40–41). This is also the position taken on the website of the International Court of Justice – www.icj-cij.org/court/index.php?p1=1&p2=1, last visited June 8, 2013); Mikaël Schinazi, *The Three Ages of International Commercial Arbitration* (Cambridge: Cambridge University Press, 2021), at pp. 51–52 (Jay Treaty as the turning point and Treaty of Washington as the high watermark of international arbitration). However, *see* Daniel J. Hellebusch, "From Imperial to International Law: Protecting Foreign Expectations in the Early United States," 65 *UCLA Law Review* 142 (2018), at p. 154: "No commissioner possessed expertise about settling the aftermath of a colonial civil war, and it was the very issues of revolution that stymied the commission" (internal citations omitted). The mixed claims commission established under the Jay Treaty (1794) did not include an independent umpire or law professionals and was, as such, more administrative in nature than legalistic. *See further* Craig B. Hollander, "'The Citizen Complains': Federal Compensation for Property Lost in the War of 1812," 38(4) *Law and History Review* 659 (2020). *See also* Bennett Ostdiek and John Fabian Witt, "The Czar and the Slaves: Two Puzzles in the History of International Arbitration," 113 *American Journal of International Law* 535 (2019), at pp. 562–564 (shows how Treaty of Ghent arbitration was a form of sovereign arbitration and in choosing the Russian Czar as arbitrator provided political assurances to both sides that they had done their best to assure domestic constituencies regarding pro- and anti-slavery issues; further, the Czar confined his analysis to an examination of the grammar in question). Others point to the Treaty of Ghent, ending the War of 1812 with Great Britain (Merle Eugene Curti, *The American Peace Crusade, 1815–1860* (New York: Octagon, 1973), at p. 4. Yet others identify the Treaty of Washington in 1871, which referred Civil War disputes with Great Britain to a Geneva tribunal as the first modern, professional international arbitration (Hersch Lauterpacht, *Private Law Sources and Analogies of International Law: With Special Reference to International Arbitration* (London: Longmans, Green and Co., 1927), at p. 216 (The Alabama arbitration stands on the threshold of modern international arbitration); Georges Abi-Saab, "Fragmentation or Unification: Some Concluding Remarks," 31 *NYU Journal of International Law & Politics* 919 (1999), at pp. 921–922).

emanated from it was an important legacy of the Lieber Tribunal, but this is clear mainly because we now have over a century of hindsight.[331]

Characterizing US legalism in terms of "highs and lows of international arbitration" helps explain why historians have associated the origins of modern international arbitration with Anglo-American diplomacy and why they have overlooked the Lieber Tribunal.[332] State responsibility was a mask for US power in the region.[333] This misperception is the result of a carefully curated US diplomatic practice that emphasized the private nature of resolving alien protection claims, and which suppressed the underlying public dimension of the international liability in the resulting awards. The last thing Lieber's tribunal looked like at the time was a mask for US hegemony.

[331] In the twentieth century, many historical works on US–Mexican arbitrations begin with a discussion of the general obligation under international law to protect aliens and the resulting responsibility for breaching that duty. For example, the first chapter of Desvernine's study on US–Mexican claims was devoted to and titled "Responsibility" – Raoul Eugene Desvernine, *Claims Against Mexico: A Brief Study of the International Law Applicable to Claims of Citizens of the United States and Other Countries for Losses Sustained in Mexico During the Revolutions of the Last Decade* (New York: Private, 1921).

[332] *See, e.g.*, Roger P. Alford, "The American Influence on International Arbitration," 19(1) *Ohio State Journal on Dispute Resolution* 69 (2003); J. G. Merrills, "The Contribution of the Permanent Court of Arbitration to International Law and to the Settlement of Disputes by Peaceful Means," in P. Hamilton, H. C. Requena, L. van Scheltinga and B. Shifman (eds.), *The Permanent Court of Arbitration: International Arbitration and Dispute Resolution* 3–30 (The Hague: Kluwer, 1999); Stephen Barcroft, "The Hague Peace Conference of 1899," 3(1) *Irish Studies in International Affairs* 55 (1989); Janis, *supra* note 1, at p. 149. On the exaggerated credit given to the US for the institutionalization of international arbitration, *see* Kevin M. Anderson, "The Venezuelan Claims Controversy at the Hague, 1903," 57(3) *Historian* 525 (1995).

[333] *See* Paolo Amorosa, *The American Project and the Politics of History: James Brown Scott and the Origins of International Law* (April 14, 2018) (Doctoral dissertation, University of Helsinki), at p. 75 (Langdellian formalism made it possible for legalists to "mask the contradiction between democratic ideals and imperial uses of American power"), as cited in Christopher R. Rossi, *Whiggish International Law: Elihu Root, the Monroe Doctrine, and International Law in the Americas* (Leiden: Brill, 2019), at p. 117; Martti Koskenniemi, "Epilogue: To Enable and Enchant – on the Power of Law," in Wouter Werner, Marieke de Hoon and Alexis Galán (eds.), *The Law of International Lawyers: Reading Martti Koskenniemi* 393 (Cambridge: Cambridge University Press, 2017): the power of law is to legitimate but also to enchant by hiding the politics of the law behind its normativity. *Although, see* Anne-Charlotte Martineau, "A Forgotten Chapter in the History of International Commercial Arbitration: The Slave Trade's Dispute Settlement System," 31 *Leiden Journal of International Law* 219 (2018) who argues against the notion that today's dispute resolution mechanism of international arbitration was conceived as a means to depoliticize international investment law because such a view is over-simplistic.

On the US Tradition of Legalism

What explains the importance of legalism to postbellum US diplomacy? Was there a US "tradition" of legalism? From its earliest days, the US exhibited an allegiance to international law. In its first international document, the Declaration of Independence (1776), the US grounded its national aspirations upon the Laws of Nature that united mankind.[334] Diplomats and political leaders in the US were typically lawyers. Of the fifty-six signers of the Declaration of Independence, thirty-five were lawyers.[335] Until the mid-nineteenth century, the majority of US Senators, about half of the US Congressmen and the majority of Governors were lawyers.[336] Virtually every foreign minister from the founding through the Second World War was a trained attorney.[337] Sir Henry Maine regarded Robert Livingston (1746–1813), the first US foreign minister, as the "finest legal genius of modern times."[338] John Jay (1745–1829), the second foreign minister, who was also the Chief Justice of the US Supreme Court, negotiated the famous Jay Treaty.[339] The list is both long and distinguished.[340] This continued through 1871, when Hamilton Fish resolved the *Alabama Claims* with Great Britain by

334 *See* David Armitage, "The Declaration of Independence and International Law," 59(1) *William and Mary Quarterly* 39 (2002).

335 Jesse S. Reeves, "Growth and Development of Law," in George Edwin Rines (ed.), *The Encyclopedia Americana* 488–493 (New York: The Encyclopedia Americana Corporation, 1920), at p. 490. Interestingly, more copies of Blackstone's Commentaries were sold in the US during the eighteenth century than in England – according to the Blackstone Institute, a Texas-based organization – *see* www.blackstoneinstitute.org.

336 Anton-Hermann Chroust, *The Rise of the Legal Profession in America, Volume 2: The Revolution and the Post-Revolutionary Era* (Norman: University of Oklahoma Press, 1965), at p. 285.

337 Few were international lawyers by profession. Edmund Randolph was an exception. *See* Bertram D. Hulen, *Inside the Department of State* (New York: McGraw Hill, 1939), at p. 43; John M. Raymond and Barbara J. Frischolz, "Lawyers Who Established International Law in the United States, 1776–1914," 76 *American Journal of International Law* 802–829 (1982), at pp. 806–807; Carl Landauer, "The Ambivalences of Power: Launching the American Journal of International Law in an Era of Empire and Globalization," 20 *Leiden Journal of International Law* 325 (2007), at p. 326.

338 Graham H. Stuart, *The Department of State: A History of Its Organization, Procedure, and Personnel* (New York: Macmillan, 1949), at p. 75.

339 The General Treaty of Friendship, Commerce and Navigation between the United States and Great Britain, commonly known as the Jay Treaty of November 19, 1794, 8 Stat. 116.

340 Similarly, John Marshall (1755–1835) who was the third "Secretary of State" (and sixth foreign minister), was also a Chief Justice of the US Supreme Court, where he rendered dozens of landmark decisions of national and international significance. For example,

establishing a "High Commission" of Anglo-American dignitaries. To John Bassett Moore, one of the first US-born international lawyers, there was a definite pattern of US foreign policy that was based on international law.[341] Moore was a State Department insider who described international law as being almost as influential on US foreign policy as the latter was on the former.[342] Indeed, as the US foreign policy historian Benjamin Allen Coates writes, the US not only popularized international arbitration in its first century, but helped codify important fields of international law such as war crimes and neutrality as well.[343]

But sanguine assertions about a tradition of US legalism[344] are somewhat misrepresentative, as Coates himself notes.[345] The relationship between the US and international law was complex, pragmatic and at times contradictory. On the one side, US diplomats relied heavily on arbitration because of the classical legalistic culture that pervaded the inner circles of American diplomacy.[346] Certainly, the shared ideology

The Exchange v. McFadden, The Nereide, Thirty Hogsheads of Sugar v. Royal, The Antelope; *see further* Stuart, *supra* note 343 at p. 36.

341 To the US, says Moore, only international *law* could ensure the stability of international politics. *See* John Bassett Moore, *The United States and International Arbitration* (Boston: American Peace Society, 1896), at p. 3 ("In the conduct of its foreign relations, the Government of the United States has exerted a potent influence upon the development of international law").

342 John Bassett Moore, "International Arbitration," reprinted in *The Collected Papers of John Bassett Moore*, Vol. III. 406–428 (New Haven: Yale University Press, 1944), at p. 406.

343 Benjamin Allen Coates, *Legalist Empire: International Law and American Foreign Relations in the Early Twentieth Century* (Oxford: Oxford University Press, 2016), at pp. 25–28 (Coates summarizes the US "tradition" in international law that was already established by the early twentieth century as comprising of three foreign policies: the promotion of international neutrality and avoidance of foreign entanglements (since George Washington's Farewell Address of 1796); the promotion of state recognition and prohibition of foreign intervention (declared by Monroe in 1823); and, relatedly, the promotion of American exceptionalism (or unilateralism) and avoidance of international institutions (articulated as Manifest Destiny in 1845)).

344 *See* Francis A. Boyle, "American Foreign Policy toward International Law and Organizations: 1898–1917," 6 *Loyola of Los Angeles International and Comparative Law Review*. 185 (1983). Further, to quote Jeffrey Dunoff, "To think in terms of 'traditions' flattens history and erases its ruptures, transformations, and incommunicabilities" (Jeffrey Dunoff, "Engaging the Writings of Martti Koskenniemi: Introduction to the Symposium," 27(2) *Temple International and Comparative Law Journal* 272 (2013), at p. 227).

345 Benjamin Allen Coates, *Legalist Empire: International Law and American Foreign Relations in the Early Twentieth Century* (Oxford: Oxford University Press, 2016), at pp. 25–28.

346 *See, e.g.*, Mark Weston Janis, *The American Tradition of International Law: Great Expectations, 1794–1914* (New York: Oxford University Press, 2004); Jonathan Zasloff,

between liberal elites in Mexico and the US helps explain the intra-American arbitration project.[347] Domestically too, the postbellum era was a time of professionalization in US legal education.[348] On the other side, many historians see US arbitration as a legalized form of imperialism.[349] In his recently published history of international arbitration, University of Toronto Professor David Schneiderman writes of the dark legacy of the US practice; he describes international legalism as an "alibi" of colonialism.[350] The US, for example, protected its nationals

"Law and the Shaping of American Foreign Policy: From the Gilded Age to the New Era," 78 *NYU Law Review* 239 (2003); Jonathan Zasloff, "Law and the Shaping of American Foreign Policy: The Twenty Years' Crisis," 77 *S. California Law Review*. 583 (2004).

347 Thomas David Schoonover, *Dollars over Dominion: The Triumph of Liberalism in Mexican–United States Relations, 1861–1867* (Baton Rouge: Louisiana State University Press, 1978), at p. xix. According to Schoonover, who wrote his doctoral dissertation on US–Mexican relations in the 1860s, the Lieber tribunal was a result of the shared liberal ideology of the two countries.

348 Especially as represented by the establishment of Columbia Law School – *see* Alan Nissel, "The Columbianization of US Legal Education," (work in progress on file with author) – regarding the significance of Columbia law professor Theodore Dwight to the professionalization of legal education. On "professionalism," *see* James A. Brundage, "The Rise of the Professional Jurist in the Thirteenth Century," 20 *Syracuse Journal of International Law and Commerce* 185–190 (1994), at p. 185; Roscoe Pound, "What is a Profession? The Rise of the Legal Profession in Antiquity," 19 *Notre Dame Law Review* 203–228 (1944); John Archer Jackson, "Professions and Professionalization," in John Archer Jackson (ed.), *Professions and Professionalization* 1–17 (Cambridge: Cambridge University Press, 1970), at pp. 4–5; G. Harries-Jenkins, "Professionals in Organizations," in Jackson (ed.), *ibid*, at pp. 51–108, 69–77; Jonathan Zasloff, "Law and the Shaping of American Foreign Policy: From the Gilded Age to the New Era," 78 *NYU Law Review* 239 (2003), at pp. 253, 277; Christopher R. Rossi, *Whiggish International Law: Elihu Root, the Monroe Doctrine, and International Law in the Americas* (Leiden: Brill, 2019), at pp. 116–117.

349 See, *e.g.*, Santiago Montt, "What International Investment Law and Latin America Can and Should Demand From Each Other. Updating the Bello/Calvo Doctrine in the BIT Generation," 3 *Res Publica Argentina* 75 (2007); Santiago Montt, "Latin American Position on State Responsibility. Looking into the Past for Lessons on the Future," LEGS seminar presentation, Princeton University, February 9, 2009 (available online at https://lapaweb.princeton.edu/sites/default/files/2009-0209_Montt_LEGS_chapter.pdf, last visited on May 9, 2010); Teemu Ruskola, *Legal Orientalism: China, the United States, and Modern Law* (Cambridge, MA: Harvard University Press, 2013).

350 *See* David Schneiderman, *Investment Law's Alibis: Colonialism, Imperialism, Debt and Development* (Cambridge: Cambridge University Press, 2022), at p. 6: "It is, indeed remarkable how salient and durable those [colonial] methods remain today." He continues: "[T]hey continue to justify the maintenance of regimes that 'lay waste' to certain peoples, social relations and environments. I characterize this matrix of practices as 'alibis' in so far as they provide for a set of rules and institutions – the investment law regime – that increasingly are indefensible" (internal citations omitted).

extraterritorially in China through the US Court for China and in Egypt through the Mixed Courts of Egypt. Why then were such forms of protection not similarly taken in Latin America? Why, indeed, did US lawyers professionalize *international* arbitration decades before *domestic* arbitration procedures?[351]

Clearly there was something more to international arbitration than a cultural disposition toward legalism, especially within the Republican Party at the time.[352] Neither liberalism nor imperialism alone explains why the US employed arbitration in Latin America and not in, for example, East Asia. The US practice was motivated more by pragmatism than by an ideology of imperialism or liberalism. American arbitration was a bit of both. The US was just as legalistic as it needed to be to achieve regionally specific policy aims. Vis-à-vis their southern neighbors, the Monroe Doctrine explains why lawyer-diplomats in the State Department wielded international law to provide better than local economic protection for their nationals in Latin America.[353] Furthermore, to combat the historic US fear of British power, every President of this period sought actively to expand US influence abroad, especially in Latin America. The idea was to carry out the inevitable "Americanization" of the entire continent.[354]

351 *See* John T. Morse, Jr., *The Law of Arbitration and Award* (Boston: Little Brown, 1872), at pp. 99–100; *see further* Frances Kellor, *American Arbitration: Its History, Functions and Achievements* (New York: Harper & Brothers, 1948).

352 For Democrats (as opposed to Republicans) legalism mostly with boundary disputes. *See* Nick Cleaver, "Grover Cleveland's General Arbitration Treaty of 1897: Legalism and Internationalism in late-19th Century US Foreign Policy," available online at www.academia.edu/3391358/Grover_Cleveland_s_General_Arbitration_Treaty_of_1897_Legalism_and_Internationalism_in_late_19th_Century_U_S_Foreign_Policy?email_work_card=view-paper, last visited May 3, 2021.

353 To take a non-arbitration example, after decades of espousing the principle of *de facto* recognition for nearly a century, the US felt comfortable denying the legal existence of the extremely effective (and almost victorious) Confederate revolutionaries to its south. Similarly, when it came to recognizing the Díaz government in Mexico, Fish instructed his Minister there to withhold US recognition until Foster was assured that the Díaz Government had "sufficient strength to carry out its international obligations" (Foreign Relations of the United States (hereinafter "FRUS") (Washington, DC: Government Printing Office, 1877), at pp. 385 et seq. as cited in Goebel, *supra* note 133, at p. 203).

354 Edward Everett, "Stability and Progress: Remarks Made on the 4th of July, 1853, in Faneuil Hall," in Edward Everett (ed.), *Orations and Speeches on Various Occasions*, Vol. 3 (Boston: Little Brown & Co., 1859), at pp. 224–231 (originally expressed by Secretary of State Edward Everett in 1853).

When the process of this Americanization began, the US was still perceived as a good neighbor.[355] Speaker of the House Henry Clay (1777–1852) could be taken seriously when he claimed that the day was coming when regional governments "[w]ould be animated by an *American* feeling, and guided by an *American* policy. They would obey the laws of the system of the New World, of which they would compose a part, in contradistinction to that of Europe."[356] These laws of the New World, it turned out, were less a source of brotherly love than of northern control. In 1895, when Secretary of State Richard Olney looked back on three decades of US foreign policy, he was not talking about regional solidarity: "Today the United States is practically sovereign on this continent, and its fiat is law upon the subjects to which it confines its interposition."[357] By then the US was no longer a regional role model or guardian. It was a hegemon, a Great Power.

An International Regime of Property Protection

By the end of the century, an international legal regime of property protection was in place.[358] The habitual use of international arbitration increasingly assured foreign investors of the availability of international protection where local remedies fail. This Western (or "international") accomplishment critically reduced the riskiness of investing capital abroad.[359] There was now a body of positive law setting out the

355 *See supra* note 60 and accompanying text.

356 James F. Hopkins (ed.), *The Papers of Henry Clay*, Vol. 2 (Lexington: University Press of Kentucky, 1961), at pp. 519–529, as quoted in Henry William Brands, *What America Owes the World: The Struggle for the Soul of Foreign Policy* (Cambridge: Cambridge University Press, 1998), at p. 5.

357 Dispatch of Secretary of State Richard Olney to Ambassador Thomas Bayard of July 20, 1895, *FRUS* (Washington, DC: Government Printing Office, 1895), at p. 558.

358 By "international regime," I have in mind here Robert Keohane and Joseph Nye's usage: "By creating or accepting procedures, rules, or institutions for certain kinds of activity, governments regulate and control transnational and interstate relations" (*Power and Interdependence* (Boston: Little Brown & Co, 1977) at p. 5. On the early protection of property as part of the *ius gentium, see* Martti Koskenniemi, *To the Uttermost Parts of the Earth: Legal Imagination and International Power 1300–1870* (Cambridge: Cambridge University Press, 2021), at pp. 88–123.

359 As political scientist Charles Lipson writes, "the juridical dominance of individual possession *on a worldwide basis* … assured the hegemony of individual appropriation, the very basis of modern capitalism" (Charles Lipson, *Standing Guard: Protecting Foreign Capital in the Nineteenth and Twentieth Centuries* (Berkeley: University of California Press, 1985), at p. 21, emphasis in original).

international protection of property and the legal consequences for violating that law. Realizing this change and seeking to promote it, the US Congress began publishing its own *Digest of International Law of the United States.* First published in three volumes in 1886, this series was first edited by Francis Wharton (1820–1889) who had served as Examiner of Claims in the State Department.[360] Hamilton Fish along with the majority of the US Supreme Court justices urged Congress to finance its publication.[361] Subsequent editions of this storied digest were edited by John Bassett Moore (1860–1947), Green Haywood Hackworth (1883–1973) and Marjorie Millace Whiteman (1898–1986) all of whom played major roles in the international legalization of such claims and whose names are mentioned throughout this book.

By 1886, international arbitration had become more than a messianic idea. And in the summer of 1898, Tsar Nicholas II was able to expect the cooperation of the diplomatic representatives in St. Petersburg in permanently institutionalizing arbitration as a pacific form of international dispute resolution.[362] It was indeed established a year later. Perhaps no aspect of the newly minted Permanent Court of Arbitration reflected its American origins more than the simple fact that its first case was the *Pious Fund of the Californias.*[363] This first case was a claim between the

[360] Wharton was the son of a prominent family of lawyers and politicians. His father, Thomas Isaac Wharton (1751–1856) who also was responsible for editing legal digests.

[361] From Hon. Hamilton Fish: "The Digest promises to supply a much needed want and could come from no other hand" (US Congress, Joint Committee on Printing, 49th Cong, 1st Session, S. Rep. (June 3, 1886)).

[362] When Tsar Nicholas II invited other nations to establish the PCA in 1898, institutionalizing international arbitration seemed like a largely European affair. The first formal change in the US foreign policy of international arbitration was initiated a few years later by President Theodore Roosevelt. Thanks in large part to the efforts of Secretary of State, Elihu Root, and his deputy, James Brown Scott – both founders of the American Society of International Law – the US began to promote international arbitration *as a matter of policy*. In addition to persuading several governments to sign on to the Hague Treaty, Root and Scott persuaded President Roosevelt and Mexican Secretary of Foreign Affairs, Ignacio Mariscal (who was still in office since the time of Fish), to send the *Pious Funds of California* dispute to the newly formed PCA. *See* John Bassett Moore, "Comment on the General Arbitration Treaties of 1911," in *Collected Papers of John Bassett Moore*, Vol. III (New Haven: Yale University Press, 1944).

[363] *The Pious Fund of the Californias (The United States of America v. The United Mexican States)*, 1902-01, Permanent Court of Arbitration, Arbitrators: Mr. Henning Matzen, The Right Hon. Sir Edward Fry, His Excellency M. de Martens, Mr. T. M. C. Asser Jonkheer and A. F. de Savornin Lohman, available online at https://pca-cpa.org/en/cases/75/, last visited June 21, 2021.

US and Mexico concerning the continuing expropriation of Jesuit property.

The *Pious Fund of the Californias* was a microcosm of the US turn to international arbitration. The underlying dispute between the US and Mexico was several decades old by the time it arrived in The Hague. It was one of the main reasons the two nations agreed to set up a mixed claims commission under the Treaty of Guadalupe Hidalgo in 1848.[364] It was also the biggest award issued by The Lieber Tribunal three decades later.[365] In 1902, the PCA Tribunal rendered its award, which was the third award in favor of the US. The primary difference in the PCA proceeding as compared to the previous two efforts was its composition; all members of the 1902 tribunal were professional arbitrators from countries *other* than those that were parties to the litigation. And it was this third award that was finally recognized and paid by Mexico.[366] Thus, at the end of the postbellum era, as at its beginning, the US successfully secured better-than-local positions for its nationals through international arbitration – whether based in Washington, DC or at The Hague.

With the establishment of the PCA, international arbitration was no longer led by US diplomacy. The Great Powers universalized the American practice of *ad hoc* professionalism and provided it with a vocabulary of communitarianism. Even the nomenclature of a "permanent" "court," as is well-known, is a manifestation of this dissonance: the PCA was neither "permanent" nor a "court." It was a beautiful building (a "Peace Palace") that was available for use by willing – if disputing – states. Much has been made of the inherency of this contradiction and the purpose here is not to expose it.[367] William Penfield, who represented

[364] Because Mexico disputed its obligation to pay any interest accruing after the period covered by the Lieber Tribunal, diplomatic negotiations between the US and Mexico continued until an arbitral agreement was finally signed on May 22, 1902. *See further* W. S. Penfield, "Hague Tribunal," 11(10) *The Michigan Alumnus* 164–170 (1905), at p. 167.

[365] *See* Francis J. Weber, "The Pious Fund of the Californias," 43(1) *Hispanic American Historical Review* 78 (1963), at p. 84: Umpire Thornton awarded the amount of $904,700.79, which was twenty-one years' interest at the rate of $43,080.99 per annum, or 6 percent of one-half the capitalized value of the Pious Fund.

[366] The *Pious Funds* award was US$ 904,070.99, representing twenty-one years of interest on half of the property value. Mexico treated this award as ending the alien claim that survived two prior claims treaties between the US and Mexico (in 1848 and 1868).

[367] Some degree of dissonance is unsurprising and even inevitable. *See* J. H. H. Weiler, "The Rule of Lawyers and the Ethos of Diplomats: Reflections on the Internal and External Legitimacy of WTO Dispute Settlement," in R. Porter *et al.* (ed.), *Efficiency, Equity, and Legitimacy: The Multilateral Trading System at the Millennium* (Washington, DC:

the US in the *Pious Funds* case in the PCA, affirmed that "In its origin and development, arbitration was resorted to rather as an expedient than upon principle."[368]

It was expedient for the US to support the PCA as a way to divert attention away from its unvoiced aims of regional hegemony. Some historians have missed this point because the promoters of international arbitration were peace activists and public philanthropists. However, the likes of David Dudley Field II (1805–1894), Ulysses S. Grant (1822–1885) and Andrew Carnegie (1835–1919) were also often spokesmen for the business community.[369] They did not represent mainstream popular views regarding arbitration in the 1890s. By then, the horrors of the Civil War were a faint memory and the "manly" ideals of war – rather than arbitration – were once again being romanticized.[370]

The promise of historical progress is palpable in the history of international arbitration. Both President Theodore Roosevelt (1858–1919) and Secretary of State Elihu Root (1845–1937) were awarded the Nobel Peace Prize for their contributions to international arbitration. In fact, *every single Nobel Peace Prize recipient prior to World War I was specifically recognized for his or her contribution to international arbitration.* That is a remarkable fact to be pondered. This narrative misplaces the actual versus the aspirational role of the PCA. Professionalized international arbitration was not the product of any one state's conduct and there is little evidence of the technique averting major military conflict. Quite the contrary.

Brookings Institution Press, 2001): "The dissonance is almost inevitable and its correction, where such correction is needed, will not be painless or without cost especially as there is, in my view, in some cases a certain zero-sum game between internal and external legitimacy" (internal citations omitted).

368 William L. Penfield, "International Arbitration," 1(2) *American Journal of International Law* 330 (1907), at p. 330.

369 Even Field, the great codifier of both US and international law, was "one of the most powerful and famous, and least-loved, American lawyers of the 19th century" (Ross E. Davies, "The Judiciary Funded: The Generosity of David Dudley Field," 14(2) *Green Bag* 435–452 (2011), at p. 435). He was very unpopular even among the members of the Association of the Bar of the City of New York (*see* Veenswijk, *supra* note 334, at pp. 75–78). Similarly, John Chandler Bancroft Davis, an important lawyer-diplomat in Fish's department was president of Newburgh and New York Railway Company (Thom Hartman, *Unequal Protection: The Rise of Corporate Dominance and the Theft of Human Rights* (New York: Rodale, 2002), at p. 107).

370 I would like to thank Professor Joyce Goldberg for pointing this out to me.

1898: From Good to Great Power

The transformation of the US standing on the world stage was readily visible by 1898, when it began formally colonizing overseas territories including Puerto Rico, just off its southeastern shores. Asserting the Monroe Doctrine in 1902, the US dictated an arbitral resolution to the Venezuelan crisis not as a local peace mediator but as a regional hegemon. This change in global status is reflected in the 1904 adaptation of the Roosevelt Corollary to the Monroe Doctrine, which more expressly asserted the US role of policing the hemisphere for various matters including property protection.[371] Latin Americans, seeking to reign in foreign intervention, formulated their own policies of non-intervention. Argentine foreign minister Luis Drago (1859–1921) argued that "the public debt of an American State cannot occasion armed intervention ... by a *European Power.*"[372] President Theodore Roosevelt agreed and in his 1904 State of the Union Address, he formally affirmed the Drago doctrine.[373] There was no longer any ambiguity about

[371] On the flexibility of the Monroe Doctrine, *see* Christopher R. Rossi, *Whiggish International Law: Elihu Root, the Monroe Doctrine, and International Law in the Americas* (Leiden: Brill, 2019), at p. 11 ("In the history of the Monroe Doctrine, and coinciding with the decades bookending the turn of the twentieth century, the meaning of the Monroe Doctrine indeed had changed dramatically." "No modern treatment of international law in the Americas can escape the omnipresent significance of the Monroe Doctrine").

[372] Note of December 29, 1902 from Señor Luis M. Drago, Minister of Foreign Relations of the Argentine Republic, to Señor Martin Garcia Mérou, Minister of the Argentine Republic to the United States, available online at https://history.state.gov/historicaldocuments/frus1903/d2, last visited June 16, 2021. *See also* Luis M. Drago and H. Edward Nettles, "The Drago Doctrine in International Law and Politics," 8(2) *The Hispanic American Historical Review* 204 (1928). *See also*, especially as concerning water boundary disputes, Peter L. Reich, "Foreign Relations Between Mexico and the United States in the Nineteenth Century, 1821–1910," 24 *PROFMEX WebJournal* 12 (2019) (Mexico pushed back against the Monroe Doctrine corollary with "Diaz Doctrine," which said that every country's sovereignty had to be respected and that each state would handle debt issues within its own legal system).

[373] Roosevelt stated that the US would ensure that states in the region fulfilled their international obligations to foreign investors or invite "foreign aggression to the detriment of the entire body of American nations." According to the doctrine articulated by President Theodore Roosevelt in his State of the Union Address in 1904, the US would intervene in conflicts with Latin American countries to enforce legitimate claims (Theodore Roosevelt, *Addresses and Presidential Messages of Theodore Roosevelt, 1902–1904* (New York: G. P. Putnam's Sons, 1904), at p. 380). For Secretary of State Richard Olney's criticism of the Roosevelt Corollary to the Monroe Doctrine, *see* Richard Olney, "The Development of International Law," 1 *American Journal of International Law* 418 (1907), at p. 424.

the US claim to use force in the region. The Roosevelt Corollary, like the original Monroe Doctrine, prohibited European intervention, but it also reserved the right for the US to use coercive action to police the Americas, except for the enforcement of public debt, that is.[374] In this sense, by the turn of the century *the US went from being a good power promoting international legalism to being a Great Power wielding its expansive authority.*

Other nations took note of the empire's new clothes. In 1906, at the Manhattan home of Oscar S. Straus (1850–1926), US lawyer-diplomats Elihu Root and James Brown Scott gathered to form the first professional US organization of international law: the American Society of International Law. In Strauss' words, "We are a world power and we must put world-power clothes on to meet the situation."[375] The turn to international arbitration was a US project that sought to protect US – not European and certainly not Latin American – interests. The US wielded arbitration to hold states in Latin America responsible for failing to meet the "internation Americanizing al minimum standard" of protection to US aliens.[376] At the center of this technical, legal practice was Hamilton Fish, the Secretary of State under President Ulysses S. Grant. As noted,

374 Poignantly, President Grant's two most important foreign policy goals ended in 1898 – war (Cuba) and peace (Britain). 1898 was the end and not the beginning of American imperialism. *See* Gregg Jones, *Honor in the Dust: Theodore Roosevelt, War in the Philippines, and the Rise and Fall of America's Imperial Dream* (New York: New American Library, 2012). Roosevelt actualized Everett's 1853 vision of "Americanizing" the New World (*see* Edward Everett, "Stability and Progress: Remarks Made on the 4th of July, 1853, in Faneuil Hall," in Edward Everett (ed.), *Orations and Speeches on Various Occasions*, Volume 3 (Boston: Little Brown & Co., 1859), at pp. 224–231 (originally expressed by Secretary of State Edward Everett in 1853)).

375 "Root Heads New Body on International Law," *New York Times*, January 13, 1906 as cited in Benjamin Coates, "Upon the Neutral Rests the Trusteeship of International Law: Legal Advisers and American Unneutrality," in Johan den Hertog and Samuël Kruizinga (eds.), *Caught in the Middle: Neutrals, Neutrality and the First World War* 35 (Amsterdam: Amsterdam University Press, 2011).

376 Regarding the eventual acceptance of the international minimum standard among tribunals, *see* Theo L. Pauthonier, *The Transition from Diplomatic Protection to Investor-State Arbitration and the Rise of Private Actors on the International Scene* (2015) (unpublished L.L.M. dissertation, Durham Law School) (on file with author), pp. 18–24; Frédéric Mégret, "Mixed Claim Commissions and the Once Centrality of the Protection of Aliens," in Ignacio de la Rasilla and Jorge E. Viñuales (eds.), *Experiments in International Adjudication: Historical Accounts* 127 (Cambridge: Cambridge University Press, 2019), at p. 127.

Fish professionalized the State Department and, in the process, expedited its resolution of diplomatic claims. From 1868 onwards, US diplomats established international arbitration as the default tool of alien protection. Although inchoate and often inconsistent, the resulting awards began to articulate rules regarding a state's responsibility for injuries to aliens, as I will discuss in the next chapter.

3

The Creation of State Responsibility in the New World

1870: The First Professional International Tribunal

The arbitration of alien protection claims was a subtle intervention into the local legal systems of host states. The US used the technique of legalism to provide an international layer of protection to its nationals sojourning abroad. This practice resulted in the creation of a new body of caselaw that, for the first time, articulated a positive doctrine of "state responsibility," for alien injuries.[1] This was a major departure from international law's origins in European diplomatic practice. By delegating international claims to professional arbitrators, the US morphed *diplomatic* protection claims into *alien* protection claims. An international regime of property law was born. Thenceforth, it was clear that states must provide an "international minimum standard" of protection to aliens, the details of which were to be determined by *international* arbitrators.[2] Jean d'Aspremont has labeled this US feat as an "invention

[1] I discuss the coining of "state responsibility" during the interwar era as an international law term of art in Chapter 5.

[2] As Edwin M. Borchard writes in 1915, "the standard of a duty of the State towards aliens and its international responsibility for violation of its obligations may be considered the result of a gradual evolution in practice, States having in their mutual intercourse recognized certain duties incumbent upon them" (*The Diplomatic Protection of Citizens Abroad or The Law of International Claims* (New York: The Banks Law Publishing Co., 1915), at p. 177). Interestingly, while outside the scope of this chapter, the premodern origins of this standard were closely related to right of hospitality (or sociability) put forward by Vitoria. In the context of arguing for the Spanish natural right to missionize the Amerindians, Vitoria states that all nations are obligated to treat foreign nationals according to an appropriate standard of hospitality. A violation of this standard triggers the right to wage a "just war" against the host nation (Franciscus de Vitoria, *De Indis et de Ivre Belli. Reflectiones, ed.* Ernest Nys, Carnegie Institute of Washington (Washington, DC: Gibson Brothers, 1917), at pp. 151–156. The classical reference on the historical origins of the standard is Gerrit Walter Gong, *The Standard of 'Civilization' in International Society* (Oxford: Clarendon Press, 1984). For a review of the standard in western literature during the late nineteenth and early twentieth centuries, *see* Charles G. Fenwick, *International Law* (2nd ed., New York: D. Appleton-Century Company, 1934), at pp. 197–216. *See also*

of international responsibility."[3] And this must certainly have been a source of satisfaction to Secretary of State Hamilton Fish.

By relying on new legal procedures, the US legitimated its claims of alien protection; but this validation came at a long-term cost. Fish and his successors did not seek an arbitration policy that would create a *general* doctrine of state responsibility for violating international law and not just for alien injuries. But this is exactly what happened. Eluding its diplomatic control, state responsibility grew into a rebellious child of the United States. In just a few decades, non-Anglo-American international lawyers effectively expanded the doctrine's limited boundaries of alien injuries into the broader realm of *general international law*. Such is the power of law. Once established as a legal form or principle, international lawyers from other states were able to progressively develop the nineteenth century doctrine into one that allowed for attributing state responsibility for *any* international wrong. The US opposed this generalized doctrine with all its diplomatic power but was unable to prevent its codification by the UN. Below, I have structured this chapter to reflect these two consequences of intra-American arbitration: (1) the legalization of alien protection and (2) the resulting creation of state responsibility.[4]

Charles Henry Alexandrowicz, *The European–African Confrontation: A Study in Treaty Making* (Leiden: Sijthoff, 1973), at p. 6 (attributes the emergence and application of the standard to the ascendancy of positive law). There were many names to the standard: the "minimum standard of civilized justice," "minimum standard of international law," "minimum standard of civilization," etc. The term "international minimum standard," however, was an early twentieth century development, as I discuss in the next chapter. As far as premodern enforcement is concerned, before the advent of the law of state responsibility, the disposition of international disputes was conceptualized as either being peacefully or forcefully resolved. Vattel, for example, discussed the peaceful settlement of disputes and the use of force in his The Law of Nations, Book II, ch. XVIII and chs. I–IV, XI–XIII, respectively. For a discussion see Vincent Chetail, "Vattel and the American Dream: An Inquiry into the Reception of the Law of Nations in the United States," in V. Chetail and P.-M. Dupuy (eds.), *The Roots of International Law. Liber Amicorum Peter Haggenmacher* 251 (The Hague: Martinus Nijhoff, 2013), at p. 263.

[3] Jean d'Aspremont, "The General Claims Commission (Mexico and the United States) and the Invention of International Responsibility," in I. de la Rasilla del Moral and J. Vinuales (eds.), *Experiments in International Adjudication: Historical Accounts* (Cambridge: Cambridge University Press, 2018) available online at https://ssrn.com/abstract=3150798, last visited on February 22, 2019.

[4] On the concept of legalization (in the sense of tribunalization, juridification or positivization), *see* Martti Koskenniemi, "The Fate of Public International Law: Between Technique and Politics," 70(1) *Modern Law Review* 1–30 (2007), at p. 16; H. L. A. Hart, *The Concept of Law* (Oxford: Clarendon Press, 1961), at pp. 229–231. On the evolution of arbitral

Protection as a Premise of International Intercourse

To the US, the protection of nationals abroad was a premise of international intercourse.[5] The promise of protection was "guaranteed by every important European state, and by the United States soon after its independence."[6] US citizens expected to retain certain fundamental rights as they crossed borders.[7] This expectation inhered from their

juridification, *see* Kenneth Smith Carlston, *The Process of International Arbitration* (New York: Columbia University Press, 1946), at pp. 3–33; Crawford Morrison Bishop, *International Arbitral Procedure* (Baltimore: King Bros., 1930, based on Ph.D. Columbia University 1930). On the *Institut de Droit International*'s "Projet de règlement pour la procédure arbitrale international" (Session de La Haye, 1875), *see* Martti Koskenniemi, "The Civilizing Mission: International Law and the Colonial Encounter in the Late 19th Century" (*Rechtshistorikertag*, Bonn, September 12–17, 2004), at pp. 17–18: (though no stable standard of civilization ever emerged from the lawyers' debates, lawyers were still deeply embedded in the language of the standard).

5 This view is shared among Anglo and Latin American commentators alike – *see* Arnulf Becker Lorca, "International Law in Latin America or Latin American International Law? Rise, Fall, and Retrieval of a Tradition of Legal Thinking and Political Imagination," 47(1) *Harvard International Law Journal* 283 (2006), at p. 290 ("Variety among Latin American textbooks might be explained by positioning them along a continuum between universalism and particularism and contrasting them with one another . . . In the naturalist mode, universality is a necessary attribute of the law of peoples. If, as a matter of definition, *ubi societas ibi ius*, the interaction between different peoples is not lawless but regulated by the natural principles of the law of peoples"). *See also* Raoul Eugène Desvernine, *Claims against Mexico: A Brief Study of the International Law Applicable to Claims of Citizens of the United States and Other Countries for Losses Sustained in Mexico during the Revolutions of the Last Decade* (Private Publication, 1921), at p. 8.

6 Charles Lipson, *Standing Guard: Protecting Foreign Capital in the Nineteenth and Twentieth Centuries* (Berkeley: University of California Press, 1985), at p. 9. Lipson continues in a footnote: "United States acceptance of these general principles was reflected in article 6 of the 1795 treaty between the United States and Spain. Some years later, Secretary of State John Quincy Adams wrote of that provision: 'There is no principle of the law of nations more firmly established than that which entitles the property of strangers with the jurisdiction of another country in friendship with their own protection of its sovereign by all efforts in his power. This *common rule of intercourse* between all civilized nations has, between the United States and Spain, the further and solemn sanction of an express stipulation by treaty.'" Mr. Adams to Mr. de Onis, Spanish minister, March 12, 1818, in US Congress, *American State Papers. Foreign Relations*, Vol. 4 (Washington, DC: Gales and Seaton, 1834), at p. 476 (emphasis added). For a history of the British promise of protection, *see* Lauren Benton and Lisa Ford, *Rage for Order: The British Empire and the Origins of International Law 1800–1850* (Cambridge, MA: Harvard University Press, 2016), ch. 4: The Promise of Protection.

7 The context of this international legalization was the US and French Revolutions. It was only in the century after the French Revolution, that European governments established diplomatic protection as "a definite practice" (Edwin Montefiore Borchard, *The Diplomatic Protection of Citizens Abroad or The Law of International Claims* (New

citizenship, which was meant to provide "a certain guarantee of security, the assurance of having some spot you can call your own and that no one can alienate from you."[8] Before 1870, this protection was limited to domestic legal enforcement actions and international diplomacy efforts.[9] After Hamilton Fish appointed his friend Francis Lieber as the umpire of the US–Mexico Mixed Claims Commission of 1868 ("Lieber Tribunal"), private injuries became justiciable claims.[10] By referring such claims to professional arbitrators, the US reformulated what was once a domestic-based diplomatic claim into a technical, international one.[11]

Hence the expression "alien protection." "Alien," as distinguished from "foreigner," is a technical term with roots in early modern legal

York: The Banks Law Publishing Co., 1915), at p. 808). *See also* Julius Goebel, Jr., "The International Responsibility of States for Injuries Sustained by Aliens on Account of Mob Violence, Insurrections and Civil Wars," 8(4) *American Journal of International Law* 802–852 (1914), at p. 819 ("The . . . responsibility for aliens injured . . . may be regarded as an outgrowth of the whole movement for individual rights which culminated in the French Revolution. When states realized that their nationals possessed domestic rights and privileges, they began to insist upon a certain observance of these rights by other states when their subjects ventured abroad").

8 Patrick Weil, *The Sovereign Citizen: Denaturalization and the Origins of the American Republic* (Philadelphia: University of Pennsylvania Press, 2012), at p. 2, internal citations omitted.

9 Conceptually, the duty of alien protection has four aspects: (1) the duty to protect nationals at home, (2) the duty to protect nationals abroad, (3) the duty to protect aliens at home and (4) the duty to protect aliens abroad. Only perspective (3) gave rise to international litigation. The extent to which a state protects its own nationals at home or abroad was considered a public domestic matter. Similarly, states were not held internationally accountable for their failure to protect their own nationals abroad. Given the exclusion of perspectives of (1), (2) and (4) from international litigation – at least prior to the institutionalization of international human rights law – I will largely omit them from my discussion below.

10 As Edwin Borchard has written, "Not until the legal position of the state toward individuals, both its own citizens and aliens, and of states between themselves, had become clearly defined in modern public law, did diplomatic protection become a factor in international intercourse" (Edwin M. Borchard, "Basic Elements of Diplomatic Protection of Citizens Abroad," 7 *American Journal of International Law* 497 (1913), at pp. 515, 518–519).

11 Governmental lawyers abstracted general principles of law to protect people going places abroad. This *lex mercatoria* formed the basis of the international laws applied to investment protection – *see* Yves Dezalay and Bryant G. Garth, *Dealing in Virtue: International Commercial Arbitration and the Construction of a Transnational Legal Order* (Chicago: University of Chicago Press, 1996), at p. 3 (the abstraction of international law is therefore closely tied to the activities of individuals and groups, who thereby give concrete meaning to the abstraction).

practice.[12] Alien protection became a formalized field of international law that gave individual investors an opportunity – beyond local courts or diplomatic intervention – to redress injuries suffered abroad. When nations agreed to establish international mixed claims commissions, individuals simply had to file a qualifying claim with their foreign office for its inclusion in the litigation proceedings. Claims would be resolved by independent, third-party tribunals, staffed by professional attorneys authorized to issue binding awards, which are based on general principles of law.[13]

Formally, the arbitration of local claims at the international level respected the political sovereignty of host states.[14] If a state was recognized as civilized, then it possessed the cultural and legal attributes of sociability. One such attribute was the duty to provide a civilized level of protection to aliens sojourning in their territories. The determination to arbitrate international claims was described as a constitutive element of statehood, rather than as a restriction to national sovereignty. Providing such a standard of care to alien property would demonstrate an acceptance of shared (Western) values and provide new states the recognition they sought by civilized nations.[15]

[12] On the origins and original usages of the term "alien," *see* M. Anderson Berry, "Whether Foreigner or Alien: A New Look at the Original Language of the Alien Tort Statute," 27 (2) *Berkeley Journal of International Law* 316 (2009), at pp. 337–367.

[13] To Cheng, general principles of law are "general propositions underlying the various rules of law which express the essential qualities of juridical truth itself, in short of Law" (Bin Cheng, *General Principles of Law as Applied by International Courts and Tribunals* (London: Stevens, 1953) at p. 24). In addition to principles of responsibility, other general principles developed by arbitrators then included res judicata, good faith, and *lex specialis generalibus derogate* (*ibid*, at pp. 25–26).

[14] So, for example, US Secretary of State Elihu Root understood international claims for alien protection to be private in nature, which paid traditional respect to Latin American sovereignty: Christopher R. Rossi, *Whiggish International Law: Elihu Root, the Monroe Doctrine, and International Law in the Americas* (Leiden: Brill, 2019), at p. 101 (sovereignty respects the distinction in municipal law systems between civil responsibility (tort) and criminal law: "If I make a contract with you and break it, it is no business of our neighbor . . . if I assault and batter you, every neighbor has an interest in having me arrested and punished, because his own safety requires that violence shall be restrained.").

[15] *See, e.g.*, the award of *Dr. Baldwin's Minatitlan Claims* (Baldwin v. Mexico), in which Umpire Baron von Róenne (Germany), approves the opinion of the US commissioner: "If Mexico wished to maintain rank and fellowship among the civilized nations of the earth she must place her laws on footing with the laws of other nations as far as related to intercourse with foreigners. What oppression they might practice upon their citizens was one thing; the practice of similar oppressions upon foreigners was another thing. The latter had the right to appeal to the protection of their government, if injured" (Award of

An Exceptional International Standard

Normally, of course, alien protection was regulated by local laws. *Exceptionally*, when such protection fell below international standards, host states could be held accountable by recourse to international litigation. But the reader of the early international awards might be forgiven for drawing the opposite conclusion – that the US-led practice became the rule of alien protection and not its exception. And the more US nationals invested in Latin America, the more Latin American governments found themselves making indemnifications for injuries. This is why I describe state responsibility as a *doctrine of exceptions* – one that was easy to manipulate by creative attorneys from its earliest usages. The early awards were professionally rendered, but they were also inconsistent. They did not establish any predictable principles of state responsibility (remedial, compliant, etc.).

The "international minimum standard" to which international lawyers made frequent reference had no meaning and was barely in use prior to the twentieth century. Its predecessor was the "standard of civilization," which can be traced back to the medieval scholastics.[16] The lawyer-diplomat Emer de Vattel (1714–1767) viewed alien injuries as constituting an "indirect injury" to a state, which then has a right of enforcement against the delinquent state.[17] For Vattel, it was important to the

the Umpire, February 23, 1842, Commission under the Convention between the United States and Mexico of April 11, 1839); John Bassett Moore (ed.), *History and Digest of the International Arbitrations to Which the United States Has Been a Party*, Vol. I (Washington, DC: Government Printing Office, 1898), at p. 3238).

16 *See* Francisco Javier Peñas Esteban, "Standard of Civilization: The History of International Relations," 40 *Relaciones Internacionales* 171 (2019), at p. 181. On the etymology of *civitas* and civilization, *see* Rossi, *supra* note 14, at p. 130.

17 As articulated by Vattel, diplomatic protection is a legal fiction that justifies international enforcement actions. To him, each harm suffered by a national as an indirect injury to the state such that the security needs of the individual are protected as the security needs of the state: "*Quiconque maltraite un Citoyen offense* indirectement *L'État, qui doit protéger ce Citoyen. Le Souverain de celui-ci doit venger son injure, obliger, s'il le peut, l'aggresseur à une entière réparation, ou le punir; puisqu'autrement le Citoyen n'obtiendrait point la grande fin de l'association Civile, que est la sûreté*" (Emer de Vattel, *Le Droit des Gens ou Principes de la Loi Naturelle, à Leiden aux Dépens de la Compagnie* I (London: Tutior, 1758), Livre II, at § 71, emphasis added. On how the Anglo-American view of international protection was based in large part on the writings of Vattel as well as the Lockean belief in ownership from labor, *see further* Martti Koskenniemi, *To the Uttermost Parts of the Earth: Legal Imagination and International Power 1300–1870* (Cambridge: Cambridge University Press, 2021), at ch. 10, "Global Law: Ruling the British Empire."

common prosperity of nations that each state be able to protect its trade and nationals abroad.[18] To be civilized meant to provide (and to expect to have provided) a basic standard of care to one's nationals.

The issue of civilized protection became more acute a century later alongside what British historian Eric Hobsbawm (1917–2012) has called the age of "new imperialism."[19] Despite the fact that this right of protection was well established by the nineteenth century, there was no clear forum within which to enforce it. As Yale Law School Professor Edwin Borchard (1884–1951) writes:

> Legally, the measure of the obligation of the state of residence to resident aliens is the measure of the national state's right. The extent of the failure to fulfill the obligation, ordinarily known as the international responsibility of the state, is in exact proportion to the amount of diplomatic pressure or protection which the national state is authorized to interpose.[20]

Hence the term "diplomatic protection."[21]

Diplomatic protection has always meant different things to different lawyers. Great Britain itself did not have a universal policy on diplomatic protection during the nineteenth century. Local conditions often dictated the ability to protect nationals abroad. Much of the world then was partitioned according to the various levels of domination of seven states: Great Britain, France, Germany, Italy, the Netherlands, Belgium and the US.[22] Many regions – Africa, the Pacific, South and Southeast Asia – were predominantly controlled by colonizing states.[23] Given the

[18] *See generally,* Isaac Nakhimovsky, "Vattel's Theory of the International Order: Commerce and the Balance of Power in the Law of Nations," 33 *History of European Ideas* 157 (2007), at pp. 160–161.

[19] Eric Hobsbawm, *The Age of Empire: 1875–1914* (New York: Vintage, 1989), at p. 56. There was a spike in its published usage after 1880 – Jean-Baptiste Michel et. al.„ "Quantitative Analysis of Culture Using Millions of Digitized Books," 331 *Science* 6014 (2014), at pp. 176–182. This is the article that announced the search tool Google Ngram, available online at https://books.google.com/ngrams.

[20] Borchard, *supra* note 10, at p. 516.

[21] Prior to the New World practice described in Chapter 2, the traditional manner of redressing injuries to nationals abroad was through "diplomatic protection." As the name suggests, the content of international rights was typically self-judged (known as the problem of "auto-interpretation"), as discussed in the previous chapter.

[22] Hobsbawm, *supra* note 19, at p. 57.

[23] *See infra* notes 35 and 36 and accompanying text. Much of this "scramble for Africa" was formalized by a treaty signed in Berlin – *see* Hobsbawm, *supra* note 19, at pp. 57–58; Antony Anghie, "Finding the Peripheries: Sovereignty and Colonialism in Nineteenth-Century International Law," 40 *Harvard International Law Journal* 1–80 (1990), at pp. 58–59.

role of the US in the Americas, that region was different from the "new imperialism." The New World was the only major region without an international frontier – lacking any serious rivalry between European powers.[24]

The Early British Practice of Diplomatic Claims

Great Britain was the greatest power of the early modern era[25] and the largest capital exporter to the Americas.[26] In contrast to US diplomats, British diplomats worked closely with private investors on policy matters relating to international trade and alien protection.[27] In the words of one British commentator,

> Whatever therefore assists, promotes and extends our Commerce, is consistent with our Interest and whatever weakens, impairs or circumscribes it, is repugnant thereto.[28]

[24] Hobsbawm, *supra* note 19, at p. 58; H. Duncan Hall, "The International Frontier," 42(1) *American Journal of International Law* 42–65 (1948), at p. 42. Despite the comparative isolation that the US enjoyed as the only Great Power in the Americas, the former feared – almost to the level of paranoia – the influence of the latter (discussed in Chapter 2).

[25] On the "greatness" of great powers, *see* Fareed Zakaria, *From Wealth to Power: The Unusual Origins of America's World Role* (Princeton: Princeton University Press, 1998), at p. 49.

[26] Great Britain promoted trade as its highest foreign policy priority – *see* Arthur Donald Innes, *England and the British Empire* (New York: Macmillan, 1913), at pp. 487–489; Michael J. Braddick, "The English Government, War, Trade, and Settlement, 1625–1688," in Nicholas P. Canny (ed.), *The Oxford History of the British Empire: The Origins of Empire* (Oxford: Oxford University Press, 1988), at pp. 292–294. On the British promotion of foreign investment by granting "sovereign rights" (which is something short of full sovereignty), *see* Martti Koskenniemi, *To the Uttermost Parts of the Earth: Legal Imagination and International Power 1300–1870* (Cambridge: Cambridge University Press, 2021), at ch. 10, "Global Law: Ruling the British Empire."

[27] Great Britain keenly appreciated the role of the state "in the service of *legitimate* trade" (David S. Landes, "Some Thoughts on the Nature of Economic Imperialism," 21(4) *The Journal of Economic History* 496 (1961), at p. 507, emphasis in original). The *legitimacy* of that trade, of course, was self-determined. The indirect manner in which the US promoted international trade is discussed in Chapter 2. *See further* Doreen Lustig, "The Enduring Charter: Corporations, States, and International Law," in Melissa J. Durkee (ed.), *States, Firms, and Their Legal Fictions Attributing Identity and Responsibility to Artificial Entities*, 87 (Cambridge: Cambridge University Press, 2024), at p. 88.

[28] John Campbell, *The Present State of Europe* (London: Longman, 1750), at p. 504, as cited in Hans Neufeld, *The International Protection of Private Creditors from the Treaties of Westphalia to the Congress of Vienna (1648–1815): A Contribution to the History of the Law of Nations* 5 (Leiden: Sijthoff, 1971).

The British government, for example, was intimately involved in the development of cotton in India, a commodity of such broad and elastic demand that "it could drive an industrial revolution."[29] In Latin America, the British provided much needed bond financing as well as infrastructure construction (especially transportation and communication). It was a "Bank of the Americas." But it did so with a lighter touch than in other regions.

A linchpin of the British imperial policy can be called liberal colonialism – that is, promoting free trade through a "rule of law" framework.[30] To accommodate the rise of British trade during the nineteenth century, British *domestic* jurisdiction expanded proportionately. The Australian legal historian William Ross Johnston details how Foreign Office lawyers struggled to cope with the rising need "to establish a sufficient jurisdiction in areas not formally part of the empire."[31] "Jurisdictional imperialism" is how Johnston describes their solution. It was a rule-based form of protection that Great Britain used in those areas of its dominion that lacked a civilized sovereign.[32] British legal counselors in its Foreign Office conceptualized territories that were either "civilised" or "colonised."[33] The latter lacked sovereignty over the territory in question such that it was the right of the English consuls and courts to exercise jurisdiction over those territories.[34]

[29] David S. Landes, *The Wealth and Poverty of Nations: Why Some Are So Rich and Some So Poor* (New York: W.W. Norton, 1998), at p. 154.

[30] *See generally* Niall Ferguson, "Globalization in Interdisciplinary Perspective," in Michael D. Bordo, Alan M. Taylor and Jeffrey G. Williamson (eds.), *Globalization in Historical Perspective* (Chicago: University of Chicago Press, 2003), at p. 559: "The British Empire in the nineteenth century . . . can be understood in part as an agency for imposing free trade and the rule of law directly on about a quarter of the world's land surface and indirectly on a great many other places, to say nothing of the world's oceans."

[31] William Ross Johnston, *Sovereignty and Protection: A Study of British Jurisdictional Imperialism in the Late Nineteenth Century* (Durham, NC: Duke University Press, 1973), at p. 328.

[32] It had two basic aspects: "One was in ensuring the provision of a duly constituted power and authority; but it also referred to an empire which was underpinned to the system of *British* law" (Johnston, *supra* note 31, at p. 328, emphasis added). For a Table on the "Rise and Decline of British Extraterritoriality," *see* Turan Kayaoğlu, *Legal Imperialism: Sovereignty and Extraterritoriality in Japan, the Ottoman Empire, and China* (Cambridge: Cambridge University Press, 2010), at p. 5.

[33] For a discussion, *see* Martti Koskenniemi, *The Gentle Civilizer of Nations: The Rise and Fall of International Law 1870–1960* (Cambridge: Cambridge University Press, 2002), at p. 108.

[34] The form of British protection depended upon the level of civilization of local authorities. For example, British policy was different in China and the Ottoman Empires (where they believed there to exist "civilised" governments) than it was in Africa and the Pacific.

Where they could, Great Britain sought to obtain a positive basis for extraterritorial jurisdiction through bilateral treaties.[35] Governmental representatives would procure treaties with local leaders. Because African leaders were often misled or coerced into signing the documents, such pacts have been labeled "unequal treaties."[36] In Africa, for example, the Berlin Conference (1884–1885) triggered a European rush to sign protectorate treaties with local leaders to demonstrate effective colonization of territories. This scramble led to a critical legal question: what was the extent to which each European state could exercise jurisdiction over territories it claimed to "protect?" Early opinions of the British Government Law Officers held that no jurisdiction could be exercised by the protecting state over nationals of other civilized states except by consent of those states, a view not adhered to by Germany and France.[37]

In "civilized" regions, when the Foreign Office was not satisfied that an injury to its national interest was redressed, a British representative often presented a claim for diplomatic protection to the host state. Not infrequently, the claim was followed by a warning – or even a reprisal – by the world's deadliest naval fleet. The British resolve to "protect its nationals abroad was famously articulated by Lord Palmerston (1784–1865) in his *Civis Romanus* speech, discussed below.[38] Local standards did not preclude the British expectation of fair treatment. However, even the British

[35] As Stephen Neff has written, "At the hands of the British and French liberal political economists, the programme was re-cast into one of global freedom of economic intercourse on a liberal capitalist basis . . . Politicians and economists negotiated an ever wider network of FCN treaties, as well as bilateral agreements for tariff reductions" (Stephen C. Neff, "A Short History of International Law," in Malcolm D. Evans (ed.), *International Law* 31 (2003), at p. 45). *See also* Douglas A. Irwin, "Multilateral and Bilateral Trade Policies in the World Trading System: An Historical Perspective," in Jaime De Melo and Arvind Panagariya (eds.), *New Dimensions in Regional Integration* 90–127 (Cambridge: Cambridge University Press, 1993), at p. 91 (nineteenth-century liberalization was attained "entirely" through bilateral agreements).

[36] *See* Gong, *supra* note 3, at pp. 66–69; Anthony Aust, *Modern Treaty Law and Practice* (Cambridge: Cambridge University Press, 2007), at pp. 320–321). In terms of statistics, 143 multilateral treaties were signed between 1851–1899; only fourteen such treaties were signed between 1648–1850 – *see* Charlotte Ku, "Forging a Multilayered System of Global Governance," in R. St. J. Macdonald and D. M. Johnston (eds.), *Towards World Constitutionalism* (The Hague: Brill, 2005), at p. 634. Even of these 143, very few were trade-related; most trade agreements were bilateral.

[37] Lord McNair, *International Law Opinions* I (Cambridge: Cambridge University Press, 1956), at pp. 41–47.

[38] Discussed further *infra* note 81 and accompanying text.

did not simply assert the preemption of British over local standards of care. The law of Great Britain governed alien treatment.

In his exhaustive study of British colonialism, Johnston concludes that the normative underpinning of jurisdictional imperialism was "legalism."[39] Several aspects of British practice support this claim, including their tribunalization of the slave trade.[40] Between 1817 and 1871, Great Britain led the effort to establish international courts for the suppression of the slave trade. Stanford University international law professor Jenny Martinez credits Great Britain for setting up "the first international human rights courts."[41] But was British diplomatic practice *legalistic*? British counselors believed that international disputes ought to be resolved by law, *but their conduct was unlegalistic*. Legalism implies the delegation of disputes to third parties. Neither the British protection of aliens nor its enforcement of the slave trade prohibition, deputized the determination of substantive disputes between states to independent (international) tribunals. Thus, despite its tribunalization, this imperialism was not a legalistic practice.

The traditional protection of aliens was a broadly recognized right, but it was not actionable as a legal claim that could be remedied by courts or tribunals.[42] Great Powers often took pains to assure their citizens that when investing abroad, the long and powerful arm of their government would protect them. This was not a legal right but a display of might. Thus, diplomatic protection "was purely a question of power."[43] Prior to the New World practice, allegations of state responsibility were often a justification for imperial force; they were rarely a legalistic yardstick by which to measure wrongs or even remedies. Great Britain may have

39 Johnston, *supra* note 31, at p. 328. Similarly, Julian Go argues that it was commonplace for both the US and Great Britain to disavow any pretensions to empire – *see* Julian Go, *Patterns of Empire: The British and American Empires, 1688 to the Present* (Cambridge: Cambridge University Press, 2011).

40 *See* Eugene Kontorovich, "The Constitutionality of International Courts: The Forgotten Precedent of Slave Trade Tribunals," 158(39) *University of Pennsylvania Law Review* 39–115 (2009), at pp. 114–115; Jenny S. Martinez, "Anti-slavery Courts and the Dawn of International Human Rights Law," 117 *Yale Law Journal* 550 (2007).

41 Martinez, *supra* note 40.

42 *See* Alphonse Rivier, *Principes du droit des gens* I (Paris: A. Rousseau, 1896), at p. 272; Georg Jellinek, *System der subjektiven öffentlichen Rechte* (2nd edn, Tübingen: J. C. B. Mohr, 1905), at pp. 119–120; Borchard, *supra* note 7, ∫138 at p. 356; Clyde Eagleton, *The Responsibility of States in International Law* (New York: New York University Press, 1928), at p. 9.

43 Hans W. Spiegel, "Origin and Development of Denial of Justice," 32 *American Journal of International Law* 63–81 (1938), at p. 71.

brought about the internationalization of criminal liability during the nineteenth century,[44] which was a milestone in the history of international criminal law. However, it was the US that internationalized civil liability, from which I trace the origins of state responsibility. The US referral of alien protection claims to international arbitration set off a widely publicized legal debate on the appropriate standard of alien protection, as I discuss in the next section.[45]

"A Confrontation of Civilizations"

The debate over the appropriate standard for alien protection was hotly contested. While no one really questioned the primacy of international over domestic law in theory, what relevance did international law have to the ordinary administration of justice? Surely this was a matter for domestic law. To the North, alien protection was ultimately regulated by international standards – that is, the "standard of civilization." To the South, the field was entirely framed by domestic law, *unless* no protection at all or discriminatory protection was provided locally.

International litigation often unearthed unspoken assumptions of litigant cultures. The debate on the "standard of civilization" was no exception. As Gerrit Gong writes, the standard is "fundamentally *a*

[44] Britain internationalized individual criminal responsibility for several illicit trades (*e.g.*, slaves and drugs) and practices (*e.g.*, piracy) – *see* Mitchel P. Roth, *An Eye for an Eye: A Global History of Crime and Punishment* (London: Reaktion, 2015), at p. 171. *See also* Anne-Charlotte Martineau, "A Forgotten Chapter in the History of International Commercial Arbitration: The Slave Trade's Dispute Settlement System," 31 *Leiden Journal of International Law* 219 (2018), at pp. 221, 233–238. Professor Martineau examines international arbitration in commercial and investment matters by examining how the Spanish crown and its concessionaires set up a mechanism to settle legal disputes regarding the slave trade. According to Martineau, the slave trade's legal basis can be found in the history of *asientos de negros*, which is the contracts by which the Spanish granted an individual, a company, or another state the privilege to supply African slaves to the Spanish colonies in America. Ultimately, the transformation of *asientos de negros* from limited royal contracts to large-scale monopolies awarded to foreign chartered companies during the sixteenth, seventeenth, and early eighteenth centuries was accompanied by the creation of an international arbitration system.

[45] The classic histories of this standard and debate are Georg Schwarzenberger, "The Standard of Civilisation in International Law," in George W. Keeton and Georg Schwarzenberger (eds.), *Current Legal Problems* (London: Stevens & Sons, 1955) and Gong, *supra* note 3. Schwarzenberger and Gong discuss the recognition of the Ottoman Empire through the Treaty of Paris as well.

confrontation of civilizations and their respective cultures."[46] This was considerably more than a theoretical – or even an economic – disagreement. It was about the very identity of emerging Latin American nations. Latin American diplomats by and large welcomed the civilization of their nations. Even the term *América Latina* – as opposed to the more neutral *Sudamérica* or *América del Sur* – was an identification with classical civilization. But civilization is a culturally specific, not a universal, idea. It is no coincidence that southern American nations chose to identify with Romantic rather than Iberian or Anglo civilization. The term "Latin America" was an overt reference to the Spanish, Portuguese and French ties of many local elites. It was also a form of resistance to the dominating Anglo-American culture.[47]

Anglo-American View: Property Rights Are Fundamental

To Anglo-American lawyers, diplomatic protection was not something that could be entrusted to diplomats to resolve effectively. There were simply too many of them. Even the term "diplomatic protection" was a misnomer. The protection of nationals abroad should be about applying shared, general principles of law to private claims that were mostly about property. States, as sovereigns, had the basic duty to maintain a domestic rule of law. Each government could accomplish this through the

[46] Gong, *supra* note 3, at p. 3; *see further* Brett Bowden, *The Empire of Civilization: The Evolution of an Imperial Idea* (Chicago: Chicago University Press, 2009), at pp. 103–105, emphasis added.

[47] Napoleon III, in his effort to install Maximillian I in Mexico in the 1860s, sought to win regional support for this intervention by establishing the local links to romantic rather than strictly Iberian (and surely not American) culture, and introduced the term "Latin America" as an alternative identity – *see* Howard Jones, *Crucible of Power: A History of American Foreign Relations to 1913* (Lanham: SR Books, 2002), at p. 212; John Charles Chasteen, *Born in Blood and Fire* (New York: W. W. Norton & Company, 2000), at p. 156; Angel R. Oquendo, "The Solitude of Latin America: The Struggle for Rights South of the Border,"43 *Texas International Law Journal* 185 (2008), at p. 190. *See also* John Bassett Moore, "Is there a Latin American?," *The Independent*, January 19, 1915 reprinted in *The Collected Papers of John Bassett Moore* (New Haven: Yale University Press, 1944), Vol. IV, pp. 26–32. Liliana Obregón, "Latin American International Law" – as opposed to Arnulf Becker Lorca's "Mestizo International Law": The author uses the term "Latin American International Law" (LAIL) and explains that it emerged and drew on the experience of the "creole" elites both during and after Spanish rule. Further, while LA regionalist perspectives (CITE, *see* pp. 154, 157–159). Another cultural distinction of course was the fact that the North was predominantly Protestant, and the South was Catholic, but this is outside the scope of the book.

implementation of internal public law within its territories. Given that "the law of nations" was theoretically a "law common to all mankind,"[48] states were bound to provide *civilized* protection to their nationals and aliens alike. The "standard of civilization" embodied this perspective, especially in the US arbitral practice.[49] No legal source was necessary to evidence a priori obligations of civilization. Protection abroad was a natural right. The open question was one of enforcement. Anglo-American governments presented alien rights as a matter of settled international practice. In an 1875 letter to his minister to Spain, Caleb Cushing (1800–1879), Secretary of State Hamilton Fish wrote:

> But we have claimed that by international law, and by the usages and customs of civilized nations, a trial at law must be conducted without unseemly haste, with certain safeguards to the accused, and in deference to certain recognized rights, in order to mete out justice.[50]

The US development of alien protection occurred within a broader regulatory framework that European nations employed in several areas of

[48] *See* Henry Wheaton, *Elements of International Law*, ed., Richard Henry Dana, Jr. (8th edn, Boston: Little, Brown, 1866), at §10; Francis Wharton, *A Digest of the International Law of the United States, Taken from Documents Issued by Presidents and Secretaries of State, and from Decisions of Federal Courts and Opinions of Attorney-General* (Washington, DC: Government Printing Office, 1886), at §9.

[49] Moore, *supra* note 15, at pp. 827 ("that *general standard of justice* upon which civilized nations are agreed"), 2377, 2947, 3041–3042. The "civilized" standard in international practice often meant customary usages of civilized nations (*i.e.*, states), *see ibid*, at pp. 357, 601, 707, 813, 839, 870, 918, 979–980, 1561, 1631, 1725–1726, 1797, 1838, 2947, 2503, 2679, 2778, 2806, 3258, 3326, 3682–3691, 3729, 3747, 3941, 4008, 4059, 4074, 4102–4105, 4355, 4545, 4950–4953, 5036.

[50] Hamilton Fish to Caleb Cushing, December 27, 1875, MS Inst. Spain, XVII. 396, as reproduced in John Bassett Moore and Francis Wharton, *A Digest of International Law as Embodied in the Diplomatic Discussions, Treaties and Other International Agreements, International Awards, the Decisions of Municipal Courts, and the Writings of Jurists and Especially in Documents, Published and Unpublished, Issued by Presidents and Secretaries of State of the United States, the Opinions of the Attorneys-General, and the Decisions of Courts, Federal and State* (Washington, DC: Government Printing Office, 1906), Vol. II, at p. 100. For a critique of the traditionality of the "rule of law" approach to internal order, *see* Federica Carugati, Gillian K. Hadfield and Barry R. Weingast, "Building Legal Order in Ancient Athens," (January 09, 2015), USC CLASS Research Papers Series No. CLASS15-1. For a discussion on the rights in property of aliens in ancient Palestine, *see* Hanan Mazeh, "Gentile Land Ownership in the Land of Israel: The Palestinian Talmud in Light of Biblical Models and Roman Law," *The Jewish Quarterly Review* (2024, forthcoming, article on file with author).

diplomacy – such as recognition.[51] European governments conditioned their recognition of statehood upon the promise of internal legal order.[52] A proto-nation that failed to meet such requirements was "uncivilized" and unrecognized. A recognized nation that did not meet the international standard could be held accountable under international law for damages or other forms of remedies.[53] Thus, the coexistence of state sovereignty and responsibility was legally possible, but only to the extent that a state could be trusted to conduct itself in a civilized manner.[54]

Nineteenth-century treaties rarely defined a legal standard of civilization.[55] As international law historian Gerrit Gong writes, "the actual task of articulating the standard of 'civilization' fell to the leading [international lawyers] of the day."[56] The most successful and important of the

[51] *See* Martins Paparinskis, *The International Minimum Standard and Fair and Equitable Treatment* (Oxford: Oxford University Press, 2013), at p. 20.

[52] Recognition in Latin America meant that visitors to those states would be subject to the laws of the land. Entrance to the club of (Christian) civilization came with the right to jurisdictional sovereignty. *See* Borchard, *supra* note 10, at pp. 515, 518–519 (only states possessing a domestic rule of law had "[T]he machinery to insure this object constitutes an essential function of state activity – within, protecting every member of society from injustice or oppression by every other member; without, protecting its citizens from violence and oppression by other states"). This idea is also discussed further in Chapter 2.

[53] *See* Wharton, *supra* note 48, at §17b (jurisdictional sovereignty only in civilized lands) *and contrast to* §223 (presentation of international claims); *see also* Alwyn V. Freeman, "Responsibility of States for Unlawful Acts of their Armed Forces," 88(2) *Recueil de Cours* 267 (1955), at p. 522 (state responsibility for the violation of the international duty to provide a minimum level of (rule of law) protection "will normally be necessary only where the territorial State's level of civilization is plainly inferior to that of average members of the international society").

[54] Heinhard Steiger, "From the International Law of Christianity to the International Law of the World Citizen – Reflections on the Formation of the Epochs of the History of International Law," 3 *Journal of the History of International Law* 180–193 (2001), at pp. 187–188 (only "civilised nations could organise themselves in the form of states, have laws and execute them" and only "sovereign states could participate in the law of nations order").

[55] An exception to the commercial treaty between the US and Chile that specified in no uncertain terms that Chile's requirement to protect US nationals was strictly limited to maintaining "the most perfect equality … between American and Chilean citizens, the former to enjoy all the rights and benefits of the present or future provisions which the laws grant to the latter in their judicial tribunals, but no special favors or privileges (Article II, of the Additional and Explanatory Convention to the Treaty of Peace, Amity, Commerce and Navigation Concluded in the City of Santiago on the 16th Day of May 1832 between the United States of America and the Republic of Chile, concluded on September 1, 1833, ratification exchanged April 29, 1834).

[56] Gong, *supra* note 2, at p. 26. Gerrit Gong's contribution to the history of this standard is significant; however, he ignores international arbitrations, which perhaps explains why he barely mentions Latin America.

doctrinalists was Henry Wheaton (1785–1848), a US diplomat and leading international publicist. Gong examined successive editions of Wheaton's *Elements of International Law* and found that Wheaton articulated the standard of civilization in the context of the US and Europe's sustained contact with increasing numbers of non-European countries.[57] To Wheaton (and even to his Spanish language translator, Carlos Calvo (1824–1906),[58] the "standard of civilization" encapsulated the ethos of Christianity.[59] In theory, the "standard of civilization" was meant to represent a cultural bond shared by Christians traveling around the globe.

However, in practice, the "standard of civilization" was an instrument of economic and political domination. German international law historians such as Georg Schwarzenberg (1908–1991) and Wilhelm Grewe (1911–2000) have long observed how Western governments relied on this standard to provide *better-than-local* protection to their nationals abroad. To Schwarzenberg, the test of civilization

> [W]as, as a rule, merely whether its government was sufficiently stable to undertake binding commitments under international law and whether it was able and willing to protect adequately the life, liberty and property of foreigners.[60]

Similarly, Grewe writes that the "principal, practical" relevance of the standard of civilization to international law was to legitimate

> [T]he system of capitulations or, in other words, the unequal treaties by which the civilised nations reserved a special jurisdiction (consular jurisdiction) over their own nationals, whom they did not wish to have subjected to the legal order and justice system of a half-civilised or uncivilised country.[61]

[57] Gong, *supra* note 2, at p. 27.

[58] Carlos Calvo, *Derecho internacional teórico y práctico de Europa y América* (Paris: D'Amyot, Durant & Pedoné-Lauriel, 1868), Vol. I, at p. 155, as cited in Liliana T. Obregón, "Writing International Legal History: An Overview," 7 *Monde(s). Histoire, Espaces, Relations* 95 (2015), at p. 107 (Calvo saw international law as being "limited to the Christian nations that marched at the head of civilization"). According to Obregón, Henry Wheaton's *A History of the Law of Nations in Europe and America from the Earliest Times to the Treaty of Washington* (New York: Gould, Banks, 1845) was translated by Calvo into Spanish and became the second most popular international law text after Bello's international law text (*ibid* at p. 104).

[59] Wheaton, *supra* note 48, at §11.

[60] Schwarzenberger, *supra* note 45, at p. 220.

[61] Wilhelm G. Grewe, *The Epochs of International Law* (transl. Michael Byers) (Berlin: Walter de Gruyter, 2000), at p. 457. For a thoughtful discussion on capitulation treaties, *see* Charles Lipson, *Standing Guard: Protecting Foreign Capital in the Nineteenth and Twentieth Centuries* (Berkeley: University of California Press, 1985), at pp. 12–16. According to Willem Theus, the first formal "modern" treaty on this matter was likely

A treaty could have spelled out such expectations as negotiated by both parties. But the US and Europe executed few treaties of capitulation in Latin America. Instead, they entered into *ad hoc* arbitration agreements that were focused primarily on procedural matters instead of legal standards or definitions.

Emergence of an International Tort

Tribunals were, therefore, left to rely on general principles of law when navigating thousands of international claims.[62] One often-used norm was reasonableness.[63] To Anglo-American lawyers, alien protection claims closely resembled private tort and property claims under domestic law.[64]

the "Capitulation" between the King of France, Francis I, and Sultan Suleiman the Magnificent in 1535/36 (Willem Theus, "There and Back Again: From Consular Courts through Mixed Arbitral Tribunals to International Commercial Courts," in Hélène Ruiz Fabri and Michel Erpelding (eds.), *The Mixed Arbitral Tribunals, 1919–1939: An Experiment in the International Adjudication of Private Rights* 29 (Baden-Baden: Nomos, 2023), at p. 34).

62 Gerald G. Fitzmaurice, "The Meaning of the Term 'Denial of Justice,'" 13 *British Year Book of International Law* 93–114 (1932), at p. 111, note 1.

63 In the *Alabama Claims* arbitration, the US and Great Britain both peppered their arguments before the Geneva panel with the rhetoric of reasonableness; *see, e.g.*, M. R. Waite, William M. Evarts and Caleb Cushing, *Alabama Claims: Argument of the United States Delivered to the Tribunal of Arbitration at Geneva, June 15, 1872* (Paris: Dubuisson & Co., 1872), at pp. 28, 110, 119, 133, 135, 166, 170, 174, 178, 181, 189, 198, 342, 369, 381, 398, 408, 461, 469, 494, 499, 521, 528, 529, 538, 556, 560; *The Case of Great Britain as Laid before the Tribunal of Arbitration Convened at Geneva under the Provisions of the Treaty between the United States of America and Her Majesty the Queen of Great Britain, Concluded at Washington, May 8, 1871* (Washington, DC: Government Printing Office, 1872), at pp. 23, 34, 44, 59, 63, 64, 75, 127, 144, 148, 260, 270, 284, 289, 395, 417, 427, 433, 439, 451, 508, 614, 705, 744, 777, 788, 841, 900, 918, 956.

64 In the early international arbitrations, US lawyers argued by analogy to domestic law that standards of reasonable care as applied in international law ought to be objectively determined. *See* Hersch Lauterpacht, *Private Law Sources and Analogies of International Law: With Special Reference to International Arbitration* (London: Longmans, Green and Co., 1927), §95 (Due Diligence), at pp. 217–218; Lauterpacht claims that this Anglo-American contention was supported by Roman as well as Continental legal sources (*ibid* at p. 217). As mentioned, intra-American arbitral tribunals were comprised largely of Anglo-American attorneys, so many the resulting awards were based on Anglo-American tort law. The manly ideal of common law practice was exemplified in the Langdellian Harvard training, a student was thrown "into a pit" without any "map" and forced "to find his way by himself" in order to provide a "*self-made knowledge of the law* and faith in his own abilities" (Benjamin Allen Coates, *Legalist Empire International Law and American Foreign Relations in the Early Twentieth Century* (Oxford: Oxford University Press, 2016), at p. 65). *See further* discussed below and in

In fact, the legalistic protection of nationals abroad occurred at around the same time as Anglo-American courts were developing modern tort laws. Both domestic and international tort laws were developing by courts and tribunals to explain the injurious relationships between strangers in the mid- to late-nineteenth century.[65] This new law of torts articulated a minimum standard of care owed "by all the world to all the world."[66] In domestic courts, the reasonableness standard was seen as an intuitive – if private – duty of care owed by individuals to individuals. But in international arbitrations, because the respondent was a sovereign, the tort principle took on a more complex and public component; at the international level, private tort laws were forming the normative basis of governmental liability for injuries to (foreign) individuals.[67]

Findings of civil liability were made by reference to an objective standard of protection.[68] Domestic judges did not deduce liability

Alan Nissel, "The Columbianization of U.S. Legal Education" (work in progress on file with author). For a counterview, *see* Marija Dordeska, "General Principles of Law Recognized by Civilized Nations: Method, Inductive-Empirical Analysis and (More) 'Scientific' Results," in Rosanna Deplano (ed.), *Pluralising International Legal Scholarship: The Promise and Perils of Non-Doctrinal Research Methods* 18 (Cheltenham: Edward Elgar, 2019), at pp. 31–32 ("It is widely believed that the Court ascertains general principles by relying solely on domestic law. The research findings, however, show quite the opposite . . . General principles may have domestic, international and/or a judicial underpinning"). However, on the differences between domestic and international tort law Pierre-Hugues Verdier, "Cooperative States: International Relations, State Responsibility and the Problem of Custom," 42(1) *Virginia Journal of International Law* 839 (2002), at pp. 854–855 (internal citations omitted).

65 *See* G. Edward White, *Tort Law in America: An Intellectual History* (New York: Oxford University Press, 1980), at p. *xi*; according to White, the shift from a writ-specific, particularized "common law" damages that were not based on pre-arranged, contractual relations occurred in part because an industrializing economy brought "strangers" into more contact with one another. J. H. H. Weiler, "The Geology of International Law – Governance," 64 *Heidelberg Journal of International Law* 547–562 (2004), at p. 551.

66 On the legal development of this general duty of care, *see* White, *supra* note 65, at pp. 92, 320. Ultimately, this idea was most famously articulated by Lord Atkin in the English case of *Donoghue v. Stevenson* [1932] AC 562 (HL Sc) (the "good neighbor" principle).

67 The law of negligence was developed to describe those occasions when such duties were breached. See White, *supra* note 65, at pp. 5, 18–19, 146. *See also* (regarding the civil origins of tort or extra-contractual private liability) Borzu Sabahi, *Compensation and Restitution in Investor–State Arbitration. Principles and Practice* (Oxford: Oxford University Press, 2011), at pp. 15–32 (traces to Roman concept of delictual obligations). Liability in the domestic context was labeled "negligent" and in the international setting "uncivilized."

68 Jennifer Pitts, *Boundaries of the International: Law & Empire* (Cambridge, MA: Harvard University Press, 2018), at p. 182 (international law was seen as in a state of "development" that was at once "both an index and a source of progress"). *See also* Robert L. Tsai, "Legal Language in Nineteenth-Century America," in Nan Goodman and Simon Stern

through empirical research; the rules of reasonableness were induced by analytically using other general principles of law.[69] Similarly, international lawyers in the nineteenth century did not believe that the basic requirements of civilization needed to be positivized in a code or treaty.[70] Arbitrators often cited the English jurist Sir Frederick Pollock (1845–1947) for the proposition that the "reasonable man" was not the subject but the object of a hypothetical analysis.[71] "He," Sir Frederick writes, "will neither neglect what he can forecast as probable, nor waste his anxiety on events that are barely possible. He will order his precaution by the measure of what appears likely in the known course of things."[72] These were the twin concepts of negligence and

(eds.), *The Ashgate Research Companion to Law and Humanities in Nineteenth-Century America* (Farnham: Ashgate, 2015); American University, WCL Research Paper No. 2014-51, available at SSRN: http://ssrn.com/abstract=2542661, at p. 3: "This more sophisticated view took most visible hold in property, torts, and contract law, helping industrialists and corporations take increasing risks in the economy by altering social expectations of responsibility and blame." In the US, many states did not allow punitive damages for tort liability because it was to be only civil in nature – Morton J. Horwitz, "The History of the Public/Private Distinction," 130 *University of Pennsylvania Law Review* 1423 (1982), at p. 1422.

69 *See generally* J. Patrick Kelly, "Customary International Law in Historical Context: The Exercise of Power Without General Acceptance," in *Reexamining Customary International Law* (Cambridge: Cambridge University Press, 2017), at p. 4 (analyzing how many customary international legal norms were put forward on the basis of inductive reasoning but that such assertions usually go unsubstantiated); Andreas Hadjigeorgiou, "Beyond Formalism: Reviving the Legacy of Sir Henry Maine for CIL," in *The Theory, Practice and Interpretation of Customary International Law* 183 (Cambridge University Press, 2022), available online at: https://ssrn.com/abstract=3864447, last visited August 22, 2021 (seeks a revival of the legacy of Sir Henry Maine regarding evolutionary conception of law beyond traditional formalistic sources of international law).

70 Eagleton put forward this argument throughout *The Responsibility of States in International Law* (*supra* note 42).

71 *See e.g.*, Francis Wharton, *A Treatise on the Law of Negligence* (2nd ed., Philadelphia: Kay and Brother, 1878), at p. 15; Paulos Alexandrou Zannas, *La responsabilité internationale des États pour les actes de négligence* (Montreux: Ganguin & Laubscher, 1952), at p. 102.

72 Sir Frederick Pollock, *A Treatise on the Law of Torts in Obligations Arising from Civil Wrongs in the Common Law* (St. Louis: F. H. Thomas Law Book Co., 1894), at p. 45. According to Pollock, the standard of liability for negligence assumes "that a person is expected to anticipate and guard against all reasonable consequences, but that he is not, by the law of England, expected to anticipate and guard against that which no reasonable man would expect to occur" (*Greenland v. Chaplin* (1850), 5 Ex. at p. 248 as reproduced in *ibid*).

due diligence.[73] The former required the establishment of a causal link between the plaintiff's injury and the respondent's conduct and the latter precluded such a relationship.[74]

The US applied this standard both as a sword and a shield.[75] Two US Civil War examples illustrate this point. In the *Alabama Claims*, the US argued that Britain was liable under international law for its failure to prevent private shipbuilders in Liverpool from outfitting Confederate raiders such as in *Alabama*. The international tribunal in Geneva concluded,

> The due diligence ... ought to be exercised by neutral Governments in exact proportion to the risks to which either of the belligerents may be exposed from a failure to fulfil the obligations of neutrality on their part.[76]

In the US–Peru Mixed Claims Commission, which also included claims arising from the Civil War, the US made the opposite argument, insisting that the US could not be held liable under international law for the acts of Confederate soldiers not under Union control. The US–Peru tribunal agreed:

[73] According to Sir Frederick, "Only that harm which falls within one of the specified categories of wrong-doing ... to abstain from wilful injury, to respect the property of others, and to use due diligence to avoid causing harm to others – are all alike of a comprehensive nature" (*The Law of Torts: A Treatise on the Principles of Obligations Arising from Civil Wrongs in the Common Law : to which is Added the Draft of a Code of Civil Wrongs Prepared for the Government of India* (London: Stevens and Sons, 1901) at p. 22). *See also* Anne Peters, Heike Krieger and Leonhard Kreuzer, "Due Diligence in the International Legal Order: Dissecting the Leitmotif of Current Accountability Debates," in Anne Peters, Heike Krieger and Leonhard Kreuzer (eds.), *Due Diligence in the International Legal Order* 1 (Oxford: Oxford University Press, 2020), at p. 2 (principles of due diligence in the nineteenth century grew out of principles of reasonableness and the law of torts in the context of alien protection claims).

[74] As Secretary of State William Seward wrote in an 1863 letter to the resident Peruvian minister in Washington, DC: "A Government is liable internationally for injury inflicted on aliens through its negligence in permitting insurgents to destroy the property of such aliens and by its subsequent implied ratification of the conduct of such insurgents, there being no redress offered in the courts of such Government" (William Seward to Federico L. Barreda, January 9, 1863 as cited in Wharton, *supra* note 48, §223). Similarly, the US Supreme Court viewed the international standard of protection in terms of due diligence. In *United States v. Arjona*, for example, it declared that: "The law of nations requires every national government to use 'due diligence' to prevent a wrong being done within its own dominion to another nation with which it is at peace, or to the people thereof" (120 U.S. 479 (1887), at p. 484). According to the Supreme Court, national governments are "*responsible to foreign nations for all violations ... of their international obligations*" (*ibid* at p. 483, emphasis added).

[75] For further discussion regarding US "double-standards," *see infra* note 255 and accompanying text.

[76] *The Case of the United States to be Laid Before the Tribunal of Arbitration* (Washington, DC: Government Printing Office, 1872), at p. 9.

> The United States Government is not liable for loss to Peruvian citizens caused by the destruction of their property on board a ship in Chesapeake Bay, in 1862, such destruction being effected by a sudden attack of insurgents, which could not by due diligence have been averted by the Government of the United States.[77]

Anglo-American insistence on international standards of care turned less on technical rule application than on the pragmatic interpretations.[78] As the State Department lawyer Marjorie Whiteman (1898–1986) notes in her exhaustive review of the early awards, the concept of reasonableness seems to have been a circular one.[79] A state was responsible to indemnify aliens for injuries when the treatment accorded them was below "the standard generally recognized by the family of nations as reasonable."[80] But if that standard was not a legal rule, how did it enter into the arbitral discussion?

"*Civis Romanus Sum*" Becomes an International Standard

Protecting one's nationals abroad was often a demonstration of political power abroad. The nature of this protection was most memorably articulated by Lord Palmerston (1784–1865). After Greece consistently failed to protect British subjects residing in Greece, the then Foreign Secretary Lord Palmerston gave his "*Civis Romanus*" speech to the House of Commons in 1850 regarding his resolution of the Don Pacifico affair.[81]

Don David Pacifico was a Jewish national of Great Britain (born in Gibraltar) who had moved to Athens as an investor and community leader. The Government of Greece at the time took out sovereign debt from the London-based Rothschild family. It had already defaulted on

[77] Seward to Barreda, January 9, 1863 as cited in Wharton, *supra* note 48, §223.

[78] Regarding the concept of fault, *see* Marjorie M. Whiteman, *Damages in International Law* (Washington, DC: Government. Printing Office, 1937), Vol. I, at pp. 38–39; Borchard, *supra* note 7, at p. 399.

[79] Whiteman, *supra* note 78, vol. III, at pp. 1766–1767.

[80] Whiteman, *supra* note 78, vol. I, at p. 307; *see also ibid* at pp. 1547–1549.

[81] British historian A. J. P. Taylor has described the House debate over Palmerston's speech as "perhaps the greatest debate on the principles of foreign policy in our parliamentary records (Alan John Percivale Taylor, *The Trouble Makers: Dissent over Foreign Policy, 1792–1939* (Bloomington: Indiana University Press, 1958), at p. 56). Taylor continues, "For, apart from Palmerston's own triumph of vindication, the debate was dominated by Radicals on both sides. The traditional themes of foreign policy – the Balance of Power, the security of India, naval supremacy – were ignored. Discussion centred, as Radicals thought it should, on morality." All that mattered during the debate was normative basis for British intervention abroad.

the loan once but was bailed out by Great Britain. Lord Lionel de Rothschild felt that a personal visit to Athens was then necessary to apply pressure on Greece to repay its debt this time around. Out of sensitivity to Lord Rothchild (who was Jewish), Greece decided to ban the burning of effigies that Easter. But, as Professor Katherine E. Flemming writes, "at the same time that the government didn't want to offend Rothschild, it resented him tremendously for the economic hold he and the great powers had over Greece."[82] The terms of the loan were extremely unfavorable to the Greeks (*e.g.*, requiring first priority of payment), creating a resentment on the streets that left many feeling that their recent independence from Ottoman control had not secured much in the way of political or economic autonomy.[83]

In this context, on Easter Day 1847, Don Pacifico was robbed by a local mob of Greek Catholics and suffered substantial property loss. What began with stone throwing, resulted in a horde beating his wife and children, ransacking his house, stealing approximately £270 of silver entrusted to him by members of the Jewish community for the sake of building Athens' first Jewish synagogue, burning down his home and other acts of vandalism.[84] Don Pacifico called for the police, who turned up but did nothing to stop the crowd (which included the son of the next Prime Minister). Thus, the international claim was not just one of theft and arson but of the police enabling the crimes to be committed "in broad daylight."[85] Don Pacifico appealed to the British Government for diplomatic protection, who took up the claim.[86] After three years without any agreement from Greece for indemnification, the Royal Navy blockaded the Piraeus Coast and seized its ships in the harbor. In response, Greece agreed to refer the matter of compensation to a foreign commission, which awarded Don Pacifico the nominal sum of £150.

Lord Palmerston (Figure 3.1) justified the blockade as the appropriate response to the denial of justice suffered by Don Pacifico. What was at

[82] K. E. Flemming, *Greece: A Jewish History* (Princeton: Princeton University Press, 2008), at pp. 24–25.

[83] Flemming, *supra* note 82, at p. 20.

[84] For discussion see Christopher A. Casey, *National Abroad: Globalization, Individual Rights, and the Making of Modern International Law* (Cambridge: Cambridge University Press, 2020), at pp. 17–21.

[85] Flemming, *supra* note 82, at p. 25.

[86] The British consul to the newly designated capital, Edmund Lyons wrote to Prime Minister John Kolettis of the incident as "one of the most barbarous outrages ever committed in modern times" (Flemming, *supra* note 82, at p. 24).

Figure 3.1 Lord Palmerston (Photo courtesy of Wikimedia Commons)

stake was not so much human rights or antisemitism, but British primacy. Anyone who was British was entitled to *civilized* treatment abroad. In a four-and-a-half-hour sermon that ended well-past midnight, Lord Palmerston proclaimed:

> Civis Romanus Sum, so also a British subject in whatever land he may be, shall feel confident that the watchful eye and the strong arm of England will protect him against injustice and wrong.

The alternative of relying on local standards of justice, he continued, was unreasonable:

> [I]f the people of the country are liable to have heavy stones placed upon their breasts, and police officers to dance upon them; if they are liable to have their heads tied to their knees, and to be left for hours in that state; or to be swung like a pendulum, and to be bastinadoed as they swing, foreigners have no right to be better treated than the natives, and have no business to complain if the same things are practiced upon them. We may be told this, but that is not my opinion, nor do I believe it is the opinion of any reasonable man.[87]

[87] Parl. Deb., vol. 62, ser. 3, cols. 380–444, June 25, 1850, quoted in Elihu Root, "The Basis of Protection to Citizens Residing Abroad," Opening Address as President of the American

It was not as though Lord Palmerston's speech repeated a long-known British refrain. His 1850 proclamation was an about face from his 1848 circular to British consulates abroad. Then, while in the same position as Foreign Secretary, Lord Palmerston stated:

> The British Government has considered that the losses of imprudent men who have placed mistaken confidence in the good faith of foreign Governments would prove a salutary warning to others, and would prevent any other foreign loans from being raised in Great Britain, except by governments of known good faith and ascertained solvency.[88]

One can only speculate as to what changed between 1848 and 1850. The matter at issue in 1848 was a series of defaulting Latin American nations. In 1850 the respondent was a local European nation. In 1848, the matter was contract law (sovereign debt) and in 1850 it was property protection. But I think it is likely that the British Foreign Office, like the US State Department, was overwhelmed with claims for diplomatic intervention. And by 1850, enough was enough. Don Pacifico may have been a watershed moment from when British diplomatic policy was to rely less on local laws and more on external (*i.e.,* British) ones. Yet, the British approach to protection, as the *Don Pacifico Affair* itself illustrates, was too military and politically intensive to sustain in the long term; it would require some American adjustments to succeed in becoming an accepted international standard of property protection.[89]

Root Adapts Palmerston's Position

The US clearly expected its nationals to be treated according to international standards and this expectation closely resembled Lord Palmerston's rhetoric of civilization. However, the US asserted its expectation of alien protection based on international law rather than on

Society of International Law, at the Fourth Annual Meeting of the Society in Washington, April 28, 1910, reproduced in 4 *American Journal of International Law* 517 (1910), at p. 522. For a general discussion, *see* Derek Taylor, *Don Pacifico: The Acceptable Face of Gunboat Diplomacy* (Elstree: Vallentine-Mitchell, 2008).

88 Quoted in James Fred Rippy, *British Investments in Latin America, 1822–1949: A Case Study in the Operations of Private Enterprise in Retarded Regions* (St. Paul: University of Minnesota Press, 1959), at p. 199.

89 *See generally* Lauren Benton and Lisa Ford, *Rage for Order: The British Empire and the Origins of International Law 1800–1850* (Cambridge: Harvard University Press, 2016), ch. 4, "The Promise of Protection"; Koskenniemi, supra note 26, at ch. 10, "Global Law: Ruling the British Empire."

Figure 3.2 Elihu Root[90]

domestic constitutional or political authority.[91] The most quoted articulation of the US was made by Secretary of State Elihu Root (1845–1937) (Figure 3.2) in a 1910 speech to his colleagues in the American Society of International Law:

> The rule of obligation is perfectly distinct and settled. Each country is bound to give to the nationals of another country in its territory the benefit of the same laws, the same administration, the same protection, and the same redress for injury which it gives to its own citizens, and neither more nor less; provided the protection which the country gives to its own citizens conforms to the established standard of civilization. There is a standard of justice, very simple, very fundamental, and of such general acceptance by all civilized countries as to form a part of the international law of the world.[92]

[90] Photo Courtesy of *Getty* Images, www.gettyimages.fi/detail/uutiskuva/american-jurist-and-statesman-elihu-root-us-secretary-of-war-uutiskuva/3072018?adppopup=true.

[91] Eugene Wambaugh, "The Place of Denial of Justice in the Matter of Protection," 4 *Proceedings of the American Society of International Law* 123 (1910), at p. 130; Gerald G. Fitzmaurice, "The Meaning of the Term 'Denial of Justice,'" 13 *British Yearbook of International Law* 93–114 (1932), at pp. 113–114.

[92] Elihu Root, "The Basis of Protection to Citizens Residing Abroad," Opening Address as President of the American Society of International Law, at the Fourth Annual Meeting of

Whereas Lord Palmerston expressed an "imperial standard of fairness,"[93] Root spoke in terms of the "standard of civilization" accepted as part "of the international law of the world." Palmerston placed Great Britain "in the role of international arbiter,"[94] whereas Root saw the issue in international legal terms. Root was subtle, like his predecessor, Hamilton Fish.[95] According to Root, *generally*, the standard of protection was a local one – no more and no less; *exceptionally*, when local laws failed to conform "verifiable" standards of justice, only then did international law apply. Both were essentially in agreement: domestic law was not the final word on of alien protection. Palmerston framed his argument as a political doctrine of British power; US lawyer-diplomats like Root articulated the basis of alien protection in terms of a minimum international standard of care.

Latin American View: International Liability Is Disgraceful

To Latin Americans, the problem with international arbitration in the late nineteenth century was not so much a critique of civilization, capitalism or the importing of other Western standards. Venezuelan jurist Andrés Bello (1781–1865), for instance, was a regional symbol for the rule of law and staunch supporter of property protection.[96] The bigger problem for Latin Americans about applying international legal standards to diplomatic protection was the disrespect of their hard-fought sovereignty.[97] It offended their sense of national pride. They disputed the contention that international law required an international

the Society in Washington, April 28, 1910, reproduced in 4 *American Journal of International Law* 517 (1910), at p. 521. According to Freeman, "Few propositions of law are supported by as much authority in international jurisprudence and literature as this one" (Alwyn V. Freeman, "Recent Aspects of the Calvo Doctrine and the Challenge to International Law," 40 *American Journal of International Law* 121, 133 (1946).

93 For a discussion of the term, *see* Benton and Ford, *supra* note 89, at p. 114.

94 Benton and Ford *supra* note 89, at p. 115.

95 Like Fish, Root was a bureaucrat and the most trusted member of the President's cabinet – Rossi, *supra* note 14, at p. 111.

96 Santiago Montt, *State Liability in Investment Treaty Arbitration: Global Constitutional and Administrative Law in the BIT Generation* (Oxford: Hart, 2009), at p. 41; Lipson, *supra* note 6, at pp. 16–17. I am grateful to Jonathan Miller of Southwestern Law School, for highlighting this point to me.

97 *See* Commissioner Palacio's dissent in *Salvador Pratts*: Palacio goes so far as to criticize the claimant for relying on earlier European diplomatic practice of seeking claims arising out of civil wars as legal precedence, since "Everybody knows what was the real and true design of those three governments and that they did not succeed in their enterprise" (in Moore, *supra* note 15, Vol. III, at pp. 2899–2900). *See also* Kate Miles, *The Origins of International Investment Law* (Cambridge: Cambridge University Press, 2013), at p. 21 (Western diplomats sought to apply standards of property protection to non-Western

standard of protection and any attempt to implicitly "civilize" them. As newly viable states, they felt that they ought to be deemed just as sovereign as other states.

To Latin Americans, domestic law was not a matter of international concern and the protection of aliens was not a matter of "reasonableness" under tort law; it was about a legal and political decision that each state must make about its own needs, abilities and will.[98] The appropriate standard of care owed to nationals and foreigners alike was exclusively a domestic one; so long as states provided the same level of protection to both, no denial of justice claim could arise.[99] This position that international law only prohibited discrimination but nothing more was most famously articulated by Carlos Calvo (1824–1906) (Figure 3.3). Calvo, an Argentinian lawyer-diplomat, was writing in the turbulent context of the first national declarations of independence from Spain (summer of 1816).[100] He argued against the Anglo-American expectation to hold successor governments liable for acts outside their control – whether it was the acts of previous administrations or those of unsuccessful rebels.[101] As there were rather few arbitrations by the middle of the nineteenth

states "that became inextricably linked with colonialism, oppressive protection of commercial interests, and military intervention").

98 The reasonable man standard was far from universally accepted and from being without criticism. Albert S. Thayer, for example, in a journal edited by Pollock, noted the circularity of the concept: "The reason of a 'reasonable man' is custom" ("Natural Law," 21 *Law Quarterly Review* 50 (1905) , at p. 62 (journal edited by Pollock); Kevin Jon Heller, "Beyond the Reasonable Man? A Sympathetic but Critical Assessment of the Use of Subjective Standards of Reasonableness in Self-Defense and Provocation Cases," 26(1) *American Journal of Criminal Law* 1 (1998), at pp. 4, 8–9.

99 As one commentator recently summarized the position: "The national treatment doctrine preaches that aliens are entitled to the same treatment granted to nationals and nothing else" (Carmen Tiburcio, *The Human Rights of Aliens Under International and Comparative Law* (The Hague: Kluwer, 2001), at p. 45).

100 Interestingly, Calvo was writing at a time of British dominance. As an Argentine, he was more scared of British rather than US pressure. The original theorist behind the "Calvo Doctrine" was the Venezuelan jurist Andrés Bello (1781–1865). In the first Latin American international law treatise – *Derecho de Jentes*, published in 1832 – Bello espoused principles of non-intervention and equality among nations. *See* Santiago Montt, "Latin American Position on State Responsibility. Looking into the Past for Lessons on the Future," LEGS seminar on February 9, 2009, available online at: http://lapa.princeton.edu/uploads/2009-0209%20Montt%20LEGS%20chapter.pdf (last visited on July 14, 2010), at p. 15.

101 Martti Koskenniemi, *The Gentle Civilizer of Nations: The Rise and Fall of International Law 1870–1960* (Cambridge: Cambridge University Press, 2002), at p. 18, note 23; Kathryn Greenman, "Aliens in Latin America: Intervention, Arbitration and State Responsibility for Rebels," 31 *Leiden Journal of International Law* 617 (2018), at p. 622 (Calvo never made such a statement explicitly).

Figure 3.3 Carlos Calvo[102]

century, Calvo viewed the arbitral application of the "standard of civilization" as undermining the legitimacy of the entire international legal system.[103]

Internally, Calvo's doctrine required states to provide equal treatment to nationals and aliens alike. Externally, it rejected the prohibition of foreign intervention even in the event of a breach of the duty to protect. To Calvo, the principles of international liability emerging from Intra-American arbitrations represented "an exorbitant and fatal privilege, essentially favorable to the powerful states and injurious to the weaker nations, establishing an unjustifiable inequality between nationals and foreigners."[104] After Calvo published the first of several editions of *Derecho internacional teórico y práctico de Europa y América* in 1863, Latin American governments adopted his doctrine as a matter of policy.[105] Its parliaments enacted domestic laws restrictively defining

[102] Photo courtesy of BNF/Société de Géographie de Paris. Avec l'aimable autorisation de la Société de Géographie, www.sfdi.org/internationalistes/calvo/.

[103] Carlos Calvo, *Derecho internacional teórico y práctico de Europa y América* (Paris: D'Amyot, Durant & Pedoné-Lauriel, 1868), at §291) discussed in Greenman, *supra* note 101, at p. 623.

[104] Carlos Calvo, *Le droit international théorique et pratique* (5th ed., Paris: A. Rousseau, 1896), I, p. 350 as cited and translated in Shea, *infra* note 104, at p. 18.

[105] The Calvo Doctrine was formally accepted by all Latin American States except Haiti at the First International Conference of American States held at Washington in 1889–1890; see Jan Paulsson, *Denial of Justice in International Law* (Cambridge: Cambridge University Press, 2005), at p. 21; Donald Shea, *The Calvo Clause: A Problem of Inter-American and International Law and Diplomacy* (Minneapolis: University of Minnesota Press, 1955), at p. 18; Wenhua Shan, "Is Calvo Dead?" 55 *American Journal of Comparative Law* 123 (2007). In fact, there was a spike in its published usage after 1895 (*see supra* note 18).

"denial of justice" as the refusal by the judiciary to grant aliens any access to the courts.[106] Diplomats included so-called "Calvo Clauses" in treaties.[107] These provisions built on the Calvo Doctrine by denying the possibility of diplomatic protection.[108] Calvo Clauses were popular in regional treaties as well as in international *contracts* with Latin American countries (especially concerning railroad concessions).[109] But they went virtually unused in treaties outside of the New World.[110]

Initial Hostility towards State Responsibility

Opposition to international standards of protection was at first conflated with hostility to the budding doctrine of state responsibility.[111] At the First Pan-American Congress in 1890, the delegates recommended

106 For some examples, *see* Fitzmaurice, *supra* note 90, at p. 99 and Goebel, *supra* note 7, at p. 833.

107 Alejandro Álvarez, "Latin America and International Law," 3(2) *American Journal of International Law* 269 (1909), at p. 307; Fitzmaurice, *supra* note 90, at p. 93; Oliver J. Lissitzyn, "The Meaning of the Term Denial of Justice in International Law," 30 *American Journal of International Law* 632–646 (1936), at pp. 635–638.

108 Montt, *supra* note 96, at p. 20.

109 Montt, *supra* note 96, at pp. 21–23. In at least three nineteenth-century cases, Calvo Clauses were held to bar international claims. Case of Beales, Novle & Garrison, US-Venezuelan Commission of 1885, in Moore, *supra* note 15, Vol. IV, at p. 3548 (question of validity of clause was not involved in the decision); Case of Flanagan, Bradley, Clark & Co., US–Venezuelan Commission of 1885, *ibid*, p. 3564; Case of Tehuantepec Ship Canal Co., US-M MCC of 1868, *ibid*, at p. 3132 as cited in Abraham Howard Feller, *The Mexican Claims Commissions 1923–1934: A Study in the Law and Procedure of International Tribunals* (New York: Macmillan, 1935), at p. 185.

110 *See* Paulsson, *supra* note 104, at p. 21; in 1873 the US rejected the Mexican reliance on Calvo's doctrine as one that was written by a young international lawyer whose theories had not gained acceptance (note from Mexican Foreign Minister to US Ambassador). Hence the need for the *Mavrommatis* case in the World Court (1925), which was one of the first (and last) institutional opportunities for the West to override Calvo's approach. And hence the political need for the Drago Doctrine (announced in 1902 by the Argentine Minister of Foreign Affairs Luis María Drago) and its response, the Roosevelt Corollary Doctrine (pronounced in 1904 by US President Theodore Roosevelt in his State of the Union).

111 Many US writers – including Richard Baxter, Edwin Borchard, Julius Goebel and Louis Sohn – have caricatured the Latin American position as one of espousing "non-responsibility" for violations of international law (*see* Montt, *supra* note 96, at p. 19). Even Latin American writers seem to have conceded this point. According to Raoul Eugène Desvernine, a legal adviser to Mexico, "Latin-American history . . . presents a consistent attempt on the part of many of the more tempestuous and revolution-ridden of the Latin-American states to evade international responsibilities through the insertion, in treaties contracted between themselves, and in their constitutional law and municipal

passing a resolution on the equality doctrine which meant denying state responsibility. The resolution had unanimous support (except the US). At the second conference in 1902, many resolutions were adopted that limited state responsibility for the denial or undue delay of justice. The end result was a treaty that was signed by all the states represented (except the US). Santiago Montt, a Chilean professor of international law, contests this historic view. To Montt, Calvo stood for the rejection of both imperialism and impunity, but he never rejected state responsibility in principle.[112] Calvo was in fact a founding member of *L'Institut de Droit international*, from which he became an early supporter of accountability for international violations. I agree with Montt in terms of Latin American doctrine; in practice, however, nineteenth century Latin American lawyers and diplomats did expressly oppose the norm of state responsibility in the nineteenth century.

Latin American arbitrators such as José Andrade expressed their dissatisfaction with state responsibility for alien protection in their articulate dissenting opinions. *The Apure* (1885) was one of the first international awards to include a lengthy analysis of state responsibility.[113] The steamer *Apure* was carrying the US Consul in Venezuela, Frederick Wipperman, when it ran aground on the Venezuelan coast. Indigenous tribes attacked the vessel and looted the Consul's belongings. US Commissioner John Little demanded reparation from Venezuela, alleging the latter's failure to protect a foreign consul. Venezuelan Commissioner Andrade disagreed, arguing that the international duty to protect aliens was a subjective standard of due diligence. Further, he wrote: "*the principle of the nonresponsibility of states for the losses and damages suffered by foreigners in times of internal trouble or civil wars* is the true principle of international law."[114] His colleagues on the tribunal, however, disagreed.[115]

law, of provisions limiting the state liability for injuries to aliens" (Desvernine, *supra* note 5, at p. 17).

112 *See* Montt, *supra* note 96, at pp. 5, 19, noting how neither Calvo nor Bello intended for their doctrines to negate the principle of state responsibility.

113 *Amelia de Brissot, No. 27, Ralph Rawdon, No. 28, Joseph Stackpole, No. 29, and Narcisa de Hammer, No. 30, v. Venezuela*, US and Venezuelan Claims Commission, convention of December 5, 1885.

114 Moore, *supra* note 15, at p. 2966, emphasis in original. To Commissioner Andrade, the obligation to protect *The Apure* had to be assessed in light of Venezuela's weakened abilities during times of civil war.

115 Citing the Italian international lawyer Pasquale Fiore (1837–1914), the tribunal affirmed in principle that "Venezuela did not neglect ... to adopt the means and measures

In *Joseph Forrest*, (the same) Commissioner Andrade again rejected the denial of justice claim put forward. Andrade argued that:

> To declare her [Venezuela] obliged besides to protect foreign property against all the risks of war, when she was unable to defend her own citizens, nor even the supreme good of her independence and political sovereignty, would be to understand justice otherwise than it has been regularly understood in the international society as well as in that of the equo bono. No nation can be required to do for others what she has not been able to do for herself.[116]

In this award, in contrast to *The Apure*, Andrade's reasoning was accepted by the tribunal.

Opposing Dollar Diplomacy

The opposition to international standards was not just a theoretical or financial one. Latin Americans opposed the reliance on the international standard of care because of how it was used to justify military interventions and other forms of European colonialism.[117] When local governments refused to arbitrate, Western governments often sent, or threatened to send warships.[118] An infamous example is the *Water Witch* affair (Figure 3.4), which involved Edward Hopkins (1822–1891),

proportionate to the gravity of the case, and is sufficient to withdraw from her the charge of voluntary omission of diligence, which is brought to-day against her" (Moore, *supra* note 15, at p. 2954). However, Umpire John V. L. Findlay still found Venezuela responsible for a denial of justice by failing to subsequently prosecute the assailants for their actions (*ibid*, at pp. 2967–2971).

116 *Joseph Forrest v. The United States of Venezuela*, No. 5 (1885), Moore, *supra* note 15, Vol. 3, at p. 2948.

117 *See, e.g.*, Edward Everett, review of Gregorio Funes, *Ensayo de la historia civil del Paraguay, Buenos-Ayres, y Tucuman*,12 *North American Review* 432–443 (1821), at p. 56 ("South America will be to North America, we are strongly inclined to think, what Asia and Africa are to Europe"). *See further* Greg Grandin, "The Liberal Traditions in the Americas: Rights, Sovereignty, and the Origins of Liberal Multilateralism," 117(1) *American Historical Review* 68–91 (2012), at p. 69.

118 Andreas H. Roth, *The Minimum Standard of International Law Applied to Aliens* (Leiden: Sijthoff, 1949), at p. 88; Alwyn V. Freeman, *The International Responsibility of States for Denials of Justice* (London: Longmans, Green & Co., 1938), at pp. 497–530; William Marion Gibson, *Aliens and the Law: Aspects of the National Treatment of Aliens in the United States* (Chapel Hill: Chapel Hill Press, 1940), at pp. 1–18; Eagleton, *supra* note 42, at pp. 82–87; Frederick Sherwood Dunn, *The Protection of Nationals: A Study in the Application of International Law* (Baltimore: The Johns Hopkins Press, 1932), at pp. 113–172.

Figure 3.4 USS Water Witch (Photo courtesy of Wikimedia Commons)

the "pioneer promoter of Paraguay."[119] Hopkins had founded the United States and Paraguay Navigation Company to take advantage of his personal relationship with Paraguayan President Carlos Antonio López (1790–1862). When that relationship soured, a series of financial difficulties set in that exposed Hopkins' investments to market risk. Without first seeking local redress, Hopkins appealed to the State Department for diplomatic protection. After President Buchanan secured Paraguay's "consent" to arbitrate through a threat of naval force, he appointed Cave Johnson, a friend and former judge, as its commissioner.[120]

The tribunal paid close attention to the fact that the claimants were familiar with the risks inherent to investing in an emerging market.[121] Paraguay was not held "responsible to the said company in any damages

[119] Harold F. Peterson, "Edward A. Hopkins: A Pioneer Promoter in Paraguay," 22(2) *The Hispanic American Historical Review* 245–261 (1942), at p. 245. I also consider the *Water Witch* at length in Chapter 2.

[120] Johnson was an interesting public personality. He shifted the postal service from a collect on delivery postage system to a prepaid postal system by introducing the stamp in 1847; he also introduced street corner mail boxes in urban areas – Clement L. Johnson, "The Public Career of Cave Johnson," 10 *Tennessee Historical Quarterly* 195 (1951).

[121] Paraguay Mixed Arbitration Tribunal, in Moore, *supra* note 15, at p. 1511.

or pecuniary compensation whatever, in all the premises."[122] On the contrary, the tribunal reprimanded the US for elevating the claim to an international forum:

> [A]s citizens of the US, they owed it to themselves and to their own country, as well as to the infant republic just emerging from tyranny and oppression, to have set an example of forbearance, moderation, and justice that would have reflected honor upon the institutions of their own country, and have inspired the people of Paraguay with new zeal and energy in their struggles to secure for themselves institutions producing such results.[123]

While the Water Witch affair demonstrated the willingness of plaintiff states to use force to encourage pacific resolutions, its vocal rejection of "dollar diplomacy" was atypical. Affirming state responsibility for breaching the "standard of civilization" entrenched an economic class system that favored Western foreigners over local investors. While Latin Americans supported liberal international norms, they opposed its inconsistent application to in the New World.[124] They viewed the turn to international arbitration as applying a double standard of international law – that is, one that applied to new but not to established states. This conclusion is eloquently phrased by Cambridge University law professor Kate Miles, "The colonial encounter created 'otherness' in the concept of the host state, excluding it from the protection principles of international investment law."[125]

Does Sovereignty Imply Liability?

Did international law require that statehood resemble a form of government that is continuously exposed to international liability? Ultimately,

[122] *Ibid*, at p. 1501.

[123] *Ibid*, at 1504.

[124] I hasten to add that Latin American writers were not the only ones who disapproved of the Western approach to state responsibility; even some Anglo-American publicists criticized the unprincipled nature of US arbitration. In his *International Law*, William Edward Hall (1835–1894), for example, accuses the US of employing double standards regarding prosecuting and defending alien protection claims. He footnoted this view for the first time in the 1904 edition. *Compare* William Edward Hall, *A Treatise on International Law* (Oxford: Clarendon Press, 1880), at p. 180 *to* William Edward Hall, *A Treatise on International Law*, J. B. Atlay, ed. (5th ed., Oxford and London: Clarendon and Stevens & Sons, 1904), at pp. 219–220, note 1 ("In other words the country which had been guilty of direct complicity with raids on a friendly state from settled country close to the seat of government did not hesitate when its own interests were involved to ask that state to undertake a distant and difficult expedition into wild and almost uninhabited regions").

[125] Miles, *supra* note 97 at p. 32.

in the debate over this question between North and South America there was no single winner.[126] On the one hand, in international legal doctrine, Latin American diplomats have prevented the US from ever codifying the international minimum standard on a multilateral basis. On the other hand, in arbitral practice, the US habit of delegating alien protection claims to international tribunals continued to allow for the application of that same standard on a regular – albeit bilateral – basis. Caught in the middle of this wrangle were the arbitrators, who were saddled with the impossible task of bridging the gap between North and South American views of international law and justice.

The name of the most popular international claim – *denial* of *justice* – seems to have "paralyzed reflection."[127] The duty itself was articulated negatively, in terms of what it was *not*: justice.[128] The many synonyms

[126] *See* Steven L. Haynes, *Alternative Vision: The United States, Latin America, and the League of Nations during the Republican Ascendancy* (doctoral dissertation submitted to Kent State University, 2012, at p. 2, available online at https://etd.ohiolink.edu/apexprod/rws_etd/send_file/send?accession=kent1353120620&disposition=inline, last visited June 30, 2021. The US achieved its aim of professionalizing international arbitration and positivizing an international protection of property. *See* Yves Dezalay and Bryant Garth Law, "Merchants of Law as Moral Entrepreneurs: Constructing International Justice from the Competition for Transnational Business Disputes," 29 (1) *Law & Society Review* 27 (1995): "Arbitration, we could say, was mistranslated. The misunderstanding was total between these litigators, on one side, who wanted to fight on their own terrain of facts with their usual weapons of adversary procedure, discovery, cross-examination; and the arbitrators on the other, for whom the noble terrain was that of law. Certainly, after the first misunderstanding, each side sought to bridge the gap. But in this private justice in the service of merchants, the relation of the forces was such that one made more inroads than the other" (at p. 53). However, as I discuss in the following chapters, the South found their revenge to these developments within the codification bodies of international institutions. Latin Americans succeeded in convincing their colleagues within the League of Nations and later, the United Nations, to codify state responsibility not based on US practice of alien protection but on the German theory of international responsibility, especially as articulated by the Italian doctrinalist and future Special Rapporteur on state responsibility Roberto Ago.

[127] Paulsson, *supra* note 104, at p. 2: "This striving towards justice is to all appearances one of man's strongest emotions which is why reason has the greatest difficulty in controlling it" (Vladimir Bukovsky, *Introduction, Arthur Koestler, Darkness at Noon* (1940; trans. Daphne Hardy, London: Folio Society, 1980)). *See also* Charles Cheney Hyde, "Review: The International Responsibility of States for Denial of Justice, by Alwyn V. Freeman," 34(2) *American Journal of International Law* 363 (1940), at p. 365: "The law today suffers grievously from various attempts to portray what it ordains through equivocal phrases that themselves demand explanation. 'Denial of justice' is one of them."

[128] Articulated as "denial" rather than "access" to justice. It is one of very few international norms defined in the negative; another example of this is the claim of "abuse of rights" – *see* Paulsson, *supra* note 104, at p. 60.

used for "denial of justice" shared this aspect: for example, justice *in re minime dubia*,[129] gross injustice,[130] substantial or gross miscarriage of justice,[131] palpable injustice,[132] notorious injustice,[133] manifest injustice,[134] substantial denial of justice.[135] US-based international arbitrator Jan Paulsson has recently commented that this doctrinal disagreement has brought on a "dialogue of the deaf" that has lasted for centuries.[136]

"Someone Ought to Pay"

As mentioned above, the obligation to protect aliens was based on natural law, a proto-human right. The lecture notes of John Bassett Moore (1860–1947) of Columbia University reflect this:

[129] *E.g.*, *E. F. W. Leichardt v. Mexico*, No. 952, Am. docket, convention of July 4, 1868, MS. Op. II 580; Moore, *supra* note 15, at p. 3134.

[130] *E.g.*, Mr. Evarts, Sec. of State, to Mr. Langston, Minister to Haiti, No. 23, April 12, 1878, MS. Inst. Hayti, II, 136, *Digest of International Law*, Vol IV, at p. 656; Mr. Evarts, Sec. of State, to Mr. Foster, Minister to Mexico, April 19, 1879, MS. Inst. Mexico, XIX 570, *Digest of International Law*, Vol. VI, at p. 696; Charles Cheney Hyde, *International Law Chiefly as Interpreted and Applied by the United States* Vol. I (Boston: Little, Brown & Co., 1922), at p. 391.

[131] *E.g.*, Hargrave J of the Privy Council in *R v. Michael Murphy*, June 22, 1869, *The English Reports*, Vol. XVI (London: W. Green & Sons, 1902), at p. 185; Award of the Hon. William R. Day, arbitrator, in the matter of the claims of *John D. Mezger & Co. v. The Republic of Hayti*, protocol of Oct. 18, 1899, For. Rel. 1901, 262, 264, 275. For the brief of the Hon. William L. Penfield, Solicitor of the Department of State, for the United States, in this case, see Mr. Hay, Sec. of State to Mr. Day, March 29, 1900, 244 MS. Dom. Let. 65; *Digest of International Law* ∫1072.

[132] *E.g.*, *Francis McManus et al. v. Mexico*, No. 348, Am. docket, per Mr. Zamacona, MS. Op. III. 361; Moore, *supra* note 15, at p. 3413.

[133] *E.g.*, Decree issued by General Guzman Blanco, provisional president of Venezuela, of February 14, 1873, For. Rel. 1883, 918; *Digest of International Law* Vol. VI (1906), at p. 319; 96 *British and Foreign State Papers*, p. 648, as cited in Goebel, infra note 177, at p. 837.

[134] *E.g.*, Abstract of a note from the minister for foreign affairs of Salvador, in relation to the law of the 29th of September, 1886, concerning the status of foreigners, naturalization, matriculation, etc., *Papers Relating to the Foreign Relations of the United States* No. 75 (Washington, DC: Government Printing Office, 1888), at p. 94

[135] *E.g.*, Award of the Hon. William R. Day, arbitrator, in the matter of the claims of *John D. Mezger & Co. v. The Republic of Hayti*, protocol of Oct. 18, 1899, For. Rel. 1901, 262, 264, 275. For the brief of the Hon. W. L. Penfield, Solicitor of the Department of State, for the United States, in this case, see Mr. Hay, Sec. of State to Mr. Day, March 29, 1900, 244 MS. Dom. Let. 65; *Digest of International Law* ∫1072.

[136] Paulsson, *supra* note 104, at p. 24.

> Every human being has rights, which civil society is bound to respect: an individual may be a mere cosmopolite, owning no permanent allegiance to any Nation whatever. Such an individual, if he come, as he may, into the limits of a civil society, has a right to full protection, of his life, liberty, property (actual and potential), health, reputation etc., and if either of these be violated, such person has a just claim, jure naturae et civile, as if he were a full subject or citizen of that nation, or of any other nation.[137]

The doctrine of sources of international law – comprised mainly of treaties, customs, and general principles – arrived only in the twentieth century. First catalogued by the celebrated positivist Lassa F. L. Oppenheim (1858–1919) in his 1905 treatise on international law,[138] it was then codified in the statutes of the Permanent Court of International Justice ("PCIJ")[139] and International Court of Justice ("ICJ").[140] From a positive law standpoint, of course, treaties are the "hardest" source of law, followed by customary laws. However, in the nineteenth century, the most relevant source for international disputes was not treaties or custom; it was general principles of law.[141]

In the *Montijo* award, the US owners of a steamer that was taken over by revolutionaries sought compensation from Colombia. Although the Colombian government had nothing directly to do with the seizure, Umpire Robert Bunch (1820–1881) was certain of one fundamental point: "It is clear, on every principle of the plainest justice, that '*some one*' *ought to pay* for this act and for its consequences."[142] Since the 'some one' would not be the actual takers of the vessel, since they had been

[137] John Bassett Moore, Columbia Law School Archives, Box 21, at p. 3 (emphasis in original).

[138] Lassa Oppenheim, *International Law: A Treatise* (2nd ed., London: Longmans, Green and Co., 1912), at pp. 20–25. But *see* Jean d'Aspremont, "What Was Not Meant to Be: General Principles of Law as a Source of International Law," in R. Pisillo Mazzeschi and P. De Sena (eds.), *Global Justice, Human Rights, and the Modernization of International Law* 1 (Cham: Springer, 2018), at pp. 3–9 (the elevation of general principles of law into a source of international law in article 38 of the PCIJ amounts to a reinvention of general principles that departed from earlier arbitral practice and legal thought).

[139] Statute of the Permanent Court of International Justice art. 38, Dec. 16, 1920, 6 *League of Nations Treaty Series* 379.

[140] Statute of the International Court of Justice art. 38, June 26, 1945, 59 Stat. 1055, 1060, T.S. No. 993.

[141] I agree with Christine Gray that arbitral tribunals did not turn in any systematic way to particular systems of law or to general principles of law; but I disagree with her assertion that arbitral tribunals rarely referred to general principles of law – Christine Gray, *Judicial Remedies in International Law* (Oxford: Oxford University Press, 1987), at p. 6.

[142] Moore, *supra* note 15, at p. 1444, emphasis added.

pardoned, responsibility was thus attributed to Colombia. Similarly, the *Emilio Roberts* tribunal confessed:

> It is much more difficult for us to fix the amount of the claim, in a reasonable manner, than to give judgment about the justice of the same claim. Claimants almost always exaggerate enormously, and try to present the facts in the light most favourable to themselves, without paying great respect to the truth ... For this reason, we, the Commissioners, are compelled to proceed solely by simple conjectures and inferences, drawn from the very few facts we have before us, and to make a very ample use of the discretionary power which pertains to our office.[143]

Tribunals ruled intuitively, broadly based on general legal principles and their own senses of justice.[144]

Protecting Property as a General Principle

"Property rights needed defending," writes US historian Benjamin Allen Coates,[145] and international arbitrators took up that role. They could draw from their prior experience in domestic practice. In the nineteenth century, lawyers were often trained as legal scientists: standing ready to process any set of facts "in the language of general principles."[146] Legal liability was not necessarily a legislated result; it was an *adjudicated*

[143] Memorial and Opinion, docket 594, MS., US Department of State as cited in Cheng, *supra* note 13, at p. 239, note 18.

[144] Whiteman conceded in the opening of her book, "The study does not purpose to be a handbook ... Rather, the cases are indicative of how reasonable men have measured damages in a variety of circumstances" (Whiteman, *supra* note 78, vol I, at p. *v*).

[145] Benjamin Allen Coates, *Legalist Empire: International Law and American Foreign Relations in the Early Twentieth Century* (Oxford: Oxford University Press, 2016), at p. 10.

[146] Koskenniemi, *supra* note 33, at p 26. *See also* John Bassett Moore, "A Brief Sketch of the Life of Francis Wharton," "Forward" to *Diplomatic Correspondence of the American Revolution*, ed. Francis Wharton (1889), Vol. I, *xi–xxvii*, reprinted in *The Collected Papers of John Bassett Moore* (New Haven: Yale University Press, 1944), Vol. I, pp. 45–64, 49; Sir Frederick Pollock, *The Law of Torts: A Treatise on the Principles of Obligations Arising from Civil Wrongs in the Common Law* (London: Stevens and Sons, 1886), at pp. 4–13; Amanda Perreau-Saussine, "Lauterpacht and Vattel on the Sources of International Law: The Place of Private Law Analogies and General Principles" in Peter Haggenmacher and Vincent Chetail (eds.), *Vattel's International Law in a XXIst Century Perspective* (The Hague: Brill, 2011). *See* d'Aspremont, *supra* note 138, at pp. 2–3 (general principles of law were used as an expansionist tool as opposed to a proper source of law; international lawyers could extract rules from them where none could otherwise be found, as *non liquet*. I discuss this point further in Chapter 2.

one.[147] If violation, then responsibility. The latter was derived from the former. International legal liability would fare no differently than its domestic counterpart. Sir Hersch Lauterpacht (1897–1960) had demonstrated in his 1925 doctoral dissertation that international arbitrations were frequently grounded in domestic legal analogies.[148] Given the lack of dispositive positive law, international arbitrators, like international lawyers of the time generally, had to become comparative lawyers.[149]

Western diplomats and lawyers believed they could codify alien protection claims without the need for public codification.[150] International arbitration was an opportunity for lawyers to do just that with the "international minimum standard" of alien protection.[151] The very first article of *L'Institut de Droit international*'s founding statute linked this purpose to its own mission of formulating and publicizing general principles of science.[152] Natural legal principles regarding the basic rights

[147] Lawyers could derive the substance of state responsibility analytically. This idea was crystallized in the *Chorzów* case, when Poland argued that even if it had violated an obligation owed to Germany, there was no treaty provision that ensured that Poland's international responsibility would be engaged in such an event. The PCIJ responded that where there is an international obligation, international responsibility may necessarily follow and this relationship does not need to be spelled out in a treaty (*Case Concerning the Factory at Chorzów (Germany v. Poland) (Claim for Indemnity) (Jurisdiction) Judgment No. 8 of 26 July 1927*, Permanent Court of International Justice, Ser. A, No. 9, Collection of Judgment, at 21). *See also* James Crawford and Simon Olleson, "The Exception of Non-performance: Links between the Law of Treaties and the Law of State Responsibility," 21 *Australian Yearbook of International Law* 55–74 (2001), at pp. 66–73 (heavy reliance on domestic analogy but described as treaty interpretation, a good illustration of how arbitrators approached state responsibility in the premodern era).

[148] Hersch Lauterpacht, *Private Law Sources and Analogies of International Law: With Special Reference to International Arbitration* (London: Longmans, Green and Co., 1927), especially at p. 210.

[149] The first journal of international law, *Revue de droit international et la législation comparée* (1869), was also of comparative law. The first US international lawyer, Henry Wheaton, was led to the study of international law through his "fondness for the discussion of general principles."

[150] *See* Johann Caspar Bluntschli, *Das moderne Völkerrecht der civilisierten Staaten als Rechtsbuch dargestellt* (2nd edn, Nördlingen: Beck, 1872); Martti Koskenniemi, "The Legacy of the 19th Century" (2007, unpublished paper on file with author), at pp. 13–14.

[151] Martins Paparinskis has argued that the international minimum standard is not a technical legal standard but shorthand for alien protection in general – *see* Paparinskis, *supra* note 51, at p. 13 as well as Chapter 2.

[152] "*De formuler les principes généraux de la science, ainsi que les règles qui en dérivent, et d'en répendre la connaissance*" (cited in Koskenniemi, *supra* note 33, at pp. 47–48).

of individuals carried considerable sway in the early arbitrations. The hard positivism of the *Lotus* Principle was several decades away.[153]

Like the underlying duty to protection, arbitrators interpreted the responsibility for its breach in terms of general principles of law. Occasionally, states pre-agreed to liability for alien injuries in a *compromis*.[154] I have largely excluded such instances of liability from this study.[155] As Bin Cheng (1921–2019) explains, pre-agreed-upon liability (or, as he calls it, "assumed liability") is distinct from adjudicated forms of responsibility.[156] I have also omitted those infrequent incidents when states made indemnifications for alien injuries not out of a sense of legal obligation but in the spirit of humanity.[157] My focus is on adjudicated forms of state responsibility. As Dr. Cheng notes,

> Responsibility properly so-called is an independent juridical concept subject to well defined principles as to its origin, scope and consequences,

[153] According to the World Court: "International law governs relations between independent States. The rules of law binding upon States therefore emanate from their own free will as expressed in conventions or by usages generally accepted as expressing principles of law and established in order to regulate the relations between these co-existing independent communities or with a view to the achievement of common aims. *Restrictions upon the independence of States cannot therefore be presumed*" (*The Case of The S.S. Lotus* (France v. Turkey), 1927 P.C.I.J. (ser. A) No. 10, (Sept. 7), at p. 18, emphasis added). *See further* Ole Spiermann, *International Legal Argument in the Permanent Court of International Justice: The Rise of the International Judiciary* (Cambridge: Cambridge University Press, 2005), at pp. 254–261.

[154] An example is the *compromis* of the US–Paraguay Mixed Claims Commission, which included the following provision: "The Government of Paraguay binds itself 'for the responsibility which may result from the decree of the commissioners.'" United States–Paraguay Mixed Commission, in Moore, *supra* note 15, at p. 1496. Similarly, in the second US–Mexico Mixed Claims Commission, Mexico sought to "unbind" itself from the tribunal's award in *La Abra Silver Mining Company*, since it was based on fraudulent evidence (*ibid* at pp. 1334–1335).

[155] For example, Claims of the Hudson's Bay and Puget's Sound Agricultural Companies: Commission under the Treaty of July 1, 1863 (1871), Moore, *supra* note 15, at pp. 247, 249.

[156] Cheng, *supra* note 13, at pp. 165–170, also uses the terminology of "assumed" versus "negotiated" responsibility and only considers the former "responsibility" in the strict sense of the term.

[157] *See, e.g.*, John Bassett Moore, "The Late Chilian Controversy," (8)3 *Political Science Quarterly* 467–494 (1893), at p. 487: On September 2, 1885, a US mob drove innocent Chinese nationals from their homes and massacred them. No attempt was made by authorities to punish those culpable. After the Chinese Government made diplomatic requests to the US, Secretary of State Bayard denied any international liability for the affair. But Bayard did express his outrage regarding the shameful miscarriage of justice rendered in Wyoming and agreed to indemnify the victims as an "act of humanity."

> while 'assumed responsibility' is in reality only a contractual obligation based on consent, the extent of the obligation being determined by the parties themselves.[158]

Even when a treaty was available as a positive source, it was usually less probative than general principles of law, as I will show in the next section.[159]

But Who Should Pay? The Attribution Problem of Mobs and Revolutions

If the idea that "someone ought to pay" for alien injuries was clear, the mechanics of imposing state responsibility for denials of justice were in flux. Legally, if the state was a composite entity, how did international law attribute responsibility to it for the illicit conduct of its separate organs? What was the wrong being remedied? And factually, what was the injury being redressed in international arbitrations?[160] Was the underlying injury to the alien a factual or legal matter (or both)? The answers to these questions cannot be gleaned from the early international awards.[161]

[158] Cheng, *supra* note 13 (emphasis added).

[159] See *The Montijo* (United States v. Colombia), Award of July 26, 1875, (per Umpire Robert Bunch) "But there is another and a stronger reason for such liability. This is that the general government of the Union, through its officers in Panama, failed in its duty to extend to the citizens of the United States the protection which, both by the law of nations and by special treaty stipulation, it was bound to afford" (Moore, *supra* note 15, at p. 1444).

[160] Later, in the twentieth century, tribunals were more precise. In *Labaree*, the commission spelled out the difference between compensating the individual victims and satisfying the claimant state (2 Foreign Relations (1907) 942–943). See also the *Lentz* case (*Digest of International Law,* Vol. VI, at p. 794). According to Hyde, these are examples of punishments for denials of justice (*supra* note 125, at p. 515 – Clyde Eagleton, "Measures of Damages in International Law," 39 *Yale Law Journal* 52 (1929), at p. 63.

[161] On the prehistory of the concept of attribution, *see* Jan Arno Hessbruegge, "The Historical Development of the Doctrines of Attribution and Due Diligence in International Law," 36 *NYU Journal of International Law & Politics* 265 (2004), at pp. 265–292: "The 18th and 19th centuries were characterized by a gradual (re-) expansion of state responsibility. The replacement of the king with the state as the subject of international law slowly took hold in the writings of the 18th century publicists and allowed them to develop new doctrines of responsibility" (*ibid* at pp. 287–288).

Results depended not only on the facts of each case, but also on the identity of the litigating parties and the arbitrators.[162]

Illustrative of this point is the case of injuries suffered by aliens during internal revolutions (civil wars, mob violence, etc.). The laws of state responsibility were expanded to provide remedies for such claims.[163] Prior to the US turn to arbitration, states were generally not liable for injuries suffered during civil wars or other occasions where local governments are not in control the situation.[164] Modern international arbitrators not only attributed liability for injuries suffered at the hands of mobs. They also imposed liability on newly formed governments *for the acts of rebel forces* – whether or not they were successful in their revolution.[165] This would be like holding the US responsible to France for alien injuries caused by Confederate soldiers well behind battle lines. This is something that never happened. By 1905, a mixed claims tribunal considered a "well-established rule of international law" that revolution-

162 At times, the awarded amounts reflected an attempt to remedy the underlying injury suffered (*e.g.*, wrongful death) as opposed to simply the denial of access to justice. Yet, in one case, Umpire Lieber awarded damages in a case where there was a clear wrong but no clear injury to be compensated. Other times, international awards seemed to reflect a tribunal's difficulty in considering both the issue of remedying a private injury and redressing a public wrong (In *Fayette Anderson and William Thompson*, Umpire Thornton concluded: "It seems proved that a certain amount of property was forcibly taken by Mexican troops . . . The evidence as to the amount and value of the property . . . is not satisfactory, though it is clear that some of their property was so taken." An award was made nonetheless (Decision of November 5, 1874, Opinion, Docket 333, MS Department of State as cited in Whiteman, *supra* note 78, vol. II, at p. 841)).

163 Hessbruegge, *supra* note 161, at pp. 302, 303; *see also* Coussirat-Coustère and Eisemann, *infra* note 165, at 307; Tal Becker, *Terrorism and the State: Rethinking the Rules of State Responsibility* (Portland: Hart, 2006), ch. 3.

164 *See* Moore, *supra* note 15, at p. 2972. I am thankful to Kathryn Greenman for highlighting the importance of this field to the fine line between the rules and exceptions of State responsibility for alien injuries (*see* her "Aliens in Latin America: Intervention, Arbitration and State Responsibility for Rebels," 31 *Leiden Journal of International Law* 617 (2018)).

165 In *William S. Shrigley vs. Chile*, regarding the destruction of alien property, the tribunal concluded: "Neutral property taken for the use of service of armies or functionaries thereunto authorized gives a right to the owner to demand compensation from the government exercising such authority . . . The same liability attaches for encroachments upon the rights of neutrals in the case of a successful revolutionary government" (Pierre Michel Eisemann and Vincent Coussirat-Coustère, *Répertoire de la Jurisprudence Arbitrale Internationale*, Vol. I 1874–1918 (Leiden: Brill, 1989), at p. 307; Moore, *supra* note 15, at pp. 3711–3712).

ary acts are deemed "acts of a *de facto* government."[166] (The tribunal offered no authority for this position.)[167]

Attributing state responsibility for omissions was a particularly knotty question and was articulated in terms of due diligence obligations.[168] While establishing liability for omissions is more difficult than for acts, when a tribunal does end up awarding damages for failures to act, they often included higher levels of damages.[169] No domestic or international

[166] *French Company of Venezuelan Railroads*, 10 R.I.A.A. 285 (France–Venezuela Mixed Claims Commission, 1905), *Dix Case*, 9 R.I.A.A. 119, 120 (U.S.–Venezuela Mixed Claims Commission, 1903), respectively, as cited in Hessbruegge, *supra* note 161, at pp. 301–302. This position was also affirmed in the award of *Salvador Commercial Company (El Salvador/US)* (1902) 15 RIAA 455. As recently as in 2013, James Crawford cites to the award in his treatise on *State Responsibility: The General Part* (Cambridge: Cambridge University Press, 2013), at pp. 116–117 regarding the concept of "authority" as including all three branches of government working in official capacity. By the turn of the twentieth century, it was also clear that states were responsible for the conduct of all their officials, including the judiciary.

[167] *See* Edwin M. Borchard, "Tort Liability of the State," 12(1) *Journal of Comparative Legislation and International Law* 1 (1930), at p. 6 (tribunals expansively interpreted attribution to hold revolutionaries vicariously responsible for the conduct of the displaced government); *see also* Award of Umpire Lieber, August 2, 1871, *Rafael M. Miller v. Mexico*, No. 490 as reproduced in Moore, *supra* note 15, at p. 2974.

[168] Becker, *supra* note 163: "harmful private conduct and State wrongdoing in relation to that conduct" (p. 24). "Rather, State responsibility is engaged solely for the State's *own* violation of a separate and distinct duty to exercise due diligence in preventing and punishing the private office" (p. 24) – emphasis in original; Hessbruegge, *supra* note 161 at pp. 268–269. This is a level of conduct that falls below active complicity. A state can be liable for mere complicity, a lower level of participation than agency, even if it sanctioned the conduct after the fact. ("Complicity" is also referred to as "condonation" or "adoption" of private acts, distinctions that are borne out with more sophistication in the twentieth century.) For example, in the *Case of Cotesworth and Powell*, Colombia was liable for damages to Great Britain for the denial of justice caused by granting an amnesty to revolutionary forces who had inflicted the underlying injury. The tribunal based its decision on "the well-established principle in international polity, that, by pardoning a criminal, a nation assumes the responsibility for his past acts" (Moore, *supra* note 15, at 2085). Arbitrators adopted this position as a general principle of law – as though no expansion was taking place at all. A similar result occurred in the *ad hoc* arbitration of the Venezuelan Steam Transportation Company claim against Venezuela (January 19, 1892, Moore, *supra* note 15, at p. 1693): "A government 'which refuses to repair the damage committed by its citizens or subjects, to punish the guilty parties, or to give them up for that purpose, may be regarded as virtually a sharer in the injury and as responsible therefore.'" The tribunal relied on both North (Wharton) and South American publicists (Calvo) for its conclusion.

[169] Whiteman, *supra* note 78, Vol. I, at pp. 36–39. In the *Case of the Brig General Armstrong*, the arbitration panel cleared Portugal of responsibility for allowing Great Britain to attack the US privateer vessel without intervening to ensure the neutrality of its port. According to the tribunal, Portugal's liability turned on the matters of due diligence and

legal rule was relied upon to increase damages for omissions. For example, during a Chilean civil war, the *Itata*, a vessel loaded with arms headed to Chile, was seized in San Diego, California. The local court released the *Itata* anyway. When the new government saw the ruling, it was viewed as a non-neutral act by the US.[170] Chile retaliated by arresting people leaving and entering its legation.[171] It was in this context that sailors on leave from the *USS Baltimore* found themselves in the coastal town of Valparaiso. Two of the sailors were on a pub crawl that developed into a brawl that devolved into a riot with stabbings, shootings and killings. Chilean police were onsite but did nothing to break up the mob.[172] After a heated exchange of diplomatic notes, Chile complied with all US demands; they agreed to bypass local courts and to submit the question of reparation to the US Supreme Court, who imposed a liability on Chile of US$ 75,000 in gold.[173] What is most interesting about this award is how John Bassett Moore, then the Third Assistant Secretary of State, describes it. He was very pleased with this US victory because, in his opinion, it was a "general and settled principle" of international law that there was *no responsibility of a government* for *mob violence*.[174]

fault, of which it found none (Moore, *supra* note 15, at pp. 1103–1105). In 1882, the US Congress passed legislation, out of a sense of "patriotism," that provided damages to the privateers (*ibid*).

170 First, there was the cutting of the cables of the Central and South American Telegraph Company as well as the visit of US Navy Admiral Brown to Quinteros Bay. Second, there was the delayed manner in which the US recognized the belligerency rights of the Congressionalist-backed forces (though the US was quick to recognize the newly established Congressionalist government). Third, there was the fact that the US Minister to Chile granted asylum from domestic prosecution to eighty previous officials of the Balmaceda administration by hosting them in the US legation in Santiago, including two assailants accused of the "barbaric" murder of youths whose bodies were subject to "frightful indignities." *See* John Bassett Moore, "The Late Chilian Controversy," 3(8) *Political Science Quarterly* 467-494 (1893), at pp. 470–471, 481; Osgood Hardy, "Was Patrick Egan a 'Blundering Minister?'" 8(1) *The Hispanic American Historical Review* 65–91 (1928), at p. 65.

171 Moore, *supra* note 152, at p. 473 (when the US heard that Chilean authorities were treating its legation with disrespect, "the scene was suddenly and completely transformed. The question became international, and the possibility of a conflict was suggested").

172 Moore, *supra* note 152, at p. 485.

173 Moore, *supra* note 152, at p. 494.

174 Moore, *supra* note 152, at p. 486; also, the sailors, says Moore, were contributorily negligent for seeking "diversion in dangerous places frequented by lawless characters" (*ibid*, at p. 489). Footnote in due diligence (lack of due diligence can be justified by mob – however, if there was an agreement for "special protection," mob violence may be no justification (*ibid*, at p. 487).

In other words, he was particularly proud of how his government muscled the gold from Chile given that the latter had no obligation to do so under settled principles international law.

Contrast this result with that in the case of *Salvador Prats*, where the Lieber Tribunal had to consider the question of US "responsibility . . . for injuries committed by rebel forces against aliens in time of civil war." Mr. Prats was a Mexican national who owned cotton on board the *M. A. Stevens*. His property was destroyed when Confederate soldiers burned the British brig, which was then docked outside of New Orleans. To Commissioner William Wadsworth, the legal answer was simple: "We have no difficulty answering that question in the negative." Confederate forces were not "authorities of the United States" since they were not authorities of or effectively controlled by the US Government.[175] Though in agreement with this result, Commissioner Gómez Palacio took pains to emphasize that the result was a general rule of international law regarding the nonresponsibility of states for the acts of rebels. To Palacio, international law should be consistent in not holding states responsible for injuries caused by conduct over which the host state lacked the ability of any control.[176]

Because civil war cases are hard cases to incorporate into consistent doctrine, Columbia Law School legal historian Julius Goebel (1892–1973) chose mob violence as the case study of his monograph on state responsibility.[177] Attributing responsibility for injuries arising out of civil war touches on the fundamental norm of assigning culpability for *controllable* conduct only. If a host state without local control were liable to pay damages for alien injuries, this would give an unfair advantage to

[175] Mixed Commission established under the Convention concluded between the United States of America and Mexico on July 4, 1868, *Case of Salvador Prats v. the United States of America*, in Moore, *supra* note 15, at p. 2889 (emphasis added).

[176] The international requirements of alien protection "[M]ust be such as to render impossible any other, better or more careful and attentive, so as not to omit anything, practical or possible, which ought to have been done in the case . . . and so the jurists and law writers, in establishing the maxim *ad impossibile nemo tenetur* [nobody can be bound to do the impossible] have merely been the interpreters of common sense. The same truth will be expressed in a more practical language by saying that the extent of the duties is to be commensurate with the extent of the means for performing the same, and that he who has employed all the means within his reach has perfectly fulfilled his duty, irrespective of the material result of his efforts" (Moore, *supra* note 15, at pp. 2893–2894).

[177] *See* Julius Goebel, Jr., "The International Responsibility of States for Injuries Sustained by Aliens on Account of Mob Violence, Insurrections and Civil Wars," 8(4) *American Journal of International Law* 802 (1914).

foreigners as compared to domestic investors.[178] Despite Goebel's attempts to prove otherwise, alien injury cases seem to have done just that; namely, they were instances not of a consistent rule of law but of arbitrary outcomes where local governments were held liable for injuries they neither caused nor had the ability to prevent. Far from being a "hard" or unusual case to study, writes Kathryn Greenman, mob violence was the "archetype" of state responsibility.[179] It was no coincidence that state responsibility rested on cases of civil unrest.

The doctrine was born in chaos. As Professor Greenman notes, "Many arbitrations, including the most influential, followed revolutions or civil wars" and were not based on injuries suffered during peacetime.[180] The foundational claims of state responsibility were not important diplomatic disputes between sovereign states or major rulings about important economic or trade matters. They were not cases of outright wrongful acts. Rather, the earliest sources of state responsibility were typically private claims arising out of civil wars, during which time there was no clear governmental control or power. Injuries were suffered, yes, but no wrongs clearly attributable. In other words, arbitrators articulated state responsibility for alien injuries as an exception to state practice rather than the rule. And that was the point.[181]

[178] Calvo, in the first volume of the newly formed *Revue de Droit International et de Legislation Comparée*, argued that state responsibility injuries caused by rebels "would create an unwarrantable inequality between foreigners and nationals to the benefit of powerful states at the expense of weaker ones and infringe the principle of territorial jurisdiction" (Carlos Calvo, "De la non-responsabilité de l'Etat à raison des pertes et dommages éprouvés par les étrangers en temps de troubles intérieurs ou de guerres civiles," 1 *Revue de Droit International et de Legislation Comparée* 417 (1869), at p. 422.

[179] Greenman, *supra* note 101, at p. 618.

[180] Greenman, *supra* note 101, at p. 622. Jean d'Aspremont has explained that the rule of attributing state responsibility for the acts of rebels "rests neither on sound precedential nor systemic grounds" but was instead "the outcome of a political choice to lessen impunity and promote accountability in case of violation of international law by non-State actors" (Jean d'Aspremont, "Rebellion and State Responsibility: Wrongdoing by Democratically Elected Insurgents," 58 *International and Comparative Law Quarterly* 427 (2009), at p. 427).

[181] From its earliest days, the doctrine of state responsibility was exceptional in nature. For example, it often addressed the unusual circumstance of injuries from civil unrest or mob violence. The legal question was whether to make the rule of state responsibility narrowly applicable to cases of discrimination only or more broadly to claims of alien injuries instances falling short international standards of protection. *See further* Greenman, *supra* note 101, at p. 618. Professor Greenman explains how nearly all Anglo- and Latin American scholars agreed that state responsibility was exception rather than rule of alien protection under international law. *But it was the scope of the exceptions* that was profoundly contested.

Quantifying Alien Injuries

Once an international tribunal established the existence of a breach that was either caused or should have been prevented by a state, the next question was that of "indemnification." The term indemnification fit the *ad hoc* approach to alien protection, which overemphasized quantifiable harms and underemphasize their qualitative or normative components. International arbitrators had little interest in philosophical speculation.[182] They were usually more preoccupied with settling claims about individuals (the private aspect) than in deciding how to attribute those wrongs to a state (the public aspect); they fixated on quantifying injuries rather than assessing culpability. In sum, tribunals took an "indemnification approach" to international claims. Awards referred to violations of international law most frequently as grounds for "reparation," "restitution" or "indemnification" rather than as "reprisals," "satisfaction," or

Whereas Anglo-American lawyers argued that states should not be allowed to avoid international liability for deliberately preferring anarchy, Latin American attorneys only recognized the relevance of international law to alien protection claims in the event there was discrimination (*ibid* at pp. 25–26). In retrospect, the doctrine of this subfield was a Rorschach test for international lawyers of the time. For example, in the 1913 and 1914 issues of the *American Journal of International Law*, future president of Panama, Harmodio Arias, and Columbia Law School historian, Julius Goebel, looked at the same body of arbitral awards and drew opposite conclusions about the possibility of state responsibility for alien injuries arising out of civil wars. Dr. Harmodio lists all the major publicists (including Anzilotti) who deny all responsibility for such injuries but repeatedly affirms the general rule of state responsibility for alien injuries *not* arising out of civil war. Goebel seems suspicious of Harmodio and other Latin American publicists' motives. They are not out to reaffirm the principles of state responsibility, but to undermine them ("The Latin American states have shown considerable ingenuity in devising schemes to avoid liability for injuries to aliens. See Harmodio Arias, "The Non-Liability of States for Damages Suffered by Foreigners in the Course of a Riot, an Insurrection, or a Civil War," 7(4) *American Journal of International Law* 724 (1913). To Goebel, "They have repudiated the theory of responsibility not only in their diplomatic correspondence, but in their statutes, their treaties, and even in their constitutions. Goebel's views are likely representative of those of his European colleagues. Perceiving how expanding the exception of injuries arising out of civil war might undermine the rule of state responsibility, the *Institut de Droit international*, at its 1900 meeting, condemned Latin American efforts to undermine state responsibility through Calvo clauses in their treaties (*see* Goebel, *supra* note 177, at p. 841).

182 As Borchard wrote, international law practitioners were "unwilling to indulge in philosophical speculation" (Borchard, *supra* note 10, at p. 520, internal citations omitted); Whiteman, *supra* note 78, Vol. 1 at p. 34: "Arbitrators are apt to agree on the amount to be allowed but to disagree on the reasons for allowing the particular amount." The idea of circumstances precluding wrongfulness (i.e., Chapter V of the Draft Articles) is a later concept. At the time, breach implied liability such that there was no additional step of wrongfulness that had to be proven or avoided, as will be discussed later in this section.

"justice."[183] Because arbitrators usually focused on injuries rather than wrongs, the resulting liability amounts often reflected an unstated normative component.[184]

Rarely but occasionally, tribunals did hint at the normative underpinning of an international award. Umpire Lieber, in the case of *Francis W. Rice*, awarded US$ 4,000 for a three-day wrongful detention even though the latter suffered no serious injury because of the deprivation of individual liberty at stake.[185] The arbitral historian and State Department lawyer Marjorie Whiteman (1898–1986) found that tribunals awarded half as much for warranted arrests made with improper procedures as compared to unwarranted arrests (with similar factual injuries).[186] A rare discussion of general principles of responsibility was the case of *Cotesworth & Powell* (1875).

Cotesworth & Powell involved the theft of property by the judge in a local bankruptcy case brought by the British tea and tobacco importer. Ultimately, the judge was caught by the Colombian authorities, but the government provided the judge with amnesty. Remedial claims against the judge therefore became impossible. The arbitrator in the case was a professional attorney and the US Minister Resident to Colombia William L. Scruggs (1836–1912). The tribunal "deduced" ten "principles of responsibility" before concluding that the Colombian government was responsible for a denial of justice that was "almost without precedent in the modern annals of judicial corruption."[187] The question posed to the

[183] One of numerous such examples is the case of the *Masonic* in Moore, *supra* note 15, at p. 1059; Lauterpacht, *supra* note 148, at p. 134 (with regards to state responsibility for international delicts, "no clear-cut rule can be laid down with regard to all cases in which the international responsibility of the State becomes engaged"); William Edward Hall, *A Treatise on International Law* (3rd ed., Oxford: Oxford University Press, 1890), at p. *vi* ("It would be very unwise of an international lawyer to indulge in the delusion, with which he is often credited, that formulas are stronger than passions").

[184] Indeed, most awards were quantified based on underlying injuries rather than attributed wrongs. Goebel noted this inconsistency: "It is worth while indicating the peculiar nature of the infraction of an international norm. The violation proceeds primarily from the injury, as I have indicated, and not from the illegal *act* itself. This explains in some measure the fact that, although the injury which gives rise to a violation is in reality objective in character, it is treated as if it were purely subjective violation of right. The subjective character arises from the dual character of any injury which gives rise to an international obligation. Similarly in municipal law we may have an act which gives rise on the one hand to a civil liability and on the other to a criminal responsibility" (Goebel, *supra* note 7, at p. 810).

[185] Commission established under the convention of July 4, 1868, docket 7 as cited in Whiteman, *supra* note 78, Vol. I, at 412.

[186] Whiteman, *supra* note 78, Vol. I, at 415.

[187] Moore, *supra* note 15, at pp. 2064–2065.

international tribunal was whether Colombia was bound by international law to indemnify Great Britain for the injury to the claimant (and, if so, by how much).[188] Scruggs explained that the underlying judicial corruption was an exclusively domestic matter, but its subsequent cover-up by the Colombian government constituted a basis for an international claim.[189] Which injury, then, was the indemnification aimed at remedying: the wrongful seizure, the subsequent cover-up or both? Of the ten "principles of responsibility" articulated by the international tribunal, none directly addresses this basic question.[190]

The indemnification approach is also reflected in contemporary doctrinal writings on alien protection. Textbooks refer to principles of "damages" or

[188] *Ibid*, at p. 2056.

[189] *Ibid*, at p. 2053. Umpire Casimir Troplong (the French *Chargé d'Affaires*) and the tribunal agreed that "by pardoning a criminal, a nation assumes the responsibility for his past acts (*ibid*, at p. 2085).

[190] This type of irregularity was later described by Hersch Lauterpacht as the central problem of borrowing principles of liability from private law. See Lauterpacht, *supra* note 148, at p. 135 ("A historical survey of the treatment of this problem shows . . . the adoption of the private law principle in the formative period of international law, its beneficial effect upon international relations, its acceptance by the common opinion of writers and by the practice of States, and, lastly, its rejection as a misleading private law analogy by a number of positivists writers on the ground of the special character of international law"). Indeed, focusing on factual issues rather than moral ones did not prevent legal inconsistencies. It was less controversial to rely on established quanta of injury than to expound upon principles of responsibility. Even when the injury under discussion was not directly related to the wrong committed by the state. As Whiteman observed: "The damages may be calculated on the basis of an extraneous matter not affecting the responsibility of the respondent state in the first instance" (Whiteman, *supra* note 78, vol. 1, at pp. 519–520). Instead, they often deduced liability from the juridical fact of breach (*ibid*, at p. 34: "Arbitrators are apt to agree on the amount to be allowed but to disagree on the reasons for allowing the particular amount."). Thus, by simply requiring states to pay a fee, tribunals refrained from blaming states for wrongs. Occasionally, international awards were issued for "non-material" damages, including intangible *private* damage (*e.g.*, wrongful death) and *public* injuries (*e.g.*, diplomatic indignities). *See ibid* at pp. 83, 519; see also *Kellett*, in Moore, *supra* note 15, Vol. 2, at pp. 1862–1864. But *see S.S. "I'm Alone" (Can. v. US), 3 R.I.A.A. 1609 (1935) (US–UK 1935).* The awards were even inconsistent regarding "material" losses ("The problem of measuring the extent of the physical or mental impairment of the claimant and of assessing an appropriate monetary indemnity for such injury is, of course, exceedingly difficult" (Whiteman, *supra* note 78, Vol. I, at 519). When assessing liability for a state's failure to prosecute wrongful death, tribunals awarded damages in amounts ranging from U.S. $5,000 (*e.g.*, US national in Mexico) (Case of *Louise O. Canahl* (United States v. Mexico), *Opinions of the Commissioners* (1929) 90, docket 593 as cited in Whiteman, *supra* note 78, Vol. 1, at p. 54) to US$ 50,000 (*e.g.*, US missionary in Persia) (Case of *Mary Schauffler Labaree* as cited in Whiteman, *supra* note 78, Vol. I, at p. 63). This irregularity is particularly noticeable in the awards issuing damages for bodily injuries (as opposed to property losses).

"remedies" rather than "liability" or "responsibility." Even when a writer attempts to induce principles of remedies, disclaimers abound regarding their dissimilarity to international practice. For example, in 1937, Green Hackworth felt comfortable stating, in his "Forward" to Marjory Whiteman's *Damages in International Law*:

> At no time in the history of the United States, if not in all history, has there been brought together such a wealth of useful material as is presented in this treatise, wherein the primary emphasis is placed upon the measurement of damages in international claims as distinguished from the general responsibility giving rise to such claims.[191]

As Whiteman concedes in the opening of her book, "The study does not propose to be a handbook … Rather, the cases are indicative of how reasonable men have measured damages in a variety of circumstances."[192] Arbitrators were careful to be seen as doing their best. It was clear to Whiteman that no one at the time – not arbitrators, foreign officers or writers – could distinguish between the reasons underlying awards (principles of responsibility) and reasons for the amounts of the award (principles of damages). The term "damage," then, was generally used in its broad sense to include any indemnity for loss, injury, costs, etc.[193] The focus on damages injuries reflected an indemnification rather than a "responsibility approach" to alien protection claims.

The Traditionality of *Chorzów*

International arbitrators were often local diplomats who happened to be lawyers (*see* Table 3.1). As attorneys they were well-equipped to resolve private remedial issues but also adept at being mindful of public sensitivities. Great efforts were taken to emphasize the dignified nature of a *compromis* and suppressed the doctrinal implications of the dispute.[194] It was this model of international remedies that the Permanent

191 Green H. Hackworth, "Foreword," in Whiteman, *supra* note 78, Vol. I, at p. *iii*.

192 Whiteman, *supra* note 78, Vol. I, at p. *v*; in the view of Jean Ho, the awards were more "harmonious than haphazard" (Jean Ho, *State Responsibility for Breaches of Investment Contracts* (Cambridge: Cambridge University Press, 2018), at p. 4).

193 *Ibid*, at p. *vi*.

194 *Ibid*, at p. 31: In a typically sanctimonious passage, Moore writes, "Among an enlightened and Christian people the spirit of revenge, discarded, as it is, in laws for the government of men in their private relations, can still less be adopted as a principle of public conduct. For, just in proportion as the responsibility of nations are greater and more solemn than those of private individuals, in that proportion are nations bound to exceed the measure of private virtue in their efforts to hasten the era of peace."

Table 3.1 *Draft list of US arbitrations of alien injuries (1794–1902)*[1]

Date of treaty	Counter-State to US	Commission	Included lawyer?	Umpire/Arbitrator
11/19/1794	Great Britain	British Claims Commission	No	John Guillemard
11/19/1794	Great Britain	Mixed Claims Commission	No	John Trumbull
7/12/1822	Great Britain	Mixed Claims Commission	No	Emperor of Russia
4/11/1839	Mexico	Mixed Claims Commission	No	Baron Von Róenne
2/26/1851	Portugal	Mixed Claims Commission	No	President of France
2/8/1853	Great Britain	Mixed Claims Commission	No	Joshua Bates
6/5/1854	Great Britain	Specific issue (fishing)	No	John Hamilton Gray
9/10/1857	New Granada	US Claims Commission	No	N. G. Upham
11/10/1858	Chile	Specific claim	No	King of Belgium
2/4/1859	Paraguay	Specific claims; treaty corrections	No	None
7/2/1860	Costa Rica	US Claims Commission	No	Chevalier Joseph Bertinatti
12/20/1862	Peru	Specific claims	No	King of Belgium
11/25/1862	Ecuador	Mixed Claims Commission	Yes	Alcides Destruge
1/12/1863	Peru	Mixed Claims Commission	No	Pedro Aleantara Herran
7/1/1863	Great Britain	Specific claims	Yes	Benjamin Robbins Curtis
4/25/1866	Venezuela	Mixed Claims Commission	No	Juan N. Machado
7/4/1868	Mexico	Mixed Claims Commission	Yes	Francis Lieber, Sir Edward Thornton
12/4/1868	Peru	Mixed Claims Commission	No	Federico Augusto Elmore, Teodoro Valenzuela
3/14/1870	Brazil	Specific Claim	Yes	Sir Edward Thornton
2/12/1871	Spain	US Claims Commission	No	M. Bartholdi

Table 3.1 (*cont.*)

Date of treaty	Counter-State to US	Commission	Included lawyer?	Umpire/Arbitrator
5/8/1871	Great Britain	Specific claims	Yes	Sir Alexander Cockburn, Charles Francis Adams, Federico Sclopis, Jakob Stämpfli, Marcos Antônio de Araújo
5/8/1871	Great Britain	Mixed Claims Commission	No	Count Louis Corti
5/8/1871	Great Britain	Specific claim	No	Maurice Delfosse
8/17/1874	Colombia	Specific claim	Yes	Robert Bunch
1/15/1880	France	Mixed Claims Commission	No	Baren de Arinos
5/24/1884	Hayti	Specific claims	Yes	William Strong
12/5/1885	Venezuela	Mixed Claims Commission	Yes	Samuel F. Phillips, John V. L. Findlay
5/24/1888	Hayti	Specific claim	Yes	Alexander Porter Morse
12/6/1888	Denmark	Specific claims	Yes	Sir Edmund J. Monson
1/19/1892	Venezuela	Specific claims	Yes	Johann Anton Wolff Grip
8/7/1892	Chile	Mixed Claims Commission	No	Alfred de Claparede
2/28/1893	Ecuador	Specific claim	No	Alfred St. John
3/2/1897	Mexico	Specific claim	Yes	Vicente G. Quesada
5/17/1898	Peru	Specific claim	Yes	Samuel Henry Strong
22/5/1902	Mexico	Specific claim	Yes	Henning Matzen, Edward Fry, Friedrich Martens, Tobias Michael Carel Asser, A. F. De Savornin Lohman

[1] For an exhaustive list of intra-American arbitration treaties, *see* William R. Manning, (ed.), *Arbitration Treaties Among the American Nations to the Close of the Year 1910* (New York: Oxford University Press, 1924). *See also* John Barrett, *The Pan American Union: Peace, Friendship, Commerce* (Washington, DC: Pan American Union, 1911), at pp. 243–249.

Court of International Justice crystalized in the *Case Concerning the Factory at Chorzów* (1928).

In *Chorzów,* one of the most frequently cited precedents of state responsibility, the Swiss judge and lawyer-diplomat Max Huber

(1874–1960) identifies a customary international law of remedies in the early international arbitrations. He states:

> [I]t is a principle of international law, even a general conception of law, that any breach of an engagement involved an obligation to make reparation.[195]

This passage summarizes the "indemnification approach" of New World arbitrations. It was based expressly on state practice without analyzing that practice and on general principles of law without evaluating those principles. It reflects the US position on state responsibility for alien protection as remedies for private injuries. How individuals were entitled to seek those remedies against states was more assumed than analyzed.[196] To *international* arbitrators, the pull of applying an *international* as opposed to a domestic standard was obvious. And given that international arbitrators were typically Western-trained, they were predisposed to viewing alien protection in domestic legal terms.[197] In listing the "various sources of international law," Wheaton ranked as first:

> 1. Text-writers of authority, showing what is the approved usage of nations, or the general opinion respecting their mutual conduct, with the definitions and modifications introduced by general consent.[198]

[195] Permanent Court of International Justice, Series A (1928), at p. 46. Similarly (and slightly earlier), in *Chapman*, the mixed (US–Mexican) tribunal stated: "Correlative rights and obligations on the part of each member of the family of nations are derived from international law" (*William E. Chapman (U.S.A.) v. United Mexican States 4 R.I.A.A.* 643 (1930), 637).

[196] Although the "Vattelian fiction" (that the individual injury was effectively transformed into the state's injury upon exhaustion of local remedies, etc.) was an oft-repeated mantra – *see* Annemarieke Vermeer-Künzli, "As If: The Legal Fiction in Diplomatic Protection," 18(1) *European Journal of International Law* 37 (2007).

[197] Martti Koskenniemi, "General Principles: Reflexions on Constructivist Thought in International Law," 18 *Oikeustiede-Jurisprudentia* 117 (1985), at p. 157 (footnotes omitted).

[198] Henry Wheaton, *Elements of International Law* (4th ed., London: Stevens & Sons Ltd., 1904), at §15, p. 24. *See also* John Westlake, "Relations between Public and Private International Law" (1865), in Lassa Oppenheim (ed.), *Collected Papers of John Westlake* (Cambridge: Cambridge University Press, 1914), at p. 287; Theodor D. Woolsey, *Introduction to the Study of International Law* (5th ed., London: Sampson, 1879), p. 13; *see further* Sabahi, *supra* note 67, at p. 39 (on common training in Roman law). *See also* Hersch Lauterpacht, *Private Law Sources and Analogies of International Law: With Special Reference to International Arbitration* (London: Longmans, Green and Co., 1927), at p. 215 (international arbitrations, "one after another . . . shatter the fiction of an international law totally independent of conception and rules of private law" (footnotes

Just as it was assumed that "someone ought to pay" for the injury, it was taken for granted that property rights were as safeguarded by international law as they were by domestic law. The protection of property, like the respect for sovereignty, was a fundamental belief.[199] Anglo-American lawyers canonized "property rights" within their domestic legal codes during the late nineteenth-century.[200] It has been said that doing the same globally was international law's "noblest triumph."[201] Of course, it has also been said that the establishment of state responsibility for alien injuries has legitimated international law's dark underbelly of imperialism.[202] A careful reading of the awards reveals imprints of both interpretations.

omitted)). On the preference of general principles over treaties or custom, *see* Frederick Pollock, "Sources of International Law," 2 *Columbia Law Review* 511 (1902), at pp. 515–517 available online at: www.google.com/books/edition/The_Law_of_Torts/atUzAAAAIAAJ?hl=en&gbpv=0 (it is generally not practicable to make a general statement regarding the Law of Nations based on treaties or conventions because they are merely binding on the parties to them). On the legal origins of the public/private distinction in Anglo-American law, *see* Morton J. Horwitz, "The History of the Public/Private Distinction," 130 *University of Pennsylvania Law Review* 1423 (1982), at p. 1424: "One of the central goals of nineteenth century legal thought was to create a clear separation between constitutional, criminal, and regulatory law-public law-and the law of private transactions-torts, contracts, property, and commercial law." An analysis on the public/private distinction of international arbitral awards is outside the scope of this project; I discuss the topic in Alan Nissel, "The Dichotomization of International Law," (unpublished paper on file with author).

199 Recourse to evaluative statements on state responsibility for alien injuries implied a background theory that either supported or opposed Western values. *See* Koskenniemi, *supra* note 26, chs. 9–10 (a legacy of British imperialism was that the capitalistic protection of property would become an element of international sovereignty); James W. Ely, Jr., "Property Rights and the Supreme Court in the Gilded Age," 38(3) *Journal of Supreme Court History* 330 (2013) (the Court was animated to protect the rights of property owners as a means of upholding individual liberty against governmental overreaching. The justices saw private property as essential for the enjoyment of liberty).

200 "Property Rights" became term of art in the postbellum era according to legal historian G. Edward White, *American Legal History: A Very Short Introduction* (New York: Oxford University Press, 2013), at p. 38.

201 Tom Bethell, *The Noblest Triumph: Property and Prosperity through the Ages* (New York: St. Martin's Press, 1998), at p. 100; *see also*, regarding international investment protection, Christopher A. Casey, *National Abroad: Globalization, Individual Rights, and the Making of Modern International Law* (Cambridge: Cambridge University Press, 2020), at p. 179.

202 Antony Anghie, "Finding the Peripheries: Sovereignty and Colonialism in Nineteenth-Century International Law," 40 *Harvard International Law Journal* 1 (1990), at p. 73.

The Lieber Tribunal itself expressly promoted the "cultivation" of foreign-owned land.[203] In the *Stückle* case, which concerned a private contract with the *de facto* government in Yucatán, the Lieber Tribunal provided a rare glimpse of the Western arbitrator's value system:

> Men are so made that the divine law of interdependence shall keep them united in society and there is no grander expression of a fundamental principle in jurisprudence than the old *Ubi Societas Ibi Jus*. Man must produce, appropriate and exchange, and he is destined, obliged and commanded to create and own individual property; the more distinctly so the further he succeeds in removing from the communistic state of the savage.[204]

Although arbitrators were rarely of the same nationality as litigant states, they all shared key Western values, especially regarding the protection of property. In two of the most famous Anglo-American awards, *Alabama Claims* and *Trail Smelter*, the tribunals were explicit about their reliance on domestic legal analogies.[205] The Alabama Tribunal defined the now famous "three rules" of international due diligence law based on general principles of the Common Law.[206] In the 1930's *Trail Smelter* case, the tribunal borrowed the Anglo-American tort of trespass to impose liability on Canada for cross-boundary environmental harm.[207] Employing general principles necessarily depended on arbitrators' backgrounds.[208] As British international lawyer Sir Humphrey Waldock

[203] Whiteman, *supra* note 78, Vol. II, at p. 1356.

[204] *Stückle's Case* of July 19, 1871, *FW Stückle v. Mexico No 901* convention of July 4, 1868, as reproduced in Moore, *supra* note 15, at p. 2936.

[205] *E.g., Trail Smelter Case (United States of America v. Canada), 3 R.I.A.A.* 1905 (1941), at p. 1950.

[206] *Alabama Claims*, *supra* note 63.

[207] *Trail Smelter*, *supra* note 206, at p. 1931.

[208] International arbitrators employed, customized or hybridized whatever rules, principles and standards to achieve this purpose – *see* Zachary Douglas, "The Hybrid Foundations of Investment Treaty Arbitration," 74 *British Yearbook of International Law* 151 (2003), at p. 185. As Lauterpacht states, the five Anglo-American nineteenth-century arbitrations demonstrate the heavy reliance of international litigation on private rules of law (*supra* note 148, at p. 215). Another example of this phenomenon is that international arbitrators would restrict damages based on Anglo-American tort law, including the distinction between "direct" and "indirect" injuries arising from a breach of a duty in question (Whiteman, *supra* note 78, Vol. III, at pp. 1767–1780. *See also* Koskenniemi, *supra* note 194, at pp. 141, 157; Michael Waibel, "Interpretive Communities in International Law," in A. Bianchi, D. Peat and M. Windsor (eds.), *Interpretation in International Law* 147 (Oxford: Oxford University Press, 2015), at p. 147: "The meaning of international law norms hinges on background principles shared by interpreters who form part of one or several interpretive communities."

(1904–1981) confided: "Truth to tell, arbitral tribunals . . . have probably done no more in most cases than take into account their own knowledge of the principles of the systems in which the arbitrators were themselves trained."[209]

However, in the process, professionalized arbitration translated the politics of capitalism and imperialism into a legal regime of investment protection. It rebranded the imperial origins of those standards and presented them as "international" instead. International tribunals regularly applied *international* standards to alien protection claims.[210] In so doing, arbitrators reformulated the "standard of civilization" into the "international law" of alien protection. This allowed twentieth-century lawyers such as Hersch Lauterpacht[211] and the UN International Law Commission[212] to reject the European "*standard of civilization*" for the purposes of recognition but to retain the *international legal* standard of alien protection. The latter was baptized as the *International Minimum Standard* (IMS).[213] By suppressing a discussion of the values of

[209] Sir Humphrey Waldock, "General Course on Public International Law," 106 *Recueil Des Cours* 1 (1962), at p. 66.

[210] This is not surprising if for no other reason that the forum in which such decisions were made was an international one. Latin Americans may have "lost" this debate the moment it was delegated to an international body.

[211] Lauterpacht said that "Modern international law knows . . . of no distinction, for the purposes of recognition, between civilised and uncivilised States within and outside the international community of civilised states" (Hersch Lauterpacht, *Recognition in International Law* (Cambridge: Cambridge University Press, 1947), at p. 31).

[212] The International Law Commission of the UN expressed that it would no longer use the term "civilized" because it was a term that "dated back to the colonial era with its concept of the 'white man's burden'" (UN ILC Yearbook (1949), at p. 170).

[213] In addition to state responsibility, another term that was coined in the interwar era was the "international minimum standard." This standard was not only applicable to the protection of aliens, but to people in general: prisoners, seamen, laborers, etc. As I explain later in the book, the move to institutions, and the corresponding project of codification, resulted in lengthy debates over legal doctrine. Although the doctrine of state responsibility for alien protection failed to be codified multilaterally, it lived on in the new, commercialized garment of "investment protection." Unlike international trade, which continued to be a fertile ground for multilateral treaty-making, investment protection would survive as a bilateral affair. After the Second World War, states entered into thousands of Bilateral Investment Treaties (BITs) with developing (including Latin American) nations, to protect the investments of their nationals abroad. The first BIT was entered into (by Germany and Pakistan) in 1959, again indicating the significance of decolonization on the law and diplomacy of both alien protection in particular and state responsibility in general.

"civilization," international arbitrators decoupled alien protection from the European "civilization" project. The latter was discredited and dropped, whereas the former continues to be affirmed as international law.[214] This remains a legacy of the Lieber Tribunal on state responsibility.[215]

New Responsibility for the New World

US investors, of course, continue to file claims against Mexico for breaching the IMS. In this sense, the arbitral history of US and Mexico during the nineteenth and twentieth centuries is a microcosm of the intra-American practice of state responsibility.[216] As time went on, the IMS became increasingly contested as well as articulated. In the first Mixed Claims Commission between the two countries (established in 1839), US arbitrators generally agreed that "if Mexico wished to maintain rank and fellowship among civilized nations of the earth, she must place

[214] The content of the standard was regularly being changed – different for the Ottoman Empire in 1856 than it was for Japan in 1905. But, according to Gong, "By 1905 [when Japan gained recognition as a 'civilized' State], at the latest, a standard of 'civilization' had emerged as an explicit legal principle and an integral part of the doctrines of international law prevailing at the time" (Gong, *supra* note 2, at p. 14). This standard only arose in the 1948 Havana convention – *see generally* Alexander Orakhelashvili, "The Normative Basis of 'Fair and Equitable Treatment': General International Law on Foreign Investment?" 46(1) *Archiv des Völkerrechts* 74 (2008). *See also* Todd Weiler, "The Interpretation of International Investment Law: Equality, Discrimination and Minimum Standards of Treatment in Historical Context" (Eduardo Valencia-Ospina and Loretta Malintoppi, eds., Leiden: Martinus Nijhoff, 2013), at p. 17 (the protection and security and fair and equitable treatment standards are both part of the customary international law minimum standard of treatment of aliens (CILMSTA), and thus, neither standard portends a meaning independent from that which is intended under CILMSTA).

[215] In his final report on the Lieber Tribunal to Hamilton Fish, the US agent, Joseph Hubley Aston, wrote: "The commissioners deemed it proper, at the outset of their labors, to give reasons for their judgments and action, in carefully prepared opinions; and this practice was followed by each of the gentlemen who acted as umpire. The opinions of the commissioners and the umpire are recorded, and they will be found to contain valuable contributions to the law of international reclamations" (Moore, *supra* note 15, at p. 1299).

[216] For a discussion of Vitoria and how the New World was historically the situs of a newly secularized law of nations, *see* Bowden, *supra* note 46, at pp. 112–124. Regarding the transition from natural to positive law in Anglo-American jurisprudence in the late nineteenth and early twentieth centuries, *see* Stuart Banner, *The Decline of Natural Law: How American Lawyers Once Used Natural Law and Why They Stopped* (Oxford: Oxford University Press, 2021).

her laws on the footing with other nations so far as related to the intercourse with foreigners."[217] In the second US–Mexico Mixed Claims Commission (established in 1868), Umpire Lieber upheld the same reasoning for attributing state responsibility for injuries to aliens.[218] Common to rulings by both of the first two commissions was a comfort level about the needlessness of explaining – let alone justifying – the international legal duty to protect aliens.[219]

However, in the third US–Mexico Mixed Claims Commission (established in 1923), Commissioner Fred K. Nielsen (1879–1963) found it necessary in the 1926 *Neer Case* to articulate the international duty in greater detail.[220] While his purported definition ("a pronounced degree of improper governmental administration") was an improvement, it was still imprecise and formulated in the negative.[221] Similarly, in the 1924 *Janes Case*, Commissioner Nielson awarded an indemnity for the death of a man when Mexico desisted from prosecuting the likely murderer. After expansively interpreting "loss" to include feelings of grief, mistrust and lack of safety, he went out of his way to reject "the old ways" of the past when exaggerated claims were made and granted. The "new" way, he

[217] *Dr. John Baldwin v. Mexico*, Award of February 23, 1842 under the convention between the United States and Mexico of April 11, 1839, in Moore, *supra* note 15, at p. 3238. The US commissioners referred (and the umpire, Baron Von Róenne, Prussian minister to Washington, agreed) to the *Meade* claim against Spain for the purpose of showing an acknowledgment by Spain of liability for the palpable misconduct of judicial tribunals.

[218] For example, in *Halstead's Case*, Lieber held that the wrongful detainment of a US businessman in Colima (for being without a passport), was "plainly not according to right and justice" (*A. H. Halstead v. Mexico*, No. 18, Convention of July 4, 1868, MS. Op. I, 231, as reproduced in Moore, *supra* note 15, at p. 3244).

[219] In the words of US Secretary of State Evarts, if the Mexican government "confesses itself unable or unwilling to conform to those international obligations which must exist between established governments of friendly states, it would thereby confess that it is not entitled to be regarded or recognized as a sovereign and independent Power" (Evarts to Foster, August 2, 1877, MS. Instructions, Mexico XIX 357, as cited in Amos J. Peaslee, "The Sanction of International Law," 10(2) *American Journal of International Law* 328 (1916), at p. 334).

[220] The international standard is really the duty to protect aliens fairly and the violation of which is termed (broadly speaking) a "denial of justice," and justifies "diplomatic intervention" (*L. F. H. Neer and Pauline Neer (U.S.A.) v. United Mexican States*, IV *Recueil des sentences arbitrales* 60–66, October 15, 1926, at p. 64). According to the *Neer* commission: "there is a long way between holding that a more active and more efficient course of procedure might have been pursued, on the one hand, and holding that this record presents such lack of diligence and of intelligent investigation as constitutes an international delinquency, on the other hand" (*ibid*, at p. 61). That "way," however, seems to have been impossible for lawyers to define (*ibid*, at pp. 61–62).

[221] *Ibid*, at p. 65.

said, was to be more precise and contextual.[222] But a yardstick by which the wrongfulness of claims could be measured predictably never materialized.

Chorzów and *Chattin*, the *Neer* and *Janes Cases* remain classical sources of state responsibility.[223] As the rate of international arbitrations increased, publicists updated their commentaries.[224] In his analysis of successive editions of Wheaton's *Elements of International Law*, Gerrit Gong found that the opaque "standard of civilization" was progressively articulated in disputes between the West and other states.[225] Resolving alien protection claims was a difficult one for legal commentators to explain.[226] Doctrinal writings reflect a normative gap between the stated purposes of international obligations and the actual arbitral awards for violating those obligations. These "responsibility gaps" reflected the ultimate purpose of state responsibility for alien protection claims – settling private claims effectively but not systematically.[227]

[222] *See Laura M. B. Janes et al.* (United States v. Mexico), *Opinions of the Commissioners* (1927) 118–119, docket 168.

[223] *Factory at Chorzów (Germany v. Poland),* 1928 P.C.I.J. (ser. A, No. 17), discussed above; *B. E. Chattin v. The United Mexican States,* 4 R.I.A.A. 282, 286–287 (1927). Interestingly there is no casebook on state responsibility and no academic study to my knowledge on the most frequently cited cases and awards in the field of state responsibility. Regarding how the international arbitration regime evolved into a tightly networked judicial system based on precedent, *see* Yarik Kryvoi, "The Path of Investor-State Disputes: From Compensation Commissions to Arbitral Institutions," 3 *ICSID Review: Foreign Investment Law Journal* 33 (2018), at pp. 743, 744.

[224] While natural lawyers such as Grotius and Vattel struggled with the difficulty of ascertaining the content of a state's international responsibility for injuries to aliens, no distinct approach can be found in the prehistory of state responsibility – *see* William Oke Manning, *Commentaries on the Law of Nations*, (Sheldon Amos, ed., London: H. Sweet, 1875), at p. 169; Goebel, *supra* note 177, at p. 811; Clyde Eagleton, "Measures of Damages in International Law," 39 *Yale Law Journal* 52 (1929), at pp. 54–55. I hasten to add that such "gaps" are not unique to international law – *see* Jeremy Waldron, "The Rule of International Law," 30 *Harvard Journal of Law & Public Policy* 15 (2006), at p. 16.

[225] Gong, *supra* note 2, at p. 27, emphasis added. See also Nicholas Onuf, "Henry Wheaton and 'The Golden Age of International Law,'" 6 *International Legal Theory* 2–9 (2000), at p. 4. As Nicholas Onuf has written, they key to his achievement was "Wheaton's doctrinal genealogy."

[226] This combination led one early commentator to remark, "It is hard to draw definite legal conclusions about a subject which is half diplomatic and half legal and about which nations feel so strongly" (Lionel Morgan Summers, "The Calvo Clause," 19 *Virginia Law Review* 459 (1933), at p. 482).

[227] *See* Alan Nissel, "Two Visions of Institutionalizing Peace: Too Much Too Soon and Too Little Too Late," (unpublished paper on file with author). Even US commentators have recognized this. For a survey of the inconsistent arbitral practice of awarding damages

To Clyde Eagleton (1891–1958), one of the first to write on the doctrine of state responsibility, the early awards looked like "a chaos of interpretation."[228] Another major US commentator on American arbitrations, Marjorie Whiteman, concluded,

> those charged with the settlement of claims frequently fail to state the basis of the responsibility in a particular claim ... there is a failure to distinguish between and explain what was measured in fixing the indemnity, as distinguished from why any amount was allowed.[229]

The fact that Whiteman, with her boss, Legal Advisor Green Hackworth's backing, wrote her treatise on *Damages in International Law* without discussing principles of responsibility reflects the unprincipled state of the practice.[230] It also signifies a distinctly US approach to state responsibility; it was *ad hoc* rather than systematic,[231] focused on indemnification more than culpability.

The early rules on state responsibility hardly comprised a coherent doctrine. They arose as a byproduct of *ad hoc* litigation rather than negotiated legislation. In fact, prior to the twentieth century, there was no State Department policy of either professionalizing arbitration or codifying international law. John Bassett Moore, the most important

see Whiteman, *supra* note 78, at pp. 383–385, 408. For a critique of the historical manner in which the law of attribution depended more on the age than on the conduct of States – *see* Hessbruegge, *supra* note 161, at pp. 292–303.

228 Eagleton, *supra* note 42, at pp. 22–23. Eagleton continues: "It is here suggested that the chief cause of the inconsistencies found in writers, and among statesmen and international tribunals as well, is uncertainty as to the exact bearing of the word responsibility itself."

229 Whiteman, *supra* note 78, Vol. I, at p. 385. Similarly, in his "Foreword" to Whiteman's just cited *Damages in International Law*, Green Hackworth (1883–1973), then the Legal Advisor the US Secretary of State (and later the first US judge on the International Court of Justice) wrote: "At no time in the history of the United States, if not in all history, has there been brought together such a wealth of useful material as is presented in this treatise, wherein the primary emphasis is placed upon the measurement of damages in international claims as distinguished from the general responsibility giving rise to such claims" (*ibid*, at p. *iii*).

230 While Whiteman does claim that general principles of damages can be extrapolated from the early international awards, her study is riddled with disclaimers to that assertion (Whiteman, *supra* note 78, Vol. I, at pp. *iii*, *v*, 276, 284, 519). *See also supra* note 187 and accompanying text.

231 For a quantified view of the inconsistent arbitral practice of awarding damages *see* Whiteman, *supra* note 78, at pp. 383–385, 408. Similarly, states were responsible for attributable violations of international law, but the manner in which those breaches were attributed often depended more on the identity than on the conduct of states – *see* Hessbruegge, *supra* note 161, at pp. 292–303.

international lawyer in the State Department at the time, seems to have been totally unaware of any such policy.[232] The US lobbied for secure effective remedies for alien injuries, but not a legal doctrine of state responsibility for violations of any international law. The purpose was simply to improve the position of its nationals abroad as and when they were injured.[233] As James Crawford and Tom Grant note:

> [I]f State responsibility was the result of a bargain between States, it was an *unspoken bargain, a jural construction*: there is little evidence of undertakings between States seen as giving rise to any *general* relation of responsibility.[234]

Creating Room for Argument

The novelty of the American practice was its legal professionalism. By delegating its international claims to third parties to be resolved, the US created new room for argument. More than creating a clear substantive doctrine of international enforcement, this professional practice produced an opportunity for peaceful dispute resolution based on binding rules of law. From the Lieber Tribunal of 1868 onwards, international claims would be increasingly resolved by recourse to third-party tribunals (*1st element*) composed of one or more professional lawyers (*2nd element*) who are authorized to issue binding awards (*3rd element*) based on legal rules (*4th element*). By relying on lawyers instead of diplomats to

232 *See, e.g.*, John Bassett Moore, *International Adjudication. Ancient and Modern History and Documents Together with Mediatorial Reports, Advisory Opinions and the Decisions of Domestic Commissions on International Claims,* Modern Series (New York: Oxford University Press, 1929), Vol. I, at p. *viii*. Moore was supposed to update Wharton's international law digest (*supra* note 48), which was anticipated to be a minor task. When it transpired that the work, because of an explosion in US arbitral practice, would be much larger in scope, Congress authorized Moore to undertake a new, broader project.

233 *See generally* Benton and Ford, *supra* note 89, at pp. 85–116 (a touchstone of the Anglo-American view of sovereignty by the nineteenth century was the global protection of nationals but the form that such protection took was sufficiently flexible to allow for an array of jurisdictional claims over the poor and oppressed at home and subjects and foreigners abroad); *see also* Lisa Ford, "Protecting the Peace on the Edges of Empire: Commissioners of Crown Lands in New South Wales," in Lauren Benton, Adam Clulow and Victoria Bain Attwood (eds.), *Protection and Empire: A Global History* 175 (Cambridge: Cambridge University Press, 2018), at p. 178.

234 James Crawford and Tom Grant, "Responsibility of States for Injuries to Foreigners," in J. P. Grant and J. C. Barker (eds), *The Harvard Research in International Law: Contemporary Analysis and Appraisal* 77–126 (Buffalo: W. S. Hein, 2007), at p. 84; James Crawford, *State Responsibility: The General Part* (Cambridge: Cambridge University Press, 2013), at p. 26 (emphasis added).

resolve disputes, the US generated an intermediary space within which to measure international wrongs.

Indeed, state responsibility is a doctrine of "second opinions" more than one of measured culpability. In one of his last articles published, NYU law professor Thomas Franck (1931–2009) highlights the significance of litigation to the development of international law. The move from dyadic diplomacy to triadic arbitration, he writes, opens up the opportunity for independent law-making – what he terms "second opinions."[235] The more states made recourse to international arbitration, the more they caused the creation of international rules: "case by case, it has shed much of its indeterminacy."[236] By the twentieth century, findings of liability signified an increasingly sophisticated framework of secondary principles that were triggered upon the event of a state breaching its international duties.[237]

As arbitration spread globally, the US lost control over its underlying legal principles. That this aspect of law-generation went unnoticed by its early promoters explains how it was that the Great Powers – at the height of their influence – accepted legal liability as an acceptable outcome of international dispute resolution.[238] The Western expectation was that attributions of international liability would be effectively limited to other

[235] The US established international arbitration as a *process* "to which a dispute can be referred for a credible opinion to trump and supplant the rival opinions expressed by the disputants" (Thomas M. Franck, "On Proportionality of Counter-Measures in International Law," 102(4) *American Journal of International Law* 715–767 (2008), at p. 717). On the *de facto* legislative role of arbitrators, *see* D. Brian King and Rahim Moloo, "International Arbitrators as Lawmakers," 46 *International Law and Politics* 891 (2014).

[236] Franck, *supra* note 236, at p. 718.

[237] Conceptually speaking, if the underlying obligation that breach was the "primary" law, the set of laws that determined that breach and its remedy were "secondary" laws and the enforcement of those remedies were "tertiary" laws. Thus, in modern terms, principles of international responsibility would no longer be associated with excuses for (*secondary*) enforcement actions but with justification for (*tertiary*) enforcement actions.

[238] According to Eagleton, "While its application to a particular set of circumstances may be disputed, the principle [of binding responsibility] itself is never questioned in the practice of states" (Eagleton, *supra* note 42, at p. 21). In a footnote, Eagleton writes that "There are some international laws that seem to contradict this, but they are not general international law but particular cases of victors' justice – *e.g.*, Article 231 of the Treaty of Versailles and the clauses attempting to hold the Kaiser Wilhelm II personally responsible: Outside of the fact that this would be *ex post facto* action, the subsequent failure of efforts to outlaw war establishes the lack of responsibility under international law." This view is inaccurate. As I discussed in Chapter 2, Great Britain rejected the principle of responsibility in the Treaty of Washington negotiations (the fourth rule).

states. That was not *their* expectation. But by entering into a network of international arbitration agreements with Latin American nations, Western governments unwittingly set themselves up to be judged in the same manner.[239]

The Power of Law

Such is the power of law. The law is not a fixed set of norms.[240] It is a fluid social instrument that is cultivated with every application.[241] Though attorneys employ legal rules to serve the specific, short-term ends of their clients, this strategy can conflict with the long-term ends of the same clients.[242] The State Department's reliance on international arbitration to further US interests in the New World was no exception. Hamilton Fish did not ask Francis Lieber to umpire a US–Mexico mixed claims commission with the intention of codifying international law. But such juridification was the inevitable result. Fish turned to international arbitration to invoke the legitimizing power of law as an instrument of US regional interests. He certainly hoped that international arbitrators would entrench primary international rules regarding alien protection, but not that they would articulate secondary rules of liability for breaching that standard.

The US mistake was in viewing international law merely as a diplomatic tool and not as a social framework. Both the North and the South employed international law to serve their particular agendas.[243] As Arnulf Becker Lorca writes,

> The term universality … describes a profound transformation in the nature and function of the international legal order itself: although

[239] US diplomats could choose the arbitrators, but they could not write the arbitral awards.

[240] A literal meaning of "law" is something "laid down" or fixed" ("Law." Oxford Dictionaries. April 2010. Oxford University Press. January 13, 2012), a quality that is manifestly present in the English term "statute" or the German "Gesetz" (which can also be translated as "laid down").

[241] For a wonderful recapitulation of his argument on the power of language and legal imagination to fuel political change, *see* the final chapter of Koskenniemi, *supra* note 26, "Conclusion and Epilogue."

[242] *See* Sally Engle Mary, *Colonizing Hawai'i: The Cultural Power of Law* (Princeton: Princeton University Press, 2000), at p. 265.

[243] The same language of international law is used to conserve and empower the position of all states. *See* Martti Koskenniemi, *Histories of International Law: Dealing with Eurocentrism*, Inaugural Lecture delivered on November 16, 2011 on the occasion of accepting the Treaty of Utrecht Chair at Utrecht University (on file with author), at p. 14; John Fabian Witt, *Lincoln's Code: The Laws of War in American History* (New York: Free Press, 2012), at p. 4.

> international law continued enabling Western powers' global, political, and economic intervention, it also began regulating and to some extent limiting the power of Western states, governing the interactions between independent political organizations on a global scale.[244]

From the Latin American perspective, as discussed, responsibility was the antithesis of sovereignty. It was capitulation. But because its protection was both *ad hoc* and legalistic, the US was able to cover up its imperial interests in a cloak of liberalism.[245] Anglo-Americans described responsibility as the correlative of sovereignty. The willingness and ability to observe preexisting international laws was viewed as a prerequisite to civilized (or international) society. To be recognized, a state had to be diplomatically, commercially and administratively viable. *It had to be trustworthy*. Property had to be protected.[246] This was the cost of entry to international society.[247]

244 Arnulf Becker Lorca, "Universal International Law: Nineteenth-Century Histories of Imposition and Appropriation," 51 *Harvard Journal of International Law* 475 (2010), at p. 478.

245 Notwithstanding US intentions – or its rhetoric of civilization, equality and lawfulness – the structure of *ad hoc* legalism included a real bias in favor of Western nationals. On "bad faith," a structural argument that is independent of consciousness/self-awareness, *see* Duncan Kennedy, *Critique of Adjudication (Fin De Siècle)* (Cambridge, MA: Harvard University Press, 1998), especially ch. 8.

246 On the protection of property as one of the core, minimalist requirements of international society, *see* Rossi, *supra* note 14, at p. 140: ("at a minimal level, international society constrained force (the jus ad bellum and the jus in bello), honored commitments (*pacta sunt servanda*), and acknowledged property in terms of ownership (dominium) and control (imperium). For these pluralists, international society upheld rules of coexistence that states accepted to maintain a functional, operational order").

247 William Edward Hall, one of the first Anglo-American writers on state responsibility, expresses a similar view. He wrote that "The ultimate foundation of international law is an assumption that states possess rights and are subject to duties corresponding to the facts of their postulated nature" (Hall, *supra* note 183, at §7). For a discussion about Great Britain's double-standard regarding state responsibility for alien protection, *see* Moore, *supra* note 15, at pp. 4950–4952; J. Patrick Kelly, "Customary International Law in Historical Context: The Exercise of Power Without General Acceptance," in Brian D. Lepard (ed.), *Reexamining Customary International Law* (Cambridge: Cambridge University Press, 2017), at p. 19 (in the context of *laissez faire* economic policies domestically but not abroad). As Frédéric Mégret writes, the West pursued a long tradition that insisted that periphery countries being "safe for business" was the price for their integration into the international community and they used mixed claims to achieve this end Frédéric Mégret, "Mixed Claim Commissions and the Once Centrality of the Protection of Aliens," in Ignacio de la Rasilla and Jorge E. Viñuales (eds.), *Experiments in International Adjudication: Historical Accounts* 127 (Cambridge: Cambridge University Press, 2019); Greenman, *supra* note 101, at pp. 15–19 (arbitration was about opening Latin American doors to commerce).

In the eyes of Anglo-American arbitrators, imposing responsibility was an implicit recognition of statehood, a diplomatic pat of assurance on the back. Thus, in the *Montijo*, Umpire Robert Bunch (1820–1881) writes:

> Holding a State responsible reflects no disgrace to the nation; on the contrary, the conduct of Colombia, is calculated to advance her reputation in the eyes of the world, as it shows her willingness to adopt, for the solution of difficulties, the enlightened course which has found favor, especially of late years, with powerful countries which could have trusted with confidence to the arbitrament of the sword.[248]

The umpire's position may sound naïve.[249] But Robert Bunch had served as the British minister at Bogotá; also, as consul (and secret agent) in Charlestown during the Civil War, when he was directly involved in the 1861 *Trent Affair*. He was appointed to the British and Spanish Mixed Commission Court in Havana for the abolition of the slave trade. Bunch was an experienced legal hand in the New World. His reasoning reflects a common bias regarding the civilizing purpose of international law.

1907: Latin Americans Move to Organizations

When arbitrators imposed international responsibility on new states, they were not applying a consistent but a double standard of international law: one for the new states and one for the old.[250] While the "standard of civilization" did not originate in Latin America, it assumed a legalistic form there for the first time in the nineteenth century.[251]

[248] *Case of The Montijo*, *supra* note 159, at pp. 1442–1443.

[249] For a more recent articulation of this expectation *see* Louis Henkin, *How Nations Behave: Law and Foreign Policy* (2nd ed., New York: Columbia University Press, 1979), at p. 52: "Every nation's foreign policy depends substantially on its 'credit' – on maintaining the expectation that it will live up to international mores and obligations."

[250] Much has been written on this topic, but mainly in the European context. *See* Grewe, *supra* note 61, at p. 446 (linkage of international law to minimum standards came through the practice of 'unequal' treaties). *See also* Anghie, *supra* note 23, at p. 7 ("The violence of positivist language in relation to non-European peoples is hard to overlook").

[251] During the nineteenth century, twenty-two American treaties mention alien protection with regards to access to courts, beginning with the treaty with Colombia of 1824 and ending with that with Peru of 1887. From 1782 to 1903, twenty-eight treaties included provisions against seizures or detentions, sometimes in relation to embargoes. The 1824 treaty with Colombia specified a "sufficient" indemnification for such cases in addition to seven more treaties (*all with Latin American* countries). See Robert R. Wilson, "Property-Protection Provisions in United States Commercial Treaties," 45 (1) *American Journal of International Law* 83–107 (1951), at pp. 92–93.

Formally, in the New World, all states had the equal obligation to maintain an internal system of legal machinery that measured up to a "vague international standard."[252] But, practically, international tribunals tended to interpret international law to apply state responsibility expansively for new states, but narrowly for established states. Worse, findings of state responsibility for a denial of justice also implied the legally inferior – "semi-civilized" or worse, "uncivilized" – nature of that state.[253] As José Gustavo Guerrero (1876–1958), the first institutional expert on state responsibility, said in 1926, "As between self-respecting states there can be no greater insult than to question the good faith of municipal magistrates in their administration of justice."[254]

By the twentieth century, the field was toxic.[255] Both the International Minimum Standard and state responsibility for its breach were under virulent attack. The historian of international relations Allison Powers Useche analyzed over a century of Mexican–US arbitration through the

[252] Clyde Eagleton, "Denial of Justice in International Law," 22 *American Journal of International Law* 538 (1928), at pp. 538–539. And because this was an *international* standard, respondent states could not use domestic law as a defense. *See, e.g.*, Secretary of State Baynard to Mr Connery, November 1, 1887, *Compilation of Reports of Committee on Foreign Relations, U.S. Senate,* 1887, 751, at p. 753: "If a Government could set up its own municipal laws as the final test of its international rights and obligations, then the rules of international law would be but the shadow of a name, and would afford no protection either to states or to individuals."

[253] But *see* Jeremy Waldron, "The Rule of Law as an Essentially Contested Concept," (March 19, 2021). NYU School of Law, Public Law Research Paper No. 21-15, available at SSRN: https://ssrn.com/abstract=3808198 (how focusing on "rule of law" can lead to a "dialogue of the deaf").

[254] League of Nations, "Report of the Sub-committee of the Committee of Experts for the Progressive Codification of International Law," 20 *American Journal of International Law Special Supplement* 177 (1926), at p. 198. Such criticism was not limited to Latin Americans. Columbia University legal historian Julius Goebel, Jr. (1892–1973) accused the US of being the worst perpetrator of double standards when it came to the legal development of international law (Goebel, *supra* note 177, at p. 851). Goebel accused the US of being "ready to press claims for injuries to its own citizens abroad ... on other hand, this same government has invariably repudiated the principle of responsibility when similar claims have been made upon it and in most instances an indemnity has been granted ... This is due, perhaps, to the traditional belief that *responsibility must first be denied before an indemnity may be paid*" (emphasis added). Hall also criticized the US for its double standards (*supra* note 124, at pp. 218–219, note 1).

[255] Discussed in Chapter 5, but *see* Katherine Van Wezel Stone, "Arbitration – From Sacred Cow to Golden Calf: Three Phases in the History of the Federal Arbitration Act," (May 7, 2021), UCLA School of Law, Public Law Research Paper No. 21-19, available at: https://ssrn.com/abstract=3841808 (how also in the domestic setting, arbitration went from a sacred cow to controversial golden calf).

use of mixed claims commissions. She observes that the diplomatic debates about the appropriate standard of international justice were "vigorous" and, ultimately, irresolvable. After Mexican lawyers persuasively demonstrated how the US legal system itself violated international law, the US sought to unwind the international structure of mixed claims commissions with Mexico. The two countries agreed to pay a lump-sum settlement, whereby Mexico avoided paying the majority of compensation originally demanded by the US, and the US prevented a ruling by an international tribunal on the inadequacy of its own domestic legal system under international law. The 1941 Global Settlement for Mexico seems, in retrospect, to elegantly bookend the early modern era of international arbitration.[256]

Latin American lawyers began the nineteenth century by supporting international arbitration, but they ended the century as its severe opponents. They grew wary of the civilizing rhetoric and especially its arbitral arm.[257] With the establishment of international institutions such as the Permanent Court of Arbitration and League of Nations, Latin Americans were increasingly able to resist US diplomatic power.[258] They did so with the help of their colleagues in Geneva by reinventing state responsibility as a general doctrine based not on the American practice but on German theory. But, as I will discuss in the next two chapters, the decision within the UN to codify state responsibility as a general doctrine of enforcement was *both a reaction to and remains a legacy of* US legalism.

[256] Allison Powers Useche, "The Standard of Civilization on Trial at the United States/Mexico Claims Commission 1923–1937," 1 *Jus Gentium: Journal of International Legal History* 391 (2016), at pp. 398–399; *see also* John Dwyer, *The Agrarian Dispute: The Expropriation of American-Owned Rural Land in Postrevolutionary Mexico* (Durham: Duke University Press, 2008), at pp. 232–266.

[257] Charles Salomon (1862–1936) seems to have been genuinely cynical about the civilizing mission: "No word is more vague and has permitted the commission of more crimes than that of civilization" (*L'occupation des territoires sans maître*. Études de droit international (Paris: Giard, 1889), at p. 195 as quoted in Koskenniemi, *supra* note 33, at p. 106).

[258] Discussed at the end of Chapter 2 and further in Chapter 5.

4

International Responsibility as German Philosophy

1848: *Ordnung* among Revolutions

It was in Germany that state responsibility grew up as an international norm. In a century of failed revolutions and, ultimately, the forging of an empire, German-speaking public lawyers struggled to construct a legal basis for state responsibility. The US practice of international arbitration yielded the first body of positive rules on liability for alien injuries, but the early awards lacked clear doctrines of responsibility. It was only with German systematization of public law that lawyers began to articulate an overarching framework for dealing with state violations of their international obligations. These two narratives of early state responsibility represent the two dominant cultures in international law: US pragmatism and German philosophy.[1]

The road from the US to Germany was not a straight one. For example, in 1871, the US established the first professional international arbitral tribunal under the auspices of Columbia law professor Francis Lieber. Then, in 1899, the Great Powers, led by Russia, founded the Permanent Court of Arbitration. And, finally, in 1920, under the leadership of

[1] Although I focus in this chapter on the distinctly "Germanic" characteristics of the theorization of state responsibility, I also consider the theories of non-Germans as well. Dionisio Anzilotti (1867–1950), an Italian law professor, wrote the first ever treatise on state responsibility in 1902 (Dionisio Anzilotti, *Teoria generale della responsabilità dello Stato nel diritto internazionale*. Parte prima, Il problema della responsabilità di diritto internazionale (Firenze: F. lumachi, 1902)). As Mónica Garcia-Salmones Rovira writes, while the positivism of Oppenheim and Kelsen are quite distinct, both "are better understood as arising from the German philosophical method" (Mónica García-Salmones Rovira, *The Project of Positivism in International Law* (Oxford: Oxford University Press, 2013), at p. 19. More generally, as regards the relationship between German theory and international law, *see* Martti Koskenniemi, *The Gentle Civilizer of Nations: The Rise and Fall of International Law 1870–1960* (Cambridge: Cambridge University Press, 2002), ch. 3, and Martti Koskenniemi, "Between Coordination and Constitution: International Law as a German Discipline," 15 *Redescriptions. Yearbook of Political Thought, Conceptual History and Feminist Theory* 45–70 (2011).

President Wilson, the League of Nations set up the Permanent Court of International Justice (1922) and organized the Committee of Experts (1924). The creation of state responsibility advanced from the US to world bodies in The Hague, but it did so *via* Germany.

In the next two chapters, I shift my focus from North America – where lawyer-diplomats continued to employ international arbitration to resolve alien protection claims – to *Mitteleuropa*, where lawyer-philosophers began to systematically construct rules and conditions for imposing international legal responsibility upon states. German-speaking lawyers constructed theories of public law to make sense of how broadly governmental powers were expanding with the political unification of the country.[2]

A common thread running through German legal thought was an obsession with methodology. There was a sense that the rigorous philosophical analysis was crucial to validating state authority. By contrast, the German strand of state responsibility showed little interest in the American practice of international arbitration. To public law academics like Heinrich Triepel (1868–1946), such arbitrations were really about *makeshift* settlements than about precedent-setting law. In Triepel's terminology, the arbitral agreements were contracts (*Verträge*) as opposed to law-making treaties (*Vereinbarung*).[3] Rather than deduce public law principles from arbitral practice, German and other continental public lawyers looked inwardly to construct a state's responsibility for violating international law.

The Quandary of Binding Sovereigns

Theories of state responsibility first surfaced in the writings of German public lawyers during the nineteenth century. That century saw the

[2] There is a rich literature on the social and philosophical history of German public law. Thankfully, I have drawn much from these secondary sources – including the works of Jochen von Bernstorff, Sandra Link, Martti Koskenniemi, Reut Yael Paz and Michael Stolleis. The goal is to synthesize the existing literature on the history of international law with my research on the practical and doctrinal histories of state responsibility. For a more lengthier version of this chapter, see Chapter 4 of my doctoral dissertation (Alan Tzvika Nissel, *A History of State Responsibility: The Struggle for International Standards (1870–1960)*, dissertation submitted to Helsinki University in satisfaction of LLD degree, 2016, available online at stateresponsibility.com, last visited February 2, 2022).

[3] I have not seen this explanation offered in the primary or secondary literature of German public legal theory. For a different, but general discussion of the topic in the primary literature, *see* Triepel, *Völkerrecht und Landesrecht*, *infra* note 81, at p. 95 and in the secondary literature, *see* Stephen C. Neff, *Justice among Nations: A History of International Law* (Cambridge: Harvard University Press, 2014), at p. 232.

dissolution of the Holy Roman Empire in 1806, the failed anti-monarchy March Revolutions of 1848 and the creation of a major European power with the establishment of the German Empire in 1870. Germans began to rethink public legal theory to explain the rising and falling of Germany. Much of their attention was focused on domestic power structures; however, in the second half of the century, German theorists examined the externalities of public authority as well.[4] In fact, it was through the lens of external public law that German thinkers began to see the possibility of legal responsibility constraining Great Powers. These theories balanced a conservative conception of sovereign power with a liberal determination to protect certain private rights.[5] As Martti Koskenniemi writes,

> Nowhere was the challenge to international law posed more strongly than in Germany. Nowhere did lawyers take more seriously the task of responding to that challenge, or develop more sophisticated theories to that effect.[6]

There was not any unified German philosophy of international law or of state responsibility. German theorizing of public law in general, and state responsibility in particular, evolved over the course of changing political scenarios as chronicled by several different men. August Wilhelm Heffter (1796–1880), Johann Kaspar Bluntschli (1808–1881) and Heinrich Triepel (1868–1946) represent the first wave of the German international lawyers. These theorists all came from comfortable Protestant backgrounds, and all had a relatively easy time securing academic appointments on the merits of their scholarship. For them, the reality of sovereignty left little room for a robust conception of state responsibility. Later German-speaking theorists did not see the state from the same perspective. Georg Jellinek (1851–1911), Hans Kelsen (1881–1973), Karl Strupp (1886–1940) and Hersch Lauterpacht (1897–1960) were all Jewish and all struggled professionally despite their internationally recognized abilities.[7] This second wave of Germanic

[4] Dirk Hanschel, "German Federalist Thinking and International Law," 4 *Goettingen Journal of International Law* 2, 363 (2012), at p. 366 (they "have themselves made suggestions for international federalism as a more or less natural extension of their national constitutional doctrine").

[5] On the centrality of property protection within the German order of private law (and the obligations of states to protect property, *see* Martti Koskenniemi, *To the Uttermost Parts of the Earth: Legal Imagination and International Power, 1300–1870* (Cambridge: Cambridge University Press, 2021), at pp. 919–924.

[6] Koskenniemi, *Gentle Civilizer*, *supra* note 1, at p. 181.

[7] Much of the creative strand within German public legal thought originated in those whom Stolleis labels the "outsiders" especially as the Viennese Jews (Michael Stolleis, *A History of*

international lawyers were more inclined to rethink the relationship between sovereignty and responsibility than were their gentile colleagues.

Prior to the late nineteenth century, holding a state *legally* accountable for its breaches was far from assured. The extent of a state's international liability was usually negotiated (as in the Treaty of Washington) or auto-interpreted (as in the Don Pacifico affair) rather than determined legalistically.[8] As a result, neither practitioners nor theorists viewed state responsibility as *intermediary* in nature. Findings of breach depended on the ability to enforce the alleged breach.[9] This changed as German theorists began cultivating the concept of state responsibility into a legal category of its own, which became primarily focused on *the conditions of attribution*.[10] Remedial enforcement actions would come into play only after a court or tribunal could establish the existence of a breach that was imputable to a state. Going forward, the state responsibility would have three layers to it:

1. Primary obligations (*e.g.*, to protect aliens);
2. Secondary obligations of responsibility (*e.g.*, to repair alien injuries); and
3. Tertiary rights of enforcement (*e.g.*, reprisals to secure reparations).[11]

Public Law in Germany 1914–1945 (Oxford: Oxford University Press, 2004), at p. 435), who usually had to "wait excessively long periods before receiving full professorships" (*ibid* at p. 140).

8 Namely, resolving international disputes by recourse to professional, third-party adjudicators who would base their binding rules on pre-existing legal principles, as discussed in Chapter 3.

9 *See* Ian Brownlie, *System of the Law of Nations: State Responsibility, Part I* (Oxford: Clarendon Press, 1983), at pp. 3–5. Classical notions of responsibility were not distinctly legal as much as they were religious or moral concepts. For so long as international law was not separated from theology and secularized into its own field, responsibility for breaching its norms was not distinct from Roman legal responsibility and ecclesiastical responsibility or natural responsibility – discussed further in Koskenniemi, *Gentle Civilizer*, *supra* note 1, at pp. 189–190.

10 For a history of attribution in international law from ancient times to modern, *see* Jan Arno Hessbruegge, "The Historical Development of the Doctrines of Attribution and Due Diligence in International Law," 36 *NYU Journal of International Law & Politics* 265 (2004).

11 Through the writings of Triepel and Anzilotti especially, the categories of primary rights, secondary duties and tertiary enforcement actions (though not described in those terms) became visible as separate subfields of state responsibility. *See further* James Crawford, *State Responsibility: The General Part* (Cambridge: Cambridge University Press, 2013), at p. 49 (the essence of modern state responsibility is the omission of preconditions such as fault or damage).

Figure 4.1 August Wilhelm Heffter[12]

Heffter Initiates a Positive Law of State Responsibility

August Wilhelm Heffter (1796–1880) (Figure 4.1) is the first theorist of state responsibility.[13] Heffter was a liberal member of Germany's academic nobility who studied in Berlin and Leipzig with Friedrich Carl von Savigny (1779–1886), father of the German historical school.[14] In the early years of his academic career, Heffter focused on domestic public law, including civil procedure, criminal and monarchical law.[15] In 1844, he published on the international law common to Christian nations in *Das Europäische Völkerrecht der Gegenwart* (The Contemporary

[12] Image courtesy of Humboldt University of Berlin, www.hu-berlin.de/de/ueberblick/geschichte/rektoren/heffter_august.

[13] Crawford, *supra* note 11, at p. 21; Ian Brownlie, "The History of State Responsibility," in R. G. Girardot, H. Ridder, M. L. Sarin, and T. Schiller (eds.), *New Directions in International Law: Essays in Honour of Wolfgang Abendroth –Festschrift zu seinem 75. Geburtstag* 19 (Frankfurt: Campus, 1982), at p. 22.

[14] On Heffter's background, Ingo J. Hueck, "Pragmatism, Positivism and Hegelianism in the Nineteenth Century. August Wilhelm Heffter's Notion of Public International Law," in Michael Stolleis and Masaharu Yanagihara (eds.), *East Asian Perspectives on International Law* 42 (Baden-Baden: Nomos, 2004), at p. 52.

[15] While teaching at Bonn, he published *Beiträge zum deutschen Staats- und Fürstenrecht* (Contributions to the German State and Princely Law) in 1829; August Wilhelm Heffter, *Beiträge zum deutschen Staats- und Fürstenrecht* (Berlin: G. Reimer, 1829) (this is a general work of public law in which Heffter sets out, *inter alia*, the conditions for a state to be responsible (*verantwortlich*) under domestic public law, *see* pp. 162–163).

European Law of Nations).[16] In the section where he discusses state responsibility (*Aus unerlaubten Handlungen*[17] and *Allgemein ahndungswürdige Verletzungen des Völkerrechts*),[18] Heffter writes generally, paying little attention to technical rules such as fault or attribution. For example, he writes that international public law requires states to remedy broken promises or face reprisals: "wherever an inequality is caused by arbitrariness, there has to be a compensation; this is the law of justice."[19] Heffter is more concerned about substantive laws such as the freedom of intercourse and the protection of foreigners.[20]

In Heffter's view, a state's liability can be cured by satisfaction. Violating states must satisfy injured states with material and, where relevant, intellectual reparations. There is no need for legalistic means such as arbitration or adjudication. The absence of any formalized international judiciary permits the possibility of immediate self-help by auto-interpretation.[21] Violations of most international laws can be enforced only by those states who are directly injured by the conduct of the wrongful state. Exceptionally, however, violations of serious international obligations can be implemented by any nation, even non-injured states.[22] Heffter's aim in *Das europäische Völkerrecht* is not to provide a detailed normative system, but rather to introduce a positive structure of

[16] August Wilhelm Heffter, *Das europäische Völkerrecht der Gegenwart* (Berlin: Müller, 1844).

[17] Heffter, *supra* note 15, at §101.

[18] Heffter, *supra* note 15, at §104.

[19] Heffter, *supra* note 15, at §101: "*denn überall, wo durch Willkühr eine Ungleichheit hervorgebracht ist, muß es auch eine Wiederausgleichung geben; dies ist das Gesetz der Gerechtigkeit.*"

[20] *See further* Christopher Szabla, "A New Foundation for Freedom of Movement in an Age of Sovereign Control: The Liberal Jurisprudence of August Wilhelm Heffter," 40 (1) *Law and History Review* 63 (2022), at p. 72 (Heffter enumerated a number of *Grundsätze* of the freedom of intercourse (*Verkehrsfreiheit*) upon which international law was based).

[21] Heffter, *supra* note 15, at §101: "*sonst ist dieser befugt, die Genugtuung zu erzwingen oder selbst zu nehmen.*" Heffter allows the state to disavow its treaty-based duties whenever they conflict with the welfare of its people (*ibid*, at §98).

[22] Heffter lists several punishable offenses under international law (*Allgemein ahndungswürdige Verletzungen des Völkerrechtes*): violations of human rights, attempts at world domination, violations of diplomatic immunity, denials of general rights, violations of *erga omnes* obligations, piracy and slavery (once it becomes prohibited by all European nations) – *supra* note 15, at §104.

international law based upon general principles of law.[23] His findings are extrapolated by analogy from domestic law or deduced analytically[24] rather than induced empirically from international practice.[25]

Heffter's high-level theory of state responsibility reflects a monarchical view that grants the sovereign broad private rights and limited public duties.[26] This conception of state responsibility was a modest one.[27] He describes external public responsibility as being similar to internal private responsibility (states *vis-à-vis* states being parallel to individuals *vis-à-vis* other individuals). Heffter frequently refers to states in the same manner as he does to individuals or persons. Because the state is not its own legal entity, state responsibility is a form of *personal collective liability*. These natural law-based positions, writes Heffter, cannot be written off as mere illusions in the international plane since they are accepted as a matter of course among individuals in domestic societies.[28]

[23] *See* Luigi Nuzzo, "History, Science and Christianity. International Law and Savigny's Paradigm," in Luigi Nuzzo and Milos Vec (eds.), *Constructing International Law: The Birth of a Discipline 25* (Frankfurt am Main: Klostermann, 2012), at p. 39 ("Heffter's international law was founded on the categories of the private law – personae, res, actiones – and could give international law the dogmatic strength that it hadn't yet and that it was looking for").

[24] *See further* Arthur Nussbaum, "Rise and Decline of the Law-of-Nations Doctrine in the Conflict of Laws," 42(2) *Columbia Law Review* 189–206 (1942), at p. 197: "What happened was not a relapse into the philosophy of Natural Law; rather it was ... subconscious transmutation of forceful tendencies into dogmas" (internal citations omitted).

[25] *See* Doreen Lustig, "The Business of International Law: International Legal Attitudes Toward the Business Enterprise, 1870–1954," paper presented to IILJ International Legal Theory Colloquium Spring 2012, p. 61, note 113 (the German codification enterprise reformulated German private law as a legal system that was internally coherent and gapless).

[26] *Ibid*, at §52. *See also* Eyal Benvenisti, "The Origins of the Concept of Belligerent Occupation," 26(3) *Law and History Review* 621 (2008), at p. 630: (his dual role kept him from pushing his ideas forward and from seeing through the chrysalis of the modern state).

[27] As Franz von Holtzendorff (1829–89) notes, Heffter's views of international law are distinctly Hegelian in that they are based on the force of history as much as on conditions of philosophy (*Handbuch des Völkerrechts* (Berlin: C. Habel, 1885), at p. 487). For example, Heffter writes that the ultimate tribunal of international law is history ("*sein Organ und Regulator ist die öffentliche Meinung und das letzte Gericht ist die Geschichte*" *ibid*, at §2). For a discussion of the influence of Hegel's student, Eduard Gans, on Heffter, *see* Benvenisti, *supra* note 26, at p. 630 (Gans was the one who convinced Heffter to write *Das Europäische Völkerrecht der Gegenwart*).

[28] Heffter, *supra* note 15, at p. 187: "*Was indessen alle Gesetzgebungen und Rechtsverwaltungen zivilisierter Völker unter Privatpersonen als ein sich von selbst*

His discussion of the content and enforcement of state responsibility is notable for its positivistic formulation and his analysis of *unerlaubten Handlungen* (unauthorized, illicit acts) – though he does not mention the word *Haftung* (liability) in the text.[29] The popularity of *Das Europäische Völkerrecht* ensured that the sections on illicit acts and their consequences would be broadly read and commented upon.[30] Robert von Mohl (1799–1875), who was both an early theorist of the *Rechtstaat* and a diplomat, praised the book as the best work on international law.[31] To Ingo Hueck of the Max Planck Institute, the 1844 publication marks a turning point in the "quiet fundamental positivism" of nineteenth-century German international law.[32]

Heffter's emphasis is on expanding state powers as he saw them in Europe; he was not focused on colonial ventures, of which there were few at the time by Germany. This may explain in part why Heffter's treatment of international law differs so markedly from that of Johann Casper

verstehendes Recht angenommen haben, kann unmöglich unter den Staatsgewalten selbst eine Chimäre sein."

29 Heffter, *supra* note 15, at §101.

30 *Das Europäische Völkerrecht* went through eight editions and was translated into French, Greek, Hungarian, Polish, Russian and Spanish. In the US, it received much attention through its incorporation in Wheaton's *Elements of International Law.* Also, through Francis Lieber, Heffter's views influenced Henry Halleck, President Lincoln's General-in-Chief during the Civil War. *See* Betsy Baker Röben, "The Method Behind Bluntschli's 'Modern' International Law," 4(2) *Journal of the History of International Law* 249 (2002), at p. 254. The book was one of the most important German international law texts of the nineteenth century. His application of scientific terminology to international law was innovative. For this reason, Stephen Neff describes Heffter as the first international law positivist (Stephen C. Neff, *Justice among Nations: A History of International Law* (Cambridge: Harvard University Press, 2014), at p. 228). *See also* Benvenisti, *supra* note 26, at p. 630 (the book was the first attempt by a "real" lawyer to tackle international law).

31 Robert von Mohl, *Die Geschichte und Literatur der Staatswissenschaft in Monographieen dargestellt* (Erlangen: Enke, 1855), Bd. 1, at p. 394. Nussbaum describes it as the most systematic work on international law of the nineteenth century (p. 230). For a discussion on contemporary German views of Heffter, *see* Ingo J. Hueck, "Pragmatism, Positivism and Hegelianism in the Nineteenth Century. August Wilhelm Heffter's Notion of Public International Law," in Michael Stolleis and Masaharu Yanagihara (eds.), *East Asian Perspectives on International Law* 42 (Baden-Baden: Nomos, 2004), at p. 51.

32 Hueck, *supra* note 13, at p. 45. On the eighteenth-century (onward) transformation of natural law at German universities and the use of ius gentium to justify, explain and limit royal power, *see* Martti Koskenniemi, "Law of Nations and the 'Conflict of the Faculties,'" *The Intersection of Theory and History* (Spring 2018), at pp. 4–28, at p. 4, available online at www.academia.edu/39100486/LAW_OF_NATIONS_AND_THE_CONFLICT_OF_THE_FACULTIES_?auto=download&email_work_card=download-paper, last visited July 4, 2020.

Bluntschli, who collaborated with Heffter on their 1857 *Staatswörterbuch*[33] and, like Heffter, was a founding member of the *Institut de Droit International* in 1873.

Bluntschli Codifies International Law as Confined to Sovereignty

Johann Caspar Bluntschli (1808–1881) (Figure 4.2) was an influential law professor within the group of German public lawyers who sought to formulate a "strictly juristic" methodology of public law (*see.* The new methodology, developed famously by Carl Friedrich von Gerber (1823–1891) in private law, sought a logical "analysis and construction of the purely legal elements."[34] In 1872, when Bluntschli wrote *Das moderne Völkerrecht der civilisierten Staten* (*The Modern International Law of Civilized States*), he excluded from it any section on state responsibility. This is noteworthy given that *Das moderne Völkerrecht* was an attempt – the first of its kind – at the complete codification of international law.[35] Bluntschli, like Heffter before him, does not seem to regard "responsibility" as adding anything more to the legal equation than the concept of international breach, which already implied the right to reparations, satisfaction or assurances of non-repetition, *etc.*[36]

[33] Szabla, *supra* note 19, at p. 65.

[34] Michael Stolleis, *Public Law in Germany, 1800-1914* (New York: Berghahn, 2001), at p. 317.

[35] Carl Friedrich von Gerber's contribution to German codification efforts is worth noting. Through his sixteen editions of *System des deutschen Privatrechts* (*System of German Private Law*) that were published between 1848 and 1891, Carl Friedrich von Gerber sought to separate the historical from the dogmatic and the political from the legal (Carl Friedrich von Gerber, *System des deutschen Privatrechts* (Jena: Friedrich Mauke, 1848). See further Stolleis, *supra* note 3636, at p. 317 (Gerber's novel theory of the state was an important intellectual moment in the history of state responsibility because he reconstructs the legal personality of the state as a legal person with exclusive, sovereign powers over all the German Länder; this view opened the door to a distinct, positive international theory of state responsibility). Bluntschli was also inspired by his friend Francis Lieber's codification of the laws of war (the "Lieber Code") to systematize a holistic conception of modern international law – Johann Caspar Bluntschli, *Das moderne Völkerrecht der civilisierten Staaten als Rechtsbuch dargestellt* (2nd edn, Nördlingen: Beck, 1872). David Dudley Field's *Outlines of an International Code* (New York: Baker, Voorhis & Co., 1872) was not put forth by its author as a complete code; hence the title.

[36] For example, regarding treaty violations: "*Wenn ein Stat seine völkerrechtliche Verbindlichkeit gegen einen andern Stat lediglich nicht erfüllt so hat der berechtigte Stat die Wahl entweder die Erfüllung beziehungsweise Schadensersatz wegen Nichterfüllung zu verlangen oder von dem Vertragsverhältniss zurückzutreten dessen Bestimmungen nicht erfüllt worden sind*" (Bluntschli, *supra* note 35, at p. 258) (quoted with original spelling).

Figure 4.2 Johann Caspar Bluntschli[37]

In *Das moderne Völkerrecht*, Bluntschli bases the source of international obligation on natural law. There is a human equality of law (*menschliche Rechtssgleichheit*) shared by people of all nations, such that no state can disavow its human duties (*Menschenpflichten*). The obligation of international law does not stem from state consent. If it were so, treaties would simply be contract law (*Vertragsrecht*). The obligatory nature of international law (*Verbindlichkeit des Völkerrechts*) arises out of necessity (*Nothwendigkeit*) rather than of arbitrariness (*Willkür*).[38] International public law, however, interestingly, does not trump domestic public law.[39] If the constitutional law of a nation requires it to contravene an international obligation, the state shall adhere to its own constitutional norms: "Before all treaties, the nations have their rights."[40] Nor

[37] Photo courtesy of Haus der Bayerischen Geschichte – Königreich, available online at https://hdbg.eu/koenigreich/index.php/objekte/xzoom/herrscher_id/2/id/806.

[38] Bluntschli, *supra* note 35, at §§2–3.

[39] Interesting, especially given Bluntschli's support for the Treaty of Washington and the Alabama Tribunal, which imposed an international law of due diligence that trumped domestic British neutrality law.

[40] Bluntschli, *supra* note 35, at §458 ("*Vor allen Tractaten haben die Nationen ihre Rechte*").

would state responsibility ensue when a breach is justified by principles of self-preservation or *ultra posse nemo tenetur.*[41]

Bluntschli's discussion of state responsibility is meager. He touches only briefly on several related issues such as alien protection, justifications for violating international law and "super" enforcement powers. If an alien is injured abroad, the state of the alien's nationality is entitled to demand that the injustice be corrected, even if the state was not directly involved, based on principles of reparation (*Reparationshaftung*), satisfaction (*Genugthuung*) and assurances of non-repetition.[42] This is precisely the position Bluntschli takes in his self-described "independent" opinion on the question of the *Alabama Claims* (which was requested by his friend, US law professor, Francis Lieber).[43] States are not generally responsible for injuries to aliens arising out of civil unrest or civil war.[44] If an agent of the host State injures an alien, then the claimant state can insist that the agent be called to account, bring an end to the injustice or punish the assailant.[45] If a host state does not administer a system of justice that is adequate to protect the interests of other states, then it may be held responsible to those states for not meeting international standards of justice.[46]

Bluntschli does not seek to define the content of a state's responsibility since this will depend on the type and extent of the underlying obligation in question. The most that one can say about its content, writes Bluntschli, is that the principle of proportionality (*Verhältnissmässigkeit*) is the yard-stick of state responsibility.[47] An example of disproportionate demands is the claim for "indirect damages" (*e.g.*, for prolonging the US Civil War)

[41] Bluntschli, *supra* note 35, at §§459, 460, 471.

[42] Bluntschli, *supra* note 35, at §380.

[43] Johann Caspar Bluntschli, *An Impartial Opinion on the Alabama Question and the Manner of Settling It* (reprinted in Washington, DC: Government Printing Office, 1871), at p. 21: "The right solution of the difficulty consists in the combination of a material reparation intended to indemnify the American owners, with a moral guarantee of the commercial and maritime relations against the return of similar injuries. The first of these objects will be attained by means of a just pecuniary indemnity, which Great Britain shall pay to the Union, to be divided among the damaged persons; the second will be attained by a fresh proclamation of the duty incumbent on *neutral* and friendly states to prevent, so far as possible, the abusing of their neutral territories for the organization of military expeditions."

[44] Johann Caspar Bluntschli, *Das moderne Völkerrecht der civilisirten Staten als Rechtsbuch dargestellt* (Nördlingen: C.H. Beck'schen, 1868 [1872]), at §380.

[45] Bluntschli, *supra* note 43, at §466.

[46] Bluntschli, *supra* note 43, at §467.

[47] Bluntschli, *supra* note 43, at §469.

brought by the US against Great Britain in the *Alabama Claims* dispute.[48] In contrast to civil and criminal law, the international legal consequences of a breach are never regulated in advance. If a state breaches a fundamental norm of international law, one that threatens world peace, then all states possess *Grossmächte* ("super" or "extraordinary" powers) to restore the legal order.[49] Bluntschli's list of breaches triggering these "super powers" is similar to (but shorter than) Heffter's. It includes piracy, deprivation and usurping of the rights of other states, plus the destruction or domination of public global transit routes.[50] Enforcement, however, could be taken unilaterally without the requirement of triadic legalism or any attempt thereof.[51]

Bluntschli was not of the same mind as Heffter about the reality of a legal doctrine of state responsibility. To the former, "The development of International Law or the institution of a universal State might organise the legal (*rechtliche*) responsibility of nations. At present this is only an ideal which the future may perhaps realize."[52] Devoted to the "monarchical principle,"[53] Bluntschli did not see international responsibility as a general possibility under the then prevailing views of sovereignty. He was writing post-Gerber but pre-Jellinek, as I will discuss in the next section.

[48] Bluntschli, *supra* note 43, at §469. The *Alabama Claims* is discussed at length in Chapter 2.

[49] Bluntschli, *supra* note 43, at §471.

[50] Bluntschli, *supra* note 43, at §472.

[51] Johan Casper Bluntschli, *Lehre vom modernen Staat* (Stuttgart: J. G. Cotta'schen, 1876), officially translated in *The Theory of the State* (Oxford: Clarendon Press, 1885), at p. 478; *see also ibid* at p. 509. On legalism, see Chapter 3.

[52] Johan Casper Bluntschli, *The Theory of the State* (Oxford: Clarendon Press, 1885), at p. 478—originally published as *Lehre vom modernen Staat* (Stuttgart: J.G. Cotta'schen, 1876).

[53] Many German lawyers at the time were still comfortable with the "monarchical principle," a contradictory notion that recognized "that the monarchy must be constrained by the needs of the day and it pushed the not yet achieved points into the future" (Michael Stolleis, *Public Law in Germany, 1800–1914* (New York: Berghahn, 2001), at pp. 61–63. German legal theory, says Stolleis, had to balance the competing interests of absolute monarchical rule and the unwieldy but inexorable momentum of popular sovereignty. In Germany, constitutions were not ratified prospectively by a government; they were conceded to on a piecemeal basis. Monarchs (who factually preexisted positive constitutions) *allowed* themselves to be partially limited by laws.). As late as 1871, the preamble to the Constitution of the Empire derived its legitimacy from the monarchs of governments of individual states – George A. Glynn (ed.), *Foreign Constitutions: Comprising the Constitution of Argentina, Belgium, Brazil (empire and Republic), Columbia, Ecuador, France, Germany, Honduras, Japan, Mexico, Prussia, Switzerland and Venezuela,* Part II, Vol. 3 (Albany: Argus, 1894), at p. 263.

While Heffter and Bluntschli provided early treatments of state responsibility, they stand out as attempts "to square the circle of statehood and an international legal order by lawyers trained in public law."[54] Both Heffter and Bluntschli died in 1880, the same year that Georg Jellinek published *Die rechtliche Natur der Staatenverträge* (*The Legal Nature of State Treaties*).

Jellinek Provides for the Theoretical Possibility of State Responsibility

The contribution of Georg Jellinek (1851–1911) (Figure 4.3) to the theory of international law was vital to a positivist theory of state responsibility.[55] This German lawyer of rabbinic Jewish origins was the first to square the circle of sovereign responsibility without relying on natural law. Jellinek was raised in a politically active and observant Jewish household, one of the most prominent Jewish families of the nineteenth century. His father, Adolf, was a liberal political activist, the Chief Rabbi of Austria and an influential scholar of Jewish mysticism and history.[56] Talmudic reasoning was second nature to the three Jellinek brothers. However, finding a tenured academic position in Germany, did not come easily to Georg – even after he attained the title of Professor of Public Law in Vienna.

Jellinek's theory is rooted in traditional German philosophy. He accepts how Georg Wilhelm Friedrich Hegel's (1770–1831) grounds the law's validity on state consent.[57] However, Jellinek argues that Hegel erred in the view that international obligations rest on the discretion of state promises (*Haltensollen*).[58] He first discusses state responsibility in

[54] Koskenniemi, *Gentle Civilizer*, *supra* note 1, at p. 181.

[55] Georg Jellinek's contribution to the theory of international law has been described as "the most influential" of the nineteenth century (Jochen von Bernstorff, "Georg Jellinek and the Origins of Liberal Constitutionalism in International Law," 4(3) *Goettingen Journal of International Law* 659 (2012), at p. 660). So dominant was Jellinek's approach that subsequent theoretical discussions on international law can be described as "footnotes" (Koskenniemi, *supra* note 1, at p. 53).

[56] *See* Reut Yael Paz, "Making it Whole: Hersch Lauterpacht's Rabbinical Approach to International Law," 4 *Goettingen Journal of International Law* 417 (2012), at pp. 137–144.

[57] Georg Wilhelm Friedrich Hegel, *Die Philosophie des Rechts: Die Mitschriften Wannenmann* (Heidelberg 1817/18) und Homeyer (Berlin 1818/19) edited and annotated by Karl Heinz Ilting (Stuttgart: Klett-Cotta, 1983), at §159 (describes international law as *äußeres Staatsrecht*).

[58] This is a realist critique that Karl Strupp's student Hans Morgenthau would develop a century later – *see* von Bernstorff *supra* note 55, at p. 665.

Figure 4.3 Georg Jellinek[59]

System der subjektiven öffentlichen Rechte (*System of Subjective Public Rights*, 1892)[60] and later in *Allgemeine Staatslehre* (*General State Theory*, 1900).[61] On its face, Jellinek's views of international law and state responsibility are more conservative than progressive. He views international law as a hierarchical system, considering state responsibility for breaching that law a primitive form of liability: "Collective liability which existed in an early level of civilization for all members of a social organization (family, kin, tribe, commune, army) continues to exist in international law, *which is the most undeveloped field of law.*"[62]

[59] Photo courtesy: Wikimedia commons, available online at https://en.wikipedia.org/wiki/Georg_Jellinek#/media/File:Georg_Jellinek.jpg, last visited May 24, 2023.

[60] Georg Jellinek, *System der subjektiven öffentlichen Rechte* (Freiburg: J. C. B. Mohr, 1892).

[61] Georg Jellinek, *Allgemeine Staatslehre* (Berlin: O. Häring, 1900). In *Allgemeine Staatslehre*, he includes a small discussion of collective liability on p. 526 (*Gesamthaftung*), which is discussed at considerably greater length in *System der subjektiven öffentlichen Rechte*.

[62] *System der subjektiven öffentlichen Rechte*, at p. 243 (emphasis added): "*Die Gesamthaftung, welche auf früher Kulturstufe für alle Angehörigen eines sozialen Verbandes: Familie, Sippe, Stamm, Gemeinde, Heer bestand, besteht im Völkerrecht, allerdings dem unentwickeltsten Rechtsgebiete noch ungeschwächt fort.*"

Jellinek sought to introduce a new, more secure, juristic method for constructing concepts of international law than prior German efforts.[63] Key to Jellinek's theory is his new conception of the state. In *Die rechtliche Natur der Staatenverträge* (1880), he departs from his predecessors by arguing that the state was far too heterogeneous and polymorphous to be described as an organic political body (especially after Bismarck's departure).[64] To make his argument, Jellinek puts forward a two-sided vision of the state that is both sociological and legal (*Zwei-Seiten-Theorie*). The sociological dimension describes the relationships between the government and its people.[65] The legal aspect regulates the formal constitutional authority of the state – in terms of its rights and its obligations.

Jellinek's *Zwei-Seiten-Theorie* views both the government and the governed as both subjects and as objects. Each has its rights and obligations. Individual rights can be compromised for the sake of national interests; similarly, sovereign powers are limited to the pursuit of national interests. Both perspectives are true and correct, but each provides a unique perspective on the state. To Jellinek, law is only one aspect of the state, and it is one of the greatest facilitators (*Hilfsmittel*) of state interests. More so than politics, sociology, theology or morality, the law is the optimal tool for managing the relations of disputing parties within a society.[66]

Jellinek questions the Hegelian concept of the state. He asks not *what the state is* but rather *how do we think about the state*?[67] Thus, he famously stresses *die normative Kraft des Faktischen* (the normative power of the factual), as I will discuss further below.[68] Norms depend on facts and *vice versa*, depending on the various positions of the

63 Georg Jellinek, *Die Lehre von den Staatenverbindungen* (Vienna: A. Hölder, 1882), at p. 4; for an excellent discussion, *see* Jochen von Bernstorff and Max Henry Mayer, "The Historical School and German 19th Century Contributions to International Legal Thought" (2022), available at https://ssrn.com/abstract=4106343, last visited June 22, 2022.

64 Georg Jellinek, *Die rechtliche Natur der Staatenverträge. Ein Beitrag zur juristischen Construktion des Völkerrechts* (Vienna: Hölder, 1880), at p. 92.

65 Jellinek, *supra* note 64, at pp. 46–49. This view is similar to those of Gerber.

66 "International law exists for States and not States for international law" (Jellinek, *supra* note 64, at p. 340, translated by Paz, *supra* note 56, at p. 147).

67 Paz, *supra* note 56, at pp. 148–149.

68 Jellinek, *supra* note 64, at pp. 337–338.

individual's relationship with the state. The individual stands directly in relation to the state in domestic politics; it is simple for domestic law to reflect this through a hierarchy of superior and inferior laws. In contrast, states are arranged horizontally in the international society, so that one state's laws do not supersede those of another.

To solve this distinctly international problem about the binding nature of law, Jellinek set forth his theory of self-obligation (*Selbstverpflichtungslehre*). It describes the reality of international life, where many apparently "easy" cases evidence examples of states binding themselves to legal obligations. To Jellinek, public law is an *a priori* restriction to state power. Legal regulations bind national sovereigns; and German sovereignty is not confined to the physicality of its sovereign. This is a move away from the mainstream German (*e.g.*, Bluntschli's) conception of the German state as distinct from, rather than comprised of, the German people.[69] A state's legitimacy under domestic and international law is based on the same will of the state. Just as internal public law stands "above" the state, so does external public law bind the state. This is the psychological basis of any legal obligation.[70] It is the empirically verifiable manifestation of a state's consent to be bound that frames a promise as a legal, binding one (*Sichverpflichtetfühlen*).

In his rethinking of sovereignty, Jellinek argues that the state is not coercing itself, a logical impossibility. Rather, the state is guaranteeing the beneficiaries of its promise – whether individuals or states – that it would keep its word.[71] Jellinek's view is not such an obvious position to take in the nineteenth-century German legal context. Hegel's view of international law as external public (or state) law (*äußeres Staatsrecht*) would still apply.[72] State autonomy was a foundational principle of international law. To Jellinek's colleagues, however, sovereignty and responsibility

[69] Johann Caspar Bluntschli, *The Theory of the State* (authorized translation of 6th edn, Oxford: Clarendon, 1885), at p. 463.

[70] "It does not exhaust the nature of law that it is the will of the State, for it is not the will of the State as such that is law but the *binding* will of the State," Jellinek, *supra* note 64, at pp. 5–6 (emphasis added).

[71] Jellinek, *supra* note 64, at p. 27.

[72] Hegel, *supra* note 59, at §159. For a discussion on this translation, *see* "The Legacy of the Nineteenth Century," in David Armstrong (ed.), *Routledge Handbook of International Law* 141 (New York: Routledge, 2009), at p. 145 ("The view of international law as 'external public law' remained influential in the German-speaking realm well into and even beyond late-19th century").

were seen as mutually exclusive options.[73] Jellinek demonstrates that states frequently bind themselves in a manner that is clearly observable. Certain general principles such as *pacta sunt servanda* and responsibility for breach are inherent components of any system of law.[74] The subtlety of this point is worth highlighting: Jellinek expressly seeks to build a new basis for constitutional authority that is not based on old ways of natural legal reasoning, but on the new theories of positivism. The alternative of framing state responsibility more traditionally to fit within Hegel's *äußeres Staatsrecht* would foreclose its efficacy.

[Enter: Jellinek's meta-principle of the normative power of the factual.]

To Jellinek, legal normativization is inherent to our natural world. International law, as a social construct, does not consist of neutral facts alone, but of normative component as well. International law possesses a proto-constitutional quality.[75] Like domestic public law, it includes norms that are not limited to or based on state will; such norms are inherent in any system of law *qua* law. While Jellinek clearly seeks to ground international public law on verifiable social facts, facts could take his theory only so far. Ultimately, Jellinek, like his predecessors, had to resort to deduced conceptions of the law in order to validate norm-creating rules such as *pacta sunt servanda* (promises shall be kept) and *rebus sic stantibus* (change in circumstances). Social beings living in conflict require legal protection. And the law means nothing in any context – domestic or international – without certain *a priori* elements. The alternative would not only be undesirable in Jellinek's view; it would not reflect the reality of domestic and international society, where individuals and states regularly and willingly subject themselves to binding commitments.

Jellinek's is not a full-throated theory of international law. However, his significance is in how he changed the terms of debate.[76]

[73] *See, e.g.*, Adolf Lasson, *Princip und Zukunft des Völkerrechts* (Berlin: Hertz, 1871), at pp. 12–31.

[74] Jochen von Bernstorff, "Georg Jellinek and the Origins of Liberal Constitutionalism in International Law," 4(3) *Goettingen Journal of International Law* 659 (2012), where this point is brought out convincingly (at pp. 669–671).

[75] Though international law, at least in Jellinek's time, was still an "anarchical law" (discussed at length in Hersch Lauterpacht, "The Nature of International Law and General Jurisprudence," 37 *Economica* 301 (1932), at pp. 308–313).

[76] Domestically, his contribution marks the beginning of the end of the monarchical principle and the Gerber–Laband school of legal methodology (discussed *supra* note 35). *See* further Arthur J. Jacobson and Bernhard Schlink, (eds.), *Weimar: A Jurisprudence of Crisis* (Berkeley: University of California Press, 2000), at Prologue–ch.1.

Selbstverpflichtungslehre's balancing of sovereignty and responsibility managed to stabilize international law theory from its Hegel-induced tailspin. Jellinek's concept of state obligation was the first of its kind in international law and it opened the door to the possibility of state responsibility. It demonstrates a philosophically plausible argument that certain components of the law can be justified not by state practice but by social necessity. As the international law historian Jochen von Bernstorff writes:

> This is the very essence of constitutional thinking in public law – the assumption that a political powerful entity limits its freedom by abiding to a set of meta-rules, be they of a procedural or substantive nature, that cannot be modified unilaterally in an ad hoc fashion.[77]

To Jellinek, international law is based on the will of the states – on both their statements and their practices. Like all other systems of law, international law emerges from the state and is binding on both because of society's needs and expectations.[78] In this way, Jellinek relates the duty to obey international law to the *interests* or *needs* (rather than the express consent) of states.[79] This deferential positivism was interpreted and adapted differently by subsequent thinkers, including Anzilotti, Kelsen and Lauterpacht. But his theoretical contribution became an identifiably lasting one. His reliance on the normative power of facts allowed for the possibility of but also the severe limitation of state responsibility. This weakness led Lauterpacht in the next generation to conclude that: "f[80]

Triepel and Concentric State Responsibilities

Heinrich Triepel (1868–1946) (Figure 4.4) was the next German law professor to theorize international responsibility of states (*die*

[77] *See* von Bernstorff *supra* note 55, at pp. 671–672.

[78] The list of sources – treaties, custom, and general principles – catalogued by Lassa Oppenheim in his 1905 treatise and eventually codified in the statutes of the Permanent Court of International Justice and its successor the International Court of Justice (ICJ), continues to serve as the focal point for discussions of international law.

[79] Jellinek, *supra* note 64, at pp. 48–50; Koskenniemi, "Between Coordination and Constitution," *supra* note 1, at p. 53.

[80] Lauterpacht, *supra* note 75, at p. 419. To Lauterpacht, Erich Kaufmann's (1880–1972) *Das Wesen des Völkerrechts und die clausula rebus sic stantibus* (Tübingen: Mohr, 1911) is "the only work in which an attempt has been made a thorough exposition of the law of co-ordination" (*ibid*, at p. 420).

Figure 4.4 Heinrich Triepel[81]

Völkerrechtliche Haftung des Staates).[82] Triepel was also the first commentator to substantively consider the issues of attribution (*e.g.*, fault) and implementation of state responsibility. The son of a lawyer and businessman, Triepel rose through the ranks to become a leading figure within the German academy. The same year in which he published *Völkerrecht und Landesrecht* (1899), he was appointed as an associate professor at the University of Leipzig. The following year he was appointed as full professor at the University of Tübingen, after which

[81] Photo courtesy of Government of Poland, www.szukajwarchiwach.gov.pl/en/jednostka/-/jednostka/7006683/obiekty/490226.

[82] Heinrich Triepel, *Völkerrecht und Landesrecht* (Leipzig: C. L. Hirschfeld, 1899), at pp. 324–371. As I discuss below, Triepel and Hall were the first international law commentators to provide special treatment of the liability of states under international law. Edwin Borchard considers Triepel's *Völkerrecht und Landesrecht* to be the first general work on international law to pay special attention to the international responsibility of states – Edwin M. Borchard, "Reviewed Work: Das Völkerrechtliche Delikt. by Karl Strupp," 15(1) *American Journal of International Law* 146 (1921), at p. 146.

he moved to Kiel and then to Berlin's law faculty. Triepel became an active leader in several professional organizations as well.[83]

Like Jellinek, Triepel does not seek a pure theory of law. He believes that a "legal explanation of the binding character of law is impossible" since any such attempt is doomed to circularity.[84] However, unlike Jellinek, Triepel does not base his theory of international public responsibility on its domestic analogue. He takes a distinctly *international* approach.[85] Triepel is best known as the "father of dualism" because of how he seeks to relate international to domestic law.[86] In *Völkerrecht und Landesrecht* (*International Law and Domestic Law*), Triepel argues that international law and domestic law are "two circles that touch at most, but that never intersect."[87] Within the international sphere, states cannot create law unilaterally; they act in coordination with other states as international co-sovereigns. Accordingly, not all international acts and events are sources of law. If a state enters into a transaction with another state without any intent to generate lasting law, this would be a matter of contract law (*Vertragsrecht*). By contrast, two or more states may enter

[83] In 1920, in the aftermath of the First World War, Triepel began publishing the *Archiv für öffentliches Recht* (Archive for Public Law), founded by Paul Laband (1838–1918) in 1895. The following year, Triepel founded the *Vereinigung der Deutschen Staatsrechtslehrer* (Association of the German Constitutional Lawyer), the purpose of which was to "provide the basis for a working group that was urgently desired under the exigencies of the present." The association was a source of impassioned debate about the Weimar constitution and met annually until 1932 (Heinrich Triepel, *Die Vereinigung der Deutschen Staatsrechtslehrer, Archiv des öffentlichen Rechts* 43 (Tübingen: Mohr, 1922), at p. 349, translated by Ralf Poscher, "Heinrich Triepel," in Arthur J. Jacobson and Bernhard Schlink (eds.), *Weimar: A Jurisprudence of Crisis* (Berkeley: University of California Press, 2000), at p. 172).

[84] Triepel, *supra* note 82.

[85] This expansive approach to state responsibility was novel in international law, especially for a conservative positivist in Germany – *see* Olivier de Frouville: "Attribution of Conduct to the State: Private Individuals," in James Crawford, Alain Pellet and Simon Olleson (eds.), *The Law of International Responsibility* (Oxford: Oxford University Press, 2011), at pp. 259–260.

[86] On the lasting impact of Triepel to contemporary Anglo-American practice, *see* Joseph G. Starke, "Monism and Dualism in the Theory of International Law," 17 *British Yearbook of International Law* 66 (1936), at pp. 68–69; Felix Lange, "Between Systematization and Expertise for Foreign Policy: The Practice-Oriented Approach in Germany's International Legal Scholarship (1920–1980)," 28(2) *European Journal of International Law* 535 (2017), at p. 538.

[87] Triepel, *supra* note 81, at p. 111: "*Sie sind zwei Kreise die sich höchstens berühren niemals schneiden.*"

into an agreement in a law-making manner (*Vereinbarung*).[88] Only in the latter did Triepel see "a common will, an international sovereign, and thus, international law."[89] This distinction was broadly accepted in Germany and explains why German theorists rarely considered the rise of *ad hoc* international arbitrations as worthy of analysis in their theories. States did not enter arbitration agreements with the intent of codifying substantive international laws. Each arbitration agreement, especially in the Americas, was a bilateral transaction that sought to address certain claims as they arose in developing economies.[90]

Like Jellinek, Triepel views the state as its own legal entity. It is not the corporate sovereign or prince; it is not the collective. It is its own personality, one with distinctly international rules of attribution. He critiques the theories of Heffter and Jellinek as being grounding in their theories of state responsibility on complicity (*Mitschuld*)[91] or collective liability (*Gesamthaftung*) rather than on direct imputation (*Zurechnung*).[92] Consistent with his dualist approach, Triepel insists that "the State does not become, as is always said, responsible for the act [of the individual] just because of its passivity, it was and remains responsible if it neglects to do what it is obliged to do by reason of that act."[93] A state is responsible only for the acts of individuals, if the latter does not interfere with the wrongful acts of the former. This is an independent, international grounding of liability – one that is not derived from private conduct but from state acts.[94] International public law imposes direct liability on states for violating its own international duties.

Interestingly, when referring to a state's responsibility, Triepel prefers to use the term "*Haftung*" (liability) over "*Verantwortlichkeit*"

88 Triepel, *supra* note 81, at pp. 49–74.

89 Ole Spiermann, *International Legal Argument in the Permanent Court of International Justice: The Rise of the International Judiciary* (Cambridge: Cambridge University Press, 2005), at p. 41, internal citations omitted.

90 An exception to this rule is that Treaty of Washington, which settled the *Alabama Claims* dispute and also set forth the "three rules" of international neutrality, discussed below.

91 Triepel, *supra* note 81, at pp. 325–328. To Triepel, state approval (*Biligung*) is not the same as state participation (p. 328). Triepel refers to Jellinek's System, p. 313 in note 1 on p. 328, and on p. 327 to Heffter's §103 in note 1.

92 *See* Triepel, *supra* note 81, at p. 325: "*Nun ist es zunächst sicher, dass die Haftung des Staats für Handlungen Einzelner ihren Grund heuten Tages nicht findet in der Zugehörigkeit des Thäters zum Staatenverbande. Der frühmittelalterliche Gedanke einer Haftung der Gemeinschaft für ihre Glieder ist dem modernen Völkerrecht fremd; nur ganz vereinzelt taucht er noch dann und wann empor.*"

93 *See* Triepel, *supra* note 81, at pp. 333–334.

94 *Ibid.*

(responsibility), which was employed by both Heffter and Jellinek.[95] This is probably because, in contrast to his predecessors, Triepel is focused on the technical rules of imputation that provide the legal connection between the acts of individuals and the liability of states.[96] These rules cannot be defined unilaterally by states (*e.g.*, by domestic law).[97] This is a departure from Jellinek's concept of *Selbstverpflictung* in that Triepel does not base the bindingness of international law on individual state will alone.[98] Triepel breaks with the accepted, Grotian requirement of fault for the establishment of responsibility in international law.[99] This objective view of state responsibility would be further fleshed out a few years later by Dionisio Anzilotti in Italy.

To Triepel, there is a fundamental distinction between a state's responsibility for acts of citizens as compared to acts of its organs. Whereas the former is based on an *objective* foundation, the second one is of *personal* basis. A state must be responsible only for its own conduct. Its responsibility must be determined not merely by the state's relation to the underlying wrongful act, but to the agent of that act.[100] There is, thus, no difference in the explanation of the content of state responsibility, whether reparation (*Reparationshaftung*) or satisfaction (*Genugthuung*).

[95] *Staatenverantwortlichkeit* (state responsibility) is not exactly synonymous with *Haftung des Staates* (liability of states). Both in the general usage of German literature as well as in the texts of German legal theory, *Verantwortlichkeit* is frequently used as the general idea of responsibility ("duty" or "culpability"). Whereas *Haftung* often conveys the technical, legal term consequences of breaching the law ("liability"). I discuss the coining of the term "state responsibility" in Chapter 5. According to Geneviève Viney, the term "responsibility" first appeared only at the end of the eighteenth century (Geneviève Viney, 'Responsabilité,' 35 *Arch Phil de droit* 277 (1990)). For another brief attempt at a genealogy of the term "responsibility" in international law, see Crawford, *supra* note 8, at p. 27, note 117).

[96] Triepel, *supra* note 81, at pp. 324–359.

[97] Conversely, neither was the international standard of alien protection to be governed by international law, but substantively by domestic law. According to Triepel, a state is liable for the well-being of a foreign citizen as long as this citizen stays in the state's territory. It is only liable within its own laws and not within the laws of the foreign citizen's state: "*denn was dem eigenen Unterthanen recht ist, wird auch dem Fremden, den ja Niemand zwingt, bei uns zu weilen, billig sein*" (*supra* note 81, at p. 343).

[98] *See* Triepel, *supra* note 81, at pp. 60–82. Once a State commits to a rule, that rule binds the State as any autonomous legal rule (*autonomer Rechtssatz*) would. For a discussion, *see* Spiermann, *supra* note 89, at p. 40.

[99] Hugo Grotius, *De jure belli ac pacis* (Oxford: Clarendon, 1926) [1625], Book II, ch. 21.

[100] Triepel, *supra* note 81, at p. 348.

The state shall be responsible for all conduct that objectively violates its international obligations.[101]

If wrongful conduct is imputable to a state, this can give rise to two types of remedies: reparations (*Reparationsverbindlichkeit*) and satisfaction (*Genugthuung*). Most commonly, *Reparationsverbindlichkeit* requires a state to pay compensation for wrongs committed by private individuals in which the responsible state was complicit (*Mitschuld*) or was additionally culpable (*Verschuldung*).[102] To support this position, Triepel relies exceptionally on the famous international arbitration of the *Alabama Claims*, in which case Great Britain violated its neutrality obligations by not diligently preventing the outfitting of rebel Confederate ships by private Liverpudlian shipbuilders.[103] Given that the underlying wrongful conduct in such cases is committed by private individuals, liability for reparations is less important to Triepel.

In contrast, liability for satisfaction arises when reparations would not sufficiently redress the injury in question. Satisfaction does not aim to cure such injuries, because they are in a sense incurable (*unheilbare Verletzung*). Neither is satisfaction a form of international criminal law. Rather, satisfaction seeks a measure of pacification (*Beschwichtigung*) of the feelings of the injured state.[104] To claim this more serious form of liability, the injured state must have been attacked from within the territory of the responsible state. This type of liability has a territorial character.[105] Even this form of international wrong does not depend on any findings of fault. It is sufficient, says Triepel that the obligation to protect was not provided. International law requires states to protect the existence of other states, their territory, their constitutions, their honor, their representatives, diplomats and citizens from attacks out of its own territory. Thus, liability and protection go "hand in hand."[106]

[101] Namely, for acts that the state itself could have done; otherwise, it would be impossible to regard those facts as being state acts (Triepel, *supra* note 81, at pp. 348–349).

[102] Triepel, *supra* note 81, at pp. 334–335.

[103] Triepel, *supra* note 81, at p. 335: "*Haftung des Staates, wenn er verhindern konnte und widerrechtlich nicht verhinderte, wenn er es an der* 'due diligence' *im Sinne der drei Regeln des Vertrags von Washington fehlen liess.*" I discuss the Treaty of Washington's resolution of the *Alabama Claims* at length in Chapter 2.

[104] Triepel, *supra* note 81, at p. 335.

[105] Triepel, *supra* note 81, at p. 336.

[106] Triepel, *supra* note 81, at p. 339: "*Haftpflicht und Schutzpflicht gehen hier eben stets Hand in Hand.*"

Triepel's theory of international law exposes the state to many actions of liability, but under domestic and international law. In the event that the concentric circles of domestic and international law shall meet, then each system must resolve for itself a method of reconciliation. In international law, international duties will trump domestic ones and *vice versa* for domestic law. To Triepel, this was not a contradiction since the two legal systems operated independently of each other.[107] Thus, his stance on the primacy of international over domestic law was not a progressive one. Triepel was conservative and even described himself as a "moderate anti-positivist."[108] As his dualism implies, Triepel was not writing with the same urgency to regulate state conduct as his older colleague, Georg Jellinek.[109] Still, the structure and methodology of his writings had a lasting influence on state responsibility, especially within Anglo-American circles.

German Theory beyond Germany

The ideas of Heffter, Jellinek and Triepel provided legal theorists with a platform from which to advance and critique budding theories of state responsibility. By the early nineteenth century, international lawyers within Germany and abroad were writing monographs on the topic. In this section, I consider the contributions of three lawyers who practiced outside of Germany: William Edward Hall (1835–1894), Dionisio Anzilotti (1869–1950) and Lassa Oppenheim (1858–1919). All three of these writers were clearly influenced by nineteenth-century German

[107] Triepel, *supra* note 81, at pp. 438–439.

[108] Michael Stolleis, *A History of Public Law in Germany 1914–1945* (Oxford: Oxford University Press, 2004), at p. 179. Triepel confesses: "I am ... neither an absolutist nor a democrat, but if someday I would have to decide unconditionally and without further ado for absolutism or democracy, I would, without thinking twice, prefer monarchic absolutism as the lesser evil ... in the certainty that it is ultimately better to live under the enlightened or unenlightened despotism of a single person than under the despotism of the never enlightened rabble" (Heinrich Triepel, *Unitarismus und Föderalismus im deutschen Reiche: Eine staatsrechtliche und politische Studie* (Tübingen: Mohr, 1907), at p. 119 as translated by Ralf Poscher, "Heinrich Triepel," *supra* note 72, at p. 173).

[109] Before he died in 1946, the Berlin public law professor sanguinely expressed that "the ugly blots that emerged in the recent past will somewhat fade" (Heinrich Triepel, *Vom Stil des Rechts: Beiträge zu einer Ästhetik des Rechts* (Heidelberg: Schneider, 1947), at p. 123, as cited in Ralf Poscher, "Heinrich Triepel," *supra* note 82, at p. 174.

theory and all of their writings have since entered the canon of state responsibility.[110]

Hall Introduces State Responsibility to Anglo-Americans

William Edward Hall was an Oxford-educated lawyer, adventurer and early member of the Alpine Club. He became an international law scholar while on an academic detour from his postgraduate studies in the arts and history.[111] Hall was the first writer in the English language to discuss a doctrine of state responsibility.[112] Like Heffter, he is noticeably cautious. Also like Heffter, Hall includes a footnote at the beginning of the section on state responsibility on the "inadequacy with which the topic is discussed in works of international law."[113] In his 1880 treatise on international law, Hall accepts the traditional Anglo-American position regarding state responsibility for alien injuries, holding that a state may claim the responsibility of host states for injuries to the former's nationals.[114] In that work, he provides an expanded section on the

[110] I situate their contributions within the context of German internationalism and the first theories of state responsibility. However, I do not consider Hall, Anzilotti and Oppenheim as part of the same professional circles as German internationalists. Further, all three were firmly rooted in actual diplomatic practice as compared to their German colleagues. Especially in the case of Anzilotti, these theorists' contributions can be seen as important extrapolations of nineteenth-century German legal theories, which based state responsibility upon state sovereignty. Hall and Anzilotti, however, were not neo-Kantians. For a somewhat contrarian discussion on whether or not Jellinek was a neo-Kantian, *see* Stanley L. Paulson, *The Very Idea of Legal Positivism* (Stuttgart: Steiner, 2013), at pp. 146–147.

[111] T. E. Holland, "Hall, William Edward (1835–1894)," rev. Catherine Pease-Watkin, *Oxford Dictionary of National Biography* (Oxford: Oxford University Press, 2004).

[112] Though Wheaton mentions the concept haphazardly in his writings – *see* Henry Wheaton, A History of the Law of Nations in Europe and America from the Earliest Times to the Treaty of Washington (New York: Gould, Banks, 1845), at pp. 44, 188, 319–320. Westlake and a few other Anglo-American publicists do acknowledge that states can be held responsible for particular breaches of international law such as injuries to aliens, but they do not provide any special treatment of the topic – *see, e.g.*, John Westlake, *International Law, Part I: Peace* (Cambridge: Cambridge University Press, 1910), at p. 329.

[113] Part II, ch. 4, §65 ("Responsibility of a state"), note 1: "The subject of the responsibility of a state is not usually discussed adequately in works upon international law. It is treated more or less completely or portions of it are commented on in Bluntschli . . . Halleck. . . Phillimore."

[114] William Edward Hall, *A Treatise on International Law* (Oxford: Clarendon Press, 1880), at p. 235: "States possess a right of protecting their subjects abroad which is correlative to

"Responsibility of a state" under the general heading of "General Principles of the Law Governing States in their Normal Relations."

Hall cautiously updated his editions of *International Law* to include new theories of state responsibility as they were being expounded in Germany. In the Preface to his 1889 edition, Hall writes that "It would be very unwise of an international lawyer to indulge in the delusion, with which he is often credited, that formulas are stronger than passions."[115] At the same time, Hall accepts that the law of state responsibility comprises an actionable legal doctrine. He had harsh words regarding Heffter's and Bluntschli's view that a state may repudiate a treaty when it conflicts with the rights and welfare of its people.[116] To Hall:

> Law is not intended to bring licence and confusion but restraint and order; and neither restraint nor order can be imposed by the principles of which the expression has just been quoted. Incapable in their vagueness of supplying a definite rule fundamentally immoral by the scope which they give to unregulated action, scarcely an act of international bad faith could be so shameless as not to find shelter behind them. High sounding generalities by which anything may be sanctioned are the favourite weapons of unscrupulousness and ambition; they cannot be kept from distorting the popular judgment but they may at least be prevented from affecting the standard of law.[117]

Hall believed in a system of international law but was vigilant about the incongruities between its theory and practice. With the publication of multiple editions of Hall's textbooks, state responsibility as a topic became increasingly studied in the Anglo-American world.

Anzilotti Completes the International Theory of State Responsibility

In 1902, Dionisio Anzilotti (1867–1950) published *Teoria generale della responsabilità dello stato nel diritto internazionale* (*General Theory of State Responsibility in International Law*), the first monograph devoted

their responsibility in respect of injuries inflicted upon foreigners within their dominions."

115 William Edward Hall, *A Treatise on International Law* (London: Macmillan, 1889), at p. vi, as reproduced in William Edward Hall and J. B. Atley, *A Treatise on International Law* (Oxford: Oxford University Press, 1904), at p. vii.

116 Heffter, *supra* note 14, at §98; Bluntschli, *supra* note 35, at §§415, 456.

117 Hall, *supra* note 114, at §116.

exclusively to the theory, doctrine or practice of this topic.[118] The importance of this work lay in Anzilotti providing a complete theory of the international responsibility of states, including all three of its major subfields: rules of attribution liability; the content of liability; and implementing that liability. In Italy, as in Germany, public law theorists were called upon relatively late in the modern era to grapple with the politics of unification.[119] Anzilotti was an active practitioner, serving as legal advisor to the Italian foreign ministry. He was a world-renowned thinker, whose positivist theories did not simply rely on earlier German studies (such as Heinrich Triepel) but shaped later German thinkers (such as Karl Strupp). He was also a founding judge and president of the Permanent Court of International Justice (PCIJ).

Anzilotti's theory of international law in general, and state responsibility in particular, are strongly statist. Like Jellinek and Triepel, Anzilotti argues that the responsibility of states shares its normative basis with the sovereignty of states: "the existence of an international legal order postulates that the subjects on which duties are imposed should equally be responsible in the case of a failure to perform those duties."[120] Just as international law grants states powers, it also imposes upon them restrictions to those powers.[121] Rights and responsibilities are simply different aspects of a state's sovereignty. However, unlike Jellinek and Triepel, Anzilotti was both a positivist and a dualist, which allowed him to develop a broader doctrine of state responsibility than his German predecessors.

[118] Dionisio Anzilotti, *Teoria generale della responsabilità dello Stato nel diritto internazionale. Parte prima, Il problema della responsabilità di diritto internazionale* (Firenze: F. lumachi, 1902).

[119] On the influence of German thought on Italian legal doctrine, *see* Annamaria Monti, "'Interdisciplinary' Legal Studies and the Emergence of New Academic Teachings: A Research Project on Law Courses in 19th–20th Century Italy," 1 CIAN - Revista de Historia de las Universidades 19 (2016), at pp. 91–97. *See further* Angelo Piero Sereni, *The Italian Conception of International Law* (New York: Columbia University Press, 1943), ch. 11. On the comparison between Italian and German contributions to international law, *see* Francesco Messineo, "Is there an Italian Conception of International Law," 2(4) *Cambridge Journal of International and Comparative Law* 879 (2013) (Italian school firmly rooted on Jellinek and the German school – *ibid*, at p. 892).

[120] Dionisio Anzilotti, *Corso di diritto internazionale* (3rd ed., Rome: Athenaeum, 1928), translated into French by Gilbert Gidel, *Cours de droit international* (Paris: Panthéon-Assas/LGDJ, 1999 [1929]), at p. 467.

[121] In an oft-quoted derivative of this formulation, de Visscher describes state responsibility as the "necessary corollary" of the equality of states – Charles de Visscher, "La responsabilité des États," in *Bibliotheca Visseriana II* (Leyden: Brill, 1924), at p. 90.

To Anzilotti, in all legal systems there is a general obligation to repair wrongs.[122] The existence of a breach triggers a new legal relationship, the duty to repair.[123] Following Triepel, Anzilotti employs distinctly international rules for state responsibility.[124] Anzilotti's express purpose in writing a treatise on state responsibility was to clarify the international principles of attribution that connect the acts of individuals to the overarching responsibilities of states.[125] For example, while fault and intent are critical elements in domestic law, they are foreign to a legal system with exclusively states as subjects. Anzilotti's rejection of the fault requirement is indicative of his overall rejection of domestic analogies as a source of international law.

Further, taking issue with Jellinek, he writes that state responsibility is not a matter of subjective psychology,[126] but only of objective fact.[127] To Anzilotti there is nothing extra-legal in the finding of an international wrong; it is comprised of two simple, verifiable facts: did specific conduct occur and did that conduct violate international law?[128] This objective

122 *See* Emmanuelle Jouannet, *Emer de Vattel et l'émergence du droit international classique* (Paris: Pedone, 1998), at p. 407.

123 Anzilotti, *supra* note 120, at p. 467. *See also* Dionisio Anzilotti, "La responsabilité internationale des États à raison des dommages soufferts par des étrangers," 13 *Revue générale de droit international public* 285 (1906), at p. 308.

124 *See* Anzilotti, *supra* note 120, at p. 498 (regarding malice and fault being different in domestic and international contexts). *See further* Roberto Ago, "Le délit international," 68 *Recueil des cours* 440 (Paris: Sirey, 1939), at pp. 491, 450 n 1; James Crawford and Tom Grant, "Responsibility of States for Injuries to Foreigners," in J. P. Grant and J. C. Barker (eds.), *The Harvard Research in International Law: Contemporary Analysis and Appraisal* 77–126 (Buffalo: W. S. Hein, 2007), at pp. 81–82.

125 *Ibid*, at p. 469 ("the act of the State is nothing but the activity of individuals that the law imputes to the State").

126 According to Anzilotti, "*le dol et la faute dans le sens propre du mot expriment des manières d'être de la volonté comme fait psychologique et on ne peut donc en parler qu'en se rapportant à l'individu*" (Anzilotti, *supra* note 120, at p. 498).

127 Anzilotti, *supra* note 120, at pp. 5–29 (especially at 14), pp. 285–309. On this transformation, from "subjective" to "objective" fault, *see* Sandra Szurek, "La force majeure en droit international" (doctoral thesis, Université Paris II Panthéon-Assas, 1996), Vol I, 293–307; Sandra Szurek, "The Notion of Circumstances Precluding Wrongfulness," in Crawford, Pellet and Olleson, *supra* note 85, at pp. 433–434. See further Pierre-Marie Dupuy, "The International Law of State Responsibility: Revolution or Evolution?," 11 *Michigan Journal of International Law* 105 (1989), at p. 110: Anzilotti, along with Basdevant, Bourquin, and Brierly, brought the notions of responsibility and liability into almost total synonymity (in French, *responsabilité* describes both).

128 Anzilotti, *supra* note 120, at p. 5: "*l'action, c'est-à-dire un fait matériel, extérieur, et sensible, et la règle de droit, avec laquelle il se trouve en contradiction.*" Attribution is objective but depends on the facts and laws underlying each case. Official acts of state

position would become the dominant one among international lawyers during the twentieth century.[129]

Anzilotti's discussion of attribution is extensive. Their purpose is to connect the dots between the content of, and a state's compliance with, its international obligations.[130] He introduces two new forms of responsibility: "direct" and "indirect."[131] To Anzilotti, "indirect responsibility" is triggered when a state has outsourced its diplomacy to another state but retains its own international personality, and thereby creates a multilateral relationship among the parties.[132] The rule of indirect responsibility is a small exception to Anzilotti's positivist conception of state responsibility.[133]

organs, even if legal under domestic law, could be breaches of international law attributable to the state. Yet, unofficial acts of private individuals, even if illegal under domestic law, could not be breaches of international law attributable to the state – "*La responsabilité internationale des États à raison des dommages soufferts par des étrangers*" (*supra* note 113, at pp. 5–29 and 285–309). *See further* Szurek, *supra* note 127 (doctoral thesis), Vol. I, pp. 293–307.

129 According to Roberto Ago, after Anzilotti, the attribution of state conduct became a positive law of international responsibility (Ago, *supra* note 124, at p. 470). James Crawford draws a line from Anzilotti through Ago to Arango-Ruiz in the progressive development of state responsibility. He labels this an "Italian tradition" of state responsibility ("The International Court of Justice and the Law of State Responsibility," in Christian J. Tams and James Sloan (eds.), *The Development of International Law by the International Court of Justice* (Oxford: Oxford University, 2013), at pp. 72, 75).

130 Anzilotti, *supra* note 120, at p. 491.

131 This distinction does not track Vattel's earlier concept of "indirect responsibility" (Emer de Vattel, *The Law of Nations, or Principles of Natural Law Applied to the Conduct and Affairs of Nations and Sovereigns* (Charles Ghequiere Fenwick, trans.) (Washington, DC: Carnegie, 1916) [1758]: "Whoever ill-treats a citizen indirectly injures the State, which must protect that citizen. The sovereign of the injured citizen must avenge the deed and, if possible, force the aggressor to give full satisfaction or punish him, since otherwise the citizen will not obtain the chief end of civil society, which is protection"). For a discussion, *see* de Visscher, *supra* note 121, at p. 94; Francisco V. Garcia Amador, "State Responsibility: Some New Problems," 94(2) *Recueil des cours* 365 (1958), at pp. 401–405.

132 Since international law prohibits injuring another State would still apply to the former, it is able to engage in delictual conduct but, as it cannot enter into relations with the injured or offended state, the delictual state "must address itself to the State which represents it, and the duty to redress the damage caused rests with that State" (Anzilotti, "*La responsabilité internationale des États à raison des dommages soufferts par des étrangers,*" *supra* note 113, at p. 301, translation and discussion in Ago, *supra* note 124, at p. 6). Although largely overlooked at the time this was written, this view of Anzilotti's became increasingly influential with the establishment of international institutions such as the League of Nations.

133 Anzilotti argues that the legal equality of states precludes the invocation by one state of the responsibility of another state for the breach of a third state (or the international community) – Anzilotti, *supra* note 821, at p. 88.

Anzilotti limits the content of state responsibility to the bilateral claim to reparation as opposed to a right of reprisal. He clearly separates the issues of attribution, remedies and enforcement in his writing.[134] Though the Italian lawyer allows for certain instances of multilateral intervention in theory, actual international practice was not there yet.[135] Thus, punitive state responsibility was impossible, given the reality of international society; such an expanded form of international responsibility would be premised on a vision of the international community as a whole that was "unknown to international law and repugnant to it."[136] This bilateralist-communitarian ambivalence[137] was present in the title to his 1906 *Revue Générale*: "*La responsabilité internationale des États.*" The article was subtitled: "*à raison de dommages soufferts par des étrangers.*"

Given his importance to early doctrinal developments, some writers have proclaimed Anzilotti to be the "founder" of state responsibility.[138] Anzilotti was certainly one of the most influential writers on state responsibility in the first half of the twentieth century. More importantly, by unpacking the concept of state responsibility into three sub-components – attribution, remedies and enforcement – Anzilotti "liberated" the procedural and substantive issues of state responsibility from

[134] To Anzilotti, the content of state responsibility, the right to reparations, included both for moral and material injury: "The breach of the international legal order committed by a State subject to that order thus gives rise to a duty of reparation, in general consisting of the restoration of the disrupted legal order" ("*La responsabilité internationale des États à raison des dommages soufferts par des étrangers,*" *supra* note 113 as translated by Dupuy in Pierre-Marie Dupuy, "Dionisio Anzilotti and the Law of International Responsibility of States," 3(1) *European Journal of International Law* 139 (1992), at p. 145). Similar to Anzilotti, de Visscher wrote that "International responsibility is a fundamental notion reducible to the obligation of a State to make reparation for the consequences for a wrongful act that is imputable to it" (Charles de Visscher, "Le déni de justice en droit international," 52 *Recueil des cours* 421 (1935)).

[135] See Roberto Ago, International Law Commission Yearbook (1976), Vol. II, Part One, at p. 42, note 219; Nolte, *infra* note 139, at p. 1087.

[136] Anzilotti, *supra* note 120, at p. 468.

[137] Anzilotti, *supra* note 120, at p. 517 (there is no international right to reparation without an injury) and p. 468 (there is no international criminal responsibility of states).

[138] *See* Dupuy, *supra* note 837, at p. 139 (Anzilotti was "the greatest and most outstanding classic author" of the Golden Age of positivist voluntarism); Max Sørenson (ed.), *Manual of Public International Law* (London: Macmillan, 1968), at p. 554 (the founder of state responsibility was Anzilotti); Hersch Lauterpacht, *Private Law Sources and Analogies of International Law: With Special Reference to International Arbitration* (London: Longmans, Green and Co., 1927), at p. 136.

the question of enforcement.[139] Still, in *Teoria generale della responsabilità dello stato*, he takes as his starting point, the German theories of state responsibility. The first three citations are to Heffter, Gerber and Jellinek.[140]

But as critical a figure as Anzilotti was, he does not represent the field's beginning or its end. His Hohfeldian-like correlating of rights and responsibilities[141] was seen as unacceptably incomplete and weak by the next generation of international lawyers.[142] The outbreak of the First World War shook the statist credo and led many international lawyers to press for international solidarity as an alternative international framework. To shore up the legal stability of the international system and to address the real needs of humanity, these lawyers would argue that state responsibility should not be tethered to decaying notions of sovereignty.

Oppenheim Popularizes State Responsibility

The German approach to state responsibility was first exported to England through Hall but most famously *via* Lassa Francis Lawrence Oppenheim (1858–1919). Oppenheim's international law treatises (published in London from 1905) were the most referenced international law texts of the past century.[143] Mónica Garcia-Salmones Rovira considers the German émigré "the inaugurator of the tradition of the

[139] Georg Nolte, "From Dionisio Anzilotti to Roberto Ago: The Classical International Law of State Responsibility and the Traditional Primacy of a Bilateral Conception of Inter-State Relations," 13(5) *European Journal of International Law* 1083 (2002), at p. 1087.

[140] Anzilotti, *supra* note 1, at pp. 1–2.

[141] I am referring to Hohfeld's system of "jural opposites" and "jural correlatives" – *see* Wesley Newcomb Hohfeld, "Some Fundamental Legal Conceptions as Applied in Judicial Reasoning," 23 *Yale Law Journal* 16 (1913): that is, liability as the opposite of immunity and the correlative of power.

[142] As Bin Cheng notes, "Anzilotti failed to pursue to its logical conclusion his new standpoint that rules ... in international law operated autonomously" (Bin Cheng, *General Principles of Law as Applied by International Courts and Tribunals* (London: Stevens, 1953), at p. 206). According to Nolte, "Anzilotti, the positivist, seems to stand against Ago, who would represent a certain renaissance of natural law. And Anzilotti, the legal defender of sovereign power politics, seems to stand against Ago, the domesticator of sovereignty" (Nolte, *supra* note 139, at p. 1084). However, *see* Anzilotti, *supra* note 120, at p. 13.

[143] Lassa Oppenheim, *International Law: A Treatise, Vol. I: Peace* (London: Longmans, Green, and Co., 1905).

economic-positivist international law."[144] Oppenheim was the son of a Jewish horse trader and educated at the Universities of Berlin, Göttingen and Heidelberg. By the age of twenty-three, he had received his doctorate in law from Göttingen. For the first two decades of his career, he seems to have not at all been interested in international but rather in criminal law. It was not until he moved to London in 1895 that he turned to international law.

In 1908, Oppenheim replaced John Westlake (1828–1913) as the Whewell Professor of International Law at Cambridge University.[145] He includes a general treatment of state responsibility in a standalone chapter of his 1905 treatise.[146] As he does in other chapters, Oppenheim begins with several citations to legal doctrine. For state responsibility, the citations are heavily weighted towards German texts, but also include Anglo-American, Latin American and French sources. Here he seeks to provide a systematic – if brief – treatment of the emerging field. It is a "combination of the German passion for organization and the English love of detail."[147]

He provides a general discussion of state responsibility but, then considers instances of state responsibility in the context of specific international norms – *e.g.*, injuries to aliens or diplomatic envoys, neutrality, *etc.*[148] While there is not yet an "International Court of Justice which could establish such responsibility," he writes that state

[144] García-Salmones Rovira, supra note 1, at p. 2. She clearly identifies and stresses the importance of his German roots. Indeed, García-Salmones Rovira traces critical roots of the Anglo-American (*e.g.*, Oppenheim, Borchard, Lauterpacht, Eagleton, Jessup) as well as Italian (*e.g.*, Anzilotti, Ago) legal schools to the German philosophical approach to public law. On Oppenheim's bridge from Germany to the US, *see ibid*, especially ch. 3.

[145] More so than any other position on any other law faculty, Whewell Professors from Lassa Oppenheim to James Crawford arguably made the greatest impact on the doctrine of state responsibility.

[146] *Ibid*, at §§148–167 (almost twenty pages).

[147] Mark Janis, "The New Oppenheim and Its Theory of International Law," 16(2) *Oxford Journal of Legal Studies* 329 (1996), at pp. 330–331, as cited in Amanda Perreau-Saussine, "A Case Study on Jurisprudence as a Source of International Law: Oppenheim's Influence," in Matthew Craven, Malgosia Fitzmaurice and Maria Vogiatzi (eds.), *Time, History and International Law* 100 (2007), at p. 95. Mónica García-Salmones Rovira describes Oppenheim as an "integrator," whose international upbringing and professional life is reflected in his scholarship (García-Salmones Rovira, *supra* note 1, at p. 50).

[148] The chapter is focused on the positive law of nations. Like Triepel before him, Oppenheim was a follower of Karl Binding and of Karl Bergbohm, who were inclined to "purify" international law of its natural legal roots (*see* García-Salmones Rovira, *supra* note 1, at p. 33).

responsibility is nevertheless a "*legal* responsibility."[149] Although there is still no legalistic procedure for ascertaining the content of a state's responsibility, the fact of its existence is not open to question. Oppenheim defines state responsibility in a manner familiar to contemporary lawyers: "For every neglect of an international legal duty constitutes an international delinquency."[150]

Oppenheim does not attempt to define the content of state responsibility. Instead, like Bluntschli, he expects this to be determined bilaterally on a case-by-case basis:

> The only rule which is unanimously recognised by theory and practice is that out of an international delinquency arises a right for the wronged State to request from the delinquent State the performance of such expiatory acts as are necessary for a reparation of the wrong done.[151]

This is because Oppenheim believed that international law at the turn of the twentieth century permitted the wronged state to exercise "such means as are necessary to enforce an adequate reparation."[152] This unfortunate fact, he writes, is clearly evidenced in the American diplomatic practice regarding alien protection.[153] The scope of implementation is reparations and compliance and excludes punitive measures, writes Oppenheim. States, as sovereigns, cannot be punished.[154] In the event of aggressive acts, defensive states can take measures of self-preservation that would not trigger its legal responsibility "however injurious it may actually be to another State" because such are committed neither willfully nor maliciously.[155]

Oppenheim makes great efforts to present the law of state responsibility as coherent and complete – even if its enforcement is still clearly in its primitive stages. The fact that he was a "pragmatist" did not preclude

149 Oppenheim, *supra* note 143, at §148 (emphasis in original).

150 Oppenheim, *supra* note 143, §148.

151 Oppenheim, *supra* note 143, at §156.

152 Oppenheim, *supra* note 143, at §156; also discussed in §148 ("the violated State can through reprisals and even war compel the delinquent State to comply with its international duties").

153 Oppenheim, *supra* note 143, at §162: In the case of the denial of justice to aliens, if a court does not provide non-discriminatory protection, it triggers the host state's responsibility. "But if a Court observes its own proper forms of justice and nevertheless pronounces a materially unjust judgment, matters become so complicated that there is hardly a peaceable way in which the injured State can successfully obtain reparation for the wrong done, and eventually war may break out between the respective States."

154 Oppenheim, *supra* note 143, at §§151, 166.

155 Oppenheim, *supra* note 143, at §154.

Oppenheim from having an overarching vision of international law, but his was a "hidden theoretical world."[156] And he did not see it as the task of international lawyers to complete its development by eliminating "old" notions of sovereignty. Like Jellinek, Triepel and Anzilotti before him, Oppenheim seeks to establish a doctrine of state responsibility within the established, positive confines of sovereignty.[157] He does not substantively develop the law of state responsibility, but the popularity of his treatises certainly served to disseminate German theories among Anglo-American audiences. Throughout its first six editions (1905–1947), Oppenheim's *Treatise* remained "by common consent the outstanding and most frequently employed systematic treatise on the subject in the English-speaking countries."[158] The writings of Lauterpacht and Arnold Duncan McNair (1885–1975) in Great Britain and of Borchard and Eagleton in the US borrowed much from the structure and approach of Oppenheim's (brief) chapter on state responsibility.

To recapitulate, early German theorists, including Heffter and Bluntschli, conceived of international law as a genus of public law and concentrated on examining treaties, customs and general principles of law. Later theorists, including Jellinek and Triepel, sought to provide a more scientific methodology to the project. This stream was based less on the actual consent of states as on the competence of experts (such as themselves). Still, with their deference to sovereignty, these lawyers did not produce expansive theories on state responsibility. However, their theories convincingly demonstrated that the existence of state responsibility was an essential attribute of sovereignty. Anzilotti took nineteenth-century German theory to its logical positivist conclusion by constructing

[156] García-Salmones Rovira, *supra* note 1, at p. 52. She continues, "The theories imported from Germany were invisible in Oppenheim's work because they were the basic tools with which he constructed his international law" (*ibid*).

[157] In *Wimbledon*, the world court interpreted that responsibility is but an attribute of sovereignty (*The SS Wimbledon*, 1923, PCIJ Series A, No. 1, p. 4, 25. *See* Oppenheim, *supra* note 143 at p. 243: "Responsibility for such [international legal] duties is . . . a quality of every State as an International Person, without which the Family of Nations could not peaceably exist." Benedict Kingsbury suggests that "Perhaps Oppenheim's most enduring impact on international law is his construction of a rigorously statist conception of international society" (Benedict Kingsbury, "Legal Positivism as Normative Politics: International Society, Balance of Power and Lassa Oppenheim's Positive International Law," 13(2) *European Journal of International Law* 401 (2002), at p. 409).

[158] Arthur Nussbaum, *A Concise History of the Law of Nations* (New York: Macmillan, 1947), at p. 277.

a framework of international responsibility. His *Teoria generale della responsabilità dello stato nel diritto* is at once broad and comprehensive as well as bilateralist and retrained in its scope. After the Great War, this would change.

After Versailles

In response to the trauma of the First World War – and especially to the Treaty of Versailles[159] – German lawyers became more engaged with current events. The interwar era saw the publication of several more monographs dedicated to state responsibility. By the late-1930s, German-speaking writers such as Hans Kelsen (1881–1973),[160] Alf Verdross (1890–1980)[161] and Karl Strupp (1886–1940)[162] and others had put state responsibility on the international law map.[163]

Roberto Ago (1907–1995), in his 1939 Hague lectures, continues Anzilotti's project of developing a system of imputation based on his state-centered conception of international law.[164] In the US, Edwin Borchard (1884–1951)[165] and Clyde Eagleton (1891–1958)[166] write extensively on state responsibility and for new audiences. Hersch Lauterpacht (1897–1960), an Austrian- and British-trained international

[159] Treaty of Peace between the Allied and Associated Powers and Germany, concluded at Versailles, 28 June 1919, 2 *Bevans* 235, 13 *American Journal of International Law Supplement* 151 (1919).

[160] Kelsen, *infra* notes 185–203 and accompanying text.

[161] Verdross, *infra* note 236.

[162] Strupp, *infra* notes 205–234 and accompanying text.

[163] For example, Fritz Benjamin wrote his dissertation on state responsibility for acts of its organs at Heidelberg: *Haftung des Staates aus dem Verschulden seiner Organe nach Völkerrecht*, Doctoral Dissertation submitted to Heidelberg University, November 4, 1909 (Breslau: Fleischmann, 1909) (like Grotius, Benjamin, who took issue with Schoen and others, believed in the requirement of fault for the imposition of state responsibility). Paul Schoen wrote an infrequently cited but substantive work on state responsibility: *Die völkerrechtliche Haftung der Staaten aus unerlaubten Handlungen* (Breslau: Kern, 1917), at pp. 35, 135–136 (new theories of state responsibility such as Anzilotti's satisfied positive conditions of law at the expense of excluding communitarian interests). Paul de Visscher wrote extensively on the topic in French (de Visscher, *supra* notes 121, 134).

[164] Ago, *supra* note 124, at p. 462 (*un fait illicite peut être imputé même à un sujet-personne juridique*). State responsibility is a system of neutral, legal rules based on states as the international personality. As I will discuss in the next chapter, "theoretical" Ago was in this regard quite distinct from "doctrinal" Ago.

[165] Borchard, *infra* notes 272–277 and accompanying text.

[166] Eagleton, *infra* notes 278–314 and accompanying text.

lawyer, not only writes extensively on the topic, but after the Second World War, drafted the UN document calling for the codification of general state responsibility.[167] Below, I demonstrate how this interwar period yielded a doctrine of state responsibility that has continued to serve as a general framework of international law enforcement actions.[168]

After the First World War, the relationship in Germany between internal and external public law was reversed. Instead of extrapolating principles of international law from domestic law, German public lawyers began to look for metaprinciples from other sources – such as natural law and international law.[169] The trauma of the Great War seems to have renewed a debate about fundamentals, and a search for a new standard by which to measure governmental conduct. The sense was that the previous generation had strayed too far from the reality of national political life. Public lawyers were being too positivist – *too gentle* – to be effective. The new generation of lawyers, many of whom were Jewish and were trained in Vienna, viewed the nineteenth-century theories as being too flimsy and easily dismissed to regulate state conduct.[170] In 1914, German Chancellor Theobald von Bethmann-Hollweg (1856–1921) notoriously disclaimed the constraints of law on necessity, "*wir sind jetzt in der Notwehr; und Not kennt kein Gebot.*"[171] Necessity knows no law.

Karl Strupp (1886–1940) is an example of a German-speaking international lawyer who appealed for change even as World War I broke out. However, Strupp in 1914 sounded different than Strupp in 1924. During that decade, Strupp morphed from a strong dualist who favored national over international laws to a strong supporter of the primacy of international over national law.[172] When the Great War broke out, Strupp was almost finished with a treatise on the laws of war; so, he rushed into

167 Lauterpacht, *infra* notes 236–272 and accompanying text.

168 As I will discuss in the next chapter, it was during this time, I believe, that "State responsibility" was coined as a term of art.

169 Stolleis, *supra* note 108, at p. 174.

170 *See* Isabel V. Hull, *A Scrap of Paper: Breaking and Making International Law during the Great War* (Ithaca: Cornell University Press, 2014), at p. 76 ("Germany's prewar international lawyers followed their government").

171 "We are now in a state of self-defense; and necessity knows no law" (cited in Shabtai Rosenne (ed.), *The International Law Commission's Draft Articles on State Responsibility, Part 1, Articles 1–35* (Dordrecht: Nijhoff, 1991), at p. 43). As Stolleis has commented, "the flood of special war law . . . drowned out all other areas of the law" (Stolleis, *supra* note 108, at p. 37, internal citations omitted).

172 Link describes Strupp's development starting in nationalism and then changing after the First World War, especially because of the invasion of Belgium (*infra* note 205, at p. 339).

print. In *Das internationale Landkriegsrecht*, Strupp tries to reconcile the mainstream German view that the Hague Regulations[173] "*in no way*" impeded the goal of "the complete defeat of the enemy" with his position on the binding nature of international law.[174] A decade later, Strupp was less concerned with appeasing nationalist sentiments than with strengthening international law into the primary normative framework governing interstitial relations. International society needed a rule-based approach if it wanted to prevent another global calamity.

Interwar lawyers like Strupp felt that international society could not wait for states to institutionalize international law through *ad hoc* treaty-making; diplomacy would have to be supplemented by a constitutional structure. A more comprehensive and legal solution was needed to safeguard international society from the perils of international politics. This disgust was felt by legal minds on both sides of the war. In a long-winded speech regarding the dangers of the Reich, Jacques Marquis de Dampierre (1874–1947) wrote of "bellicose Germanism" as coming into "inevitable conflict" with existing principles of international law.[175] German violations "had been so blatant, and the law had been so defenseless, that most French politicians felt uneasy speaking of German guilt in positive–legal terms at all; it was an almost metaphysical guilt that was thrust upon Germany, a guilt inadequately encompassed in terms of violations of the Hague treaties."[176]

The Versailles peace treaty did not just end the war; it did so by holding Germany morally and financially responsible for the losses sustained during the war. According to Article 231 of the treaty, "The Allied and Associated Governments affirm and Germany accepts the *responsibility* of Germany and her allies for causing all the loss and damage to which the Allied and Associated Governments and their nationals have been subjected as a consequence of the war imposed upon them by the aggression of Germany and her allies."[177]

That an international treaty could name the "responsibility" of a civilized state for its internationally wrongful conduct was a milestone

[173] Convention (IV) Respecting the Laws and Customs of War on Land, The Hague, October 18, 1907, entered into force, January 26, 1910.

[174] Karl Strupp, *Das internationale Landkriegsrecht* (Frankfurt: J. Baer & Co., 1914), at p. 3 (emphasis in original); Hull, *supra* note 170, at p. 77 (internal citations partially omitted).

[175] Jacques Marquis de Dampierre, *German Imperialism and International Law* (London: Constable & Co., 1917), at p. 15.

[176] Koskenniemi, *Gentle Civilizer*, *supra* note 1, at p. 293.

[177] *Supra* note 159, emphasis added.

in the history of state responsibility. This was a rare occurrence. The form of responsibility in the Versailles treaty was not a legalistic one; it was not a dispute that was delegated to a third party for adjudication; rather, it was an imposed capitulation (or settled negotiation at best). However, it was an important step in the general acceptance of international legal responsibility as an attribute of rather than an obstacle to state sovereignty. However, it was not Article 231's inclusion of state responsibility that inspired German and other interwar lawyers to further theorize the topic.

Even Walther Schücking (1875–1935), the longstanding German pacifist who was also a delegate and negotiator of the Versailles treaty, saw it as a personal affront and voted against it in the German Reichstag.[178] Schücking's response to the trauma of Versailles was to focus on future multilateral treaties such as the Covenant of the League of Nations as well as international codification efforts including the League's Codification Committee.[179] Led by Schücking, interwar lawyers sought to reengage the international community by pressing for Germany's participation in multilateral efforts, such as the 1925 Locarno treaties.[180] They hoped to mitigate the injustice of Versailles through additional treaties and arbitrations and, ultimately, participation in the League of Nations.[181] Although Schücking's writings do not focus on state responsibility,[182] he played a leadership role, along with Kelsen and Strupp, in attacking the "old" assumptions of sovereignty's power.[183] These lawyers "saw themselves as part of a modernization movement in international law."[184]

178 *See* Mónica García-Salmones Rovira, "Walther Schücking and the Pacifist Traditions of International Law," 3 *European Journal of International Law* 755 (2011), at p. 760 (pacifistic idealism unshattered by injustice).

179 For a discussion, *see* Jost Delbrück, "Law's Frontier: Walther Schücking and the Quest for the Lex Ferenda," 22(3) *European Journal of International Law* 801 (2011), at p. 808.

180 Treaty of Mutual Guarantee between Germany, Belgium, France, Great Britain and Italy; October 16, 1925 (The Locarno Pact), available online at https://avalon.law.yale.edu/20th_century/locarno_001.asp, last visted August 7, 2021.

181 Karl Strupp, *Das Werk von Locarno* (Berlin and Leipzig: de Gruyter, 1926), pp. 92–93.

182 For example, his 1927 Hague Lectures, "*Le développement du Pacte de la Société des Nations*," 20 *Recueil des Cours* (1927) and his article on sanctions by the League of Nations, "*Die Organisation der Völkerbundexekution gegen den Angreifer*," 16 *Zeitschrift für Völkerrecht* 529 (1932), both focused on institutional mechanisms for peaceful dispute resolution rather than on the substance of that legalism – that is, state responsibility.

183 Jochen von Bernstorff, *The Public International Law Theory of Hans Kelsen: Believing in Universal Law* (Cambridge: Cambridge University Press, 2010), at pp. 61–70.

184 *Ibid*, at p. 5.

Kelsen Brings Coherence to the Doctrine

Hans Kelsen (1881–1973) (Figure 4.5) was the most influential German-speaking theorist to emerge from the interwar era. He reconceptualized international law as part of a pure, unitary system (*Reine Rechtslehre*).[185] This was a methodical rejection of Triepel's dualism, which had become widely accepted by the turn of the twentieth century.[186] Kelsen was born to Jewish parents in Prague and converted to Christianity in 1905 with the publication of his first book (on the political theory of Dante).[187] In 1911, Kelsen published his doctoral dissertation, *Hauptprobleme der Staatsrechtslehre entwickelt aus der Lehre vom Rechtssatze* (*Main Problems in Theory of Public Law, Developed from Theory of the Legal Statement*), which triggered a public Austro-German debate on the nature of legal theory.[188] In 1920, a year after Kelsen was appointed to a full professorship at the University of Vienna, he published *Das Problem der Souveränität und die Theorie des Völkerrechts*, which expanded his views to encompass international public law.[189] Kelsen's "Vienna School" was a dominant influence at the time. Its main periodical was the *Zeitschrift für öffentliches Recht* (*Journal of Public Law*), which was established in 1914 under a different title and then again in 1919. Kelsen's theories spread into many continents, especially Latin America.[190]

185 Hans Kelsen, *Reine Rechtslehre* (Wien: Deuticke, 1934).

186 For a discussion of Kelsen's reaction to Triepel's dualism see Spiermann, *supra* note 89, at p. 43.

187 Hans Kelsen, *Die Staatslehre des Dante Alighieri* (Vienna: F. Deuticke, 1905).

188 Hans Kelsen, *Hauptprobleme der Staatsrechtslehre entwickelt aus der Lehre vom Rechtssatze* (Tübingen: Mohr, 1911).

189 Hans Kelsen, *Das Problem der Souveränität und die Theorie des Völkerrechts* (Tübingen: Mohr, 1920).

190 Josef L. Kunz, *Latin-American Philosophy of Law in the Twentieth Century* (New York: New York University Press, 1950); H. B. Jacobini, *A Study of the Philosophy of International Law as Seen in Works of Latin American Writers* (The Hague: Martinus Nijhoff, 1954), at p. 111 ("There is considerable indication that the Pure Theory of Law has been an important factor in ... Latin American legal philosophy"); Wolfgang Stegmüller, *Hauptströmungen der Gegenwartsphilosophie* (6th ed., Stuttgart: Alfred Kröner Verlag, 1978), at p. 346; Stolleis, *supra* note 108, at p. 156 (Kelsenian scholarship, with its sharp distinction between law and politics, was a safe and effective outlet for activism in the shadow of the clergy, both for Jewish academics in Austria as well as secular-leaning scholars in Latin America).

Figure 4.5 Hans Kelsen[191]

Kelsen agrees with the fundamental view of his former teacher, Georg Jellinek: states are bound by law. But this juridical fact is not proven by *Selbstverpflichtungslehre*, which is yet another fiction. Why replace a legal fiction with a sociological one? To Kelsen:

> The problem of the so-called auto-obligation of the State is one of those pseudo-problems that result from the erroneous dualism of State and law. This dualism is, in turn, due to a fallacy of which we meet numerous examples in the history of all fields of human thought. Our desire for the intuitive representation of abstractions leads us to personify the unity of a system, and then to hypostasize the personification. What originally was only a way of representing the unity of a system of objects becomes a new object, existing in its own right . . . Then the pseudo-problem arises as to the relationship between these two objects.[192]

The idea of sovereignty that previous German theorists had worked so hard to protect was in fact a logical redundancy. The norm had no separate value from the more general and fundamental question

[191] Photo courtesy of Getty Images, www.gettyimages.no/detail/news-photo/jurist-%C3%B6sterreich-usaum-1930-news-photo/541040891?adppopup=true.

[192] Hans Kelsen, *General Theory of Law and State* (Anders Wedberg, trans., Cambridge: Harvard University Press, 1945), at p. 198, emphasis added. The book was originally published as *Allgemeine Staatslehre* (Berlin: Springer, 1925).

regarding international law's primacy over domestic law. In the monistic conception, sovereignty is simply the sum total of competences allowable under international law.[193]

Kelsen sparred heatedly with Triepel and his coterie during annual meetings of the Association of German Teachers of State Law.[194] For Triepel, statutes alone were unable to measure public actions. Additionally, courts had to consider historical facts as a necessary part of their process of adjudication. For Kelsen only pure, positive law could assess political authority. Pure law, of course, did not mean politically neutral law. As the German legal historian Jochen von Bernstorff explains, Kelsen's interwar project sought to weaken traditional notions of sovereignty and to strengthen new institutions of international law.[195] His methodology was to "free" the law from the ideological baggage of contemporary discourse.[196] Further, based on his experience in drafting the Austrian Constitution of 1920[197] and his membership in the Constitutional Court of Austria (*Verfassungsgerichtshof VfGH*), Kelsen believed a court that was independent and removed from party influences was both possible and desirable.[198]

Kelsen's conception of state responsibility corresponds to his view of "International Law as Primitive Law."[199] To the Vienna School, international law was not yet necessarily "law." But it was in the process of becoming such law. Until that time, international law permits reprisals and war as a sanction of legal rights, but it does not contain sophisticated rules of attribution, reparation and enforcement. Kelsen contrasts state responsibility to "civil" conceptions: "In international law, responsibility

[193] Martti Koskenniemi, "Sovereignty. Prolegomena to a Study of International Law as Discourse," *Kansainoikeus/Jus Gentium* 71–106 (1987), at p. 78 (footnotes omitted). Strupp would share this view. Strupp wants to ban the term "sovereignty" (*Souveränität*) from international law: "*Il faut éliminer du Droit international public la notion de la souveraineté, notion erronée et donnant lieu a de dangereux malentendus*" (Link, *infra* note 205, at p. 332; Karl Strupp, *Éléments du droit international public universel, européen et américain* (Paris: Rousseau, 1927), at p. 24).

[194] Stolleis, *supra* note 108, at pp. 181–195.

[195] von Bernstorff, *supra* note 183, at pp. 2–3. The Vienna School, he continues, "set out to destroy what they felt were the detrimental tenets of classical international law theory" (*ibid*, at p. 6).

[196] von Bernstorff, *supra* note 183, at p. 61.

[197] *Österreichische Bundesverfassung*, enacted October 1, 1920.

[198] Stolleis, *supra* note 108, at p. 188.

[199] Kelsen, *supra* note 191, at pp. 355–357.

is neither civil nor criminal."[200] According to the "pure" view of state responsibility, the only legal consequence of a wrongful act was the right of the injured state to impose a sanction on the respondent state.[201]

To Kelsen, state responsibility takes its rightful place within a coherent system of rules. It is a doctrine that regulates states because *law* regulates states and not because of state will. Legal obligation derives from pure, internal legal norms. To Kelsen, who considered Jellinek both his teacher and his foil, the law was not a way of describing the state, *it was the state.* It was legally impossible to impute the conduct of an individual to the state unless that act was somehow legally constituted. The law is the law no matter how awful.[202] Accordingly, state responsibility was no longer a concept to tap dance around. As with the domestic law, international law necessarily includes a doctrine of public responsibility. If international law was not yet fully developed, this did not preclude the existence of law's inherent (if weak) features.[203] This took much pressure off sovereignty-focused doctrines of state responsibility. International law was law because it had a coercive component – legal recourse to force.[204] This created room for his students to rethink the field in broader terms, especially outside Germany. Kelsen trained some of the most influential international lawyers, including Alf Verdross, Hersch Lauterpacht, Karl Strupp, Alwyn Freeman (1910–1983) and Hans Morgenthau (1904–1980).

[200] Hans Kelsen, "Théorie du droit international public," 84 *Recueil des cours* 1 (1953-III), at p. 87.

[201] To Kelsen, state responsibility exclusively consisted of the specific sanctions of reprisals and war – *see ibid* at p. 87.

[202] Even if an individual official commits the most heinous of acts, this conduct can be attributable to a state. In a memorandum to Justice Robert H. Jackson on the prosecution of Axis criminality, Kelsen writes that individual criminal conduct is attributable to states and that liability at the collective, state level was more suitable than at the individual level, unless the individual committed the conduct on his own initiative and not under the color of governmental authority (as cited and discussed in García-Salmones Rovira, *supra* note 1, at p. 364).

[203] This position is likely to have been influential on a later US scholar, James Brown Scott, who studied in Heidelberg when Kelsen taught there, between 1891 and 1894.

[204] "These sanctions like the sanctions of national law, consist in the forcible deprivation of life, liberty, and other goods, notably economic values. In a war human beings are killed, maimed, imprisoned and national or private property is destroyed; by way of reprisals national or private property is confiscated and other legal rights are infringed" (Hans Kelsen, "The Essence of International Law," in Karl W. Deutsch and Stanley Hofffmann (eds.), *The Relevance of International Law Essays in Honor of Leo Gross* (transl. Max Knight, Cambridge: Schenkman, 1968), at p. 87, as cited in Paz, *supra* note 56, at p. 222).

Strupp Seeks Balance in State Responsibility

Karl Strupp (1886–1940) (Figure 4.6) was the next major writer on state responsibility after Anzilotti. Strupp represents the apex of the German approach to state responsibility. Not only did he write his *Habilitation* and several more monographs on the topic,[205] he lectured internationally (including several courses at the Hague Academy of International Law)[206] and drafted a treaty on state responsibility in 1927.[207] Motivated as he was to reconcile the ideals of public law with the realities of German politics, Strupp was somewhere in the middle of the international law theory spectrum. This is not surprising given that, on the one hand, it was Jellinek who inspired Strupp to take up the field of international law and to view it from a historical perspective; on the other hand, Walther Schücking (1875–1935), the first German justice on the PCIJ, was Strupp's thesis advisor at Marburg University. Schücking, one of the few German pacifists within the German legal academy, infused Strupp with a sense of international law's role in the peace movement (*internationale Friedenssicherung*).[208] This balance is reflected in Strupp's *Habilitation*, in which he tackles not only the general ideal of state responsibility but its exception of *Notrecht* as well.[209]

205 *See e.g.*, Karl Strupp, *Das völkerrechtliche Delikt* (Berlin: Kohlhammer, 1920); Karl Strupp, *Die völkerrechtliche Haftung des Staates, insbesondere bei Handlungen Privater* (Kiel: Institut für Internationales Recht, 1927). He studied history and law (majoring in *Völker-* and *Staatsrecht*) in Heidelberg and Marburg between 1905 and 1909. Georg Jellinek had significant influence on Strupp. Sandra Link points out the international atmosphere of Jellinek's seminars, his rhetoric, and the fact that he dedicated a lot of his time to his students were characteristics that Strupp took as role models for his own career. After graduating in Marburg under Walther Schücking, Strupp wanted Jellinek as his dissertation advisor. But Jellinek was unwell at that time, so that Strupp wrote his dissertation with Karl Heinsheimer (Sandra Link, *Ein Realist mit Idealen, der Völkerrechtler Karl Strupp (1886–1940)* (Baden-Baden: Nomos, 2003), at p. 21).

206 In 1925 and again in 1930 – *see further infra* notes 211 and 219.

207 Strupp, *Die völkerrechtliche Haftung des Staates*, *supra* note 205.

208 Link, *supra* note 205, at p. 47.

209 Link agrees with Verdross that Strupp is the first author who treated the question of emergency law with reference to positivism and not to natural law: "*Man kann sogar noch einen Schritt weiter gehen und mit Verdross behaupten, daß Strupp der erste Schriftsteller [ist], der dieses Problem nicht naturrechtlich, sondern positivrechtlich behandelt*" (Link, *supra* note 205, at p. 157).

Figure 4.6 Karl Strupp[210]

Strupp's focus on state responsibility reflects his view that the doctrine was necessary to complete the project of positivizing international law; inspired by Anzilotti's internationalizing of state liability, Strupp sought to complete what Anzilotti began.[211] The Great War, however, moderated his expectations about the potential of public law theory to restrain actual political (not to mention military) power. Clear doctrine was needed, and it had to reflect state practice.[212]

After the Outbreak of the First World War, Strupp became convinced both of international law's primacy over national law and of its interstitial nature. To him, international law's protection of aliens too, was principally concerned with state interests rather than individual rights.[213]

[210] Photo courtesy of Universitätsarchiv Frankfurt am Main (UAF Best. 854 Nr. 1705).

[211] In the decades that passed between Anzilotti and Strupp, the notion of sovereignty had been sufficiently pierced. To Strupp, the idea of sovereignty was not tied to absolute power, but to independence – *see* Karl Strupp, "Les règles générales du droit de la paix," 47 *Recueil des Cours* 263 (1934), at p. 494.

[212] Karl Strupp, "Review: The International Responsibility of States for Denial of Justice, by Alwyn V. Freeman," 18(5) *International Affairs* 689 (1939), at p. 689.

[213] Strupp reviews arbitrations regarding the rights of alien protection but only to substantiate the positivist claim regarding the state-centered international system, wherein only states possess rights and responsibilities – "*C'est à juste titre qu'on a affirmé ici le droit d'action de l'État car l'individu ne peut renoncer à un droit qui, à la vérité, au point de vue juridique, n'est pas le sien, mais appartient à son État. Celui-ci, seul, détermine dans*

He develops the ideas of *Das völkerrechtliche Delikt* against this state-centered background. Strupp argues that state practice is more important than legal logic (*Rechtslogik*). And state practice is very much in existence. Even during times of emergency and war, all states always claim to be invoking and adhering to international law.[214]

Strupp balanced his fidelity to positive law with his desire for a robust system of international law by combining his writings with instances of state practice along with general statements on international theory.[215] Strupp disapproved of the overhauling of international law without intergovernmental support. His approach had to be balanced. He proposed a public treaty on state responsibility, rather than codifying the field *via* private codification. Strupp's draft treaty takes a relatively abstract approach to codifying state responsibility.[216] He seeks to articulate rules of international law that could form the basis of *future* international dispute resolutions.

In *Das völkerrechtliche Delikt*, Strupp writes that the violation of an international obligation triggers the inherent "international responsibility of States."[217] In the first provision of Strupp's 1927 draft treaty on state responsibility, he writes: "A State is responsible to other States for the acts of persons or groups whom it employs for the accomplishment of its purposes (its 'organs'), in so far as these acts conflict with the duties which arise out of the State's international legal relations with the injured State."[218] The 1927 draft treaty opens with generalizations regarding state

quelles conditions il exercera son droit de protection" (Karl Strupp, "L'intervention en matière financière," 8 *Recueil des cours* 1 (1925), at p. 80).

214 Strupp, *Das völkerrechtliche Delikt*, *supra* note 205, at pp. 139–142.

215 Discussed in the next chapter.

216 Strupp, *Die völkerrechtliche Haftung des Staates*, *supra* note 205 (his draft was one of only two interwar codification proposals of state responsibility that approached the topic deductively from the perspective of general principles).

217 Strupp, *Das völkerrechtliche Delikt*, *supra* note 205, at pp. 13–14 (rather than an "international delict").

218 Strupp, *Die völkerrechtliche Haftung des Staates*, *supra* note 205, translation by the Harvard Law School, Research in International Law: Nationality, Responsibility of States, Territorial Waters (Drafts of Conventions prepared in anticipation of the first Conference on the Codification of International Law, The Hague, 1930) (Cambridge Mass., 1929) Part II, Appendix No. 8, pp. 235–236. The draft is not entirely comprised of secondary principles. So, for example, he incorporates the international minimum standard of alien protection in Article 4(2): "Such care is required as may be demanded from a civilized or constitutional State (*Kultur- oder Rechtsstaat*)."

responsibility for any violation attributable to it. For Strupp, as for Anzilotti and in contrast to the then dominant view, no fault had to be imputed to the state to incur its liability. The question of how much the state would have to do to prevent injuries – that is, its duty of diligence, covered by Article 4(2) – would depend on the facts of each case.

Strupp largely ignores the caselaw of state responsibility that was generated by the New World arbitrations. In his Hague Lectures on "The right of the international judge to rule in equity,"[219] he describes international arbitration as an important source of international equity but not of law. This approach is similar to those of many French writers on international arbitration.[220] There is not one citation in this lecture series to the arbitration digests of John Bassett Moore. Strupp is more concerned with reviewing theory and doctrine such as Calvo and Drago rather than practice such as the Lieber Tribunal.[221] This is the same approach that he takes in his books on international arbitrations,[222] on arbitration treaties,[223] and on the German practice of international arbitration.[224] His treatment of the *Alabama Claims* was an exception to this rule.[225]

219 Karl Strupp, "Le droit du juge international de statuer selon l'équité," 33 *Recueil des cours* 351 (1930).

220 *See* Strupp, *supra* note 205, at p. 383. During the period of 1856–72, as Lapradelle and Politis write, the tribunals were: *Composée le plus souvent de membres qui, s'ils ne sont pas des diplomates … , ou des mandataires munis d'instructions …, n'ont ni la préparation juridique du juge, ni sa mentalité, elle a la tendance de préférer la transaction au jugement et la solution de fait à la décision du droit. Parfois, le compromis semble l'y pousser en l'invitant à statuer d'après les principes de la justice et de l'équité, ce qui aboutit à l'exclusion systématique du droit international*" (Albert Geouffre de Lapradelle and Nicolas Politis, *Recueil des arbitrages internationaux* (Paris: Pedone, 1905)). *See also* Henri La Fontaine, *Pasicrisie Internationale: Histoire Documentaire des Arbitrages Internationaux (1794–1900)* (Berne: Imprimerie Stampelli & CIE, 1902), at p. *ix*; Hans Wehberg, *The Problem of an International Court of Justice* (Charles G. Fenwick, trans., Oxford: Clarendon, 1918), at pp. 12–29.

221 The Convention between the United States of America and United States of Mexico (signed in Washington, DC on July 4, 1868, 15 Stat. 679) was umpired by Francis Lieber.

222 Karl Strupp, *Die internationale Schiedsgerichtsbarkeit* (Berlin: Rothschild, 1914).

223 Karl Strupp, *Die wichtigsten Arten der völkerrechtlichen Schiedsgerichtsverträge* (Munich: Duncker & Humblot, 1917).

224 Karl Strupp, *Die Schiedsgerichts-, Gerichts- und Vergleichsverträge des Deutschen Reiches* (Berlin: G. Stilke, 1919). For a discussion of Strupp's approach to international arbitration, *see* Link, *supra* note 205, at pp. 263–269 (*Die Institutionen internationaler Schiedsgerichts- und Gerichtsbarkeit in Strupps Werk*).

225 Strupp discusses the arbitration in the context of state responsibility for acts and omissions of its organs (*Haftung des Staates für kompetenzgemäßes Handeln seiner Organe*). He cites the *Alabama Claims* to disprove the strict liability of Anzilotti and

In retrospect, Strupp is rarely mentioned even in the footnotes of most twentieth century doctrinal texts.[226] Even in his own time, Strupp was more popular *outside* of Germany than he was inside of it.[227] In Sandra Link's biography of Strupp, she notes that although his views became broadly accepted in international doctrine and later even in practice, Strupp is rarely given credit for having put them forward.[228] Prior to the establishment of the UN International Law Commission (ILC), no one else had written as much on state responsibility as Karl Strupp. Even the structure of the UN's codification of state responsibility – its lack of preconditions and its hybrid bilateral-multilateral form – are all reflected in Strupp's writings.[229]

Strupp is also known for supervising the doctorate of Hans Morgenthau (1904–1980).[230] Morgenthau further developed Strupp's realistic positivism by writing his doctoral thesis on the political frontiers of international law.[231] In his dissertation, Morgenthau argues that not all types of international disputes could usefully be submitted to international legal dispute resolution. Some – that is, those not based on well-defined particular issues – were simply matters for political or diplomatic settlement. Morgenthau's realism was fostered by Strupp's ambivalent approach to international law.[232] Morgenthau dismissed the ideals of Strupp as incorrect conflations of norms with facts.[233]

the fault-based view of Schoen (Strupp, *supra* note 226, at sec. 52; Schoen, *supra* note 163, at sec. 54).

226 However, *Das völkerrechtliches Delikt* was cited approvingly in the Italian-United States Conciliation Commission in the *Armstrong Cork Company* case, Decision No. 18 of 22 October 1953, *Recueil Des Sentences Arbitrales*, Vol. 14, at p. 163.

227 Link, *supra* note 205, at pp. 29, 165, 764.

228 Link, *supra* note 205, at pp. 123–125.

229 Discussed in Chapter 5.

230 Strupp commented officially that it satisfied "not only the requirements of a summa cum laude dissertation but could have fully met the requirements of a good *Habilitation*. Its scholarly level is extremely high" (Strupp's evaluation in HJM-B65, Frankfurt University, as cited in Christoph Frei, *Hans J. Morgenthau: An Intellectual Biography* (Baton Rouge: Louisiana State University Press, 2001), at p. 33).

231 Hans Joachim Morgenthau, *Die internationale Rechtspflege. Ihr Wesen und ihre Grenzen* (Leipzig: Noske, 1929).

232 It was likely also a reaction to the tragic fate of his other international law mentor, Karl Neumeyer (1869–1941), who committed suicide with his wife just before they were to be transported from their *Koeniginstrasse* home – *see* Hans Joachim Morgenthau, "An Intellectual Autobiography," 15(2) *Society* 63 (1978), at p. 65.

233 For taking "the appropriateness of the devices for granted and [tending] to blame the facts for the failure" (Hans Joachim Morgenthau, "Positivism, Functionalism and International Law," 34 *American Journal of International Law* 266 (1940), at note 22,

To realists such as Morgenthau, international law, like the emperors before, had no clothes on.[234] The contrasting legacies of Strupp and his colleague Hersch Lauterpacht could not have been more stark.

Lauterpacht Institutionalizes State Responsibility

Hersch Lauterpacht (1897–1970) (Figure 4.7) was also one of Kelsen's best students.[235] Like Kelsen's rebellious protégé, Alfred Verdross (1890–1980),[236] Lauterpacht emphasizes that international law needs to include those norms that, as an integral part of the *ordre public* of the international community, are not subject to the disapproval of states. As recent scholars have noted, Lauterpacht's cultural background was heavily influenced by his Jewish upbringing: he was taught to read texts critically, even religious ones. He believed in the interpretative power of legal scholars as being "more relevant than that of God, the sovereign and the lawgiver. God, the lawgiver, is himself bound by law."[237] Accordingly, while Lauterpacht shared Kelsen's constructivism, he was dissatisfied with positive legal theory. International society needed firmer footing – not for the sake of preserving primitive notions of sovereignty but of protecting people, like Lauterpacht's family of origin, all of whom were slaughtered during the Holocaust.[238] He grounds the law on the fact of the community, which precedes the will of the state.[239]

Lauterpacht demonstrates that the practice of international law is no different in nature from domestic law. The former also borrows handily

as cited in Hatsue Shinohara, *US International Lawyers in the Interwar Years: A Forgotten Crusade* (Cambridge: Cambridge University Press, 2012), at p. 173).

234 Shinohara, *supra* note 233, at p. 172.

235 Hans Kelsen, "Tributes to Sir Hersch Lauterpacht," 10 *International and Comparative Law Quarterly* (1961) reprinted in 2 *European Journal of International Law* 309 (1997), at p. 309.

236 Alf Verdross broke with Kelsen in 1923 to develop a radically different approach. With Verdross we see a clear return by interwar international lawyers to the sources of natural law. Verdross joined the debate in a series of articles published in the mid-1930s. *See* Alf Verdross, "Forbidden Treaties in International Law," 31 *American Journal of International Law* 571 (1937), at note 3.

237 Yael Paz, *supra* note 56, at p. 441.

238 *See ibid*, at p. 423 (Lauterpacht's conceptualization of international law as based on the natural law tradition was chosen to protect the individual, not the sovereign).

239 Hersch Lauterpacht, *The Function of Law in the International Community* (Oxford: Clarendon Press, 1933), at p. 423.

Figure 4.7 Hersch Lauterpacht[240]

from the latter, as seen in the caselaw of international tribunals.[241] In *Private Law Sources and Analogies in International Law*, Lauterpacht rejects German positivism as deviating from traditional legal norms.[242] He attacks Triepel's restricted view of international law as based on incorrect assumptions about the publicness and positiveness of international law.[243] Like Kelsen, Lauterpacht seeks to provide a complete "textbook" of international law. Incomplete chapters would be updated in future editions, by which time international society will

[240] Photo courtesy of The Lauterpacht Centre for International Law, University of Cambridge, UK.

[241] Lauterpacht, *supra* note 132 at p. 210. *See also* (more recently), An Hertogen, "The Persuasiveness of Domestic Law Analogies in International Law," 29(4) *European Journal of International Law* 1127 (2018).

[242] Lauterpacht, *supra* note 132 at p. 51. This work was the publication of his (second) doctoral dissertation, (this one) written under the supervision of Sir Arnold McNair at the London School of Economics. His departure from Vienna is clearly indicated by the subtitle to that book: *With Special Reference to International Arbitration*. In England, as in America, international arbitration was a thriving practice of international law.

[243] Lauterpacht, *supra* note 132 at p. 137: Opponents of this "orthodoxy" based their views upon Triepel and his later follower Anzilotti and on "the usual argument on the inapplicability of private law" to international law (Anzilotti, *supra* note 821, at pp. 179, 180).

have evolved accordingly.[244] However, unlike Kelsen, Lauterpacht believes in the fluidity of positive and natural law.[245] He articulates his preference for "the uncertainty of 'higher law' . . . to the arbitrariness and insolence of naked force."[246] In so doing, Lauterpacht builds upon Kelsen's approach of a complete international law, albeit impure.[247] This pragmatism provided international theory with the tendons and ligaments needed to connect the pieces of existing practice.[248]

Lauterpacht was progressive in how he insisted that international law is just as law-like as domestic systems of law. But he made this argument by recourse to traditional hermeneutical methods. His strategy is for publicists to privately codify fundamental fields like state responsibility by reinterpreting existing laws in radical ways.[249] So for international law to function as effectively as other legal systems, it must also include

244 Paz, *supra* note 237, at p. 430 ("Lauterpacht's modern natural law approach to natural international law owes much to Kelsen's influence as his Doktorvater").

245 Hersch Lauterpacht, "The Grotian Tradition in International Law" 23 *British Yearbook of International Law* 1 (1946); Koskenniemi, *Gentle Civilizer*, *supra* note 1, at pp. 406–411; Renée Jeffery, "Hersch Lauterpacht: The Realist Challenge and the 'Grotian Tradition' in 20th-Century International Relations," 12(2) *European Journal of International Relations* 223 (2006); Benedict Kingsbury, "A Grotian Tradition of Theory and Practice?: Grotius, Law, and Moral Skepticism in the Thought of Hedley Bull," 17(1) *Quarterly Law Review* 3 (1997); A. Claire Cutler, "The 'Grotian Tradition' in International Relations," 17 *Review of International Studies* 41 (1991), at pp. 1–3.

246 Lauterpacht, *supra* note 262, at p. 24.

247 This is an example of how the writings of Lauterpacht, who was not German, are meaningfully rooted in the German tradition of public law systematization. I note that, to Martti Koskenniemi, Hersch Lauterpacht was a Victorian and a German in his double program of scientism and individualism – *see* Martti Koskenniemi, "Lauterpacht: The Victorian Tradition in International Law," 8 *European Journal of International Law* 215 (1997), at p. 218; Martti Koskenniemi, "The Function of Law in International Community: 75 Years After," 79 *British Yearbook of International Law* 353 (2008), at p. 356; *see also* Koskenniemi, *Gentle Civilizer*, *supra* note 1, at p. 373, (Lauterpacht was more British than he was German in his approach to international law). For a recent conference on Lauterpacht's early years, *see* Felix Lange, "Conference Report: Lauterpacht and Beyond: Jewish/German Authorship and the History of International Law," 13 *German Law Journal* 793 (2012), available at germanlawjournal.com/index.php?pageID=11&artID=1441, last visited December 3, 2014.

248 This perceived progress in the development of international law is reflected in the series of editions of Oppenheim's *International Law* treatise. In the 1905 edition, as discussed, there is already an entire chapter devoted to state responsibility (pp. 198–216). The 1912 and 1920 editions are not substantially unchanged; however, in Lauterpacht's edition in 1955, there is a drastic departure from Oppenheim's positivism – *see* Hersch Lauterpacht, *Oppenheim's International Law* (8th ed., London: Longmans, Green & Co., 1955).

249 Nolte, *supra* note 139, at p. 1098.

certain peremptory norms that were an integral part of the public order of the international community.[250] Accordingly, the establishment of an "obligation" is sufficient to imply the corollary possibility of responsibility for its breach.[251] No additional source of responsibility (*e.g.*, a *compromis* agreement) was necessary. The combined boldness and humility of this approach is a subtle departure from previous theory with fundamental consequences.

Thus, Lauterpacht no longer looked, as the previous generation of German public lawyers had, to sovereignty to ground state responsibility. State responsibility is a corollary of law rather than of sovereignty. Accordingly, responsibility – properly so-called – is a general principle of law rather than a provision of an international contract or treaty.[252] The question of fault, thus, is not a general precondition of responsibility, but could be relevant in certain cases.[253] In this way, Lauterpacht expands the theory of state responsibility, while, at the same time, managing to package his approach as "orthodox."[254] For example, in

[250] *See* Koskenniemi, *Gentle Civilizer*, *supra* note 1, at pp. 42–47.

[251] *See* Wilhelm G. Grewe, *The Epochs of International Law* (Michael Byers, trans., Berlin: Walter de Gruyter, 2000), at p. 474.

[252] For a similar view, *see* Alain Pellet, "The Definition of Responsibility in International Law," in Crawford, Pellet, Olleson, *supra* note 85, at p. 14: "The objectivization of responsibility for internationally wrongful acts which results from the excision of damage as a precondition for responsibility is at the origin of a transformation of the function which responsibility is called upon to fulfill in an international society which has less a purely inter-State character and is better integrated than formerly."

[253] To Lauterpacht, states are "moral entities accountable for their acts and omissions in proportion to the *mens rea* of their agents, the real addressees of international duties – a conception which must form the foundation of any legal theory of responsibility" (Lauterpacht, *supra* note 132 at p. 137). In a footnote, Lauterpacht continues: "Attempts have been made to prove that the recent practice of States dispenses with the requirement of culpable negligence, and that it adopts the principle of absolute liability."

[254] Lauterpacht, *supra* note 132 at p. 137. Lauterpacht's position on *culpa* was a critique of those who, like Justice Holmes in the United States, held that it was both immoral and unscientific to base responsibility on subjective psychologies (for a discussion, *see* Martti Koskenniemi, "Doctrines of State Responsibility" in Crawford, Pellet and Olleson, *supra* note 85, at pp. 49–50). Oliver Wendell Holmes Jr. is the same person who, earlier in his career pressed law schools not to include international law in the curriculum because "International law, of course, has little to do in any sense, with the practice of the profession" (cited in Benjamin Allen Coates, *Legalist Empire: International Law and American Foreign Relations in the Early Twentieth Century* (Oxford: Oxford University Press, 2016), at p. 59).

his 1937 Hague lectures, Lauterpacht demonstrates that state sovereignty did not preclude state crimes.[255] Any contrary position, he argues, would defy "logic, justice and practice."[256]

Lauterpacht's broad view of state responsibility was well ahead of his time. Most theorists still viewed state responsibility in strictly bilateralist terms.[257] Lauterpacht also sees international law as operating within a gapless process that addresses every manner of social need (hence the increasing importance of international lawyers). He readily acknowledges the inchoateness of contemporary international theory. But the existence (or law-ness) of international law is another matter altogether – one that includes in its sources an abundance of international practice as well as writings of recognized jurists.[258]

Lauterpacht believed in "the tradition of idealism and progress,"[259] which viewed the primitivity of international theory and practice as transient.[260] Like Strupp, Lauterpacht studied the Anglo-American practice of international arbitration. The full title of his dissertation, supervised by his longtime mentor and friend Arnold McNair, is *Private Law Sources and Analogies of International Law: With Special Reference to*

[255] Hersch Lauterpacht, "Règles générales du droit de la paix," 62 *Recueil des cours* 99 (1937).

[256] Nolte, *supra* note 139, at p. 1091. In his postwar writings, Lauterpacht takes an even firmer stance regarding the possibility of subjecting states to penal responsibility. For a discussion *see* Philippe Sands, "Twin Peaks: The Hersch Lauterpacht Draft Nuremberg Speeches," 1(1) *Cambridge Journal of International and Comparative Law* 37 (2012), at pp. 41–42.

[257] *See, e.g.*, Lassa Oppenheim, *International Law* (Ronald F. Roxburgh, ed., 3rd ed., London: Longmans, Green & Co., 1920), at p. 249; William Edward Hall, *A Treatise of International Law* (A. Pearce Higgins, ed., 8th ed., Oxford, Clarendon Press, 1924), p. 65; for a discussion *see* Nolte, *supra* note 139, at pp. 1089–1095. Georg Nolte refers to this as the "traditional primacy of a bilateral conception of inter-state relations" (*supra* note 139).

[258] Lauterpacht, *supra* note 132 at p. 134: "no clear-cut rule can be laid down with regard to all cases in which the international responsibility of the State becomes engaged." Thus, responsibility in international law is not limited to German public legal theory or Anglo-American arbitral practice. International law is more than theory or practice and must be able to address any set of conflicting considerations (Lauterpacht, *supra* note 273 at p. 383).

[259] Lauterpacht, *supra* note 262, at pp. 307–396.

[260] Martti Koskenniemi, "Between Apology and Utopia: The Politics of International Law," in Martti Koskenniemi, *The Politics of International Law* 35 (Oxford: Hart, 2011), at pp. 53, 477; Lauterpacht, *supra* note 258, at pp. 403–407, 431–434.

International Arbitration (1927). As the title suggests, Lauterpacht was more focused on the sources of international law, including state responsibility, than he was on the substance of the laws themselves.[261] Lauterpacht exhaustively demonstrated in *Private Law Sources* that actual international arbitrations, "one after another . . . shatter the fiction of an international law totally independent of conception and rules of private law."[262] He fought his colleagues' objections of *non liquet* (lacking applicable law) arguing that the ongoing practice of international arbitration has revealed an international legal system that is gap-free.[263]

In *The Function of Law in the International Community* (1933), Lauterpacht considers state responsibility from the standpoint of "Filling the Gaps by the Application of General Principles of Law and of Principles of Private Law."[264] Here, as in *Private Law Sources*, Lauterpacht makes no effort to treat the laws of state responsibility systematically. This fact may be explained by Lauterpacht's view that the arbitrations do not point to any clear principles. After reviewing the awards of the international arbitrator and judge Max Huber (1874–1960), Lauterpacht comments on the "unprincipled" nature of state responsibility in practice.[265] Arbitration is a fitting form of international dispute resolution but not a productive source of international doctrine.[266] Lauterpacht viewed state responsibility as being practiced as a "twin" discipline to tort law.[267] As such it was the product of *ad hoc* litigation – a rather undisciplined basis for doctrine. Still, "[t]he judicial character of international arbitration is a matter of historical

[261] For example, when discussing the *British Claims in the Spanish Zone of Morocco* after discussing the reliance on general principles of law at length, Lauterpacht writes that Umpire Huber "then proceeded to lay down the various rules of State responsibility in regard to aliens" and leaves it at that (*supra* note 258, at p. 127).

[262] Lauterpacht, *supra* note 132, at p. 215, footnotes omitted.

[263] Yael Paz, *supra* note 56, at p. 432.

[264] Lauterpacht, *supra* note 258, at p. 123.

[265] Lauterpacht, *supra* note 258, at p. 127. For example, the *Island of Palmas* and *British Claims in the Spanish Zone of Morocco*, discussed *infra* notes 384–385 and accompanying text.

[266] Lauterpacht, *supra* note 258, at pp. 127–130: "In such cases the judicial function asserts itself by performing the essential task of the law-creating process, namely, by effecting either a judicial compromise between two conflicting claims or, if that is not possible, by giving effect to the claim which is stronger in law."

[267] Randall Lesaffer, "Argument from Roman Law in Current International Law," 16 *European Journal of International Law* 25 (2005), at p. 27.

fact and of positive international law."[268] Judicial, of course, does not necessarily mean precedent-worthy.[269]

Like Oppenheim, for Lauterpacht, the important conclusion to draw from the fact of international arbitrations is that tribunals are practicing law, and their iterations of state responsibility are consistently based on general principles of law. One of Lauterpacht's most lasting intellectual legacies is that the lack of international law's behavior-regulating rules creates a situation where adjudicators must overly (and suspiciously) rely on general principles of law. The antidote to this problem is increased institutionalization, which will lead to the production of satisfactory secondary rules of interpretation.[270] The ILC would later adopt a similar approach to state responsibility as general principles of international law: "Today one can regard responsibility as a general principle of international law, a concomitant of substantive rules and of the supposition that acts and omissions may be categorized as illegal by reference to the rules establishing rights and duties."[271]

Borchard Fails to Limit the Theory of State Responsibility

Across the Atlantic, American international lawyers were split about the possibility of an overarching theory of state responsibility. The traditionalists, led by Edwin M. Borchard (1884–1951), John Bassett Moore (1860–1947), and Elihu Root (1845–1937), were proponents of neutrality laws as the most effective basis for international cooperation. They opposed the idea of codifying international law based on logic and supported the view of basing it on experience.[272] The progressives, led

[268] Lauterpacht, *supra* note 258, at p. 389, internal citations omitted.

[269] On the judicial character of international arbitration, see Moore in the Preface to his *International Adjudications* (1929) and by Strupp, *Das Recht des internationalen Richters, nach Billigkeit zu statuieren* (1930); Lauterpacht, *Analogies*, section 28.

[270] Lauterpacht, *supra* note 258, at pp. 78–92; on this point, *see further* Eliav Lieblich and Yoram Shachar, "Cosmopolitanism at a Crossroads: Hersch Lauterpacht and the Israeli Declaration of Independence," 84 *British Yearbook of International Law* 1 (2014), at p. 19 (this diagnosis and its remedy permeates all of Lauterpacht's writings).

[271] Lauterpacht, *supra* note 258, at p. 423.

[272] *See further* Shinohara, *supra* note 233, at p. 34. In this section, I adopt Shinohara's categorization of traditional and progressive US interwar international lawyers. For a similar grouping (into realists and idealists) and analysis, see Stephen Wertheim, "The League That Wasn't: American Designs for a Legalist-Sanctionist League of Nations and the Intellectual Origins of International Organization, 1914–1920," 35(5) *Diplomatic History* 797(2011).

by Clyde Eagleton (1891–1958), Charles G. Fenwick (1880–1973) and Quincy Wright (1890–1970), were constitutionalists who saw international law as unifying an international community; they supported efforts to codify state responsibility based on international needs rather than its meager instances of practice.[273] Neither group succeeded in doing anything more than provide additional sources on the doctrine of state responsibility.

Borchard's determination to root state responsibility in international practice reflects the approach of his mentor and closest colleague, John Bassett Moore,[274] whose compilations of international arbitration are critical records of the early history of state responsibility. Moore supervised Borchard's doctoral studies (in the Department of Political Sciences) at Columbia University. As Chief Librarian for the Law Department of the Library of Congress, Borchard was proficient in comparative law. He was a multilingual scholar familiar with Latin American constitutional law as well as German public legal theory. This knowledge is reflected in Borchard's dissertation, *The Diplomatic Protection of Citizens Abroad* which is a broad synthesis of intercontinental theory and practice.[275] Borchard's views broadly reflect those of the US Government, which was at the time steeped in a culture of classical legalism.[276] (What other country's foreign affairs department would poach a head librarian to become its chief legal officer?) Borchard questioned "nineteenth century's individualistic notions of liberty,

[273] See John Hepp, "James Brown Scott and the Rise of Public International Law," 7(2) *Journal of the Gilded Age and Progressive Era* 151 (2008), at p. 153: "Mirroring changes in the domestic legal community, international lawyers began to shift from the legal formalism so beloved by Elihu Root and Scott, to a more interdisciplinary approach known as sociological jurisprudence." I have largely omitted Alwyn V. Freeman, also an important of writer on state responsibility in English, from the discussion here since his works are more surveys in nature and not meant to be original theoretical or doctrinal contributions; *see* Alwyn V. Freeman, *The International Responsibility of States for Denials of Justice* (London: Longmans, Green & Co., 1938), at p. *ix* (he also states that he wants "to construct a consistent theory of State responsibility" but then just puts it together by way of survey with the theoretical section in under fifteen pages (pp. 15–27)).

[274] Justus D. Doeneck, "Edwin M. Borchard, John Bassett Moore, and Opposition to American Intervention in World War II," 6(1) *Journal of Libertarian Studies* 1 (1982), at pp. 1–2.

[275] According to James Crawford, Borchard's structure resembles that of Triepel (*supra* note 11, at p. 24), but I am not quite certain of this except insofar as they both are very concerned with the relations between international and domestic law and begin with fundamental questions about international law.

[276] I discuss this point further in Chapter 2.

contract and property."[277] Yet he remained steadfast in his bilateralist beliefs. During both world wars, he advocated for isolationist foreign policies that precluded any breach of neutrality laws. Borchard was out of touch, even in his own time, with the *Zeitgeist*. Despite his massive output, he failed to stay the German-led push for an overarching theory of state responsibility.

I note that, in contrast to Borchard's writings, Clyde Eagleton's *The Responsibility of States in International Law* (1928) was very well received on both sides of the Atlantic.[278] The book was a published version of the doctoral dissertation Eagleton completed for the Department of Political Sciences at Columbia University. To Eagleton, state responsibility is a norm of natural law.[279] As a practitioner of international law who consulted for the United States as well as the United Nations, Eagleton readily admitted that "a chaos of interpretation reigns" over state responsibility.[280] However, this chaos neither undermines the lawness of, nor is even the fault of, international law. Its chief cause is the "uncertainty as to the exact bearing of the word responsibility itself."[281] The chaos was a "purely theoretical" problem.[282] Surely, the progressive sentiment implied, the international legal system's actual needs were more important than its theoretical ones.[283] Eagleton, thus, looked to strengthen the

[277] Edwin M. Borchard, "Recent Developments in International and Municipal Law," 10 *Law Library Journal* 21 (1917), at p. 22.

[278] Eagleton's publications on the topic include *The Responsibility of States in International Law* (New York: New York University Press, 1928); "Denial of Justice in International Law," 22 *American Journal of International Law* 538–559 (1928); Eagleton, *infra* note 282.

[279] "If one inquires as to the origin of obligation in jurisprudence, he is forced back to moral axioms" (Eagleton, *supra* note 278, at p. 3).

[280] Eagleton, *supra* note 278, at p. 23.

[281] Eagleton, *supra* note 278, at p. 23.

[282] States are not interested in theories but "the actual rules of law" (Clyde Eagleton, "Measures of Damages in International Law," 39 *Yale Law Journal* 52 (1929), at p. 58).

[283] The doctrine of state responsibility was to play a critical function: "to maintain a reasonable standard of civilized justice." Eagleton states that: "It is obvious that the community of nations can not permit a respondent state to say: We have observed all the forms of our local law, and therefore have no responsibility. To admit this would mean to admit that international law is impotent to protect aliens. There is, and must be, an international standard for the administration of local justice for aliens, demanding the promulgation of laws, and their proper enforcement, and the creation of machinery, and its efficient operation, for the protection of aliens" (Clyde Eagleton, "Denial of Justice in International Law," *supra* note 278, emphasis added). As his colleague, Quincy Wright, writes: the establishment of international institutions such as the League of Nations confirmed that "a shifting of emphasis from the rights of state to responsibilities of state

doctrine of state responsibility for the sake of preventing more war,[284] to which Edwin Borchard actually responded, this was "the doctrine of making faces."[285]

State Responsibility as *Buchrecht*

In sum, for many interwar legal thinkers, international law was a complete legal system – even if some excused it as being only *temporarily* primitive. To be sure, international law had its weaknesses, but these were not fundamental. They were temporary hurdles to be overcome by creative lawyering. The existence of state responsibility was as axiomatic to international law as individual responsibility was to domestic law.[286] Many interwar lawyers also believed that state responsibility could be penal. In 1939, Roberto Ago (1907–1995) gave his first Hague Lecture on *Le délit international*, in which he rejected the civil law framework of state responsibility.[287] This was a sign of doctrine to come. Ago, the future ILC *Special Rapporteur* on state responsibility, would incorporate this departure from Anzilotti's positivist framework into the UN's codification project, as I will discuss in the next chapter.

The Anglo-American and German approaches to state responsibility seem to have existed in parallel universes. One was practiced *ad hoc* while the other was articulated methodically.[288] One focused on individual

is the fundamental change of international law" (Shinohara, *supra* note 233, at p. 28. Similarly, according to James Garner, the League's Covenant has established a new international obligation: it has "shifted emphasis more and more from the right of states to obligations and responsibilities" (James Garner, Recent Developments in International Law (Calcutta: University of Calcutta, 1925), at pp. ix, 397–398 as cited in Shinohara, *supra* note 233, at p. 57).

284 Eagleton, *supra* note 278, at pp. 743–746.

285 194 *Proceedings of the American Society of International Law* 96 as cited in Shinohara, *supra* note 233, at p. 167.

286 *See* Thomas Atkins Street, *The Foundations of Legal Liability: A Presentation of the Theory and Development of the Common Law* (Northport: Edward Thompson, 1906), at p. 67; Eagleton, *supra* note 88, at pp. 3–5.

287 Ago, *supra* note 124. Ago criticizes Anzilotti for assuming that the concept of crime would violate the positivist nature of international law because it is based on a pre-existing legal community. To Ago, the primary characteristic of a crime was not punishment but its repressive character as a countermeasure. Sanctions were neither as regular as Kelsen argued nor as illusory as Anzilotti claimed. Sometimes state responsibility included the obligation to make reparations and other times it allowed for reprisals.

288 *See* Martins Paparinskis, "Investment Arbitration and the Law of Countermeasures," 79 *British Yearbook of International Law* 264–352 (2008), at p. 273 (the apparently

liberties, the other on the preservation of national sovereignty. It was the German language of international law that the ILC chose to employ in its codification of state responsibility. On one level, this was the result of the tireless efforts of German-speaking lawyers such as Lauterpacht. They succeeded in publishing a corpus of literature that softened the differences between international and domestic law. But Lauterpacht was just one person. His view, as influential as it was, does not alone explain the ILC's approach to codifying state responsibility, which became a UN project for the next six decades. His initial 1949 outline for the UN's codification of international law included the field of state responsibility, especially for alien injuries.[289] The ILC only took up the codification of state responsibility in general after Lauterpacht's passing in May 1960. During his lifetime – even while he was a judge on the ICJ – Lauterpacht's writings were a matter of *Buchrecht* (textbook law).[290]

When Lassa Oppenheim coined the term "*Buchrecht*," he had in mind a "system erected by greater or smaller authorities on the foundations of state practice, and in its details often uncertain and contested."[291] German jurists had remarkable success in theorizing state responsibility, but their efforts had only a marginal impact on international practice

ineffective customary law of diplomatic protection and the treaty law of investment arbitration seemed to be developing independently from one another).

289 UN Doc. A/CN.4/Rev.1 (1949), available on the website of the International Law Commission, at http://untreaty.un.org/ilc/documentation/english/a_cn4_1_rev1.pdf (last visited February 28, 2012), at pp. *iii–iv*. It begins with the codification of sources and subjects and ends with that of international dispute resolution and state responsibility. (It may surprise some readers how apt Lauterpacht's introduction to the field remains.) Lauterpacht gave two reasons for his focus on alien injuries: The "treatment of aliens and injuries to aliens have constituted in practice the most conspicuous application of the law of responsibility of States." Also, the general principles of state responsibility could be clarified through a close study of its main arena of practice. See ILC Programme of work (1949), A/CN.4/1/Rev. 1, 56 (para 97); James Crawford and Tom Grant, "Responsibility of States for Injuries to Foreigners," in Grant and Barker, *supra* note 124, at p. 89.

290 Lassa Oppenheim, *Die Zukunft des Völkerrecht* (Leipzig: W. Engelmann, 1911), at p. 11; *Buchrecht* is translated as book-law in the English edition: Lassa Oppenheim, *The Future of International Law* (Oxford: Clarendon, 1921), at p. 5. Oppenheim writes that "the law of nations was, until the first of the Peace Conferences, essentially a book-law. Treatises depicted the law such as it was growing, in the form of custom, out of the practice of states in international intercourse. There were only a few international enactments, and there was no international court practice" (*ibid*, at p. 67).

291 Spiermann, *supra* note 89, at p. 23.

during their day.[292] Georg Jellinek himself observed at the opening of the 1899 Hague Peace Conference that it was peculiar for his Emperor to appoint to the German delegation two lawyers: one of whom had only recently published a pamphlet ridiculing the idea of perpetual peace, while the other had just denied the law-ness of international law![293] Indeed, German theory was loosely linked to the most practiced field of international law, alien protection.[294] International arbitrators, in turn, largely ignored the German theorization of state responsibility; they continued to resolve alien protection claims based on private law conceptions of tort.[295] The Anglo-American approach to international law continued to dominate discourse within international institutions until the 1960s.[296]

None of the seminal interwar cases of the PCIJ yielded Lauterpacht-like opinions.[297] They were either narrowly tailored treaty interpretations

[292] Koskenniemi, *Gentle Civilizer*, *supra* note 1, at p. 210 ("Little of the positive law had emerged from German sources").

[293] Georg Jellinek, "*Zur Eröffnung der Friedenskonferenz*" (1899), in Ausgewählte Schriften, II, pp. 542–543, 547–548 as cited in Koskenniemi, *Gentle Civilizer*, *supra* note 1, at p. 208.

[294] Spiermann, *supra* note 89, at p. 23. In his doctoral dissertation (*Étude sur la jurisprudence de la Cour Permanente de Justice Internationale*), Max Sørensen writes that, "when one categorises *dicta* of the Permanent Court along the lines of Article 38 and sources theory in general, one is not using theory to describe the decisions but the decisions to describe the theory" (cited in *ibid*, at p. 25). Indeed, "It takes a long time to find international law mentioned in most of the voluminous books written by former foreign ministers and their advisors" (Wilhelm G. Grewe, "The Role of International Law in Diplomatic Practice," 1(1) *Journal of History of International Law* 22 (1999), at p. 31).

[295] States continued to balk at the idea of compulsory (or even general) jurisdiction for international disputes. For an excellent discussion on the topic, *see* Spiermann, *supra* note 89, at p. 9.

[296] This can be seen in both postwar conferences in Versailles and San Francisco.

[297] In fact, no international cases before *Barcelona Traction* (1970) made general statements on the law of state responsibility. *See Barcelona Traction, Light and Power Company, Limited* (Belgium v. Spain), Judgment of 5 February 1970 (Second Phase), ICJ Reports pp. 3–53, especially at para. 33. On the conceptual ambiguity of the decision, *see* dissent by future ILC *Special Rapporteur* Judge Willem Riphagen, *ibid*, at pp. 334–357. Interestingly, the Court's approach later turned out to have been beneficial for investors as it showed the inadequacy of customary law-making efforts in the area; pushing the law-making resources into treaty-making, discussed further below in Chapter 6; *see* Stephen Schwebel, "Some Aspects of International Law in Arbitration between States and Aliens," in Stephen Schwebel (ed.), *Justice in International Law* (Cambridge: Cambridge University Press, 1994), at pp. 196, 210–211. As an example of pre-Ago practice in the ICJ, *see Interpretation of Peace Treaties with Bulgaria, Hungary and Romania, Second Phase,* ICJ Reports 221 (1950), at p. 228: "the refusal to fulfill a *treaty* obligation involves international responsibility" (emphasis added).

or arbitration-like pronouncements on civil reparations.[298] The *Wimbledon* case (1923), the first contentious case decided by the first permanent court of international law,[299] was an alien protection case. In it, the PCIJ stresses the sovereignty of states while omitting any *general* role of responsibility.[300] This result was intentional. At the inaugural meeting of the PCIJ in 1922, Dionisio Anzilotti stated:

> This and no other is the raison d'être and the function of the Court: to facilitate and develop the solution according to law, not of the great international conflicts, but of the ordinary disputes which today are less adequately dealt with by diplomacy, an organization little suited for the purpose.[301]

Even in the oft-cited *Chorzów* case (1927), the PCIJ seemed to be making a grand statement on the law-ness of international law: "It is a principle of international law that the breach of an engagement involves an obligation to make reparation in an adequate form."[302] However, the continuation (and less famously quoted portion) of the passage is: "Reparation therefore is the indispensable complement of a failure to apply a *convention* and there is no necessity for this to be stated in the convention itself."[303] The PCIJ explicitly restricted its decision to the scope of treaty interpretation; it avoided any mention of discussing general questions of responsibility and opted instead to interpret the bilateral treaty between Germany and Poland that gave rise to its

[298] As Huber wrote to Moore re: the *Island of Palmas*: "[I]t was a most interesting case from a legal point of view, a case of pure law of nations, not, as most of the cases decided by the Court, a question of interpretation of some badly drafted class of a convention, or a civil case, as Chorzow, international only by some connection with a treaty" (Spiermann, *supra* note 89, at p. 296). *See also ibid*, at p. 396. *See also* Robert Y. Jennings, "The International Court of Justice after Fifty Years," 89 *American Journal of International Law* 493 (1995), at p. 493; Åke Hammarskjold, "The Permanent Court of International Justice and the Development of International Law," 14 *International Affairs* 797 (1935), at p. 797.

[299] *S.S. Wimbledon* (U.K. v. Japan), 1923 PCIJ (ser. A) No. 1 (Aug. 17). According to the PCIJ, responsibility is but an attribute of sovereignty (at pp. 4, 25).

[300] *S.S. Wimbledon* (U.K. v. Japan), 1923 PCIJ (ser. A) No. 1 (Aug. 17), at para. 35: "the right of entering into international engagements is an attribute of State sovereignty." *See further* Jan Klabbers, "Clinching the Concept of Sovereignty: Wimbledon Redux," 3 *Austrian Review of International and European Law* 345 (1998).

[301] Cited in Spiermann, *supra* note 89, at p. 146.

[302] *Factory at Chorzów* (Germany v. Poland), 1927 PCIJ (ser. A) No. 9 (July 26), at para. 55.

[303] *Factory at Chorzów* (Germany v. Poland), 1927 PCIJ (ser. A) No. 9 (July 26), at para. 55, emphasis added.

jurisdiction.[304] This pronouncement was expressly based on early professional arbitrations rather than published theories.

1919: The Kitchen and the Christmas Tree

During the interwar era, German-speaking lawyers were dissatisfied with their predecessors' progress. Some sought to shamelessly combine pragmatic reformism with German *Rechtslehre*; others dipped deeper into the well of positivism for a more pure, reliable result. These lawyers sought to downplay the differences between domestic and international law. They untethered state responsibility from state sovereignty and sought pragmatic (if less theoretically coherent) solutions to the problems of international relations. As Martti Koskenniemi writes,

> Lauterpacht's modernity lies in his constant stress on the primacy of interpretation to substance, of process to rule in a fashion that leads him into an institutional pragmatism that is ours, too. Such nominalism liberates lawyers to create international order by imagining that it already exists.[305]

Kelsen, Strupp, Lauterpacht and many of their contemporaries were unwilling to rely on either state will or popular understanding to enforce international law. The "old" liberal internationalism, with its "knowledge is virtue" approach to educating public opinion,[306] had given way to the reality that more was needed to bring peace.[307] These lawyers developed sophisticated doctrines that served to establish theoretical conditions and practical relevance of attributing state responsibility. Strupp drafted a treaty on the topic and Lauterpacht advised the ILC on its codification. Yet, prior to the 1960s, these theoretical approaches had little actual impact on either international diplomacy or adjudication.

304 Convention concerning Upper Silesia, concluded at Geneva on May 15, 1922 (Germany and Poland). For an interesting discussion on how Roberto Ago successfully employed general concepts of state responsibility (though the PCIJ did not mention any of these principles in its final decision) in *Phosphates in Morocco* (Morocco v. France), 1938, Series C No. 85 at pp. 1024, 1295, *see* Spiermann, *supra* note 89, at pp. 376–377.

305 Koskenniemi, *Gentle Civilizer*, *supra* note 1, at p. 358.

306 The opening article of the first volume of the *American Journal of International Law*, was Elihu Root, "The Need of Popular Understanding of International Law," 1 *American Journal of International Law* 1 (1907).

307 Stephen Wertheim, "The League That Wasn't: American Designs for a Legalist-Sanctionist League of Nations and the Intellectual Origins of International Organization, 1914–1920," 35(5) *Diplomatic History* 797(2011), at p. 803.

German lawyers readily appreciated the problem: state power lacked sufficient validation and regulation. However, their solutions yielded drastic departures from existing practices.[308] What explains this divergence between theory and practice – between *Rechtstaat* and *Machtpolitik*? German public lawyers were not simply apologists; they cared about protecting liberal values and regulating power: "Issues like the political character of state law, the state of emergency, the process of state integration, the functional preconditions of democracy, and the scientific character of jurisprudence were discussed and debated with an intellectual energy and professional passion that have not been equaled since."[309]

Nor were German theorists mere armchair philosophers.[310] Many were active at the highest levels of national politics, including Kelsen, Schücking, Strupp and Triepel.[311] Public law was a popular and active field in Germany. The number of German public law professors doubled in the period from 1914 to 1932 (to approximately one hundred).[312] How could German internationalist optimism be at its height on the eve of the Great War, when Chancellor Bethmann Hollweg referred to a treaty guaranteeing Belgian neutrality as but a "scrap of paper?"[313] What explains Reich Justice Minister Otto Thierack (1889–1946) threatening to remove the training of lawyers entirely from academia?[314] Such facts suggest that something was wrong with its underlying assumptions.[315]

308 According to Stolleis, the level of legal abstraction in public law theory was inversely proportionate to the confidence public lawyers had in their own epistemologies – Stolleis *supra* note 108, at p. 432.

309 Stolleis, *supra* note 108, at p. 447.

310 Although, as Kammerhofer writes, "*Rechtsdogmatik* is a German obsession – nowhere has more been written on the proper role and limits of doctrinal legal scholarship than there. The term is untranslatably German and the debate is culturally specific and cannot be transposed to the level of international legal scholarship without more" (Jörg Kammerhofer, "The Interaction of Doctrine and Theory in (International) Legal Scholarship," in Pauline Westerman, Kostiantyn Gorobets and Andreas Hadjigeorgiou (eds.), *Conceptual (De)Constructions of International Law* (Cheltenham: Edward Elgar, 2022), available online at SSRN: https://ssrn.com/abstract=3777918, last visited May 3, 2021, at p. 2, internal citations omitted).

311 Stolleis, *supra* note 108, at p. 100.

312 Stolleis, *supra* note 108, at pp. 101, 145.

313 *See* Isabel V. Hull, *A Scrap of Paper: Breaking and Making International Law during the Great War* (Ithaca: Cornell University Press, 2014), at p. 42.

314 Stolleis, *supra* note 108, at p. 443.

315 Koskenniemi, *Gentle Civilizer*, *supra* note 1, at p. 228; "Nothing demonstrates the isolation and helplessness of the German international law community better than its

It is beyond the scope of this chapter to even attempt to resolve law's relationship to politics. I mention it here simply to highlight the contrasting futures of domestic and international conceptions of public law. Of course, both domestic and international law suffer from the same legitimation crisis. The German faith in positive law has long since given way to other, more constitutional, approaches to international law. But before the Second World War, German public lawyers sought a measure of validity from philosophy – validity, alas, that would never come from actual practice.[316] They felt that they had to be something more than apologists. Their solutions, general theories of state responsibility, were robust and comprehensive but almost irrelevant to the contemporary practice of states, including Germany.

Die völkerrechtliche Haftung des Staates went on to live a long and fruitful life through postwar UN codification efforts, but this did not stop the untimely death of the Weimar Republic in the twentieth century. Nor did it ensure the success of the political reforms of the mid-nineteenth century. Heinrich Heine (1797–1856), whose spirits rose and fell with the March Revolutions, captures the meekness of German idealism in his *Germany – A Winter's Tale*:

> The wind's asleep, that howled so wild;
> At home it's quiet as could be;
> Germania, the great big child,
> Plays happily around his Christmas tree . . .
> The wood and stream rest cozily,
> By gentle moonlight comforted;
> But – on a sudden – can it be
> A shot? – perhaps it is a friend shot dead . . .
> Poet, be still; your anguish grows –
> You are so so sick . . . 'twere wiser not to speak.[317]

turn inwards, and backwards, into nineteenth-century debates about the basis of the law's binding force" (*ibid*, at p. 229).

316 Koskenniemi, *Gentle Civilizer*, *supra* note 1, at p. 194: "What the profession sought from philosophy was reassurance that its normative project was still valid and might perhaps finally devise a correct relationship between cosmopolitan community and patriotism."

317 Heinrich Heine, reprinted in Frederic Ewen (ed.), *Heroic Imagination: The Creative Genius of Europe from Waterloo (1815) to the Revolution of 1848* (Edinburgh: Edinburgh University Press, 2004), at pp. 595–595.

5

State Responsibility as World Order

1947: Transformation with the UN

Even though it played only a minor role in international litigation, the German theory of public law has had a lasting impact on international legal doctrine. The mark of German approaches to international law on state responsibility was most felt within international organizations such as the International Law Commission (ILC) of the United Nations, established in 1947. After the Great War, Latin American legal experts promoted a codification strategy within newly formed world bodies that would reject the US practice of arbitration and approve instead the German theory of state responsibility. Prior to the advent of the ILC, these efforts failed. As I discuss in Chapter 3, the "North" dominated the hemispheric debate over the appropriate legal standard for protecting aliens. However, the US failed to codify an international standard of care based on that practice. Instead, from 1920 to 1960, Latin American and other semi-peripheral lawyers succeeded in reconceptualizing the field of state responsibility based on German public law as a general regime of international enforcement actions, leaving the protection of aliens as a separate, specialized field.

However, in the codification debate of state responsibility, the "South" found their revenge on the "North." State responsibility, which was born in intra-American arbitrations, was reformulated to have outgrown its colonial origins. It was based on abstract principles of public responsibility instead of haphazard rules resulting from alien protection arbitrations. These rules could be applied to the breach of any international obligation by any state. It took several decades for this codification vision to be accepted as the majority view. But by the early 1960s, the ILC began codifying state responsibility as "secondary" rules that are triggered whenever a "primary" international duty was breached. The ILC distinction between primary and secondary rules of international law embodied the German focus on general conditions of responsibility as opposed to specific remedies that may ensue, as discussed in the previous chapter.

Going forward, the rules of state responsibility would become a space for legalism – one in which professional arbitrators could separate allegations of breach from enforcement actions. In premodern times, before the advent of state responsibility, once states invoked the liability of another state for breaching its rules, it was up to the claimant state to enforce those rights on its own. The responsibility of states was not a doctrinal part of any international legal order. Once German law professors reframed the concept in terms of the nature of sovereignty, with rules about authority, control, fault and imputation, state responsibility became a doctrine of in between – one that connected the dots between allegations of international breach and actions of international enforcement.[1]

1930 was a turning point in the codification history of state responsibility. That year, the US control over the future doctrine of state responsibility – based on the arbitral practice of alien protection – ended. At the

[1] This shift within world bodies – codifying state responsibility as secondary rather than primary rules – is often described as a doctrinal "revolution" (*see, e.g.*, Pierre-Marie Dupuy, "The International Law of State Responsibility: Revolution or Evolution?," 11 *Michigan Journal of International Law* 105 (1989); Alain Pellet, "The Definition of Responsibility in International Law," in James Crawford, Alain Pellet and Simon Olleson (eds.), *The Law of International Responsibility* (Oxford: Oxford University Press, 2011), at p. 4). It is widely acknowledged that *Special Rapporteur* Roberto Ago (Italy) played a critical role in transforming the ILC's codification of state responsibility. Ago's combination of legal erudition, political savvy and amiable personality was virtually unparalleled. Indeed, in honor of his eightieth birthday, friends submitted articles that filled four complete volumes – *International Law at the Time of Its Codification: Essays in Honour of Roberto Ago* (Milan: Giuffre, 1988). See also Pellet, *supra* note 1, at p. 80. Recently, Jan Klabbers commented on Ago's effective codification style: he "managed to have all key positions (chair of the committee of the whole, chair of the drafting committee, etc.) occupied by fellow ILC members: this way, the influence of states could be kept to a minimum" (Jan Klabbers, "Review of Antonio Cassese, Five Masters of International Law: Conversations with R-J Dupuy, E *Jimenez* de Arechaga, R Jennings, L Henkin and O Schachter (Oxford: Hart, 2011)," 22(4) *European Journal of International Law* 1175–1177 (2011), at p. 1177). One aim of this chapter is to demonstrate that the ILC doctrine of state responsibility is as much a narrative of (pre-1960) continuity as it is one of rupture. The legal doctrine underlying Ago's eight reports on state responsibility can be categorized as within the positivist tradition of German public law as interpreted by Dionisio Anzilotti. Even Ago's idea of codifying "secondary" rather than "primary" rules of responsibility was likely borrowed from Herbert Hart's, *The Concept of Law* (Oxford: Oxford University Press, 1961), at p. 79; *see further* Anastasios Gourgourinis, "General/ Particular International Law and Primary/Secondary Rules: Unitary Terminology of a Fragmented System," 22(4) *European Journal of International Law* 993 (2011); Eric David, "Primary and Secondary Sources," in Crawford, Pellet, Olleson, *supra* note 1, at p. 80 (it was the US ILC member, Herbert Briggs, who first used the expression "primary and secondary" rules).

League of Nations codification conference on international law held in The Hague from 13 March to 12 April 1930 ("Codification Conference"),[2] delegates had two very different codification choices: to base the doctrine of state responsibility on (1) the past practice of alien protection or (2) the future needs of the international community. The first option turned on the perceived legitimacy of the international minimum standard of care to aliens; the traditional remedy for breaching the standard was damages. The second was a progressive vision of a world governed by a new international rule of law with state responsibility as its core doctrine.

Thus, there was broad acknowledgement by the US and other conference delegates about the need to codify state responsibility.[3] But how the doctrine should be codified was very much in dispute. For example, in a telegram to Secretary of State Henry L. Stimson (1867–1950), the chairman of the US delegation, David Hunter Miller (1875–1961) wrote that he anticipated that the conference would proceed with US rather than Latin American proposals: "There is likelihood of a general agreement on a limited number of articles which will not cover various questions presented by the original proposals. I think that so far as these articles are generally agreed on, they will be entirely satisfactory to us and in accord with our policy."[4] As we will see, however, Latin Americans had been waiting three decades for an international platform from which to oppose this policy.

A Shift within World Bodies

The interwar *Zeitgeist* within world bodies lent itself to ambitious codification efforts. Harvard Law School professor David Kennedy has described this political shift as a "move to international institutions."

[2] The Codification Conference was held at The Hague from March 13, to April 12, 1930.

[3] Among Western international lawyers, there was also the expectation that this would come about at the 1930 Codification Conference. Interestingly, 1930 is also the same year that Hersch Lauterpacht delivered his Hague lecture series on "*La théorie des différends non justiciables en droit international*" (34 *Recueil des cours* 493 (1930-IV)).

[4] National Archives, Washington, DC, Record Group 43 Records of International Conferences, Commissions, and Expositions, International Conference Records United States Delegation to Conference for Codification of International Law, General Records, 1930, 019-110.021, Box No. 3, Entry 178, Folder unnumbered (American Delegation-Organization, Instructions, Etc.). Reading through the correspondence between the delegates and public officials as well as private citizens, there is a sense that state responsibility should be codified as alien protection and not more.

After the First World War, diplomats imagined these institutions as defending international society from the shared fear of war. Lawyer-diplomats drafted treaties such as the Covenant of the League of Nations[5] and the Pact of Locarno[6] to shepherd the move from chaos to order.[7] These treaties were live efforts to institutionalize an international rule of law that would spell the end of war.[8] By transforming military and political clashes into legal "disputes," these treaties provided opportunities for an international bureaucracy.[9] Below, I build upon Professor Kennedy's account by illustrating the impact of this move to institutions on the codification of state responsibility.

Decolonization (and the consequent creation of new states) brought with it broader representation within world bodies. This new reality affected the procedures and substance of international codification. In terms of procedure, as new states participated in international conferences, their increased representation ended the Western dominance of such bodies and made multilateral codification impracticable during the interwar era.[10] In terms of substance, especially after the Second World War, international codifiers reframed state responsibility as abstract principles of attribution. German theory fitted this new codification strategy well because it presented a comprehensive (and politically new) foundation upon which to build.

[5] The Covenant of the League of Nations (Including Amendments adopted to December 1924), available online at https://avalon.law.yale.edu/20th_century/leagcov.asp, last visited August 4, 2021.

[6] The Treaty of Mutual Guarantee between Germany, Belgium, France, Great Britain and Italy, signed at Locarno, October 16, 1925, available online at https://avalon.law.yale.edu/20th_century/locarno_001.asp, last visited August 4, 2021.

[7] To David Kennedy, "The use of a text to signal the move, and indeed to move, from chaos to order is part of the genius of modern institutional practice" (David Kennedy, "The Move to Institutions," 8(5) *Cardozo Law Review* 841 (1987), at p. 848; *see also* Antal Berkes, "The League of Nations and the International Law of State Responsibility," 22 *International Community Law Review* 331 (2020), at p. 335.

[8] Kennedy, *supra* note 7, at pp. 866–867, internal citations omitted.

[9] One that Kennedy describes as "radically decontextualized" (*supra* note 7, at p. 982).

[10] *See* Laurence R. Helfer and Timothy Meyer, "The Evolution of Codification: A Principal-Agent Theory of the International Law Commission's Influence," in Curtis Bradley (ed.), *Custom's Future: International Law in a Changing World* (Cambridge: Cambridge University Press, 2016), at pp. 13–14 (bypassing the treaty-making process was deemed the best approach, both because it denied states the opportunity to formally express disagreement with aspects of the draft articles and because it opened other avenues – the disaggregated and relatively uncoordinated actions of states and international tribunals and organizations – for the ILC's work to gain traction," internal citations omitted).

Expanded world bodies provided a forum in which Latin American lawyers could voice their opposition to the international minimum standard.[11] Whereas private attempts to codify international law had begun in earnest during the late nineteenth century,[12] public efforts commenced only in the twentieth century, after The Hague Conventions of 1899 and 1907.[13] While neither Hague treaty directly

[11] According to Becker Lorca, after the first Hague Conferences, Latin American lawyers globalized their cause of codifying international law as a shield against the hegemonic and colonial interests of the US and Europe – *see* Arnulf Becker Lorca, "International Law in Latin America or Latin American International Law? Rise, Fall, and Retrieval of a Tradition of Legal Thinking and Political Imagination," 47(1) *Harvard International Law Journal* 283 (2006), at pp. 298–299, 305. Further, writes Arnulf Becker Lorca, by the late-1920s, the move to institutions had provided a platform for a more international, or "*mestizo*," doctrine of state responsibility (Arnulf Becker Lorca, *Mestizo International Law: A Global Intellectual History 1842–1933* (Cambridge: Cambridge University Press, 2015), at pp. 22, 317). Legal historian Christopher Rossi has recently written on how the Latin American turn to international institutions such as the Central American Court of Justice (CACJ) came in response to the US turn to international arbitration: "However, a counter-narrative already had developed, beginning in the mid-nineteenth century [that] projected darker implications of the United States' hemispheric rise beginning with the annexation of Texas (1845), the Mexican-American War (1846–1848), which sparked the rise of Latin Americanism among critical factions of South America's intelligentsia, and the mid-nineteenth century competition with Great Britain over the control or neutral status of the isthmus (resulting in the Bidlack-Mallarino Treaty with Colombia (1846), and the Clayton-Bulwer Treaty with Great Britain (1850)). In Central America, the counter-narrative would influence a judgment of the CACJ that would attempt to reformat the language of international law as a prophylactic against the application of the Monroe Doctrine. In attempting to reshape international law, the CACJ ended up forwarding its own whiggish interpretation of international legal history" (Christopher R. Rossi, *Whiggish International Law Elihu Root, the Monroe Doctrine, and International Law in the Americas* (Leiden: Brill, 2019), at p. 120).

[12] The *Institut* had a "*Projet de règlement pour tribunaux arbitraux internationaux*" but Geneva session presentation in 1874 intended to regulate only the procedural aspects of arbitration and did not provide explicitly for executive rules – Session de Genève, 1874, par L. Goldschmidt, in 4 *Revue de droit international et de legislation comparée* 421 (1874); *see* Kristina Lovrić-Pernak, "The concept of international arbitration in 19th century International Law – Legal authority reduced to moral peace," 1st Meeting of the Working Group "Paradoxes of Peace in the 19th Century Europe," Research Project Europe 1815–1914, Helsinki, November 16–17, 2010 (paper on file with author), at p. 6.

[13] *See* the Avalon Project on the Laws of War, https://avalon.law.yale.edu/subject_menus/lawwar.asp, last visited August 3, 2021. Prior to the twentieth century, however, states did enter into multilateral codification treaties – *e.g.*, the 1864 Convention for the Amelioration of the Condition of the Wounded in Armies in the Field. *See further* Ernest Nys, "The Codification of International Law," 5 *American Journal of International Law* 871–900 (1911); James Crawford, "The Progressive Development of International Law: History, Theory and Practice," in Denis Alland, Vincent Chetail, Olivier de Frouville & Jorge E. Viñuales (eds.), *Unité et diversité du droit international:*

addressed the doctrine of state responsibility, it was at these conferences that Latin Americans began to solidify their opposition to Western codification.[14] As committees of international experts convened to legislate fundamental rules of international law, divisions began to emerge between Western and other delegates concerned with how and how much to codify, bit by bit, based either on past practice or wholistically to address systemic needs.[15]

Effective codification would hinge upon the ability to secure voting blocs within world bodies. For example, 1956 and 1961 were important dates because it was then that the ILC expanded its membership from fifteen to twenty-one and then to twenty-five.[16] These expansions

Écrits en l'honneur du Professeur Pierre-Marie Dupuy (Leiden: Martinus Nijhoff, 2014). Neither the *Institut de droit international* nor the International Law Association made any effort to codify state responsibility in the nineteenth century (in the context of alien protection or otherwise). The concept is not mentioned in David Dudley Field's *Draft Outline of an International Code* (New York: Baker, Voorhis & Co., 1872) and only obliquely referred to in Johann Caspar Bluntschli's *Le droit international codifié* (Charles Édouard Lardy, trans., Paris: Librairie Guillaumin, 1886) – *see, e.g.*, at p. 274. At the First International Conference of American States, held in Washington (1889–1890), diplomats adopted a recommendation concerning "Claims and Diplomatic Intervention," which referred to the enjoyment by foreigners of the civil rights and legal remedies open to natives. At the Second Conference in Mexico City (1901–1902), diplomats adopted the "Convention Relative to the Rights of Aliens," which dealt, *inter alia*, with the problem of state responsibility for the acts of individuals, the question of diplomatic protection, and rules concerning the exhaustion of local remedies (*see* Carnegie Endowment for International Peace, *The International Conferences of American States, 1889-1928* (New York, Oxford University Press, 1931), pp. 45, 90–91).

14 *See* Arnulf Becker Lorca, "Codifying American International Law: The End of the Classical Legal Order" (unpublished paper on file with author); Becker Lorca, *supra* note 11, at pp. 298–299, 305.

15 Professor Spinedi and Judge Simma open their book with: "The work on State responsibility for wrongful acts is, without doubt, the most ambitious codification project in the history of the UN International Law Commission" (Marina Spinedi and Bruno Simma (eds.), *United Nations Codification of State Responsibility* (New York: Oceana, 1987), at p. *xii*. See also Shabtai Rosenne, "The Codification of the Law of State Responsibility 1924–1990," in Shabtai Rosenne, (ed.), *The International Law Commission's Draft Articles on State Responsibility, Part 1, Articles 1–35* (Dordrecht: Nijhoff, 1991), at p. *vi*: "State Responsibility is one of the most difficult and delicate questions to be examined by the Commission, and I believe that for a proper understanding of this set of draft articles (and of those to follow), a description of the vicissitudes of the history of its official codification is necessary."

16 In 1956, the Sixth Committee of the General Assembly reached an agreement regarding the allocation of seats among the regional groups to ensure distribution between different forms of civilization and legal systems in connection with increasing the membership of the Commission from fifteen to twenty-one. *See* Official Records of the General Assembly, Eleventh Session, Annexes, agenda item 59, document A/3427, para. 13; and

reversed the Anglo-American balance of institutional power and, consequently, quashed the effort to base state responsibility on alien protection. Accordingly, I divide the history of codifying state responsibility into two phases: before and after the 1960s.[17]

Codification Begins where Arbitration Ends

The most important effect of the League of Nations on the development of state responsibility did not emerge from the case law of the Permanent Court of International Justice (PCIJ). It derived from a group of international law professionals meeting sporadically as the Committee of Experts for the Progressive Codification of International Law (Committee of Experts).[18] The League of Nations established the committee in 1924 to represent the "main forms of civilization" so as to prepare a list of subjects that were sufficiently "ripe" for codification by a multilateral treaty.[19] The first chairman of that committee was Hjalmar Hammarskjöld (1862–1953), the former Swedish Prime Minister (and father of Dag, the second UN Secretary General). At the very first session in April 1925, Hammarskjöld created a subcommittee on state responsibility that focused on codifying the field based on the US-led arbitral practice of alien injuries.[20]

ibid, Sixteenth session, Annexes, agenda item 17, document A/4779, paras. 4 and 5. In 1961, different views were expressed concerning the continuation of this arrangement when the membership of the Commission was increased from twenty-one to twenty-five. *See* Official Records of the General Assembly, Sixteenth Session, Annexes, agenda item 77, document A/4939, paras. 9–12; and document A/36/371, paras. 4–6.

17 Rosenne divides the history of codifying state responsibility into three eras: under Guerrero (1924–1930), García Amador (1947–1961) and Ago (1962–2001). See, e.g., Rosenne, *supra* note 15, at pp. 7–8, 19–27.

18 In my view, The PCIJ had a limited impact on the development of international law in general and on state responsibility in particular. The change in the composition of the ICJ during the 1960s enabled it to employ reasoning based more on doctrine than practice. For the perspective on the non-Eurocentric nature of the PCIJ, *see* Ole Spiermann, "Judge Wang Chung-Hui at the Permanent Court of International Justice," 5(1) *Chinese Journal of International Law* 115 (2006).

19 Resolution of 24 July 1920, reproduced in 41 *American Journal of International Law Supplement* 104 (1947).

20 Specifically:

1. whether, and in what cases, a state may be liable for injury caused on its territory to the persons or property of foreigners;
2. whether and, if so, in what terms it would be possible to contemplate the conclusion of an international convention providing for the ascertainment of the facts which may

All the experts on the subcommittee for state responsibility – José Gustavo Guerrero (1876–1956) (El Salvador), Charles de Visscher (1884–1973) (Belgium) and Wang Chung-Hui (1881–1958) (China) – were leaders of the international bar who served as judges on the PCIJ. Both Guerrero and de Visscher were authors of commentaries on state responsibility.[21] The formation of such a distinguished group of international lawyers lent immediate legitimacy to the new international codification project on state responsibility.[22] Indeed, most histories of state responsibility begin with this Committee of Experts.[23]

The main figure to emerge from the first phase of codification is the Salvadoran international lawyer José Gustavo Guerrero (Figure 5.1), who in many ways was the intellectual successor to Carlos Calvo (1824–1906).[24] Guerrero was the Chairman of the subcommittee, the last President of the PCIJ as well as the first President of the ICJ as well. Guerrero too was also a "post-sovereignty" liberal for whom international law was not the accidental outcome of alien injuries, but the

> involve liability on the part of a state, and forbidding in such cases recourse to measures of coercion before the means to pacific settlement have been exhausted"

(Records of the Fifth Assembly (1924), LNOJ, 5th year, Sp. Sup. 23 at pp. 82–83, 87, 121–125; Minutes of the First Committee, Sp. Sup. 24, at pp. 14, 25–28, 97–98 as reproduced in in Rosenne, *supra* note 15, at pp. 2–3).

21 José Gustavo Guerrero, *La responsabilidad internacional de los estados por los daños causados en su territorio a la persona o bienes de los extranjeros* (Paris: Imprimerie Lahure, 1926); Charles de Visscher, "La responsabilité des États," in Bibliotheca Visseriana II (Leyden: Brill, 1924); Charles de Visscher, "Le déni de justice en droit international," 52 *Recueil des cours* 421 (1935); on the success of Wang Chung-Hui as an international judge, *see* Spiermann, *supra* note 18.

22 As Jean Monnet has said "Nothing is possible without men, but nothing is lasting without institutions" (quoted in Roger Cohen, "The Beauty of Institutions," *The New York Times*, November 25, 2011).

23 A similar historical comment was made regarding international adjudication. *See* Shabtai Rosenne, *The World Court: What It is and How It Works* (2nd ed., Leyden: A. W. Sythoff, 1963), at pp. 19, 26: "The real significance of the experience of the Permanent Court seems to lie . . . From its experimental beginnings it established the point that a permanent international judicial organ is both feasible and necessary, even without going so far as to be accompanied by any true compulsory jurisdiction."

24 *See generally* José Gustavo Guerrero, *La codification du droit international: la première conférence, La Haye, 13 mars–12 avril 1930* (Paris: Pedone, 1930); *La responsabilidad internacional de los estados por los daños causados en su territorio a la persona o bienes de los extranjeros* (Paris: Imprimerie Lahure, 1926); "*La responsabilité internationale des États*," in *Academie Diplomatique Internationale, Seances et Travaux*, March 12, 1928, pp. 18–30; José Gustavo Guerrero and Wang Chung Hui, "Report of the Sub-Committee of the Committee of Experts for the Progressive Codification of International Law," 20 *American Journal of International Law Special Supplement* 177 (1926).

Figure 5.1 José Gustavo Guerrero[25]

intentionally designed construction of Great Powers within the international community.[26]

Guerrero circulated a 1926 report co-written with Wang Chung-Hui (1881–1958) that included twelve tentative conclusions for discussion among the committee.[27] The Guerrero report is cleverly drafted to refer to the established doctrine of state responsibility without referring to its controversial origins. It limits the sources of state responsibility for breaches of either a specific treaty provision of "a duty recognized by customary law in a clear and definite form."[28] The international

[25] Photo courtesy of Wikimedia Commons, https://en.wikipedia.org/wiki/Jos%C3%A9_Gustavo_Guerrero#/media/File:EEBldDDW4AELtVo1929._In_Geneva,_Switzerland,_Salvadoran_lawyer_and_diplomat_Dr._Jos%C3%A9_Gustavo_Guerrero_places_the_first_stone_of_the_Palais_des_Nations,_the_headquarters_of_the_League_of_Nations,_today_UN.jpg.

[26] *See* Kathryn Greenman, "Aliens in Latin America: Intervention, Arbitration and State Responsibility for Rebels," 31 *Leiden Journal of International Law* 617 (2018), at p. 628; Becker Lorca, *supra* note 11, at p. 221.

[27] League of Nations, "Report of the Sub-Committee of the Committee of Experts for the Progressive Codification of International Law," 20 *American Journal of International Law Special Supplement* 177 (1926). For example, the first conclusion was that state responsibility is triggered only upon the event of a wrongful act committed by one state against another (*ibid*).

[28] As reproduced in Rosenne, *supra* note 15, at p. 4.

minimum standard of care is not mentioned in any of the conclusions or, indeed, in the report at all. At the same time, the Guerrero report does not reject the practice of international arbitration or require that international claims be submitted to international courts. No mention is made of recourse to the newly formed PCIJ at all.[29]

The Guerrero Report was met with considerable opposition from members who expected a more traditional report that supported Western views of state responsibility as the remedy for alien injuries.[30] This is because it was balanced in its approach. On the one hand, Guerrero opposed imperialism and sought to codify state responsibility more flexibly.[31] He appreciated the broader significance of international responsibility[32] as the "constitutive order" and "collective will" of states.[33] On the other hand, Guerrero was a modern liberal for whom the sanctity of property is central.[34] In sum, his report suffers from the curse of compromise.[35] Guerrero actually sought a path of "in between," a *via media* that would bridge the differences between Latin and

[29] *See further* Rosenne, *supra* note 15, at p. 8.

[30] The responses of the governments and commissioners are reproduced in Shabtai Rosenne, The League of Nations Conference for the Codification of International Law 1930, Vol. II 342–441 (New York: Oceana, 1975). For example, to Borchard, the Guerrero Report was a key cause of failure in The Hague – see Edwin M. Borchard, "'Responsibility of States,' at the Hague Codification Conference," 24 *American Journal of International Law* 517 (1930), at p. 517.

[31] For a contrary view, *see* Santiago Montt, *State Liability in Investment Treaty Arbitration: Global Constitutional and Administrative Law in the BIT Generation* (Oxford: Hart, 2009), at p. 53 (the Guerrero Report played a key role in articulating the position of capital importing countries at the Conference).

[32] Note that Guerrero used the term "international responsibility" based on the assumption that the rule of international law only applies to the persons of states – *see* Guerrero Report, *supra* note 24, at p. 180.

[33] Guerrero, *supra* note 24, at p. 89.

[34] He recognizes that general rule of domestic protection levels but allows for exceptions for acts of rebels in the event of appropriation of property and denial of justice. *See* Guerrero Report, *supra* note 24, at pp. 197, 202; *see also* Greenman, *supra* note 25, at p. 631.

[35] See Guerrero Report, *supra* note 24, at p. 197: "Treaties concluded between certain European States, and between several of the American States, which contain provisions disclaiming responsibility in case of damage occasioned by revolt and civil war, have often been the subject of criticism. We think that these criticisms ought rather to be leveled against the nations which, in defiance of all international rules, have sought to impose on other States a responsibility which the latter could never really have incurred. The States of Latin America have acted wisely in endeavouring to secure protection for their legitimate rights by means of treaty provisions."

Anglo-Americans.[36] Guerrero's goal was not revolutionary but gradual progress.[37] However, his approach was rejected by both sides.[38] (So much for moderation.) Anglo-American lawyers declined to deduce principles from German theory. Continental European and Latin American (or, "Latin European")[39] lawyers refused to induce norms from international (read: Anglo-American) awards.

The 1930 conference was a highly anticipated event in the field.[40] The League's call to codify international law was met with enthusiasm not only internally by the Committee of Experts but externally as well, by Harvard Law School, the *Institut de Droit international* and other professional bodies. Western lawyers especially held out high expectations

[36] *See* Martti Koskenniemi, *The Gentle Civilizer of Nations: The Rise and Fall of International Law 1870–1960* (Cambridge: Cambridge University Press, 2002), at p. 307.

[37] Codification was an opportunity for discussing the basic tenets of the classical legal order and the "Semi-peripherals, and in particular Latin Americans, rose up to the challenge" – *Junta Internacional de Jurisconsultos, Actas, Resoluciones y Documentos: Primera Reunión En Rio De Janeiro*. 26 De Junio–19 De Julio De 1912. Rio de Janeiro, 1914 at pp. 47–51, 51–76; Alejandro Álvarez, *La codificacion del derecho internacional en América: trabajos de la tercera Comisión de la Asamblea de Jurisconsultos reunida en Santiago de Chile* (Santiago: Imprenta Universitaria, 1923), at pp. 26–27 as cited in Becker Lorca, *supra* note 14. *See also* Todd Weiler, *The Interpretation of International Investment Law: Equality, Discrimination and Minimum Standards of Treatment in Historical Context* (Leiden: Martinus Nijhoff, 2013), at p. 10 ("Francisco Garcia-Amador was one of the first publicists to grasp the transformative potential of such a mechanism [of granting standing to individuals to sue states for international wrongs], especially if combined with a set of substantive norms requiring some kind of judicial review mechanism for State conduct"). On the backlash of strategies by semi-peripheral and other states to the US-led investment arbitration regime, *see* Malcolm Langford, Daniel Behn and Ole Kristian Fauchald, "Backlash and State Strategies in International Investment Law," in T. Gammeltoft-Hansen and T. Aalberts (eds.), *The Changing Practices of International Law: Sovereignty, Law and Politics in a Globalising World* (Cambridge: Cambridge University Press, 2017).

[38] This cleavage was raised by the very first speaker (Dr. José Lobo d'Avila Lima of Portugal), who expressed fear about the inability to codify within an institution that is comprised by two such different codification approaches – "Anglo-American" and "Continental" (League of Nations, *Acts of the Conference for the Codification of International Law, Held at The Hague from March 13th to April 12th 1930, Meetings of the Committees, Vol. IV, Minutes of the Third Committee, Responsibility of States for Damage caused in Their Territory to the Person or Property of Foreigners* (Geneva, 1930), League of Nations, doc. C. 351.M.145.1940.IV, at p. 18). *See also* Becker Lorca, *supra* note 14.

[39] As discussed below, for lack of a better term, Latin Europeans refers to the member bloc comprised of Latin Americans and "Latin" Europeans (mainly French and Italian).

[40] I note that in 1929, the Paris Conference on the Treatment of Foreigners attempted to codify alien protection without any success at all, *see* further Berkes, *supra* note 7, at p. 6.

for its success.[41] The most influential of the private efforts, the Harvard Research in International Law project, prepared draft conventions on state responsibility in 1929.[42]

These two draft conventions incorporated a view of state responsibility that was essentially a doctrine about the remedies for alien injuries.[43] They were meant as a restatement of existing law to be circulated to and studied by all participating governments prior to the Codification Conference. Led by Hackworth and Borchard, the draft conventions were not simply apologies for US policy.[44] The Acting Secretary of State himself instructed Hackworth and Borchard when at The Hague *not* to approve the Harvard Draft "as a whole."[45] Hackworth himself would go on to serve as President of the ICJ and was active on the Executive Council of the American Society of International Law, writing extensively on international law.[46] Borchard, besides serving as an Assistant Solicitor of the State Department, was a liberal pacifist who advocated publicly to keep the US neutral in both world wars. While these men's views usually

[41] Green Hackworth, a conference delegate and attorney in the US State Department, is clear on these points: "To the international lawyer . . . the Responsibility of States for Damage Caused in Their Territory to the Person or Property of Foreigners, involves principles that underlie the whole fabric of public international law. There is perhaps no subject of international law so constantly and so actively before the nations, nor one which so vitally affects them, as that of Responsibility of States" (Green H. Hackworth, "Responsibility of States for Damages Caused in Their Territory to the Person or Property of Foreigners," 24 *American Journal of International Law* 500–516 (1930), at p. 500).

[42] Harvard Law School, "Draft Convention on Responsibility of States for Damage Done in Their Territory to the Person or Property of Foreigners," 23 *American Journal of International Law Special Supplement* 133 (1929). This draft was the first of two conventions drafted by the Harvard Law School; the second was in 1961, discussed below.

[43] It even, in the first provision, *defined* "the responsibility of States" as the "duty to make reparation to another state for the injury sustained by the latter state as a consequence of an injury to its national" (Article 1).

[44] Indeed, the 1929 Harvard Draft Convention also departed from past US practice in certain areas in order to propose moderate changes that would be necessary to secure acceptance by other countries (Crawford and Grant, *infra* note 122, at p. 140).

[45] Acting Secretary of State JP Cotton in a letter of 27 February 1930 to David Hunter Miller the Chairman of the US delegation to the codification conference: "You will understand, of course, that the delegates are in no sense to approve the Harvard drafts as a whole or to approve the League bases as a whole" (National Archives, Washington, DC, Record Group 43, *supra* note 4, Entry 178, Folder unnumbered (American Delegation-Organization, Instructions, Etc. 110.021).

[46] Most famously, his eight-volume *Digest of International Law* (Washington, DC: Government Printing Office, 1940–1944).

tracked those of the US Government, they were also genuine and judicious in their own right.[47]

In Germany, the *Deutsche Gesellschaft für Völkerrecht*, under the leadership of the lawyer-diplomat Walther Schücking (1875–1935), also published a draft convention on state responsibility for alien injuries.[48] The German draft is rather expansive in its approach. It does not so much disagree with the Harvard Draft Convention, as much as provide substantially more detail. Regarding the international duty to protect aliens, the German draft provides several rules that comprise the international minimum standard (which could be preempted by treaty obligations).[49] The draft is systematic as well as expansive in its approach. It provides not only the substance of the duty to protect aliens but also specifies the conditions and consequences of breaching that duty. The final provision also implicitly permits reprisals once all reasonable forms of pacific dispute resolution have been attempted and have failed.

[47] Still, as Jonathan Zasloff has written, the State Department at that time was itself a bastion of "classical legalism" (Jonathan Zasloff, "Law and the Shaping of American Foreign Policy: From the Gilded Age to the New Era," 78 *New York University Law Review* 239 (2003), at p. 255; Jonathan Zasloff, "Law and the Shaping of American Foreign Policy: The Twenty Years' Crisis," 77 *Southern California Law Review* 583 (2004), at p. 585).

[48] *Institut für Internationalen Recht an der Universität Kiel, Zeitschrift für Völkerrecht* (Breslau, 1930), vol. XV, pp. 359–364; see Chapter 4 for a discussion of Karl Strupp's draft treaty on state responsibility.

[49] According to Article 2 (as reproduced in Annex II to Francisco Victor García Amador, "First Report on International Responsibility," Report of 20 January 1956, U.N. Doc. A/CN.4/96, reprinted in 2 *Yearbook of the International Law Commission* 173 (1956), Vol. II):

1. In the absence of special agreements or other rules of international law, every State is obligated to protect the life, freedom and property of aliens in its territory.
2. This obligation means, in particular, that:
   a) An alien may not be wrongfully deprived of his freedom. Wrongful deprivation of freedom is deemed to include, in particular, the upholding of an unlawful arrest, detention in provisional custody for a manifestly unnecessary or inadmissible length of time, and imprisonment without due cause or in conditions of unnecessary hardship.
   b) Expropriation of duly acquired rights is admissible only for reasons of the general welfare and against appropriate compensation.
   c) Concessions granted to aliens or rights conferred by contract on aliens may be withdrawn only for compelling reasons of public welfare and against full compensation.
   d) The obligations of indebtedness of a State toward an alien may not be annulled by that State and performance of them may not be refused by that State without lawful cause. Payments of interest and repayments of principal may be suspended or modified only in the event of financial necessity.

Interestingly, the draft does not call such actions "reprisals," but "measures of self-defence."[50]

The *Institut de Droit international* also drafted a separate convention on state responsibility that closely mirrored the Harvard research project.[51] At its Lausanne meeting in 1927, the *Institut* had adopted a resolution on the international responsibility of states for damage caused in their territory to the person and property of foreigners that was drafted by the Viennese law professor and international arbitrator Leo Strisower (1857–1931).[52] The resolution resembles the Harvard draft in that it limits its scope to alien injuries in its substance. For example, it affirms the arbitral pronouncement that the general standard of alien protection is non-discrimination.[53] It also modifies the 1926 Guerrero report by calling for all alien protection disputes to be resolved pacifically – if not by an international commission of inquiry, then by the Permanent Court of Arbitration or World Court.[54]

50 Article 16(2): "Measures of self-defence shall not exceed the bounds of necessity and shall not be disproportionate to the injury. In the event of disagreement on whether this is the case, the States shall endeavor to settle the disagreement by peaceful means."

51 This is not the first time the *Institut* promoted the issue of state responsibility, but it was its first codification attempt. Under the leadership of Nobel Peace Prize nominee Emilio Brusa, the *Institut* produced an 1898 report on state responsibility for injuries arising out of mob violence and civil wars (Emilio Brusa, "Responsabilité internationale des États à raison des dommages causés sur leur territoire à la personne et aux biens des étrangers," 33 *Annuaire de l'Institut de droit international* 330 (1927)) and a 1900 resolution negating the promotion of "Calvo Clauses" in treaties (Emilio Brusa and Ludwig von Bar (Rapporteurs), "Règlement sur la responsabilité des Etats à raison des dommages soufferts par des étrangers en cas d'émeute, d'insurrection ou de guerre civile," 18 *Annuaire de l'Institut de droit international* 254).

52 Brusa, *supra* note 51, at pp. 330–335). *See also* the report by Leo Strisower, *ibid*, Vol. I, at pp. 455–562, and general discussion, *ibid*, Vol. III, at pp. 81–168, available online at www.idi-iil.org/idiF/resolutionsF/1927_lau_05_fr.pdf, last visited on March 28, 2012. Like Jellinek, Kelsen, Strupp and Lauterpacht, Strisower was a German-speaking Jew. *See further* James Loeffler and Moria Paz (eds.), *The Law of Strangers Jewish Lawyers and International Law in the Twentieth Century* (Cambridge: Cambridge University Press, 2019): "nineteenth- and twentieth-century European Jews turned to international law as a vision for concrete legal protection against state violence and official discrimination on the one hand and a post-traditional utopian revisioning of international community on the other" (p. 8); Ari Mermelstein, Victoria Saker Woeste, Ethan Zadoff and Marc Galanter (eds.), *Jews and the Law* (New Orleans: Quid Pro Quo Books, 2014), especially chs. 9–12.

53 "*Réserve faite des cas où le droit international appellerait un traitement de l'étranger préférable à celui du national*" (Article 4).

54 Article 13.

1930: Year of Promise, Year of Crisis

Forty-seven governmental delegations attended the 1930 codification conference at The Hague. Even the Soviet Union sent its first foreign delegation, as an "observer," to the international conference. Despite the excitement, the conference was unable to come even close to meeting its stated aims of codification. Notwithstanding the appointments of three committees and numerous subcommittees, no majority – let alone consensus – could be reached on any of the codification topics.[55] Discussions about the legal sources of codification alone took up five of the available twelve days.[56] This not only seemed to waste precious time, but also set the tone of disappointment for the duration of the conference.[57]

On the opening day, fundamentally opposing views were put forth. A French delegate thought he could begin discussions with a statement about the basis of international responsibility to which all could be expected to agree:

> [A]ny failure to comply with the international obligations of a State, owing to the act of its organs, whether legislative, executive or judiciary does involve the responsibility of that State.[58]

The Anglo-American delegates – especially the US, led by Green Hackworth and Edwin Borchard – wanted a more expansive statement that included the secondary obligation to repair. Latin American delegates wanted a more restrictive provision.[59] Guerrero, in attendance as the Salvadoran delegate, demanded that responsibility could arise only

[55] See Borchard, *supra* note 30, at p. 539.

[56] Guerrero, representing El Salvador, stated that, unless he knew what the international obligations were to which he was expected to subscribe, he could not sign the convention on behalf of his government. *See* Borchard, *supra* note 30, at p. 520.

[57] Rosenne, *supra* note 15, at pp. 1442, 1583; Martins Paparinskis, "Sources of Law and Arbitral Interpretations of Pair Matéria Investment Protection Rules," in Ole Kristina Faucal and André Nollkaemper (eds.), *Unity or Fragmentation of International Law: The Role of International and National Tribunals* (London: Hart Publishing, 2011), at p. 94.

[58] Hackworth, *supra* note 41, at pp. 501–502. The gist of this provision was to base international responsibility squarely upon the civil law notion of fault (as opposed to risk). This proposal was supported by the argument that it carries out the theory of Articles 1382 and 1384 of the French Civil Code to the effect that a person is responsible for the damages that by fault he or his employees cause to another – Borchard, *supra* note 30, at p. 518. On private law theories of governmental responsibility in tort, see Edwin Borchard, "Theories of Governmental Responsibility in Tort," 28 *Columbia Law Review* 577 (1928), at pp. 577, 597 et seq., 607, note 82.

[59] Hackworth, *supra* note 41, at p. 501.

for breaches of "recognized" and "established" international laws.[60] In other words, any violation of a rule of international law that was not universally accepted would be insufficient to trigger state responsibility.[61]

Latin Americans pushed for equality of foreigners' and locals' rights based on domestic standards of law. Anglo-Americans insisted that the "fact that a foreigner is invested with a recognised public status imposes upon the State a special duty of vigilance."[62] The former sought to consider responsibility in the general sense (as the principles underlying international law enforcement) but the latter saw it simply as the international basis for claims of reparation.[63] These positions informed committee votes. When it came to voting on international responsibility for mob violence, the final tally was twenty-one to seventeen and split along discernible socioeconomic lines (*see* Table 5.1).[64]

Agreement in any lasting form had eluded the conference.[65] Of the four conference topics, the least amount of progress was made in the field of state responsibility. This surprised and disappointed many participants who felt that the topic was ripe for codification in 1930.[66] The League's inability to codify international law was also perceived as a structural failure within the design of international institutions. In an undated letter, US delegation Chairman Miller writes that "I think the general result of this Convention will be a blow to the whole idea of the codification of international law."[67]

Many explanations have been offered for the codification failure in The Hague.[68] According to Borchard, the conference was preordained to fail because it sought to base the codification of state responsibility on the 1926 Guerrero report, which represented the Latin American – rather

[60] Hackworth, *supra* note 41, at pp. 502–503.

[61] Hackworth, *supra* note 41, at p. 504, emphasis added.

[62] Hackworth, *supra* note 41, at pp. 509, 512.

[63] Hackworth, *supra* note 41, at pp. 511–513.

[64] The vote was on what was to be Article 10 – Hackworth, *supra* note 41, at p. 514.

[65] As Shabtai Rosenne wrote: "from the outset the work of the Committee was marked by formidable differences of approach" (Rosenne, *supra* note 15, at p. 13). *See also* Becker Lorca, *supra* note 14: "Everyone realized that semi-peripheral states had congealed into a strong minority block that prevented reaching the two-thirds majority required on a second reading of the draft articles. Everyone realized that the codification of international responsibility had failed" (internal citations omitted).

[66] *See* Becker Lorca, *supra* note 11, at p. 317 (Hague Conference again blocked by the semi-peripherals).

[67] National Archives, Washington, DC, Record Group 43, *supra* note 4, Entry 178, Folder unnumbered (American Delegation-Organization, Instructions, Etc.).

[68] For a contrary view on the importance of the 1930 conference *see* Berkes, *supra* note 7.

Table 5.1 *Votes by delegations on Article 10*

21 states voted for Article 10	17 states voted against Article 10
Austria	Chile
Australia	China
Belgium	Colombia
British Empire	Czechoslovakia
Canada	Free City of Danzig
Estonia	Hungary
Finland	Kingdom of Yugoslavia
France	Mexico
Germany	Nicaragua
Greece	Persia
India	Poland
Irish Free State	Portugal
Italy	Rumania
Japan	Salvador
Netherlands	Turkey
Norway	United States of Brazil
Spain	Uruguay
Sweden	
Switzerland	
Union of South Africa	
United States of America	

than the "majority" or Anglo-American – approach.[69] Writing decades later, the Israeli international lawyer Shabtai Rosenne (1917–2010) (shown in Figure 5.2) explained the failure of the conference on three practical grounds. First, it was the first such public experiment; prior to 1930, international codification had been the task of "learned societies" rather than of convention delegates. Second, the "Bases for Discussion" were insufficient texts for codification purposes, leaving too much open for debate. Third – and in my opinion, inaccurately – Rosenne argues

[69] Borchard, *supra* note 30, at pp. 517–540, 517 (the draft departed materially from the subsequent Bases of Discussion); Percy Corbett, *Law and Society in the Relations of States* (New York: Harcourt, Brace and Company, 1951), at p. 49 ("A strong minority of the Latin American and certain European States, refused to subscribe to a general standard of civilized justice and instead that no injury was suffered by an alien who received the same treatment as nationals"); Becker Lorca, *supra* note 14 (Borchard's bitter tone might be explained because the failure of the Committee was also a personal defeat).

Figure 5.2 Shabtai Rosen (center) speaks with Israeli Foreign Minister Abba Eban and Director of the Mossad Reuven Shiloah[70]

that the Codification Conference failed because of the Preparatory Committee's insufficient consultation with governments prior to 1930.[71] The Preparatory Committee's communication with states may not have been thorough, but it was certainly not haphazard.[72] Even Germany admitted: "The problem of the responsibility of States for

[70] Photo courtesy of the Wiki Commons: available online at https://en.wikipedia.org/wiki/Shabtai_Rosenne#/media/File:Rozen_aven.jpeg, last accessed May 5, 2024.

[71] Rosenne, *supra* note 15, at pp. 16–17. Compare his comments to those on p. 12, where he describes the high level of communication with states. Yuen-Li Liang (who represented China at the conference) seems to take a different position, describing the preparations to the 1930 conference as a notable departure from previous Hague conferences – *see* International Law Commission, *United Nations Documents on the Development and Codification of International Law*, Supplement to 41(4) *American Journal of International Law Special Supplement* 36 (1947).

[72] For example, Austria and Czechoslovakia believed that alien protection was not governed by any special regime of state responsibility (Rosenne, *supra* note 29, at p. 433). The Netherlands was adamant about not impinging on national criminal law, which Guerrero's report seemed to do and that the laws should only be confined to times of peace – to the exclusion of the situations of war and neutrality (*ibid* at p. 435). By far, the most contentious issue was the juridical or normative basis of state responsibility (*see ibid* at pp. 444–445).

damage done to the person or property of foreigners is not clearly defined in the theory of international law."[73]

The political subtext of state responsibility during that conference is also instructive. The goal to codify the "responsibility of States" was more challenging to the delegates than the other subjects of codification.[74] The substance of state responsibility for alien protection remained divisive. Even prior to the codification conference, Clyde Eagleton (1891–1958) was worried that the differences of opinion between Anglo-Americans and Latin Americans regarding the level of alien protection would torpedo any possibility of codification success.[75] More importantly, by 1930, Anglo-Americans no longer controlled the discourse within international institutions. Latin American delegates had by then coalesced as a voting bloc opposed to the international standard of protection.[76] During the first three decades of international codification, Latin American delegates solidified their cause of codifying international law as a shield against Anglo-American hegemonic and colonial interests. Whereas in 1907 they left the Hague conference feeling frustrated,[77] by 1930, they could sense their increasing clout.[78]

[73] Rosenne, *supra* note 15, at p. 432 (emphasis added to highlight the circularity of the statement). Japan and Roumania agreed with this proposition as well.

[74] Delegates were unable to codify the two other topics considered in The Hague – nationality and territorial waters. Three of the four other topics deemed "ripe" for codification by the League's codification Committee in 1927 – diplomatic privileges and immunities, procedure of international conferences and the drafting of treaties, piracy and the law of the sea – were all successfully codified relatively soon thereafter. *See* League of Nations Doc. C/196/M/70/1927/V. Only the codification of state responsibility took several more decades to complete.

[75] Clyde Eagleton, "Measures of Damages in International Law," 39 *Yale Law Journal* 52 (1929), at p. 52.

[76] From Andrés Bello to Carlos Calvo and Luis María Drago, an argument can be made that Latin American states were persistent objectors during the nineteenth century formation of the international standard of protection – *see* Dino Kritsiotis, "On the Possibilities of and for Persistent Objection," 21 *Duke Journal of Comparative & International Law* 121 (2010), at pp. 127–134. This argument, however, would only be of historic relevance for Latin American countries (except Brazil), given their subsequent entry into bilateral investment treaties, as I discuss below and in the final chapter (Epilogue).

[77] Secretary Root worked hard diplomatically to ensure that Latin American countries would be invited to the 1907 Hague Peace Conference, a greatly appreciated gesture. *See* Christopher R. Rossi, *Whiggish International Law Elihu Root, the Monroe Doctrine, and International Law in the Americas* (Leiden: Brill, 2019), at p. 62; Lars Schoultz, *Beneath the United States: A History of U.S. Policy toward Latin America* (Cambridge: Cambridge University Press, 1988), at p. 195.

[78] Becker Lorca, *supra* note 11, at p. 326. As UCL law professor Gerry Simpson writes in *Great Powers and Outlaw States*, this influence reflected a substantial change in world affairs, reversing the "legalized hegemony" of the Old World as set out by the Congress of

The ease with which the *Institut de Droit international* succeeded in passing its draft convention on state responsibility provides a conspicuous contrast to the League's earlier effort. In the eyes of its President, the US professor James Brown Scott (1866–1943), the importance of the 1927 Lausanne resolution was so great that its existence justified the entire establishment of the *Institut*. To Scott:

> [T]he project [on codifying state responsibility] is worthy of the Institute whose declaration it is, and that it would of itself go far to justify the creation of the Institute if it were not already in existence. It is a well-nigh *perfect piece of codification*, in the sense of stating the law as it is and of developing it and transmuting it into what it should be in accordance with the fundamental and recognized principles of justice. It was a triumph, not of officials, but of *men of good will*.[79]

Scott, like many other international lawyers of his time, understood that the codification of state responsibility was central to the overall efficacy of international law. The President of the *Institut* was particularly proud of Leo Strisower, the Reporter for the resolution. Strisower's resolution included several clear positions on state responsibility for injuries to aliens, including the internationality of minimum standards, denials of justice, due diligence and the prohibition of forceful intervention until peaceful alternatives were exhausted. Despite their doctrinal differences, the *Institut* managed to agree on twelve principles of state responsibility for alien injuries.

Why was a similar compromise not open to the delegates at The Hague? I do not believe it was because of a lack of preparation.[80] Numerous individuals, institutions, societies and states made abundant preparations for the conference. The conference failed because there were essentially two disparate groups of delegates when it came to state responsibility: *litigants* and *respondents*. These two groups had irreconcilably opposed views on its substantive codification. The practicable approach, or so it seemed at the time, was to base the codification on the actual practice of states. Of all the pre-conference draft codifications, only two and both

Vienna (1815) – *see* Gerry Simpson, *Great Powers and Outlaw States: Unequal Sovereigns in the International Legal Order* (Cambridge: Cambridge University Press, 2004), at p. 94; Rossi, *supra* note 77, at p. 95.

79 James Brown Scott, "The Institute of International Law," 21 *American Journal of International Law* 716 (1927), at p. 724.

80 According to Rosenne, this was a widely held view and resulted in an improved situation with the ILC, wherein which greater opportunities for governmental involvement occurred directly with the ILC and indirectly through the General Assembly (and the Sixth Committee) – Rosenne, *supra* note 15, at pp. 18–19.

private efforts (*i.e.*, Karl Strupp[81] of Germany and Anton Roth[82] of France) addressed state responsibility in general terms. A substantial minority of states (mainly Latin American) regarded the caselaw as having been effectively imposed upon them.[83] Even terminology such as the "denial of justice" could not be agreed upon in committee.[84] As a result, the Latin American bloc, "sustained by a common vision of international law, turned out to be relentless interveners during the negotiations."[85]

The Legacy of 1930

While the League did not succeed in codifying international law that year, it did succeed in crystallizing state responsibility as *the* doctrine regulating the conditions and consequences of breaching international law. Before the 1930s, state responsibility was not a term of art, and was only haphazardly addressed in the writings of publicists. Only a decade earlier, the 1920 edition of Oppenheim's *International Law*, contrasted the political nature of "responsibility" with the legal quality of "delinquency."[86] Similarly, Article 231 of the Versailles Treaty, in which Germany accepted "responsibility" for the First World War, the word was used in a conspicuously moralistic sense.[87] By 1930, "state

[81] Discussed in Chapter 4.

[82] *See* Anton Roth, *Das völkerrechtliche Delikt vor und in der Verhandlungen auf der Haager Kodifications Konferenz 1930* (Leipzig: Universitatsverlag von Robert Noske, 1932), at pp. 177–178. The text of Roth's draft convention is available online at http://legal.un.org/docs/?path=../ilc/documentation/english/a_cn4_217.pdf&lang=EFS, last visited November 10, 2015.

[83] Daniel Müller, "The Work of García Amador on State Responsibility for Injury Caused to Aliens" in Crawford, Pellet and Olleson, *supra* note 1, at pp. 69–74, 70.

[84] *See* Borchard, *supra* note 30, at p. 534: "The representatives of Rumania, Mexico, Salvador, and other Latin-American countries objected so vigorously to the term 'denial of justice,' which they contended had been misconstrued by many international tribunals, that it was decided to endeavour to find a definition sufficiently broad to cover the conception of denial of justice without using the term."

[85] Clémentine Bories, "The Hague Conference of 1930" in Crawford, Pellet, Olleson, *supra* note 1, at pp. 61–67, 63, internal citations omitted.

[86] Lassa Oppenheim, *International Law: A Treatise,* I (Ronald F. Roxburgh, ed., 3rd ed., London: Longmans, Green & Co., 1920), at p. 246.

[87] *See* Philipp Siegert, *Staatshaftung im Ausnahmezustand: Doktrin und Rechtspraxis im Deutschen Reich und in Frankreich, 1914–1919* (Frankfurt-am-Main: Klostermann Vittorio, 2020)) (Siegert examines state liability for the First World War as based on progressive conceptions of state responsibility that in some cases contracdicted preexisting international law). See *also* Crawford and Grant, *infra* note 122, at p. 85. Although the provision was not a legalistic application of state responsibility, the impact was lasting. According to James Crawford, after the First World War, "virtually no book . . . lacked a

responsibility" had become equated with the consequences of breaching international law. The drafting committee debated the nomenclatures of "liability," "responsibility" and other options. Some preferred the word "responsibility" as an accurate translation of the French *responsabilité*, whereas others favored "liability," because of the overly broad meanings of the English word "responsibility." In the end, the delegates chose "state responsibility" because of its "convenience."[88] Perhaps it was the ambiguity of the phrase that lent itself so well to international law. Either way, in retrospect, the 1930 conference effectively coined the term "state responsibility" as a technical doctrine regulating international law enforcement.

García Amador Takes a New Approach

After the Second World War, the next international codification project was led by the UN, which established the International Law Commission (ILC) in 1947 to foster the "progressive development of international law and its codification."[89] Hersch Lauterpacht (1897–1960), then the Whewell Professor of International Law at Cambridge University, was tapped by the ILC to select the most suitable topics ripe for codification. In his anonymously submitted *Survey of International Law in relation to the Work of Codification of the International Law Commission*, Lauterpacht recommended that the ILC learn from the 1930 Conference and address the issues of alien protection and general state responsibility separately. He believed that the 1930 convention was correct to focus on state responsibility for alien protection.[90] However, state responsibility was also much more than the legal consequences of economic loss:

> [I]t is clear that that branch of international law transcends the question of responsibility for the treatment of aliens. Its codification must take into

separate chapter on the subject" (James Crawford, *State Responsibility: The General Part* (Cambridge: Cambridge University Press, 2013), at p. 28). Other treaty mentions of the international legal "responsibility" of states during the first half of the twentieth century are: Article 3, Convention (IV) respecting the Laws and Customs of War on Land: Regulations concerning the Laws and Customs of War on Land. The Hague, 18 October 1907; Article 12, Convention (III) relative to the Treatment of Prisoners of War. Geneva, 12 August 1949; and Article 29, Convention (IV) relative to the Protection of Civilian Persons in Time of War. Geneva, 12 August 1949.

88 Borchard, *supra* note 30, at p. 520.

89 Article 13, United Nations Charter. To this end, the General Assembly in Resolution 174 (II) of November 21, 1947, established the International Law Commission.

90 Hersch Lauterpacht, *Survey of International Law in relation to the Work of Codification of the International Law Commission: preparatory work within the purview of article 18, paragraph 1, of the Statute of the International Law Commission,* UN Doc. A/CN.4/Rev.1 (1949), at para. 97.

> account the problems which have arisen in connexion with recent developments such as the question of the criminal responsibility of States as well as that of individuals acting on behalf of the State.[91]

The ILC approved of Lauterpacht's recommendation to change the codification approach to state responsibility and listed alien protection and state responsibility as two *separate* topics of codification.[92] "Already by 1949," writes James Crawford regarding the codification of state responsibility, "it was unfinished business."[93] And so it was to remain for several more decades.

Codification was incomplete and continuing at different paces. International lawyers on the ILC from the US and Europe were keen on codifying alien protection but patient about general state responsibility.[94] Those from Latin America, however, remained adamant about pursuing the opposite strategy.[95] By 1953, the latter group also had the ear of their own governments and a growing number of other countries within the UN General Assembly. In a 1953 session of the General Assembly, Cuba submitted a draft resolution that included a request that the Commission "prioritize" its codification of state responsibility "as soon as possible."[96] The following year in Geneva, Francisco Victor García Amador (Cuba) submitted the first memorandum on the topic for the ILC and, in so doing, set himself up to be appointed its first *Special Rapporteur* on state responsibility.[97]

91 Lauterpacht, *supra* note 90, at para. 98. The protection of aliens was dealt with under the fourth heading "The Individual in International Law" (*ibid*, at pp. 45–48) and state responsibility on its own as the eight heading "The Law of State Responsibility" (*ibid*, at pp. 56–57).

92 Yearbook of the International Law Commission, 1949, at pp. 46, 53.

93 James Crawford, *The International Law Commission's Articles on State Responsibility: Introduction, Text and Commentaries* (Cambridge: Cambridge University Press, 2002), at p. 1. Indeed, that same year, Judge Álvarez (Venezuela) wrote in a separate opinion in the *Corfu Channel* decision: "Like sovereignty, the responsibility of States is an ancient conception and holds a very important place in international law. It is a delicate matter, and is a constant subject of controversies, because it is not regulated by any well-established precepts. That was evident at the Codification Conference at The Hague in 1930" (*Corfu Channel Case* (UK v. Albania) (Merits), Judgment of April 9, 1949, 4 ICJ Reports 39 (1949) at pp. 43–44).

94 *See* comments of Georges Scelle in *Yearbook of the International Law Commission*, 1949, at pp. 49–50.

95 *See, for instance*, the observations of Judge Álvarez in *Annuaire de l'Institut de Droit international* (1947), pp. 53, 54, 60, 61.

96 UN. Doc. A/C.6/L.311.

97 Francisco Victor García Amador, "Memorandum on the question of State Responsibility," UN Doc. A/CN.4/80 (Spanish only). In the context of UNGA Resolution 799, and in what must frankly be described as an overly technical and petty

And García Amador, like Guerrero before him, was motivated to craft a doctrine of state responsibility that was cleansed of the US-imposed "international standard of justice."[98] Unlike Guerrero, however, García Amador packaged his project as a "new" doctrine – even granting procedural standing (*locus standi*) to individuals within international courts and tribunals. In his 1954 memorandum, García Amador argues for a "modern" approach to codification, since "traditional" international law did not sufficiently address the fundamental position of the individual,[99] who has "human rights" beyond those of investment protection. Just as alien protection claims give rise to international litigation, so should human rights violations, argues García Amador.[100] The fact that this view was progressive, ought not to have prevented the ILC from codifying the field based on the *needs* of international society.[101] While García Amador clearly opposed US imperialism, he was steeped in its legal culture. He was a potential bridge between developed and developing worlds.[102] He had been able to do so with regard to codifying the law of the sea, but state responsibility was a thornier task.

In 1955, García Amador published an article titled "State Responsibility in the Light of the New Trends of International Law" in, of all places, the *American Journal of International Law*.[103] The "new" trends to which he referred did not arise from international arbitral practice, but from institutional design.[104] In this, the early dawn of international human rights, García Amador saw the establishment of the United Nations and the decolonization of states as heralding a

manner, García Amador repeatedly stresses the importance of codifying state responsibility as soon as possible. (Roberto Ago joined only in 1957.)

98 García Amador, *infra* note 102, at p. 343–344.

99 García Amador, "*supra* note 97, at para. 9. The *Special Rapporteur*, like many other writers in the field, contrasts "traditional" to "modern" doctrines of state responsibility – *see, e.g.*, Visscher, *supra* note 21 at p. 421.

100 *See* García Amador, *supra* note 97, at para. 11: To the Cuban international lawyer, "[t]he international recognition and protection of human rights are facts whose consequences must necessarily affect the right or ability to bring international claims" (my translation).

101 García Amador, *supra* note 97, at para. 14.

102 *See* Burton A. Landy, Victor Miguel Marroquín-Merino, Francisco Orrego Vicuña, and Keith S. Rosenn, "In Memoriam: Francisco V. Garcia-Amador," 25 *University of Miami Inter-American Law Review* 1 (1993), at p. 7: "His writings are abundantly clear that his thinking was aimed, not at impeding a rightful evolution of the law, but rather at ensuring that international law should meet the legitimate concerns of both developed and developing nations."

103 Francisco Victor García Amador, "State Responsibility in the Light of the New Trends of International Law," 49 *American Journal of International Law* 339 (1955).

104 García Amador relied heavily on recent writings from Columbia Law School professor Philip Jessup, especially his *A Modern Law of Nations* (New York: Macmillan, 1948).

Figure 5.3 Francisco V. García Amador, seen with V. I. Sapozhnikov (Ukraine) on the left and Fereydoun Adamiyat (Iran) on the right (October 18, 1954)[105]

"transformation in contemporary international law" that dethroned states from their central, Westphalian position.[106] This *new* international law viewed individuals as its real subjects and human rights as its primary purpose.[107] Thus, it would be impossible to codify state responsibility based on existing law since "obviously neither doctrine nor case-law has yet adopted a conclusive position as to the basis of international responsibility."[108] To the US, those were provocative words and they fought to oppose this progressive agenda for state responsibility (Figure 5.3).

[105] Photo courtesy of the United Nations, General Assembly's Sixth Legal Committee. They are, from left to right: Mr. V. I. Sapozhnikov, of the Ukrainian SSR, Vice Chairman; Dr. Francisco V. Garcia Amador, of Cuba, Chairman; and Dr. Fereydoun Adamiyat, of Iran, Rapporteur 10/18/1954.

[106] García Amador, *supra* note 103, at p. 339.

[107] García Amador, *supra* note 103, at p. 342. On how this line of reasoning behind state responsibility laid the basis for international human rights as well as international investment law *see* Frédéric Mégret, "Mixed Claim Commissions and the Once Centrality of the Protection of Aliens," in Ignacio de la Rasilla and Jorge E. Viñuales (eds.), *Experiments in International Adjudication: Historical Accounts* 127 (Cambridge: Cambridge University Press, 2019), at pp. 12–14.

[108] Fifth Report of the Special Rapporteur of the International law Commission on International Responsibility, UN Doc. A/CN.4/125 (1960).

Is Responsibility Derived from Private or Public Law?

The two visions of state responsibility – as tortious remedies for alien injuries or constitutional framework for all international enforcement actions – continued to be debated within the ILC. While García Amador succeeded in being appointed as the first *Special Rapporteur* of the ILC for state responsibility, he never got very far with his annual reports. Officially, the ILC blamed its "heavy agenda" as the reason or delaying further study "on the subject for the time being."[109] Unofficially, this was the first of several excuses that the ILC would make for its unwillingness to discuss the new approach to state responsibility. Behind the scenes, the two rival groups were digging in their heels for a protracted battle. On the one hand, García Amador was the ILC's *Special Rapporteur* on the topic. On the other hand, the ILC's secretariat requested that Harvard law professors Louis Sohn (1914–2006) and Richard Baxter (1921–1980) revise Harvard's 1929 draft convention on state responsibility.

The 1961 Harvard draft actually closely resembles the *Deutsche Gesellschaft für Völkerrecht*'s draft of 1930.[110] Here we see a further example of German thought informing attitudes on international law; it is a restatement of alien protection as well as a framework that sets the conditions for attributing responsibility for breaching those laws. In the Harvard draft, *alien protection* is not associated with *human rights.*[111] Rather, *alien protection* meant *foreign investment protection.*[112] The draft is in many ways the crystallization of the US approach to alien protection and, as Cambridge law professor Philip Allott writes, it established "a new international law of torts" for investors.[113] However, by 1961, the US controlled only a minority of views within the ILC, which did not even

[109] Report of the International Law Commission Covering the Work of its Sixth Session, 3, July 28, 1954, Official Records of the General Assembly, Ninth Session, Supplement No. 9 (A/2693), Extract from the Yearbook of the International Law Commission, 1954, vol. II, at p. 162, para. 74. Based on Roberto Ago's first report (Report of the International Law Commission, 21st Session, *ILC Yearbook 1969*, vol. II, 203, 229–230, at para. 67), contemporary commentators are content to rely on this as the explanation for García Amador's failure – *see e.g.*, Müller, *supra* note 83, at p. 72.

[110] *See infra* note 116.

[111] *See supra* note 103 and accompanying text.

[112] *See supra* note 85; as Kathryn Greenman writes, it also continues to mean investment protection – *see* "The Law of State Responsibility and the Persistence of Investment Protection," in *Contingency in International Law: On the Possibility of Different Legal Histories* 389 (Oxford: Oxford University Press, 2021).

[113] Philip Allott, "State Responsibility and the Unmaking of International Law," 29(1) *Harvard International Law Journal* 1–26 (1988), at p. 5.

submit Harvard's draft treaty to governments for comment. Like García Amador's reports, the ILC paid little attention to Sohn and Baxter's draft convention.

García Amador tried but failed to get the ILC's attention by stressing the practical and theoretical transformation occurring within the field of state responsibility.[114] To him, codification had "to bring the 'principles governing State responsibility' into line with international law at its present stage of development," which included the protection of human rights.[115] Remarkably, the first ILC *Special Rapporteur* did not appreciate the political risk of this expanded codification scope. He stressed that "[t]he legal content of international responsibility did not give rise to any major difficulties in traditional doctrine and practice."[116] However, in 1956, the ILC was already too divided for such an ambitious plan.[117]

114 Summary record of the 370th meeting, UN Doc. A/CN.4/SR.370, Extract from the Yearbook of the International Law Commission, 1956, vol. I, at p. 228, para. 19. In the previous year, he had written that the "international standard of justice" requires aliens and nationals to be treated alike. He cited in his support the US international lawyer, Philip Jessup, who had recently argued that the international law of responsibility for injuries to aliens should be called for injuries to individuals (Jessup, *supra* note 104, at p. 97); García Amador, *supra* note 103, at p. 343–344.

115 García Amador, *supra* note 49, at para. 10. He cites the American international lawyer Phillip Jessup (1897–1986): "[T]he history of this branch of international law during the nineteenth and twentieth centuries exemplifies the way in which a body of customary law develops in response to the need for adjustment of clashing interests. He stresses that the driving force behind the legal phenomenon was the desire of Governments for political influence in certain countries, the scramble for markets and for sources of raw materials. 'The history of the development of international law on the responsibility of States for injuries to aliens is thus an aspect of the history of imperialism, or dollar diplomacy'" (Jessup, *supra* note 104, at pp. 95–96 and 105 (also discussed in Philip C. Jessup, "Responsibility of State for Injuries to Individuals," 46(6) *Columbia Law Review* 903 (1946)).

116 García Amador, *supra* note 49, at para. 35. However, see, somewhat in contrast, his remarks in para. 6. Citing *Chorzów* (1928), Anzilotti's *Corso di diritto internazionale* (*supra* note 104), Eagleton's *The Responsibility of States in International Law* (New York: New York University Press, 1928), the Harvard Research Draft (1929) the Third Committee of the Codification Conference (1930) and other Interwar literature, García Amador put forward a consensus view on state responsibility. The Second World War, however, shifted the focus to the position of individuals such that they could possess rights and could even be held criminally responsible for their actions (*see ibid* at paras. 35–50).

117 According to Todd Weiler: "Francisco Garcia-Amador was one of the first publicists to grasp the transformative potential of such a mechanism [of granting standing to individuals to sue states for international wrongs], especially if combined with a set of substantive norms requiring some kind of judicial review mechanism for State conduct" (Todd Weiler, *The Interpretation of International Investment Law: Equality,*

After García Amador was finally able to present his findings, he was flayed by his ILC colleagues. Future ICJ judge Sir Gerald Fitzmaurice (1901–1982) (Great Britain) argued that "[t]he primary consideration was not the general responsibility of all international obligations, but, in particular, the responsibility of states for damage caused to the person or property of aliens."[118] Sergei B. Krylov (1888–1958) (Soviet Union) disagreed, saying that only an expansive treatment of state responsibility would address contemporary needs.[119] Radhabinod Pal (1886–1967) (India) roundly disapproved of García Amador's treatment of "*International* Responsibility," noting that the General Assembly had made it clear in Resolution 799 that the ILC was to codify "*State* Responsibility" which was not the same thing as alien protection.[120]

I list these disagreements not because of the importance of each comment but to demonstrate the petulance that prevailed during the only sessions in which the ILC considered García Amador's reports. It is difficult to imagine any progress emerging from such an atmosphere of intellectual bickering. The ILC's own summary of the meetings is misleading: "Without taking any decisions on the particular points the Commission requested the special rapporteur to continue his work in the light of the views expressed by the members."[121]

The following year, García Amador tried to respond substantively to all of his colleague's comments.[122] He tried not to get weighed down in

Discrimination and Minimum Standards of Treatment in Historical Context (Leiden: Martinus Nijhoff, 2013), at p. 10). Weiler continues: "There is little doubt that Garcia-Amador's ILC colleagues fully grasped the transformative potential of this mechanism, which is precisely why they would have apparently felt so incredibly threatened by it. Garcia-Amador would be replaced, as Special Rapporteur, by a conventional thinker who would not cause such tumult" (*ibid* at p. 11).

118 Summary record of the 371st meeting, UN Doc. A/CN.4/SR.371, Extract from the Yearbook of the International Law Commission, 1956, vol. I, at p. 233, para. 4.

119 Summary record of the 371st meeting, *supra* note 118, at pp. 233–234, paras. 5–9.

120 Summary record of the 371st meeting, *supra* note 118, at p. 236, para. 24. Interestingly, Pal is mainly remembered for his dissenting opinion in the Tokyo War Crimes Trial – *see* Assaf Likhovski, "Jurisprudence and Nationalism in the British Empire in the Early Twentieth Century: India, Egypt, and Palestine Compared," *The English Historical Review* (Forthcoming 2024), available online via SSRN https://ssrn.com/abstract=4475214 last visited July 20, 2023.

121 Report of the International Law Commission on the Work of its Eighth Session, 23, Doc. A/CN.4/104, 4 July 1956, Official Records of the General Assembly, Eleventh Session, Supplement No. 9, (A/3159), Extract from the Yearbook of the International Law Commission, 1956, vol. II, at p. 301, para. 35.

122 UN Doc. A/CN.4/SR.413, Summary record of the 413th meeting, Extract from the Yearbook of the International Law Commission, 1957, vol. I, at p. 154, para. 36.

controversial details and concentrated on "general principles."[123] But it was too late. During the ensuing discussion (briefly held over the course of three meetings), members of the ILC undiplomatically asserted their reservations regarding his Second Report. Luis Padilla Nervo (1894–1985) (Mexico) famously opined:

> As far as Latin America was concerned, the history of the institution of State responsibility was the history of the obstacles placed in the way of the new Latin American countries – obstacles to the defence of their (at that time) recent independence, to the ownership and development of their resources, and to their social integration . . . The vast majority of new States had taken no part in the creation of the many institutions of international law which were consolidated and systematized in the nineteenth century . . . With State responsibility . . . international rules were established, not merely without reference to small States but against them, and were based almost entirely on the unequal relations between great Powers and small States.[124]

This impression was reflected throughout the United Nations. In its General Assembly's Sixth Committee (Legal Division), a Hungarian delegate (Endre Ustor), referring to Mr. Padilla Nervo's comments, expressed "in view of the development of a socialist economic system coexisting with the capitalist system and the attainment of independence by many former colonial territories, the concept of state responsibility, in so far as concerned the protection of aliens, had become entirely obsolete."[125]

Perhaps the most hollow comment came from the Italian international lawyer Roberto Ago (1907–1995), who said that "he was all the more grateful to Mr. García Amador for his report because the problems it

According to James Crawford and Tom Grant, García Amador and Ago fundamentally disagreed about the scope of codification. The former sought to limit it to civil responsibility and the latter to criminal as well. "Responsibility of States for Injuries to Foreigners," in J. P. Grant and J. C. Barker (eds), *The Harvard Research in International Law: Contemporary Analysis and Appraisal* 77–126 (Buffalo: W. S. Hein, 2007), at p. 90). I disagree, as I discuss *infra* notes 130 and 173.

123 Yearbook of the International Law Commission, 1957, vol. I, p. 154. An exception to this rule was his study regarding the equal protection of aliens and nationals (*ibid, supra* note 122).

124 Summary record of the 413th meeting, *supra* note 122, at p. 155, paras. 45–46 (emphasis added).

125 As cited in Yoshiro Mastui, 'The Transformation of the Law of State Responsibility," 20 *Thesaurus Acroasium* 5 (1993), at p. 60.

dealt with had interested him for years."[126] Then Ago proceeded to position himself as García Amador's replacement. Without any official reason for doing so, Ago summarized the views of his colleagues and posed three options to them: (1) the Commission could do nothing; (2) it could take the approach espoused by the current *Special Rapporteur*; or (3) as Lauterpacht had first suggested, it could codify the field on its own in general terms – that is, without touching upon the political controversies raised over the previous few days.[127]

The next day, when it was time for the *Special Rapporteur* to respond, García Amador made it clear how he was ambushed by Ago.[128] Yet, at the end of the session, Padilla Nervo asked his colleagues to refrain from even voting on the report.[129]

Codifying within a New Institutional Reality

Once the Latin American commissioners had forged an alliance with other semi-peripheral and Soviet delegates within the UN,[130] a new institutional reality emerged.[131] State responsibility was not the only

126 Summary record of the 413th meeting, *supra* note 122, at pp. 156–157, para. 61.

127 UN Doc. A/CN.4/SR.415, Summary record of the 415th meeting, Extract from the Yearbook of the International Law Commission, 1957, vol. I, at pp. 167–168, paras. 38–43.

128 UN Doc. A/CN.4/SR.416, Summary record of the 416th meeting, Extract from the Yearbook of the International Law Commission, 1957, vol. I, at pp. 169, para. 18: "He found himself . . . in an unenviable position because of the contradiction between certain criticisms. On the one hand, he had been commended for abandoning the somewhat revolutionary approach of his first report . . . in favour of a more realistic attitude. On the other, he had been taxed with introducing revolutionary elements belonging to the sphere neither of codification nor of development of international law, but to municipal law. Equally disconcerting was Mr. Ago's observation that he had neglected to consider the penal element in state responsibility. For the Commission would recall that in his previous report he had devoted a whole chapter to criticizing the limitation of the concept of state responsibility to civil liability, and had reluctantly excluded the penal element at the express request of the Commission."

129 *Ibid*, at p. 172, para. 39.

130 The Soviet approach to state responsibility in the 1960s was to expand its scope to include its codification for international crimes such as aggression and colonization. *See* F. J. Ferdinand Joseph Maria Feldbrugge, Gerard Pieter Van den Berg, William Bradford Simons, *Encyclopedia of Soviet Law* (The Hague: Brill, 1985) at p. 388. I thank Lauri Mälksoo for aiding me in researching the Soviet Union's promotion of state responsibility during the 1960s.

131 The alliance is evident in the plenary discussions. *See, e.g.*, Summary record of the 415th meeting, *supra* note 127, at p. 165, para. 25.

international project to be affected by this.[132] The Latin Americans now had a strong political platform from which to oppose US diplomatic pressure. In this environment, García Amador's attempted compromise failed to gain even Latin American support for his reports; on the contrary, they accused him of being complicit with US oppression of Latin Americans.[133] This was not the collegiality of Strisower's *L'Institut de Droit international.* It was the United Nations. And within post-War international bodies, as the 1957 summer plenary sessions make clear, agreement over codification was no longer about whose legal argument was most persuasive, but rather which political bloc made up the membership on the ILC.[134]

García Amador, brought up within the culture of "Pan-Americanism," was now an outsider.[135] He was a member of the previous generation of international lawyers: educated in the West, a practitioner of Anglo-

[132] Marina Spinedi, in "From One Codification to Another: Bilateralism and Multilateralism in the Genesis of the Codification of the Law of Treaties and the Law of State Responsibility," 13(5) *European Journal of International Law* 1099 (2002), writes of how the 1960s saw the communitarianization of both the law of state responsibility and the law of treaties.

[133] In fact, García Amador suggests the ILC collaborate with the Inter-American Juridical Committee. *See* UN Doc. A/CN.4/88, Report of the International Law Commission Covering the Work of its Sixth Session, *supra* note 109, at p. 77. Perhaps years later, when García Amador published a book on the codification of state responsibility, he did so in collaboration with US international lawyers. *See* Francisco Victor García Amador, Louis B. Sohn and R. Baxter, *Recent Codification of the Law of State Responsibility for Injuries to Aliens* (Leiden: Sijthoff, 1975). His graduate legal degrees were awarded by Ivy League, US law schools: Francisco Victor García Amador y Rodríguez, *The Academic Discussion Concerning the Existence of an American International Law* (1944) (unpublished M.A. thesis, Harvard Law School); Francisco Victor García Amador y Rodríguez, *The Exploitation and Conservation of the Resources of the Sea* (1960) (doctoral dissertation submitted to Columbia Law School) (dissertation is dated after two editions on the same topic were published by Sijthoff).

[134] García Amador made it clear in the 1961 plenary (in context of treaties) that he was given no guidance till after his first report (*supra* note 49). It was rejected and he did nothing to change course. For the Special Rapporteur that would have been in 1956.

[135] *See* Elihu Lauterpacht, *The Life of Hersch Lauterpacht* (Cambridge: Cambridge University Press, 2010) at p. 357: Lauterpacht seems not to have been much of a team player, and that he did not enjoy his time on the International Law Commission. During May 1952, Sir Hirsch wrote to his wife, Rachel that "I'm not sure whether I will wish to remain with them. I am much respected, and people are very friendly, but it is an egregious bit of humbug; the majority do not know any international law; and the method of work is bad. The result is that after three hours – this is the normal period of the daily meeting – I am quite exhausted and have a splitting headache. There is really no reason for me to expose myself to that." In June, he wrote to Rachel: "*They are an ignorant lot.* Sometimes I think that they appreciate what I am doing. Sometimes it

American legalism and a believer in economic liberalism.[136] He was not alone in this Latin American perspective, but was increasingly out of touch with the postcolonial era.[137] The ILC ignored the remainder of the *Special Rapporteur's* reports (officially, to "make time" to discuss its codification of treaties).[138]

The same was true for updating of the Harvard Draft Convention by Louis Sohn and Richard Baxter. China's delegate, Yuen-Li Liang, who ran

seems that they are angry at being treated like members of my seminar. However, members of my class are much better" (emphasis added).

136 In preparing his first report on state responsibility, García Amador visited Harvard to confer with the project directors (García Amador *supra* note 129, at p. 176, at para 14). Earlier drafts of the eventual 1961 Harvard Research Draft were noted in the 1959 and 1960 meetings of the ILC (Yearbook of the International Law Commission, 1959/1 147 54; *ibid*, 1960/1 266 70, 276 83, as noted, Sohn and Baxter, *infra* note 169, at p. 546, n 7. According to James Crawford and Tom Grant, "the Garcia-Amador draft was influenced by external work more, perhaps, than any other output by an ILC special rapporteur on any topic" (*supra* note 122, at p. 90).

137 Also in 1958, the Inter-American Juridical Committee (IAJC), an advisory body to the Organization of American States, issued its report on the American contribution to the law of state responsibility (Inter-American Juridical Committee, *Contribution of the American Continent to the Principles of International Law that Govern the Responsibility of States: Observations Made by the Inter-American Juridical Committee concerning Resolution VI approved at the Third Meeting of the Inter-American Council of Jurists, to be considered at the Fourth Meeting of the Council to be held in Santiago de Chile* (Washington, DC: Pan American Union, 1958)). As the IAJC's report makes clear, the American experience of international arbitration was critical to the development of state responsibility. It was both an important legal source and the seedpod of doctrinal disagreement over state responsibility. The report prefaces its conclusion as follows "[T]he following principles … have been accepted by a majority of our countries, and … in our opinion, form part of Latin American international law as well as, in certain aspects, of American international law" (Inter-American Juridical Committee, *ibid*, at p. 8). Appended to the report was the separate opinion of the Member from the United States, who stated that "In view of the foregoing, I believe that the alleged 'principles' set forth … are subject to objection" (*ibid* at p. 14). The majority of states in the IAJC saw codification as restricting the role of responsibility in international relations, whereas the US saw it as a means of solidifying inroads achieved in past arbitrations.

138 Francisco Victor García Amador, "Third Report on International Responsibility: Responsibility of the State for Injuries Caused in its Territory of the Person or Property of Aliens," UN Doc. A/CN.4/111 (1958); Francisco Victor García Amador, "Fourth report on International Responsibility: Responsibility of the State for Injuries Caused in its Territory to the Person or Property of Aliens. Measures Affecting Acquired Rights," UN Doc. A/CN.4/119 (1959). UN Doc. A/CN.4/117, Report of the International Law Commission covering the work of its Tenth Session, 28 April–4 July 1958, Official Records of the General Assembly, Thirteenth Session, Supplement No. 9 (A/3859), Extract from the Yearbook of the International Law Commission, 1958, vol. II, at p. 110, para. 172. On this "delay" tactic, *see supra* note 108 and accompanying text.

the UN's international law codification division, had actually requested that Harvard retool its earlier draft.[139] Liang was steeped in the codification history of state responsibility. He served as technical adviser to the Chinese delegation at the 1930 Hague codification conference. He was also personally connected to Harvard Law School, where he was a Carnegie Teachers Fellow that same year. If anyone could bridge the doctrine gap that was growing within the ILC, it seemed it could be Yuen-Li Liang. However, the second Harvard draft was anything but warmly received in Geneva. Grigory I. Tunkin (1906–1993) (Soviet Union) hid nothing of his disapproval of the draft as well as the *Special Rapporteur*'s approach, neither of which adequately considered the disparate international economic systems developing at the time.[140] Ahmed Matine-Daftary (1897–1971) (Iran) added that the ILC would not give any further treatment of codification efforts that were "based on purely European standards of justice."[141]

Sensing an opportunity, Roberto Ago reminded his colleagues that there still remained his "third option" of separating the contentious codification project of alien protection from the progressive development of general principles of state responsibility, which need not be based on past arbitral practice.[142] Surprisingly, even Liang then withdrew his support from the codification project that he himself had commissioned to endorse Ago's "third option."[143] Now on the defensive, Anglo-American members of the ILC had to turn back to history to justify alien protection as a precolonial enterprise. In the words of British chairman Sir Gerald Fitzmaurice:

> some members had seemed to take the view that practically all the law relating to the treatment of aliens was a product of colonialism. That, of

[139] They felt that they could not update Baxter's draft because of how much had changed in the previous three decades – UN Doc. A/CN.4/SR.512, Summary record of the 512th meeting, Extract from the Yearbook of the International Law Commission, 1959, vol. I, at p. 147, paras. 2–7.

[140] Summary record of the 512th meeting, *supra* note 139. I, at p. 149, para. 24.

[141] Summary record of the 512th meeting, *supra* note 139, at p. 149, para. 25. Tunkin and Matine-Daftary's approaches were then endorsed by Bartoš (*ibid*, at para. 27).

[142] Summary record of the 512th meeting, *supra* note 139, at pp. 150–151, paras. 33–38.

[143] Summary record of the 512th meeting, *supra* note 139, at p. 151, para. 46. Liang clearly regretted having introduced the second Harvard Draft Convention to the ILC and quickly back-pedaled, stating that he "wished to make it clear that the Harvard draft had been prepared entirely on the responsibility of its authors under the general auspices of the Harvard Law School and that there had been no responsibility on the part of the United Nations Secretariat so far as the financing and the substance of the draft were concerned" (*ibid*, at para. 42).

> course, was quite incorrect historically as everyone knew who had read e.g. the chapter on the historical and legal foundations of the law relating to the denial of justice in Alwyn V. Freeman's standard work.[144] The law relating to the treatment of aliens had come into being, long before the era of colonialism, out of conditions in Europe soon after the Middle Ages, when foreigners had had very little status and in many cases no rights before the law or access to the court.[145]

This backpedaling notwithstanding, it was too late. Alien protection was radioactive from a legislative standpoint and basing a representative codification effort on nineteenth-century international arbitration was a non-starter.[146]

The fate of García Amador's "traditional" approach was sealed by 1960. That year, the ILC spent a few sessions discussing – not the *Special Rapporteur*'s report, but another revision to the Harvard Draft Convention and the Inter-American Juridical Committee's report on the American contribution to state responsibility.[147] In the comments following these two presentations, the division in the Commission was sharply drawn between those wishing to limit the ILC's study of state responsibility to alien protection and those who wished to entirely remove the topic of alien protection from the ILC's work on state responsibility.[148] The first group consisted largely of the Anglo-American members of the Commission and the *Special Rapporteur*. The second group consisted of almost everyone else and was led by Roberto Ago (Italy) and, to a lesser extent, Luis Padilla Nervo (Mexico)

[144] Alwyn V. Freeman, *The International Responsibility of States for Denial of Justice* (London: Longmans, Green & Co., 1938).

[145] UN Doc. A/CN.4/SR.513, Summary record of the 513th meeting, Extract from the Yearbook of the International Law Commission, 1959, vol. I, at p. 152, paras. 8–9.

[146] As Professors Crawford and Grant explain, by overly associating his work with the Anglo-American approach, "García Amador sidelined his work and himself" (Crawford and Grant, *supra* note 122, at p. 102).

[147] Gómez Robledo, observer for the IAJC, noted his institution's difficulty in assisting the ILC (UN Doc. A/CN.4/SR.566, Summary record of the 566th meeting, Extract from the Yearbook of the International Law Commission, 1960, vol. I, at pp. 264–265, paras. 2–24.

[148] In its 1960 report (*ibid*), some representatives of the Commission expressed regret that the Commission had not found time to undertake a thorough study of state responsibility. They maintained that confining state responsibility to alien protection would violate the spirit of General Assembly resolution 799 (VIII); the subject should therefore be extended to include the principles governing state responsibility for violation of the national sovereignty, independence and national integrity of other states, and of the right of nations to self-determination and the use of their natural resources.

and Grigory Tunkin (Soviet Union). This second group, it must be stressed, did not share a view on the substance of state responsibility, but agreed that it should be approached in a radically new way that was divorced from the US protection of its nationals in Latin America.

At the ILC's thirteenth session (1961), García Amador submitted his final report.[149] In it, he continues his longstanding critique of "traditional" state responsibility.[150] Despite its erudition, the report was clearly ignored by García Amador's colleagues in Geneva. Worse, the UN General Assembly's Sixth Committee (Legal) paid considerable negative attention to García Amador's reports during that winter in New York.[151] In the process of negotiating Resolution 1505 (XV) of 12 December 1960,[152] the General Assembly was the scene of acrimonious debates on the topic of international law and unsuccessful codification.[153] The

[149] Francisco Victor García Amador, Fifth Report on International Responsibility, UN Doc. A/CN.4/134, reprinted in 2 *Yearbook of the International Law Commission* 1 (1961), Vol. II.

[150] *See, e.g.*, García Amador, *supra* note 149, para. 176. In 1955, García Amador published his view that "It is not difficult to understand why this codification cannot be undertaken as a pure and simple restatement of existing rules. These rules were created and have developed according to some fundamental views and concepts which have undergone a profound transformation in contemporary international law" (García Amador, *supra* note 97, at p. 339). Note the source: the *American* Journal of International Law. García Amador did not believe in codifying American international awards, but he was guilty by association.

[151] *See* Official Records of the General Assembly, Fifteenth Session, Sixth Committee, 649th to 672nd meetings as well as Annexes, agenda item 65, (1960/1961) Doc. A/4605, sections II and III and paras. 12, 45–49; ST/LIB/SER.B/A.11 (61.I.18).

[152] The text of the resolution was not subversive of past codification efforts. But the surrounding debates were rancorous. According to the resolution, the General Assembly:

1. "*Decides* to place the question entitled Future work in the field of the codification and progressive development of international law on the provisional agenda of its sixteenth session in order to study and survey the whole field of international law and make necessary suggestions with regard to the preparation of a new list of topics for codification and for the progressive development of international law;
2. *Invites* Member States to submit in writing to the Secretary General, before 1 July 1961, any views or suggestions they may have on this question for consideration by the General Assembly."

[153] The Secretary General's report on the resolution already made it clear that, by 1961, two groups were already entrenched in the ILC codification process. *See* Secretariat of the United Nations, "Planning of Future Work of the Commission. Resolution adopted by the General Assembly regarding future work in the field of the codification and progressive development of international law – Note by the Secretariat," UN Doc. A/CN.4/138, available online at http://untreaty.un.org/ilc/documentation/english/a_cn4_138.pdf.

Legal Office of the UN actually complained about the ILC to the Sixth Committee for violating the principle of geographical distribution in the staff recruitment, allegedly collaborating with US law schools, and for the procedure and substance of the ILC reports.[154] García Amador was singled out for his visits to Harvard Law School, which was described as a "reactionary" institution.[155]

In his final appearance on the ILC, García Amador expressed his personal sadness and even anger at his colleagues for their reception of his reports:

> [I]t was . . . regrettable that the resolution had been so closely associated with one of the most aggressive and demagogic propaganda campaigns in the history of the United Nations. It was quite obvious to anyone who had heard the discussions in the Sixth Committee or who had read the summary records and the Committee's report to the plenary that a group of countries which had never been concerned with the development and codification of international law, but had customarily opposed them, had suddenly tried to pose as the champion of the progress of international law and as the defender of its principles.[156]

The Special Rapporteur continued:

> It was the same group of countries which repeatedly and consistently had subordinated and were subordinating the validity of international law to the principle of national sovereignty and had opposed and continued to oppose compulsory arbitration . . . While he would not dwell on the details, he must raise the question of the unfair – when they were not wholly unfounded – attacks on the Secretariat, the Special Rapporteur and even the Commission itself in connexion with the topic of State responsibility.[157]

While the *Special Rapporteur* was conveying his grief, Chairman Grigory Tunkin (Soviet Union) interrupted him. According to the official record:

[154] Report of the International Law Commission on the work of its Thirteenth Session, UN Doc. A/CN.4/141, 1 May to July 1961, Official Records of the General Assembly, Sixteenth Session, Supplement No. 10 (A/4843), Extract from the Yearbook of the International Law Commission, 1961, vol. II, at p. 208, para. 55.

[155] See 657th meeting of Sixth Committee, para. 27, referred to and cited by García Amador in *ibid.*

[156] Report of the International Law Commission on the work of its Thirteenth Session, *supra* note 154, at, pp. 207–208, para. 51, respectively.

[157] *Ibid,* at p. 208, at para. 52 (emphasis added).

> The CHAIRMAN, observing that the Commission was not discussing the work of the Sixth Committee, but the future codification of international law, requested Mr. García Amador to keep within the limits of the subject under consideration.[158]

García Amador changed his tone. He explained that he had simply done what he thought his colleagues had asked him to do: in response to General Assembly Resolution 799 (VIII), he had submitted his first report in 1956, which the Commission had not had time to consider seriously since discussion had focused on the Law of the Sea. Since that time, noted García Amador, there had only been two items on its agenda for which the Assembly had specifically requested new codification: diplomatic immunities and state responsibility. "How was it then that the Commission, which had produced such fruitful work in its first six years, had continually deferred the study and codification of the topic of State responsibility?"[159]

Chairman Tunkin then ended the conversation by noting that:

> the Commission was not expected to make any recommendation or take any decision on the subject. The debate had been initiated only because some members of the Commission had wished to put on record their views on future work in the field of the codification and progressive development of international law."[160]

Those "members" were García Amador and Ago.[161] In invoking Resolution 799, Chairman Tunkin sought to establish a new atmosphere in the ILC. To Tunkin and the new guard, a *de novo* review of the UN's codification program was fully justified.[162] After suggesting that the *Special Rapporteur* "should be modest,"[163] García Amador fired back that he "regretted to note that the criticisms to which he had referred came from those quarters least sympathetic to the concept of international human rights as accepted by the United Nations as a whole."[164] García Amador was dejected. His goal had been to fight the international

[158] *Ibid*, at p. 208, at para. 58.
[159] *Ibid*, at p. 208, at para. 59.
[160] *Ibid*, at p. 209, para. 62.
[161] *See e.g.*, the heated exchanges in *ibid*, at pp. 208–218, paras. 58–59, 76–77.
[162] *Ibid*, at p. 221, para. 35.
[163] *Ibid*, at p. 222, para. 37.
[164] *Ibid*, at p. 223, para. 45.

standard of justice; instead, he was fending off criticism for promoting it.[165] This was indeed a sad outcome for such a worthy publicist.

Both Guerrero and García Amador had struggled for years to forge a compromise between the doctrinal positions of the North and South Americans.[166] Even though the two experts were actually from Latin America and between them produced seven scholarly reports and two preliminary memoranda, no common ground could be found between them and their colleagues on the ILC. Whilst in the interwar era, when the balance of institutional power still favored the US, Guerrero was soundly rejected by the diplomatic and legal establishment for his overly restrictive codification of the field. He was dismissed from the preparatory efforts for the Hague Codification Conference and from his diplomatic post (at the behest of the US).[167] During the early postwar period, as the balance of institutional power shifted, García Amador was at times ignored and at others openly rebuked. Although the labors of both international lawyers were comprehensively rejected by their colleagues, their work product *continued to frame all subsequent codification efforts.*

What explains their failure? One common interpretation is the workload of the ILC,[168] which was simply overloaded at the time. It was working simultaneously on the laws of the sea, treaties and state responsibility. The contrasting history of these projects, however, is striking. The ILC successfully codified law of the sea first in 1956. The law of treaties took a bit longer but was formally codified by 1966. The ILC did not complete its codification of its Draft Articles on state responsibility

[165] *Ibid*, at p. 258, para. 53.

[166] García Amador focused on individual and human rights, a tradition that goes back to Alejandro Álvarez. Both were tragic figures: well-intentioned internationalists who were spurned by their fellow Latin Americans. This phenomenon was a general one in world bodies, wherein which internationalists (including German, Chinese lawyers) were rejected by their countrymen.

[167] In 1927, Gustavo Guerrero returned to El Salvador as Minister of Foreign Affairs, and as we will see, headed the Salvadoran delegation to the Habana Conference. At Habana, Guerrero led the anti-imperialist legal backlash against the US, which cost him his position as Minister. *See* "Gustavo Guerrero, 1876-1958, in Memoriam," *Revue Internationale Française du Droit Des Gens*, 28, 1959; A Martínez Moreno, "José Gustavo Guerrero, caballero andante de derecho," in A. Cançado Trindade and A. Martínez Moreno (eds.), *Doctrina Latinoamericana del derecho internacional* 9–32 (San José: Corte Interamericana de Derechos Humanos, 2003), as cited in Becker Lorca, *supra* note 14.

[168] This explanation is at least implied throughout both Crawford, *supra* note 93, and Crawford, Pellet and Olleson, *supra* note 1, at pp. 53–59.

until 2001 (Draft Articles).[169] Interestingly, the ILC completed its codification of its Draft Articles on diplomatic protection soon thereafter, in 2006. In a twist of historic irony, the ILC's codification of diplomatic protection was based on Ago's approach to general state responsibility (as opposed to the ongoing – and current – practice of international arbitration![170]

Commentators often highlight the relationship between the doctrine of state responsibility and its problematic history within international arbitrations.[171] When he issued his first report as *Special Rapporteur*, Roberto Ago quickly conceded how the ILC's early failures were tied to the "*the quicksand of aliens' rights*."[172] As the ICJ Judge Georg Nolte (Germany) writes:

[169] The Responsibility of States for Internationally Wrongful Acts: Text adopted by the Commission at its fifty-third session, in 2001, and submitted to the General Assembly as a part of the Commission's report covering the work of that session. The report, which also contains commentaries on the draft articles, appears in Yearbook of the International Law Commission, 2001, vol. II (Part Two). Text reproduced as it appears in the annex to General Assembly resolution 56/83 of December 12, 2001, and corrected by document A/56/49(Vol. I)/Corr.4. I hasten to comment that this time suggests that the problem of codifying state responsibility was not simply one of scheduling.

[170] Draft Articles on Diplomatic Protection: Text adopted by the International Law Commission at its fifty-eighth session, in 2006, and submitted to the General Assembly as a part of the Commission's report covering the work of that session. The report, which also contains commentaries on the draft articles, appears in Official Records of the General Assembly, Sixty-first Session, Supplement No. 10 (A/61/10), available online at https://legal.un.org/ilc/texts/instruments/english/draft_articles/9_8_2006.pdf, last visited on May 24, 2023. Note that what I call irony is what insiders like Professor Sean D. Murphy, who is a former member of the ILC (United States), refer to as the "heritage of state responsibility" and find that there "is no surprise that the ILC drew heavily on the ASR [Articles on State Responsibility] when completing the diplomatic protection topic" (Sean D. Murphy, "The Heritage of the Articles on State Responsibility for the International Law Commission," in Patrícia Galvão Teles and Pierre Bodeau- Livinec (eds.), *Article-by-Article Commentary of the Articles on State Responsibility* (Oxford: Oxford University Press, forthcoming, 2024), at p. 5, available online at https://ssrn.com/abstract=4412555, last visited May 25, 2023.

[171] Shabtai Rosenne *vii:* "The work on State responsibility for wrongful acts is, without doubt, the most ambitious codification project in the history of the UN International Law Commission (ILC). While all the former and other current topics studied by the Commission deal with certain, defined 'primary' rules of international law, State responsibility, in a sense, embraces the entire 'other side of the medal,' the totality of legal rules and consequences linked to the breach of any international obligation of the State. No other codification project goes so deeply into the 'roots,' the theoretical and ideological foundations of international law, or has created comparable problems." Rosenne would know as he was there. But his is only a partial explanation.

[172] Yearbook of the International Law Commission, 1969, vol. I, p. 106 (emphasis added).

> The mandate for ... Ago, was the result of a compromise between the traditional Western approach of viewing the law of state responsibility as primarily one of responsibility for injuries to aliens, and the demand by representatives from the socialist and some Third World states to codify the rules of responsibility for the violations of the most important rules of international law ... The compromise ..., consisted in a mandate to codify the general rules, that is, the secondary rules of state responsibility."[173]

This is certainly correct. But Ago's codification success is not explained by this compromise. Earlier efforts were compromises as well. The nature of institutional decision-making is always one of compromise.

Former ILC commissioner Alain Pellet (France) blames the political tactlessness of García Amador and credits the tactfulness of his successor, Roberto Ago.[174] Certainly, García Amador failed to grasp the difference between what his colleagues were saying *officially* and what they were seeking *unofficially*. (As is well known, this one strategic error – ignoring the unspoken – can and has derailed several codification projects and countless professional careers.)

Pellet is correct to focus on the individual contributions of the *Special Rapporteurs*, which must have made an impact.[175] The Law of the Sea was successfully codified under a single *Special Rapporteur*, Jean Pierre Adrien François (1889–1978) (Netherlands), who had written his doctoral dissertation in 1919 on the Law of the Sea. Although the treaties project was not completed by a single person, all of the *Special Rapporteurs* appointed – James L. Brierly, Sir Hersch Lauterpacht, Sir Gerald Fitzmaurice, and Sir Humphrey Waldock (1904–1981) – were products of the same community of British international law.[176] In contrast, state responsibility was codified by F. V. García Amador (Cuba), Roberto Ago (Italy), Willem Riphagen (Netherlands), Gaetano Arangio-Ruiz (Italy) and James Crawford (Australia). In relative terms, the state responsibility project lacked cohesiveness and continuity.

173 Georg Nolte, "From Dionisio Anzilotti to Roberto Ago: The Classical International Law of State Responsibility and the Traditional Primacy of a Bilateral Conception of Inter-State Relations," 13(5) *European Journal of International Law* 1083 (2002), at p. 1097, internal citations omitted.

174 Pellet, *supra* note 1, at p. 78.

175 Pellet, *supra* note 1, at p. 6.

176 *See also* Shabtai Rosenne, "Some Diplomatic Problems of Codification of the Law of Treaties," 41 *Washington Law Review* 261–281 (1966), at pp. 267–268 (until 1960, the General Assembly did not take much interest in the ILC's work on treaties and, in general, in having the ILC prepare treaties to be approved in international conferences rather than as expository codes).

To these explanations, I will note once again, that the change in the composition of the ILC had tilted the balance of institutional power from Anglo- to Latin America. Their increasing representation in international organizations allowed Latin American international lawyers to finally avenge the disgrace of their earlier losses in the fora of international arbitrations. Further, the context of decolonization precluded any substantive consensus on the law of state responsibility, a doctrine that was born in the imperialism of the New World. Ago's winning strategy of decontextualizing codification efforts had the advantage of appearing politically neutral – and was, therefore, a brilliantly acceptable option for the ILC.[177]

Ago and the End of US Dominion

The appointment of Roberto Ago as Chairman of the subcommittee on state responsibility represents the end of an era; no longer did the US dictate the direction of world bodies. In his approach to state responsibility, Ago, like Anzilotti and Strupp, emphasizes the internationality of the rules of attribution. More than anything else, state responsibility is a system of imputation, derived from the state's special position as international subject: "*un fait illicite peut être imputé même à un sujet-personne juridique.*"[178] This is not to say that state responsibility deals exclusively with the conditions of imposing liability. The doctrine is more than about attribution rules; it also has substantive, intrinsic meaning.[179]

[177] On this intentional design of this neutrality, *see* Jean d'Aspremont, *International Law as a Belief System* (Cambridge: Cambridge University Press, 2017), pp. 72–79 (discussing Ago's "Second report on state responsibility," in the Yearbook of the International Law Commission, 1970, Vol. II, UN Doc A/CN.4/233, at p. 185). *See also* Jean d'Aspremont, "Canonical Cross-Referencing in the Making of the Law of International Responsibility," in Serena Forlati, Makane Mbengue and Brian McGarry (eds.), *The Gabčíkovo-Nagymaros Judgment and Its Contribution to the Development of International Law* (Leiden: Brill/Nijhoff, 2020), at pp. 3–5; Jean d'Aspremont, "The General Claims Commission (Mexico and the United States) and the Invention of International Responsibility," in I. de la Rasilla del Moral and J. Vinuales (eds.), Experiments in International Adjudication - Historical Accounts (Cambridge: Cambridge University Press, 2018), at p. 9, available online at https://ssrn.com/abstract=3150798, last visited on February 22, 2019.

[178] Roberto Ago, "Le délit international," 68 *Recueil des cours* 440 (Paris: Sirey, 1939), at p. 462.

[179] Ago, *supra* note 178, at pp. 532–533, where the *Special Rapporteur* criticized the prevailing view and argued that exceptions and exonerations apply to illegality rather than to responsibility or, put in crude common law terms, that they are defenses, in the strict sense, rather than pleas in mitigation.

Ago was interested in the nature of a state's liability: was it a delict, a crime, a tort, *etc.*?[180] His view is clearly evidenced by the title of his 1939 Hague lecture series: *Le délit International.*

Ago's doctrine was motivated by his fear of war. To Ago, as Professors Crawford and Grant write, state responsibility:

> [M]ay be seen as a response to the ruinous world of the Great War, and a recall of the practice of responsibility as applied in the last decades of the 19th century, from the Alabama arbitration to the Venezuela claims and the two Hague Peace Conferences.[181]

The League of Nations failed for lack of legal and institutional robustness. So, the UN could succeed only if international law could stand up to states. The society of states needed an international rule of law, including rules of enforcement, if it were to avoid world wars. Thus, Ago directed the ILC to "give priority to the definition of the *general* rules governing the international responsibility of States."[182] State responsibility is about both fixing individual breaches of international law as well as providing for "the systemic consequences of international wrongs.[183]

I do not here dwell on the substance of Ago's doctrine of state responsibility. But it is important to note that by broadening the scope of codification, Ago was the first to articulate a doctrine of state responsibility that was both inspirational and progressive as well as sufficiently

180 Gilles Cottereau, "Resort to International Courts in Matters of Responsibility," in Crawford, Pellet and Olleson, *supra* note 1, at p. 80, 1115, at p. 1125. For a contrary view – that Ago was mostly concerned with the consequences rather than the content of responsibility, *see* Ago, *supra* note 178, at p. 420; however, as Pellet points out, even Ago was not consistent about this claim – *see* Pellet, *supra* note 1, at p. 80, at pp. 77–78.

181 Crawford and Grant, *supra* note 122, at p. 85.

182 *Supra* note 109, at p. 139 (para 90), emphasis added. This idea can be traced back to Gustavo Guerrero's Questionnaire of 1926, which states that "international responsibility arises not from the injury sustained by foreigners, but from an action or inaction imputable to a state" – *see* Gustavo Guerrero, "Questionnaire No. 4: Responsibility of States for Damage Done in Their Territories to the Person or Property of Foreigners," 20 *American Journal of International Law Supplement* 176 (1926), at p. 201. It is also visible in Ago's 1939 Hague course, in which he emphasizes that international wrongfulness implies more than reparations; it is an international delict. International wrongs cause not only injuries to individuals but necessarily a break in the international order as well. The concept of individual injury is integrally linked to the concept of legal order: "*Puisqu'aucune qualification juridique n'a de valeur que par rapport à un système, à un ordre juridique particulier, et dans le cadre de celui-ci, il en résulte que la qualité de fait illicite est essentiellement relative à un ordre juridique donné*" (Ago, *infra* note 206, at p. 423).

183 Ago, *infra* note 206, at p. 429.

Table 5.2 *Composition of Codification Committees in 1925 and 1962*

Committee of Experts (1925)	International Law Commission (1962)
Hjalmar Hammarskjöld (Sweden)	Roberto Ago (Italy)
Giulio Diena (Italy)	Gilberto Amado (Brazil)
Cristobal Botella (Spain)	Milan Bartos (Yugoslavia)
James Brierly (United Kingdom)	Herbert W. Briggs (USA)
Henri Fromageot (France)	Marcel Cadieux (Canada)
Jose Gustavo Guerrero (Salvador)	Erik Castrén (Finland)
Bernard C. J. Loder (Netherlands)	A. El-Erian (United Arab Republic)
Vilhena Barboza de Magalhaes (Portugal)	Taslim O. Elias (Nigeria)
Adelbert Mastny (Czechoslovakia)	André Gros (France)
Michikazu Matsuda (Japan)	Eduardo Jiménez de Aréchaga (Uruguay)
Simon Rundstein (Poland)	Victor Kanga (Cameroon)
Walter Schücking (Germany)	Manfred Lachs (Poland)
Jose Leon Suarez (Argentina)	Liu Chieh (China)
Charles de Visscher (Belgium)	Antonio de Luna García (Spain)
Chung Hui Wang (China)	Luis Padilla Nervo (Mexico)
George W. Wickersham (USA)	Radhabinod Pal (India)
	Angel M. Paredes (Ecuador)
	Obed Pessou (Dahomey)
	Shabtai Rosenne (Israel)
	Abdul Hakim Tabibi (Afghanistan)
	Senjin Tsuruoka (Japan)

diplomatic to attract a majority of votes within the codifying committees. Ago had the overwhelming support of ILC members, who regularly approved his reports, whereas García Amador could not even get his colleagues to support his votes. The simplest explanation of this uncomfortable fact is the aforementioned change in composition of the ILC.[184]

The numbers are instructive. In 1925, thirteen of the sixteen members of the Committee of Experts represented Western countries (including Czechoslovakia, Japan and Poland). In 1962, only ten of twenty-five members of the ILC represented Western countries (*see* Table 5.2). That is a reduction from seventy-seven percent to forty percent of the

[184] As Shabtai Rosenne has noted, "*Grosso modo* the change of direction adopted by the International Law Commission . . . coincides with the great expansion in the membership of the United Nations following the rapid process of decolonization of the 1960s" (Rosenne, *supra* note 15, at p. 2).

Table 5.3 *Growth in membership of UN*

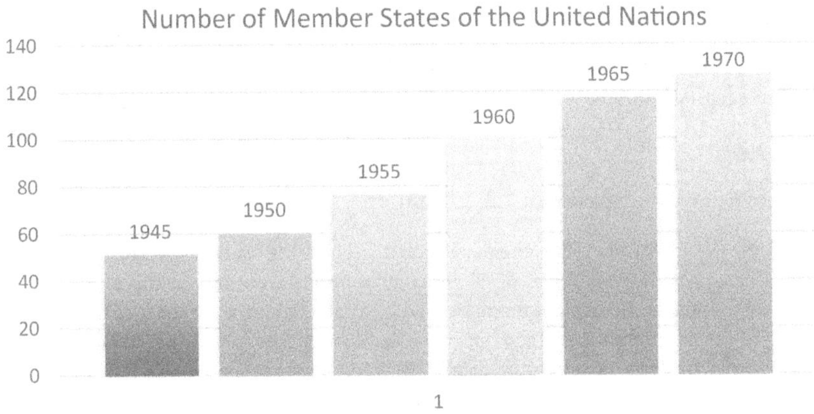

committees' composition. New states and fresh alignments were also added to the matrix. In 1962, twenty-four percent of ILC members came from states that *did not even exist* in 1925. Additionally, twenty-four percent of them came from cultures that were entirely unrepresented on the Committee of Experts. Finally, the Committee of Experts predated the Cold War, when American codification enemies teamed up with the Soviet Union, as discussed above, to defeat efforts to codify state responsibility within the framework of the American regional practice of alien protection.[185]

What Anglo-American international lawyers thought international law needed most, the minimum protection of aliens, is precisely what Latin Americans demanded be excluded from the discussion. Latin Americans resisted the US approach as patronizing and argued instead for a standard of equality applicable to nationals and foreigners alike. Thus, if the US won the debate over international standards within the international arbitration forum, it had now lost the debate when it came to international codification within the ILC.

Latin Americans Find Their Place within World Bodies

It is easy to understand the divergent opinions of Anglo-American and Continental European international lawyers to state responsibility. But

[185] At The Hague Peace Conference of 1899 there were twenty-six states in total – of which eighteen states were European.

what explains the fact that it was the Latin American members of the International Law Commission who rejected the Latin American *Special Rapporteurs'* reports? The earlier generation of Latin American international lawyers took a regionalist approach; the later generation adopted a universalist stance.[186] As Arnulf Becker Lorca writes, "[R]oughly from the 1880s to the 1950s, a distinguished group of authors and texts fought over the affirmation or negation of a distinct Latin American international law."[187] However, he continues,

> By the end of the 1950s, the particularistic sensibility was harnessed to the Latin American national-developmentalist project, resulting in the abandonment of the explicit discussion of, and reliance on, the existence of a regional international law for the development of other professional projects, such as providing legal justification for the nationalization of national resources, expropriation in general, and regional schemes of integration.[188]

Latin American representatives employed a two-pronged strategy within international institutions. First, they sought to increase their presence on international commissions of codification. Second, they abandoned their original position of absolute domestic sovereignty (*soberanía absoluta*)[189] in support of a new one of strengthening the overall international legal system (*solidaridad internacional*).[190] In terms

[186] On "American international law" as the origin of modern international law *see* Alejandro Álvarez, "Latin America and International Law," 3(2) *American Journal of International Law* 269–353 (1909), at pp. 311–312 (American international law was the origin even of multilateralist international law). On the fictitiousness of the American origins of international law, *see* Carl Landauer, "The Ambivalences of Power: Launching the American Journal of International Law in an Era of Empire and Globalization," 20 *Leiden Journal of International Law* 325 (2007), at p. 340 ("The American ideal of self-reliance … comes with ambivalences, ironies, and countercurrents, and … so did the mythologies surrounding the image of international law as ultimately American international law"). On international legal myths as literature, *see* Chnxi Tang, Imagining World Order: Literature and International Law in Early Modern Europe, 1500-1800 (Ithaca, NY: Cornell University Press, 2018).

[187] Becker Lorca, *supra* note 11, at p. 287; *see also ibid*, at p. 299.

[188] Becker Lorca, *supra* note 11, at p. 305.

[189] *See* Greg Grandin, "The Liberal Traditions in the Americas: Rights, Sovereignty, and the Origins of Liberal Multilateralism," 117(1) *American Historical Review* 68–91 (2012), at p. 71.

[190] As Arnulf Becker Lorca writes, "Vernacular cosmopolitans did not try to limit state responsibility by deducing rules from sovereignty. They rather defended their claims within and not against the language of internationalism" (Becker Lorca, *supra* note 14). On the "irony" of this move, *see* Koskenniemi, *supra* note 36, at p. 175; Borchard, *supra* note 30, at p. 521.

of the history of state responsibility, the first wave of Latin American regionalists overwhelmingly espoused a doctrine of "non-responsibility" and the second wave of universalists advocated one of "general responsibility."[191] The former denied the international liability of their governments for breaches of *international minimum standards.* The latter sought to interpret state responsibility expansively as applicable to breaches of *all international standards.*

The swing from regionalism to universalism among Latin Americans coincided with another shift – from anti-formalism to formalism – among Continental international lawyers.[192] Early international lawyers were less concerned with the technical binding dimension of law than they were with its civilizing mission.[193] Theirs was an anti-formalist view less interested in sources than in results.[194] As discussed in the previous chapter, cosmopolitan German writers excogitated doctrines of international law that were coherent and systematic – a transformational grammar that was well suited to Latin American codification needs. Accordingly, with the change in national make-up of the ILC, Latin Americans supported Roberto Ago's "third option" of codifying state responsibility along the lines of German theory.

With García Amador out of the way, the ILC rethought its agenda in light of General Assembly resolution 1686 (XVI) of December 18, 1961. The consensus was that García Amador's reports were worthless and that the project had to be uprooted and started anew. In fact, the ILC spent more time discussing the topic in 1962 than in all previous years (and by a wide margin). Alfred Verdross (1890–1980) (Austria) suggested that, like the *Institut*, the ILC appoint a subcommittee (in addition to a *Special Rapporteur*) to study state responsibility for codification purposes.[195]

191 For a recent discussion by a Latin American scholar, *see* Santiago Montt, "Latin American Position on State Responsibility. Looking into the Past for Lessons on the Future," LEGS seminar on February 9, 2009; for an older view as expressed by a US scholar, *see* Julius Goebel, Jr., "The International Responsibility of States for Injuries Sustained by Aliens on Account of Mob Violence, Insurrections and Civil Wars," 8(4) *American Journal of International Law* 802 (1914), at p. 831.

192 *See* Becker Lorca, *supra* note 14.

193 Koskenniemi, *supra* note 36, at p. 51.

194 Koskenniemi, *supra* note 36, at p. 52: As Martti Koskenniemi has said, "Emphasis was less on the construction of rational systems – this was an old-fashioned idea – than on the development and cultivation of appropriate personal attitudes – on becoming 'civilized,' in a word" (*ibid*, at p. 53).

195 UN Doc. A/CN.4/SR.631, Summary record of the 631st meeting, Extract from the Yearbook of the International Law Commission, 1962, vol. I, at p. 15, para. 2.

Ago agreed but wanted to appoint the subcommittee before the new *Special Rapporteur.*[196] He intuited that the ideas outlined in the report were not enough. He needed committee support first.[197] Tunkin and then Chairman Pal (India) agreed to the modified version of Verdross' proposal.[198] The bloc was aligned, leaving the minority to reluctantly capitulate to the seemingly neutral act of appointing a subcommittee. They remained opposed to "an abstract approach to the subject of state responsibility divorced from its roots in actual international life."[199] However, whether through ignorance or weakness, this is exactly what the majority on the Commission, including its chairman, was indirectly proposing. It was all but stated that the new subcommittee was to rethink the approach (and, per Ago's suggestion, divorce the substance of international obligations from the consequences in the event of their breach) before a new *Special Rapporteur* was appointed. Verdross' move muffled the minority.

Despite protests by Anglo-American members of the ILC, the consensus was to appoint a sub-committee on state responsibility.[200] The next day, without consulting ILC members, Chairman Pal proposed that the committee be chaired by Ago and composed of Aréchaga, Briggs, El-Erian, Gros, Lachs, de Luna, Paredes, Tsuruoka and Tunkin.[201] When Ago was appointed the chairman just a month later, the Latin American coup was complete. In its single meeting, it was "agreed that, in a study of the topic of state responsibility, *it was necessary to separate the essential principles of responsibility from all the subjects with which it had been traditionally associated.*"[202]

[196] Summary record of the 631st meeting, *supra* note 195, at p. 17, para. 15.

[197] Ago's idea was to postpone the topic of state responsibility for after 1962 because it was not clear what the composition of the ILC would be was accepted (p. 99, para. 29).

[198] Summary record of the 631st meeting, *supra* note 195, at p. 21, para. 71; p. 18, para. 27.

[199] UN Doc. A/CN.4/SR.632, Summary record of the 632nd meeting, Extract from the Yearbook of the International Law Commission, 1962, vol. I, at p. 27, para. 59 (Herbert W. Briggs, US).

[200] UN Doc. A/CN.4/SR.636, Summary record of the 636th meeting, Extract from the Yearbook of the International Law Commission, 1962, vol. I, at p. 45, para. 1.

[201] UN Doc. A/CN.4/SR.637, Summary record of the 637th meeting, Extract from the Yearbook of the International Law Commission, 1962, vol. I, at p. 45, para. 1. Immediately, one member complained that he was not included (Yasseen) and was then included (*ibid*, at p. 45, paras. 2–5).

[202] UN Doc. A/CN.4/SR.668, Summary record of the 668th meeting, Extract from the Yearbook of the International Law Commission, 1962, vol. I, at p. 267, para. 166, emphasis added. That same year, the subcommittee's recommendations were approved by the General Assembly in Resolution 1803 (Passed December 11, 1962).

Ago underscored the common goals of codification and simultaneously deemphasized the divisive elements of international practice. He positioned his efforts as codifying state responsibility as an instrument of peace.[203] This rhetoric, as noted above, began to change with decolonization around the 1960s. In 1961, the UN General Assembly passed Resolutions 1236 and 1505, recommending that the ILC continue its codification and progressive development of state responsibility and that states make every effort to strengthen international peace.[204] A new path had been cleared. Several members of the subcommittee submitted papers. *Significantly, none of them came from an Anglo-American.*

Ago's submission, his first to the ILC on state responsibility, is elegant, simple and prescient. He argues that, as long as efforts to codify state responsibility were derived from alien protection, they were doomed to fail.[205] The ILC had to approach codification more systematically, based on German theories of state responsibility. His colleagues agreed. They praised his work almost without qualification. Terms like "excellent" (Castrén), "fully adequate" (Rosenne), "fully endorsed" (Lachs), and "full agreement" (Pal) were commonly used.[206] That summer, the ILC appointed him as its second *Special Rapporteur* for state responsibility (Figure 5.4).[207]

203 To Ago, whereas state responsibility was historically most closely associated with the protection of aliens' property, it may now be progressively developed for the purpose of the protection of peace (Yearbook of the International Law Commission, 1969, vol. I, pp. 110, 114, vol. II, p. 136).

204 Resolution 1505 (XV) of December 12, 1960, Resolutions 1236 (XII) of December 14, 1957 and 1301 (XIII) of December 10, 1958 – available from the UN website, www.un.org/documents/resga.htm, last visited January 10, 2014. In contrast, García Amador based his codification project more narrowly on Resolution 799 (Resolution 799 (VIII) of December 7, 1953, simply considered it "desirable for the maintenance and development of peaceful relations between States" that the principles of state responsibility be codified (available from the UN website, www.un.org/documents/resga.htm, last visited January 10, 2014); *see further* García Amador, *supra* note 97, at p. 21).

205 Roberto Ago, "Working Paper," UN Doc A/CN.4/SC.1/WP.6 (in Yearbook of the International Law Commission, 1963, vol. II, UN Doc. A/5509, annex I, appendix II, at p. 263).

206 UN A/CN.4/SR.686, Summary record of the 686th meeting, Extract from the Yearbook of the International Law Commission, 1963, vol. I, at pp. 80–85.

207 The UN General Assembly, in Resolution 2272 (XXII) of December 1, 1967, not only approved of Ago's approach but also asked that his work be "expedited."

Figure 5.4 Fifteenth session of the ILC (May 27, 1963)[208]

1960: The Tongue If Not the Arm of International Enforcement

The UN and, before it, the League of Nations, created institutional opportunities to codify state responsibility beyond the US-led practice of alien protection. At first, Anglo-American delegates within world bodies expected to crystallize arbitral gains through international codification. Latin Americans, often on the respondent side of international arbitrations, resisted attempts to base the law of state responsibility upon what they viewed as a century of imperialistic practice. Codification, they claimed, should proceed systematically, based more closely on German theory than on the American practice. In the 1960s context of decolonization, as international institutions became more representatives of global cultures and politics, the US approach became a minority view and impossible to codify.

The decade of the 1960s was a critical turning point in the history of state responsibility. There was a changing of the guard globally and within world bodies. Decolonization ensured that US dominance within world bodies would never be the same as when the US forged a post-war

[208] Photo courtesy of the United Nations, available at: https://dam.media.un.org/archive/-2AM9LO0A9JWY.html.

neoliberal order. Similarly, when Roberto Ago replaced García Amador as *Special Rapporteur* for state responsibility in 1962, the International Law Commission would fully uncouple its codification efforts from the intra-American arbitrations.

Thus, Ago's "revolutionary" doctrine of state responsibility[209] was no such thing. The ILC's treatment of state responsibility under Ago's leadership was the predictable result of a changing composition within world bodies. The codification of state responsibility as a general framework of international law enforcement did not begin in 1969, when Ago submitted his first report on the topic "State Responsibility" to the ILC.[210] Nor had it begun in 1956, when García Amador published his first report on "International Responsibility."[211] The ILC's doctrine was a form of what Chilean law professor Arnulf Becker Lorca calls *mestizo* international law.[212] It is a hybrid of Anglo- and Latin American contributions born of a secularized imperialism that arose within the New World.[213]

The new doctrine was both a reaction to the US practice of alien protection and an extension of Continental theories of state responsibility. It was a traditional tool of international litigation but, at the same time, a progressive element within that world. From its first usages in the late nineteenth century, state responsibility was a battle of legal cultures (Anglo-American vs. Continental European), of power blocs (North America vs. South America) and of intellectual constructs (Continental European vs. Anglo-American). The field was dominated by US voices from 1870 until 1930. The US failure to codify state responsibility at The Hague in 1930 was one turning point. And the appointment of Roberto Ago in 1962 was another one in the history of the struggle for international standards.

Ago's ability to codify state responsibility in general terms was a testament to his capacity to construct a language of state responsibility that resembled US and German doctrines, but without connecting them.

209 *See supra* note 1; but for a more critical view, *see* Martins Paparinskis, "The Once and Future Law of State Responsibility," 114(4) *American Journal of International Law* 618 (2020), at p. 621.

210 Roberto Ago, "First Report on State Responsibility (Review of Previous Work on Codification of the Topic of the International Responsibility of States)," United Nations Document A/CN.4/217.

211 *See supra* note 49.

212 *See supra* note 11.

213 As discussed in Chapter 3.

Indeed, by codifying a general doctrine of state responsibility based on German theory rather than US practice, the ILC bifurcated the field into two. One doctrine of state responsibility is Ago's general system of international law enforcement, which would flourish in international institutions such as the ILC and the World Court. The other doctrine is the uncodified body of law arising from international arbitrations, which would continue to thrive – though not without controversy – within the world of investor protection claims and international trade law.[214] In the next chapter (Epilogue), I describe how these two developments, the "codified" and "uncodified" doctrines of state responsibility, have continued to coexist.

214 *Compare* Anna Ventouratou, "The Law on State Responsibility and the World Trade Organization," 22(5–6) *Journal of World Investment & Trade* 759 (2021), at p. 761 *to* Regis Yann Simo, "The Law of International Responsibility: The Case of the WTO as a 'Lex Specialis" or the Fallacy of a 'Self-Contained' Regime," 22 *African Journal of International & Comparative Law* 184 (2014), at p. 204.

Epilogue

From State Responsibility to the Responsibility of States

Enforcing Hospitality in 1870

Whatever else it is, state responsibility is the backbone (or "femur," if you will) of international law.[1] Improbably, the international community has an accepted doctrine of international law even though it lacks any international government or police force. The existence of this doctrine sustains our faith in the reality of international law.[2] This is exactly the

[1] I am indebted to Tami Shiffman for this point. In Ian Brownlie's first edition of *International Law* (Oxford: Oxford University Press, 1966), he writes: "Today one can regard responsibility as a general principle of international law, a concomitant of substantive rules and of the supposition that acts and omissions may be categorized as illegal by reference to the rules establishing rights and duties" (at pp. 353–354). On its critical rule for international law, *see* Martti Koskenniemi, "Doctrines of State Responsibility," in James Crawford, Alain Pellet and Simon Olleson (eds.), *The Law of International Responsibility* 45–51 (Oxford: Oxford University Press, 2011) ("most lawyers would not hesitate to affirm that 'State responsibility' is a necessary aspect of international law's being 'law', perhaps an indispensable element of the legal personality of States" (internal citations omitted)). On the foundational myth of state responsibility, see Jean d'Aspremont, *International Law as a Belief System* (Cambridge: Cambridge University Press, 2017), at p. 4 (the ILC doctrine is one of four foundational myths about the fundamental doctrines of international law (others are doctrines of sources, statehood and *jus cogens*), which are based on what d'Aspremont calls "fictive histories" (imaginary genealogies) of international law doctrines). For more on this point, *see* the introduction to Chapter 1.

[2] The codified doctrine is a cornerstone of international law. Today, it is almost redundant to say that state responsibility "is a necessary aspect of international law's being 'law,' perhaps an indispensable element of the legal personality of States" (Koskenniemi, *supra* note 1); *see also* W. E. Hall, *A Treatise on International Law* (4th edn., Oxford: Clarendon, 1898), at p. 56; Lassa Oppenheim, *International Law: A Treatise, Vol. I (Peace)* (3rd ed., Sir Ronald Roxburgh, ed., London: Longmans, Green, and Company, 1920), at p. 195; Roberto Ago, "Third Report on State Responsibility," Yearbook of the International Law Commission, Vol. II-1, at pp. 205–206, 224). This need not be understood as an unacceptably state-centered position. As Max Huber explained in the *Island of Palmas* arbitration of 1928, sovereignty involves protective duties towards one's own population as well as

type of success for which the postwar promoters of state responsibility within the United Nations had wished. In this final chapter, I consider the nature of this success, as well as some themes that are shared by the three historic narratives – American, German and institutional – in this book and, finally, offer some concluding thoughts about the dual role of state responsibility in international relations today.

Since 1870, the doctrine of state responsibility grew out of the century old practice of *lex mercatoria* – namely, the protection of strangers. It first arose in the New World as a rule about the legal consequences of Latin American states who failed to provide a minimum level of hospitality to Western foreigners in their territories. While the international obligation to protect strangers is as old as the Bible, it was transformed into an actionable claim by US lawyer-diplomats who began delegating international claims for alien injuries to professional international arbitral tribunals from 1870 onwards.[3] This turn to international arbitration resulted in the first body of positive laws on state responsibility. In the twentieth century, progressive international lawyers developed this relative narrow doctrine regarding aliens into a more general one that regulates the enforcement of all international breaches attributable to states. The evolution of state responsibility over the past century and a half has been a lengthy attempt to expand the nineteenth century US practice into an overall rule of international law.

Understood in this civilizational context, state responsibility has emerged as a modern iteration of international love. Yes, international love. Paraphrasing Martti Koskenniemi, state responsibility is a lot like love, as it is both necessary and impossible. We cannot live without them, but we cannot have them either.[4] In a flat world, where all states have equal say in the creation of international law, the goal of creating a doctrine to ensure an international rule of law has been as necessary as it has been illusory. The doctrine sits uncomfortably on the fence dividing the apologia of self-help and the utopia of solidarity; while state practice has usually followed the former, international doctrine is more

towards the persons and property of foreigners and other states (*Island of Palmas Case*, II UNRIAA, p. 839).

3 *See, e.g.*, Leviticus 19:34: "But the stranger that dwelleth with you shall be unto you as one born among you, and thou shalt love him as thyself; for ye were strangers in the land of Egypt: I am the Lord your God" (King James version).

4 Martti Koskenniemi, "Human Rights, Politics and Love," in *The Politics of International Law* 153 (Oxford: Hart, 2011), at p. 153. A 1987 song by an Irish rock band comes to mind as well (U2, "With or Without You," *The Joshua Tree* (Island Records, 1987)).

closely correlated to the latter. After a century of codification effort, one would be hard-pressed to argue that international law is more consistently complied with today than it was beforehand. Yet, international lawyers cling to the doctrine with the loyalty of longtime lovers. In the ups and downs of an international history marked as much by war as by peace, the doctrinalists have become the international romantics, promoting a disposition of progressive codification and political optimism that runs counter to most of the state practice we read about in *The New York Times.*

Fittingly, James Crawford (1948–2021) (Figure 6.1), who, along with Ago, was the most important codifier of state responsibility, opens his textbook on the topic with a quote from the poem "Sailing to Byzantium" by W. B. Yeats:

> *And louder sing*
> *For every tatter in its mortal dress.*[5]

Judge Crawford might be forgiven for seeing himself as Yeats' "aged man" in a "tattered coat" yelling for every mortal to hear about the spiritual journey that is state responsibility. It was the optimistic and resourceful efforts of norm entrepreneurs like himself that state responsibility was spoken into existence in the twentieth century. The project of codifying state responsibility represents the power of hope among international lawyers. It demonstrates how lawyers were able to reformulate the same rules of international hospitality that were first used to impose reparative duties upon weak states into broad principles that could be wielded by those same weak states against the Great Powers.[6] This transition did not happen overnight; nor was it ever really completed. I describe this development in terms of three overlapping phases: (1) prelegalism (2) *ad hoc* legalism and (3) institutional legalism. From 1870 to 1960, international lawyers formulated increasingly idealistic doctrines of state responsibility about how to judge states who misbehave in a world without international police.[7]

[5] James Crawford, *State Responsibility: The General Part* (Cambridge: Cambridge University Press, 2013), at p. 1.

[6] As Martti Koskenniemi writes, "International law's energy and hope lies in its ability to articulate existing transformative commitment in the language of rights and duties and thereby to give voice to those who are otherwise routinely excluded" (*The Gentle Civilizer of Nations: The Rise and Fall of International Law 1870–1960* (Cambridge: Cambridge University Press, 2002), at pp. 516–517).

[7] Relatedly, Michaël Schinazi identifies three different "ages" in the history of international investment protection: the Age of Aspirations (1870s–1920s); the Age of

Figure 6.1 James Richard Crawford[8]

Three Phases of State Responsibility

Pre-legalism

Prior to the late nineteenth century, international law was enforced dyadically and without regular recourse to adjudication. While I have not focused on historic events before the middle of the nineteenth century, I have contrasted that era as one lacking a customary practice of international legalism. States resolved their international disputes in many ways but without recourse to professional, third-party adjudicators who would base their binding rules on preexisting legal principles. This began to change with the US turn to international arbitration in the New World. Then, with the twentieth-century move to institutions, state responsibility became formulated as a framework for an international rule of law that was generally applicable to all international disputes. This institutional development did not replace prior usages (mainly within

Institutionalization (1920s–1950s), which ended with establishment of 1958 Convention on the Recognition and Enforcement of Foreign Arbitral Awards, and; the Age of Autonomy (from 1950s to date) – *see* Michaël Schinazi, *The Three Ages of International Commercial Arbitration* (Cambridge: Cambridge University Press, 2021), at pp. 14–15.

[8] Photo courtesy of Lauterpacht Centre for International Law, www.lcil.cam.ac.uk/memoriam-he-judge-james-crawford-ac-sc-fba.

international arbitration) of state responsibility. Both modern "phases" of state responsibility – *ad hoc* and institutional legalism – continue to coexist.

Centuries ago, accusing a state of bearing international responsibility was often a legal cover for war or an otherwise non-actionable norm. Premodern international law permitted states to enforce rights through interventions. Since there was no legal requirement of peaceful dispute resolution, "findings" of international responsibility were either unilaterally asserted (*e.g.*, letters of marque, declarations of war) or bilaterally negotiated (*e.g.*, diplomatically or by treaty). Occasionally, states relied on third parties such as the Pope or other sovereigns to resolve international disputes, but this was infrequent and unlegalistic. International law did not require a third-party's disposition and each state could assert for itself the extent of its own enforcement protocols. The legality of international claims – to the extent that such legitimization mattered – was often judged by how effective the enforcement action was in retrospect.

Ad Hoc *Legalism*

The function of responsibility in international law changed as imperial powers vied for economic influence in the New World. Beforehand, there was little need to professionalize the diplomatic claims system due to the colonial monopolization of trade with, and effective prohibition of, immigration to the region. Within the Spanish and Portuguese empires, colonial governments addressed property protection as a matter of internal (colonial) law. With the advent of the industrial revolution, new forms of international travel and the independence of Latin American nations, foreign investors were invited to invest in the region. And they did, but they were often disappointed with the results. And, as they did, they called on their governments to provide them with diplomatic protection at a pace with which governments such as the US were not able to keep up. The backlog of claims created a diplomatic crisis between Western nations and newly formed Latin American governments; often, the former withheld recognizing the legitimacy of the latter until promised a resolution to outstanding diplomatic claims for protection.[9] As Kathryn Greenman astutely notes, the doctrine of state

[9] *See further* Kathryn Greenman, "Aliens in Latin America: Intervention, Arbitration and State Responsibility for Rebels," 31 *Leiden Journal of International Law* 617 (2018), at p. 636, where Professor Greenman summarizes this vicious cycle of foreign dependence

responsibility arose to redress the explosive combination between the unraveling of Spanish colonialism and expansion of Western capitalism in Latin America.[10]

In the late nineteenth century, the US invented the most effective tool to address this diplomatic crisis. The US approach of invoking international law and arbitration formally respected local sovereignty yet practically provided sufficient redress to alien protection claims. US lawyer-diplomats, such as Secretary of State Hamilton Fish, were confronted with the need to respond to these calls for protection without undermining the Monroe Doctrine's prohibition of intervention. He found that new paradigm in international legalism.[11] By relying on the technique of international arbitration, the US could reap the benefits of colonial rule – for example, economic protection – without some of its costs – for example, political domination.

The professionalism of this turn was novel in that it relied pragmatically on third-party attorneys to resolve international claims. While the European arbitrations, such as the *Alabama Claims* in Geneva between the US and Great Britain, garnered worldwide press and fanfare, it was the American practice of international arbitration that resulted in the establishment of a new doctrine of state responsibility, one that began to outline the extent to which one could hold an international sovereign accountable for its conduct. By relying on lawyers to resolve international claims, the US practice generated an intermediary space – between the allegation of breach and its remedial enforcement – for professional dispute resolvers to articulate rules of liability. As the US practice of litigating diplomatic claims gained ground, the right of a state to forcefully intervene in another state became correspondingly restricted.

as follows: "They perceived foreign investment as vital for economic recovery and nation-building as well as a means to shore up their own internal authority and wealth. It was not in their short-term interest, however, to rebalance their economies. Being chronically on the verge of bankruptcy, governments were susceptible to the demands of foreign finance to maintain or create economic and legal systems which served their (foreign finance's) interests and yet which only reinforced economic instability."

10 *Ibid.*

11 Here I take issue with Kathryn Greenman's conclusion that "The doctrine of state responsibility for rebels can thus be understood as a response to the decolonization of Latin America: that is, a response to the need to 'externalise what had been internal aspects of colonial law and governance'" (Greenman, supra note 9, at p. 637, internal citations omitted). I think that the turn to international law was much more than externalizing the previously internal aspects of colonial law.

By employing legalism, US diplomats established a new legal field of "alien protection," which ultimately transformed the traditional practice of "diplomatic protection" in international law. This was not a pacific gesture to the international community. Nor was it an attempt to introduce a general framework of accountability to international law. By insisting on professional (white Anglo-Saxon Protestant male) lawyers to act as arbitrators, the US ensured that its assumptions about the relevance of minimum standards of legal protection were reflected in the international tribunals.[12] The *telos* of this *techne* was not impartial judgment or equal protection under the law. It was the special protection of US economic interests. However, the unintended consequence of this practice was the establishment of general rules of state liability applicable to claimant and respondent states alike.

At first, for Latin American nations, the costs of agreeing to international arbitration were offset by other benefits such as recognition of statehood, the prohibition on the use of force and attracting investment. However, after a few decades, the logic of more investment-protection-responsibility began to undermine the hard-fought sense of independence in the region. At the same time, with the establishment of new world bodies within which to plead their case collectively, Latin American lawyers would no longer be forced to accept the Anglo-American pill of alien protection. Within international conventions and institutions, they would seek and develop a progressive doctrine of international law that would stymie instead of strengthen US diplomatic power.

Institutional Legalism

During the twentieth century, international lawyers began to speak increasingly of a broad framework of state responsibility under international law. This doctrine was a construction of German philosophy. In the contexts of national military victories and defeats, German lawyers struggled to articulate the relationship between state power and public law. A disproportionate number of these theorists were German-speaking Jews (e.g., Georg Jellinek, Karl Strupp, Hersch Lauterpacht) or

[12] From the late 1860s onwards, the best appellate lawyers of the DC Circuit Court were regularly retained for international arbitrations. For example, Caleb Cushing, Samuel F. Phillips and James Mandevile Carlisle were selected four times each as an attorney or commissioner; Alexander Porter Morse and George S. Boutwell were selected three times each as an attorney or commissioner, etc.

of Jewish origins (e.g., Hans Kelsen).[13] They envisioned an international law that was complete and completely necessary. Instead of trying to induce rules from international awards, they preferred to deduce principles to address the needs of political life. Every violation of international law triggered international responsibility. International life required such a basic law.

The fact that international practice did not clearly support such a comprehensive doctrine was not critical. The "primitive" state of international law was dismissed as temporary in nature; international lawyers were free to draw from the sophisticated practice of domestic law to fill in the gaps of international doctrine. In other words, international lawyers excogitated international laws into existence. As such, German theorization was an intellectual transformation. It was an *intellectual* but not a *practical* transformation. During the lifetimes of these (mainly Jewish) international lawyers, their theories were essentially a type of *Buchrecht*, textbook law that largely ignored and was ignored by state practice. Where their work achieved great purchase, however, was within world bodies.

The establishment of international institutions after two world wars coincided with ambitious efforts to codify international law. The early attempts to codify state responsibility – all based on the US practice – failed to win committee approval. It was only with the wave of decolonization in the 1960s that the International Law Commission (ILC) would be able to find codification consensus, one based on German theory. This institutional success reflected a shift in the composition of experts within the UN as well as a reconceptualization of the topic from (or "primary") to auxiliary (or "secondary") rules, as discussed in the previous chapter. This was a strategy of abstraction (from substantive to conceptual rules), and it was effective. The ILC finalized its codification of state responsibility in 2001, after almost eight decades of effort.

[13] See generally James Loeffler and Moria Paz, *The Law of Strangers Jewish Lawyers and International Law in the Twentieth Century* (Cambridge: Cambridge University Press, 2019); Reut Yael Paz, "From Rosa Luxemburg to Hersch Lauterpacht: An Ostjüdische Heritage in International Law?," in Dawid Bunikowaki and Alberto Puppo (eds.), *Why Religion? A Critical Philosophy of Law, Peace and Religion* 221 (Berlin: Springer, 2020) (Lauterpacht's *Ostjüdische* ancestry bound him to a lineage of critically minded Jews who transcended national, ethnic and religious particularism, and worked towards a cosmopolitan and intellectual legal culture).

This third "phase" of institutional legalism coincided with but did not replace the second one of *ad hoc* legalism.[14] The US has led the practice of international arbitration well into the current century.[15] Great Britain too has been a leading practitioner in the field. Anglo-American litigants comprised a majority of early PCA and PCIJ disputes involving state responsibility. A common law developed with the initial consent of states (the *compromis*), but without any intent to positivize the field.[16] As a result, Judge James Crawford has referred to the jural development of state responsibility as the "unspoken bargain" between states.[17] This lawyer-created bargain that resulted in the general, codified doctrine also begot an unspoken *doctrine* of state responsibility, which was always naturally more inchoate. Sociologies of international arbitration have referred to this unspoken doctrine as the new *lex mercatoria*.[18] It relies on lawyers more than on law and on *ad hoc* consent more than on institutionalized procedures.[19]

[14] The introductions of *ad hoc* legalism and, later, institutionalized legalism, were just that. The Lieber Tribunal of 1868 and the German theories of state responsibility introduced new mechanisms for resolving international disputes. However, the arbitral protection of aliens did not replace their diplomatic protection. Both forms – legalistic and diplomatic – continue to be practiced. Similarly, even after the ILC codification, certain disputes have continued to be managed in premodern (e.g., self-defense) and *ad hoc* (e.g., alien protection) manners of enforcement.

[15] The first disputes resolved by the Permanent Court of Arbitration (1902) and the World Trade Organization (1995) involved US litigants.

[16] Alwyn V. Freeman has written on this development of "international common law" regarding state responsibility. *See* Alwyn V. Freeman, "Responsibility of States for Unlawful Acts of their Armed Forces," 88(2) *Recueil de Cours* 267 (1955), at pp. 5–31; Alwyn V. Freeman, *The International Responsibility of States for Denials of Justice* (London: Longmans, Green & Co., 1938), at pp. 497–503. See also Jan Paulsson, "International Arbitration and the Generation of Legal Norms: Treaty Arbitration and International Law" (Draft), Presentation, ICCA Annual Congress May 21, 2006, at p. 13, as cited in Jeffrey P. Commission, "Precedent in Investment Treaty Arbitration: A Citation Analysis of a Developing Jurisprudence," 24(2) *Journal of International Arbitration* 129–158 (2007), at p. 156 (arbitrators pick out certain "good" awards as precedents that set standards and contributed "to a higher level of consistent quality").

[17] James Crawford and Tom Grant, "Responsibility of States for Injuries to Foreigners," in J. P. Grant and J. C. Barker (eds.), *The Harvard Research in International Law: Contemporary Analysis and Appraisal* 77–126 (Buffalo: W. S. Hein, 2007), at p. 84.

[18] Yves Dezalay and Bryant G. Garth, *Dealing in Virtue: International Commercial Arbitration and the Construction of a Transnational Legal Order* (Chicago: University of Chicago Press, 1996), at pp. 39–42.

[19] Anthea Roberts, "Clash of Paradigms: Actors and Analogies Shaping the Investment Treaty System," IILJ International Legal Theory Colloquium Spring 2012, at p. 6: "the investment treaty system is in the early stages of a major recalibration that will result in a significant revaluation of the importance of different paradigms for understanding the

Some Themes

Consequentiality of Breach

What then can be said generally by way of conclusions regarding a doctrine that is primarily *ad hoc* and remains stubbornly uncodified? In retrospect, while no singular doctrine of state responsibility is discernable, certain themes are present in all three narratives about state responsibility in this study. I believe that one can point to a spectrum of state responsibility, with different purposes for the doctrine, including systemic and transactional ones.[20]

Most obviously, responsibility in international law means "answerability." As NYU law professor J. H. H. Weiler has said: "At the heart of state responsibility is a regime of consequence."[21] As its etymology suggests, the core of responsibility is the possibility of liability.[22] It is this sense of state responsibility that makes it common for international lawyers to refer to the doctrine as the "heart" or "soul" of international law.[23] Most

field" (available online at https://law.yale.edu/system/files/documents/pdf/sela/Roberts_-_Clash_of_Paradigms_-_4_Dec_2012-1.pdf, last visited November 14, 2018).

20 While it is outside the scope of the current work, I hope that I will be able to consider some of the practical consequences that have ensued to the practice of international dispute resolution as a result of the ILC and ICJ projecting a view of state responsibility as solidarity and the maintenance of an international rule of law; see also Martti Koskenniemi, "Solidarity Measures: State Responsibility as a New International Order?," 72 *British Yearbook of International Law* 337 (2001). See also Natasha Wheatley, "Spectral Legal Personality in Interwar International Law: On New Ways of Not Being a State," 35(3) *Law and History Review* 753 (2017) available online at https://doi.org/10.1017/S0738248017000256 last visited October 10, 2021. A related analysis of sovereignty was recently offered in Ronald A. Brand, "The Vulnerable Sovereign," University of Pittsburgh Law Review (Forthcoming, U. of Pittsburgh Legal Studies Research Paper No. 2021-21), available online at https://ssrn.com/abstract=3869708, last visited October 30, 2021 (proposes a different focus in the analysis of "sovereign" relationships, viewing sovereignty as a quality to be exercised, not a quantity of authority to be used to "rule over" others, at p. 18).

21 Joseph H. H. Weiler, "Editorial: Crime and Punishment: The Reification and Deification of the State (A Footnote to the Syria Debate)," 24(4) *European Journal of International Law* 993 (2013), at p. 993. See also Chapter 1, where I discuss a similar view held by James Crawford.

22 James Crawford and Jeremy Watkins, "International Responsibility," in Samantha Besson and John Tasioulas (eds.), *The Philosophy of International Law* 283 (Oxford: Oxford University Press, 2010), at p. 283.

23 The very idea of state responsibility as the consequence of breaching international law is as axiomatic as it is ancient. *See, e.g.*, the opening sentence of one of the most famous books on the topic: "As Paul Reuter remarked, 'responsibility is at the heart of international law … it constitutes an essential part of what may be considered the

frequently, the consequentiality of state responsibility takes the form of damages.[24] Between 1794 and 1972, out of the 435 inter-state arbitrations, 261 of them dealt with damages; the remaining awards concerned the interpretations of boundaries, title to land and a few other disputes.[25] Occasionally, international courts such as the International Court of Justice (ICJ or World Court) can blame states for committing international wrongs, a public shaming that is more weighty than damages; however, this result is atypical, even within the ICJ.[26]

Constitution of the international community'" (Alain Pellet, "The Definition of Responsibility in International Law," in James Crawford, Alain Pellet and Simon Olleson (eds.), *The Law of International Responsibility* (Oxford: Oxford University Press, 2011), at p. 3). According to Martti Koskenniemi, "most lawyers would not hesitate to affirm that 'State responsibility' is a necessary aspect of international law's being 'law,' perhaps an indispensable element of the legal personality of States" (Martti Koskenniemi, "Doctrines of State Responsibility," in Crawford, Pellet and Olleson, *ibid*, at p. 46). Similarly, see Vaughan Lowe, "State Responsibility: Who? What? When?" The Josephine Onoh Memorial Lecture 2002 (Hull: The University of Hull, 2003), at p. 1 (the framework of moral responsibility of states); James Crawford, "State Responsibility," in Rüdiger Wolfrüm (ed.), *Max Planck Encyclopedia of Public International Law* (Oxford: Oxford University Press, 2012), at §1 (cardinal institution of international law). Katja Creutz, *State Responsibility in the International Legal Order: A Critical Appraisal* (Cambridge: Cambridge University Press, 2020), at p. 1 (The first sentence of the book is: "State responsibility has for long been at the core of the international legal order with roots in state practice, legal theorizing and judicial pronouncements"). Creutz also cites other authors who view state responsibility as the "metalanguage," "glue," etc. of the international legal order (*ibid*, at p. 24).

24 As Jan Klabbers writes, "The raison d'être of the legal institution of state responsibility . . . is that states provide a guarantee to other subjects of international law that their rights will be protected" (Jan Klabbers, *The Concept of Treaty in International Law* (The Hague: Kluwer, 1996), at p. 101, internal citation omitted). See also *supra* note 20 and accompanying text. In the early international arbitrations, tribunals were more focused on the quantity of the remedy than on the quality of the wrong in question. This "indemnification approach" led to a host of legal inconsistencies, but focusing on factual issues rather than moral ones also facilitated further arbitration. This tradition of quantifying wrongs is most evident in the PCIJ's *Chorzów* decision of 1928.

25 Christine Gray, *Judicial Remedies in International Law* (Oxford: Oxford University Press, 1987), at p. 11, as cited in James Crawford and Jeremy Watkins, "International Responsibility," in Samantha Besson and John Tasioulas (eds.), *The Philosophy of International Law* 283 (Oxford: Oxford University Press, 2010), at p. 292.

26 For a discussion, *see* James Crawford, "The International Court of Justice and the Law of State Responsibility," in Christian J. Tams and James Sloan (eds.), *The Development of International Law by the International Court of Justice* (Oxford: Oxford University, 2013), at p. 72; to Crawford, this suggests that "damages are not necessarily the best measure of responsibility."

Legalism as Method

Since the late nineteenth century, legalism has played an increasingly critical role in the resolution of international disputes. Whether conceived as the specific duty to repair alien injuries or the general duty to remedy any violation, international lawyers have regarded state responsibility as a midway station between the allegation of breach and the right of enforcement. That space – between allegation and enforcement – was filled by professional lawyers articulating binding opinions based on general principles of law. Within international arbitrations, state responsibility arose *ad hoc* to redress alien injuries as they arose. German-speaking theorists later expanded the idea of state responsibility into a general framework of enforcement, which became widely accepted by international law professionals.

Legitimating Political Interests

The story of state responsibility is one of law entrepreneurs struggling to establish international norms and their enforcement. For US lawyer-diplomats, the doctrine justified imposing international law upon Latin American nations for injuries suffered by Western aliens. For Latin American lawyer-diplomats, allowing for the possibility of state responsibility was a tradeoff for generating Western recognition of new governments as well as defensively staving off the continuous threat of foreign interventions. For German public lawyers, state responsibility explained how to tame the unprecedented power of their colonializing governments. All three of these narratives employed state responsibility as a legitimating doctrine – or at least as a lens though which to assess the authority of state conduct.

Exceptional Rules

State responsibility is more a doctrine of exceptions than of general rules. This is so on several levels of analysis. *Generally*, for law to be law, it would have to be regulated by a sovereign power that has the ability and authority to do so. *Exceptionally*, other legal systems, lacking sovereign power, such as international law, must rely on doctrines of legality such as state responsibility. *Generally*, imposing liability upon a state would imply a hierarchical relation to that state and therefore violate its sovereignty. *Exceptionally*, imposing responsibility for alien injuries to Latin

American states was in fact a constitutive recognition of their newfound sovereignty.[27] *Generally*, the violation of international law did not trigger a right to demand international litigation. *Exceptionally*, the protection of aliens in the New World became the legal basis for requesting professional international arbitration (under the threat of force).[28] *Generally*, the international minimum standard of property protection does not require a state to be responsible for actions outside of its control. *Exceptionally*, states are responsible for the acts of rebels in its territories.[29] *Generally*, state responsibility is governed by the *lex generalis* of the ILC doctrine. *Exceptionally*, it is governed by regimes of *lex specialis* such as alien protection, diplomatic protection, investment protection, due diligence, *etc*.

These examples demonstrate that certain patterns are visible within the theory, doctrine and practice of state responsibility. But what they do not explain is the substantive content or strategic purpose of state responsibility – for example, civil or criminal, retrospective or prospective, deontic or consequentialist, *etc*. This was and remains an open question. Both the US practice and the ILC codification avoided answering the question. In both narratives, lawyers sought to validate their doctrines by minimizing exposure to background questions of politics. The US did so by focusing on quantifying wrongs. It is only within the theories of German philosophers that the purposes and functions of state responsibility are spelled out, usually in deontic terms. The ILC avoided such statements, opting instead to use a system of secondary rules that are politically neutral and context dependent.

ILC's Success in Geneva

In creating the World Court and International Law Commission, the United Nations established two mutually reinforcing powers in the

[27] Contrast the view of Adolf Lasson, *Princip und Zukunft des Völkerrechts* (Berlin: Hertz, 1871), at pp. 12–31 with the finding in the Claim of the Venezuela Steam Transportation Company: Convention between the United States and Venezuela of January 19, 1892, in John Bassett Moore, *History and Digest of the International Arbitrations to which the United States Has Been a Party, Together with Appendices Containing the Treaties Relating to Such Arbitrations, and Historical Legal Notes* (Washington, DC: Government Printing Office, 1898), at p. 1717.

[28] Contrast the Virginius affair and accompanying text with the intra-American arbitrations, beginning with the Lieber Tribunal, as discussed in Chapter 2.

[29] See Greenman, supra note 9.

development of international doctrine.[30] Within a few decades of World War II, the ILC crafted a framework of state responsibility to which the ICJ has made frequent and influential reference. As *Special Rapporteur* tasked with codifying state responsibility, Roberto Ago provided a unified restatement of state responsibility that would be applicable as a matter of general law to any violation of international law attributable to states. He also drafted the ILC code of state responsibility to be solidaristic; since every state has an interest in the maintenance of an international rule of law, Ago provided for the possibility of both injured and non-injured states to uphold the sanctity of international law.

One year after issuing Ago's first report on state responsibility,[31] the ICJ provided the first glimpse in practice of state responsibility in its expanded form with the *Barcelona Traction* case in 1970.[32] This was the first case in which an international court affirmed that states have obligations *erga omnes* – that is, owed to the international community as a whole.[33] At the same time, *Barcelona Traction* was a dispute about alien protection and not the protection of global commons. This was no coincidence and is consistent with most international litigations, which usually involve the resolution of private claims. In 1902, the first case of the Permanent Court of Arbitration (PCA) was a typical alien protection claim by the US against Mexico.[34] In 1924, the second case of the Permanent Court of International Justice (PCIJ) was also an alien

[30] On their symbiotic relationship, including the cross-referencing between "mutually reflecting mirrors" between the ILC and ICJ, see Serena Forlati, Makane Moïse Mbengue and Brian McGarry (eds.), *The Gabčíkovo-Nagymaros Judgment and Its Contribution to the Development of International Law* (Leiden: Brill, 2020), at p. ix and see further Jean d'Aspremont, "Canonical Cross-Referencing in the Making of the Law of International Responsibility," in *ibid*, at pp. 29–33 (how both UN institutions cite to each other as evidence of existing practice).

[31] Roberto Ago, "First report on State responsibility," 1969, *Yearbook of the International Law Commission*, vol. II., UN Doc. A/CN.4/217.

[32] *Barcelona Traction, Light and Power Company, Limited* (Belgium v. Spain), Judgment of 5 February 1970, ICJ Reports 1970, at p. 3; *see further* Martti Koskenniemi, "Solidarity Measures: State Responsibility as a New International Order?," 72 *British Yearbook of International Law* 337 (2001).

[33] *Ibid*, at paras. 33–34. For *Special Rapporteur* Willem Riphagen's critique of the Court's dicta regarding erga omnes obligations, *see ibid*, at p. 340. *See generally* Ben Juratowitch, "Diplomatic Protection of Shareholders," 81 *British Year Book of International Law* 281 (2011).

[34] *The Pious Funds Case* (United States of American v. Mexico), October 14, 1902, 9 Recueil des sentences arbitrales 1.

protection dispute between Greece and the United Kingdom.[35] In 1949, the third case of the International Court of Justice (ICJ) was an alien protection claim brought by France against Egypt.[36]

The most litigated field of state responsibility has not been environmental harm, cybercrimes or aggression; it has been investor or alien protection claims. And even within the latter field, the ILC doctrine has not played a dispositive as much as a legitimating role – citing to the Draft Articles to support arbitral conclusions rather than to establish them.[37] This should not be surprising since, as we have seen, most of the early international awards affirmed that consequentiality of breaching international law without naming "state responsibility" as the framework that regulated those consequences.[38] The most cited state responsibility case is probably the *Case Concerning the Factory at Chorzów* (1928),[39] in which Germany petitioned the PCIJ for reparations from Poland for taking possession of two German nitrate factories in Chorzów.[40] The PCIJ saw the outcome in that case as turning on three issues: the legal existence of an international duty to repair, the factual existence of injuries and assessing the extent of those injuries.[41] That was it.

[35] *See The Mavrommatis Palestine Concessions* (Greece v. Britain), Judgment of August 30, 1924, Permanent Court of International Justice, PCIJ Series A, No. 2 (1924).

[36] *The Protection of French Nationals and Protected Persons in Egypt* (France v. Egypt) 1950 ICJ Reports 59.

[37] *See further infra* note 75. This conclusion supports that of USC Law School Dean Andrew Guzman, who writes that state responsibility is and was always governed by state practice and customary international law – as opposed to the ILC doctrine (Andrew T. Guzman, "Saving Customary International Law," 27 *Michigan Journal of International Law* 115 (2005), at p. 116 note 1). Indeed, even to the extent that the ILC doctrine is invoked repeatedly as representative of customary international law, that is more of a formal than a substantive assertion (as Martins Paparinskis writes, "Not every actor agrees with everything, as shown by criticisms in the Sixth Committee's 2019 session of erga omnes claims by China and Iran and of the silence on special circumstances of small island developing states by Micronesia. But the arc of the legal process bends toward positivizing the ILC work" (Martins Paparinskis, "The Once and Future Law of State Responsibility," 114(4) *American Journal of International Law* 618 (2020), at p. 620, internal citations omitted)).

[38] This, however, has changed since the 1960s. International arbitrators today are more willing to not only quantify indemnification but to analyze state responsibility as well.

[39] *See, e.g.*, Google Ngram Viewer, available online at https://books.google.com/ngrams.

[40] For a concise summary of the *Chorzów Factory* proceedings, see Manley O. Hudson, "The Seventh Year of the Permanent Court of International Justice," 23 *American Journal of International Law* 1 (1929), at pp. 14–15.

[41] *Factory at Chorzów* (Germany v. Poland), Judgment No. 13, September 13, 1928, Series A, No. 17, at p. 29.

No mention of state responsibility. The PCIJ disposed of the first point succinctly:

> The Court observes that it is a principle of international law . . . and even *a general conception of law*, that any breach of an engagement involves an obligation to make reparation.[42]

The specific legal issue at hand was *reparation*, a basic legal principle that was not unique to international law; it was a general conception of law rooted in international arbitral practice.[43] A line of jurisprudence can be traced from the early American awards to this seminal statement.

Yet, state responsibility as an idea has come to mean so much more than alien protection. This is why, in the literature on the topic, most commentaries track its history alongside that of the ILC's codification rather than as a non-linear thread of cases running from the Lieber Tribunal to the World Court. Since the postwar era, however, narrative of state responsibility as alien protection has been reformulated in evolutionary terms – namely, before the ILC codified state responsibility, it was largely bilateralist and since then it has evolved into a multilateralist framework. Today state responsibility is increasingly spoken of as a general doctrine of international law enforcement.[44] This shift from the narrow bilateralism to expanded solidarism is symbolized by the *Barcelona Traction* case,[45] as mentioned above, in which the World Court agreed with the ILC that the doctrine of state responsibility was broader than the practice of alien protection.[46] No longer would state

[42] *Ibid*, emphasis added. The contradiction of its last sentence seems to have been lost on the PCIJ.

[43] Redressing international violations was more about repairing physical injuries than about satisfying moral wrongs – *Factory at Chorzów*, Jurisdiction, 1927, PCIJ, Series A, No. 9, at p. 21: "The essential principle contained in the actual notion of an illegal act – a principle which seems to be established by international practice and in particular by the decisions of arbitral tribunals is that reparation must, as far as possible, wipe out all the consequences of the illegal act and reestablish the situation which would, in all probability, have existed if that act had not been committed" (emphasis added).

[44] When Special Rapporteur cum Judge James Crawford published his influential treatise on the topic, he dubbed it State Responsibility: The General Part; similarly, when his mentor, Ian Brownlie published the first textbook on state responsibility, he titled it Ian Brownlie, System of the Law of Nations: State Responsibility, Part I.

[45] *Supra* note 15, at p. 3.

[46] There was no need to base the legal doctrine of state responsibility on actual practice. According to the Barcelona Court: "In seeking to determine the law applicable to this case, the Court has to bear in mind the continuous evolution of international law. Diplomatic protection deals with a very sensitive area of international relations, since

responsibility be just associated with quantifying damages for direct harms; it would also be relevant to the analysis of redressing systemic wrongs and maintaining an international rule of law. The new trend of *Barcelona Traction* bookends the time period of this history, demonstrating the transition from bilateralist to solidaristic conceptions of state responsibility. But it also illustrates well the duality of state responsibility, as I discuss in the next section.[47]

The Duality of State Responsibility

State responsibility represents both the rule of international law as well as the of *ad hoc* legalism of international arbitrations. As mentioned, it is the field of alien protection that remains the mainstay of international practice when it comes to state responsibility. One reason for this result is that the predominance of US law firms in international arbitration has ensured that investment protection claims continue to be treated as the primary source of international litigation.[48] While this practice is based on *ad hoc* arbitrations and remains uncodified, it is repeatedly affirmed in bilateral investment treaties (BITs) and multilateral treaties.[49] A few

the interest of a foreign State in the protection of its nationals confronts the rights of the territorial sovereign, a fact of which the general law on the subject has had to take cognizance in order to prevent abuses and friction" (*Barcelona Traction*, at para. 37).

[47] On the concept of duality, *see further* Alan Tzvika Nissel, "The Duality of State Responsibility," 44(3) *Columbia Human Rights Law Review* 793 (2013).

[48] Yves Dezalay and Bryant G. Garth, *Dealing in Virtue: International Commercial Arbitration and the Construction of a Transnational Legal Order* (Chicago: University of Chicago Press, 1996), at p. 55. While outside the scope of this work, it is worth mentioning that another reason for the rise of bilateralist solutions is simply the declining will of states to use multilateral solutions – *see* Richard H. Steinberg, "The Rise and Decline of a Liberal International Order," in David L. Sloss (ed.), *Is the International Legal Order Unraveling?* (Oxford: Oxford University Press, 2022). UCLA School of Law, Public Law Research Paper No. 21-28 (on the domestic and international blowback from the "hyperliberalism" that preceded the Great Recession, and a dispersion of global power that makes governance of multilateral regimes increasingly difficult; this has combined to weaken the liberal international order and political support for it – at p. 25). On this effect on China and international trade, see Gregory Shaffer, *Emerging Powers and the World Trading System: The Past and Future of International Economic Law* (Cambridge: Cambridge University Press, 2021), at p. 11 and throughout the book.

[49] From their inception, BITs incorporated the international standard of alien protection as the "fair and equitable treatment" (FET) standard of protection – see further Ioana Tudor, *The Fair and Equitable Treatment Standard in the International Law of Foreign Investment* (Oxford: Oxford University Press, 2008), at p. 66. On the stratified evolution of BITs, see Herman Walker, Jr., "Treaties for the Encouragement and Protection of

important litigations arising out of these treaties include *Mondev*,[50] *Azurix*[51] and *Saluka Investments*.[52] The fact that each of these tribunals included the late James Crawford as arbitrator or counsel indicates both the vitality of the US practice within mainstream international law and its functional compatibility with the ILC doctrine.[53]

The ILC's codification success occurred despite US opposition within world bodies. But what the US failed to accomplish within the multilateral codification, it secured through bilateral treaties.[54] As Santiago Montt writes:

Foreign Investment: Present United States Practice" 5 *American Journal of International Law* 229, 243 (1956) (explaining that FCN treaties – the US equivalent of BITs during the 1950s – "illustrate the feasibilities of bilateralism"). On the norm of full protection and security – including variations such as "protection and security" and "the most constant protection and security," which were recurring clauses in the nineteenth-century Friendship, Commerce and Navigation treaties – *see* Robert R. Wilson, "Property-Protection Provisions in United States Commercial Treaties," 45(1) *American Journal of International Law* 83–107 (1951). On the diplomatic and political motivation for the US to use BITs instead of FCNs, *see generally* Kenneth J. Vandevelde, *The First Bilateral Investment Treaties: US Postwar Friendship, Commerce, and Navigation Treaties* 1 (Oxford: Oxford University Press, 2017).

50 *Mondev International LTD v. United States of America*, ICSID Case No. ARB (AF)/99/2. October 11, 2002.

51 www.worldbank.org/icsid/cases/pdf/ARB0112_Azurix-Award-en.pdf.

52 *Saluka Investments BV (The Netherlands) v. The Czech Republic*, Partial Award dated March 17, 2006, available online at www.pca-cpa.org/showpaged5fc.html?pag_id=1149, last visited November 13, 2015.

53 I could add here that in fact, the two fields offer each other cross-legitimation. The international doctrinalists provide Anglo-American practitioners with *lettres de nobles* and the latter offer the former additional data points from which to progressively develop their doctrines (*see further* Dezalay and Garth, supra note 48, at p. 42).

54 On how the US began promoting the FET standard as its efforts to promote *ad hoc* legalism within international institutions faltered, *see* Yves Dezalay and Bryant G. Garth, *Dealing in Virtue: International Commercial Arbitration and the Construction of a Transnational Legal Order* (Chicago: University of Chicago Press, 1996), at p. 45. On the depoliticized nature of the FET *see* Mona Pinchis, "The Ancestry of 'Equitable Treatment' in Trade: Lessons from the League of Nations During the Inter-War Period," 15(1) *Journal of World Investment & Trade* 13 (2014), at p. 15. The minimum standard of international law would become based upon new investor treaties rather than old imperial awards. This finding corresponds to Mona Pinchis' history of FET. Professor Pinchis finds that Western states advanced the FET as a way of promoting legal protection of new investments within emerging markets. I think it noteworthy that Professor Pinchis does not substantiate her conclusion about the new US approach to investment protection by reference to historical documents (*ibid*, at p. 19); no doubt, the US was more self-conscious about the foreign perception of its approach to investment protection during the twentieth century and stopped linking the FET to the nineteenth century arbitrations (regarding which see Georg Schwarzenberger, "The Protection of British

> A careful historical review of the field of state responsibility for injuries to aliens and their property in the 20th century demonstrates that by signing BITs, developing countries have finally managed to adhere to IMS ... In other words, history has spiraled full circle, with the result that we now find ourselves in a position somewhat similar to that of the 19th century.[55]

International lawyers, such as Professor Montt, have come to reconcile the coexistence of codified and uncodified doctrines of state responsibility – with the ILC Articles seen as a *lex generalis* and alien protection as an example of *lex specialis*. What is less clear is the relationship between the two doctrines.[56] At the very least, it is clear that the codified doctrine is not the final say on state responsibility. Likely, it is also hierarchically inferior to the uncodified doctrine.[57]

Property Abroad," 5(1) *Current Legal Problems* 295 (1952), at p. 323: the most effective way to internationally protect property is to avoid "even any appearance of a new type of 'imperialism.'" This repackaging worked and the FET has gained broad acceptance in both bilateral and regional instruments.

55 Santiago Montt, "Latin American Position on State Responsibility. Looking into the Past for Lessons on the Future," LEGS seminar on February 9, 2009, available online at http://lapa.princeton.edu/uploads/2009-0209%20Montt%20LEGS%20chapter.pdf (last visited on July 14, 2010), at p. 5. See also Santiago Montt, *State Liability in Investment Treaty Arbitration: Global Constitutional and Administrative Law in the BIT Generation* (Oxford: Hart, 2009) at pp. 62–73 ("US strikes back" with international minimum standards).

56 Discussed further below. On the relationship between *lex specialis* and the problem of creating too much room for argument, *see* Martti Koskenniemi, "International Law as 'Global Governance,'" in J. Desautels-Stein and C. Tomlins (eds.), *Searching for Contemporary Legal Thought* 199 (Cambridge: Cambridge University Press, 2017); Loris Marotti and Paolo Palchetti, "Of Restoring Compliance, Lex Specialis and Intersecting Wrongs: the Question of 'Remedies'" in Gabčíkovo-Nagymaros, in *The Gabčíkovo-Nagymaros Judgment and Its Contribution to the Development of International Law* (*supra* note 30).

57 This was seen in the World Court in *Gabčíkovo-Nagymaros Project (Hungary/Slovakia)*, the International Court of Justice left open the question of when specific and when general doctrines of state responsibility apply; if an attorney invokes treaty law, then the case may be governed by *lex specialis* and need not fit within the "general" parameters of the ILC code (Draft Article 55) – *see* Marotti and Palchetti, *supra* note 30, at p. 147. *See also* Martti Koskenniemi, "Study on the Function and Scope of the *Lex Specialis* Rule and the Question of 'Self-Contained Regimes,'" UN Doc. A/CN.4/ILC(LVI)/SG/FIL/CRD.1, para. 36, available online at https://digitallibrary.un.org/record/573157?ln=en, last visited November 30, 2021; Andreas Kulick and Michael Waibel, "General International Law in International Investment Law," in Andreas Kulick and Michael Waibel (eds.), *Commentary on General International Law in International Investment Law* (Oxford: Oxford University Press, 2023), at pp. 7, 17.

Codifying an Unspoken Doctrine

Roberto Ago's grand vision of state responsibility was both optimistic and opportunistic.[58] On the verge of the Second World War, with the demise of the League of Nations all but assured, Ago called for a broad international legal enforcement regime; but he would base this new doctrine on public legal theory and very loosely tie it to an arbitral practice that had already been critiqued as legalized imperialism.[59] Ago's solution was to create an abstraction rather than a continuation of the past arbitral practice. Ago was so careful, writes Belgian international law professor Jean d'Aspremont, that the genealogy between Ago's doctrine and past precedents is "imaginary."[60] This approach allowed for broad applicability as well as institutional acceptance within the United Nations. Ago designed the ILC code to be easy to use and to have broad application.[61]

Since Ago and the ILC designed state responsibility as a regime of *default rules*, it also provided for the possibility of primary rules such as alien protection to override them. This approach provides the benefit of flexibility.[62] In the final part of the ILC code, Draft Article 55 (Lex Specialis) provides as much:

58 Roberto Ago, "Le délit international," 68 *Recueil des cours* 440 (Paris: Sirey, 1939).

59 For a great analysis of the ILC's reliance on the US–Mexico General Claim Commission, see Jean d'Aspremont, "The General Claims Commission (Mexico and the United States) and the Invention of International Responsibility," in I. de la Rasilla del Moral and J. Vinuales (eds.), *Experiments in International Adjudication: Historical Accounts* (Cambridge: Cambridge University Press, 2018), at pp. 18–20.

60 *Ibid*, at p. 8.

61 Roberto Ago, "Second report on state responsibility," in *Yearbook of the International Law Commission*, 1970, Vol. II, UN Doc A/CN.4/233, at p. 185; Jean d'Aspremont, *International Law as a Belief System* (Cambridge: Cambridge University Press, 2017), pp. 72–79 ("this was the "product of a carefully orchestrated design process" regarding the architects of international responsibility (presumably including State, organization and individual criminal responsibilities under international law").

62 *See* Federica Paddeu and Christian Tams, "Dithering, Trickling Down, and Encoding: Concluding Thoughts on the 'ILC Articles at 20' Symposium," *EJIL: Talk!* August 9, 2021, available online at www.ejiltalk.org/dithering-trickling-down-and-encoding-concluding-thoughts-on-the-ilc-articles-at-20-symposium, last visited November 3, 2021: "Has this affected the Articles; have they evolved in their 20-year journey? It seems to us that, for the most part, developments so far have left the ILC's framework and even its rules largely unchanged. This is no doubt in part because of their flexibility. What is more, deviations from the ILC's framework can easily be explained away as lex specialis, leaving the residual regime unaffected. Whatever the GA ultimately decides, the Articles are not the final word on State responsibility. But if individual rules on responsibility may change over time, the blueprint provided by the Articles is likely to endure."

> These articles do not apply where and to the extent that the conditions for the existence of an internationally wrongful act or the content or implementation of the international responsibility of a State are governed by special rules of international law.

The "special rules of international law" referred to are those substantive (or primary) rules that already provide for remedies and enforcement actions.[63] The ILC did not intend for the Draft Articles to be an overarching constitutional regime but to be default rules that applied whenever special rules were not applicable. This was the only way to successfully codify the field in under a century given the international debate between Anglo- and Latin American international lawyers over the future of state responsibility.

In my doctoral dissertation, I described the intra-American legal rift as a "Struggle for International Standards."[64] The idea behind the title was that norm entrepreneurs from the North and South both agreed on the need for international standards but struggled to mold them in their own image.[65] The doctrine of state responsibility took over eighty years to codify. But, as we have seen in previous chapters, the history of state responsibility has a longer arc than this hemispheric debate. When described as a struggle, the narrative seems like one with a happy conclusion: codification. But codification has clarified very little in the way of international practice since it allows for so many exceptions and such broad interpretation. The ILC code was purified of its imperial heritage while validating the continuation of that practice.[66]

[63] Although "it is often hard to distinguish what is 'general' and what is particular'" when it comes to general rules and their exceptions– see International Law Commission, "Fragmentation of International Law: Difficulties Arising from the Diversification and Expansion of International Law," Finalised by Martti Koskenniemi, April 13, 2006, UN Doc. A/CN.4/L.682., at para. 58 (p. 35).

[64] Alan Tzvika Nissel, *A History of State Responsibility: The Struggle for International Standards (1870-1960)*, Dissertation submitted to Helsinki University in satisfaction of LLD degree, 2016.

[65] More recently, in a collection of essays published by Oxford University Press' History of International Law series, Jochen von Bernstorff and Philipp Dann describe this conceptual dispute as "The Battle for International Law" between the North and the South – Jochen von Bernstorff and Philipp Dann (eds.), *The Battle for International Law South-North Perspectives on the Decolonization Era* (Oxford: Oxford University Press, 2019).

[66] In other words, while the ILC codified state responsibility, it simultaneously cultivated its replacement by specific regimes. *See also* Koskenniemi, *supra* note 1, at p. 49: "Like any good compromise, the ILC text can be cited as a victory of the 'bilateralist' as well as the 'communitarian' school. The debate that polarizes 'bilateralism' and community interests survives because it plays on the indeterminacy of both notions."

Indeed, although state responsibility is codified, it is also uncodifiable. Meaning, even though the field has been codified, the final code has not fostered a unification but a fragmentation of doctrine. When modern problems such as global pandemics arise, lawyers are decreasingly turning to the ILC's code.[67] As Katja Kreutz of the University of Helsinki has recently written, "the general law of state responsibility is not as uniformly relevant across the spectrum of international obligations as it once was, and that the importance of this law has diminished over time."[68] This is partially due to the strengthening of specialty responsibility regimes.[69] The nature of this duality of doctrines becomes clearer when we consider the context within which Roberto Ago was operating in the 1960s.

The Men of 1963

In *The Gentle Civilizer of Nations*, Martti Koskenniemi recounts the legacy of the eleven men who established the *Institut de droit*

[67] Some influential, recently published articles on the future of state responsibility no longer even mention the ILC's role or its codified product. *See, e.g.*, Sienho Yee, "To Deal with a New Coronavirus Pandemic: Making Sense of the Lack of Any State Practice in Pursuing State Responsibility for Alleged Malfeasances in a Pandemic—Lex Specialis or Lex Generalis at Work?," 19 *Chinese Journal of International Law* 237 (2020); Riddhi Josh, "Force Majeure under the ILC Draft Articles on State Responsibility: Assessing Its Viability against COVID-19 Claims," 24 (24) *ASIL Insights* 17 September 2020, available online at www.asil.org/insights/volume/24/issue/24/force-majeure-under-ilc-draft-articles-state-responsibility-assessing, last visited October 30, 2021; Ntina Tzouvala and Robert Knox, "International Law of State Responsibility and COVID-19: An Ideology Critique," *Australian Yearbook of International Law* (online, 2021), available at https://brill.com/view/journals/auso/39/1/article-p105_9.xml?language=en ANU College of Law Research Paper No. 21.25, available online at https://ssrn.com/abstract=3930470, last visited October 13, 2021.

[68] Creutz, *supra* note 23, at p. 302; *see also ibid*, at p. 15 ("This fragmentation of responsibility has resulted in the coexistence of multiple responsibility regimes in international law. These developments challenge the position of state responsibility as the primary responsibility system").

[69] So much so that it is often difficult to discern where one ends and the other begins. As Martti Koskenniemi, then the ILC Commissioner studying the fragmentation of international law, writes: "it is often hard to distinguish what is 'general' and what is 'particular' in international law" ("Study on the Function and Scope of the *Lex Specialis* Rule and the Question of 'Self-Contained Regimes,'" UN Doc. A/CN.4/ILC(LVI)/SG/FIL/CRD.1, para. 23 available online at https://digitallibrary.un.org/record/573157?ln=en, last visited November 30, 2021). Regarding the uncertain hierarchy between two *lex specialis* regimes such as investment protection and the law of the sea, *see* Alberto Pecoraro, "Law of the Sea and Investment Protection in Deep Seabed Mining," 20(2) *Melbourne Journal of International Law* 530 (2019).

international on September 8, 1873, in the Ghent Town Hall. These "men of 1873" shared an underlying sensibility regarding their role as international lawyers. They saw themselves as the juridical conscience-consciousness of the civilized world.[70] They were the *gentle* civilizers of their client-governments' foreign policies. It was the regular practice, for example, of Columbia law professor Francis Lieber (1800–1872) to communicate with leading US politicians such as Secretary of State Hamilton Fish (1808–1893) about using law and law professors to resolve international disputes. As international institutions grew in size and diversity, decision-making depended more on consensus-building and less on sensibility-sharing. The growth of world bodies created the need for a new actor: the institutional international lawyer.[71]

Roberto Ago (1907–1995), who in 1963 submitted his first written report to the ILC, is paradigmatic of this new lawyer. Unlike the "men of 1873" who focused their efforts on influencing national governments, the "men of 1963" had a different decision-making audience: fellow international lawyers.[72] As Harvard law professor David Kennedy writes, these lawyers seek votes by avoiding openly political acts or statements: "Where they govern, they aspire to do so with clean hands, detached from the messy business of arbitrating among political groups."[73] The fortunes of these two groups diverged in the mid-twentieth century. The European gentle civilizers never recovered from the Second World War; whereas institutional international lawyers continued to thrive and prosper.

Hersch Lauterpacht (1897–1960) and Roberto Ago were contemporaries. Lauterpacht belonged to the earlier generation of international lawyers and Ago to the later one. While each represented his country

[70] Koskenniemi, supra note 1, at p. 47. Koskenniemi also notes how they also knew the limits of their influence as *gentle* civilizers.

[71] A prototypical institutional lawyer was actually from the US: James Brown Scott. See further Benjamin Allen Coates, Transatlantic Advocates: American International Law and US Foreign Relations, 1898–1919 (Doctoral Dissertation submitted to Columbia University, 2010), at p. 406: Scott maintained considerable "institutional power." He served as President of the Institut, the American Society of International Law, and directed the Carnegie Endowment's Division of International Law.

[72] Both groups, however, were still exclusively comprised of men. It was not until 2001 that the first women were appointed by the UN General Assembly to the International Law Commission.

[73] David Kennedy, "The Twentieth-Century Discipline of International Law in the United States," in Austin Sarat, Bryant Garth and Robert A. Kagan (eds.), *Looking Back at Law's Century* 386 (Ithaca: Cornell University Press, 2002), at p. 392. Professor Kennedy in this quote is referring to international lawyers generally.

(England and Italy, respectively) within the ILC during the postwar era, they did so in distinct ways. Lauterpacht, who was among the last of the gentle civilizers, still sought to impose his liberal sensitivity of international law upon his colleagues.[74] In *Private Law Sources and Analogies*, Lauterpacht described how he viewed his role as an international lawyer: an heroic gap-filler who wields maxims of municipal jurisprudence and general principles of law to adjudicate claims.[75] The Polish-born and Austrian-trained British Jewish international lawyer died in 1960. By that time, moralizing visions could no longer be effectively embraced in the committee room, even Lauterpacht's theory of non-theory.

Both men were norm entrepreneurs offering progressive laws to the international community. But while only ten years separated the two, Lauterpacht and Ago represented two different generations of international law. Whereas Lauterpacht strived to balance inchoate international practice with progressive doctrine, Ago was willing to codify law afresh, without the need for precedents or domestic analogues. The thrust of Ago's international legal energies was directed toward his colleagues within international institutions (especially the United Nations), where he wielded a persuasive theory of positivism to shape an expansive but thin doctrine of state responsibility.[76]

A Signpost of International Law

Ago's vision of state responsibility was a doctrine of *international law* enforcement. Ago rejected Lauterpacht's reliance on domestic analogies. He viewed international law as a distinctly unique regime of law and worthy of its own *sui generis* doctrine of responsibility. He was also very much aware of the toxicity that the US role inserted into the history of state responsibility. He therefore rejected Lauterpacht's reliance on past

[74] Martti Koskenniemi describes Lauterpacht's *The Function of Law* as "the last book on international theory – the theory of non-theory, the acceptable, sophisticated face of legal pragmatism" (Koskenniemi, supra note 1, at p. 369).

[75] *See* especially the series of case analyses in Hersch Lauterpacht, *Private Law Sources and Analogies of International Law: With Special Reference to International Arbitration* (London: Longmans, Green and Co., 1927), at pp. 215–296; Koskenniemi, supra note 1, at p. 369.

[76] As discussed in Chapter 1, this was an international doctrine of responsibility that served a fundamentally different role than in domestic law. Indeed, the whole concept of codifying state responsibility would be bizarre within the context of domestic law – especially in common law systems where there is no general statute or restatement on the law of remedies or enforcement.

arbitrations and domestic analogues. To Ago, the administration of international law uses an atypical form of legal enforcement. *Typically*, the idea of liability is associated with being subject to someone else's normative power; this is structural lacking in international society.[77] The existence of state responsibility as a general doctrine comes to compensate for lacking that enforcement process.

Thus, state responsibility is not only a set of international rules about attribution and remedies. It is evidence of the consequentiality of international law.[78] Both the men of 1873 and of 1963 were clear about this power. In contrast to domestic lawyers, international lawyers saw themselves as possessing a disproportionate power to influence the content of the law within international society.[79] Ago had both the vision and skill to set state responsibility on the track to successful codification. He believed that the costs associated with abstracting the doctrine into secondary rules – that is, legal ambiguity – were worth baring to establish state responsibility as the signpost of international law.[80] Others feared it would mark the end of international law.

[77] As Joseph Raz writes about the normativity of responsibility: "Typically, unlawfully causing harm places one under a legal obligation to compensate the harmed people. But again, typically, the law makes enforcement of that duty dependent on an enforcement process" (Joseph Raz, *From Normativity to Responsibility* (Oxford: Oxford University Press, 2011), at p. 255).

[78] James Crawford, "Investment Arbitration and the ILC Articles on State Responsibility," 25 *ICSID Review* 127 (2010), at p. 132 (all international lawyers cite to rules of state responsibility often "by way of signposting rather than actually integrating the substance of the [ILC] Articles into the decision").

[79] Lacking an international congress or legislature, the doctrines of lawyers like Lauterpacht and Ago are particularly impactful. This is not limited to the topic of state responsibility – *see* Simon Chesterman, "Herding Schrödinger's Cats: The Limits of the Social Science Approach to International Law," 22(1) *Chicago Journal of International Law* (2021), at p. 56: "The reason is that the international law academic – more, I would argue, than perhaps any other discipline – has the potential to affect the subject matter of his or her study."

[80] On how state responsibility is a blunt tool that can be used a sword or shield, to attack or defend legal norms, *see* Scott Veitch, *Law and Irresponsibility: On the Legitimation of Human Suffering* (Oxford: Routledge-Cavendish, 2007) (legitimates human suffering by demonstrating how legal institutions operate as much to deflect responsibility for harms suffered as to acknowledge them); Katja Creutz, *supra* note 23, at p. xi ("State responsibility is a blunt tool"). The functional point here is a psychological one, about perceiving and believing in the law-ness of international law; *see further* Federica Paddeu and Christian Tams, "The ILC Articles at 20: Introduction to the Symposium," EJIL: Talk! August 2, 2021, available online at www.ejiltalk.org/the-ilc-articles-at-20-introduction-to-the-symposium, last visited November 3, 2021: The Draft Articles today are mainly used "as rules that operate in the background: necessary to international law's functioning, at

1960 and the Unmaking of International Law

In 1988, Cambridge law professor Philip Allott predicted that the ILC's abstraction of state responsibility into general rules was a major setback:

> The long quest by the International Law Commission for a substantive system of state responsibility is a search for a mythical creature, the hunting of a snark. It threatens the incremental creation of a true international legal system in a true international society and reveals the long-term destructive effect of a government-dominated commission on the development of international law.[81]

To Allot, the ILC unmoored state responsibility from the unpleasant but effective limitations of international practice. By expanding the doctrine to cover all enforcement actions in general, the ILC pushed the project from one within its mandate of progressive codification into a rabbit hole paved with utopian intentions.[82] As the title to his 1988 article makes clear, Allott went so far as to predict that the generalization of the rules on state responsibility would be the "unmaking of international law." By disconnecting the doctrine of state responsibility from the politics of its history, the ILC abstracted so much from the doctrine that it left much space for debate. And, as Philip Allott writes: "When lawyers leave room for argument there is much room for injustice."[83]

least as far as claims and disputes are concerned, but often fairly general – so that their impact on the outcome of such claims and disputes is not always felt."

81 Philip Allott, "State Responsibility and the Unmaking of International Law," 29(1) *Harvard International Law Journal* 1–26 (1988), at p. 2. Without considering the politics of state responsibility, we risk reinforcing the invisibility of its norms. On the invisibility of background norms, see David W. Kennedy, "Background Noise? - the Politics Beneath Global Governance," 21 *Harvard International Law Review* 52 (1999), at p. 57: "By reinforcing the invisibility of background norms and private arrangements, mainstream commentators have taken important areas of political contestation out of the internationalist's vision precisely as the disaggregation of the state makes these norms and institutions the most significant sites for international policymaking." See also Prosper Weil, "Towards Relative Normativity in International Law," 77 *American Journal of International Law* 413 (1983).

82 Some have criticized the "doctrinal utopianism" of the UN which sought to, in Martti Koskenniemi's words, "achieve logical consistency at the cost of applicability in the real world of state practice" ("Between Apology and Utopia: The Politics of International Law," in Martti Koskenniemi (ed.), *The Politics of International Law* 35 (Oxford: Hart, 2011), at p. 40.

83 The full quote is worth duplicating: "[I]f responsibility exists as a legal category, it must be given legal substance. In particular, general conditions of responsibility have to be created which are then applicable to all rights and duties. The net result is that the deterrent effect of the imposition of responsibility is seriously compromised, not only by

Yet, when diplomats leave room for argument, there is also much room for "second opinions." The late NYU law professor Thomas Franck (1931–2009) writes in his last published article "that it may well be that the surprising jurisprudential success of some broad principles, despite their vagueness, is simply due to their having provided what turns out to be an efficient process for rendering such second opinions."[84] It was precisely the delegation of disputes to professional tribunals that provided the first opportunity to articulate positive rules on state responsibility based on general principles of law.[85] The doctrine of state responsibility was never confined to the annual reports of the UN's International Law Commission. It also thrives within international arbitral seats and international law journals.

There is so much more to say about state responsibility's paradoxical past. The dance between theory and practice – as between rules and their exceptions – has long characterized the field. This book is but a single attempt to provide a history that is inclusive of both the codified and uncodified doctrines of state responsibility. It is offered as a useful source for international practitioners.[86] But it is hoped that the work will also

nationalizing it (the first vicious consequence) but also by leaving room for argument in every conceivable case of potential responsibility (the second vicious consequence). When lawyers leave room for argument there is much room for injustice" (*supra* note 81, at p. 14).

[84] Thomas M. Franck, "On Proportionality of Counter-Measures in International Law," 102 (4) *American Journal of International Law* 715–767 (2008), at p. 718, discussed further in Chapter 3.

[85] Thus, while Allott's critique of the ILC doctrine is as prescient today as when it was first published in 1988, I believe that international standards were always based as much on natural as on positive legal sources. For example, an understudied sociological element of international law compliance is the factor of shared cultural values among state parties to a rule, which often times plays a more important role to source of international obligation – be it an agreement or an *a priori* rule. As Nehal Bhuta writes in his review of *To the Uttermost Parts of the Earth*, "*Civilization*, rather than natural law-derived *Staatsklugheit*, becomes the true foundation of international law" (Nehal Bhuta, "'Like a Tree in the Garden of State Sciences': From Staatswissenschaften to External Public Law," 32(3) *European Journal of International Law* 1035 (2021), at p. 1040).

[86] *See* Todd Weiler, *The Interpretation of International Investment Law: Equality, Discrimination and Minimum Standards of Treatment in Historical Context* (Leiden: Martinus Nijhoff, 2013); in the first sentence of the book, on p. 1, Weiler writes: "It is a fundamental premise of this book that anyone who attempts to interpret the provisions of an investment treaty, without first establishing a proper historical grounding, risks embarking upon a rudderless excursion in subjective analysis." On the related importance of retrospectivity and historical analysis, *see* Jean d'Aspremont, "Time Travel in the Law of International Responsibility," in Samantha Besson (ed.), *Theories of International Responsibility Law* (Cambridge: Cambridge University Press, 2022), at p. 5: "In modern

serve as a helpful resource for us to imagine more ways for the law to prevent injustices to strangers, a goal that has, for at least 15,000 years, been a goal of our socialization.[87]

Between the years 1870 and 1960, lawyers like Hamilton Fish, Georg Jellinek and Roberto Ago have established state responsibility as a constitutional element of international law.[88] While it is impossible to define the exact contours of that responsibility from the past, it is clear that they inaugurated an "argumentative tradition"[89] that continues to serve as a platform for political discourse on the relevance of international law to the problem of state responsibility. These lawyers were practitioners, philosophers and publicists. They all dreamt of a world governed by law.

I will end the chapter as I began it, with W. B. Yeats. In his 1914 poem, "Responsibilities," the Irish poet and politician quotes an anonymous epigraph, "in dreams begins responsibility."[90] The poet concludes:

> *You most of all, silent and fierce old man*
> *Because you were the spectacle that stirred*
> *My fancy, and set my boyish lips to say*

temporality, the past is thus affirmed in the present and by the present, for the sake of the present's self-formation, self-identification, and self-congratulation. Yet, once affirmed in the present by the present, the past is immediately demoted to a defunct status. This instant 'killing' of the past which the present has just affirmed is precisely what, in modern temporality, allows the present to be present" (internal citations omitted).

87 For example, within the Jewish tradition, *see* James Loeffler and Moria Paz (eds.), *The Law of Strangers Jewish Lawyers and International Law in the Twentieth Century* (Cambridge: Cambridge University Press, 2019).

88 As Jean d'Aspremont of the University of Manchester writes, "[F]undamental doctrines … are designed by reference to imaginary precedents with a view to staging the authority of those modes of legal reasoning in judicial and decision-making processes" ("The General Claims Commission (Mexico and the United States) and the Invention of International Responsibility," in I. de la Rasilla del Moral and J. Viñuales (eds.), *Experiments in International Adjudication: Historical Accounts* 150 (Cambridge: Cambridge University Press, 2018), at p. 153 (internal citations omitted)).

89 d'Aspremont, *ibid*, at p. 2. *See also* Federica Paddeu and Christian Tams, "The ILC Articles at 20: Introduction to the Symposium," *EJIL: Talk!* August 2, 2021, available online at www.ejiltalk.org/the-ilc-articles-at-20-introduction-to-the-symposium, last visited November 3, 2021: "The UN General Assembly 'noted' the Articles and commended them to the attention of Governments in December of that same year. Since then, the Articles have become the obvious reference point for debates about State responsibility: they are invoked, applied, cited, criticised, studied by nearly everyone working in or with international law, from undergraduate students to investment tribunals, and even domestic courts."

90 William Butler Yeats, *The Collected Works of W. B. Yeats, Vol. I: The Poems* 100 (2nd ed., New York: Simon and Schuster, 1997 [1914]). Yeats cites an "Old Play" as the source of this aphorism.

'Only the wasteful virtues earn the sun ... '
I have no child, I have nothing but a book,
Nothing but that to prove your blood and mine.

Yeats describes responsibility as originating in dreams. State responsibility did not originate in a treaty or textbook. It was spoken into existence as part of the creative process that continuously unmakes and remakes international law. I expect that lawyers will continue to sail to Byzantium and back to legitimate their political projects of mending broken femurs, of demanding hospitality to strangers and of improving our world through law. On these journeys, they will do well to recall that the doctrine of state responsibility is a pliable one that has been continuously made, unmade and remade to address the specific needs of those invoking its name.

BIBLIOGRAPHY

A. Claire Cutler, "The 'Grotian Tradition' in International Relations," 17 Review of International Studies 41 (1991)

A. Curtis Wilgus, "James G. Blaine and the Pan American Movement," 5(4) The Hispanic American Historical Review 662 (1922)

A. Martínez Moreno, "José Gustavo Guerrero, caballero andante de derecho" in A. Cançado Trindade and A. Martínez Moreno (eds.), Doctrina Latinoamericana del derecho internacional 9–32 (San José: Corte Interamericana de Derechos Humanos, 2003)

A.A. Cançado Trindade, "Origin and Historical Development of the Rule of Exhaustion of Local Remedies in International Law," 12 Belgian Review of International Law 499 (1976)

Abraham Howard Feller, The Mexican Claims Commissions 1923–1934: A Study in the Law and Procedure of International Tribunals (New York: Macmillan, 1935)

Adolf Lasson, Princip und Zukunft des Völkerrechts (Berlin: Hertz, 1871)

Adrian Cook, The Alabama Claims (Ithaca, N.Y.: Cornell University Press, 1975)

Åke Hammarskjold, "The Permanent Court of International Justice and the Development of International Law," 14 International Affairs 797 (1935)

Alain Pellet, "The Definition of Responsibility in International Law," in James Crawford, Alain Pellet and Simon Olleson (eds.), *The Law of International Responsibility* (Oxford: Oxford University Press, 2011)

Alan John Percivale Taylor, The Trouble Makers: Dissent over Foreign Policy, 1792–1939 (Bloomington: Indiana University Press, 1958)

Alan McPherson, "Forget the Maine! The Legacy of 'The United States and the Americas,'" 35(4) Diplomatic History 709–728 (2011)

Alan Tzvika Nissel, "The Columbianization of U.S. Legal Education" (unpublished paper on file with author)

"The Dichotomization of International Law" (unpublished paper on file with author)

"The Duality of State Responsibility," 44(3) Columbia Human Rights Law Review 793 (2013)

A History of State Responsibility: The Struggle for International Standards (1870–1960), dissertation submitted to Helsinki University in satisfaction of LLD degree, 2016, available online at stateresponsibility.com

"The ILC Articles on State Responsibility: Between Self-Help and Solidarity," 38 N.Y.U. Journal of International Law & Politics (2006)

Albert Geouffre de Lapradelle and Nicolas Politis, Recueil des arbitrages internationaux (Paris: Pedone, 1905)

Albert S. Thayer, "Natural Law," 21 Law Quarterly Review 50 (105)

Alberto Pecoraro, "Law of the Sea and Investment Protection in Deep Seabed Mining," 20(2) *Melbourne Journal of International Law* 530 (2019)

Alejandro Álvarez, American Problems in International Law (New York: Baker, Voorhis & Co., 1909)

La codificacion del derecho internacional en América: trabajos de la tercera Comisión de la Asamblea de Jurisconsultos reunida en Santiago de Chile (Santiago: Imprenta Universitaria, 1923)

"Latin America and International Law," 3(2) American Journal of International Law 269 (1909)

The Monroe Doctrine: Its Importance in the International Life of the States of the New World (Oxford: Oxford University Press, 1924)

Alexander Marie Stuyt, Survey of International Arbitrations, 1794–1989 (3rd ed, The Hague: Martinus Nijhoff, 1990)

Alexander Orakhelashvili, "The Normative Basis of 'Fair and Equitable Treatment': General International Law on Foreign Investment?" 46(1) Archiv des Völkerrechts 74 (2008)

Alexandre Mérignhac, Traité théorique et pratique de l'arbitrage international (Paris: Larose, 1895)

Alexis Galán, "The Search for Legitimacy in International Law: The Case of the Investment Regime," 43 Fordham International Law Journal 79 (2019)

Alexis Mourre, "Perspectives of International Arbitration in Latin America," 17 American Review of International Arbitration 597 (2006)

Alf Verdross, "Forbidden Treaties in International Law," 31 American Journal of International Law 571 (1937)

Allan Nevins, Hamilton Fish: The Inner History of the Grant Administration (New York: Dodd, Mead & Co., 1936)

Allison Powers Useche, "The Standard of Civilization on Trial at the United States/Mexico Claims Commission 1923–1937," 1 Jus Gentium: J. Int'l Legal Hist. 391 (2016)

Alphonse Rivier, Principes du droit des gens I (Paris: A. Rousseau, 1896)

Alwyn V. Freeman, The International Responsibility of States for Denial of Justice (London: Longmans, Green & Co., 1938)

"Recent Aspects of the Calvo Doctrine and the Challenge to International Law," 40 American Journal of International Law 121 (1946)

"Responsibility of States for Unlawful Acts of their Armed Forces," 88(2) Recueil de Cours 267 (1955)

Amanda Perreau-Saussine, "A Case Study on Jurisprudence as a Source of International Law: Oppenheim's Influence" in Matthew Craven, Malgosia Fitzmaurice and Maria Vogiatzi (eds.), Time, History and International Law 100 (2007)

"Lauterpacht and Vattel on the Sources of International Law: The Place of Private Law Analogies and General Principles" in Peter Haggenmacher and Vincent Chetail (eds.), Vattel's International Law in a XXIst Century Perspective (The Hague: Brill, 2011)

Amos Elwood Corning, Hamilton Fish (New York: Lanmere Publishing Co., 1918)

Amos J. Peaslee, "The Sanction of International Law," 10(2) American Journal of International Law 328 (1916)

An Hertogen, "The Persuasiveness of Domestic Law Analogies in International Law," 29(4) European Journal of International Law 1127 (2018)

Anastasios Gourgourinis, "General/Particular International Law and Primary/ Secondary Rules: Unitary Terminology of a Fragmented System," 22(4) European Journal of International Law 993 (2011)

Andreas H. Roth, The Minimum Standard of International Law Applied to Aliens (Leiden: Sijthoff, 1949)

Andreas Kulick and Michael Waibel, "General International Law in International Investment Law," in Andreas Kulick and Michael Waibel (eds.), *Commentary on General International Law in International Investment Law* (Oxford: Oxford University Press, 2023)

Andrew T. Guzman, "Saving Customary International Law," 27 Michigan Journal of International Law 115 (2005)

"Why LDCs Sign Treaties That Hurt Them: Explaining the Popularity of Bilateral Investment Treaties," 38 Va. J. Int'l L. 639 (1998)

Angel R. Oquendo, "The Solitude of Latin America: The Struggle for Rights South of the Border,"43 Texas International Law Journal 185 (2008)

Angelo Piero Sereni, The Italian Conception of International Law (New York: Columbia University Press, 1943)

Anna Ventouratou, "The Law on State Responsibility and the World Trade Organization," 22(5–6) Journal of World Investment & Trade 759 (2021)

Annamaria Monti, "'Interdisciplinary' Legal Studies and the Emergence of New Academic Teachings: A Research Project on Law Courses in 19th–20th Century Italy," 1 CIAN - Revista de Historia de las Universidades 19 (2016)

Anne Orford, "Food Security, Free Trade, and the Battle for the State," 11(2) Journal of International Law and International Relations 1 (2015)

International Law and the Politics of History (Cambridge: Cambridge University Press, 2021)

Anne Peters, Heike Krieger and Leonhard Kreuzer (eds.), Due Diligence in the International Legal Order 1 (Oxford: Oxford University Press, 2020)

Anne-Charlotte Martineau, "A Forgotten Chapter in the History of International Commercial Arbitration: The Slave Trade's Dispute Settlement System," 31 Leiden J. of Intl. L. 219 (2018)

Annemarieke Vermeer-Künzli, "As If: The Legal Fiction in Diplomatic Protection," 18(1) European Journal of International Law 37 (2007)

Anthea Roberts, "Clash of Paradigms: Actors and Analogies Shaping the Investment Treaty System," IILJ International Legal Theory Colloquium Spring 2012

Anthony Aust, Modern Treaty Law and Practice (Cambridge: Cambridge University Press, 2007)

Anthony J. Bellia Jr. and Bradford R. Clark, "The Federal Common Law of Nations," 109(1) Columbia Law Review 1–93 (2009)

Anthony Townsend Kronman, "Hart, Austin, and the Concept of a Legal System: The Primacy of Sanctions," 84(3) Yale Law Journal 584 (1975)

Anton Roth, Das völkerrechtliche Delikt vor und in der Verhandlungen auf der Haager Kodifications Konferenz 1930 (Leipzig: Universitatsverlag von Robert Noske, 1932)

Anton-Hermann Chroust, The Rise of the Legal Profession in America, Volume 2: The Revolution and the Post-Revolutionary Era (Norman: University of Oklahoma Press, 1965)

Antony Anghie, "Finding the Peripheries: Sovereignty and Colonialism in Nineteenth-Century International Law," 40 Harvard International Law Journal 1 (1990)

Ari Mermelstein, Victoria Saker Woeste, Ethan Zadoff and Marc Galanter (eds.), Jews and the Law (New Orleans: Quid Pro Quo Books, 2014)

Arnulf Becker Lorca, "Codifying American International Law: The End of the Classical Legal Order" (unpublished paper on file with author)

"International Law in Latin America or Latin American International Law? Rise, Fall, and Retrieval of a Tradition of Legal Thinking and Political Imagination," 47(1) Harvard International Law Journal 283 (2006)

Mestizo International Law: A Global Intellectual History 1842–1933 (Cambridge: Cambridge University Press, 2015)

"Universal International Law: Nineteenth-Century Histories of Imposition and Appropriation," 51 Harvard Journal of International Law 475 (2010)

Arthur Donald Innes, England and the British Empire (New York: Macmillan, 1913)

Arthur J. Jacobson and Bernhard Schlink (eds.), Weimar: A Jurisprudence of Crisis (Berkeley: University of California Press, 2000)

Arthur Nussbaum, A Concise History of The Law of Nations (New York: Macmillan, 1947)

(ed.), Internationales Jahrbuch für Schiedsgerichtswesen in Zivil- und Handelssachen (Berlin: Carl Heymanns, 1926–1934)

"Rise and Decline of the Law-of-Nations Doctrine in the Conflict of Laws," 42 (2) Columbia Law Review 189–206 (1942)

Arthur P. Whitaker, The United States and the Independence of Latin America, 1800–1830 (New York: W. W. Norton & Co., 1964 [1941])

Assaf Likhovski, "Jurisprudence and Nationalism in the British Empire in the Early Twentieth Century: India, Egypt, and Palestine Compared," The English Historical Review (Forthcoming 2023), available online via SSRN https://ssrn.com/abstract=4475214 last visited July 20, 2023.

August Wilhelm Heffter, Beiträge zum deutschen Staats- und Fürstenrecht (Berlin: G. Reimer, 1829)

Das europäische Völkerrecht der Gegenwart (Berlin: Müller, 1844)

Aviva Chomsky, West Indian Workers and the United Fruit Company in Costa Rica, 1870–1940 (Baton Rouge: Louisiana State University Press, 1996)

Awalou Ouedraogo, "La neutralité et l'émergence du concept de due diligence en droit international. L'affaire de l'Alabama revisitée," 13(2) Journal of the History of International Law 307–346 (2011)

Bardo Fassbender, "The United Nations Charter as Constitution of the International Community," 36(3) Columbia Journal of Transnational Law 529 (1998)

Ben Juratowitch, "Diplomatic Protection of Shareholders," 81 British Yearbook of International Law 281 (2011)

Benedict Kingsbury, "A Grotian Tradition of Theory and Practice? Grotius, Law, and Moral Skepticism in the Thought of Hedley Bull," 17(1) Quarterly Law Review 3 (1997)

"Legal Positivism as Normative Politics: International Society, Balance of Power and Lassa Oppenheim's Positive International Law," 13(2) European Journal of International Law 401 (2002)

Benjamin Allen Coates, Legalist Empire: International Law and American Foreign Relations in the Early Twentieth Century (Oxford: Oxford University Press, 2016)

Transatlantic Advocates: American International Law and U.S. Foreign Relations, 1898–1919 (Doctoral Dissertation submitted to Columbia University, 2010)

"Upon the Neutral Rests the Trusteeship of International Law: Legal Advisers and American Unneutrality," in Johan den Hertog and Samuël Kruizinga (eds.), Caught in the Middle: Neutrals, Neutrality and the First World War 35 (Amsterdam: Amsterdam University Press, 2011)

Benjamin Brake and Peter J. Katzenstein, "The Transnational Spread of American Law: Legalization as Soft Power," Institute of International Law & Justice Presentation of June 2010

Benjamin Perley Poore, Congressional Directory, 1st ed. (Washington, DC: Government Printing Office, 1881)

Bennett Ostdiek and John Fabian Witt, "The Czar and the Slaves: Two Puzzles in the History of International Arbitration," 113 American Journal of International Law 535 (2019)

Bertram D. Hulen, Inside the Department of State (New York: McGraw Hill, 1939)

Betsy Baker Röben, Johann Caspar Bluntschli, Francis Lieber und das modern Völkerrecht 1861–1881 (Baden-Baden: Nomos, 2003)

"The Method Behind Bluntschli's 'Modern' International Law," 4(2) Journal of the History of International Law 249 (2002)

Bin Cheng, General Principles of Law as Applied by International Courts and Tribunals (London: Stevens, 1953)

Borzu Sabahi, Compensation and Restitution in Investor-State Arbitration (Oxford: Oxford University Press, 2011)

Brett Bowden, The Empire of Civilization: The Evolution of an Imperial Idea (Chicago: Chicago University Press, 2009)

Brian Loveman, No Higher Law: American Foreign Policy and the Western Hemisphere since 1776 (Chapel Hill: University of North Carolina, 2010)

Bruce Benson, "An Exploration of the Impact of Modern Arbitration Statutes on the Development of Arbitration in the United States," 11 Journal of Law, Economics and Organization 479 (1995)

Burdette Gibson Lewis, "Our Trade Relations with Latin America," 14(10) Journal of Political Economy 602 (1906)

Burton A. Landy, Victor Miguel Marroquín-Merino, Francisco Orrego Vicuña and Keith S. Rosenn, "In Memoriam – Francisco V. Garcia-Amador," 25 *University of Miami Inter-American Law Review* 1 (1993)

C. G. Roelofsen, "'The Jay Treaty and All That': Some Remarks on the Role of Arbitration in European Modern History and its 'Revival' in 1794," in Alfred H. A. Soons (ed.), International Arbitration: Past and Prospects 201–210 (Leiden: Martinus Nijhoff, 1990)

Camilo Barcia Trelles, Doctrina de Monroe y cooperación internacional (Madrid: Editorial Mundo Latino, 1931)

Carl Friedrich von Gerber, Das moderne Völkerrecht der civilisirten Staten (Nördlingen: C. H. Beckschen, 1872)

System des deutschen Privatrechts (Jena: Friedrich Mauke, 1848)

Carl Landauer, "The Ambivalences of Power: Launching the American Journal of International Law in an Era of Empire and Globalization," 20 Leiden Journal of International Law 325 (2007)

Carlos Calvo, "De la non-responsabilité de l'Etat à raison des pertes et dommages éprouvés par les étrangers en temps de troubles intérieurs ou de guerres civiles," 1 Revue de Droit International et de Legislation Comparée 417 (1869)

Derecho internacional teórico y práctico de Europa y América (Paris: D'Amyot, Durant & Pedoné-Lauriel, 1868)

Le droit international théorique et pratique (5th ed., Paris: A. Rousseau, 1896)
Carlos Wiesse, Reglas de Derecho Internacional Aplicables a las Guerras Civiles (Lima: Viuda Galland, 1893)
Carmen Tiburcio, The Human Rights of Aliens Under International and Comparative Law (The Hague: Kluwer, 2001)
Carnegie Endowment for International Peace, The International Conferences of American States, 1889–1928 (New York: Oxford University Press, 1931)
Cass R. Sunstein, "Social Norms and Social Roles," 96 Columbia Law Review 903 (1996)
Catherine A. Rogers, "Fit and Function in Legal Ethics: Developing a Code of Conduct for International Arbitration," 23 Michigan Journal of International Law 341 (2002)
Céline Spector "The Plan for Perpetual Peace: From Saint-Pierre to Rousseau," 39 (3) History of European Ideas 371 (2013)
Cesare P. R. Romano, Karen J. Alter and Chrisanthi Avgerou, The Oxford Handbook of International Adjudication (Oxford: Oxford University Press, 2013)
Charles A. and Mary R. Beard, The Rise of American Civilization (New York: Macmillan, 1927)
Charles I. Bevans, Treaties and Other International Agreements of the United States of America 1776–1949 (Washington, DC: Government Printing Office, 1971)
Charles Cheney Hyde, International Law Chiefly as Interpreted and Applied by the United States Vol. I (Boston: Little, Brown & Co., 1922)
"Review: The International Responsibility of States for Denial of Justice, by Alwyn V. Freeman," 34(2) American Journal of International Law 363 (1940)
Charles De Benedetti, "Peace History, in the American Manner," 18(1) The History Teacher 75–110 (1984)
Charles de Visscher, "La responsabilité des États," in Bibliotheca Visseriana II (Leyden: Brill, 1924)
Charles de Visscher, "Le déni de justice en droit international," 52 Recueil des cours 421 (1935)
Charles Francis Adams, Before and After the Treaty of Washington: The American Civil War and the War in the Transvaal (New York: New York Historical Society, 1902)
Jr., "A Chapter of Erie," 109 North American Review 38 (1869)
Charles G. Fenwick, International Law (2nd ed., New York: D. Appleton-Century Company, 1934)
Charles H. Brower, II, "The Functions and Limits of Arbitration and Judicial Settlement under Private and Public International Law," 18(2) Duke Journal of Comparative & International Law 259–309 (2008)

Charles Henry Alexandrowicz, The European–African Confrontation: A Study in Treaty Making (Leiden: Sijthoff, 1973)

Charles Lipson, Standing Guard: Protecting Foreign Capital in the Nineteenth and Twentieth Centuries (Berkeley: University of California Press, 1985)

Charles R. Morris, The Tycoons: How Andrew Carnegie, John D. Rockefeller, Jay Gould, and J. P. Morgan Invented the American Supereconomy (New York: Times Books, 2005)

Charles S. Campbell, The Transformation of American Foreign Relations 1865–1900 (New York: Harper & Row, 1976)

Charles Salomon, L'occupation des territoires sans maître. Études de droit international (Paris: Giard, 1889)

Charlotte Ku, "Forging a Multilayered System of Global Governance," in R. St. J. Macdonald and D. M. Johnston (eds.), Towards World Constitutionalism (The Hague: Brill, 2005)

Chester Lloyd Jones, The Consular Services of the United States: Its History and Activities (Philadelphia: The John C. Winston Co., 1906)

Chester Squire Phinney, Francis Lieber's Influence on American Thought (Philadelphia: International Printing Company, 1918)

Chittharanjan Felix Amerasinghe, Local Remedies in International Law (2nd ed., Cambridge: Cambridge University Press, 2004)

Chnxi Tang, Imagining World Order: Literature and International Law in Early Modern Europe, 1500–1800 (Ithaca: Cornell University Press, 2018)

Christian G. Samito, Changes in Law and Society during the Civil War and Reconstruction (Carbondale: Southern Illinois University Press, 2009)

Christian J. Tams and James Sloan (eds.), The Development of International Law by the International Court of Justice (Oxford: Oxford University, 2013)

Christine Chinkin and Freya Baetens (eds.), Sovereignty, Statehood and State Responsibility: Essays in Honour of James Crawford 287 (Cambridge: Cambridge University Press, 2015)

Christine Gray, Judicial Remedies in International Law (Oxford: Oxford University Press, 1987)

Christoph Frei, Hans J. Morgenthau: An Intellectual Biography (Baton Rouge: Louisiana State University Press, 2001)

Christopher A. Casey, National Abroad: Globalization, Individual Rights, and the Making of Modern International Law (Cambridge: Cambridge University Press, 2020)

Christopher R. Rossi, Whiggish International Law: Elihu Root, the Monroe Doctrine, and International Law in the Americas (Leiden: Brill, 2019)

Christopher Szabla, "A New Foundation for Freedom of Movement in an Age of Sovereign Control: The Liberal Jurisprudence of August Wilhelm Heffter," 40(1) Law and History Review 63 (2022)

Christopher Whytock. "From International Law and International Relations to Law and World Politics," Oxford Research Encyclopedia of Politics, 2018; UC Irvine School of Law Research Paper No. 2018-29, available at: https://ssrn.com/abstract=3170066

Clement L. Johnson, "The Public Career of Cave Johnson," 10 Tennessee Historical Quarterly 195 (1951).

Clyde Eagleton, "Denial of Justice in International Law," 22 American Journal of International Law 538 (1928)

"Measures of Damages in International Law," 39 Yale Law Journal 52 (1929)

The Responsibility of States in International Law (New York: New York University Press, 1928)

Craig B. Hollander, "The Citizen Complains: Federal Compensation for Property Lost in the War of 1812," 38(4) Law and History Review 659 (2020)

Crawford Morrison Bishop, International Arbitral Procedure (Baltimore: King Bros., 1930, based on PhD, Columbia University 1930)

Cynthia Nicoletti, "The American Civil War as a Trial by Battle," 28(1) Law and History Review 71 (2010)

D. Brian King and Rahim Moloo, "International Arbitrators as Lawmakers," 46 International Law and Politics 891 (2014)

Daniel J. Hellebusch, "From Imperial to International Law: Protecting Foreign Expectations in the Early United States," 65 UCLA Law Review 142 (2018)

David Armitage, "The Declaration of Independence and International Law," 59(1) William and Mary Quarterly 39 (2002).

David Armstrong (ed.), Routledge Handbook of International Law 141 (New York: Routledge, 2009)

David D. Caron, "The ILC Articles on State Responsibility: The Paradoxical Relationship between Form and Authority," 96 American Journal of International Law 857 (2002)

David Dudley Field, Draft Outline of an International Code (New York: Baker, Voorhis & Co., 1872)

David Golove and Daniel Hulsebosch, "The Law of Nations and the Constitution: An Early Modern Perspective" (NYU Sch. of Law Pub. Law & Legal Theory Research Paper Series, Working Paper No. 18-45, 2018)

David J. Bederman, "The Foundations of Law: World Law Transcendent," 54 Emory Law Journal 53 (2005)

David Kennedy, "The Move to Institutions," 8(5) Cardozo Law Review 841 (1987)

"The Twentieth-Century Discipline of International Law in the United States," in Austin Sarat, Bryant Garth and Robert A. Kagan (eds.), Looking Back at Law's Century 386 (Ithaca: Cornell University Press, 2002)

David W. Kennedy, "Background Noise? - The Politics Beneath Global Governance," 21 Harvard International Law Review 52 (1999)

David S. Landes, "Some Thoughts on the Nature of Economic Imperialism," 21(4) The Journal of Economic History 496 (1961)

The Wealth and Poverty of Nations: Why Some Are So Rich and Some So Poor (New York: W. W. Norton, 1998)

David Schneiderman, Investment Law's Alibis: Colonialism, Imperialism, Debt and Development (Cambridge: Cambridge University Press, 2022)

Derek Roebuck, "Sources for the History of Arbitration: A Bibliographical Introduction," 14(3) Arbitration International 237 (1998)

Derek Taylor, Don Pacifico: The Acceptable Face of Gunboat Diplomacy (London: Vallentine-Mitchell, 2008)

Dino Kritsiotis, "On the Possibilities of and for Persistent Objection," 21 Duke Journal of Comparative & International Law 121 (2010)

Dionisio Anzilotti, Corso di diritto internazionale (3rd ed., Rome: Athenaeum, 1928)

"La responsabilité internationale des États à raison des dommages soufferts par des étrangers," 13 Revue générale de droit international public 285 (1906)

Teoria generale della responsabilità dello Stato nel diritto internazionale. Parte prima, Il problema della responsabilità di diritto internazionale (Florence: F. lumachi, 1902)

Dirk Hanschel, "German Federalist Thinking and International Law," 4 Goettingen Journal of International Law 2 (2012)

Donald Shea, The Calvo Clause: A Problem of Inter-American and International Law and Diplomacy (Minneapolis: University of Minnesota Press, 1955)

Doreen Lustig, "The Business of International Law: International Legal Attitudes Toward the Business Enterprise, 1870–1954," paper presented to IILJ International Legal Theory Colloquium, Spring 2012

"The Enduring Charter: Corporations, States and International Law," in Melissa J. Durkee (ed.), The Law and Logics of Attribution: Constructing the Identity and Responsibility of States and Firms (Cambridge University Press, forthcoming)

Doris W. Dashew, "The Story of an Illusion: The Plan to Trade Alabama Claims for Canada," 15(4) Civil War History 332 (1969).

Douglas A. Irwin, "Multilateral and Bilateral Trade Policies in the World Trading System: An Historical Perspective," in Jaime De Melo, Arvind Panagariya (eds.), New Dimensions in Regional Integration 90-127 (Cambridge: Cambridge University Press, 1993)

Duncan Kennedy, Critique of Adjudication (Fin de Siècle) (Cambridge, MA: Harvard University Press, 1998)

Edmond Pittard, La protection des nationaux à l'étranger (Geneva: W. Kündig, 1896)

Edmund Morris, "A Matter of Extreme Urgency: Theodore Roosevelt, Wilhelm II, and the Venezuela Crisis of 1902," 55(2) Naval War College Review 73–85 (2002)

Edward Digby Baltzell, Puritan Boston and Quaker Philadelphia (New Brunswick: Transaction Publishers, 1996)

Edward Everett, "Stability and Progress: Remarks Made on the 4th of July, 1853, in Faneuil Hall," in Edward Everett (ed.), Orations and Speeches on Various Occasions, Volume 3 (Boston: Little Brown & Co., 1859)

Edwin Borchard, "Theories of Governmental Responsibility in Tort," 28 Columbia Law Review 577 (1928)

Edwin M. Borchard, The Diplomatic Protection of Citizens Abroad or The Law of International Claims (New York: The Banks Law Publishing Company, 1915)

"Recent Developments in International and Municipal Law," 10 Law Library Journal 21 (1917)

"'Responsibility of States,' at the Hague Codification Conference," 24 American Journal of International Law 517 (1930)

"Reviewed Work: Das Völkerrechtliche Delikt, by Karl Strupp," 15(1) American Journal of International Law 146 (1921)

"Tort Liability of the State," 12(1) Journal of Comparative Legislation and International Law 1 (1930)

Eleanor Louisa Lord, "International Arbitration," 2(4) Annals of the American Academy of Political and Social Science (1892)

Eliav Lieblich and Yoram Shachar, "Cosmopolitanism at a Crossroads: Hersch Lauterpacht and the Israeli Declaration of Independence," 84 British Yearbook of International Law 1 (2014)

Elihu Lauterpacht, The Life of Hersch Lauterpacht (Cambridge: Cambridge University Press, 2010)

Elihu Root, "The Basis of Protection to Citizens Residing Abroad," Opening Address as President of the American Society of International Law, at the Fourth Annual Meeting of the Society in Washington, April 28, 1910, reproduced in 4 American Journal of International Law 517 (1910)

"The Need of Popular Understanding of International Law," 1 American Journal of International Law 1 (1907)

Ellen C. Collier, Instances of the Use of Force by United States' Forces Abroad, 1783–1993 (Washington, DC: Congressional Research Services, 1993)

Emer de Vattel, Le Droit des Gens ou Principes de la Loi Naturelle, à Leiden aux Dépens de la Compagnie I (London: Tutior, 1758)

The Law of Nations, or Principles of Natural Law Applied to the Conduct and Affairs of Nations and Sovereigns (Charles Ghequiere Fenwick, trans.) (Washington, DC: Carnegie, 1916 [1758])

Emilio Brusa, "Responsabilité internationale des États à raison des dommages causés sur leur territoire à la personne et aux biens des étrangers" 33 Anmiaire de l'lnstitut de droit international 330 (1927)

Emilio Brusa and Ludwig von Bar (Rapporteurs), "Règlement sur la responsabilité des Etats à raison des dommages soufferts par des étrangers en cas d'émeute, d'insurrection ou de guerre civile," 18 Annuaire de l'Institut de droit international 254 (1900).

Emmanuelle Jouannet, Emer de Vattel et l'émergence du droit international classique (Paris: Pedone, 1998)

Erasmus Peshine Smith, A Manual of Political Economy (Philadelphia: Baird, 1872)

Eric Bruggink, "The 'Alabama' Claims," 57 The Alabama Lawyer 339 (1996)

Eric Hobsbawm, The Age of Empire: 1875–1914 (New York: Vintage, 1989)

Eric T. L. Love, Race over Power: Racism and US Imperialism, 1865–1900 (Chapel Hill: University of North Carolina Press, 2004)

Erich Kaufmanns, Das Wesen des Völkerrechts und die clausula rebus sic stantibus (Tübingen: Mohr, 1911)

Ernest Nys, "The Codification of International Law," 5 American Journal of International Law 871–900 (1911)

Eugene Kantorovich, "The Constitutionality of International Courts: The Forgotten Precedent of Slave Trade Tribunals," 158(39) University of Pennsylvania Law Review 39–115 (2009)

Eugene Schuyler, American Diplomacy and the Furtherance of Commerce, Vol. III (New York: Scribner, 1886)

Eyal Benvenisti, "The Origins of the Concept of Belligerent Occupation," 26(3) Law and History Review 621 (2008)

F. Peter Phillips, "Ancient and Comely Order: The Use and Disuse of Arbitration by New York Quakers," 2016 Journal of Dispute Resolution 81 (2016)

F. R. Coudert, "Arbitration," 87 Harper's Monthly 918–927 (1893)

Fareed Zakaria, From Wealth to Power: The Unusual Origins of America's World Role (Princeton: Princeton University Press, 1998)

Federica Paddeu and Christian Tams, "Dithering, Trickling Down, and Encoding: Concluding Thoughts on the 'ILC Articles at 20' Symposium," EJIL: Talk! August 9, 2021

"The ILC Articles at 20: Introduction to the Symposium," EJIL: Talk! August 2, 2021

Felix Lange, "Between Systematization and Expertise for Foreign Policy: The Practice-Oriented Approach in Germany's International Legal Scholarship (1920–1980)," 28(2) European Journal of International Law 535 (2017)

"Conference Report: Lauterpacht and Beyond: Jewish/German Authorship and the History of International Law," 13 German Law Journal 793 (2012)

Fernando Lusa Bordin, "Reflections of Customary International Law: The Authority of Codification Conventions and ILC Draft Articles in International Law," 63 (3) International and Comparative Law Quarterly 535 (2014)

Filip Batselé, "Foreign Investors of the World, Unite! The International Association for the Promotion and Protection of Private Foreign Investments (APPI) 1958–1968" European Journal of International Law

(2023 forthcoming), available online at https://doi.org/10.1093/ejil/chad017 last visited July 5, 2023.
Foreign Office, "The Right Hon. Sir Edward Thornton, K.C.B.," in Foreign Office, Diplomatic and Consular Sketches (London: W. H. Allen & Co., 1883)
Frances Kellor, American Arbitration: Its History, Functions and Achievements (New York: Harper & Brothers, 1948).
Francesco Messineo, "Is there an Italian Conception of International Law," 2(4) Cambridge Journal of International and Comparative Law 879 (2013)
Francis A. Boyle, "American Foreign Policy toward International Law and Organizations: 1898–1917," 6 Loyola International & Comparative Law Review 185 (1983)
Francis Anthony Boyle, Foundations of World Order: The Legalist Approach to International Relations (1898–1922) (Durham: Duke University Press, 1999)
Francis J. Weber, "The Pious Fund of the Californias," 43(1) Hispanic American Historical Review 78 (1963)
Francis Lieber, Essays on Property and Labour: As Connected with Natural Law and the Constitution of Society (New York: Harper & Brothers, 1841)
The Miscellaneous Writings of Francis Lieber (Philadelphia: J. B. Lippincott & Co., 1881)
On the Idea of the Latin Race and Its Real Value in International Law – Fr. translation also, (1871), Special Collections, The Johns Hopkins University, Container: 2. Francis Lieber papers, MS-0071. Special Collections.
Francis Lieber Papers, American History Division, Huntington Library
Special Collections, The Johns Hopkins University
Francis Wharton, A Digest of the International Law of the United States, Taken from Documents Issued by Presidents and Secretaries of State, and From Decisions of Federal Courts and Opinions of Attorney-General (Washington, DC: Government Printing Office, 1886)
A Treatise on the Law of Negligence (2nd ed., Philadelphia: Kay and Brother, 1878)
Francisco Javier Peñas Esteban, "Standard of civilization: The history of international relations," 40 Relaciones Internacionales 171 (2019)
Francisco Victor García Amador, The Academic Discussion Concerning the Existence of an American International Law (1944) (unpublished MA thesis, Harvard Law School)
The Exploitation and Conservation of the Resources of the Sea (1960) (doctoral dissertation submitted to Columbia Law School)
"Memorandum on the question of State Responsibility," UN Doc. A/CN.4/80
"State Responsibility in the Light of the New Trends of International Law," 49 American Journal of International Law 339 (1955)
"State Responsibility: Some New Problems," 94(2) Recueil des cours 365 (1958)
Francisco Victor García Amador, Louis B. Sohn and R. Baxter, Recent Codification of the Law of State Responsibility for Injuries to Aliens (Leiden: Sijthoff, 1975)

Franciscus de Vitoria, De Indis et de Ivre Belli. Reflectiones, ed. Ernest Nys, Carnegie Institute of Washington (Washington, DC: Gibson Brothers, 1917)

Frank Freidel, Francis Lieber: Nineteenth-Century Liberal (Baton Rouge: Louisiana State University Press, 1947)

Frank Griffith Dawson, "The Influence of Andres Bello on Latin-American Perceptions of Non-intervention and State Responsibility," 57 British Yearbook of International Law 253 (1987)

Frank Griffith Dawson and Ivan L. Head, International Law, National Tribunals, and the Rights of Aliens (Syracuse: Syracuse University Press, 1971)

Franz von Holtzendorff, Handbuch des Völkerrechts (Berlin: C. Habel, 1885)

Frédéric Mégret, "Mixed Claim Commissions and the Once Centrality of the Protection of Aliens," in Ignacio de la Rasilla and Jorge E. Viñuales (eds.), Experiments in International Adjudication: Historical Accounts 127 (Cambridge: Cambridge University Press, 2019)

Frederick Edwin Smith (The Right Honourable Lord Birkenhead), International Law (4th ed., London: J. M. Dent & Sons, Ltd, 1911)

Frederick Pollock, "Sources of International Law," 2 Columbia Law Review 511 (1902)

Frederick Sherwood Dunn, The Protection of Nationals: A Study in the Application of International Law (Baltimore: Johns Hopkins University Press, 1932)

Frederick Waymouth Gibbs, Recognition: A Chapter from the History of the North American & South American States (London: W. Ridgway, 1863)

G. Edward White, American Legal History: A Very Short Introduction (New York: Oxford University Press, 2013)

Tort Law in America: An Intellectual History (New York: Oxford University Press, 1980)

Gaillard Hunt, The Department of State of the United States: Its History and Functions (New Haven: Yale University Press, 1914)

Gary B. Born, International Arbitration: Cases and Materials (Alphen aan den Rijn: Kluwer, 2010)

Geneviève Viney, 'Responsabilité,' 35 Arch Phil de droit 277 (1990)

Georg Jellinek, Allgemeine Staatslehre (Berlin: O. Häring, 1900)

Die Lehre von den Staatenverbindungen (Vienna: A Hölder, 1882)

Die rechtliche Natur der Staatenverträge. Ein Beitrag zur juristischen Construktion des Völkerrechts (Vienna: Hölder, 1880)

System der subjektiven öffentlichen Rechte (Freiburg: J. C. B. Mohr, 1892)

Georg Nolte, "From Dionisio Anzilotti to Roberto Ago: The Classical International Law of State Responsibility and the Traditional Primacy of a Bilateral Conception of Inter-State Relations," 13(5) European Journal of International Law 1083 (2002)

Georg Wilhelm Friedrich Hegel, Die Philosophie des Rechts: Die Mitschriften Wannenmann (Heidelberg 1817/18) und Homeyer (Berlin 1818/19), edited and annotated by Karl Heinz Ilting (Stuttgart: Klett-Cotta, 1983)

Georg Schwarzenberger, "Present-Day Relevance of the Jay Treaty Arbitrations," 53 Notre Dame Law Review 715 (1977–1978)

"The Protection of British Property Abroad," 5(1) Current Legal Problems 295 (1952)

'The Standard of Civilisation in International Law,' in George W. Keeton and Georg Schwarzenberger (eds.), Current Legal Problems (London: Stevens & Sons, 1955)

George A. Finch, "The American Society of International Law 1906–1956," 50 American Journal of International Law 293–312 (1956)

George A. Glynn (ed.), Foreign Constitutions: Comprising the Constitution of Argentina, Belgium, Brazil (empire and Republic), Columbia, Ecuador, France, Germany, Honduras, Japan, Mexico, Prussia, Switzerland and Venezuela Part II, Vol. 3 (Albany: Argus, 1894)

George L. Ridgeway, Merchants of Peace: Twenty Years of Business Diplomacy through the International Chamber of Commerce 1919–1938 (New York: Columbia University Press, 1938)

Georges Abi–Saab, "Fragmentation or Unification: Some Concluding Remarks," 31 NYU Journal of International Law & Politics 919 (1999)

Georges Berlia, "Jurisprudence, des tribunaux internationaux en ce qui concerne leur competence," 88 Recueil de cours 105 (1955)

Gerald Fitzmaurice, "Legal Advisers and Foreign Affairs," 59 American Journal of International Law 72 (1965)

Gerald G. Eggert, Richard Olney: Evolution of a Statesman (University Park: Pennsylvania State University Press, 1974)

Gerald G. Fitzmaurice, "The Meaning of the Term 'Denial of Justice,'" 13 British Yearbook of International Law 93–114 (1932)

Gerrit Walter Gong, The Standard of 'Civilization' in International Society (Oxford: Clarendon Press, 1984)

Gerry Simpson, Great Powers and Outlaw States: Unequal Sovereigns in the International Legal Order (Cambridge: Cambridge University Press, 2004)

Gilbert Gidel, Cours de droit international (Paris: Panthéon-Assas/LGDJ, 1999 [1929])

Glanville Williams, "International Law and the Controversy Concerning the Word 'Law,'" 22 British Yearbook of International Law 146 (1945)

"The Logic of 'Exceptions,'" 47 Cambridge Law Journal 261 (1988)

Gonzalo de Quesada, Arbitration in Latin America (Rotterdam: Wyt, 1907)

Graham H. Stuart, The Department of State: A History of Its Organization, Procedure, and Personnel (New York: Macmillan, 1949)

Gráinne de Búrca, Robert O. Keohane and Charles Sabel, "New Modes of Pluralist Global Governance," 45(3) New York University Journal of International Law & Politics 723 (2013)

Green Haywood Hackworth, Digest of International Law (Washington, DC: Government Printing Office, 1940–1944)

"Responsibility of States for Damages caused in their Territory to the Person or Property of Foreigners," 24 American Journal of International Law 500 (1930)
Green Haywood Hackworth and Margorie M. Whiteman, Digest of International Law (Washington, DC: Government Printing Office, 1963–1973)
Greg Grandin, Empire's Workshop: Latin America, the United States, and the Rise of the New Imperialism (New York: Henry Holt and Co., 2007)
"The Liberal Traditions in the Americas: Rights, Sovereignty, and the Origins of Liberal Multilateralism," 117(1) American Historical Review 68–91 (2012)
Gregg Jones, Honor in the Dust: Theodore Roosevelt, War in the Philippines, and the Rise and Fall of America's Imperial Dream (New York: New American Library, 2012)
Gregory Shaffer, Emerging Powers and the World Trading System: The Past and Future of International Economic Law (Cambridge: Cambridge University Press, 2021)
"Theorizing Transnational Legal Ordering," 12 Annual Review of Law and Social Science 231 (2016)
Guerra Everett, "International Arbitration in the Americas," 17 New York University Law Quarterly Review 617 (1939–1940)
Gustavo Guerrero, "Questionnaire No. 4: Responsibility of States for Damage Done in their Territories to the Person or Property of Foreigners," 20 American Journal of International Law Supplement 176 (1926)
H. B. Jacobini, A Study of the Philosophy of International Law as Seen in Works of Latin American Writers (The Hague: Martinus Nijhoff, 1954)
H. Duncan Hall, "The International Frontier," 42(1) American Journal of International Law 42–65 (1948)
Hamilton Fish Papers, American History Division, Huntington Library
Hamilton Fish Papers, Manuscript Division, Library of Congress, Washington, DC
Hanan Mazeh, "Gentile Land Ownership in the Land of Israel: The Palestinian Talmud in Light of Biblical Models and Roman Law," The Jewish Quarterly Review (2023, forthcoming, article on file with author)
Hans Joachim Morgenthau, "An Intellectual Autobiography," 15(2) Society 63 (1978)
Die internationale Rechtspflege. Ihr Wesen und ihre Grenzen (Leipzig: Noske, 1929)
"Positivism, Functionalism and International Law," 34 American Journal of International Law 266 (1940)
Hans Kelsen, Allgemeine Staatslehre (Berlin: Springer, 1925)
"The Essence of International Law," in Karl W. Deutsch and Stanley Hofffmann (eds.), The Relevance of International Law Essays in Honor of Leo Gross (transl. Max Knight, Cambridge: Schenkman, 1968)
General Theory of Law and State (Anders Wedberg, trans., Cambridge, MA: Harvard University Press, 1945)

Hauptprobleme der Staatsrechtslehre entwickelt aus der Lehre vom Rechtssatze (Tübingen: Mohr, 1911)

Das Problem der Souveränität und die Theorie des Völkerrechts (Tübingen: Mohr, 1920)

Reine Rechtslehre (Wien: Deuticke, 1934)

Die Staatslehre des Dante Alighieri (Vienna: F. Deuticke, 1905)

"Théorie du droit international public," 84 Recueil des cours 1 (1953–III)

"Tributes to Sir Hersch Lauterpacht," 10 International and Comparative Law Quarterly (1961)

Hans Neufeld, The International Protection of Private Creditors from the Treaties of Westphalia to the Congress of Vienna (1648–1815): A Contribution to the History of the Law of Nations 5 (Leiden: Sijthoff, 1971)

Hans W. Spiegel, "Origin and Development of Denial of Justice," 32 American Journal of International Law 63–81 (1938)

Hans Wehberg, The Problem of an International Court of Justice (Charles G. Fenwick, trans., Oxford: Clarendon, 1918)

Harmodio Arias, "The Non-Liability of States for Damages Suffered by Foreigners in the Course of a Riot, an Insurrection, or a Civil War," 7(4) American Journal of International Law 724 (1913)

Harold F. Peterson, "Edward A. Hopkins: A Pioneer Promoter in Paraguay," 22(2) The Hispanic American Historical Review 245 (1942)

Harvard Law School, Convention on the international responsibility of states for injuries to aliens; draft no. 12 / with explanatory notes by Louis B. Sohn and R. R. Baxter, reporters (Cambridge: Harvard Law School, 1961)

"Draft convention on 'Responsibility of States for Damage Done in Their Territory to the Person or Property of Foreigners,'" 23 American Journal of International Law Special Supplement 133 (1929)

Hatsue Shinohara, US International Lawyers in the Interwar Years: A Forgotten Crusade (Cambridge: Cambridge University Press, 2012)

Heinhard Steiger, "From the International Law of Christianity to the International Law of the World Citizen: Reflections on the Formation of the Epochs of the History of International Law," 3 Journal of the History of International Law 180–193 (2001)

Heinrich Heine, reprinted in Frederic Ewen (ed.), *Heroic Imagination: The Creative Genius of Europe from Waterloo (1815) to the Revolution of 1848* (Edinburgh: Edinburgh University Press, 2004)

Heinrich Lammasch, Die lehre von der schiedsgerichtsbarkeit in ihrem ganzen umfange (Stuttgart: W. Kohlhammer, 1914)

Heinrich Triepel, "Die Vereinigung der Deutschen Staatsrechtslehrer," 43 Archiv des öffentlichen Rechts 349 (Tübingen: Mohr, 1922)

Unitarismus und Föderalismus im deutschen Reiche: Eine staatsrechtliche und politische Studie (Tübingen: Mohr, 1907)

Völkerrecht und Landesrecht (Leipzig: C. L. Hirschfeld, 1899)
Vom Stil des Rechts: Beiträge zu einer Ästhetik des Rechts (Heidelberg: Schneider, 1947)
Henri La Fontaine, Pasicrisie Internationale: Histoire Documentaire des Arbitrages Internationaux (1794–1900) (Berne: Imprimerie Stampelli & CIE, 1902)
Henry Adams, "The Session," North American Review 29–62 (July 1870)
Henry Salmon Fraser, "A Sketch of the History of International Arbitration," 11 Cornell Law Quarterly 179 (1925–1926)
Henry Sumner, "Opinion Impartiale sur la Question de l'Alabama et sur la Maniére de la Résoudre," 2 Revue de droit international et de législation comparé 452–479 (1870)
Henry Wheaton, *Elements of International Law* (4th ed., London: Stevens & Sons Ltd., 1904)
Elements of International Law (8th ed., Richard Dana, ed., Philadelphia: Carey, Lea & Blanchard, 1866 [1836])
History of the Law of Nations in Europe and America: From the Earliest Times to the Treaty of Washington (New York: Gould, Banks & Company, 1845)
Henry William Brands, What America Owes the World: The Struggle for the Soul of Foreign Policy (Cambridge: Cambridge University Press, 1998)
Herbert Lionel Adolphus Hart, The Concept of Law (Oxford: Oxford University Press, 1961)
Herman Walker, Jr., "Treaties for the Encouragement and Protection of Foreign Investment: Present United States Practice," 5 American Journal of International Law 229 (1956)
Hersch Lauterpacht, The Function of Law in the International Community (Oxford: Clarendon Press, 1933)
"The Grotian Tradition in International Law," 23 British Yearbook of International Law 1 (1946)
Oppenheim's International Law (8th ed., London: Longmans, Green & Co., 1955)
Private Law Sources and Analogies of International Law: With Special Reference to International Arbitration (London: Longmans, Green & Co., 1927)
Recognition in International Law (Cambridge: Cambridge University Press, 1947)
"Règles générales du droit de la paix," 62 Recueil des cours 99 (1937)
Survey of International Law in relation to the Work of Codification of the International Law Commission: preparatory work within the purview of article 18, paragraph 1, of the Statute of the International Law Commission, U.N. Doc. A/CN.4/Rev.1 (1949)
"La théorie des différends non justiciables en droit international," 34 Recueil des cours 493 (1930–IV)

Hersch Lauterpacht and C. H. M. Waldock (eds.), *The Basis of Obligation in International Law and other Papers by the late James Leslie Brierly* (Oxford: Oxford University Press, 1958)

Horacio A. Grigera-Naon, "Arbitration and Latin America: Progress and Setbacks," 21 Arbitration International 27 (2005)

Hugo Grotius, De jure belli ac pacis (Oxford: Clarendon: 1926 [1625])

Hunter Miller (ed.), Treaties and Other International Acts of the United States of America (Washington, DC: Government Printing Office, 1931)

Ian Brownlie, "The History of State Responsibility," in R. G. Girardot, H. Ridder, M. L. Sarin, and T. Schiller (eds.), New Directions in International Law: Essays in Honour of Wolfgang Abendroth –Festschrift zu seinem 75. Geburtstag 19 (Frankfurt: Campus, 1982)

International Law (Oxford: Oxford University Press, 1966)

System of the Law of Nations: State Responsibility, Part I (Oxford: Clarendon Press, 1983)

Ian Hurd, "The Empire of International Legalism," 32 Ethics & International Affairs 265 (2018)

ICRC, "Geneva Convention Commemoration," 42 International Review of the Red Cross 466 (1964)

Ingo J. Hueck, "Pragmatism, Positivism and Hegelianism in the Nineteenth Century. August Wilhelm Heffter's Notion of Public International Law," in Michael Stolleis and Masaharu Yanagihara (eds.), East Asian Perspectives on International Law 42 (Baden-Baden: Nomos, 2004)

International Law Commission, Reports of the Special Rapporteur on state responsibility:

Report of the Special Rapporteur, Mr. F. V. García-Amador (8th session of the ILC (1956)), A/CN.4/96 (in Yearbook, 1956, vol. II).

Second report of the Special Rapporteur, Mr. F. V. García-Amador (9th session of the ILC (1957)), A/CN.4/106 (in Yearbook, 1957, vol. II)

Third report of the Special Rapporteur, Mr. F. V. García-Amador (10th session of the ILC (1958)), A/CN.4/111 (in Yearbook, 1958, vol. II)

Fourth report of the Special Rapporteur, Mr. F. V. García-Amador (11th session of the ILC (1959)), A/CN.4/119 (in Yearbook, 1959, vol. II)

Fifth report of the Special Rapporteur, Mr. F. . García-Amador (12th session of the ILC (1960)), A/CN.4/125 (in Yearbook, 1960, vol. II)

Sixth report of the Special Rapporteur, Mr. F. V. García-Amador (13th session of the ILC (1961)), A/CN.4/134 and Add.1 (in Yearbook, 1961, vol. II)

First report of the Special Rapporteur, Mr. Roberto Ago (21st session of the ILC (1969)), A/CN.4/217, Corr.1 and Add.1 (in Yearbook, 1969, vol. II) and Add.2 (in Yearbook, 1971, vol. II(1))

Second report of the Special Rapporteur, Mr. Roberto Ago (22nd session of the ILC (1970)), A/CN.4/233 (in Yearbook, 1970, vol. II)

Third report of the Special Rapporteur, Mr. Roberto Ago (23rd session of the ILC (1971)), A/CN.4/246 and Add.1–3 (in Yearbook, 1971, vol. II(1))

Fourth report of the Special Rapporteur, Mr. Roberto Ago (24th session of the ILC (1972)), A/CN.4/264 and Add.1 (in Yearbook, 1972, vol. II)

Fifth report of the Special Rapporteur, Mr. Roberto Ago (28th session of the ILC (1976)), A/CN.4/291, Add.1 and Add.2 (in Yearbook, 1976, vol. II(1))

Sixth report of the Special Rapporteur, Mr. Roberto Ago (29th session of the ILC (1977)), A/CN.4/302 and Add.1–3 (in Yearbook, 1977, vol. II(1))

Seventh Report of the Special Rapporteur, Mr. Roberto Ago (30th session of the ILC (1978)), A/CN.4/307, Add.1–2 and Add.2/Corr.1 (in Yearbook, 1978, vol. II(1))

Eighth Report of the Special Rapporteur, Mr. Roberto Ago (31st session of the ILC (1979)), A/CN.4/318 and Add.1–4, Add.5–7 and Add.8 (in Yearbook, 1979, vol. II(1))

Eighth Report (Addendum) of the Special Rapporteur, Mr. Roberto Ago (32nd session of the ILC (1980)), A/CN.4/318/Add.5–7 (in Yearbook, 1980, vol. II(1))

Preliminary Report of the Special Rapporteur, Mr. Willem Riphagen (32nd session of the ILC (1980)), A/CN.4/330 and Corr.1–3 (in Yearbook, 1980, vol. II(1))

Second Report of the Special Rapporteur, Mr. Willem Riphagen (33rd session of ILC (1981)), A/CN.4/344 and Corr.1–2 (in Yearbook, 1981, vol. II(1))

Third Report of the Special Rapporteur, Mr. Willem Riphagen (34th session of ILC (1982)), A/CN.4/354, Corr.1, Add.1 and Add.2 (in Yearbook, 1982, vol. II(1))

Fourth report of the Special Rapporteur, Mr. Willem Riphagen (35th session of the ILC (1983)), A/CN.4/366, Add.1 and Add.1/Corr.1 (in Yearbook, 1983, vol. II(1))

Fifth Report of the Special Rapporteur, Mr. Willem Riphagen (36th session of the ILC (1984)), A/CN.4/380 and Corr.1 (in Yearbook, 1984, vol. II (1))

Sixth Report of the Special Rapporteur, Mr. Willem Riphagen (37th session of the ILC (1985)), A/CN.4/389 and Corr.1 (in Yearbook, 1985, vol. II (1)

Seventh Report of the Special Rapporteur, Mr. Willem Riphagen (38th session of the ILC (1986)), A/CN.4/397, Corr.1–2, Add.1 and Add.1/Corr.1 (in Yearbook, 1986, vol. II(1))

Preliminary Report of the Special Rapporteur, Mr. Gaetano Arangio–Ruiz (40th session of the ILC (1988)), A/CN.4/41, Corr.1–2, Add.1 and Add.1/Corr.1–2 (in Yearbook, 1988, vol. II(1))

Second Report of the Special Rapporteur, Mr. Gaetano Arangio–Ruiz (41st session of the ILC (1989)), A/CN.4/425, Corr.1, Add.1 and Add.1/Corr.1 (in Yearbook, 1989, vol. II(1))

Third Report of the Special Rapporteur, Mr. Gaetano Arangio–Ruiz (43rd session of the ILC (1991)), A/CN.4/440 and Add.1 (in Yearbook, 1991, vol. II(1))

Fourth Report of the Special Rapporteur, Mr. Gaetano Arangio–Ruiz (44th session of the ILC (1992)), A/CN.4/444, Add.1, Corr.1 and Add.2–3 (in Yearbook, 1992, vol. II(1))

Fifth Report of the Special Rapporteur, Mr. Gaetano Arangio–Ruiz (45th session of the ILC (1993)), A/CN.4/453, Add.1, Add.1/Corr.1–3 and Add.2–3

Sixth Report of the Special Rapporteur, Mr. Gaetano Arangio-Ruiz (46th session of the ILC (1994)), A/CN.4/46, Add.1, Add.2 and Add.2/Corr.1 and Add.3

Seventh Report of the Special Rapporteur, Mr. Gaetano Arangio-Ruiz (47th session of the ILC (1995)), A/CN.4/469, Corr.1, Add.1 and Add.2

Eighth Report of the Special Rapporteur, Mr. Gaetano Arangio-Ruiz (48th session of the ILC (1996)), A/CN.4/476, Corr.1 and Add.1

First report of the Special Rapporteur, Mr. James Crawford (50th session of the ILC (1998)), A/CN.4/490, Add.1, Add.2, Add.2/Corr.1, Add.3, Add.4, Add.4/Corr.1, Add.5, Add.6, Add.7 and Add.7/Corr.1

Second report of the Special Rapporteur, Mr. James Crawford (51st session of the ILC (1999)), A/CN.4/498, Add.1, Add.2, Add.3 and Add.4

Third report of the Special Rapporteur, Mr. James Crawford (52nd session of the ILC (2000)), A/CN.4/507, Add.1, Add.1/Corr.1, Add.2, Add.2/Corr.1, Add.2/Corr.2, Add.3, Add.3/Corr.1 and Add.4

Fourth report of the Special Rapporteur, Mr. James Crawford (53rd session of the ILC (2001)), A/CN.4/517 and Add.1

International Law Commission, "United Nations Documents on the Development and Codification of International Law," Supplement to 41(4) *American Journal of International Law Special Supplement* 36 (1947)

Responsibility of States for Internationally Wrongful Acts 2001, Text adopted by the Commission at its fifty-third session, in 2001, UN Doc A/56/49(Vol. I)/Corr.4

Draft Articles on Diplomatic Protection: Text adopted by the International Law Commission at its fifty-eighth session, in 2006, and submitted to the General Assembly as a part of the Commission's report covering the work of that session. The report, which also contains commentaries on the draft articles, appears in Official Records of the General Assembly, Sixty-first Session, Supplement No. 10 (A/61/10)

Ioana Tudor, The Fair and Equitable Treatment Standard in the International Law of Foreign Investment (Oxford: Oxford University Press, 2008)

Isaac Nakhimovsky, "Vattel's Theory of the International Order: Commerce and the Balance of Power in the Law of Nations," 33 History of European Ideas 157 (2007)

Isabel V. Hull, A Scrap of Paper: Breaking and Making International Law during the Great War (Ithaca: Cornell University Press, 2014)

J. Fred Rippy, The United States and Mexico (New York: Alfred A. Knopf, 1928)

J. Patrick Kelly, "Customary International Law in Historical Context: The Exercise of Power Without General Acceptance," in Brian D. Lepard (ed.), Reexamining Customary International Law (Cambridge: Cambridge University Press, 2017)

J. Verzijl, International Law in Historical Perspective (Leiden: A. W. Sijthoff, 1973, 1974)

J. C. Bancroft Davis, Mr. Fish and the Alabama Claims: A Chapter in Diplomatic History (Cambridge: Riverside Press, 1893)

J. H. H. Weiler, "The Geology of International Law Governance," 64 Heidelberg Journal of International Law 547 (2004)

"The Rule of Lawyers and the Ethos of Diplomats: Reflections on the Internal and External Legitimacy of WTO Dispute Settlement," in R. Porter et al. (eds.), Efficiency, Equity, and Legitimacy: The Multilateral Trading System at the Millennium (Washington, DC: Brookings Institution Press, 2001)

Jack M. Balkin, "The Rhetoric of Responsibility," 76(2) Virginia Law Review 197 (1990)

Jackson H. Ralston, International Arbitrations from Athens to Locarno (Stanford: Stanford University Press, 1929)

Jacques Marquis de Dampierre, German Imperialism and International Law (London: Constable & Co., 1917)

James A. Brundage, "The Rise of the Professional Jurist in the Thirteenth Century," 20 Syracuse Journal of International Law and Commerce 185–190 (1994)

James Brown Scott, "The Institute of International Law," 21 American Journal of International Law 716 (1927)

The Spanish Conception of International Law and of Sanctions (Washington, DC: Carnegie Endowment for International Peace, 1934)

James Burke Chapin, Hamilton Fish and American Expansion (Ph.D. dissertation, Cornell University, 1971)

James Crawford, "Continuity and Discontinuity in International Dispute Settlement," 1(1) Journal of International Dispute Settlement 3 (2010)

The Creation of States in International Law (2nd ed., Oxford: Oxford University Press, 2016)

"The International Court of Justice and the Law of State Responsibility," in Christian J. Tams and James Sloan (eds.), The Development of International Law by the International Court of Justice (Oxford: Oxford University Press, 2013)

"The International Law Bar: Essence Before Existence?," ESIL 2013, 5th Research Forum: International Law as a Profession Conference Paper No. 11/2013, Available at SSRN: http://ssrn.com/abstract=2364104 or http://dx.doi.org/10.2139/ssrn.2364104

The International Law Commission's Articles on State Responsibility: Introduction, Text and Commentaries (Cambridge: Cambridge University Press, 2002)

"Investment Arbitration and the ILC Articles on State Responsibility," 25 ICSID Review 127 (2010)

"The Progressive Development of International Law: History, Theory and Practice," in Denis Alland, Vincent Chetail, Olivier de Frouville and Jorge E. Viñuales (eds.), Unité et diversité du droit international: Écrits en l'honneur du Professeur Pierre-Marie Dupuy (Leiden: Martinus Nijhoff, 2014)

"State Responsibility," in Anne Peters (ed.), Max Planck Encyclopedia of Public International Law (Oxford: Oxford University Press, 2006)

"State Responsibility," in Rüdiger Wolfrüm (ed.), Max Planck Encyclopedia of Public International Law (Oxford: Oxford University Press, 2012)

State Responsibility: The General Part (Cambridge: Cambridge University Press, 2013)

James Crawford, Alain Pellet and Simon Olleson (eds.), The Law of International Responsibility (Oxford: Oxford University Press, 2011)

James Crawford and Jeremy Watkins, "International Responsibility," in Samantha Besson and John Tasioulas (eds.), The Philosophy of International Law 283 (Oxford: Oxford University Press, 2010)

James Crawford and Simon Olleson, "The Exception of Non-performance: Links between the Law of Treaties and the Law of State Responsibility," 21 Australian Yearbook of International Law 55–74 (2001)

"The Nature and Forms of International Responsibility," in Malcolm Evans (ed.), International Law (2nd ed., Oxford: Oxford University Press, 2006)

James Crawford and Tom Grant, "Responsibility of States for Injuries to Foreigners," in J. P. Grant and J. C. Barker (eds), The Harvard Research in International Law: Contemporary Analysis and Appraisal 77–126 (Buffalo: W. S. Hein, 2007)

James Crawford, Thomas Grant and Francesco Messineo, "Towards an International Law of Responsibility: Early Doctrine," in Laurence Boisson de Chazournes and Marcelo Kohen (eds.), International Law and the Quest for its Implementation 377–402 (Leiden: Brill, 2010)

James F. Hopkins (ed.), The Papers of Henry Clay, Vol. 2 519–529 (Lexington: University Press of Kentucky, 1961)

James Fred Rippy, British Investments in Latin America, 1822–1949: A Case Study in the Operations of Private Enterprise in Retarded Regions (St. Paul: University of Minnesota Press, 1959)

James Garner, Recent Developments in International Law (Calcutta: University of Calcutta Press, 1925)

James Leslie Brierly, The Basis of Obligation in International Law, and Other Papers (Hersch Lauterpacht and C. H. M. Waldock, eds., Oxford: Clarendon Press, 1958)

James Loeffler and Moria Paz (eds.), The Law of Strangers Jewish Lawyers and International Law in the Twentieth Century (Cambridge: Cambridge University Press, 2019)

James Monroe, The Monroe Doctrine and Other Addresses (Alfred A. Stockton, ed., London: MacMillan, 1898)

James Morton Callahan, Evolution of Seward's Mexican Policy (West Virginia University Studies in American Diplomatic Relations, 1909)

James W. Ely, Jr., "Property Rights and the Supreme Court in the Gilded Age," 38 (3) Journal of Supreme Court History 330 (2013)

Jan Arno Hessbruegge's "The Historical Development of the Doctrines of Attribution and Due Diligence in International Law," 36 New York University Journal of International Law & Politics 265 (2003–2004)

Jan Klabbers, "Clinching the Concept of Sovereignty: Wimbledon Redux," 3 Austrian Review of International and European Law 345 (1998)

The Concept of Treaty in International Law (The Hague: Kluwer, 1996)

"Review of Antonio Cassese, *Five Masters of International Law: Conversations with R-J Dupuy, E Jimenez de Arechaga, R Jennings, L Henkin and O Schachter* (Oxford: Hart, 2011)," 22(4) European Journal of International Law 1175–1177 (2011)

Jan Paulsson, "International Arbitration and the Generation of Legal Norms: Treaty Arbitration and International Law" (Draft), Presentation, ICCA Annual Congress, May 21, 2006

Denial of Justice in International Law (Cambridge: Cambridge University Press, 2005)

Jay Sexton, "The United States, the Cuban Rebellion, and the Multilateral Initiative of 1875," 30(3) Diplomatic History 335–365 (2006)

Jean-Baptiste Michel, Yuan Kui Shen, Aviva Presser Aiden, Adrian Veres, Matthew K. Gray, The Google Books Team, Joseph P. Pickett, Dale Hoiberg, Dan Clancy, Peter Norwig, Jon Oorwant, Steven Pinker, Martin A. Nowak, and Erez Lieberman Aiden, "Quantitative Analysis of Culture Using Millions of Digitized Books," 331 *Science* 6014 (2014)

Jean Bodin, Les Six Livres de la République (Paris: J. Du Puys, 1576)

Jean d'Aspremont, "Canonical Cross-Referencing in the Making of the Law of International Responsibility," in Serena Forlati, Makane Mbengue and Brian McGarry (eds.), The Gabčíkovo–Nagymaros Judgment and its Contribution to the Development of International Law (Leiden: Brill, 2020)

"The General Claims Commission (Mexico and the United States) and the Invention of International Responsibility," in I. de la Rasilla del Moral and J. Viñuales (eds.), Experiments in International Adjudication: Historical Accounts (Cambridge: Cambridge University Press, 2018)

"International Law and the Rage against Scienticism. Review of Anne Orford, *International Law and the Politics of History*," 33(2) European Journal of International Law 679 (2021)

International Law as a Belief System (Cambridge: Cambridge University Press, 2017)

"Rebellion and State Responsibility: Wrongdoing by Democratically Elected Insurgents," 58 International and Comparative Law Quarterly 427 (2009)

"Three International Lawyers in a Hall of Mirrors," 32(3) Leiden Journal of International Law 367 (2019)

"Time Travel in the Law of International Responsibility," in Samantha Besson (ed.), Theories of International Responsibility Law (Cambridge: Cambridge University Press, 2022)

"What Was Not Meant to Be: General Principles of Law as a Source of International Law," in R. Pisillo Mazzeschi and P. De Sena (eds.), Global Justice, Human Rights, and the Modernization of International Law 1 (2018)

Jean d'Aspremont and S. Singh (eds.), Fundamental Concepts for International Law (Cheltenham: Edward Elgar, 2016)

Jean Ho, State Responsibility for Breaches of Investment Contracts (Cambridge: Cambridge University Press, 2018)

Jeffrey Dunoff, "Engaging the Writings of Martti Koskenniemi: Introduction to the Symposium," 27(2) Temple International and Comparative Law Journal 272 (2013)

Jeffrey P. Commission, "Precedent in Investment Treaty Arbitration: A Citation Analysis of a Developing Jurisprudence," 24(2) Journal of International Arbitration 129–158 (2007)

Jennifer Pitts, Boundaries of the International: Law & Empire (Cambridge, MA: Harvard University Press, 2018)

Jenny S. Martinez, "Anti-Slavery Courts and the Dawn of International Human Rights Law," 117 Yale Law Journal 550 (2007)

Jeremy Bentham, An Introduction to the Principles of Morals and Legislation (Burns and Hart, eds., Oxford: Clarendon, 1970 [1789])

Jeremy Waldron, "The Rule of International Law," 30 Harvard Journal of Law & Public Policy 15 (2006)

Jesse S. Reeves, "Growth and Development of Law," in George Edwin Rines (ed.), The Encyclopedia Americana 488–493 (New York: The Encyclopedia Americana Corporation, 1920)

Jochen von Bernstorff, "Georg Jellinek and the Origins of Liberal Constitutionalism in International Law," 4(3) Goettingen Journal of International Law 659 (2012)

The Public International Law Theory of Hans Kelsen: Believing in Universal Law (Cambridge: Cambridge University Press, 2010)

Jochen von Bernstorff and Max Henry Mayer, "The Historical School and German 19th Century Contributions to International Legal Thought," (2022), available at https://ssrn.com/abstract=4106343, last visited June 22, 2022.

Jochen von Bernstorff and Philipp Dann (eds.), The Battle for International Law South-North Perspectives on the Decolonization Era (Oxford: Oxford University Press, 2019)

Johann Caspar Bluntschli, "An Impartial Opinion on the Alabama Question and the Manner of Settling It," II Revue de droit international et de législation comparée (1870) Part IIID, (reprinted in Washington, DC: Government Printing Office, 1871)

Das moderne Völkerrecht der civilisierten Staaten als Rechtsbuch dargestellt (2nd edn., Nördlingen: Beck, 1872)

Le droit international codifié (Charles Édouard Lardy, trans., Paris: Librairie Guillaumin, 1886)

Johann Casper Bluntschli, Lehre vom modernen Staat (Stuttgart: J. G. Cotta'schen, 1876)

Johann Casper Bluntschli, "Lieber's Service to Political Science and International Law," in Francis Lieber (ed.), Miscellaneous Writings 7 (Philadelphia: J. B. Lippincott, 1880)

The Theory of the State (authorized translation of 6th ed., Oxford: Clarendon, 1885)

John Archer Jackson, "Professions and Professionalization," in John Archer Jackson (ed.), Professions and Professionalization 1–17 (1970) (Cambridge: Cambridge University Press, 1970)

John Austin, "The Province of Jurisprudence Determined," in The Province of Jurisprudence Determined and the Uses of the Study of Jurisprudence (Introduction by H. L. A. Hart, Indianapolis: Hackett, 1954 [1832])

John Barrett, The Pan American Union: Peace, Friendship, Commerce (Washington, DC: Pan American Union, 1911)

John Bassett Moore, The Collected Papers of John Bassett Moore (New Haven: Yale University Press, 1944)

History and Digest of the International Arbitrations to which the United States Has Been a Party, Together with Appendices Containing the Treaties Relating to Such Arbitrations, and Historical Legal Notes (Washington, DC: Government Printing Office, 1898)

International Adjudication. Ancient and Modern History and Documents Together with Mediatorial Reports, Advisory Opinions and the Decisions of Domestic Commissions on International Claims, Modern Series (New York: Oxford University Press, 1929)

"The Late Chilian Controversy," (8)3 Political Science Quarterly 467–494 (1893)

Papers, Columbia Law School Archives

The United States and International Arbitration (Boston: American Peace Society, 1896)

John Bassett Moore and Francis Wharton, A Digest of International Law as Embodied in the Diplomatic Discussions, Treaties and Other International Agreements, International Awards, the Decisions of Municipal Courts, and the Writings of Jurists and Especially in Documents, Published and Unpublished, Issued by Presidents and Secretaries of State of the United States, the Opinions of the Attorneys-General, and the Decisions of Courts, Federal and State (Washington, DC: Government Printing Office, 1906)

John Campbell, The Present State of Europe (London: Longman, 1750)

John Charles Chasteen, Born in Blood and Fire (New York: W. W. Norton & Company, 2000)

John D. Rosero, Private v. Public Authority in NAFTA: The Procyclicality of Investor Protections and Global Governance Issues (PhD diss., Rutgers the State University of New Jersey, 2010)

John Dwyer, The Agrarian Dispute: The Expropriation of American-Owned Rural Land in Postrevolutionary Mexico (Durham: Duke University Press, 2008)

John Eugene Harley, The League of Nations and the New International Law (New York: Oxford University Press, 1921)

John Fabian Witt, Lincoln's Code: The Laws of War in American History (New York: Free Press, 2012)

John Hepp, "James Brown Scott and the Rise of Public International Law," 7(2) Journal of the Gilded Age and Progressive Era 151 (2008)

John M. Belohlavek, Broken Glass: Caleb Cushing and the Shattering of the Union (Kent: Kent State University Press, 2005)

John M. Raymond and Barbara J. Frischolz, "Lawyers Who Established International Law in the United States, 1776–1914," 76 American Journal of International Law 802–829 (1982)

John Norton Pomeroy, "The Virginius," 17 Nation 332–334 (1873)

"The Virginius Case," 8 American Law Review 470 (1874)

John R. Crook, "Practicing International Law for the United States," 6 Journal of Transnational Law & Policy 1 (1996)

John T. Morse, Jr., The Law of Arbitration and Award (Boston: Little Brown, 1872)

John Westlake, International Law, Part I: Peace (Cambridge: Cambridge University Press, 1910)

"International Arbitration," 7 International Journal of Ethics (October 1896)

"Relations between Public and Private International Law," in Lassa Oppenheim (ed.), Collected Papers of John Westlake (Cambridge: Cambridge University Press, 1914)

John Y. Simon (ed.), The Papers of Ulysses S. Grant, Vol. 30, 156–1157 (Carbondale: Southern Illinois University Press, 1967)

Jonathan Zasloff, "Law and the Shaping of American Foreign Policy: From the Gilded Age to the New Era," 78 New York University Law Review 239 (2003)

"Law and the Shaping of American Foreign Policy: The Twenty Years' Crisis," 77 Southern California Law Review 583 (2004)

Jörg Kammerhofer, "The Interaction of Doctrine and Theory in (International) Legal Scholarship," in Pauline Westerman, Kostiantyn Gorobets and Andreas Hadjigeorgiou (eds.), Conceptual (De)Constructions of International Law (Cheltenham: Edward Elgar, 2022)

José Gustavo Guerrero, La codification du droit international: la première conférence, La Haye, 13 mars–12 avril 1930 (Paris: Pedone, 1930)

La responsabilidad internacional de los estados por los daños causados en su territorio a la persona o bienes de los extranjeros (Paris: Imprimerie Lahure, 1926)

"La responsabilité internationale des États," in Academie Diplomatique Internationale, Seances et Travaux, March 12, 1928

José Gustavo Guerrero and Wang Chung Hui, "Report of the Sub-Committee of the Committee of Experts for the Progressive Codification of International Law," 20 American Journal of International Law Special Supplement 177 (1926)

José Gustavo Prieto Muñoz, "The Mexican Claims Commissions and the Mixed Arbitral Tribunals in the 1920s: Lessons on Legitimacy and Legacy in International Adjudication," in Hélène Ruiz Fabri and Michel Erpelding (eds.), The Mixed Arbitral Tribunals, 1919–1939: An Experiment in the International Adjudication of Private Rights 91 (Baden-Baden: Nomos, 2023)

Josef L. Kunz, Latin-American Philosophy of Law in the Twentieth Century (New York: New York University Press, 1950)

Joseph A. Fry, "Phases of Empire: Late Nineteenth-Century U.S. Foreign Relations," in Charles W. Calhoun (ed.), The Gilded Age: Perspectives on the Origins of Modern America 283 (Lanham: Rowman & Littlefield, 2007)

Joseph G. Starke, "Monism and Dualism in the Theory of International Law," 17 British Yearbook of International Law 66 (1936)

Joseph R. Stromberg, "Sovereignty, International Law, and the Triumph of Anglo-American Cunning," 18(4) Journal of Libertarian Studies 29 (2004)

Joseph Raz, "The Law's Own Virtue," Columbia Public Law Research Paper No. 14–609, at p. 1

From Normativity to Responsibility (Oxford: Oxford University Press, 2011)

Joseph H. H. Weiler, "Editorial: Crime and Punishment: The Reification and Deification of the State (A Footnote to the Syria Debate)," 24(4) European Journal of International Law 993 (2013)

Joseph Smith, Illusions of Conflict: Anglo-American Diplomacy Toward Latin America, 1864–1896 (Pittsburgh: University of Pittsburgh Press, 1979)

Joshua Leavitt, The Monroe Doctrine (New York: Sinclair Tousey, 1863)

Jost Delbrück, "Law's Frontier: Walther Schücking and the Quest for the Lex Ferenda," 22(3) European Journal of International Law 801 (2011)

Judge Stephen W. Schwebel, "The Reality of International Adjudication and Arbitration," 12 Willamette Journal of International Law and Dispute Resolution 359 (2004)

Judith Ewell, Venezuela and the United States: From Monroe's Hemisphere to Petroleum's Empire (Athens: University of Georgia Press, 1996)

Judith Shklar, Legalism: Law, Morals, and Political Trials (2nd ed., Cambridge: Harvard University Press, 1986)

Julian Go, Patterns of Empire: The British and American Empires, 1688 to the Present (Cambridge: Cambridge University Press, 2011)

Julius Goebel, Jr., "The International Responsibility of States for Injuries Sustained by Aliens on Account of Mob Violence, Insurrections and Civil Wars," 8(4) American Journal of International Law 802 (1914)

Jr., The Recognition Policy of the United States (New York: Columbia University Press, 1915)

Justus D. Doeneck, "Edwin M. Borchard, John Bassett Moore, and Opposition to American Intervention in World War II," 6(1) Journal of Libertarian Studies 1 (1982)

K. E. Flemming, Greece: A Jewish History (Princeton: Princeton University Press, 2008)

K. J. Tromp, "Aliens and Strangers in the Old Testament," 76 Vox Reformata 4–24 (2011)

Kaj Hobér, "State Responsibility and Attribution," in P. Muchlinski, F. Ortino and C. Schreuer (eds.), The Oxford Handbook of International Investment Law (Oxford: Oxford University Press, 2008)

Kaja Harter-Uibopuu, "Anthropological and Historical Foundations: Ancient Greek Approaches toward Alternative Dispute Resolution," 10 Willamette Journal of International Law and Dispute Resolution 47 (2002)

Kal Raustiala, Does the Constitution Follow the Flag? The Evolution of Territoriality in American Law (Oxford: Oxford University Press, 2009)

Karl Strupp, "Le développement du Pacte de la Société des Nations," 20 Recueil des cours (1927)

"Le droit du juge international de statuer selon l'équité," 33 Recueil des cours 351 (1930)

Éléments du droit international public universel, européen et américain (Paris: Rousseau, 1927)

Das internationale Landkriegsrecht (Frankfurt: J. Baer & Co., 1914)

Die internationale Schiedsgerichtsbarkeit (Berlin: Rothschild, 1914)

"L'intervention en matière financière," 8 Recueil des cours 1 (1925)

"Die Organisation der Völkerbundexekution gegen den Angreifer," 16 Zeitschrift für Völkerrecht 529 (1932)

"Les règles générales du droit de la paix," 47 Recueil des cours 263 (1934)

"Review: *The International Responsibility of States for Denial of Justice*, by Alwyn V. Freeman," 18(5) *International Affairs* 689 (1939)

Die Schiedsgerichts-, Gerichts- und Vergleichsverträge des Deutschen Reiches (Berlin: G. Stilke, 1919)

Das völkerrechtliche Delikt (Berlin: Kohlhammer, 1920)

Die völkerrechtliche Haftung des Staates, insbesondere bei Handlungen Privater (Kiel: Institut für Internationales Recht, 1927)

Das Werk von Locarno (Berlin and Leipzig: de Gruyter, 1926)

Die wichtigsten Arten der völkerrechtlichen Schiedsgerichtsverträge (Munich: Duncker & Humblot, 1917)

Karl W. Deutsch and Stanley Hofffmann (eds.), The Relevance of International Law: Essays in Honor of Leo Gross (transl. Max Knight, Cambridge, MA: Schenkman, 1968)

Kate Miles, The Origins of International Investment Law (Cambridge: Cambridge University Press, 2013)

Kathryn Greenman, Aliens in Latin America: Intervention, Arbitration and State Responsibility for Rebels (Cambridge: Cambridge University Press, 2018)

"Aliens in Latin America: Intervention, Arbitration and State Responsibility for Rebels," 31 Leiden Journal of International Law 617 (2018)

"The Law of State Responsibility and the Persistence of Investment Protection," in Contingency in International Law: On the Possibility of Different Legal Histories 389 (Oxford: Oxford University Press, 2021).

State Responsibility and Rebels: The History and Legacy of Protecting Investment Against Revolution (Cambridge: Cambridge University Press, 2021)

Katja Creutz, State Responsibility in International Law: From Paradigm to Periphery (Doctoral Thesis Submitted to the Faculty of Law at the University of Helsinki, August 2015)

State Responsibility in the International Legal Order: A Critical Appraisal (Cambridge: Cambridge University Press, 2020)

Kenneth J. Vandevelde, The First Bilateral Investment Treaties: US Postwar Friendship, Commerce, and Navigation Treaties 1 (Oxford: Oxford University Press, 2017)

Kenneth Smith Carlston, The Process of International Arbitration (New York: Columbia University Press, 1946)

Kevin Jon Heller, "Beyond the Reasonable Man? A Sympathetic but Critical Assessment of the Use of Subjective Standards of Reasonableness in Self–Defense and Provocation Cases," 26(1) American Journal of Criminal Law 1 (1998)

Kevin M. Anderson, "The Venezuelan Claims Controversy at the Hague, 1903," 57 (3) Historian 525 (1995).

Kristina Lovrić–Pernak, "The concept of international arbitration in 19th century International Law: Legal authority reduced to moral peace," 1st Meeting of the Working Group "Paradoxes of Peace in the 19th Century Europe," Research Project Europe 1815–1914, Helsinki, November 16–17, 2010 (paper on file with author)

L. W. King, Harry Reginald Hall, Egypt and Western Asia: In Light of Recent Discoveries (London: Society for Promoting Christian Knowledge, 1907)

Larry D. Kramer, The People Themselves: Popular Constitutionalism and Judicial Review (New York: Oxford University Press, 2000)

Lars Schoultz, Beneath the United States: A History of U.S. Policy Toward Latin America (Cambridge: Cambridge University Press, 1988)

Lassa Oppenheim, The Future of International Law (Oxford: Clarendon, 1921)

International Law (Ronald F. Roxburgh, ed., 3rd ed., London: Longmans, Green and Co., 1920)

International Law: A Treatise (2nd ed., London: Longmans, Green, & Co., 1912)

International Law: A Treatise, Vol. I: Peace (London: Longmans, Green, & Co., 1905)

Die Zukunft des Völkerrecht (Leipzig: W. Engelmann, 1911)

Lauren Benton and Lisa Ford, Rage for Order: The British Empire and the Origins of International Law 1800–1850 (Cambridge, MA: Harvard University Press, 2016)

Laurence R. Helfer and Timothy Meyer, "The Evolution of Codification: A Principal–Agent Theory of the International Law Commission's Influence," in Curtis Bradley (ed.), Custom's Future: International Law in a Changing World (Cambridge: Cambridge University Press, 2016)

League of Nations, "Report of the Sub–Committee of the Committee of Experts for the Progressive Codification of International Law," 20 American Journal of International Law Special Supplement 177 (1926)

Leandro Prados de la Escosura, "Lost Decades? Economic Performance in Post–independence Latin America," 41 Journal of Latin American Studies 279 (2009)

Leo Gross, "States as Organs of International Law, and the Problem of Auto-Interpretation," in G. A. Lipsky (ed.), Law and Politics in the World Community (Berkeley: University of California Press, 1953)

Liliana Obregón, Completing Civilization: Nineteenth Century Criollo Interventions in International Law, SJD Dissertation submitted to Harvard Law School (September 2002), on file with author

"Latin American International Law," in Routledge Handbook of International Law 154 (London: Routledge, 2008)

Liliana T. Obregón, "Writing International Legal History: An Overview," 7 Monde (s). Histoire, Espaces, Relations 95 (2015)

Lionel M. Summers, "Arbitration and Latin America," 3 California Western International Law Journal 1 (1972)

Lionel Morgan Summers, "The Calvo Clause," 19 Virginia Law Review 459 (1933)

Lisa Ford, "Protecting the Peace on the Edges of Empire: Commissioners of Crown Lands in New South Wales," in Lauren Benton, Adam Clulow, and Victoria, Bain Attwood (eds.), Protection and Empire: A Global History 175 (Cambridge: Cambridge University Press, 2018)

Lorand Bartels and Federica Paddeu (eds.), Exceptions in International Law (Oxford: Oxford University Press, 2020)

Lord McNair, International Law Opinions (Cambridge: Cambridge University Press, 1956)

Louis Henkin, How Nations Behave: Law and Foreign Policy (2nd ed., New York: Columbia University Press, 1979),

Louise E. Matthaei, "The Place of Arbitration and Mediation in Ancient Systems of International Ethics," 4(2) The Classical Quarterly 241–264 (October 1908)

Luigi Nuzzo and Milos Vec (eds.), Constructing International Law: The Birth of a Discipline 25 (Frankfurt-am-Main: Klostermann, 2012)

Luis M. Drago and H. Edward Nettles, "The Drago Doctrine in International Law and Politics," 8(2) The Hispanic American Historical Review 204 (1928)

M. Anderson Berry, "Whether Foreigner or Alien: A New Look at the Original Language of the Alien Tort Statute," 27(2) Berkeley Journal of International Law 316 (2009)

M. R. Waite, William M. Evarts and Caleb Cushing, Alabama Claims: Argument of the United States Delivered to the Tribunal of Arbitration at Geneva, June 15, 1872 (Paris: Dubuisson & Co., 1872)

Malcolm Langford, Daniel Behn and Ole Kristian Fauchald, "Backlash and State Strategies in International Investment Law," in T. Gammeltoft–Hansen and T. Aalberts (eds.), The Changing Practices of International Law: Sovereignty, Law and Politics in a Globalising World (Cambridge: Cambridge University Press, 2017)

Manley O. Hudson, "The Seventh Year of the Permanent Court of International Justice," 23 American Journal of International Law 1 (1929)

Marcus Niebuhr Tod, International Arbitration amongst the Greeks (Oxford: Clarendon Press, 1913)

Marija Dordeska, "General Principles of Law Recognized by Civilized Nations: Method, Inductive-Empirical Analysis and (More) 'Scientific' Results," in Rosanna Deplano (ed.), Pluralising International Legal Scholarship: The Promise and Perils of Non–Doctrinal Research Methods 18 (Cheltenham: Edward Elgar, 2019)

Marina Spinedi, "From One Codification to Another: Bilateralism and Multilateralism in the Genesis of the Codification of the Law of Treaties and the Law of State Responsibility," 13(5) European Journal of International Law 1099 (2002)

Marina Spinedi and Bruno Simma (eds.), United Nations Codification of State Responsibility (New York: Oceana, 1987)

Marjorie M. Whiteman, Damages in International Law I (Washington, DC: Government Printing Office, 1937)

Mark Janis, "The New Oppenheim and its Theory of International Law," 16(2) Oxford Journal of Legal Studies 329 (1996)

Mark Weston Janis, The American Tradition of International Law: Great Expectations, 1794–1914 (New York: Oxford University Press, 2004)

Marshall C. Eakin, The History of Latin America: Collision of Cultures (New York: Palgrave, 2007)

Martins Paparinskis, "Circumstances Precluding Wrongfulness in International Investment Law," 31 ICSID Review: Foreign Investment Law Journal 484 (2016)

The International Minimum Standard and Fair and Equitable Treatment (Oxford: Oxford University Press, 2013)

"Investment Arbitration and the Law of Countermeasures," 79 British Yearbook of International Law 264–352 (2008)

"The Once and Future Law of State Responsibility," 114(4) American Journal of International Law 618 (2020)

"Sources of Law and Arbitral Interpretations of Pair Matéria Investment Protection Rules," in Ole Kristina Faucal and André Nollkaemper (eds.), Unity or Fragmentation of International Law: The Role of International and National Tribunals (London: Hart Publishing, 2011)

Martti Koskenniemi, From Apology to Utopia: The Structure of International Legal Argument (Helsinki: Finnish Lawyers' Publishing Company, 1989)

"Between Apology and Utopia: The Politics of International Law," in Martti Koskenniemi, The Politics of International Law 35 (Oxford: Hart, 2011)

"The Civilizing Mission: International Law and the Colonial Encounter in the Late 19th Century" (*Rechtshistorikertag*, Bonn, September 12–17, 2004)

"Between Commitment and Cynicism: Outline of a Theory of International Law as Practice," in Collection of Essays by Legal Advisors of States, Legal Advisors of International Organizations and Practitioners in the Field of International Law 495 (New York: United Nations, 1999)

"Between Coordination and Constitution: International Law as a German Discipline," 15 Redescriptions. Yearbook of Political Thought, Conceptual History and Feminist Theory 45–70 (2011)

"Doctrines of State Responsibility," in James Crawford, Alain Pellet and Simon Olleson (eds.), The Law of International Responsibility 45–51 (Oxford: Oxford University Press, 2011)

"Epilogue: To Enable and Enchant: On the Power of Law," in Wouter Werner, Marieke de Hoon and Alexis Galán (eds.), The Law of International Lawyers Reading Martti Koskenniemi 393 (Cambridge: Cambridge University Press, 2017)

"The Fate of Public International Law: Between Technique and Politics," 70(1) Modern Law Review 1–30 (2007)

"The Function of Law in International Community: 75 Years After," 79 British Yearbook of International Law 353 (2008)

"General Principles: Reflexions on Constructivist Thought in International Law," 18 Oikeustiede-Jurisprudentia 117 (1985)

The Gentle Civilizer of Nations: The Rise and Fall of International Law 1870–1960 (Cambridge: Cambridge University Press, 2002)

Histories of International Law: Dealing with Eurocentrism Inaugural Lecture delivered on November 16, 2011 on the occasion of accepting the Treaty of Utrecht Chair at Utrecht University (on file with author)

"Histories of International Law: Dealing with Eurocentrism," Zeitschrift des Max–Planck–Instituts für europäische Rechtsgeschichte, Rg 19 (2011)

"Human Rights, Politics and Love," in The Politics of International Law 153 (Oxford: Hart, 2011)

"International Law as 'Global Governance,'" in J. Desautels-Stein and C. Tomlins (eds.), Searching for Contemporary Legal Thought 199 (Cambridge: Cambridge University Press, 2017)

"Lauterpacht: The Victorian Tradition in International Law," 8 European Journal of International Law 215 (1997)

"Law of Nations and the 'Conflict of the Faculties,'" The Intersection of Theory and History (Spring 2018), at pp. 4–28, at p. 1

"The Legacy of the 19th Century" (2007, unpublished paper on file with author)

"The Politics of International Law: 20 Years Later," 20 European Journal of International Law 7(2009)

Report on "Fragmentation of International Law: Difficulties Arising from the Diversification and Expansion of International Law," April 13, 2006, UN Doc. A/CN.4/L.682

"Solidarity Measures: State Responsibility as a New International Order?," 72 British Yearbook of International Law 337 (2001)

"Sovereignty. Prolegomena to a Study of International Law as Discourse," Kansainoikeus/Jus Gentium 71–106 (1987)

"Study on the Function and Scope of the Lex Specialis Rule and the Question of 'Self-Contained Regimes," UN Doc. A/CN.4/ILC(LVI)/SG/FIL/CRD.1 para. 36

To the Uttermost Parts of the Earth: Legal Imagination and International Power, 1300–1870 (Cambridge: Cambridge University Press, 2021)

Maureen M. Robson, "Liberals and 'Vital Interests': The Debate on International Arbitration, 1815–72," 32(85) Bulletin of the Institute of Historical Research 38 (1959)

Max Sørenson (ed.), Manual of Public International Law (London: Macmillan, 1968)

Max Weber, Economy and Society: An Outline of Interpretive Sociology (Guenther Roth and Claus Wittich, eds., Ephraim Fischoff, et al., trans. Berkeley and Los Angeles: University of California Press, 1968 [1921], reprinted 2012)

Maximilien de Béthune duc de Sully, Grand Design of Henry IV (reprinted, London: Sweet & Maxwell, 1921)

Melissa Durkee, "Interpretive Entrepreneurs," 107(3) Virginia Law Review 431 (2021)

Melissa J. Durkee (ed.), The Law and Logics of Attribution: Constructing the Identity and Responsibility of States and Firms (Cambridge: Cambridge University Press, forthcoming)

Merle Eugene Curti, The American Peace Crusade, 1815–1860 (New York: Octagon, 1973)

Michael J. Braddick, "The English Government, War, Trade, and Settlement, 1625–1688," in Nicholas P. Canny (ed.), The Oxford History of the British Empire: The Origins of Empire (Oxford: Oxford University Press, 1988)

Michael J. Powell, From Patrician to Professional Elite: The Transformation of the New York City Bar Association (New York: Russell Sage, 1988)

Michael K. Young, "The Role of the Attorney-Adviser in the U.S. Department of State: Institutional Arrangements and Structural Imperatives," 61 Law and Contemporary Problems 133 (1998)

Michael Levenson, Modernism (New Haven: Yale University Press, 2011)

Michael P. Scharf and Paul R. Williams, Shaping Foreign Policy in Times of Crisis: The Role of International Law and the State Department Legal Adviser (Cambridge: Cambridge University Press, 2010)

Michael Stolleis, A History of Public Law in Germany 1914–1945 (Oxford: Oxford University Press, 2004)

Public Law in Germany, 1800–1914 (New York: Berghahn, 2001)

Michael Stolleis and Masaharu Yanagihara (eds.), East Asian and European Perspectives on International Law (Baden-Baden: Nomos, 2004)

Michael Waibel, "Interpretive Communities in International Law," in A. Bianchi, D. Peat and M. Windsor (eds.), Interpretation in International Law 147 (Oxford: Oxford University Press, 2015)

Mikaël Schinazi, The Three Ages of International Commercial Arbitration (Cambridge: Cambridge University Press, 2021)

Milton Pelsur, America's Outward Thrust: Approaches to Foreign Affairs, 1865–1890 (Dekalb: Northern Illinois University Press, 1971)

Minnie McDonald Paisley, Relations between the United States and Mexico from 1868 to 1882 (Masters Dissertation, UC Berkeley, September 1913)

Mona Pinchis, "The Ancestry of 'Equitable Treatment' in Trade: Lessons from the League of Nations During the Inter-War Period," 15(1) Journal of World Investment & Trade 13 (2014)

Mónica García-Salmones Rovira, The Project of Positivism in International Law (Oxford: Oxford University Press, 2013)

"Walther Schücking and the Pacifist Traditions of International Law," 3 European Journal of International Law 755 (2011)

Morton J. Horwitz, "The History of the Public/Private Distinction," 130 University of Pennsylvania Law Review 1423 (1982)

The Transformation of American Law, 1780–1848 (Cambridge, MA: Harvard University Press, 1977)

Moshe Hirsch, Invitation to the Sociology of International Law (Oxford: Oxford University Press, 2016)

N. D. Gowda, State Responsibility in the Present Context: A Critical Study with Reference to the Contemporary Issues under International Law (Thesis Submitted to University of Mysore, May 2010)

Naomi R. Lamoreaux and John Joseph Wallis, "States, Not Nation: The Sources of Political and Economic Development in the Early United States," 1 American Capitalism 1 (2016)

Natasha Wheatley, "Spectral Legal Personality in Interwar International Law: On New Ways of Not Being a State," 35(3) Law and History Review 753 (2017)

Nehal Bhuta, "'Like a Tree in the Garden of State Sciences': From Staatswissenschaften to External Public Law," 32(3) European Journal of International Law 1035 (2021)

Niall Ferguson, "Globalization in Interdisciplinary Perspective," in Michael D. Bordo, Alan M. Taylor and Jeffrey G. Williamson (eds.), Globalization in Historical Perspective (Chicago: University of Chicago Press, 2003)

Nicholas Onuf, "Henry Wheaton and 'The Golden Age of International Law,'" 6 International Legal Theory 2 (2000)

Nick Cleaver, Grover Cleveland's New Foreign Policy: Arbitration, Neutrality, and the Dawn of American Empire (New York: Palgrave MacMillan, 2014)

"Wagging the Dog: The Influence of American Representatives Overseas on the Evolution of US Foreign Policy in the Late 19th Century" (2013), available at www.academia.edu/3391328/Wagging_the_Dog_The_Influence_of_American_Representatives_Overseas_on_the_Evolution_of_US_Foreign_Policy_in_the_Late_19th_Century

Norman B. Ferris, Desperate Diplomacy: William H. Seward's Foreign Policy, 1861 (Knoxville: University of Tennessee Press, 1976)

Ntina Tzouvala and Robert Knox, "International Law of State Responsibility and COVID-19: An Ideology Critique," Australian Yearbook of International Law (online, 2021), ANU College of Law Research Paper No. 21.25, available online at https://ssrn.com/abstract=3930470

Official Opinions of the Attorneys General of the United States Advising the President and Heads of Departments in Relation to their Official Duties, Opinions of Hon. Caleb Cushing (C. C. Andrews, ed., Washington, DC: W. H. & O. H. Morrison, 1871)

Ole Spiermann, International Legal Argument in the Permanent Court of International Justice: The Rise of the International Judiciary (Cambridge: Cambridge University Press, 2005)

"Judge Wang Chung-Hui at the Permanent Court of International Justice," 5(1) Chinese Journal of International Law 115 (2006)

Oliver J. Lissitzyn, "The Meaning of the Term Denial of Justice in International Law," 30 American Journal of International Law 632–646 (1936)

Olivier de Frouville, "Attribution of Conduct to the State: Private Individuals," in James Crawford, Alain Pellet and Simon Olleson (eds.), The Law of International Responsibility (Oxford: Oxford University Press, 2011)

Osgood Hardy, "Ulysses S. Grant, President of the Mexican Southern Railroad," 24 (2) Pacific Historical Review 111 (1955)

"Was Patrick Egan a 'Blundering Minister?'" 8(1) The Hispanic American Historical Review 65–91 (1928)

Paolo Amorosa, The American Project and the Politics of History: James Brown Scott and the Origins of International Law (April 14, 2018) (Doctoral dissertation, University of Helsinki)

Patrick Weil, The Sovereign Citizen: Denaturalization and the Origins of the American Republic (Philadelphia: University of Pennsylvania Press, 2012)

Paul R. Milgrom, Douglass C. North and Barry R. Weingast, "The Role of Institutions in the Revival of Trade: The Law Merchant, Private Judges, and the Champagne Fairs," 2(1) Economics and Politics 1 (1990)

Paul Schoen, Die völkerrechtliche Haftung der Staaten aus unerlaubten Handlungen, 10 Zeitschrift für Völkerrecht, Ergänzungsheft 2 (Breslau: Kern, 1917)

Paulos Alexandrou Zannas, La responsabilité internationale des États pour les actes de négligence (Montreux: Ganguin & Laubscher, 1952)

Percy Corbett, Law and Society in the Relations of States (New York: Harcourt, Brace and Company, 1951)

Peter Bridges, "An Appreciation of Alvey Adee," 10(1) Diplomacy and Statecraft 31 (1999)

Peter L. Reich, "Foreign Relations Between Mexico and the United States in the Nineteenth Century, 1821–1910," 24 PROFMEX WebJournal 12 (2019)

P. Hamilton, H. C. Requena, L. van Scheltinga and B. Shifman (eds.), The Permanent Court of Arbitration: International Arbitration and Dispute Resolution (The Hague: Kluwer, 1999)

Philip Allott, "State Responsibility and the Unmaking of International Law," 29(1) Harvard International Law Journal 1–26 (1988)

Philip Jessup, A Modern Law of Nations (New York: Macmillan, 1948)

Philip C. Jessup, "Responsibility of States for Injuries to Individuals," 46(6) Columbia Law Review 903 (1946)

Philipp Siegert, Staatshaftung im Ausnahmezustand: Doktrin und Rechtspraxis im Deutschen Reich und in Frankreich, 1914–1919 (Frankfurt-am-Main: Klostermann Vittorio, 2020)

Philippe Sands, "Twin Peaks: The Hersch Lauterpacht Draft Nuremberg Speeches," 1(1) Cambridge Journal of International and Comparative Law 37 (2012)

Pierre-Hugues Verdier, "Cooperative States: International Relations, State Responsibility and the Problem of Custom," 42(1) Virginia Journal of International Law 839 (2002)

Pierre-Marie Dupuy, "Dionisio Anzilotti and the Law of International Responsibility of States," 3(1) European Journal of International Law 139 (1992)

"The International Law of State Responsibility: Revolution or Evolution?," 11 Michigan Journal of International Law 105 (1989)

Prosper Weil, "Towards Relative Normativity in International Law," 77 American Journal of International Law 413 (1983).

R. Kent Newmyer, "Daniel Webster as Tocqueville's Lawyer: The Dartmouth College Case Again," 11(2) American Journal of Legal History 127–147 (1967)

Randall Lesaffer, "Argument from Roman Law in Current International Law," 16 European Journal of International Law 25 (2005)

Raoul Eugène Desvernine, Claims against Mexico: A Brief Study of the International Law Applicable to Claims of Citizens of the United States and Other Countries for Losses Sustained in Mexico during the Revolutions of the Last Decade (Private Publication, 1921)

Regis Yann Simo, "The Law of International Responsibility: The Case of the WTO as a 'Lex Specialis' or the Fallacy of a 'Self-Contained' Regime," 22 African Journal of International & Comparative Law 184 (2014)

Renée Jeffery, "Hersch Lauterpacht: The Realist Challenge and the 'Grotian Tradition' in 20th-Century International Relations," 12(2) European Journal of International Relations 223 (2006)

Reut Yael Paz, "From Rosa Luxemburg to Hersch Lauterpacht: An Ostjüdische Heritage in International Law?," in Dawid Bunikowaki and Alberto Puppo (eds.), Why Religion? A Critical Philosophy of Law, Peace and Religion 221 (Berlin: Springer, 2020)

"Making it Whole: Hersch Lauterpacht's Rabbinical Approach to International Law," 4 Goettingen Journal of International Law 417 (2012)

Richard Abel, "Speaking Law to Power: Occasions for Cause Lawyering," in Austin Sarat and Stuart Scheingold (eds.), Cause Lawyering: Political Commitments and Professional Responsibilities (Oxford: Oxford University Press, 1998)

Richard B. Bilder, "The Office of the Legal Adviser: The State Department Lawyer and Foreign Affairs," 56 American Journal of International Law 633–684 (1962)

Richard H. Steinberg and Jonathan Zasloff, "Power and International Law," 100 American Journal of International Law 64 (2006)

Richard H. Steinberg, "The Rise and Decline of a Liberal International Order," in David L. Sloss (ed.), Is the International Legal Order Unraveling? (Oxford: Oxford University Press, 2022)

Richard Olney, "The Development of International Law," 1 American Journal of International Law 418 (1907)

Robert Clark Morris, International Arbitration and Procedure (New Haven: Yale University Press, 1911)

Robert H. Bates, Avner Greif, Margaret Levi, Jean-Laurent Rosenthal, Analytic Narratives (Princeton: Princeton University Press, 1998)

Robert Kagan, Dangerous Nation: America's Foreign Policy from Its Earliest Days to the Dawn of the Twentieth Century (New York: Alfred A. Knopf, 2006)

Robert Keohane and Joseph Nye, Power and Interdependence (Boston: Little Brown, 1977)

Robert Kolb, The International Law of State Responsibility: An Introduction (Cheltenham: Edward Elgar, 2017)

Robert L. Beisner, From the Old Diplomacy to the New 1865–1900 (2nd ed., Arlington Heights: Harlan Davidson, 1986)

Robert L. Tsai, "Legal Language in Nineteenth–Century America," in Nan Goodman and Simon Stern (eds.), The Ashgate Research Companion to Law and Humanities in Nineteenth-Century America (Farnham: Ashgate, 2015)

Robert R. Wilson, "Property-Protection Provisions in United States Commercial Treaties," 45(1) American Journal of International Law 83–107 (1951)

Robert von Mohl, Die Geschichte und Literatur der Staatswissenschaft in Monographieen dargestellt (Erlangen: Enke, 1855)

Robert W. Gordon, "'The Ideal and the Actual in the Law': Fantasies and Practice of New York City Lawyers,1870–1910," in Gerard W. Gawalt (ed.), The New High Priests: Lawyers in Post-Civil War America 53 (Westport: Greenwood Press, 1984)

"The Legal Profession," in Austin Sarat, Bryant Garth and Robert A. Kagan (eds.), Looking Back at Law's Century 287 (Ithaca: Cornell University Press, 2002)

Robert Y. Jennings, "The International Court of Justice after Fifty Years," 89 American Journal of International Law 493 (1995)

Roberto Ago, "Le délit international," 68 Recueil des cours 440 (1939)

(ed.), International Law at the Time of its Codification: Essays in Honour of Roberto Ago (Milan: Giuffrè, 1988)

International Law Commission Yearbook, Vol. II, Part One (New York: United Nations, 1976)

L'origine de la responsabilité internationale, Yearbook of the International Law Commission, 1970, Vol. II, UN Doc. A/CN.4/233

"Working Paper," UN Doc A/CN.4/SC.1/WP.6 (in Yearbook of the International Law Commission, 1963, vol. II, UN Doc. A/5509, annex I, appendix II

Roger Cohen, "The Beauty of Institutions," The New York Times, November 25, 2011.

Roger P. Alford, "The American Influence on International Arbitration," 19(1) Ohio State Journal on Dispute Resolution 69 (2003)

Ronald A. Brand, "The Vulnerable Sovereign," University of Pittsburgh Law Review (Forthcoming, University of Pittsburgh Legal Studies Research Paper No. 2021–21)

Roscoe Pound, "What Is a Profession? The Rise of the Legal Profession in Antiquity," 19 Notre Dame Law Review 203–228 (1944)

Ross E. Davies, "The Judiciary Funded: The Generosity of David Dudley Field," 14 (2) Green Bag 435–452 (2011)

Sally Engle Mary, Colonizing Hawai'i: The Cultural Power of Law (Princeton: Princeton University Press, 2000)

Samuel Flagg Bemis, The Latin American Policy of the United States: An Historical Interpretation (New York: Harcourt, Brace and Company, 1943)

Sandra Link, Ein Realist mit Idealen, der Völkerrechtler Karl Strupp (1886–1940) (Baden-Baden: Nomos, 2003)

Sandra Szurek, "La force majeure en droit international" (doctoral thesis, Université Paris II Panthéon–Assas, 1996)

Santiago Montt, "Latin American Position on State Responsibility. Looking into the Past for Lessons on the Future," LEGS seminar of February 9, 2009

State Liability in Investment Treaty Arbitration: Global Constitutional and Administrative Law in the BIT Generation (Oxford: Hart, 2009)

"What International Investment Law and Latin America Can and Should Demand From Each Other. Updating the Bello/Calvo Doctrine in the BIT Generation" 3 Res Publica Argentina (2007)

Scott Veitch, Law and Irresponsibility: On the Legitimation of Human Suffering (Oxford: Routledge-Cavendish, 2007)

Sean D. Murphy, "The Heritage of the Articles on State Responsibility for the International Law Commission," in Patrícia Galvão Teles and Pierre Bodeau-Livinec (eds.), Article-by-Article Commentary of the Articles on State Responsibility (Oxford: Oxford University Press, forthcoming, 2023)

Serena Forlati, Makane Moïse Mbengue and Brian McGarry (eds.), The Gabčíkovo-Nagymaros Judgment and Its Contribution to the Development of International Law (Leiden: Brill, 2020)

Shabtai Rosenne (ed.), The International Law Commission's Draft Articles on State Responsibility, Part 1, Articles 1–35 (Dordrecht: Nijhoff, 1991)

The League of Nations Conference for the Codification of International Law 1930 (New York: Oceana, 1975)

"Some Diplomatic Problems of Codification of the Law of Treaties," 41 Washington Law Review 261–281 (1966)

The World Court: What it is and How it Works (2nd ed., Leyden: A. W. Sythoff, 1963)

Sienho Yee, "To Deal with a New Coronavirus Pandemic: Making Sense of the Lack of Any State Practice in Pursuing State Responsibility for Alleged Malfeasances in a Pandemic: Lex Specialis or Lex Generalis at Work?,"19 Chinese Journal of International Law 237 (2020)

Simeon Andonov Simeonov, "The United States' First Global Bureaucrats: Consuls and the Making of the Global American State, 1833–1856," SHAFR 2020 Annual Conference Panel 60: Citizens Without Borders: Extraterritoriality, Citizenship, and the Origins of the Global American State, 1815–1860

Simon Chesterman, "Herding Schrödinger's Cats: The Limits of the Social Science Approach to International Law," 22(1) Chicago Journal of International Law (2021)

Sir Arthur Watts, "The International Rule of Law," 36 German Yearbook of International Law 15 (1993)

Sir Frederick Pollock, The Law of Torts: A Treatise on the Principles of Obligations Arising from Civil Wrongs in the Common Law to which is Added the Draft of a Code of Civil Wrongs Prepared for the Government of India (London: Stevens and Sons, 1886)

A Treatise on the Law of Torts in Obligations Arising from Civil Wrongs in the Common Law (St. Louis: F. H. Thomas Law Book Co., 1894)

Sir Humphrey Waldock, "General Course on Public International Law," 106 Recueil des cours 1 (1962)

Stanley L. Paulson, The Very Idea of Legal Positivism (Stuttgart: Steiner, 2013)

Stephen Barcroft, "The Hague Peace Conference of 1899," (3)1 Irish Studies in International Affairs 55 (1989)

Stephen C. Neff, Justice among Nations: A History of International Law (Cambridge, MA: Harvard University Press, 2014)

Stephen C. Neff, "A Short History of International Law," in Malcolm D. Evans (ed.), International Law 31 (Oxford: Oxford University Press, 2003)

Stephen Schwebel, "Some Aspects of International Law in Arbitration between States and Aliens," in Stephen Schwebel (ed.), Justice in International Law (Cambridge: Cambridge University Press, 1994)

Stephen Wertheim, "The League That Wasn't: American Designs for a Legalist-Sanctionist League of Nations and the Intellectual Origins of International Organization, 1914–1920," 35(5) Diplomatic History 797(2011)

Steve Harris, "Arbitration at Vienna: Recasting the History of International Dispute Resolution," 3 Jus Gentium: Journal of International Legal History 391 (2018)

Steven C. Bennett, Arbitration: Essential Concepts (New York: ALM Publishing, 2002)

Steven L. Haynes, Alternative Vision: The United States, Latin America, and the League of Nations during the Republican Ascendancy (doctoral dissertation submitted to Kent State University, 2012)

Stuart Banner, The Decline of Natural Law: How American Lawyers Once Used Natural Law and Why They Stopped (Oxford: Oxford University Press, 2021)

T. de Kay, The Rebel Raiders: The Warship "Alabama," British Treachery and the American Civil War (London: Pimlico, 2003)

T. E. Holland, "Hall, William Edward (1835–1894)," rev. Catherine Pease-Watkin, Oxford Dictionary of National Biography (Oxford: Oxford University Press, 2004)

T. J. Stiles, The First Tycoon: The Epic Life of Cornelius Vanderbilt (New York: Knopf, 2009)

Tal Becker, Terrorism and the State: Rethinking the Rules of State Responsibility (Portland: Hart, 2006)

Teemu Ruskola, Legal Orientalism: China, the United States, and Modern Law (Cambridge, MA: Harvard University Press, 2013)

The Rt Hon Lord Bingham of Cornhill, "The Alabama Claims Arbitration," 54 International and Comparative Law Quarterly 1 (2005)

Theo L. Pauthonier, The Transition from Diplomatic Protection to Investor-State Arbitration and the Rise of Private Actors on the International Scene (2015) (unpublished LLM dissertation, Durham Law School)

Theodor D. Woolsey, Introduction to the Study of International Law (5th ed., London: Sampson, 1879)

Theodore Roosevelt, Addresses and Presidential Messages of Theodore Roosevelt, 1902–1904 (New York: G. P. Putnam's Sons, 1904)

Thom Hartman, Unequal Protection: The Rise of Corporate Dominance and the Theft of Human Rights (New York: Rodale, 2002)

Thomas Atkins Street, The Foundations of Legal Liability: A Presentation of the Theory and Development of the Common Law (Northport: Edward Thompson, 1906)

Thomas Balch, "International Courts of Arbitration," 3 The Law Magazine and Review 1026–1046 (1874)

Thomas David Schoonover, Dollars over Dominion: The Triumph of Liberalism in Mexican–United States Relations, 1861–1867 (Baton Rouge: Louisiana State University Press, 1978)

Thomas F. O'Brien, The Century of U.S. Capitalism in Latin America (Albuquerque: University of New Mexico Press, 1999)

Thomas J. McSweeney, Priests of the Law: Roman Law and the Making of the Common Law's First Professionals (Oxford: Oxford University Press, 2020).

Thomas M. Franck, "On Proportionality of Counter-Measures in International Law," 102(4) American Journal of International Law 715–767 (2008)

Thomas Sergeant Perry (ed.), Life and Letters of Francis Lieber (Boston: James R. Osgood and Co., 1882)

Todd Weiler, The Interpretation of International Investment Law: Equality, Discrimination and Minimum Standards of Treatment in Historical Context (Eduardo Valencia-Ospina and Loretta Malintoppi, eds., Leiden: Martinus Nijhoff, 2013)

Tom Bethell, The Noblest Triumph: Property and Prosperity through the Ages (New York: St. Martin's Press, 1998)

Turan Kayaoğlu, Legal Imperialism: Sovereignty and Extraterritoriality in Japan, the Ottoman Empire, and China (Cambridge: Cambridge University Press, 2010)

United Nations Treaty Series, available online at https://treaties.un.org/pages/AdvanceSearch.aspx?tab=UNTS&clang=_en, last checked May 2, 2023

V. Coussirat-Coustère and P. M. Eisemann, Répertoire de la Jurisprudence Arbitrale Internationale 1874–1918 (Dordrecht: Martinus Nijhoff, 1989)

V. R. Berghahn and Simone Lässig (eds.), Biography between Structure and Agency. Central European Lives in International Historiography (Oxford: Oxford University Press, 2008).

Van Hulle, Britain and International Law in West Africa: The Practice of Empire (Oxford: Oxford University Press, 2020)

Vaughan Lowe, "State Responsibility: Who? What? When?" The Josephine Onoh Memorial Lecture 2002 (Hull: The University of Hull, 2003)

Vincent Chetail and Pierre-Marie Dupuy, The Roots of International Law. Liber Amicorum Peter Haggenmacher (The Hague: Martinus Nijhoff, 2013)

Virginia Kays Veenswijk, Coudert Brothers: A Legacy in Law: The History of America's First International Law Firm: 1853–1993 (New York: Dutton, 1994)

Vladimir Bukovsky, Introduction, Arthur Koestler, Darkness at Noon (1940; trans. Daphne Hardy, London: Folio Society, 1980)

W. E. Butler and V. S. Ivanenko, "Fedor Fedorovich Martens: Russian Legal Scholar, Diplomat, Arbitrator," 4 Jus Gentium: Journal of International Legal History 145 (2019)

W. E. Hall, A Treatise on International Law (4th ed., Oxford: Clarendon, 1898)

W. S. Penfield, "Hague Tribunal," 11(10) The Michigan Alumnus 164–170 (1905)

Walter LaFeber, The New Empire: An Interpretation of American Expansion 1860–1898 (Ithaca: Cornell University Press, 1963)

Walter Stahr, Seward: Lincoln's Indispensable Man (New York: Simon & Schuster, 2012)

Wenhua Shan, "Is Calvo Dead?," 55 American Journal of Comparative Law 123 (2007)

Wesley Newcomb Hohfeld, "Some Fundamental Legal Conceptions as Applied in Judicial Reasoning," 23 Yale Law Journal 16 (1913)

Wilhelm G. Grewe, The Epochs of International Law (Michael Byers, trans., Berlin: Walter de Gruyter, 2000)

"The Role of International Law in Diplomatic Practice," 1(1) Journal of History of International Law 22 (1999)

Will Durant, The Story of Civilization: Our Common Heritage (New York: Simon and Schuster, 1935)

William Barnes and John Heath Morgan, The Foreign Service of the United States: Origins, Development, and Function (Washington, DC: Department of State, 1961)

William Butler Yeats, The Collected Works of W. B. Yeats, Vol. I: The Poems 100 (2nd ed., New York: Simon and Schuster, 1997 [1914])

William Edward Hall, A Treatise on International Law (Oxford: Clarendon Press, 1880)

A Treatise on International Law (London: Macmillan, 1889)

A Treatise on International Law (3rd ed., Oxford: Oxford University Press, 1890)

A Treatise of International Law (A. Pearce Higgins, ed., 8th ed., Oxford: Clarendon Press, 1924)

A Treatise on International Law (J. B. Atlay, ed., 5th ed., Oxford and London: Clarendon and Stevens & Sons, 1904)

William Edward Hall and J. B. Atley, A Treatise on International Law (Oxford: Oxford University Press, 1904)

William Henry Michael, History of the Department of State of the United States (Washington, DC: Government Printing Office, 1901)

William L. Penfield, "International Arbitration," 1(2) American Journal of International Law 330 (1907)

William Marion Gibson, Aliens and the Law: Aspects of the National Treatment of Aliens in the United States (Chapel Hill: Chapel Hill Press, 1940)

William O. Scroggs, Filibusters and Financiers (New York: Macmillan, 1916)

William Oke Manning, Commentaries on the Law of Nations (Sheldon Amos, ed., London: H. Sweet, 1875)

William R. Manning (ed.), Arbitration Treaties Among the American Nations to the Close of the Year 1910 (New York: Oxford University Press, 1924)

William Ross Johnston, Sovereignty and Protection: A Study of British Jurisdictional Imperialism in the Late Nineteenth Century (Durham: Duke University Press, 1973)

Willem Theus, "There and Back Again: From Consular Courts through Mixed Arbitral Tribunals to International Commercial Courts," in Hélène Ruiz Fabri and Michel Erpelding (eds.), The Mixed Arbitral Tribunals, 1919–1939: An Experiment in the International Adjudication of Private Rights 29 (Baden-Baden: Nomos, 2023)

Wolfgang Stegmüller, Hauptströmungen der Gegenwartsphilosophie (6th ed., Stuttgart: Alfred Kröner Verlag, 1978)

Yarik Kryvoi, "The Path of Investor–State Disputes: From Compensation Commissions to Arbitral Institutions," 3 ICSID Review: Foreign Investment Law Journal 33 (2018)

Yoshiro Mastui, 'The Transformation of the Law of State Responsibility," 20 Thesaurus Acroasium 5 (1993)

Yves Dezalay and Bryant G. Garth, Dealing in Virtue: International Commercial Arbitration and the Construction of a Transnational Legal Order (Chicago: University of Chicago Press, 1996)

Yves Dezalay and Bryant Garth, "Merchants of Law as Moral Entrepreneurs: Constructing International Justice from the Competition for Transnational Business Disputes," 29(1) Law & Society Review 27 (1995)

Zachary Douglas, "The Hybrid Foundations of Investment Treaty Arbitration," British Yearbook of International Law 151 (2003)

INDEX

CAMBRIDGE STUDIES IN INTERNATIONAL AND COMPARATIVE LAW

Books in the Series

190 *Merchants of Legalism: A History of State Responsibility (1870–1960)*
Alan Tzvika Nissel

189 *The Functions of International Adjudication and International Environmental Litigation*
Joshua Paine

188 *Demystifying Treaty Interpretation*
Andrea Bianchi and Fuad Zarbiyev

187 *International Law-Making by the International Court of Justice and International Law Commission: Partnership for Purpose in a Decentralized Legal Order*
Omri Sender

186 *The Rebirth of Territory*
Gail Lythgoe

185 *Reimagining Sustainable Development in International Law: Perspectives from African Legal Cosmologies*
Godwin Eli Kwadzo Dzah

184 *Collective Self-Defence in International Law*
James A. Green

183 *Weaponising Evidence: A History of Tobacco Control in International Law*
Margherita Melillo

182 *The Justice Factory: Management Practices at the International Criminal Court*
Richard Clements

181 *A Communitarian Theory of WTO Law*
Chi Carmody

180 *Drones and International Law: A Techno-Legal Machinery*
Rebecca Mignot-Mahdavi

179 *The Necessity of Nature: God, Science and Money in 17th Century English Law of Nature*
Mónica García-Salmones

178 *Making the World Safe for Investment: The Protection of Foreign Property 1922–1959*
Andrea Leiter

177 *National Governance and Investment Treaties*
Josef Ostřanský and Facundo Pérez Aznar

176 *Who Owns Outer Space? International Law, Astrophysics, and the Sustainable Development of Space*
Michael Byers and Aaron Boley

175 *Intervening in International Justice: Third States before Courts and Tribunals*
Brian McGarry

174 *Reciprocity in Public International Law*
Arianna Whelan

173 *When Environmental Protection and Human Rights Collide*
Marie-Catherine Petersmann

172 *The International Law of Sovereign Debt Dispute Settlement*
Kei Nakajima

171 *The Everyday Makers of International Law: From Great Halls to Back Rooms*
Tommaso Soave

170 *Virtue in Global Governance: Judgment and Discretion*
Jan Klabbers

169 *The Effects of Armed Conflict on Investment Treaties*
Tobias Ackermann

168 *Investment Law's Alibis: Colonialism, Imperialism, Debt and Development*
David Schneiderman

167 *Negative Comparative Law: A Strong Programme for Weak Thought*
Pierre Legrand

166 *Detention by Non-State Armed Groups under International Law*
Ezequiel Heffes

165 *Rebellions and Civil Wars: State Responsibility for the Conduct of Insurgents*
Patrick Dumberry

164 *The International Law of Energy*
Jorge Viñuales

163 *The Three Ages of International Commercial Arbitration*
Mikaël Schinazi

162 *Repetition and International Law*
Wouter Werner

161 *State Responsibility and Rebels: The History and Legacy of Protecting Investment Against Revolution*
Kathryn Greenman

160 *Rewriting Histories of the Use of Force: The Narrative of 'Indifference'*
Agatha Verdebout

159 *The League of Nations and the Protection of the Environment*
Omer Aloni

158 *International Investment Law and Legal Theory: Expropriation and the Fragmentation of Sources*
Jörg Kammerhofer

157 *Legal Barbarians: Identity, Modern Comparative Law and the Global South*
Daniel Bonilla Maldonado

156 *International Human Rights Law Beyond State Territorial Control*
Antal Berkes

155 *The Crime of Aggression under the Rome Statute of the International Criminal Court*
Carrie McDougall

154 *Minorities and the Making of Postcolonial States in International Law*
Mohammad Shahabuddin

153 *Preclassical Conflict of Laws*
Nikitas E. Hatzimihail

152 *International Law and History: Modern Interfaces*
Ignacio de la Rasilla

151 *Marketing Global Justice: The Political Economy of International Criminal Law*
Christine Schwöbel-Patel

150 *International Status in the Shadow of Empire*
Cait Storr

149 *Treaties in Motion: The Evolution of Treaties from Formation to Termination*
Edited by Malgosia Fitzmaurice and Panos Merkouris

148 *Humanitarian Disarmament: An Historical Enquiry*
Treasa Dunworth

147 *Complementarity, Catalysts, Compliance: The International Criminal Court in Uganda, Kenya, and the Democratic Republic of Congo*
Christian M. De Vos

146 *Cyber Operations and International Law*
François Delerue

145 *Comparative Reasoning in International Courts and Tribunals*
Daniel Peat

144 *Maritime Delimitation as a Judicial Process*
Massimo Lando

143 *Prosecuting Sexual and Gender-Based Crimes at the International Criminal Court: Practice, Progress and Potential*
Rosemary Grey

142 *Capitalism as Civilisation: A History of International Law*
Ntina Tzouvala

141 *Sovereignty in China: A Genealogy of a Concept Since 1840*
Adele Carrai

140 *Narratives of Hunger in International Law: Feeding the World in Times of Climate Change*
Anne Saab

139 *Victim Reparation under the Ius Post Bellum: An Historical and Normative Perspective*
Shavana Musa

138 *The Analogy between States and International Organizations*
Fernando Lusa Bordin

137 *The Process of International Legal Reproduction: Inequality, Historiography, Resistance*
Rose Parfitt

136 *State Responsibility for Breaches of Investment Contracts*
Jean Ho

135 *Coalitions of the Willing and International Law: The Interplay between Formality and Informality*
Alejandro Rodiles

134 *Self-Determination in Disputed Colonial Territories*
Jamie Trinidad

133 *International Law as a Belief System*
Jean d'Aspremont

132 *Legal Consequences of Peremptory Norms in International Law*
Daniel Costelloe

131 *Third-Party Countermeasures in International Law*
Martin Dawidowicz

130 *Justification and Excuse in International Law: Concept and Theory of General Defences*
Federica Paddeu

129 *Exclusion from Public Space: A Comparative Constitutional Analysis*
Daniel Moeckli

128 *Provisional Measures before International Courts and Tribunals*
Cameron A. Miles

127 *Humanity at Sea: Maritime Migration and the Foundations of International Law*
Itamar Mann

126 *Beyond Human Rights: The Legal Status of the Individual in International Law*
Anne Peters

125 *The Doctrine of Odious Debt in International Law: A Restatement*
Jeff King

124 *Static and Evolutive Treaty Interpretation: A Functional Reconstruction*
Christian Djeffal

123 *Civil Liability in Europe for Terrorism-Related Risk*
Lucas Bergkamp, Michael Faure, Monika Hinteregger and Niels Philipsen

122 *Proportionality and Deference in Investor-State Arbitration: Balancing Investment Protection and Regulatory Autonomy*
Caroline Henckels

121 *International Law and Governance of Natural Resources in Conflict and Post-Conflict Situations*
Daniëlla Dam-de Jong

120 *Proof of Causation in Tort Law*
Sandy Steel

119 *The Formation and Identification of Rules of Customary International Law in International Investment Law*
Patrick Dumberry

118 *Religious Hatred and International Law: The Prohibition of Incitement to Violence or Discrimination*
Jeroen Temperman

117 *Taking Economic, Social and Cultural Rights Seriously in International Criminal Law*
Evelyne Schmid

116 *Climate Change Litigation: Regulatory Pathways to Cleaner Energy*
Jacqueline Peel and Hari M. Osofsky

115 *Mestizo International Law: A Global Intellectual History 1842–1933*
Arnulf Becker Lorca

114 *Sugar and the Making of International Trade Law*
Michael Fakhri

113 *Strategically Created Treaty Conflicts and the Politics of International Law*
Surabhi Ranganathan

112 *Investment Treaty Arbitration as Public International Law: Procedural Aspects and Implications*
Eric De Brabandere

111 *The New Entrants Problem in International Fisheries Law*
Andrew Serdy

110 *Substantive Protection under Investment Treaties: A Legal and Economic Analysis*
Jonathan Bonnitcha

109 *Popular Governance of Post-Conflict Reconstruction: The Role of International Law*
Matthew Saul

108 *Evolution of International Environmental Regimes: The Case of Climate Change*
Simone Schiele

107 *Judges, Law and War: The Judicial Development of International Humanitarian Law*
Shane Darcy

106 *Religious Offence and Human Rights: The Implications of Defamation of Religions*
Lorenz Langer

105 *Forum Shopping in International Adjudication: The Role of Preliminary Objections*
Luiz Eduardo Salles

104 *Domestic Politics and International Human Rights Tribunals: The Problem of Compliance*
Courtney Hillebrecht

103 *International Law and the Arctic*
Michael Byers

102 *Cooperation in the Law of Transboundary Water Resources*
Christina Leb

101 *Underwater Cultural Heritage and International Law*
Sarah Dromgoole

100 *State Responsibility: The General Part*
James Crawford

99 *The Origins of International Investment Law: Empire, Environment and the Safeguarding of Capital*
Kate Miles

98 *The Crime of Aggression under the Rome Statute of the International Criminal Court*
Carrie McDougall

97 *'Crimes against Peace' and International Law*
Kirsten Sellars

96 *Non-Legality in International Law: Unruly Law*
Fleur Johns

95 *Armed Conflict and Displacement: The Protection of Refugees and Displaced Persons under International Humanitarian Law*
Mélanie Jacques

94 *Foreign Investment and the Environment in International Law*
Jorge E. Viñuales

93 *The Human Rights Treaty Obligations of Peacekeepers*
Kjetil Mujezinović Larsen

92 *Cyber Warfare and the Laws of War*
Heather Harrison Dinniss

91 *The Right to Reparation in International Law for Victims of Armed Conflict*
Christine Evans

90 *Global Public Interest in International Investment Law*
Andreas Kulick

89 *State Immunity in International Law*
Xiaodong Yang

88 *Reparations and Victim Support in the International Criminal Court*
Conor McCarthy

87 *Reducing Genocide to Law: Definition, Meaning, and the Ultimate Crime*
Payam Akhavan

86 *Decolonising International Law: Development, Economic Growth and the Politics of Universality*
Sundhya Pahuja

85 *Complicity and the Law of State Responsibility*
Helmut Philipp Aust

84 *State Control over Private Military and Security Companies in Armed Conflict*
Hannah Tonkin

83 *'Fair and Equitable Treatment' in International Investment Law*
Roland Kläger

82 *The UN and Human Rights: Who Guards the Guardians?*
Guglielmo Verdirame

81 *Sovereign Defaults before International Courts and Tribunals*
Michael Waibel

80 *Making the Law of the Sea: A Study in the Development of International Law*
James Harrison

79 *Science and the Precautionary Principle in International Courts and Tribunals: Expert Evidence, Burden of Proof and Finality*
Caroline E. Foster

78 *Transition from Illegal Regimes under International Law*
Yaël Ronen

77 *Access to Asylum: International Refugee Law and the Globalisation of Migration Control*
Thomas Gammeltoft-Hansen

76 *Trading Fish, Saving Fish: The Interaction between Regimes in International Law*
Margaret A. Young

75 *The Individual in the International Legal System: Continuity and Change in International Law*
Kate Parlett

74 *'Armed Attack' and Article 51 of the UN Charter: Evolutions in Customary Law and Practice*
Tom Ruys

73 *Theatre of the Rule of Law: Transnational Legal Intervention in Theory and Practice*
Stephen Humphreys

72 *Science and Risk Regulation in International Law*
Jacqueline Peel

71 *The Participation of States in International Organisations: The Role of Human Rights and Democracy*
Alison Duxbury

70 *Legal Personality in International Law*
Roland Portmann

69 *Vicarious Liability in Tort: A Comparative Perspective*
Paula Giliker

68 *The Public International Law Theory of Hans Kelsen: Believing in Universal Law*
Jochen von Bernstorff

67 *Legitimacy and Legality in International Law: An Interactional Account*
Jutta Brunnée and Stephen J. Toope

66 *The Concept of Non-International Armed Conflict in International Humanitarian Law*
Anthony Cullen

65 *The Principle of Legality in International and Comparative Criminal Law*
Kenneth S. Gallant

64 *The Challenge of Child Labour in International Law*
Franziska Humbert

63 *Shipping Interdiction and the Law of the Sea*
Douglas Guilfoyle

62 *International Courts and Environmental Protection*
Tim Stephens

61 *Legal Principles in WTO Disputes*
Andrew D. Mitchell

60 *War Crimes in Internal Armed Conflicts*
Eve La Haye

59 *Humanitarian Occupation*
Gregory H. Fox

58 *The International Law of Environmental Impact Assessment: Process, Substance and Integration*
Neil Craik

57 *The Law and Practice of International Territorial Administration: Versailles to Iraq and Beyond*
Carsten Stahn

56 *United Nations Sanctions and the Rule of Law*
Jeremy Matam Farrall

55 *National Law in WTO Law: Effectiveness and Good Governance in the World Trading System*
Sharif Bhuiyan

54 *Cultural Products and the World Trade Organization*
Tania Voon

53 *The Threat of Force in International Law*
Nikolas Stürchler

52 *Indigenous Rights and United Nations Standards: Self-Determination, Culture and Land*
Alexandra Xanthaki

51 *International Refugee Law and Socio-Economic Rights: Refuge from Deprivation*
Michelle Foster

50 *The Protection of Cultural Property in Armed Conflict*
Roger O'Keefe

49 *Interpretation and Revision of International Boundary Decisions*
Kaiyan Homi Kaikobad

48 *Multinationals and Corporate Social Responsibility: Limitations and Opportunities in International Law*
Jennifer A. Zerk

47 *Judiciaries within Europe: A Comparative Review*
John Bell

46 *Law in Times of Crisis: Emergency Powers in Theory and Practice*
Oren Gross and Fionnuala Ní Aoláin

45 *Vessel-Source Marine Pollution: The Law and Politics of International Regulation*
Alan Khee-Jin Tan

44 *Enforcing Obligations Erga Omnes in International Law*
Christian J. Tams

43 *Non-Governmental Organisations in International Law*
Anna-Karin Lindblom

42 *Democracy, Minorities and International Law*
Steven Wheatley

41 *Prosecuting International Crimes: Selectivity and the International Criminal Law Regime*
Robert Cryer

40 *Compensation for Personal Injury in English, German and Italian Law: A Comparative Outline*
Basil Markesinis, Michael Coester, Guido Alpa and Augustus Ullstein

39 *Dispute Settlement in the UN Convention on the Law of the Sea*
Natalie Klein

38 *The International Protection of Internally Displaced Persons*
Catherine Phuong

37 *Imperialism, Sovereignty and the Making of International Law*
Antony Anghie

36 *Principles of the Institutional Law of International Organizations*
C. F. Amerasinghe

35 *Necessity, Proportionality and the Use of Force by States*
Judith Gardam

34 *International Legal Argument in the Permanent Court of International Justice: The Rise of the International Judiciary*
Ole Spiermann

33

32 *Great Powers and Outlaw States: Unequal Sovereigns in the International Legal Order*
Gerry Simpson

31 *Local Remedies in International Law (second edition)*
Chittharanjan Felix Amerasinghe

30 *Reading Humanitarian Intervention: Human Rights and the Use of Force in International Law*
Anne Orford

29 *Conflict of Norms in Public International Law: How WTO Law Relates to Other Rules of International Law*
Joost Pauwelyn

28

27 *Transboundary Damage in International Law*
Hanqin Xue

26

25 *European Criminal Procedures* Edited by Mireille Delmas-Marty and J. R. Spencer

24 *Accountability of Armed Opposition Groups in International Law*
Liesbeth Zegveld

23 *Sharing Transboundary Resources: International Law and Optimal Resource Use*
Eyal Benvenisti

22 *International Human Rights and Humanitarian Law*
René Provost

21 *Remedies against International Organisations*
Karel Wellens

20 *Diversity and Self-Determination in International Law*
Karen Knop

19 *The Law of Internal Armed Conflict*
Lindsay Moir

18 *International Commercial Arbitration and African States: Practice, Participation and Institutional Development*
Amazu A. Asouzu

17 *The Enforceability of Promises in European Contract Law*
James Gordley

16 *International Law in Antiquity*
David J. Bederman

15 *Money Laundering: A New International Law Enforcement Model*
Guy Stessens

14 *Good Faith in European Contract Law*
Reinhard Zimmermann and Simon Whittaker

13 *On Civil Procedure*
J. A. Jolowicz

12 *Trusts: A Comparative Study*
Maurizio Lupoi and Simon Dix

11 *The Right to Property in Commonwealth Constitutions*
Tom Allen

10 *International Organizations before National Courts*
August Reinisch

9 *The Changing International Law of High Seas Fisheries*
Francisco Orrego Vicuña

8 *Trade and the Environment: A Comparative Study of EC and US Law*
Damien Geradin

7 *Unjust Enrichment: A Study of Private Law and Public Values*
Hanoch Dagan

6 *Religious Liberty and International Law in Europe*
Malcolm D. Evans

5 *Ethics and Authority in International Law*
Alfred P. Rubin

4 *Sovereignty over Natural Resources: Balancing Rights and Duties*
Nico Schrijver

3 *The Polar Regions and the Development of International Law*
Donald R. Rothwell

2 *Fragmentation and the International Relations of Micro-States: Self-Determination and Statehood*
Jorri C. Duursma

1 *Principles of the Institutional Law of International Organizations*
C. F. Amerasinghe